Pro Android UI

■ ■ ■

Wallace Jackson

Apress®

Pro Android UI

ISBN-13 (pbk): 978-1-4302-4986-3

ISBN-13 (electronic): 978-1-4302-4987-0

President and Publisher: Paul Manning
Lead Editor: Steve Anglin
Development Editors: James Markham, Chris Nelson, Anne Marie Walker
Technical Reviewer: Chád Darby
Editorial Board: Steve Anglin, Mark Beckner, Ewan Buckingham, Gary Cornell, Louise Corrigan,
    James T. DeWolf, Jonathan Gennick, Jonathan Hassell, Robert Hutchinson, Michelle Lowman,
    James Markham, Matthew Moodie, Jeff Olson, Jeffrey Pepper, Douglas Pundick, Ben Renow-Clarke,
    Dominic Shakeshaft, Gwenan Spearing, Matt Wade, Steve Weiss
Coordinating Editor: Anamika Panchoo
Copy Editor: Linda Seifert
Compositor: SPi Global
Indexer: SPi Global
Artist: SPi Global
Cover Designer: Anna Ishchenko

Distributed to the book trade worldwide by Springer Science+Business Media New York, 233 Spring Street, 6th Floor, New York, NY 10013. Phone 1-800-SPRINGER, fax (201) 348-4505, e-mail orders-ny@springer-sbm.com, or visit www.springeronline.com. Apress Media, LLC is a California LLC and the sole member (owner) is Springer Science + Business Media Finance Inc (SSBM Finance Inc). SSBM Finance Inc is a Delaware corporation.

For information on translations, please e-mail rights@apress.com, or visit www.apress.com.

Apress and friends of ED books may be purchased in bulk for academic, corporate, or promotional use. eBook versions and licenses are also available for most titles. For more information, reference our Special Bulk Sales–eBook Licensing web page at www.apress.com/bulk-sales.

Any source code or other supplementary materials referenced by the author in this text is available to readers at www.apress.com. For detailed information about how to locate your book's source code, go to www.apress.com/source-code/.

This book is dedicated to everyone in the ever-expanding open source community who is working diligently to make professional level software and new media development tools available for everybody to use to achieve their dreams and goals. Last, but certainly not least, to my loving family, life-long friends, and rancher neighbors for all their help, assistance, laughs, and those fabulous late night BBQs.

Contents at a Glance

Contents

About the Author

Wallace Jackson has been writing for leading new media publications regarding his production work in new media content development since the advent of *Multimedia Producer Magazine*, more than two decades ago, when he wrote about computer processor architectures for the magazine's centerfold distributed at SIGGRAPH.

Since then, Wallace has written for several other leading publications about his work in interactive 3D and new media brand and advertising campaign design, including *3D Artist, Desktop Publishers Journal, CrossMedia, AV Video,* and *Kiosk Magazine*.

A COBOL and RPG2 programmer since he was in his early teens, Wallace has also written several popular application programming books covering the use of Eclipse, Java, and XML for the Android development environment for Apress (Springer Scientific) over the past decade.

Wallace Jackson is also the CEO of Mind Taffy Design, a new media content production and digital marketing and branding campaign design and development agency located in Northern Santa Barbara County, halfway between their clientele in the Silicon Valley in Northern California, and in the Hollywood, Irvine, and San Diego areas of Southern California.

Mind Taffy Design has created digital new media content deliverables using open source technology (HTML5, CSS, JavaScript, Java, JavaFX, XML, and Android) over the past two decades for many of the leading branded manufacturers in the world, including Sony, Tyco, Samsung, Nokia, Epson, Compaq, IBM, TEAC, CTX, KDS, Sun, Micron, SGI, EIZO Nanao, Techmedia, ArtMedia, KFC, and Mitsubishi.

Mr. Jackson received his undergraduate degree in Business Economics from the University of California at Los Angeles (UCLA), and his graduate degree in MIS Design and Implementation from the University of Southern California (USC). His post-graduate degree, in Marketing Strategy, is also from USC. Wallace also attended and completed the USC Graduate Entrepreneurship Program.

About the Technical Reviewer

Chád Darby is an author, instructor, and speaker in the Java development world. As a recognized authority on Java applications and architectures, he has presented technical sessions at software development conferences worldwide (U.S., U.K., India, Russia, and Australia). In his 15 years as a professional software architect, he's had the opportunity to work for Blue Cross/Blue Shield, Merck, Boeing, Red Hat, and a handful of startup companies.

Chád is a contributing author to several Java books, including *Professional Java E-Commerce* (Wrox Press), *Beginning Java Networking* (Wrox Press), and *XML* and *Web Services Unleashed* (Sams Publishing). Chád has Java certifications from Sun Microsystems and IBM. He holds a B.S. in Computer Science from Carnegie Mellon University.

Acknowledgments

I would like to acknowledge all the fantastic editors and their support staff at Apress who worked so very long and hard on this book, making it the ultimate all-around Pro Android User Interface Design application production book.

Steve Anglin, for his work as the Lead Editor on the book, and for his acquisition of myself as an author for Apress, as well as his experience and guidance during the process of writing this book.

James Markham, for his work as the Development Editor on the book, and for his experience and guidance during the process of making Pro Android UI truly great.

Anamika Panchoo, for her work as the Coordinating Editor on the book, and for her diligence in making sure I either hit my deadlines, or that I surpassed them.

Linda Seifert, for her work as the Copy Editor on the book, and for her attention to detail and conforming the text to Apress writing standards.

Chád Darby, for his work as the Technical Reviewer on the book. Chád made sure I didn't make any mistakes, because code with mistakes does not run properly, if at all, unless they are very lucky mistakes, which is quite rare in computer programming.

Finally I'd like to acknowledge Oracle for acquiring Sun Microsystems, and for continuing to enhance Java, as well as JavaFX, so that they remain the premiere open source programming languages.

I would also like to acknowledge Google for making Android OS the premiere open source operating system, and for acquiring ON2's VP8 video codec, and for making the VP8 WebM and WebP formats available to all of us open source platform multimedia content producers.

Introduction

Google's Android Operating System continues to gain market share, making it one of the most often utilized OSes internationally. Android currently powers everything from smartwatches to iTV sets to smartphones to smartglasses to touchscreen tablets to e-book readers to game consoles and now homes, appliances, audio products, car dashboards, and more.

One of the most important design considerations for any Android application is the UI Design (User Interface Design), as this defines how the Android application user interfaces with the objective of the application itself. An Android application that features a streamlined, simple, and elegant UI Design will please users and enhance sales volumes within the Android applications marketplace.

The Android OS contains a plethora of UI Design classes that have been specifically created to help Android developers implement creative UI designs, as well as to conform their UI Design to Android OS UI Design standards. This book covers those primary UI Layout Container classes and methods, as well as all the Android UI Design standards and guidelines, which every Android developer should understand and follow in their application design work process.

I wrote *Pro Android UI* to help readers delve into the inner workings of the Android UI Design standards, to explore the most popular UI layout classes and methods, and to be a complimentary title to my recent *Pro Android Graphics* title. *Pro Android UI* targets those readers who are already technically proficient, that is, those who are familiar with computer programming concepts and techniques. This title covers the latest Android 4.x Operating System revisions (4.0, 4.1.2, 4.2.2, 4.3.1, and 4.4.2), as well as covering earlier Android OS versions.

This book also covers the usage of a wide variety of related open source software packages that can be used in the Android application development work process. Such packages include seasoned open source new media applications like GIMP, Lightworks, Pencil, Blender, and Audacity. We take a look at how the usage of these packages fits into the overall Android application development work process. We also take a look at new media elements and supported formats, how they work, and how to leverage them in your UI Design process.

Using a multiple open source software package implementation approach will serve to set *Pro Android UI* distinctly apart from the other Android user interface design titles currently on the market. This book starts out with the reader installing the latest Java SE and Android SDKs using the Eclipse Kepler IDE, with the Android ADT Bundle, and then many of the most popular open source new media production applications for digital imaging, digital audio editing, digital video production, user interface wireframing and prototyping, and more.

The book then progresses through creating Menu UI Designs, ActionBar UI Designs, Android UI Rules and Guidelines, and then finally through the primary types of UI Layout Containers that developers specifically implement for their Android application UI Design.

We look at static user interface design using XML mark-up, dynamic user interface design using Java, using digital imaging within your user interface design, using digital video and animation in your user interface design, Android OS user interface design rules and standards , as well as other advanced new media concepts and multimedia application features that are currently popular in Android UI Design for Android application development.

We look at the core Android UI Design areas, including UI layout containers, UI widgets, ActionBar UI Design, New Media formats, codecs, concepts and implementations, and advanced concepts such as Fragments, all in fine detail. If you want to get an overview of and a handle on Android UI Design, this title is a great place to start that process.

Introduction to the Core Classes for Android UI Design: Development Tools, Layout Containers and Widgets

Part 1

Introduction to the Core
Classes for Android UI Design:
Development Tools, Layout
Containers and Widgets

Android UI Design Tools: Setting Up Your Android Development System

In this first chapter, we will set-up your Android Application Development workstation. I recommend using at least a hexa-core Intel or AMD 64-bit PC with 64-bit Windows 8.1 (or at least Windows 7) operating system installed on this workstation, preferable using an SSD (Solid State Drive) for your primary C:\ disk drive. An SSD will provide your workstation with a vastly accelerated overall system performance, especially at software load-time.

Fortunately, you can get a hexa-core (or octa-core) online at PriceWatch, or walk into Walmart and pick one up for just a few hundred dollars. Then, simply install all this open source software that I am going to expose you to in this chapter, which is worth thousands (actually, it's priceless if you factor in the power that it gives you), and you can then create or develop anything that you can imagine—right out of thin air.

For those readers who have just purchased their new Pro Android UI Design workstation, and who are going to put an entire development software suite together from scratch, I will go through this entire process. Essentially, these are the steps that I would go through to put together a powerful UI development workstation from scratch with zero expenditure on software.

The first objective is to get the entire Oracle Java software development kit (SDK), which Oracle currently calls **JavaSE 6u45 JDK** (Java Development Kit). Android uses Java Version 6u45, as of Android 4.4, but there is also a Java Version 7u45, and later on this year there will be a Java Version 8 released, which will contain the powerful JavaFX 2.2.45 new media engine, and so great things are coming in the future for Pro Android UI developers!

The second thing that we will download and install is Android's Developer Tools (ADT) that we get from Google's developer.android.com website.

The Android Developer Tools (ADT Bundle) consists of: the **Eclipse Kepler** 4.4 IDE (Integrated Development Environment), along with the **ADT plug-ins** which accesses the **Android 4.4 KitKat API Level 19 SDK** (Software Development Kit), which is also part of this 480MB ADT Bundle download.

After that, we'll download and install software development tools that we will utilize in conjunction with Android for things such as UI wireframing (Pencil), digital image editing (GIMP2), digital audio editing (Audacity), digital video editing (Lightworks 11.5) and 3D modeling (Blender 2.69).

All these software development tools which we download and install match the primary feature sets of expensive paid software packages, such as those from Microsoft (Visual Studio), Apple (Logic, Avid, and Final Cut Pro) and Adobe (Photoshop, Premiere, and After Effects), each of which would cost thousands of dollars to purchase.

Java 6: Download and Install the Foundation for Android

The first thing that you want to do is to visit **Oracle's Tech Network Java** archives website, which is currently located at the following URL:

`http://www.oracle.com/work/java/javasebusiness/downloads/java-archive-downloads-javase6-419409.html`

You need to download and install the latest **Java 6 JDK** environment, which, at the time of writing this book is **Java SE 6u45**, as shown in Figure 1-1.

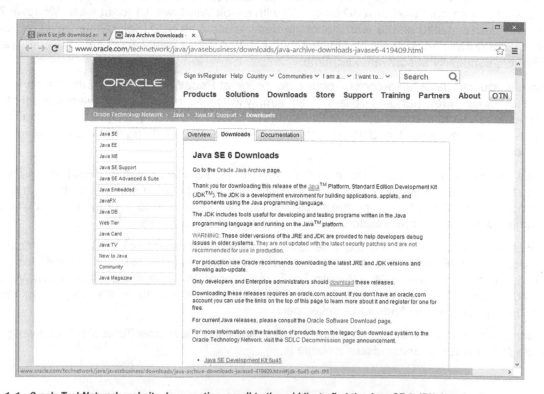

Figure 1-1. Oracle TechNetwork website Java section, scroll to the middle, to find the Java SE 6 JDK download

The URL is also shown in the address bar of Figure 1-1, or, you can simply Google **Java 6 SE JDK Download Archive 6U45,** as shown in the Google tab in the screenshot.

You can see the **Java SE Development Kit 6u45 download** link for this Java SE 6u45 JDK shown at the bottom of Figure 1-1. Make sure to use this **JDK** download link, and not the **JRE 6u45** (Java Runtime Edition) download link.

The JRE is that part of Java which "runs" or executes your Java code, once it is compiled into an interim "Java ByteStream" format, and this will not allow you to develop Java code, only to run it once it has been developed.

To develop the Java (and thus Android, which uses Java) program logic for your applications, you will need to download the JDK, as well as the JRE.

Fortunately, the JDK download also includes the JRE, which is logical, as it would be needed as part of the development and testing work process.

The reason the JRE is also available separately is that others who want to run your Java apps will need the JRE installed on their system, but do not need the entire JDK, as they are not developers.

Make sure **not** to download the JDK 7u45 JDK or the Java7u45 Bundle, which includes NetBeans 8.0, because Android uses the Eclipse IDE, and not the NetBeans IDE for the ADT plug-ins. NetBeans 8.0 is what I use for Java 8 and HTML5 development, but is not currently compatible with Android ADT.

Thus, if you see any Java 7 downloads, you are on the wrong webpage, for the current Java 7 (or Java 8) downloads, not the Java 6 "archive" page.

The Java 6 version is "archived," which means that it is still available, but is not the current version. Once Google and Oracle settle their legal positions regarding the use of Java in Android, Android OS may eventually be upgraded to utilize Java 7 or even Java 8, which would make the JavaFX new media engine available to Android developers.

What makes this something to watch out for and also somewhat confusing, is that Oracle made the Java 7 **update** or **version numbering** parallel with Java 6, so one is Java 6u45 and one is Java 7u45, making them more similar than they actually are. Java 7 has not had 45 updates, but for some reason, the version numbers have been jumped on Java 7 to parallel between the two and will most likely remain in sync from now on, so make sure to use JavaSE 6!

Once you click on the Java SE Development Kit 6u45 download link, you will be taken to a JDK6 Download section shown in Figure 1-2, where you can select the OS you're using (I'm using Windows 8.1 64-bit Windows).

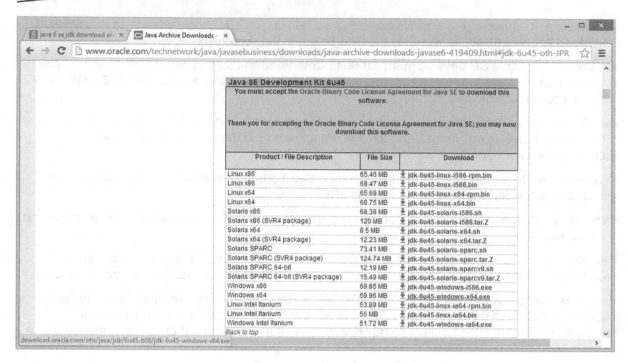

Figure 1-2. Java SE Development Kit 6u45 download links after Accept License Agreement Radio Button clicked

Once you click the **Accept License Agreement** radio button, which will be on the **top-left** of the download links table, as seen in Figure 1-2, the links will become **bolded** and you will be able to click on the link that you wish to use. If you are on Windows, and your OS is 64-bit, as my Windows 8.1 OS is, then use the **Windows x64** link, otherwise you would use the **Windows x86** link if you have Windows XP, a 32-bit OS such as Windows Vista 32-bit, or Windows 7 32-bit or even Windows 8.1 32-bit.

It is important to use 32-bit versions of Java and Eclipse if your OS is a 32-bit OS version, and similarly use a 64-bit version of Java and Eclipse, if your OS is a 64-bit version. An OS that is 64-bit can access more than 3GB of system memory. You can find out what your OS version is by dropping down your **Start** menu and **right-clicking** on the **Computer** selection and then selecting the **Properties** menu option, located at the bottom of that menu.

Once the installation executable has downloaded, open it, and install the latest Java JDK on your system. You can remove any older versions of Java using the Windows Control Panel, and Change or Remove Programs utility if your workstation is not new, so only the latest JDK and JRE are installed.

Once Java 6u45 (or later) JDK is installed on the workstation you can then download and install the **Android ADT Bundle** from the developer.android.com website. You can use the Change or Remove Programs utility in your Control Panel that you used to remove older Java versions to confirm installation.

Android ADT Bundle: Find and Download Android's IDE

The second thing that we want to do is to visit the `developer.android.com` website, and download and install the Android Development Environment ADT Bundle ZIP file. On the homepage, click the **Get the SDK** button, on the bottom left of the site, to navigate to this website's SDK section, which is shown in Figure 1-3. The URL for this section of the website can also be seen in Figure 1-3 and you can type it in directly as well if you want to:

```
https://developer.android.com/sdk/index.html
```

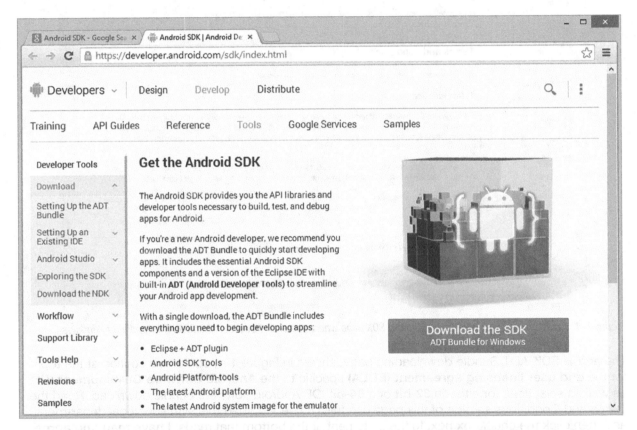

Figure 1-3. The `developer.android.com/sdk/` website download page, and the Download the SDK button, on the right

Once you are on the **Get the Android SDK** page click the **Download the SDK ADT Bundle for Windows** (a big blue button on the middle-right of the page) to download an ADT Bundle for Windows, as is shown in Figure 1-3.

This takes you to the actual downloads page, where you can select your OS bit-level version (32-bit or 64-bit) and agree to the terms of the product licensing, as is shown in Figure 1-4. Since I'm running the Windows 8.1 64-bit OS, I selected the 64-bit software version radio button.

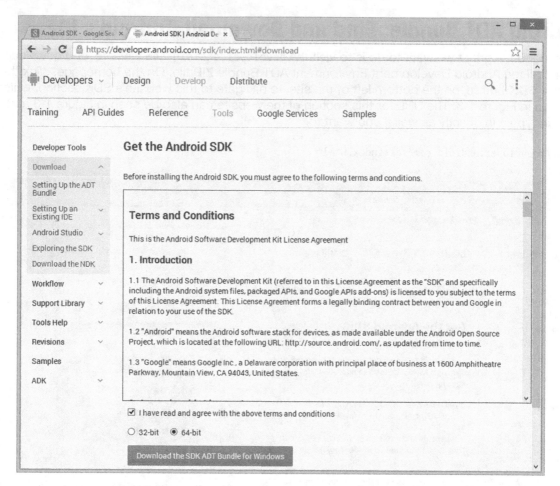

Figure 1-4. Android Developer site Get the Android SDK page where you click Download the SDK ADT Bundle for Windows

The actual SDK ADT Bundle downloading page, shown in Figure 1-4, contains a section at the top for the **end user licensing agreement (EULA)** specific to the **Android Software Development Kit**, as well as selections for either a **32-bit** or a **64-bit** IDE Android software bundle download. Read the Terms and Conditions section of this page carefully! If needed, read this with your legal department, and then click the checkbox next to the statement at the bottom that reads: **I have read and agree with the above terms and conditions**. This enables the rest of this download page functionality.

Once the checkbox has been activated (checked), you should then can select either the **32-bit** or the **64-bit** version of Eclipse 4.4's ADT Bundle that is contained inside of a **.ZIP format** software installation package.

If you downloaded the Java 6u45 JDK for Windows x64 or Linux x64 you would select the 64-bit version; conversely if you selected Java 6u45 for an x86 OS you would select the 32-bit version of this SDK ADT bundle of software.

Once this selection has been made, the actual **Download the SDK ADT Bundle** blue button will be activated and you may click it to begin a download.

Once this 480MB download is complete, which may take a while depending on your Internet connection; we'll **unzip** the files in a development directory and set-up Android for use on our Pro Android UI development workstation.

Android ADT Bundle: Installing the Android IDE

The first thing we need to do after the download is complete is to find the file that we just downloaded, which should be in your operating system's Downloads folder. Usually you can right-click on a downloaded file in your browser's download progress window, and select the **View in Folder** option.

I downloaded my software on a different workstation, so I copied this file into a Software folder on my USB thumbdrive, which is shown in Figure 1-5.

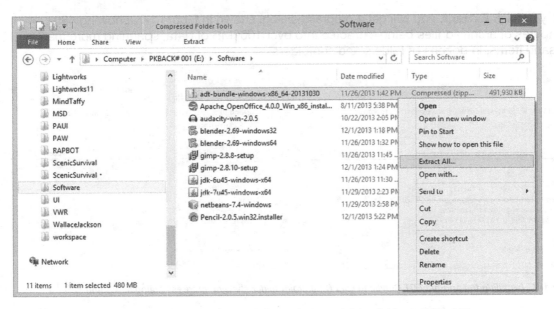

Figure 1-5. Finding the adt-bundle-windows ZIP file in my Software folder, and right-clicking to Extract All

Once you locate either the **adt-bundle-windows-x86** (32-bit Windows XP, Win7, or Vista), or the **adt-bundle-windows-x86_64** (64-bit Windows Vista, Win7 or Win8) **ZIP** file in your Downloads folder, **right-click** it, and select the **Extract All** option from the menu, as is shown in Figure 1-5.

Also shown in Figure 1-5 are a number of the software packages that I use, downloaded and installed on my Android development workstation to bring it to a fully functioning content production workstation capability, for both Android (Java 6 and Eclipse) as well as HTML5 (Java 7 and NetBeans) work.

In the **Select a Destination and Extract Files** dialog shown in Figure 1-6, place your cursor before the adt-bundle-windows part of the file name and then backspace over the Downloads folder. We are doing this because we do not want to install our development environment in our Software Downloads folder but rather under an Android folder in our primary hard drive, which is designated as **C:\Android,** and thus a resulting installation folder path would be **C:\Android\adt-bundle-windows-x86_64** as shown in Figure 1-6. Once your installation folder has been specified, click the **Extract** button.

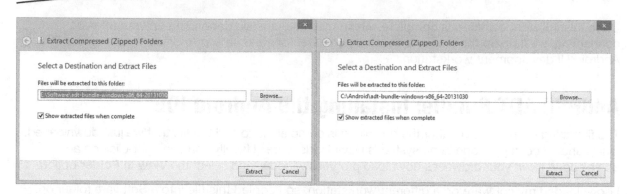

Figure 1-6. *Edit Install Folder to place it in the C:\Android\ folder that you created under your C:\ HDD root dir*

Once you click **Extract**, you will get a progress dialog, shown in Figure 1-7, showing 480+ megabytes of archived files being extracted into over 1000MB of data, spanning more than ten thousand items, in dozens of folders and subfolders.

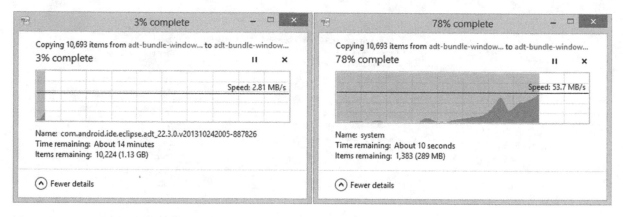

Figure 1-7. *Installing the Android ADT Bundle to your C:\Android\ folder showing progress dialog at 3% and 78%*

Once everything is extracted, which may take a little while depending on the data access (and write) speed of your hard disk drive and the computer processor speed as well, we'll be ready to create a **shortcut** for Eclipse.

Once this extraction process is completed, open your operating system file management utility; for Windows this would be called **Windows Explorer**, and is shown in use, in Figure 1-8. As you can see I have installed the latest Android OS 4.4 right next to the Android 4.2.2 OS that I used to write the *Pro Android Graphics* title earlier in 2013, as well as much of this title.

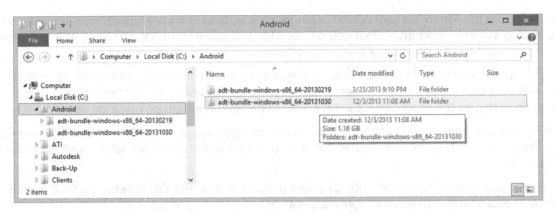

Figure 1-8. Showing the ADT Bundle for Android 4.4 (20131030) next to an ADT Bundle for OS 4.2.2 (20130219)

We need to locate our **adt-bundle-windows-x86_64-20131030** folder as well as its subfolders, in your root C:\Android\ hard disk drive in the left side of the Explorer utility, in the hard disk drive navigation pane.

Find your **eclipse** sub-folder where your application icon is located. This is located under your **adt-bundle-windows-x86_64-20131030** folder, and then click it. This shows the **contents** (files and sub-folders) for this particular folder, in your **file management pane**, located on the right side of your Windows Explorer (or other OS file management utility).

Find the **eclipse.exe** program **executable** file; it will have a **purple sphere** (program icon) on the left side of it, as shown in Figure 1-9. Right-click this eclipse executable file, and select the **Pin to Taskbar** option from the context sensitive menu, which is brought up via your right-click.

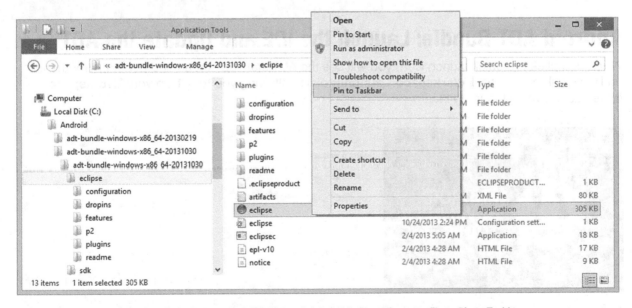

Figure 1-9. Find the C:\adt-bundle-windows install folder and right-click the eclipse.exe file to Pin to Taskbar

Once you select the Pin to Taskbar option, a single-click Eclipse software launch icon is installed on the operating system **Taskbar**, so that you can quickly and easily launch the Eclipse ADT software anytime you want to develop Android 4.4 applications.

It is important to note that we did not need to install quick launch icons (shortcuts) for Java 6u45, as the JDK that we installed exists underneath the other application development tools, and is not accessed directly, as the other open source software packages we are going to be installing are.

Java SE is a development environment infrastructure component, and is thus not directly accessed, or run, like Eclipse ADT or like other new media software development tools, which we'll be installing a bit later on.

We'll be creating launch icon short-cuts for these tools as well on our OS Taskbar so that we can quickly and easily launch them at a moment's notice!

Figure 1-10 shows a Windows Taskbar with your quick launch icons installed with key system utilities (Character Map, Calculator, Notepad, Explorer), as well as some of the apps that we are going to install in this chapter, including Eclipse ADT, Pencil, GIMP, Lightworks, Blender 3D, and Audacity (Digital Audio Editing). Why do you need audio for UI Design? You may want to create audio feedback effects for button click or app background music.

Figure 1-10. *Windows Taskbar shows the applications and utilities we are installing in this chapter*

Now we are ready to launch the Eclipse ADT IDE, and to make sure that we have all the very latest plug-ins, APIs, tools, and utilities installed.

Android ADT Bundle: Launch the IDE and Update the ADT

When you click the quick launch icon, you will see the ADT start-up screen and Loading Workbench progress bar, as well as a **Workspace Launcher** dialog allowing you to set-up your **\workspace** folder, as shown in Figure 1-11.

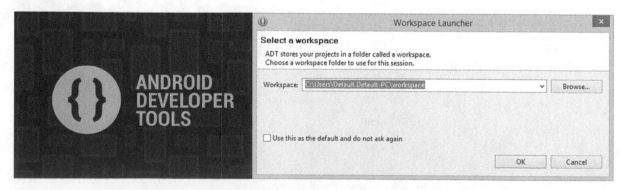

Figure 1-11. *Loading Android Developer Tools and the Workspace Launcher dialog showing Workspace folder*

On first launch Eclipse ADT may ask you for permission to use the software usage data to help them improve their product. I said Yes but you can also say No if you wish. When Eclipse starts for the first time, you will see a **Welcome!** screen, allowing you to create a **New Android Application** or to go through tutorials, such as Build Your First App, Design Your App, and Test Your App, as is shown in Figure 1-12.

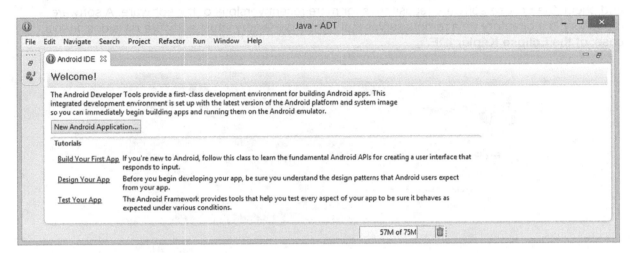

Figure 1-12. *On first launch of Eclipse ADT you will see a Welcome! screen which can be exited using the X icon*

Click the X (or cross) in the Android IDE tab, at the top of this Welcome! screen to close this and show the Eclipse ADT IDE, which is initially empty. Your IDE contains the functional panes, but no project files or data, as shown in Figure 1-13. The left pane is the **Package Explorer**, and is used for project hierarchy navigation, the middle pane is your **editing pane**, and the right pane is the **Outline** pane for getting a bird's-eye view of the project. The bottom pane contains Problems, Errors, and LogCat tabs.

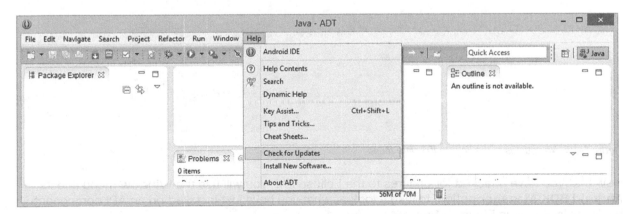

Figure 1-13. *Use the Eclipse ADT Help menu on first launch to Check for Updates to the IDE, plug-ins, API tools*

Once your Eclipse IDE has started up, select the **Help ➤ Check for Updates** menu sequence, as is also shown in Figure 1-13. This goes out over the Internet to the **Eclipse software repository** and checks for version updates.

It is important to note that for this to work properly, you must have an active connection to the Internet. If you do, Eclipse will open the **Contacting Software Sites** dialog, shown in Figure 1-14, and check the Eclipse software repositories for more recent versions of the software. A software repository is a directory on a remote server that contains the very latest software revisions, in this case, of the **Eclipse Kepler IDE**.

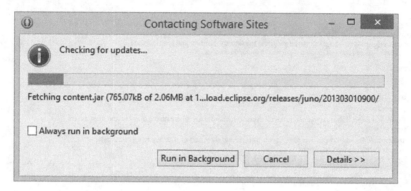

Figure 1-14. Checking for updates to the Eclipse Kepler IDE

In this case, we already have the latest version of Eclipse, which is to be expected, since we just downloaded and installed the ADT Bundle, and thus you should receive the **"No updates were found"** Information dialog.

This dialog can be seen in Figure 1-15, and informs you that no new updates for the Eclipse ADT IDE (Integrated Development Environment) have been found, which is to be expected, but we'll just make sure anyway!

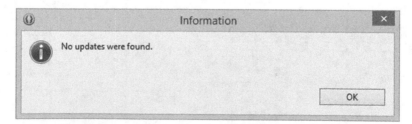

Figure 1-15. No updates to the Eclipse IDE were found

Now that you have checked for updates to the Eclipse IDE, you will use the **Window** menu and its **Android SDK Manager** option, to take a look at what you have just installed on an API component basis, as is shown in Figure 1-16.

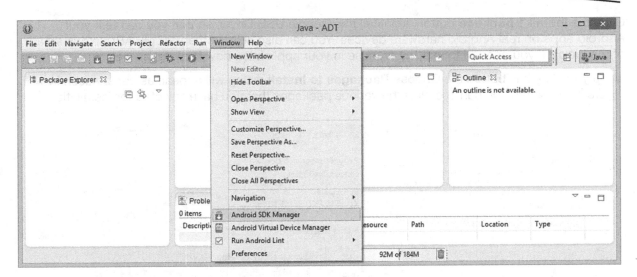

Figure 1-16. The Android SDK Manager, invoked using Window ➤ Android SDK Manager

Figure 1-17 shows this entire Android SDK Manager dialog, as well as the Eclipse-installed (default) check selection next to the **Google USB Driver**.

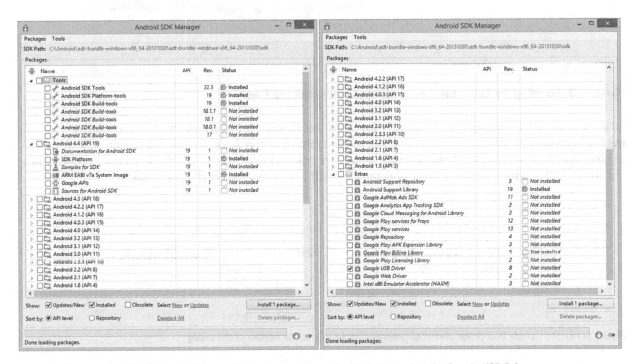

Figure 1-17. Android SDK Manager dialog and the components you just installed; select the Google USB Driver

Click the **Install 1 package** button, to install this Google USB Driver, so that you can test your Android apps on real Android hardware devices. You can also select other Google APIs in this area of the dialog if you needed to use any of these in your application development as well.

Once you click this button the **Choose Packages to Install** dialog will appear, as can be seen in Figure 1-18, where you can see all of the various packages that you have selected for installation.

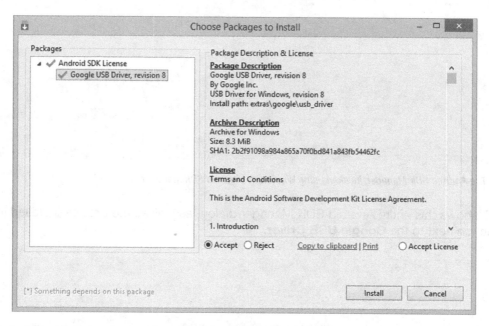

Figure 1-18. Accepting the license terms and conditions for the Google USB Driver

Once you click the **Accept** radio button to accept the **license agreement**, and then click the **Install** button, you will get the progress bar at the bottom of the Android SDK Manager dialog, shown in Figure 1-19, that shows which package is being downloaded, the revision, the percentage completed, the data transfer speed, and the time left until the download's completion.

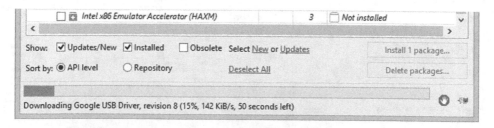

Figure 1-19. The Google USB Driver download progress bar located at the bottom of the dialog

Once the download of the Google USB Driver is complete, this progress bar will turn grey once more, and a **Done loading packages** message will appear.

Notice in Figure 1-20 that the Google USB Driver is now showing inside your Android SDK Manager dialog as being installed, and is also showing a version number (8) so that you know what version you have installed.

Figure 1-20. *Done loading packages message, and showing the Google USB Driver as Installed*

Now that you have Android ADT for KitKat 4.4 installed, let's install some other useful open source software packages that we may want to use during the book, and for your Android development endeavors in the future.

UI Wireframing Tool: Downloading and Installing Pencil

Since this is a Pro UI book, we'll download the leading open source user interface **wireframing tool**, called **Pencil 2.0.5,** as shown in Figure 1-21.

Figure 1-21. *Going to the pencil.evolus.vn website homepage to download Pencil 2.0.5 for Windows*

Go to **pencil.evolus.vn** or simply Google "Pencil Wireframe Tool," and click the orange download button on the homepage. Once the file is downloaded, launch the installer and review the license agreement as shown in Figure 1-22, and then click the **I Agree** button, to accept the licensing agreement. Then click the **Next ➤** button, and accept a default installation folder, by clicking on the **Next ➤** button again, in the third dialog.

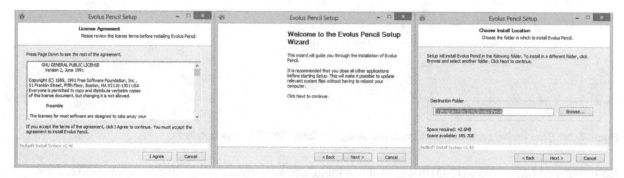

Figure 1-22. *Setting up Pencil 2.0.5; agree to the license agreement, choose installation location for the software*

Next accept the default Start Menu Folder and click the Install button, which brings up the installation progress dialog shown in Figure 1-23. If you want to see details regarding the install, click the Show Details button. When the installation is finished be sure that the **Launch Pencil** checkbox is checked and the software will launch so that you can make sure that it works on your system.

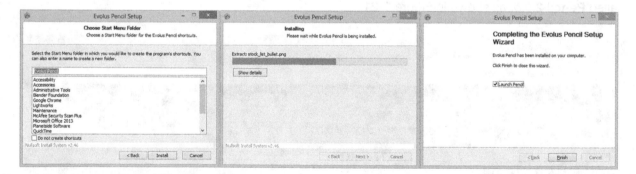

Figure 1-23. *Choosing your Start Menu Folder, Installing the software, Launch Pencil 2.0.5 to make sure it runs*

When the software launches, you should see a blank wireframe design area on the right side and several stacked palettes of wireframing tool icons on the left side of the screen, as shown in Figure 1-24.

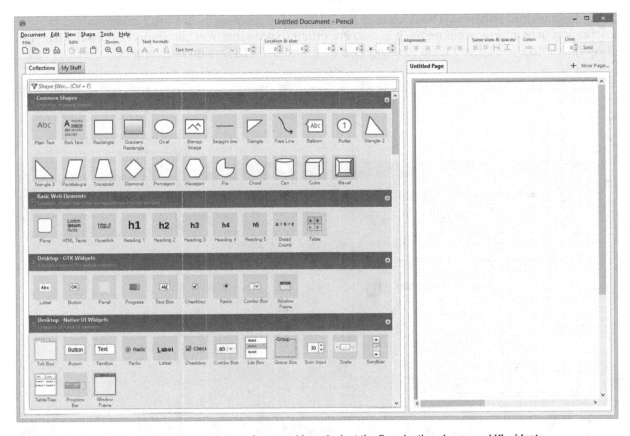

Figure 1-24. *Launching Pencil 2.0.5 to make sure it runs; taking a look at the flowcharting shapes and UI widgets*

The first section common shapes might be better suited for creating flow-charts than user interface designs, but there are some icons in that group that might be usable for basic UI Design. The second group is targeted at basic HTML website design UI elements, and the third section is targeted at UI design for Linux GTK desktop UI programmers. The fourth section is native UI design desktop widgets for OSes such as Windows and Macintosh.

Let's take a look at the user interface design widgets for the Android 4.0 ICS section of Pencil, before we exit the software and continue installing our other open source software packages that we will use for UI Design.

Grab the scrollbar handle, shown on the right side of the Pencil User Interface widget collections pane in Figure 1-24, and drag it halfway down to the center (or middle) of the slider bar range.

You will see the section come into view labeled **Mobile Android ICS** and that contains **Android 4.0 UI widgets**, which we will be using later on in the book in the chapter on UI design and wireframing techniques.

Currently, there are almost 80 different UI widgets we can drag and drop on the right side of the screen to prototype UI designs, as shown in Figure 1-25. We'll be learning about many of these UI widgets in Chapter 3 of this book on the View class, which is used to create subclasses in the android.widget package. These classes are instantiated as objects, are then implemented as functioning user interface elements. It is also important to note that you can import Android 3.0 style UI widgets into Pencil if you want to design via an Android 3.0 UI Design appearance.

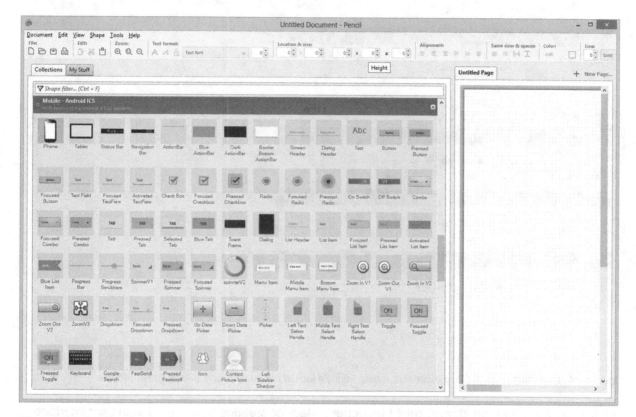

Figure 1-25.   Scrolling down to the Android 4.0 ICS Mobile UI Design widget section that we are going to utilize

Next we need to download and install the professional digital imaging software called GIMP 2.8.10, which is similar to the popular Photoshop digital imaging software package except that it's free for commercial use.

Digital Image Editing: Download and Install GIMP 2.8.10

Digital Image Editing software is important for Android development, as well as for User Inferface Design. The reason for this is that Android allows developers to integrate their own graphic elements into the Android widgets by referencing an image source, using a background image, or using an alpha value (transparency).

Alpha channels, which we'll be learning more about later, are an attribute of the UI element, which will allow digital image assets to "show through" the User Interface element. This allows a UI element to be integrated into the overall application's "User Experience" with 100% seamless results.

Open your browser and go to www.gimp.org. You are taken to the GIMP homepage, shown in Figure 1-26.

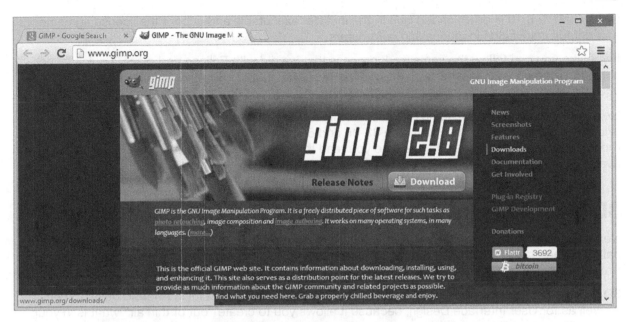

Figure 1-26. Go to the www.gimp.org website homepage, and click the Download button, or Downloads link

You could also use Google and the search term "GIMP 2" if you prefer. Once you're on the GIMP homepage you can then click on their Downloads link, or the Download button, to visit the Downloads page, as shown in Figure 1-27.

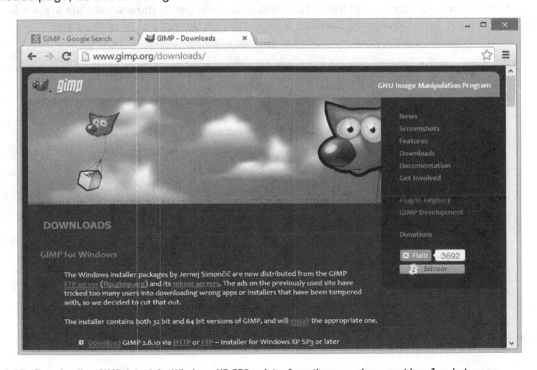

Figure 1-27. Downloading GIMP 2.8.10 for Windows XP SP3 or later from the www.gimp.org/downloads/ page

Once GIMP 2.8.10 is downloaded launch the installer executable and accept the license agreement and default installation locations and parameters.

If you like you can follow the same work process that we did with Eclipse and place a quick launch short-cut icon on your Taskbar by right-clicking the GIMP 2.8.10 icon, and selecting **Pin to Taskbar**. You can reposition launch icons by dragging them into any position you prefer on the Taskbar.

Next, let's go and get the leading open source 3D software, Blender 2.69, which is available for Windows, Linux, and Macintosh in both 32-bit and 64-bit versions. Blender updates its software monthly, and, for that reason, by the time you read this, version 2.70, or even 2.80, might be available!

3D Modeling and Animation: Download and Install Blender

Next we will need to download and install the professional 3D modeling and animation software called Blender 2.69, which is similar to the popular 3D software packages out there such as 3D Studio MAX, Maya, Cinema 4D, and Lightwave, except that it's completely free for commercial use.

3D modeling, design, rendering or animation software can be very useful in Android development, as well as for User Interface Design, because it allows you to create "out of thin air" what is in your head as a designer.

Since the Android OS allows developers to integrate their own UI graphics design elements into the Android OS, having a professional 3D tool such as Blender 3D 2.69 on your Android app development workstation is important.

Go to www.blender.org, or Google "Blender 3D," and when you get to the website (as shown in Figure 1-28), click the blue **Download Blender 2.69** button on the right side of the page.

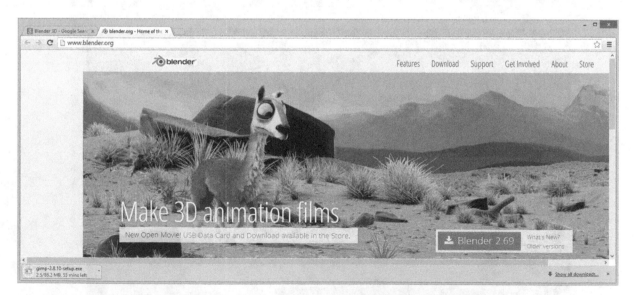

Figure 1-28. Going to the www.blender.org *website homepage, and then clicking on the blue Blender 2.69 button*

Once you do this you'll be taken to a "Download Blender" page, which has Blender versions for a plethora of different operating systems, including Windows, Macintosh, Linux, and Unix.

Since my operating system is Windows 8.1 64-bit, I downloaded the 64-bit version for Windows, as shown in Figure 1-29, at the bottom of the screenshot in the dark blue area.

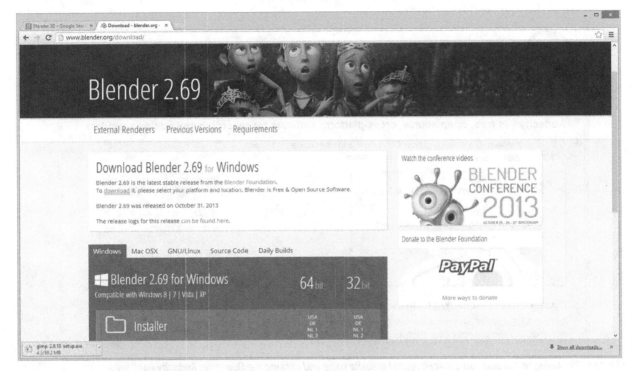

Figure 1-29. Downloading Blender 2.69 for Windows 64-bit or 32-bit from the www.blender.org/download/ *page*

I chose the .EXE installer version, because it was easier to install than a ZIP and smaller in filesize, resulting in a faster download.

Once your installer file has been downloaded, launch it, and install this impressive 3D software package, using its default settings.

If you like, you can follow the same work process that we did with Eclipse and place a quick launch shortcut icon on your Taskbar by right-clicking the Blender 2.69 icon and selecting Pin to Taskbar. You can reposition launch icons by dragging them into any position you prefer on the Taskbar.

Next, let's download the leading open source Digital Audio software package, Audacity 2.0.5, which is available for Windows, Macintosh, Linux, and other operating systems, in a 32-bit format version.

Digital Audio Editing: Downl oad and Install Audacity 2.0.5

The Audacity project is hosted on **sourceforge.net**, an open source software development website, which you might find extremely interesting, to search for software that interests you if you didn't know about the site already, that is!

To reach the Audacity project, go to the **audacity.sourceforge.net** URL, and you will see the **Download Audacity 2.0.5** link, shown in Figure 1-30.

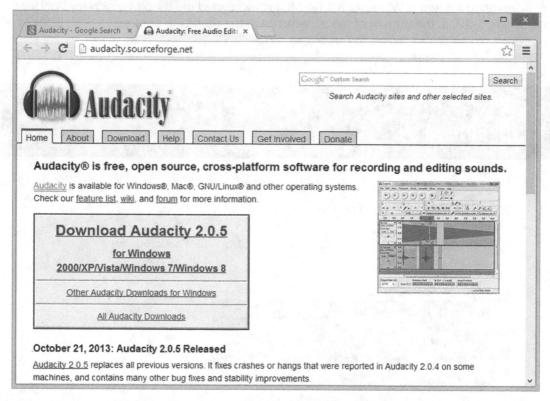

Figure 1-30.   Going to the audacity.sourceforge.net website page and clicking the Download Audacity link

Notice that the 32-bit Audacity supports decades-ancient operating systems such as Windows 2000, well over a decade old, and Windows XP, now almost a decade old. I am hoping that you are using either a Windows 7 or a Windows 8 operating system for your Android development workstations, as these newer two OSes, especially Windows 8.1, which at this point is now almost as memory efficient as Linux OSes are.

Once your Audacity installer file has been downloaded, you can launch it, and proceed to install this feature-filled digital audio editing software.

The first thing that it will ask you is in what language you want to run the software, I selected the default, English, as is shown in Figure 1-31.

Figure 1-31. *Selecting an installation language, starting the Audacity installation, reading the licensing agreement*

Then I clicked the Next button and read the information given and then I clicked the Next button again, accepted a default installation location, as shown in Figure 1-32, and Created a desktop icon, in the next dialog.

Figure 1-32. *Selecting Install Location, Creating a desktop icon and beginning the installation process*

Finally, I clicked **Install**, and got the **Installing** progress bar dialog, as shown in Figure 1-33, as well as more information regarding the Audacity project, and a final dialog where I could click the **Finish** button to exit the installer software. Now that Audacity 2.0 is installed, we can launch the software, and make sure that it's working on our system.

Figure 1-33. *Extracting installation files, reviewing open source information, finishing the install, and launching Audacity*

If you like you can follow the same work process that we did with Eclipse and place a quick launch short-cut icon on your Taskbar by right-clicking on the Audacity 2.0 icon and selecting Pin to Taskbar. You can reposition launch icons by dragging them into any position you prefer on the Taskbar.

Launch Audacity via your quick launch icon, or by double-clicking the icon on your desktop or in your Windows Explorer utility. You should see a new blank project screen, as shown in Figure 1-34, open up on your desktop. We will be using Audacity later on in the book to add sound effects to your Android UI element objects, such as your Buttons and ImageButton objects.

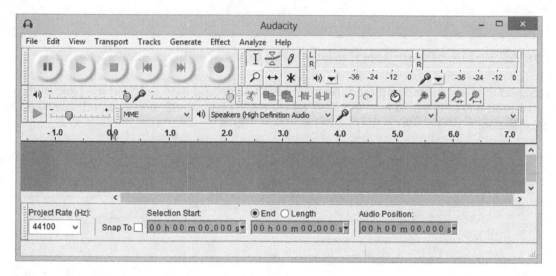

Figure 1-34. Launching Audacity 2.0.5 for Windows, to make sure that it will run properly on your workstation

Next, let's go and download the leading open source digital video software package, EditShare Lightworks 11.5, which is available for Windows, Linux, and Macintosh, in both 32-bit and 64-bit versions.

Digital Video Editing: Download and Install Lightworks 11.5

EditShare Lightworks used to be (expensive) paid digital video editing and special effects software, and to this day, it competes "head-to-head" with the leading digital video editing packages (FinalCutPro and AfterEffects).

You can find out more about this leading digital video editing FX software package on the EditShare website, at: www.editshare.com, or the Lightworks website, at www.lwks.com where you can also sign-up to get a copy of the software and then download it. When EditShare made Lightworks open source, it became the second free open source software (the first was Blender) to compete "feature-for-feature" with paid software in its genre.

Once you register on the Lightworks website, you can create a video editor profile for your company and log-in to download a copy of Lightworks 11.5 for your content development workstation that you are putting together in this chapter. Since Lightworks is such a valuable piece of software, you need to register to get it, which is fine with me, given that this software used to have a four-figure price tag.

Once you are signed-up as a proud Lightworks 11 user, you can click the **Downloads** button, shown in Figure 1-35, which is located at the top-right of the site menu, and you'll see all the different versions and documentation for the software. Click the Downloads button to initiate the download of the installer software, and once you download it, install it using the default settings, create a quick launch icon for it, and run it to make sure it is working properly with your system, as we've done with our other software.

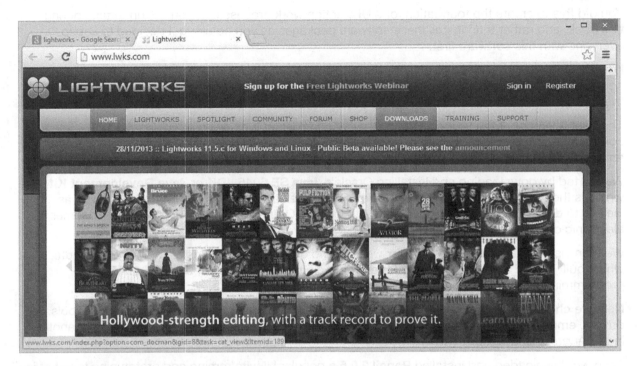

Figure 1-35. Downloading Lightworks 11.5 for Windows 32-bit or Windows 64-bit from the lwks.com *website*

Congratulations, you have assembled a professional grade Android Apps and New Media Content Development Workstation that you can now use to create Pro Android UI Designs and develop user experiences hitherbeforeto unseen!

In case you are wondering what additional open source software I have installed on my workstation besides these mainstays, I have Apache OpenOffice 4.1 (a business suite), Rosegarden (music composition and scoring), InkScape (vector illustration), POV Ray 3.7 (3D raytracing), TrueSpace (a 3D suite), and several of the DAZ products, such as Bryce 7.1, Hexagon 2.5, DAZ Studio Pro 4.6 (character modeling), and a plethora of open source utilities.

Summary

In this first chapter, you focused on setting up your 100% complete, Pro Android UI development workstation. From JavaSE 6, to Eclipse ADT, to UI prototyping and leading-edge new media content production tools, you have downloaded and installed the most impressive open source software packages that can be found anywhere on this planet.

You did this to create the foundation for a UI creation work process that you will undertake during this book, and rather than install these software packages as you go along, I decided to set up everyone with this software first.

I did this in case you wanted to explore some of the many features of these powerful, exciting, content production software packages, before actually using some of them during this book. I think that's only fair!

The best thing about the process was that we accomplished it by using open source, 100% free for commercial usage, and professional-level application software packages, which is pretty darned amazing, if you think about it.

We started by downloading and installing Oracle's **Java SE** 6u45 **JDK** or **Java Development Kit**, which is the Java 6 Programming Language's SDK. This Java JDK is required to run Eclipse, as well as to develop application software for the Android Operating System Platform for consumer electronic devices.

We then visited the **Android Developer** website and downloaded and installed the **ADT Bundle**, which built an **IDE** and **Android Developer Tools** plug-ins on top of our Java SE 6u45 JDK programming software development environment.

Next we **checked for updates** and updated our APIs and Android SDKs as well as various tools, drivers, emulators, and similar software packages, all of which will be used at some point or another in our Android UI development.

Then we downloaded and installed **Pencil 2.0.5** a popular UI wireframing and prototyping tool that is available for Windows, Linux, and Macintosh OSes.

Then we downloaded and installed **GIMP 2.8.10**, which is a powerful digital image editing package, available for Windows, Linux, and Macintosh OSes.

Next we downloaded and installed **Blender 2.69** a professional 3D modeling, rendering, and animation tool, available for Windows, Linux, and Mac OSes.

Then we downloaded and installed **Audacity 2.0.5** open source digital audio editing and sweetening tool available for the Windows, Linux, and Mac OSes.

Lastly we downloaded and installed **Lightworks 11.5,** an expensive digital video editing package recently made open source, and available for all the OSes.

In the next chapter, we'll learn about Android's **ViewGroup** Superclass, and how it is used to subclass and create **layout containers**, and we'll take a look at some of the types of layouts that we'll be using in our UI Design.

Chapter 2

Android UI Layouts: Layout Containers and the ViewGroup Class

In this second chapter, we will set-up our **Android Application Development Project**. Now that we have Eclipse ADT installed, along with Java SE 6, and a plethora of impressive open source new media design and content creation software packages, which would make anyone envious, we're ready to code!

One of the things that Eclipse sets up for us when we create a new Android project, using the Eclipse **New Android Project** creation series of dialogs, which we will master during this chapter, is an Android **layout container**.

Android layout containers are a central and key concept for UI Design within Android. The foundation for every layout container class that is in Android, and there are a dozen or more, is the **ViewGroup** Superclass.

For this reason, we dedicate one of our early foundational chapters to this ViewGroup Superclass, just to make sure you have all your basic knowledge regarding it.

While we are at it, we will get some practice in using one of the popular layout container classes (a ViewGroup subclass) in Android, called the **RelativeLayout** container.

We will see exactly how everything is set up in Android using **XML mark-up,** which we cover in this chapter, as well as Java programming logic, which we cover during the next two chapters, so we can focus on XML mark-up here.

In this way, we can learn about XML layout containers and get some work in creating the foundation for our **pro.android.ui** package, and **UserInterface** application, which we're going to create and expand as this book unfolds.

Layout Containers: Using XML for Tag-based UI Design

In Android, the majority of your User Interface, or UI, Design is created using **XML mark-up**. For this reason, during this book, you will be getting very familiar with this XML, or **eXtensible Markup Language**, and its **naming schema**, along with all its **tags** and **parameters** that allow you to define and customize your user interfaces to any desired level of complexity.

XML tags are used to define both the layout container, as well as the user interface elements, which Android calls **widgets**, which exist inside the layout container. Widgets are subclassed from the Android View Superclass, and we cover this View Superclass and its widget subclasses in the next chapter of this book, so no worries about covering UI elements!

Since widgets exist **inside of** layout containers, I had to put this chapter first. Also, since widgets always exist inside of a layout container, this makes widgets "**children**" of their "**parent**" layout containers. Android even has "**tweens**," but let's save that for the chapter on procedural animation.

In Android, we thereby use **parent tags** to define our layout container, and **child tags** to populate that layout container with user interface widgets.

A layout container tag can be a child tag if you create complex UI layouts by **nesting** layout container tags. There are many different types of layout container classes, however, so, you should never have to use nested layout containers. Nested layout containers generally use more system memory than using a single layout container. That's why this book focuses on how to design a UI efficiently and effectively by using a single layout container for your user interface design.

UI Design in Android starts with the UI layout container, and this is the reason this book is "layout container centric" in its approach to developing optimal UI designs, and is not "widget centric," as other UI design books might be. UI design is about how things are laid out, not the contents of what is inside that layout, although we will be covering those pesky little widgets as well, but only as a secondary level consideration.

Let's get back to our discussion regarding tags. In each of your XML files that define a UI layout, or anything else for that matter, such as image button states or animation parameters or value constants, the outermost parent tag must have a reference to the XML namespace, which in Android is represented by the xmlns:android parameter, which stands for XML name space.

This tag contains an HTTP reference to the server that contains all the tag definitions, so Eclipse can **validate** your tags as you use them in your XML mark-up. The parameter looks like this in a LinearLayout:

```
<LinearLayout xmlns:android="http://schemas.android.com/apk/res/android" >
```

The XML naming schemas are kept at a **schemas.android.com** virtual server in a folder structure that starts with **apk** (Android Package), with a **res** (resource) subfolder, and an **android** sub-subfolder with the XML schema.

Using Parameters: Refining and Customizing the UI Tags

Inside your XML tags, it is possible to define **parameters**, also called: **properties**, or **attributes**. As seen in the previous section with the **xmlns:android** parameter, parameters live inside every parent and child tag, in every XML file that is defined within an Android application.

If the xmlns:android parameter is not included in your parent tag, each of your child tags will be have a **wavy red underline** underneath it, which, in Eclipse, signifies that there is an error somewhere in your editing pane.

Besides the **xmlns:android** and **xmlns:tools** repository reference parameters, which live in your parent tag, most Android parameters are prefaced using **android:** not xmlns. In fact, the xmlns:android is the reason for this, as the xmlns:android actually **defines** what the android: that prefaces every parameter needs to equate to (expand to).

In the previous section we saw that xmlns:android was set to reference the `http://schemas.android.com/apk/res/android` **schema referencing path**, and so every time you see a parameter that starts with an android: it's short for **http://schemas.android.com/apk/res/android:** so that if you want to use the **android:id** parameter you can just write **android:id="@+id/myId"** instead of:

```
http://schemas.android.com/apk/res/android:id="@+id/myId"
```

This can save a lot of time and effort! And that's all that's really going on here, nothing mysterious or complicated, simply XML referencing back to a centralized XML naming schema definition repository that lives on Google Android's repository server in a virtual URL called: **schemas.android.com**.

As we go through development in this book using Eclipse I am going to show you all the tricks in the Eclipse IDE XML editing pane, such as typing the **android:** inside any tag, to get a **pop-up helper dialog** containing every possible parameter that can be utilized with that particular tag.

I will show you some other Eclipse tricks as well along the way, which can make exploring Android development easier and more enjoyable. I'll do this more during the earlier chapters, just to make sure everyone has a similar knowledge base regarding the optimal work process to take developing apps.

Parameters allow you to **fine-tune** and **configure** your UI tags to do exactly what you want them to do, which is important when designing user interface elements that contain IDs, fonts, text, graphics, size parameters, layout parameters, digital image asset references, and so on.

Android has dozens of layout containers, hundreds of widgets, and thousands of parameters, so certainly we are not going to cover this in a section of a chapter introducing layout containers, but rather over the duration of a book that contains more than a dozen in-depth chapters on Pro Android UI design.

So, let's get right into some technical jargon and Java class hierarchies.

Android ViewGroup: Our Layout Container's Superclass

The foundation for our UI design in Android is the layout container, and the foundation for layout container classes for Android is the **ViewGroup** class. I like to call it a Superclass, as it is utilized to create layout container classes, but is not used directly, unless you are creating your own customized layout container subclasses.

Fortunately with dozens of custom layout container classes already part of the Android API, all that work has been done already, and you can focus on developing your applications and on the UI design and user experience.

The ViewGroup class is a subclass of the Android **View** class, also a Superclass and used to create UI elements, or widgets, which we will cover in detail in our widget chapter (Chapter Three). View was used to create ViewGroup because certain **properties** of View need to be **inherited** by the ViewGroup subclass.

Since a View (class or constructed object) needs to be a Java **Object** that class is a subclass of the **java.lang.Object** Superclass, or, as I prefer to call it, the Java Object Masterclass. Thus, the hierarchy of ViewGroup is

```
java.lang.Object
  > android.view.View
    > android.view.ViewGroup
```

So View objects inherit all the properties that a Java Object can have, and a ViewGroup inherits all those Object properties, plus properties that have been added via the View class definition. Java is structured and logical!

The ViewGroup has two **nested classes** that encapsulate and handle two very important layout functions: **layout parameters** and **margins**. We discuss details regarding each of these nested classes in the next two sections of this chapter. There is one Java **interface** in the ViewGroup class called an **OnHierarchyChangeListener** that "listens" for hierarchy changes within the ViewGroup, and allows developers to implement their own Java program logic for when this occurs.

The **direct subclasses** of ViewGroup that we are going to cover in this book include **LinearLayout** (Chapter 12), **RelativeLayout** (Chapter 13), **FrameLayout** (Chapter 11), **GridLayout** (Chapter 14), **DrawerLayout** (Chapter 15), **ViewPager** (Chapter 17), **PagerTitleStrip** (Chapter 18), and **SlidingPaneLayout** (Chapter 16).

As you can see, we're going to take a logical, top-down approach, learning about direct subclasses of ViewGroup first, and we'll do it in their order of complexity and popularity (most often implemented to least implemented) so that we are always building on knowledge gained in a previous chapter.

There are also **indirect subclasses** of ViewGroup, which are just subclasses of direct subclasses, or **two class levels down** from ViewGroup, which we are going to cover in the book as well, spanning Chapter 11 through Chapter 18 We'll also get into even more advanced UI design using the ActionBar and Fragment classes.

ViewGroup.LayoutParams: Nested Class Controls Layout

Since we're covering all the viable ViewGroup subclasses during this book, we'll focus here on those characteristics of the ViewGroup class that are inherited by the layout container subclasses, since these are the UI layout classes we'll actually be implementing during this book.

The most important of these characteristics are those that relate to how the layout container acts relative to the parent View screen above it and to the child View widget below it. This is handled via **LayoutParams nested classes** in Android, which is short for, you guessed it: layout parameters.

This class contains two XML **attributes** (I like to call them **parameters**) or **properties** called **android:layout_width** and **android:layout_height,** which are **required** for every View (and thus ViewGroup) object that you define using XML mark-up inside a UI layout container screen definition XML file.

The class contains three **constants. FILL_PARENT** is **deprecated** and not in use anymore since API Level 8. **MATCH_PARENT** replaced it, and is used since API Level 8. What the FILL_PARENT or MATCH_PARENT do is tell the current View object to FILL or MATCH the PARENT View object's layout dimensions. If the parent tag is the layout container, and its tag specifies both the parameters: **android:layout_width="MATCH_PARENT"** as well as **android:layout_height="MATCH_PARENT",** then your UI design will fill the screen itself, minus any of the Android OS UI elements, that is!

You may be wondering, which of these two constants should I use? The answer is **MATCH_PARENT**. One of the things that the **Android Support Library** (which we upgraded to version 19 during Chapter 1) does is to watch for and change things like this automatically, so that your API Level 19 XML mark-up works Pre API Level 8, at least as far as this constant declaration goes.

The third constant is called **WRAP_CONTENT,** and It does the **exact opposite** of the MATCH_ PARENT constant, in that instead of expanding the View object boundaries (container) to fit what is above it (its parent), it **contracts** (**wraps**) around the child object below it, that is, around the current View object's **content** (what is inside your UI element container View itself).

Layout parameters are generally set in your XML UI definition, which would be termed **static** layout parameter settings. You can also use Java to set a layout parameter **dynamically** using the **Public Constructor** for the class, a **ViewGroup.LayoutParams(int width, int height)** line of Java would do this.

The ViewGroup class also has a **Public Method** called **resolveLayoutDirection**, which takes the format resolveLayoutDirection(int layoutDirection) and has two constants **LAYOUT_DIRECTION_ LTR** or **LAYOUT_DIRECTION_RTL**. LTR stands for **Left To Right**, and RTL stands for **Right To Left**. RTL support was recently added in Android 4.2 JellyBean, and thus this Public Method may not yet be implemented in many layout container subclasses. If it is, we will cover it in each layout container subclass specific chapter where it is supported.

ViewGroup.MarginLayoutParams: Nested Class for Margin

The ViewGroup.MarginLayoutParams is the second nested class in ViewGroup and this nested class is a subclass of the ViewGroup.LayoutParams nested class, which is itself a subclass of the java. lang.Object Superclass.

Just because a class is annotated as ViewGroup.LayoutParams does not mean that it is a subclass of ViewGroup, because it is actually a subclass of java.lang.Object, and not a subclass of ViewGroup. Rather it is a nested class within ViewGroup. The class hierarchy for these nested classes is

```
java.lang.Object
  > android.view.ViewGroup.LayoutParams
    > android.view.ViewGroup.MarginLayoutParams
```

This class contains six XML **attributes** (I like to call them **parameters**) or **properties** called **android:layout_marginBottom** and **android:layout_marginTop,** as well as **android:layout_ marginLeft** or **android:layout_marginStart,** and **android:layout_marginRight** or **android:layout_ marginEnd** for each side.

With the **.resolveLayoutDirection()** method we learned about in the previous section, and the **RTL support** added in Android 4.2 you may want to start to use **marginStart** and **marginEnd** parameters, rather than using marginLeft and marginRight. UI designers need to do this as of Android 4.2, so that their UI designs can seamlessly **"mirror,"** when the newly supported RTL languages such as **Arabic**, **Persian**, **Hebrew**, **Yiddish**, **Farsi**, **Urdu**, **Chinese,** or **Japanese** are utilized by your Android application end-users.

The class defines none of its own constants, but as a subclass it inherits the LayoutParams constants and attributes. It does contain 4 **data fields**, including: **bottomMargin**, **leftMargin**, **rightMargin,** and **topMargin**.

Margin parameters are generally set in your XML UI definition, which would be termed **static** margin parameter settings. You can also use Java to set a margin parameter **dynamically** using one of the nine **Public Methods** for this class. There are **getLayoutDirection()** and **setLayoutDirection()** methods, as well as **setMarginStart()** and **getMarginStart()**, and matching **setMarginEnd()** and **getMarginEnd()** methods. All these relate to this new **RTL capability** that has been added to Android 4.2, and are used to determine which layout direction is being used, and to get and set the **marginLeft** and **marginRight** data fields to the appropriate values (i.e., swap the values if RTL becomes LTR) when .resolveLayoutDirection() implements a layout direction change.

The primary method is **setMargins(int left, int top, int right, int bottom)** which takes **integer values** specified in **pixels**, and an **.isMarginRelative()** method that equates to **true** if you are using **marginStart** and **marginEnd** to define your margins, which as of Android 4.2, you should be.

The ninth public method is the **.resolveLayoutDirection()** method which will be called by the **requestLayout()** method, which is a public method of View.

The Difference Between Margins and Padding Parameters

There are actually two different parameters for adding spacing around a UI element or within or around a layout container. We first looked at **margins** in the previous section, because the **MarginLayoutParams** nested class is an integral part of the ViewGroup Superclass, enhancing its layout containing functionality. Margins aren't the only way we can control layout spacing.

The other important parameters for controlling UI spacing are the **padding** parameters. The padding parameters are not defined in the ViewGroup class, but rather are **inherited** from the **View** Superclass, which means that widget View subclasses cannot have margins, and only have padding parameters.

Since the ViewGroup class has been subclassed from the View class, it has access to the padding parameters it inherits from the View class, as well as the margin parameters, which it defines one level down in the ViewGroup class. This means that Android wishes to give layout containers access to both margins and padding, and UI widgets will only have access to padding.

You might be wondering why margins were not defined at the View Superclass level, are excluded from utilization by UI widgets (View objects), and are only included as a part of the ViewGroup classes (layout container subclasses can obviously inherit the layout_margin parameters). The reason for this is because margins control spacing on the **outside** of a View container, and leave the View container (inside) dimensions intact, whereas a padding parameter places the specified spacing on the **inside** of that View container, and thus pushes the boundaries of that View container outward. This is true whether or not you can see the boundaries for your View container; sometimes, you just have to imagine what is happening to the boundary of your View (widget) container.

Later in this chapter when we create an initial **pro.android.ui** package and **UserInterface** project, I'll make sure to add a few parameters here and there to the View widgets that we use to get you familiar with XML mark-up that provides a visual demonstration of the difference between the two types of UI layout spacing parameters.

This difference between margins and padding and when to use either of them is far more important than you might be thinking that it is at this point. This is because Android UI layout designs must support many different sizes and shapes of Android devices. One of the "low-level" ways this can be achieved optimally is by using margins and padding together in a way that allows your UI design to "morph" to fit its layout container.

An entire chapter in this book describes how to design alternate layouts. This is because of the widely disparate types of Android devices currently on the market—from watches to iTVs to tablets of all sizes to smartphones of every resolution. One of the major challenges I have as author for this book is conveying the proper work process to achieve layout independence.

Next we will take a look at the **LayoutAnimationController** class that allows you to animate your UI using the ViewGroup subclass layout container with the Android **Animation** class. We'll cover animation in detail here in the book and use this class to animate some UI widgets.

Animating Your ViewGroup: LayoutAnimationController

You might be wondering if there's a way to animate the UI layout container contents. There is indeed, and even though we won't be covering animation in depth in this book, I will go over the **LayoutAnimationController** class in this chapter, because it relates to ViewGroups directly, and I want to give you a comprehensive overview here, including everything that's connected with (related to) a ViewGroup class. If you want to get into animation at a much greater depth, check out the Apress Pro Android Graphics book title.

A layout animation controller is used to animate the layout container, or a ViewGroup object's child View widgets. It does this by referencing your Animation class XML definition, which I have an entire chapter dedicated to in the Apress Pro Android Graphics book.

Each of your layout child View widgets executes the same XML animation instruction definition as to how you want the widgets to animate. What is cool about this class is that for every one of these widgets, you can have the animation start at a different time offset.

This LayoutAnimationController class is utilized by a ViewGroup to compute the delays by which each child View widget's animation starting times need to be offset. The delay value is computed by using characteristics of each child, such as its index position within your ViewGroup layout container.

The standard implementation of a LayoutAnimationController class computes your delay by multiplying a specified amount of milliseconds by the index value of the child View widget in its parent ViewGroup layout container.

If you wanted to implement your own customized way of computing this delay value, you would subclass the LayoutAnimationController class and override the .**getDelayForView(android.view. View)** method, replacing its Java program logic with your own delay value generation algorithm.

For example, the LayoutAnimationController already has one **direct subclass** that has already been created for you; this **GridLayoutAnimationController** class computes delay values based on the column and row indices of the child View widget in its parent ViewGroup.

The LayoutAnimationController class has one nested class, which is called: **AnimationParameters** and contains the information that is utilized to compute animation delays for child View widget. There are four XML attributes, including **android:delay** to specify the delay value, **android:animation** to specify the animation definition XML file reference, **android:interpolator** to specify types of motion interpolation to use, and **android:animationOrder** to specify the order in which the animation is applied.

The class has three **AnimationOrder constants**, which can be used with your **android:animationOrder** XML parameter. The constants include: **ORDER_NORMAL**, **ORDER_ RANDOM,** and **ORDER_REVERSE**.

I cover the Android Animation class and procedural animation in the Pro Android Graphics book, where I'll make sure to show you how to define and reference this animation XML file and utilize LayoutAnimationController to animate your UI elements.

Now it's time to get into some real hands-on XML mark-up and create our UserInterface project, which we will build on during the book and turn into a full-fledged Android application. So let's fire up Eclipse and start our journey to creating a Pro Android UI application!

Create a UserInterface Project and pro.android.ui Package

Use the quick launch icon on your taskbar that you created in Chapter 1, and launch Eclipse ADT, right-click under the Package Explorer tab, and click **New** menu, and then click **Android Application Project** from the fly-out sub-menu sequence, as shown in Figure 2-1. You can ignore (pretend that it is not there at all) the GraphicsDesign (closed) folder in Figure 2-1 as it is from another book that I was writing prior to this one called *Pro Android Graphics*. The book would actually be a good companion to this one if you plan on creating custom graphic design elements for your Pro Android UI designs.

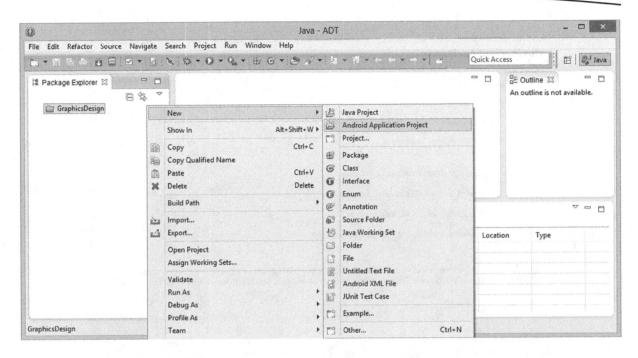

Figure 2-1. Right-click and select the New ➤ Android Application Project menu sequence to create a new project

Once you invoke this menu sequence, it brings up a series of dialogs. Each of these dialogs implements a functional area that sets-up different aspects of your application bootstrap that Eclipse will create for you once you are finished with the series of dialogs.

The New Android Application Dialog

The first dialog is named after the menu command New Android Application, and it allows you to name your Application (Project) and Package, as shown in Figure 2-2. When you type in the **Application Name**, the dialog will then mirror-type the Project Name for you automatically. I took this to signify that Android (Eclipse ADT) wants the Application Name and the Project Name to be the same. Since this is the Pro Android UI book, I decided that User Interface would be a logical name for the application, and since the space character is not allowed, I used **CamelCase** and I named it **UserInterface**.

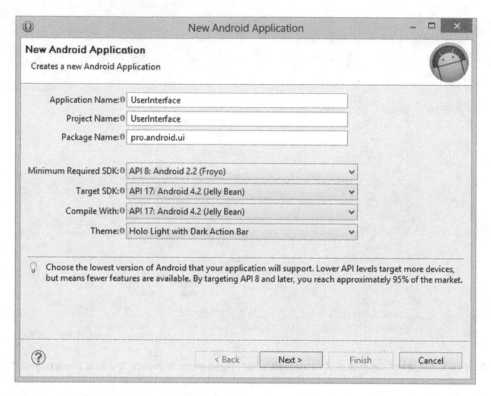

Figure 2-2. Naming our project UserInterface and our package pro.android.ui

Next I named the Java package after the book **pro.android.ui**, in all lowercase, as is the convention for package names.

The next section in the middle of this dialog features four drop-down menu selectors. The first three list all the Android API Level selections, and a fourth one lists all the existing Android OS themes.

We will use the default (suggested) **API Level 8 Froyo Android OS 2.2** for a **Minimum Required SDK** specification as that will give us a **95% market share** coverage, and support devices manufactured several years ago in product age.

Next, for our **Target SDK**, we'll select the latest **API Level 17 Jelly Bean Android OS 4.2.2** so that we are using the latest software currently available for UI development in this book. If a later version of Android has come out since this book has been published, you can use the Android version if you wish. There have been no UI class changes between 4.2.2 and 4.3.1 and 4.4.2 so you can use any of these with the same result. The majority of the 4.3 and 4.4 OS additions were performance enhancements and cloud-based service additions which could be said to be "user-facing" and not developer-facing (API) enhancements.

We also want to **Compile With** the latest API software, so we'll also select **Level 17** or later from the third drop-down selector.

Finally, we will also use the default Theme **Holo Light with Dark Action Bar** as we can always change this later and it's the theme that matches API 17 or later.

New Android Application – Configure Project Dialog

Once you click **Next** you'll get the second dialog in the series, which is the **Configure Project** dialog, as shown in Figure 2-3. We are going to accept the suggested (default) settings in this dialog as well.

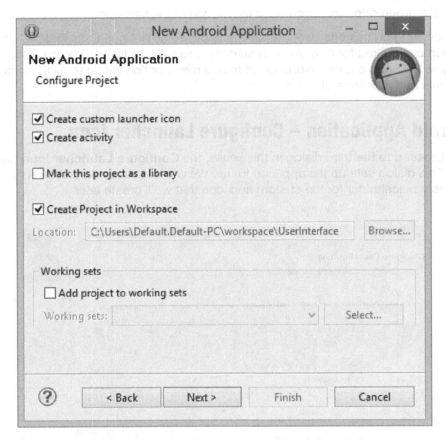

Figure 2-3. New Android Application Configure Project dialog

We want to **Create a custom launcher icon** to use as a placeholder, until we design and implement our own custom application launcher icon, so we will leave that option checked.

We definitely want to **Create an Activity** because that is what holds our Java code and **inflates** our XML UI layout definitions, so we will want to leave that option checked as well.

We do not need to **Mark this project as a library,** because it is not a part of a larger project with multiple libraries, but is rather its own self-contained (single) library, in its own (single) application package.

You can always convert your existing application project into a library at any time if you wish. To do so, you would open a **Properties** dialog for the project, and select the **is Library** checkbox, and the code you had written so far would then become a library in a larger application project that spans more than one code library.

Next make sure the **Create Project in Workspace** checkbox is selected, as we want this project to open up in Eclipse once we create it so we can start to learn about View, ViewGroup, and XML mark-up for UI design.

Finally, be sure to leave the **Add project to working sets** option unchecked since we are not using **working sets** for this Android Development project.

A working set is a group of projects you want to work on at the same time.

Since we are focusing on this one UserInterface project, we do not need this feature, so we can leave this option unchecked for now. As with Mark the project as a library, you can also go back later on inside Eclipse ADT and create a working set from a menu option within the IDE, so no worries about setting this option incorrectly here.

New Android Application – Configure Launcher Icon

Click **Next** to proceed to the third dialog in this series, the **Configure Launcher Icon** dialog, shown in Figure 2-4. This dialog sets up the app icon for us. We will let Eclipse do this for us as we need an icon to serve as a placeholder for the custom app icon that we'll create later.

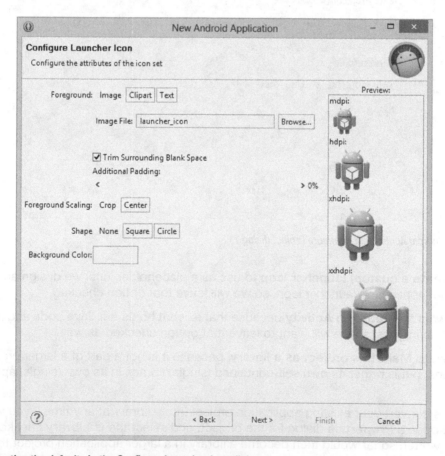

Figure 2-4. Accepting the defaults in the Configure Launcher Icon dialog

As you can see in Figure 2-4, if you have your application's icon designed already, you can specify it via this **Image File** field, but since we do not have ours created yet, I'm going to leave the **launcher_icon** file that is a default for this dialog in place until we talk about icons and images at a later time in this book.

There are also optional buttons to use **Clipart** and **Text** as the application icon. Since this is your application brand I suggest using digital imagery as it gives you the most opportunity to create the greatest visual impact, which is a lot of what this book is all about.

There are also options to **Trim Surrounding Blank Space** or **Add Padding** (the opposite of Trim Surrounding Blank Space) if you want Eclipse ADT to do this for you, personally I advocate using professional software such as GIMP 2.8.10 to do these work processes, which we will look at later on in the book.

Leave Foreground Scaling set as is and set Shape to none as we are using an alpha channel (pixel transparency) for our icon as Eclipse ADT is doing here, with its supplied graphic. We learn about alphas later when we cover digital imaging new media. Leave the background color swatch as is as well and click Next to proceed.

New Android Application – Create Activity Dialog

The fourth dialog in this series is the **Create Activity** dialog, which is shown in Figure 2-5. In this dialog, we tell Eclipse ADT that we want it to create some "bootstrap" Java code and XML mark-up for us to use for our Main Application Activity subclass. So leave this **Create Activity** checkbox selected, and select Blank Activity from the center selection area, as we want to learn by creating our own Activity UI designs within this book.

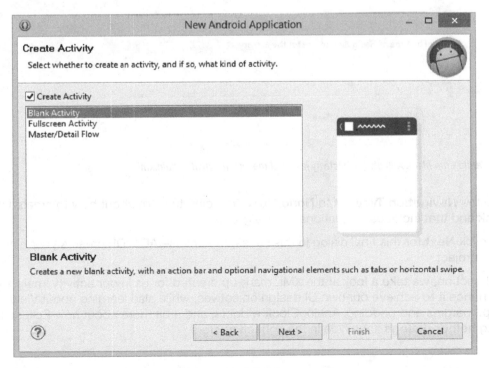

Figure 2-5. Using the Create Activity dialog to create a new blank Activity

Once you click **Next**, you will be taken to the fifth dialog in the series, the Blank Activity dialog, where we can name our Activity subclass Java and XML files.

New Android Application – Blank Activity Dialog

Let's name our Java Activity subclass MainActivity.java since it is the primary (main) Activity for our application and we name the XML file activity_main.xml using the naming convention suggested by Android, as shown in Figure 2-6.

Figure 2-6. Naming the blank Activity MainActivity.java and the layout activity_main.xml

We'll leave the **Navigation Type** set to **None**, as we're going to learn about how to create UI designs in this book and that includes navigational UI design.

Once you click **Next** for this final dialog in this series, the Eclipse ADT IDE creates your new Android application project.

In the next section, we take a look at the XML mark-up created for us in our activity_main.xml file and enhance it to achieve our own UI design objectives, while also learning about View and ViewGroup, margins and padding, AnalogClock widgets, and a bit more about how Eclipse helps us by showing **helper dialogs** if we type in the right characters.

ViewGroup XML Attributes: Configuring the RelativeLayout

Let's take a look now at what we have in the Eclipse IDE by looking in the **Package Explorer** pane on the left side of the IDE, as shown in Figure 2-7.

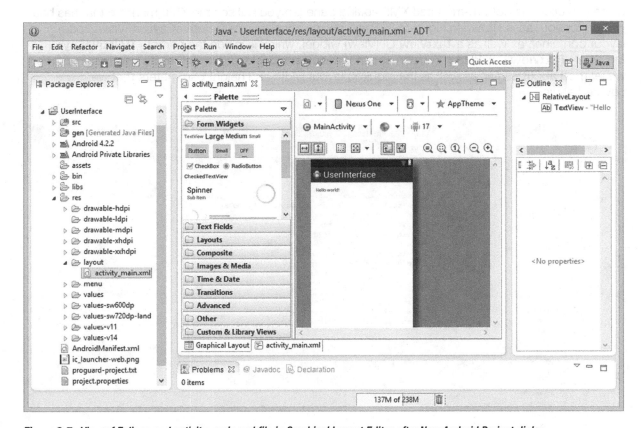

Figure 2-7. View of Eclipse and activity_main.xml file in Graphical Layout Editor after New Android Project dialog

As you can see, we now have a plethora of subfolders and files, an entire project in fact, created for us in Eclipse under the UserInterface folder.

Our Java code is in the **/src** (source code) folder and our new media assets and XML files are in the **/res** (resources) folder. UI layouts are held in a subfolder called **/res/layout**, and, as you can see, a newly created XML UI definition file that we named **activity_main.xml** is in this folder, waiting for us to edit it, which we are going to do next.

As you can see in Figure 2-7, Eclipse ADT opens up your **activity_main.xml** file for you first, assuming (correctly) that you will want to tweak your UI design. It also opens up the XML mark-up in the **Graphical Layout Editor**, which provides a preview of how the mark-up will render, and allows you to do UI editing by using a drag-and-drop visual environment, if you want to design visually instead of using XML mark-up.

Since this is a Pro Android UI book, we will be using the Graphical Layout Editor (GLE) to preview our XML mark-up, but we will be working primarily in the XML editing pane, which is accessed by clicking the bottom tab, shown in Figure 2-7 and labeled activity_main.xml. Click it to bring up your XML mark-up for this UI layout container that was generated for us.

Once you click the bottom-mounted XML editing pane tab you will see the XML mark-up that has been written for you, as is shown in Figure 2-8. The mark-up consists of a **RelativeLayout** (ViewGroup) layout container, as well as a **TextView** UI (View) widget, which is inside the parent **<RelativeLayout>** tag as a **<TextView>** child tag. You can see those **xmlns:android** and **xmlns:tools** parameters that we learned about earlier, as well as the required layout width and height parameters that we covered earlier.

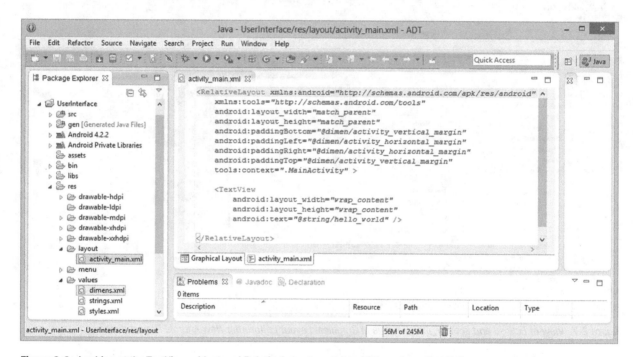

Figure 2-8. *Looking at the TextView widget and RelativeLayout container XML mark-up that Eclipse wrote for us*

After those lines of XML mark-up, there are four **android:padding** parameters that reference presets in the **dimens.xml** file, which is located in the /res folder in a subfolder called **/values**, which contains three XML constants files **dimens.xml**, **strings.xml,** and **styles.xml**. These files contain your app constants that are used for your app in a centralized locale, so constant values for dimensions, text strings, and styles can be more easily changed.

The final line of mark-up uses the **tools:context** parameter obtained using the xmlns:tools reference and sets the context for the activity_main.xml file to point back to the MainActivity.java file, which as we will see in the next chapter also references this activity_main.xml file in Java code, so, essentially, the Java and the XML files will be "wired together."

As you can see from the indentation of the XML mark-up that I have used, and which Eclipse will do automatically for you, as you will soon learn, there is a **TextView** child tag UI widget, which is a View subclass object, inside of this RelativeLayout parent layout container tag.

So a <RelativeLayout> tag has its parameters specified in its **opening tag**, which as you can see ends with a > character, and underneath (surrounding) the nested <TextView> child tag is the **</RelativeLayout>** closing tag.

The TextView tag uses a different format, as it does not need to contain a child tag, but is the child tag, so, it uses the **/>** alternate format for its closing tag. This format is used for tags that have no nested child tags, but need to contain configuration parameters, as a widget (View) object always has due to a layout_width and layout_height parameter requirement, which we learned about earlier, and will revisit throughout this book.

As you can see our TextView specified the **WRAP_CONTENT** constant for both these required layout parameters, and as you can see in Figure 2-8, the constants can be written in uppercase or lowercase, it's your choice. We also have an **android:text** parameter, which references a **strings.xml** file.

The way that you reference a strings.xml file **<string>** tag text constant definition is to drop the "s" from the strings.xml and preface it with an @ symbol, so a **<string>** constant named **hello_world** would be referenced as **@string/hello_world.** We edit this value a bit later on, so that you can see exactly how this referencing actually works.

Let's add an **ID** to this RelativeLayout so that if we want to reference and instantiate it as an object in our Java code in MainActivity.java, we can. This is done via the **android:id** parameter, and here is a cool trick so you can see all the parameters that are available to a RelativeLayout container tag in one location.

Place your cursor after the end-quote in the tools:context=".MainActivity" parameter and hit the return key, which will give you a new-line and also auto-indent your next line of XML mark-up for you. Then, type in the word **android**, and when you hit the **colon** key, a **helper dialog** pops-up that contains all the possible parameters that can be used with a Relative Layout type of layout container tag, as is shown in Figure 2-9.

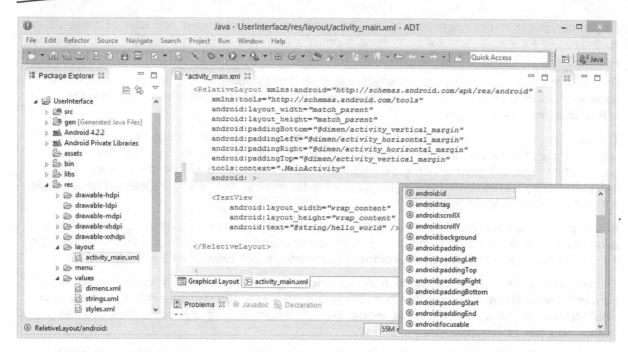

Figure 2-9. *Using the android: work process to invoke the parameter helper dialog, and selecting the android:id parameter*

Double-click the android:id parameter, the code is inserted for you, waiting for you to type in an ID value. We call our RelativeLayout **mainLayout** and use the **@+id/** referencing preface so the complete reference would be written using the following XML mark-up:

```
android:id="@+id/mainLayout"
```

The parameter can be seen in Figure 2-10.

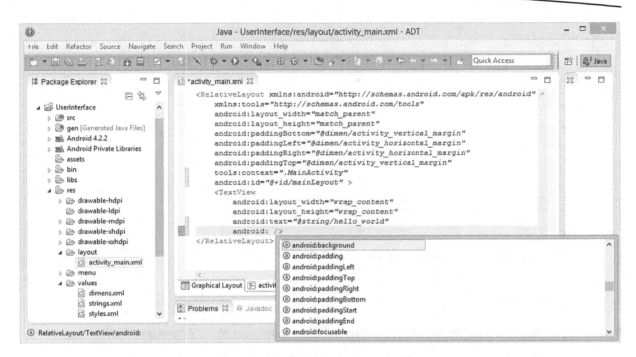

Figure 2-10. Adding an android:background parameter to our TextView tag via TextView tag parameter helper dialog

View XML Attributes: Configuring the TextView UI Widget

Now let's add some parameters to the TextView child UI widget View object so we can visualize the difference between margins and padding. The first thing we need to set to see where the boundaries of this View object container are is a nice, cornstarch blue **background color**.

Let's use the same exact work process that we just learned in the previous section for our RelativeLayout ViewGroup object, and type in **android:** and bring up a helper dialog containing all the parameters that can be used for the TextView UI element View object. Find and then double-click the **android:background** parameter to insert it into your XML mark-up after the android:text parameter, as shown in Figure 2-10.

Once that is done, we can insert a hexadecimal color value inside the empty parentheses for this tag. Android hexadecimal values begin with the pound sign or hash tag, whichever reference you prefer, followed by six or eight alphanumeric characters that represent your 24-bit or 32-bit color value.

The hexadecimal string for cornstarch blue would be **#AACCFF**. We will get into color theory in a later chapter (Chapters 7 and 10) in the book where we'll cover digital imaging new media concepts in detail. Enter #AACCFF inside the empty parentheses, as is shown in Figure 2-11, and you will be ready to "render" the UI design using the Graphical Layout Editor tab. Rendering a design is the process of turning your XML mark-up into an actual visual result.

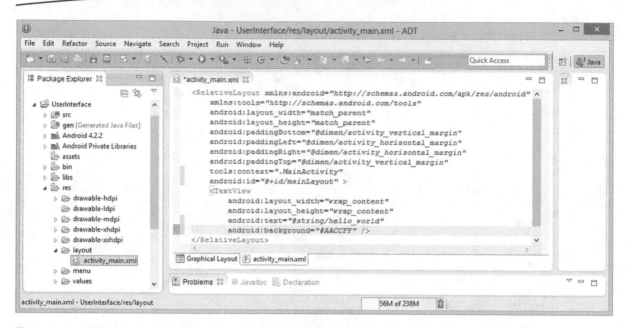

Figure 2-11. *Configuring the android:background parameter with hexidecimal value #AACCFF (cornstarch blue)*

Click the Graphical Layout Editor tab at the bottom of your XML editing pane, which switches you into a graphical development environment, shown in Figure 2-12. As you can see, you can now view your UI layout container.

Figure 2-12. *Using the Graphical Layout Editor tab to preview a background color value for the TextView container*

Now you can visualize how the **WRAP_CONTENT** constant tells the UI widget to conform to its content, as the View container is literally almost touching the ends of our Hello world text string and is almost touching this text's baseline or **descender** as well as the top of this font's **ascender**.

You can also see the cornstarch blue color that our hexadecimal color value provided, and if you are wondering why the TextView widget is **selected** with a blue outline with **control handles** on it in the GLE view, it is because we left an **editing cursor** inside the TextView XML mark-up in the XML editing pane.

Next, let's add a **padding** value to this TextView, to visualize how padding affects the relationship between this View container and its text content.

View Padding Parameter: Add Space Inside the Container

Utilize the **return-to-indent** and **android:** work process by placing a cursor right after the background parameter and press the Return key. In the helper dialog that appears, find and double-click the **android:padding** parameter, as shown in Figure 2-13. Notice that all those other padding parameters we discussed earlier in the chapter are also right there at your disposal in the help dialog, so feel free to add them and play around with them using different padding values now that our blue background color allows you to visualize exactly what each padding value is doing to your View container. Experiment with parameters–it's a good way to get a feel for what they do!

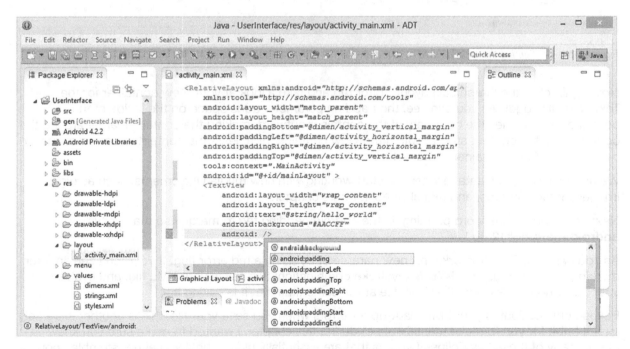

Figure 2-13. Adding an android:padding parameter to demonstrate adding space on the inside of a TextView widget

Once you double-click the android:padding parameter, and add it in your XML mark-up, enter the **12 DIP** value into the empty parentheses as shown in Figure 2-14. You can use **12dip** or **12dp**–either is acceptable to Android OS.

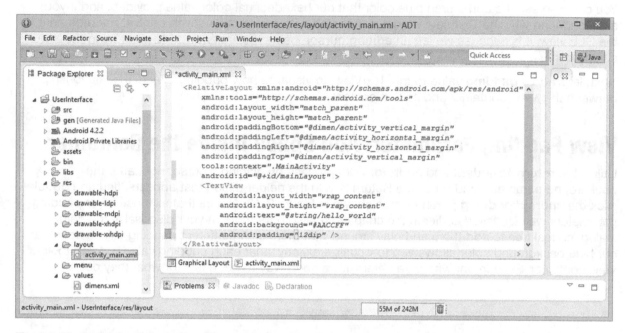

Figure 2-14. *Configuring the android:padding parameter with a 12dip data value to push out the View container*

Now again click the Graphical Layout Editor tab and take a look at your View container for the TextView UI widget. As you can see, the padding parameter adds space on the inside of the container and pushes the boundary of the container outward, making the container larger around the content, and the content smaller within the View container or at least the content becomes a smaller percentage of the container's total volume.

We use this to our advantage when we start working with new media UI elements, such as digital imagery, ImageButtons, and digital video in future chapters.

Next, let's change the word padding, in the android:padding tag to margin, so that it says **android:margin="12dip."**

As you can see, Eclipse marks this new parameter by using a red error flag. If you don't see an error marking in the IDE, use a **CRTL-S** keystroke combination; this saves your XML file, and evaluates your mark-up that is inside that XML file at the same time that it is saving it.

Eclipse only evaluates your XML mark-up for errors when you save your file; this is another extremely useful tidbit for you to make mental note of during this chapter. I wanted to make sure you knew about many of these key Eclipse features that are essentially hidden until you either stumble upon them, or somebody explicitly points out the work process behind them!

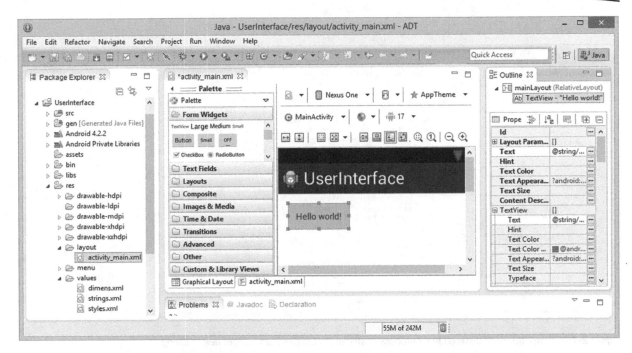

Figure 2-15. Using the Graphical Layout Editor tab to preview a 12dip padding data value for TextView container

Now we need to add more than one UI widget to our RelativeLayout container, so that we can show multiple nested child tags, as well as showing why it is called a RelativeLayout UI container. Since we will be covering all sorts of standard UI widgets in this book, let's add a cooler, more fun UI widget that Android offers: the **AnalogClock** widget.

The AnalogClock Widget: Adding a View to the ViewGroup

Next I'm going to show you how to invoke another Eclipse ADT helper dialog that shows you exactly which child tags, or View widget objects, can be added to any given parent tag, or ViewGroup, layout container object.

Place your cursor after the <TextView> closing tag, which looks like this: /> and then press the Return key on your keyboard to get Eclipse ADT to indent the next child tag line of code for you. This lines up the <AnalogClock> child tag's indenting with the first <TextView> child tag, as is shown in Figure 2-16.

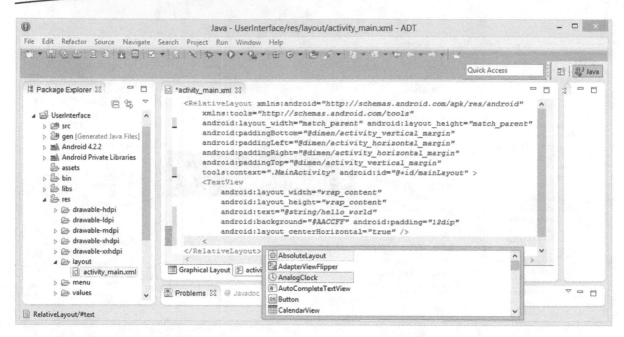

Figure 2-16. Using the < left chevron work process to invoke the Eclipse View widget helper dialog

For the first character, type a left-facing chevron or < character, which pops-up a **child tag View widget selector helper dialog**. Now I want you to say "**child tag View widget selector helper dialog**" three times, extremely fast, which will greatly disturb anyone who is within earshot, but will help you remember what this useful helper dialog is, as you will surely be using it dozens of times in this book. Find and double-click the **AnalogClock** widget to add this UI widget child tag to the RelativeLayout UI container.

Next, copy the **android:layout_centerHorizontal** parameter and ending **/>** tag from the <TextView> UI element tag above it, so that you have a parameter that centers your Analog Clock, as well as a closing element for your child tag for your new AnalogClock UI widget that we are adding to the UI design.

You might at this point also notice that the Eclipse ADT helper dialog did not provide your closing tag element for this <AnalogClock> widget tag. Nobody's perfect, not even an IDE. I'm sure this oversight will be fixed very soon.

Next, copy the two required **android:layout_width** and **android:layout_height** parameters from the TextView tag as well, since they are required, and to save you some monotonous parameter typing.

Fast coders are smart coders, and leverage their IDE and their OS features and programming environments to their maximum potential. This means using copy and paste for XML parameters that are identical between different UI tags, especially those required ones that do not change their format.

Once you are finished, you should have an initial <AnalogClock> child UI tag, which looks like what you see in Figure 2-17.

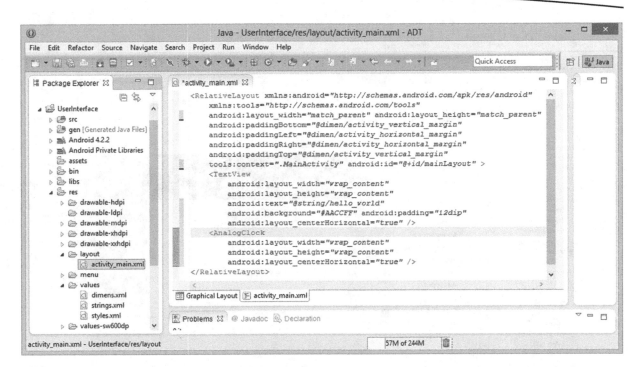

Figure 2-17. Copy layout_width, layout_height, layout_centerHorizontal, and closing /> from TextView tag into AnalogClock tag

We now have a ViewGroup layout container <RelativeLayout> parent tag, and two View widget <TextView> and <AnalogClock> child tags, nested inside of it. As you can see in Figure 2-17, due to our XML mark-up indenting it's easy to visualize the structure of our user interface design. Next, we will use the Graphical Layout to render (or visualize) how our UI design looks.

Next click the Graphical Layout Editor (GLE) tab, and review how the UI looks, shown in Figure 2-18.

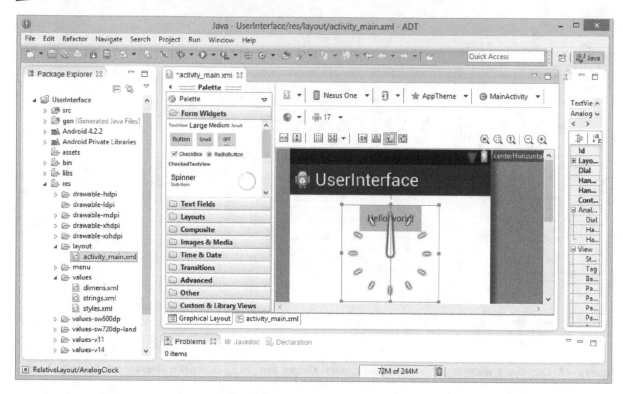

Figure 2-18. Using the Graphical Layout Editor to preview the AnalogClock widget and initial parameter settings

As you can see in Figure 2-18, we have a problem with our UI design layout, as the AnalogClock widget overlaps the TextView widget. Fortunately, we're using a RelativeLayout container, which is Android's most popular, widely used layout container.

It is also the layout container that's used by the New Android Application Project series of dialogs when you specify a blank slate for your UI design, as we are seeing here.

This RelativeLayout container, as its name belies, allows us to layout our UI widgets relative to each other. This is going to allow us to solve this UI layout problem that we see in Figure 2-18 by allowing to specify how we want the TextView and the AnalogClock View widgets to be laid out relative to each other.

Use your newly found knowledge to invoke the AnalogClock parameters helper dialog, and find the **android:layout_below** parameter and double-click it to add it underneath your android:centerHorizontal parameter, as shown in Figure 2-19.

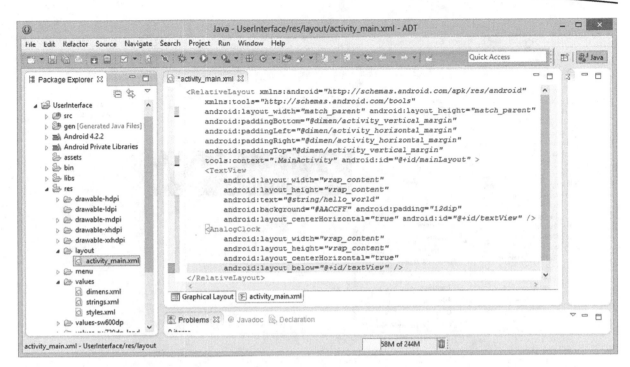

Figure 2-19. Add a RelativeLayout ViewGroup specific android:layout_below parameter referencing the textView TextView ID

The layout_below parameter references an ID for one of the other widgets that you want to lay it out relative to (below). Thus, the first thing that we need to do is to add an android:id parameter to our TextView object, as shown in Figure 2-19. I named it **textView** using the XML mark-up **android:id="@+id/textView"** to accomplish this.

Once the TextView widget has an ID value attached to it, we can reference that ID in the AnalogClock widget using an **android:layout_below** parameter, configured to point to our TextView widget via the following XML mark-up:

```
android:layout_below="@+id/textView"
```

This tells the Android OS that the AnalogClock widget should layout below the TextView widget. Once you have this one simple parameter in place, the UI design looks like it is supposed to, as you can see in Figure 2-20.

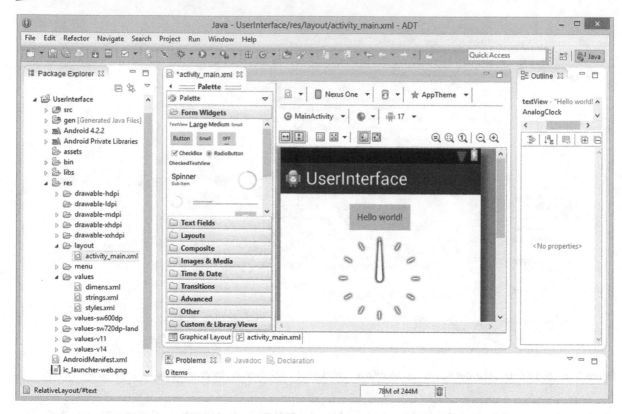

Figure 2-20. *Using the Graphical Layout Editor tab to preview AnalogClock widget and relative layout parameter*

Next, since we are not creating a simple Hello World application, rather a more complex Hello World Here's the Time App, let's go in our strings.xml file, and edit the <string> constant tag that Eclipse created for us named **hello_world** and change its text value to be something more appropriate for our enhanced UI design.

Using the Values Folder: Finish Your UI Design Using XML

Right-click the **strings.xml** file, in the **/res/values** folder, and select **Open** from the menu, or select the file, and use the **F3** key to open it up.

Next, change the value of the tag named **hello_world** to read "**Hello World Here's the Time!**" as shown in Figure 2-21. Notice while you are in this file there are also string constants defined for your **app_name**, and **action_settings** menu, both of which we will be modifying at an appropriate time. We'll adjust our application name when we work with Android Manifest XML files and our menu in the upcoming chapters (Chapters 4 and 5) on using the Menu classes in Android.

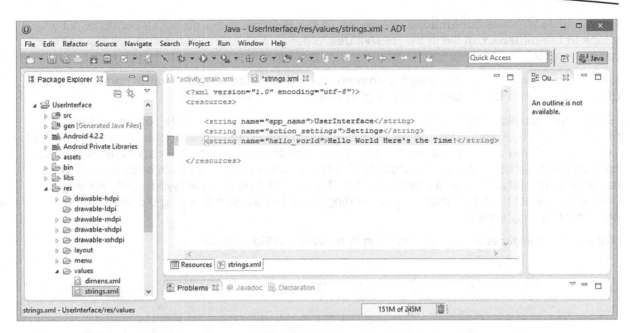

Figure 2-21. Editing your <string> XML constant for hello_world in the strings.xml file in your /res/values folder

Next we can go into our Graphical Layout Editor tab, as shown in Figure 2-22, and see the final UI design for the chapter. As you can see, now the TextView makes a lot more sense as the **screen caption** that relates to the AnalogClock that is located underneath it.

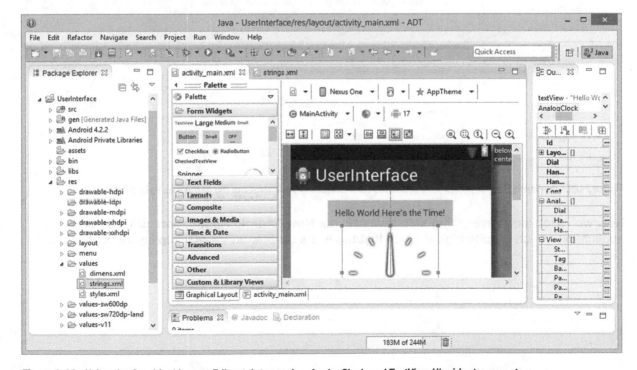

Figure 2-22. Using the Graphical Layout Editor tab to preview AnalogClock and TextView UI widget parameters

Finally, since we have **dimensions** referenced, in our RelativeLayout parent UI container, let's take a look at the **dimens.xml** file in the **/res/values** folder as well, just to make sure we have all our bases covered.

A dimension value is created using the **<dimen>** tag, which usually takes a **name** parameter, and a dimension value in **DIP** or **DP** (or dip or dp) format.

Notice that XML files in the /res/values folder do not use tags which need the **xmlns:android** or parameters such as android:name because they are just programming shortcuts to setting constant values, just as you would use at the top of your Java code. The default **dimens.xml** file, which was created when we used the New Android Application series of dialogs, defines a constant of **16dp** for both horizontal and vertical margin settings. The constant pushes the layout container edges (because widgets have no margins, only padding values) away from touching the sides of the end-user's display screen.

Right-click your **dimens.xml** file, and open it, as shown in Figure 2-23.

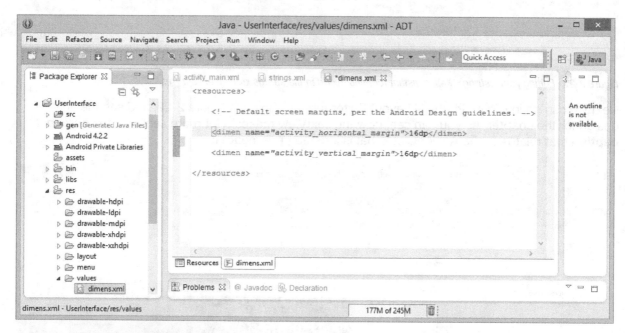

Figure 2-23. Previewing the <dimen> XML constants for MainActivity in dimens.xml file in the /res/values folder

Now we've looked at everything XML-related in our **New Android Application** dialog's bootstrap application, which is quite logical, given that this is the chapter on **ViewGroup** layout containers!

Summary

In this chapter, we took a look at the foundation of UI design in Android, the **ViewGroup** Superclass, and its layout container subclasses. First, we looked at the concept of the **UI layout container** in Android, and how Android allows us to use **XML mark-up** to define our UI designs, so that designers can work alongside of programmers without having to learn Java. We learned about **parent tags** and **child tags**, about **XML naming schemas**, and about how the **xmlns:android** schema needs to be declared and referenced in your parent tag for your Android ViewGroup layout container subclasses.

Next, we learned about using **parameters** inside these tags to customize and configure the various attributes of View widget containers, as well as to customize and configure the parent ViewGroup layout container itself. We took a closer look at the Android ViewGroup class and its many layout subclasses, as well as its origin Superclasses and its **nested classes.** We then looked at the nested class **ViewGroup.LayoutParams** and its layout constants **MATCH_PARENT** and **WRAP_ CONTENT,** which are fundamental to UI design in Android. We learned the difference between the two constants, and also covered the concept of **layout direction** (RTL and LTR) in Android.

Next, we looked at the nested class **ViewGroup.MarginLayoutParams**, and the six margin layout parameters, which are also fundamental to Android UI design. We learned that due to the new concept of **layout direction** (RTL or LTR) in Android 4.2 that we should start using **marginStart** or **marginEnd** instead of marginLeft or marginRight, in case our users switch layout directions. We also learned which of the major languages that use RTL layout direction. We took a look at how margins differ from padding, and how ViewGroup classes allow margin values, but View classes only allow padding values. We looked at the ViewGroup specific **LayoutAnimationController** class, and how it allows us to animate our UI designs onto the display screen.

Finally, we got down to business, and fired up **Eclipse ADT** and created our **pro.android.ui** package and **UserInterface** application foundation so that we could start looking at XML parent tags, child tags, and parameters, and get our hands dirty playing with magic mark-up (that's a weak joke relating to magic markers). We used XML to visualize what padding does to a UI widget. In the next chapter, we will learn about the Android **View** Superclass, and how it is used to subclass and create **widgets**, and we will take a look at some of the more popular widgets that we will be using in our UI designs.

Chapter 3

Android UI Widgets: User Interface Widgets and the View Class

In this chapter, we will learn more about the Android **View** class, as well as continuing our exploration of the Android Application development framework that was created for us by Eclipse ADT in Chapter 2, using the New Android Application series of dialogs that we recently utilized.

Now that we have a better foundation for understanding how those ViewGroup layout containers contain Android View UI widgets, and how to use XML file UI layout definitions to add UI elements using tags and configure those UI elements using parameters, we can concentrate our efforts in this chapter on learning about the View Superclass and all the advanced User Interface Design features that it currently supports.

View and ViewGroup instantiated objects are both complicated for different reasons. ViewGroup layout container objects are complicated because device screens vary in size and in shape, and thus to put together a design that works well across different display sizes and shapes can be an exceptional challenge. In fact, we have an entire chapter on this challenge coming up!

View widgets are a complicated topic because they have many **attributes**, or **properties**, as you will see in this chapter. The properties are set using **parameters**, via an XML definition in a file in the **/res/layout** subfolder. Not only do View UI elements have a ton of properties, but they also have **event listeners** that allow them to respond to user interaction, so we have a lot to cover in this chapter, between looking at all the key View object properties, and then learning how to implement your event listener so that your View object UI widget can respond to the user's interaction with it.

The Android View Class: The Superclass for UI Widgets

If the foundation for our UI designs in Android OS is an Android ViewGroup layout container, then the structure that is built on that foundation is comprised of UI element widgets that are based on the Android **View** class.

ViewGroup layout containers may hold, structure, organize, and reorient the View UI widgets, but it is those View subclass UI widgets themselves which are actually used by your users to interface with your Android application functionality and ultimately create your application UX (user experience).

The View class is itself a subclass of the Java Language's **Object** class, I like to call that class the Masterclass, because ultimately, everything in Java is an object! Thus, this View Superclass is about as high on the Java food chain as a class can get, its class hierarchy can be seen as follows:

```
java.lang.Object
 > android.view.View
```

The View Superclass is primarily used in Android to create our UI elements that are called **widgets** in Android.

As we learned in the previous chapter, this View Superclass was even used to create the ViewGroup class, because the **properties** that are a part of this View class need to be **inherited** by the ViewGroup subclass, as well as by all the different widget subclasses.

There are so many UI widget subclasses that are subclassed from this View Superclass, that there is an entire package in Android chock full of them.

This is called the **android.widget** package, and we will be using it a lot in our Java code, via **import statements** that are used to **declare** our widgets and other Android classes for usage in our application Java program logic.

The View class has **11 direct subclasses**, which we'll take a look at in the next section, as well as **70 indirect subclasses**, many of which we will implement during this book, as we learn how to utilize Android layout containers (ViewGroup subclasses), such as the RelativeLayout container, which we already had exposure to in the previous chapter on layout containers.

The View class is part of an **android.view** package, which collects subclasses that expose user interface element classes that handle screen layout and UI elements and their interaction with your application's user.

There are 50 Java classes, 47 Java interfaces, and 6 Java exceptions in the android.view package. If you want to review these individually, you can do that on the Android Developer site View package page at the following URL:

```
http://developer.android.com/reference/android/view/package-summary.html
```

Next let's take a look at the direct subclasses of View to get an overview regarding which of the key widget classes in Android are View subclasses.

Android View Direct Subclasses: Key Widgets and Utilities

Let's take a look at some of the direct subclasses of the View class. Most of the 11 direct subclasses are what I'd term "core" UI design widgets or utilities, so I think you'll find this section interesting. We will get a chance to use all these during the book, but since this chapter is to give you a comprehensive overview of View widgets, this will give you some perspective as to how far underneath View your widgets are subclassed. The widgets we'll talk about in this section are thus directly underneath the View class, and all others are at least two subclass levels under View.

Let's start with the two direct subclass widgets that we used in the previous chapter, **AnalogClock** and **TextView**. Obviously, TextView is one of your core UI elements as Text is used more than any other element in an application.

AnalogClock on the other hand is one of the least used core UI elements, and is quite specialized as it is a full working analog clock simulation. It is a fun UI widget to be sure. It is quite robust and allows you to "skin" the clock in different ways with image graphics and color values. That's why I included it in a previous chapter, as I am trying to cover as many widgets in this book as I can, and we won't have a lot of time to fool around with the fun ones and still get you up to a Pro Android UI Design proficiency.

Another mission critical direct subclass of View is your **ImageView** widget, which is used to hold and display digital image assets, which if you're in the graphics design business is going to be one of your favorite widgets!

ImageView and its **ImageButton** subclass, which means that an ImageButton UI widget is an **indirect subclass** of this View superclass, are used to display custom digital image and animation content for your application UI design.

We spent an entire chapter already on **ViewGroup**, another one of the direct subclasses which is used to create layout containers, as you already know.

A **Space** direct subclass is one of the **utility subclasses**, and, no, it does not create starfields (unfortunately), but rather it can be used to create "**spacers**," which allow you to fine-tune your UI design spacing, using **gaps** that you can insert in your UI layout designs, to control how they render.

Another utility subclass is the **ProgressBar** direct subclass, which, as its name suggests, is used to implement progress bars within your application. There is a **determinate** progress bar, which is an actual bar, and shows the actual progress, and an **indeterminate** spinning wheel progress bar option.

An even more complex utility is the **KeyboardView** direct subclass, which as you may have guessed renders a virtual keyboard on the screen for the user to use to provide text input. This is especially useful for touchscreen as most touchscreen smartphones and tablets these days do not have keyboards.

The last two direct subclasses I'm going to mention here are significantly more advanced, the **SurfaceView** and the **TextureView**. The TextureView direct subclass is essentially a hardware accelerated SurfaceView, so, I'll focus here on the SurfaceView direct subclass, as it is supported across Android devices, not just those featuring the hardware (3D or video) acceleration.

The SurfaceView class is more suited to the *Pro Android Graphics* book, but suffice it to say that this direct subclass provides the foundation for two important indirect subclasses. One is the **VideoView**, which handles digital video in Android, and the other is the **GLSurfaceView**, which handles the 3D

OpenGL rendering pipeline in Android. Both of these direct subclasses are well-suited for advanced graphics applications featuring real-time, OpenGL 3D, and streaming (or captive inside an App APK file) Digital Video assets.

Using View Properties: Important Parameters

There are 65 XML parameters that are defined in the View class that can be inherited by any of its subclasses. Clearly I can't cover every single one of them in detail here, but we will go over several of the most often used parameters in this section, and cover why each of them are important.

Some of these key parameters you have already used in the previous chapter such as the **android:id** to give your tag (object) a name. The reason that I say (object), is because, as we will see later on in this chapter, when we get into the Java side of things, that the XML definitions are "**inflated**," which means that Java methods take the tags and parameters and instantiate objects and set attributes in those objects based on the XML definition.

We also used the **android:background,** which is another very useful parameter for implementing color, imagery, or animation in your View object widget. A closely related parameter to the background parameter is the **android:alpha** parameter, which sets the alpha (transparency) value for the entire widget View object. This parameter can also be animated if you want to fade your widgets in or out. If you just want transparency in your background, then use the eight place **#AARRGGBB** hexadecimal value where the first two slots are the alpha value, with #00FFFFFF being transparent (white) and #FFFFFFFF is opaque (I am using a white color value here, in the other six slots).

We also looked at the **android:padding** parameters, which add spacing inside of a widget (View) container, as we demonstrated in the previous chapter.

Some of the View parameters that we have not looked at yet, but which we will during this book, include the **android:rotation** parameter, which can be used to rotate a view around its center (pivot) point, as well as rotation parameters targeting each of the X and Y axes. These are **android:rotationX** and **android:rotationY**. These parameters match up with an Android Animation class **rotate** transform, as do the **alpha**, **scale** and **translation** parameters.

These four parameters are used in conjunction with the **LayoutAnimationController** class that we looked at in the previous chapter.

Now let's take a look at the other animation compatible parameters in this View class. There is **android:scaleX** and **android:scaleY**, which allow you to **scale** any widget View object, using a float (floating point) data value of **0.0** (zero percent) to **1.0** (100%).

Finally, there are the **android:translateX** or **android:translateY** parameters, which allow you to **translate** or **move** the UI widget View object anywhere in the 2D screen dimension. Now we have looked at all the View attributes, or properties, which can be set in XML as parameters and which can also be accessed by the Android Animation class to perform procedural animation.

I mentioned the rotation or **pivot point** earlier, which can also be used to skew scale operations. This is set by using an **android:transformPivotX** and **android:transformPivotY** parameter. In 2D space this pivot point would have two coordinates, so these two parameters are usually utilized together.

In addition to the android:alpha parameter, there is an **android:visibility** parameter, which has three constants that it supports: **VISIBLE, INVISIBLE,** and **GONE**. Thus you would want to use android:alpha to create a fade-out or fade-in effect, and the android:visibility parameter to turn the UI widget **on** (VISIBLE) or **off** (INVISIBLE).

In case you're wondering what the GONE parameter does, it tells the layout container to calculate your layout positioning of your UI widgets in your layout container as if the widget set with **android:visibility="GONE"** were not even there, whereas the INVISIBLE parameter tells the layout container that the View object is there taking up its space but is not visible, that is, its alpha value could be considered to be zero, or fully transparent.

There are also **android:scrollX, android:scrollY,** and an **android:scrollbars** parameter that turns scrollbars on and off for View widgets that support scrolling. There are also ten android:scrollbar configuration parameters, such as **android:scrollbarSize** and **android:scrollbarStyle**. We don't really need to get into scrollbars at this point in the book, so I'm not going to go into these in detail at this point.

There are also seven parameters that relate to controlling the **focus** of a View object widget, two are **android:focusable,** and five **android:nextFocus** parameters, all of which we will cover in the next section on focus, and what it is, and why it is important to our View object widget subclasses.

The rest of the parameters are mostly specialized parameters for keeping the View object turned on (for video playback) or enabling one hardware feature or another. If you want to go through all 65 XML parameters in detail, you can find them listed on the Android Development website on the View class information summary page which is located at the following URL:

http://developer.android.com/reference/android/view/View.html

Next we're going to discuss the concept of UI widget focus, which is a key concept in any UI design workflow, whether it is Android or HTML5 or C# or C++. How users progress from one UI element to the next is very important.

Focus of a View: Which UI Widget has the User's Attention

The **focus** of a UI element, or View object widget, is simply a "state." If a UI element is being actively used by the user it is said to **have focus**. If the UI element state is idle, because one of your other UI elements **has the focus** of the user, that UI element is said to have **lost the focus**.

The ability to control focus in the XML mark-up and Java code is important to your user experience (UX) design, because your software (code) can tell exactly where in the UI that the user's focus is at any time, and react to that, if you need to do so, or choose to do so, as a software feature.

This is usually done by using an **event listener** which we're going to cover in the next section. This code "listens," for **View.OnFocusChangeListener()** methods and their invocation, which will happen when a View object widget **gets the focus**, or **loses the focus**. Once an OnFocusChangeListener() method is invoked the Java code that is written inside it is then executed.

The code that you write inside this OnFocusChangeListener() method will be executed when a focusChange event comes through your application, which signifies that focus has changed for one of your UI element View widgets.

The OnFocusChangeListener() is the only focus-related event listener; most of the others deal with user input types, such as **key** input or **click** input or **touch** input, for instance. The focus change Listener applies to each of these, because no matter what methodology you are using for hardware input (interfacing) with your application, your user is always going to progress (change focus) from one UI element to the next, in one way or another.

The most basic focus-related XML parameter is android:focusable and if set to a "true" value the View widget in question will be able to take focus. So inside of your UI widget if you want it to receive focus when the user accesses it you would include the parameter android:focusable="true", then it would generate focusChange events because it would be focusable.

Android usually determines automatically (or as a default) whether a UI widget can take focus. Obviously a data field UI widget, called the <EditText> widget child tag in XML, is one of the most prone to have focus, indicated by a blinking vertical text insertion bar.

There is a similar parameter, for touchscreen devices, which does the same thing only in **Touch mode**, called **android:focusableInTouchMode** and when set to "true" the widget in question can take focus in Touch mode.

The **android:nextFocus** parameters, including **nextFocusForward**, **nextFocusUp**, **nextFocusDown**, **nextFocusLeft,** and **nextFocusRight**, determine the **order** that focus is transferred from one user interface element to the next one. The Android OS automatically determines nextFocus order for your UI layout container, so these parameters are for overriding that, and implementing a custom UI element to UI element focus order progression.

View Listeners: Making a UI Widget Respond to the User

Of **16 nested classes** that the View class contains, **12** of them are **Listener** interfaces, commonly called **event listeners**. A reason they are called this is because data that they're listening for is commonly termed an **event**.

The other four nested classes are classes and not interfaces, and are more specialized, utility-related nested classes, and we will cover those later in the book if we need to utilize them, or you can review them at a later time on that Android Developer website View page we referenced earlier.

Android's most often utilized event listener interface nested class is an **View.OnClickListener(),** which listens for "clicks," which can be a mouse, touchscreen events, or navigation hardware events, such as depressing the trackball or a hardware selector key of one type or another.

A related event listener to .OnClickListener() is **.OnLongClickListener()**, which is when a **Long Click** is invoked by the user, instead of the regular click. A Long Click is a click that is held down for **one second** or longer, and is the Android equivalent of a right-click button in Windows or Linux.

Related to Long Click, which like a right-click brings up context sensitive menus, Android has an **OnCreateContextMenuListener()** that's called when you build a **ContextMenu** that is Android's equivalent of a right-click context sensitive menu in Windows. We will be taking a closer look at menus in the next chapter, so stay tuned for more about this event listener interface.

Another event listener related to OnClickListener() is **OnTouchListener()**, which is used for touchscreen displays.

> **Note** If you are sure your audience and devices only use touchscreen, you can use OnTouchListener()—just be aware that OnClickListener() supports both touch and click (hardware) interfaces.

For keyboard and keypad support, there is the **OnKeyListener(),** which as you might guess listens for different keystrokes and responds to them with the appropriate code. This Listener supports hardware keyboards and keypads. A KeyboardView class, which we learned about earlier, is the correct way for you to implement software keyboards, if that is what you want to do. The onKeyUp() and onKeyDown() methods are also supported in Android, if you need that level of keypress control, but implementing these is trickier.

For drag and drop functionality there is the OnDragListener(), which is used when you are dragging things around the touchscreen. In fact, Android has an entire drag and drop framework, so if you are interested in using a drag-drop framework, be sure to take a look at the following website URL:

http://developer.android.com/guide/topics/ui/drag-drop.html

For detecting when your layout (ViewGroup) container changes, such as when a user turns a device from portrait orientation to landscape orientation, there's an **OnLayoutChangeListener()** interface.

There is a new **OnHoverListener()** as of Android 4.0, which I suspect belies Google's plan to use Android for ChromeBook, because the **hover** is specific to using a mouse pointer or cursor, and is used to invoke certain features that happen when a mouse is **over an object** (UI widget) but is **not clicking** it, which is why it is called hovering, like a helicopter over its target.

It is also interesting to note that you can't hover with a touchscreen, as you are already touching it. A hover Listener won't work at all on devices prior to Android 4.0, so for now, at least, it's a niche Listener at best.

There is also an **OnGenericMotionListener()** that is triggered (your code is executed) when a movement (trackball, mouse, pen, fingers) event, which is handled by a **MotionEvent** class in Android, are detected by the Android OS.

MotionEvent objects hold two different types of movement data; absolute or relative movement, and may also contain other data with this movement data as well, depending on the type of Android device hardware that is used to generate the motion data. A MotionEvent can be used to implement advanced features such as gestures, and MotionEvent objects are also utilized with UI features such as scrollbars, which is why we are covering them here.

MotionEvent objects contain movement data that is defined in terms of its **action code** along with a set of **axis values**. The action code specifies the **state change** that occurred for the MotionEvent, such as the pointer going up or down. The 2D X and Y axis values record the position information and any other movement properties that may be occurring.

There are also Android devices that will record multiple MotionEvent data sets in parallel, at the exact same point in time. These devices feature a technology called Multi-Touch, and they feature display screens that will transmit one finger movement MotionEvent dataset for each finger utilized.

Individual fingertips and physical objects that generate movement tracing data would be referred to as "**pointers**." MotionEvent objects carry all the information about currently active pointers. This pointer information data is included even if a pointer hasn't moved since the last event was sent.

The way a MotionEvent works is when your user initially touches their touchscreen device the Android OS will deliver the touch event to the View object in question, along with an action constant **ACTION_DOWN** and a set of 2D X and Y axis values, which include the X and Y location coordinates for the touch along with information regarding touch pressure, gesture sizing, and the orientation within the touchscreen contact area. If you wanted to research MotionEvent in detail you can find its page at the following URL:

http://developer.android.com/reference/android/view/MotionEvent.html

Because this is a UI book, there is one final Listener we should cover here and that is the **OnAttachStateChangeListener(),** which is triggered when View objects are added or removed from a UI layout container. This UI designing approach, of attaching UI elements using Java, is called **dynamic** UI creation, whereas creating a layout via XML is called **static** UI creation.

UI Layout Creation: Using the setContentView() Method

Now let's get back into Eclipse ADT and our **UserInterface** project and this time we'll take a look at Java code for a change. Open your project's **/src** source code folder, and right-click the **MainActivity.java** file, in your **pro.android.ui** subfolder. This opens a MainActivity.java tab in the central editing page inside Eclipse ADT as is shown in Figure 3-1.

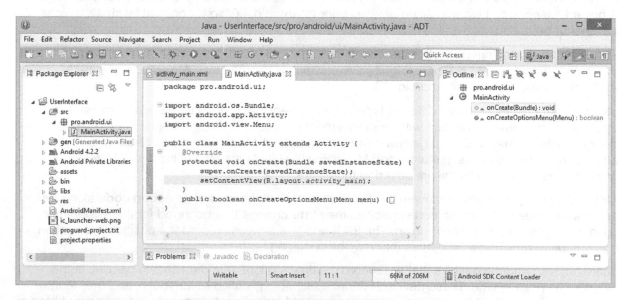

Figure 3-1. Opening and examining the MainActivity.java code that Eclipse ADT generated for us in Chapter 2

As you can see the Eclipse ADT New Android Application series of dialogs wrote the bootstrap Java code for us that was needed to put an Activity on the device display screen and references our RelativeLayout UI definition.

The first line of Java code declares our **package pro.android.ui,** followed by three import statements importing **android.os.Bundle**, **android.view.View,** and **android.app.Activity**.

Our **public class** MainActivity **extends** the Activity class declared in the android.app.Activity import statement, and the **protected void** onCreate() method utilizes the android.os.Bundle class declared in the first import statement to save a Bundle of Activity settings in a **Bundle** object named **savedInstanceState**.

The next line of code calls the **super.onCreate()** method inside an Activity Superclass, and references the .onCreate() method one level up, inside the Activity Superclass level, by using the super keyword, put in front of the .onCreate() method call, and then passing up the savedInstanceState Bundle object as its parameter. Now all we have to do is reference our XML design for our user interface layout definition and we're ready to edit some XML.

The way we reference an XML layout container definition in the /res/layout folder is using the setContentView() method with parameters that reference this layout definition file. This is done via this **R.layout.activity_main** path, where **R** stands for Android's Resources area and layout is the folder name and activity_main references the activity_main.xml file UI definition inside it. So the Java method call and path would be written like this:

```
setContentView(R.layout.activity_main);
```

Notice in Eclipse that there are little **minus** and **plus** signs, on the left side of the editing page, where you can **collapse** and **expand** the code for your methods. I have closed the method that relates to Menu creation, as we are covering the Menu classes in the next chapter of the book. Next, let's add a UI element that is another of the cornerstone UI elements for UI design: the **Button** widget View class in Android.

Adding a Button UI Widget to Our RelativeLayout Container

Click the **activity_main.xml** editing tab at the top of Eclipse and use the < left chevron work process, to add a **Button** tag to our <RelativeLayout> parent tag container, along with a **/>** closing tag, as shown in Figure 3-2.

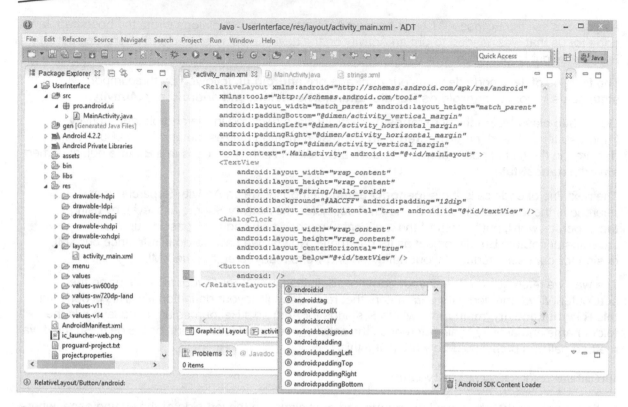

Figure 3-2. Add a Button UI widget child tag, the use an android: work process to open a parameter helper dialog

Next, use the android:work process to bring up the Button parameter helper dialog, and peruse through the parameters that are available for use with the Button UI object, as shown in Figure 3-2.

Since we are going to instantiate the Button using Java code and add event handlers for the Button object later in the chapter, we need an **android:id** parameter, so that we will be able to reference this Button in our code.

Double-click on the android:id parameter when you locate it in the helper dialog, and notice that when you are taken back to Eclipse's central edit pane that there are error flags in the XML markup, as shown in Figure 3-3.

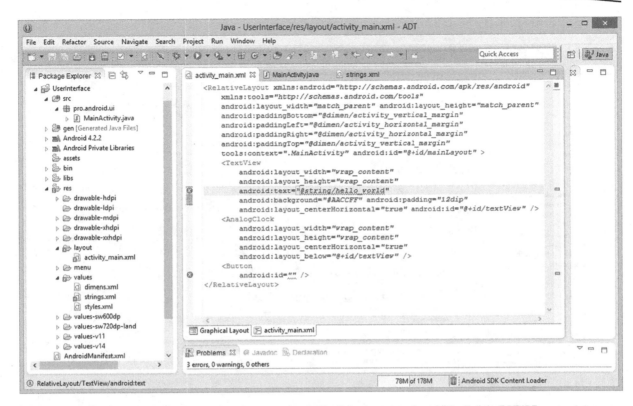

Figure 3-3. Adding our android:id parameter reference value and noticing two error flags in the Eclipse ADT IDE

The second one is to be expected, as you can't have a **null** (empty quotes) value for an android:id parameter, but the first one is strange as we have not seen that error before.

Let's take this as an excellent opportunity to explore another area of the Eclipse ADT IDE called the **Problems tab**, which is located at the bottom of the central editing pane.

Up until now we have left the Problems tab in its closed or collapsed state, so that we can have more edit room in our primary code and mark-up editing area. In the next section, we'll see exactly how to use this Problems tab.

Eclipse ADT Problems Tab: Debugging XML Errors in ADT

At the bottom of the Eclipse central editing pane you can see the GLE and XML editing tabs, and underneath these you will see another section of tabs separated by a grey border.

Place your mouse cursor over this grey border area, until the cursor turns into a double-ended arrow. Then click and drag this border upward, which will reveal the Problems tab section of the IDE, as shown in Figure 3-4.

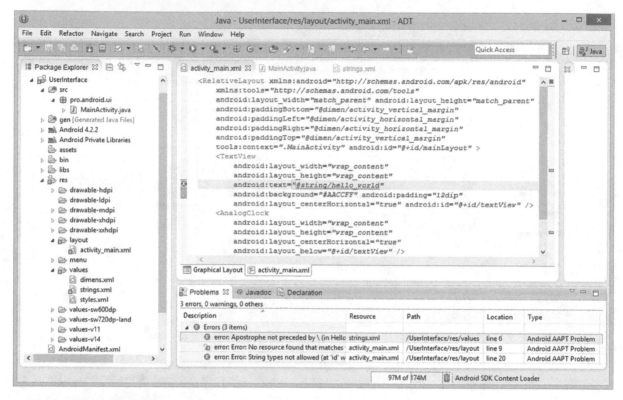

Figure 3-4. Opening the Eclipse ADT Problems tab by dragging up the separator to open up the tab display area

As you can see, Eclipse ADT wants us to escape the apostrophe character in our modified hello_world <string> constant, so this error should be pretty easy to fix.

All we have to do is simply place a \ backslash character, in front of the ' apostrophe character inside the word *Here's* in our TextView caption text constant. Once we do that and then use the **Ctrl-S** keystroke combination or the **File ➤ Save** menu sequence we can again validate the XML code and the error flags disappear, as shown in Figure 3-5.

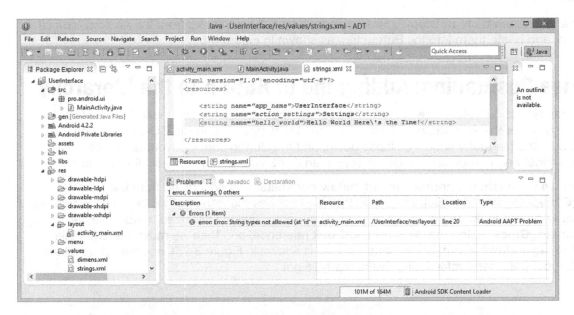

Figure 3-5. *Fixing the Apostrophe not preceded by \ error on the hello_world <string> constant to remove error*

To remove the other error we'll give our android:id parameter a reference!

Once we reference our ID, our IDE is error-free, as shown in Figure 3-6.

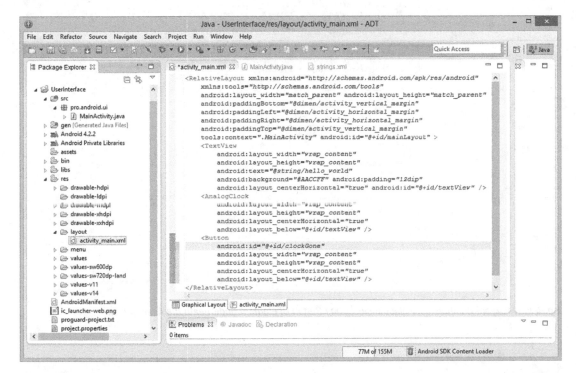

Figure 3-6. *Eliminating error flags in RelativeLayout and copying all android:layout parameters from AnalogClock*

Next, let's take a shortcut, and copy your four android:layout parameters from the AnalogClock UI widget tag, and paste them into the Button tag, as shown in Figure 3-6.

Relative Positioning: Adding the UI Button to the Hierarchy

Now we can adjust our relative layout hierarchy so that the AnalogClock is under the TextView and the Button is under the AnalogClock. That way, when we remove (using the GONE constant) the AnalogClock, the hierarchy should collapse down, and the Button should layout underneath the TextView widget and demonstrate a GONE versus an INVISIBLE parameter visibility setting.

To do this we must edit the **android:layout_below** parameter that we copied from the <AnalogClock> tag into the <Button> tag so that it references the <AnalogClock> tag ID parameter. Since this <AnalogClock> tag does not have an ID currently, first we will need to add one, let's name it **analogClock**, using the **@+id/analogClock** reference, and then we must reference this in a Button tag android:layout_below parameter, as is shown in Figure 3-7. Once we set up all the RelativeLayout parameter referencing, we're ready to go!

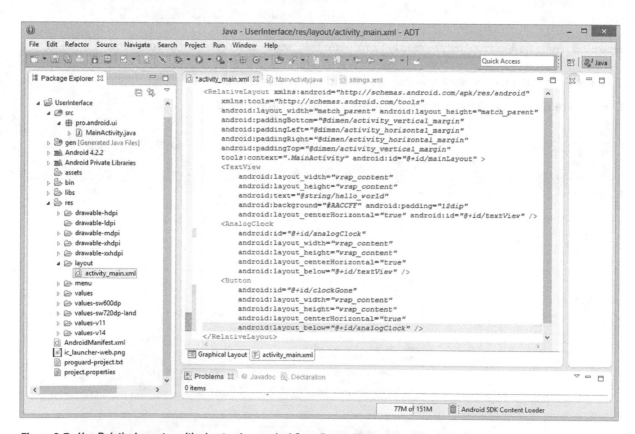

Figure 3-7.   Use RelativeLayout positioning to place a clockGone Button UI element underneath the AnalogClock

Let's click the Graphical Layout Editor tab at the bottom of the edit pane (I assume you have collapsed the Problems tab/pane back down) and see how our relative layout referencing is working.

As you can see in Figure 3-8, everything is laying out as it should, your only problem is that the Button UI element has no label. The parameter to fix this problem is the **android:text** parameter, the same one that we used in our TextView UI element, in fact.

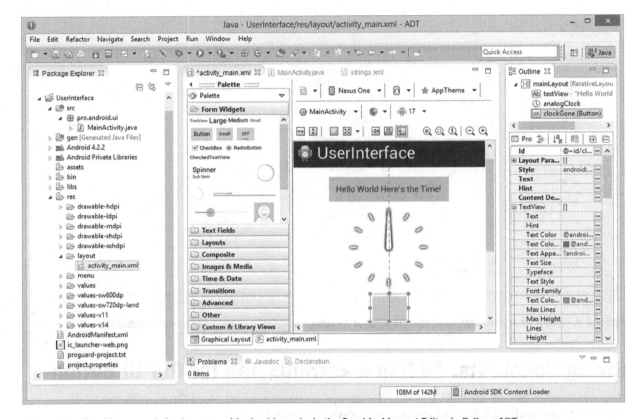

Figure 3-8. *Checking our relative layout positioning hierarchy in the Graphical Layout Editor in Eclipse ADT*

If you like, you can just copy and paste a parameter from the TextView UI element into the Button UI element, to save you some typing time.

Let's call the android:text parameter <string> constant **clockGone** as this button is going to disappear the AnalogClock UI element entirely from the layout container. The XML mark-up for this parameter thereby reads:

```
android:text="@string/clockGone"
```

As you can see in Figure 3-9 our RelativeLayout parent container and three child tags for a TextView caption, AnalogClock widget, and UI Button, which will remove the AnalogClock from this layout container, are all error-free, as well as coded using less than two dozen lines of XML mark-up.

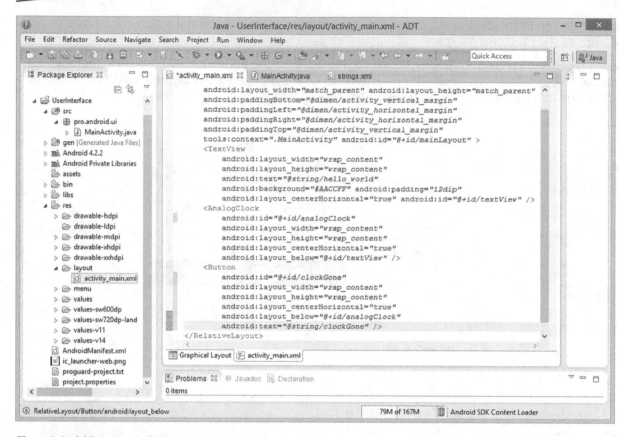

Figure 3-9. Adding an android:text parameter to reference a <string> constant named clockGone with Button text

String Constants: Adding a <string> Tag for Our UI Button

Now open your strings.xml tab and add a <string> constant named **clockGone** with the label "**Remove AnalogClock From Layout**," as shown in Figure 3-10.

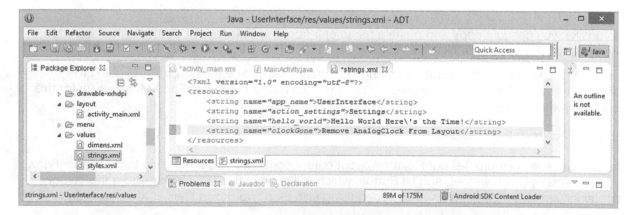

Figure 3-10. Adding the clockGone <string> constant tag to our strings.xml file in our project's /res/values folder

Now you can use the Graphical Layout Editor tab to preview the UI design, and as you can see in Figure 3-11, everything is in place and quite nicely balanced. We have done enough XML mark-up editing now to be able to jump into some Java code editing for a change, and make some of these UI widget elements interactive, and even effect parameter changes on one another.

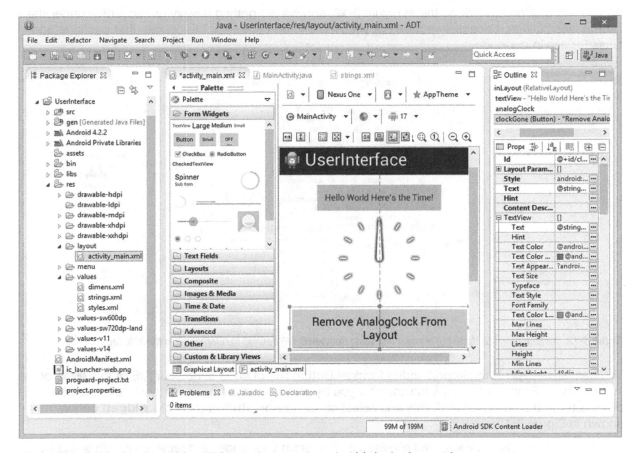

Figure 3-11. Previewing our clockGone UI Button element and new text label value from <string> constant

Next, we are going to learn how to instantiate a UI element in Java code, and attach an **event handler** to it so that we can do something with the UI element with our program logic.

Event Handling: Adding an OnClickListener in Java Code

As we learned in an earlier section in the chapter the View class has many Java **Interfaces**, each of which performs a different kind of event handling function. The logical one to start with, and to use with UI Button objects is an **onClick()** event handler, which lives inside of an **OnCLickListerner()** method. We'll go through the Java logic for this in this chapter section.

Before we can attach an event handler to a UI element, we must **instantiate** that UI element as a **Java Object**, as you probably well know. This is done by declaring the object (using its class and constructor) and name, on one side of an equal sign, and in the case of a UI element, referencing its

XML definition via the ID you assigned to it for this purpose using the findViewById() method, in one line of Java code, in the following format:

```
Button goneButton = (Button)findViewById(R.id.clockGone);
```

As you can see we have done this in Figure 3-12, and we are getting a wavy red underline under the Button class usage, because we have not yet used a import statement to declare that package and class for use in our code.

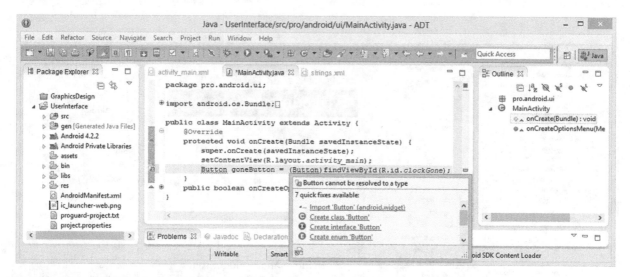

Figure 3-12. Instantiating the Button UI element and using findViewById() method to reference it to the XML tag

You can either type in the import android.widget.Button line of code to rid your IDE of this error, or you can have Eclipse ADT write the code for you by putting your mouse over (hover over, to use the precise term) the wavy red underline and selecting the **Import Button (android.widget)** option, as shown in Figure 3-12.

This removes all this red ink (or red pixels as it were) from your code, and replaces it with some wavy yellow warning underline highlighting, under the goneButton object name. If you hover your mouse pointer over the highlighted warning (or icon in the left margin), you will find that your IDE is simply letting you know that there is an object declared that is not currently in use, which is a waste of system memory until rectified.

As you can see in Figure 3-13, the import android.widget.Button statement has been written for you at the top of your Java code, and the warning pop-up helper dialog has informed you (reminded you) that your new instance of Button named goneButton needs to be used to accomplish something.

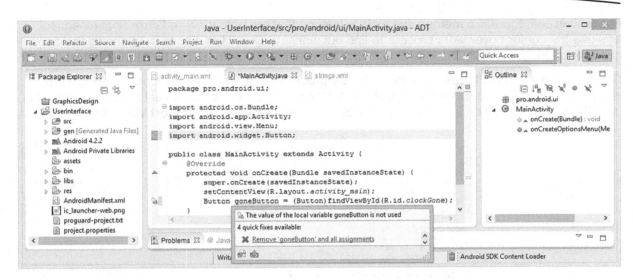

Figure 3-13. Importing the android.widget.Button class and revealing the warning with the quick fix helper dialog

Let's do that next, and use an **.setOnClickListener()** method on **goneButton**.

Once we call .setOnClickListener() off the goneButton object by using dot notation, as shown in Figure 3-14, the warning will also disappear. The full line of code to set up an OnClickListener in Android is as follows:

```
goneButton.setOnClickListener(new View.OnClickListener(){code goes here});
```

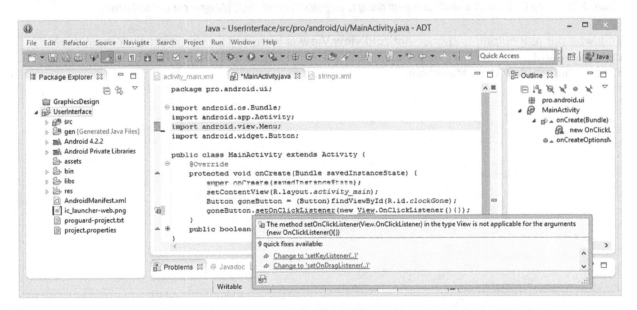

Figure 3-14. Attach a new OnClickListener() method to our goneButton Button object using .setOnClickListener()

As you can see, there is a method and class reference that are both wavy red error underlined, so let's use the cursor hover work process to find out where the error lies. Figure 3-14 shows the error highlighting for the .setOnClickListener() method, saying setOnClickListener is not applicable!

Since we know that Button objects can definitely process OnClickListener() events, our next step would be to then look at this error highlight under View, as maybe that is the real error and is causing both the errors! A solution is shown in Figure 3-15 in a quick fix pop-up—**Import View** class.

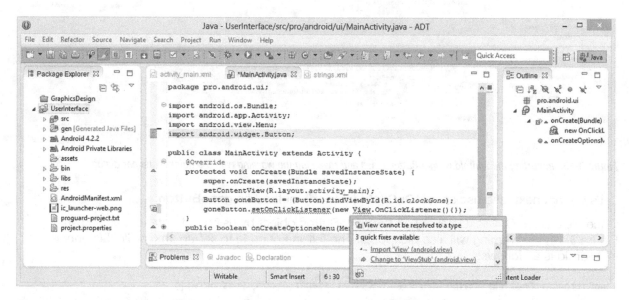

Figure 3-15.   Using Eclipse ADT's quick fix pop-up dialog to diagnose the error highlighting in our OnClickListener

This was our real culprit, and once **android.view.View** is imported for use, both error messages disappear, and a brand new one appears, as is shown in Figure 3-16, along with our brand new import android.view.View statement.

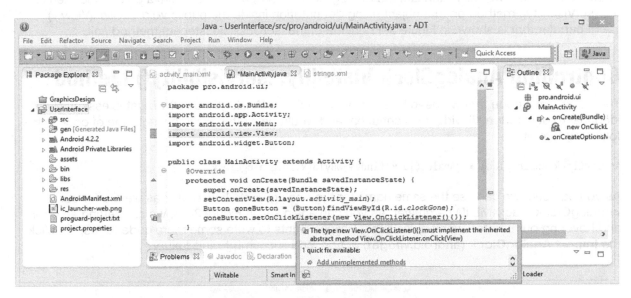

Figure 3-16.   Importing android.view.View and using the quick fix helper dialog to code the Java method

This is the type of quick fix I like, as it writes a bunch of code, simply by clicking the **Add unimplemented methods** option shown in the dialog. As you can see in Figure 3-17 we do not have a complete (empty) event handling Java code block set up for us and ready to handle and Java code processing that we need to place inside it (replacing TODO comment).

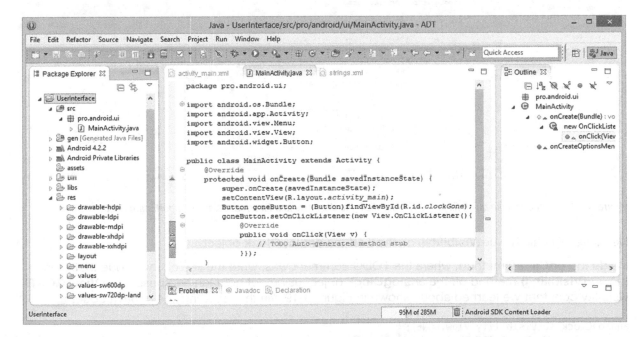

Figure 3-17.   Final OnClickListener code and public void onClick() method ready to hold our setVisibility() method

In the next section we will instantiate the AnalogClock UI widget XML as a Java object and then call the .setVisibility() method on that object using dot notation inside the public void onClick(View v) event handler that is shown in Figure 3-17, inside of the .setOnClickListener() method call.

Controlling AnalogClock Visibility: .setVisibility() Method

The line of Java code that we need to use to instantiate our AnalogClock UI widget is essentially identical to our Button UI widget instantiation, and would be written using a single line of code in the following format:

```
AnalogClock analogClock = (AnalogClock)findViewById(R.id.analogClock);
```

As you can see, we can use the same name for the AnalogClock Java object as we did for our <AnalogClock> tag XML ID parameter. As you can again see in Figure 3-18, we are getting an error and hovering our pointer over it reveals that Eclipse wants to write some more code for us, so, click the **Import AnalogClock (android.widget)** option, and succumb to this luxury.

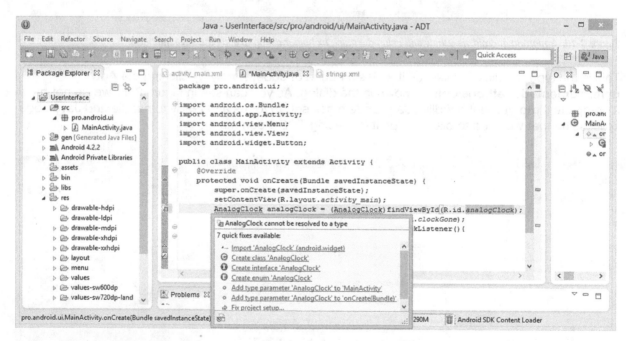

Figure 3-18. Use the Eclipse quick fix pop-up helper dialog to diagnose and fix errors using an Import statement

Next, we will call the **.setVisibility()** method off the **analogClock** object.

Inside the **onClick()** method, where the TODO comment was, write the line of Java code that calls the **.setVisibility()** method off the **analogClock** object using dot notation and pass it the **View.GONE** visibility constant we learned about, shown in Figure 3-19, via the following line of Java code:

```
analogClock.setVisibility(View.GONE);
```

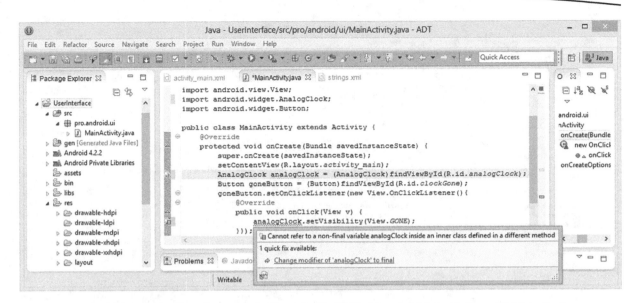

Figure 3-19. Use Eclipse's quick fix to diagnose why the analogClock object is not visible inside the onClick() method

As you can see in Figure 3-19 the .setVisibility() method is having a hard time seeing the analogClock object, which has been declared outside of its sphere of reference.

> **Tip**   To make the analogClock object "accessible" inside the onClick() method inside of the goneButton object's .setOnClickListener method, we need to declare the object instantiation using **final** access. This was suggested within the quick fix dialog, as shown in Figure 3-19.

Our Java code declaring the two UI elements to utilize in our UI design, as well as wiring them up together via event handlers and parameter changing method calls, is now in place and is error free, as shown in Figure 3-20.

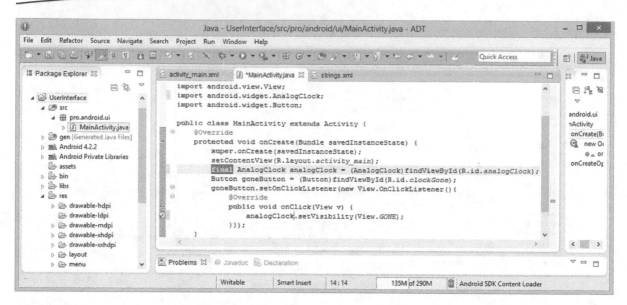

Figure 3-20. Final Java code to set visibility of the AnalogClock UI widget to GONE when goneButton is clicked

Next we need to test our code in the Android emulator, and since I need to make sure that you have at least one device emulator set-up in your IDE, we are going to get into how to install and configure Android device emulators that can be used to test our application code.

Install and Configure an Emulator: Testing Our Java Code

Open the **Window** menu in Eclipse and select the **Android Virtual Device Manager** menu option, which we saw back in Chapter 1 (see Figure 1-27).

This opens up the Android Virtual Device Manager dialog, shown in Figure 3-21. As you can see I already have an AVD (Android Virtual Device) installed in my IDE, but I will show you the work process in this section, in case your AVD Manager dialog is currently empty! On the top-right side of this dialog, you will see the **New** button, click on it, which opens a dialog allowing us to create an Android Virtual Device (AVD) definition.

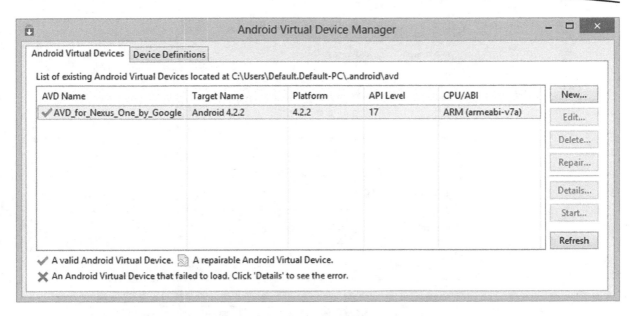

Figure 3-21. Android Virtual Device Manager accessed via the Window menu

Under the **Device** drop-down menu at the top of the **Create New AVD** dialog, find the popular **Galaxy Nexus** Android device definition, and then, in the **AVD Name** field, type a name for it such as **AVD_for_Galaxy_Nexus**. Next give it a 16MB SD card by placing a value of 16 in the **SD Card** field at the bottom, and then check the **Use Host GPU** option on the bottom right.

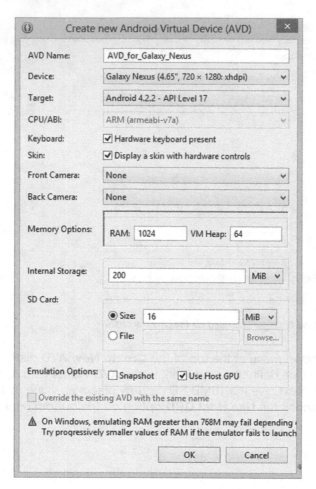

Figure 3-22. Create a new AVD dialog

We will use our workstation graphics card to do any graphics co-processing in the emulator–since we have advanced technology we might as well use it to our advantage. Once you are done, click **OK** to create the AVD.

As you can see in Figure 3-23, the AVD_for_Galaxy_Nexus is now in the AVD list in the center part of the dialog. I am going to use the Nexus One for screenshots in this book as it is a bit more reasonable in size. You can add an AVD_for_Nexus_One AVD emulator also, using this same work process.

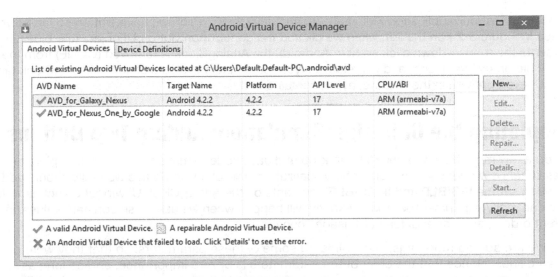

Figure 3-23. Selecting the Galaxy Nexus AVD, which was just added

To generate the AVD emulator screens shown in Figure 3-24, I selected the Nexus One emulator in the AVD Manager and used the Start…button to launch that emulator. Then, in Eclipse ADT, I **right-clicked** the project folder and selected a **Run As ➤ Android Application** menu sequence to run our app!

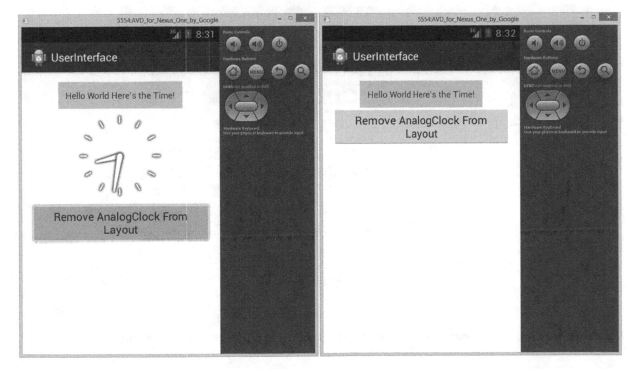

Figure 3-24. App shown running in a Nexus One emulator, with AnalogClock=VISIBLE, and AnalogClock=GONE

Now we can test our application XML mark-up and Java logic, which we have written so far. As you can see in Figure 3-24 on the left, when we clicked the goneButton Button UI object (the blue color represents the mouse-down click event in Android), the AnalogClock is removed (GONE) from the View UI hierarchy evaluation, and our relative layout parameters evaluate as if the AnalogClock tag were not even present in the RelativeLayout container.

Completing the UI Design Simulation: Adding Two Buttons

Let's do a few more things to our XML mark-up and Java code to make this a more complete or professional UI widget visibility parameter visualization simulation. To do this we really should add buttons to set the **VISIBLE** and **INVISIBLE** constants on the AnalogClock UI widget object as well, so we can really experiment with what exactly will happen when we use these constant values, in different orders, and under different UI usage scenarios.

Since we are adding more tags, I consolidated some of these parameters, so that they were on the same lines. Notice that the order of the parameters is of zero importance, and as long as they are separated by a single space character, we can add them to our tags as they best fit, as I have done in Figure 3-25. I removed the background color from the TextView, placing it into the AnalogClock tag instead, because we don't need it in TextView for demonstration purposes. It's bad user experience form to make a UI element look like it is a Button UI element, when it is in fact a Text UI element!

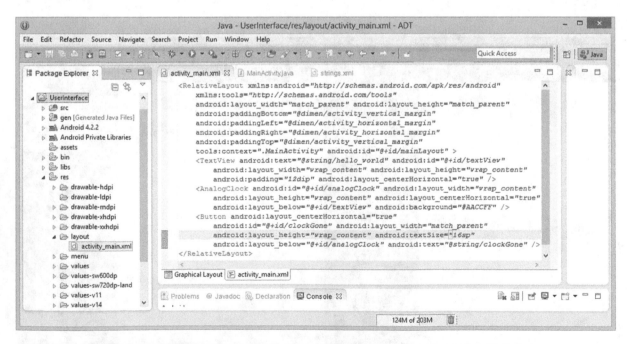

Figure 3-25. Adjusting Button parameters to get ready to copy and paste two more times to create more buttons

I also did a couple of things to stop our button label from wrapping, and thus making our button larger than it needs to be, especially since we're about to replicate it two more times, so it needs to be much more compact.

I did this by using the **android:textSize** parameter and setting it to a **16 SP** or standard pixels value, which is what you need to use for font sizes.

I also changed the **android:layout_width** constant for the Button child tag to be **MATCH_PARENT** so that the height of the button uses the WRAP_CONTENT constant, and the width uses the MATCH_PARENT constant. This is to point out to you that you can use different constants for these in the same UI element to achieve different effects, and to fit the button width to the screen width. Once we copy this UI element, then the other two will match the first Button and the button bank will look uniform in its formatting.

Before we copy and paste our more compact Button tag, let's use the GLE tab at the bottom of the editing pane and preview our changes. As you can see in Figure 3-26, our AnalogClock is now blue, our screen title does not look like it is a Button, and the Button label fits the Button far better.

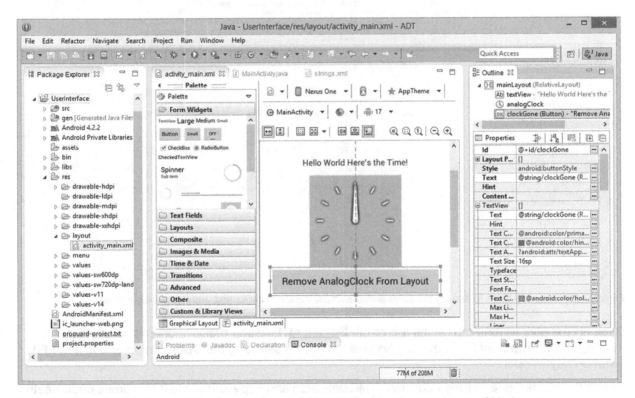

Figure 3-26. Use Graphical Layout Editor to review the new background and match_parent layout_width changes

Now we are ready to copy and paste the Button tag underneath itself twice to create another two buttons. Change the **ID** to **vizButton** and **invizButton** and **android:text** parameter to reference **clockViz** and **clockInviz** constants.

Next we will need to change that **android:layout_below** relative positioning parameter to reference the correct UI object hierarchy, or we will get all three buttons stacked on top of each other all laid out below AnalogClock and not looking too professional.

Change your clockVisible Button to reference the clockGone button and your clockInvisible Button to reference the clockVisible Button, as is shown in Figure 3-27. Now the only thing left to fix are two errors in the mark-up, these relate to not having created <string> tag constants for text labels for our two new buttons, which we have referenced, but not yet created.

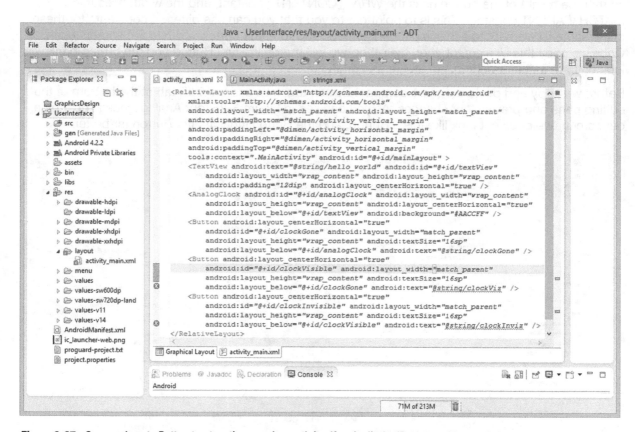

Figure 3-27. Copy and paste Button tag two times underneath itself and edit the ID, text, and layout_below values

Click on the **strings.xml** tab, at the top of the Eclipse ADT editing pane, or open it up by right-clicking the **strings.xml** file in the **/res/values** folder and selecting the **Open** option or using the **F3** function key to open.

Select the **clockGone** <string> constant XML definition and copy and paste it two times underneath itself. Give the first <string> constant copy name **clockViz** and a value of "**Restore AnalogClock Visibility**" and the second a name of **clockInviz** and a value of "**Render AnalogClock Invisible**" and then use the **Ctrl-S** keystroke combination to **Save** and validate your strings.xml file, as shown in Figure 3-28. Now, we are ready to add these new buttons!

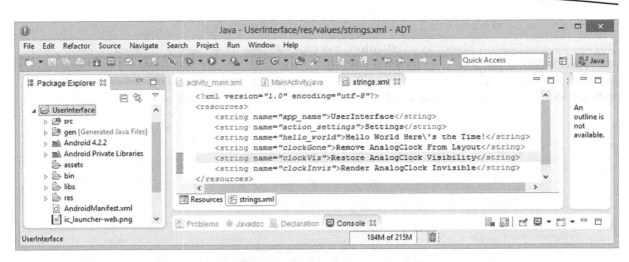

Figure 3-28. Add two <string> values for clockViz and clockInviz to label the two new buttons with their functions

Click the MainActivity.java tab, and select your goneButton instantiation Java code and .setOnClickListener() event handling structure below it and then copy and paste it underneath itself. Next, change your **goneButton** to **vizButton**, the **clockGone** ID reference to **clockVisible**, and your **View.GONE** to **View.VISIBLE**, inside of the .setVisibility() method parameter passing parenthesis, as shown in Figure 3-29.

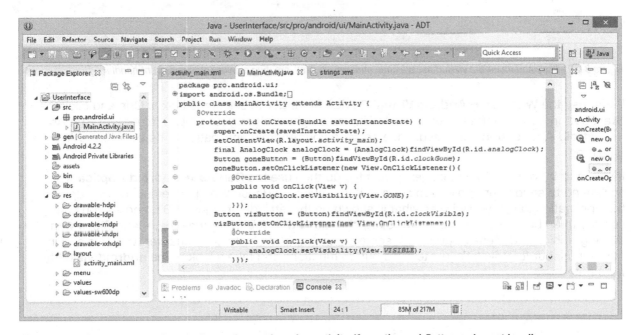

Figure 3-29. Copy and paste the goneButton Java code underneath itself, creating a vizButton and event handler

Finally, let's copy and paste this vizButton code block underneath itself.

Change your **vizButton** object to in**vizButton**, the **clockVisible** ID reference to **clockInvisible,** and your **View.VISIBLE** parameter to be **View.INVISIBLE**, inside of the .setVisibility() method parameter passing parenthesis, as is shown in Figure 3-30. Now we are ready to test our Java code and XML mark-up in the Nexus One emulator, which we set up in the previous section.

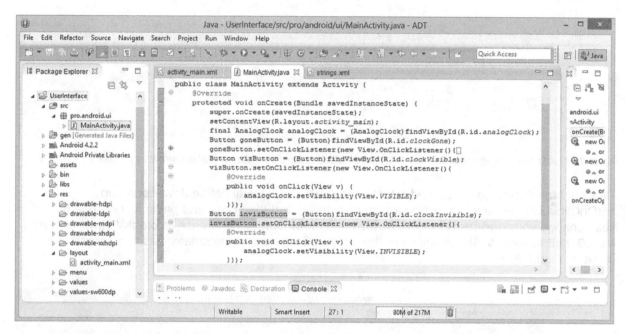

Figure 3-30. Copy and paste the vizButton Java code underneath itself, creating a invizButton and event handler

Either use the **Window ➤ Android Virtual Device Manager** to select the Nexus One and click the **Start** button, or if you have already started it, use a right-click on your project folder and **Run As ➤ Android Application** menu sequence, to send your Android application code over to the AVD emulator.

If you start it from the AVD Manager once it fire up then use the **Run As ➤ Android Application** command to send your application code to it to emulate and test. When the emulator fires up and the application loads, you will see what is shown on the left side of Figure 3-31, and as you can see our three buttons line-up and group together quite well. We'll fine-tune the AnalogClock with some graphics and these buttons with some custom spacing in the next chapter when we add in our menus, but for now let's just test the button functions and take a look at the **android:visibility** parameter.

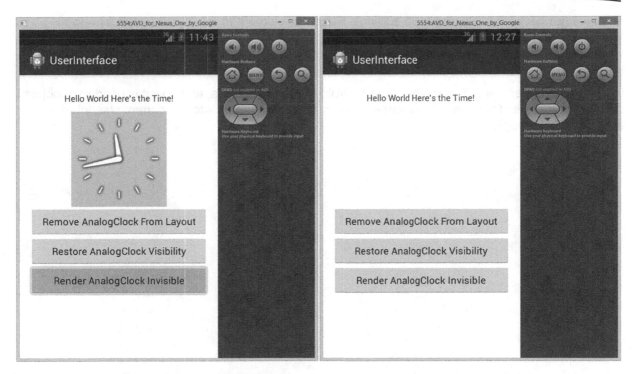

Figure 3-31. Testing VISIBLE, INVISIBLE, and GONE visibility constants, using Buttons and AnalogClock widgets

Since we already tested the GONE parameter, click on the last button that renders the AnalogClock UI widget INVISIBLE but still taking up UI layout space in the ViewGroup hierarchy. As you can see in the emulator screen on the right, the result is as expected, and the AnalogClock is gone, but its View container is still accounted for in the ViewGroup layout calculation. Click these buttons in different order to see what this **android:visibility** parameter does when widgets go from **GONE** to **VISIBLE** or **INVISIBLE** and back!

We'll leave the menu coding for the next chapter on the Android Menu class and summarize what we learned in this chapter regarding the View class.

Summary

In this third chapter, we took a look at the foundation for **UI elements** or **widgets** in Android, the **View** Superclass, as well as its direct subclasses, and even some of the more important indirect subclasses of View widgets.

Next we looked at some of the key View class **properties** or attributes, and then we learned about the concept of **focus**. Then we learned about **Listener** classes, and how they allow us to implement **event handling**, as well as how to use the **setContentView()** method, to implement our XML UI definitions.

Then we got back into XML mark-up adding a Button UI element to our layout container and then finally into Java coding, **instantiating** UI objects and attaching onClick **event listeners**. We learned how to add **Android Virtual Devices**, or **AVD**s, to our IDE so that we can better test our applications.

In the next chapter, we will learn about the Android **Menu** Superclass, and how it is used to subclass and create **menus**. Then we will implement menus of differing types into our current UserInterface application's UI Design.

Part 2

Introduction to the Android Menu Classes for UI Design: OptionsMenu, ContextMenu, PopupMenu and ActionBar

Chapter 4

Android UI Options Menus: OptionsMenu Class and the Action Bar

Now that we have covered the ViewGroup (UI layouts) and View (UI widgets) classes in Android OS, in this chapter we learn more about the Android **Menu** class. The Menu class allows us to create different types of menu structures in Android–from OptionsMenus to ActionBar menus to ContextMenus to PopUpMenus.

We focus on Android OptionsMenu class in this chapter, as they are the most important type of menu in Android, and then later on we will work with more localized PopupMenu and ContextMenu classes in the next chapter.

Implementing menus in Android is not all that different from implementing UI widgets and layout designs. The menu design work is done using XML, in the **/res/menu** folder, and then **inflated** in the Java code, and program logic is then added in to make the menu items functional, via menu event handlers.

There are two primary types of menus in Android, just like there are on a desktop computer system. **Options Menu** items are more like the top-mounted menus that you see in a PC application, and **Context Menu** items are called-up in a local context, just like the right-click context-sensitive menus in Windows and Linux OS.

Android menus can still be a complicated topic, because menus can feature **icons**, **shortcuts**, and **checkmarks**, as well as complex submenu structures, and as of Android 3.0, an **ActionBar** that you must also have a UI design for. And that's just for Options menus, then, we also have Context menus, and Pop-Up menus, both of which are different than Options menus in their design, code implementation, and even their usage within your UI designs. That is why we cover menus in three chapters, instead of just one chapter! These different menu classes in Android, OptionsMenu, PopupMenu and ContextMenu, all pull from the Android Menu master class, which we will learn about next, so that we start at the top of the Menu class code hierarchy.

Android Menu Class: A Public Interface for Making Menus

The Android Menu class, unlike the View and ViewGroup Superclasses we just covered, is actually a public interface, which was developed specifically for managing the items in a menuing system.

The Android Menu class is found in the android.view package, so if you need to import the Menu class you would use the **import android.view.Menu** statement. The Menu class has two indirect subclasses, the **ContextMenu** class and the **SubMenu** class.

Every Activity created in Android supports an **Options Menu**, containing **Actions** (Android 3.0 and later) or **Options** (Android 2.3 and earlier). This is why our blank Activity bootstrap code, which we created back in Chapter 2, contained both XML assets and Java methods for implementing the Options Menu for us automatically.

Later on in this chapter, we will edit both of these and implement our own custom Options Menu using this code and mark-up that was provided for us. We will add **menu items** to this Options Menu, as well as handling clicks on these menu additions.

The easiest way to add menu items is inflating an XML file kept in your **/res/menu** folder. This process takes your XML menu definition and turns it into a **Menu object** by using the **MenuInflater** class, which is a subclass of java.lang.Object, and it has no subclasses. Its class hierarchy is:

```
java.lang.Object
 > android.view.MenuInflater
```

Just as in the previous chapter, when we designed UI layouts using XML and then referenced that UI design using Java methods to turn it into a screen layout and then attached interactivity to that via event handling, the work process with menus is quite similar. We design the menus in XML, inflating them in the Java code, and then attaching custom code to the user's clicks via the .onOptionsItemSelected() or .onContextItemSelected() method.

Menus for Android User Interface Design: An Overview

Menus have become a necessary user interface design element, across every type of digital application, from paid applications for desktop computers to websites to HTML5 apps to JavaFX apps to Android apps and beyond.

To offer your users a unified, consistent user experience, or UX, you will utilize the Android Menu API to present your users with ActionBar menu items and menu options inside of your Activity-based user interface screens.

Beginning with Android OS version 3.0, known as Honeycomb, or API Level 11, Android device manufacturers are no longer required to provide a hardware menu button, due to more common and prolific use of touchscreen displays.

With this change, Android apps should need to move away from a dependence on the legacy five-item Android Options Menu "panel," and instead provide an **Android Action Bar** navigation methodology to present common user actions.

Of course, I will show you how to develop across both of these types of menu implementations, as with the Kindle Fire running Android 2.3.7, and a significant market share for 2.3.x devices still out there, Options Menu panels are still going to be needed by a good portion of your user base.

There are three different core types of menus, all based on an Android Menu API. There is the **Options Menu**, which places menu items in a **Menu Panel** on the bottom of the screen or on an Android **Action Bar**, the **Context Menu** and its **Contextual Action** Bar Items, and the **Pop-Up Menu**, which is local to a View that calls it and unrelated to or unassociated with the Action Bar.

The Options Menu

The Options Menu is the most important and highest level menu structure in Android, so we'll start with this type of menu in this chapter. An Options Menu is a collection of menu selections, known as **items** in Android OS. There is one Options Menu available for each of your Java Activity subclasses.

The Options Menu for each Activity is where you should place menu actions that have the most global impact on your app, such as "Index," "Bookmark," or "Settings."

If you are developing applications for Android 2.3.7 or earlier versions, your users can reveal the Options Menu at the bottom of the device display simply by pressing the **hardware Menu button** on their Android devices.

With the advent of **Android 3.0**, items from your Options Menu XML mark-up and Java code are presented on an Android **Action Bar** as a combination of on-screen action items and overflow icon (three vertical dots) menu options.

Beginning with Android 3.0, the hardware Menu button is no longer required to be provided by hardware manufacturers, so, some devices won't have one.

Android thus suggests that you should migrate toward using this Action Bar exclusively, to provide access to menu selections, and other menu options.

As we will see in this chapter, in your Options Menu XML definition files, you can specify an Options Menu Panel or Action Bar support, but generally one option will turn off the other option. For this reason, creating just the right combination of Menu support for pre-Android 3.0 users and post-Android 3.0 users becomes a very tricky thing to accomplish successfully.

For this reason, we are going to go into detail regarding menus for this chapter, look at all the XML parameter options and design options, and implement these things gradually, in our UserInterface application, as we build more and more complexity into our Options Menu structure for our pro. android.ui package UserInterface application.

The Context Menu

The next most important menu to use for your applications in Android is the **Context Menu**. A Context Menu is a free-floating menu that appears when a user performs a **long-click** on a user interface element (a View object).

You learned about the **OnLongClickListener()** in the previous chapter on View classes, and soon, you will get some experience with this event handler in triggering some Context Menus within our Android application. You also just learned about the **OnCreateContextMenuListener(),** and you'll get a chance to use that class as well in the next chapter in the book.

The Context Menu provides menu selection actions that affect your related content that you have attached the ContextMenu object to. Similar to the Options Menu object, the Context Menu was also enhanced in Android 3.0 to be able to place **contextual action bar items** onto the Android Action Bar.

For this reason, when developing for Android 3.0 or later OS versions, you would want to consider using the **contextual action mode**, to enable actions on selected content to appear in the on-screen Android Action Bar UI area.

The contextual action mode displays action items that affect the selected content in an Action Bar UI area located at the top of the display screen. Using this Action Bar UI area allows your user to select from multiple menu items, in the form of icons–if you have supplied the proper artwork.

The Popup Menu

Finally, the **Popup Menu** displays a list of menu items inside a **vertical list** UI element, which is anchored to the View that invoked this **PopupMenu** object. The PopupMenu class was introduced in Android 3.0 Honeycomb API Level 11 and may have been added because Action Bar was introduced and ContextMenu, which is quite similar to PopupMenu, became more likely to be implemented as **contextual action bar items**, as this is the current Android Menu trend.

This may have been the reason that the PopupMenu class was introduced–to pop-up menus relative to UI elements that needed on-screen localized menu support, but which did not require Android Action Bar text items or icons.

A PopupMenu object is appropriate for providing your users with pop-up menus populated with options that directly relate to specific content, or to provide menu options for the input phase of a UI-based command.

Menu options in a Popup Menu should not directly affect the corresponding content, as that is what the ContextMenu class, and contextual Action Bar items are designed for use with. So be sure to use the PopupMenu class for menu items that invoke extended actions that relate to logical regions or genres of content in your apps Activity subclasses.

A good rule of thumb would be if the Menu subclass you are invoking is local to the UI element in your screen design, it should be a ContextMenu object or a PopupMenu object. If your MenuItem objects control the actual content which the UI element controls, then simply use the ContextMenu class and not the PopupMenu class. On the other hand, if the MenuItems control the Navigation, Features or User Experience, and are not directly connected to the content being viewed or worked on, then utilize the PopupMenu class.

There is also a type of Menu subclass in Android called a **Sub Menu**, but this is a collection of nested menu items. A SubMenu object allows you to increase the complexity of your menu definitions for any given type of Menu subclass, and is implemented in your XML menu definitions, which we will get into in detail in the next section.

Using XML to Define a Menu: <menu> and <item> Tags

For all three types of Menu objects in Android, the OS provides a standard XML format to define a Menu object and its MenuItem sub-objects. Rather than having to build app menus in your application's Java code, it is far easier to define a Menu object and its MenuItem sub-object menu option items, structure, or hierarchy using an XML menu definition file resource, just like we design UI layouts, string constants, and so forth.

In this way, all you have to do in your Java code is to **inflate** this Menu object definition resource, which **instantiates** a Menu object and loads it with your exact menu structure definition, inside of your Activity subclass code.

For a number of key reasons, Android recommends using XML to create your Menu object definitions. The most important one is that by extracting a Menu definition into one XML resource (file), it allows you to design different menu structures and levels of complexity for different Android environment scenarios, including different device types, OS versions or levels, screen sizes, orientations or densities, OS themes, and similar considerations. This is achieved by having more than one menu definition XML file in your project's /res/menu resource folder.

As we have also seen, over the past couple of chapters, using XML tags and parameters makes it easier to visualize designs, whether that is UI widget structures, UI layouts, or complex, multilevel menu structures.

Defining a menu structure in XML also serves to separate the menu content design elements from your application programming logic, which, in a team environment, allows the designers who are not programmers to craft highly detailed menu structures with zero knowledge of Java classes or methods.

To define the Menu object, or <menu> in XML, you would create the XML file inside of your project's **/res/menu** directory, which as we saw in Chapter 2 was done for us, using the New Android Application series of dialogs.

The **main.xml** menu XML definition that was created for us contains the following XML menu UI definition parent and child tags: **<menu>, <item>,** and **<group>**. The <menu> tag is the **parent tag** and is declared once as follows:

```
<menu xmlns:android="http://schemas.android.com/apk/res/android">
```

This parent tag element defines your Menu object and its XML Naming Schema address, and serves as your container for the rest of your menu definition XML child tags, which consist of menu **items**, **groups,** and **sub-menus**.

This <menu> element **must** be the parent tag container for the menu XML file and needs to hold one or more <item> and optionally <group> menuing design elements. An **<item>** child tag creates a **MenuItem** object, which, as you might have guessed, represents one single item inside of the Options Menu.

To create a **sub-menu** structure, you would use this <item> child tag design element, and **nest** another <menu> element underneath it, to create that sub-menu structure.

To add MenuItem objects to this sub-menu, you would add <item> child tags, which were nested underneath that <menu> child tag, to create the sub-menu's MenuItem objects (MenuItem Selection Options are Java Objects).

The Menu **<group>** tag is an **invisible container** for **logically grouping** menu <item> elements. It allows you to group your menu items, so they share properties such as **active state** and **visibility**. You can create the <group> by nesting <item> elements inside a <group> element in your menu resource.

A menu <group> allows you to define a logical collection of menu items for your Activity subclass that shares certain traits. Once you define a group, you can, for instance, enable or disable all the grouped menu items by using the **.setGroupEnabled()** method.

Similarly, you could show or hide all your grouped menu items by using the **.setGroupVisible()** method, or specify whether all the grouped menu items are checkable, by using the **.setGroupCheckable()** Java method.

The difference between <group> and sub-menus is that the sub-menu (nested) items exist on different (lower or sub) levels of the menu structure, whereas <item> tags nested in a <group> parent tag container appear to be on exactly the same level as any other (non-group) MenuItem objects underneath the parent <menu> tag. Grouping these <item> tags allows other Java methods to be applied to these MenuItem objects all at the same time, as specified in the previous two paragraphs.

Android OS will never separate your grouped menu items. What this means is if you declare an <item> parameter **android:showAsAction="ifRoom"** (which we will be covering next) for each <item> tag, each of these MenuItem objects in this group will either **both appear in the Action Bar** or **both appear in the Action Bar Overflow Icon Menu Panel** (three stacked square dots icon).

Defining the Menu Attributes: Using Child Tag Parameters

The <item> element supports several attributes in the form of parameters, which you can use to define a MenuItem object's appearance and behavior.

The **android:id** parameter is the most important parameter, as it allows the application's Java code to recognize which MenuItem the user is selecting by assigning a unique, text-based resource ID to each MenuItem object.

The next most important parameter to declare would be the **android:title** as this parameter defines this MenuItem object's text label, which identifies what it does to the user. This parameter references a <string> constant.

Another closely related parameter to this **android:title** parameter is the **android:titleCondensed** parameter, which defines this MenuItem object's truncated or condensed text label, which allows the developer to specify a shorter or abbreviated menu title label. This parameter also references a <string> constant, and we'll implement it later on in the chapter.

The next most important parameter, especially if you plan on using an icon in Android's Action Bar for the MenuItem object, would be the **android:icon** parameter. This parameter references a **drawable** (digital image) asset, and uses it as an icon for display in the Android Action Bar.

The next most important parameter is the **android:showAsAction** parameter, introduced in Android 3.0 Honeycomb API 11, which specifies when and how this MenuItem object should appear, as an action item in the Action Bar.

There are five constants that can be utilized with the **android:showAsAction** parameter, and I discuss what each one does here. The default, as you will see later in the chapter, is **never**, and this forces a **Menu Panel** to pop up with the text titles (labels). If you are targeting pre-3.0 versions of Android, then you would want to use this constant value setting exclusively.

The most popular Menu constant for the ShowAsAction parameter is an **ifRoom** value, as this specifies to show the MenuItem on the Action Bar if there's room to fit it there; otherwise it displays under the Overflow Icon.

The next most popular constant is the **withText** constant, which if you have an icon specified, will display both the text title (label) and the icon's graphic. As with the **always** constant, which I will cover here because it is similar, this can result in a **crowded** Action Bar, which might be confusing to the end-user. Note that using the always option can also lead to text title (label) **overlap**, which would thus result in a poor user experience.

Another parameter that was introduced in Android 3.0 Honeycomb API 11 is the **android:onClick** parameter, which is pretty darned cool, because it is an **event handler** in the form of a parameter! All you do is specify your method name, and when the user clicks that element, that method is called.

It is important to note that android:onClick also works with View objects (is a global widget parameter). So, android:onClick is a useful XML option all around, for designers to be able to call their programmers Java code, as long as they know the method name.

There are also two useful **shortcut key definition** parameters, one for an **alpha shortcut** and one for a **numeric shortcut**. These two parameters are often overlooked, and yet, they can enhance user experience significantly.

- The **android:alphabeticShortcut** takes a **char** data value and defines the key on an alphabetic keyboard or keypad that is the shortcut for the MenuItem.

- An **android:numericShortcut** takes an **integer** data value and defines the key on the numeric keypad (0 through 9) that is the shortcut for the MenuItem.

There are also several MenuItem parameters for defining the **states** of menu items, such as **checked**, **enabled**, **visible,** and so on. The **android:checkable** parameter defines whether the MenuItem is checkable, that is, if it can display a checkmark next to a text title (label). There is also an **android:checked** parameter that sets the default (checked or unchecked) for the MenuItem. There are also **android:visible** and **android:enabled** parameters, to control these MenuItem attributes. All these parameters use **true** or **false** values.

Options Menu Design: Using the main.xml Menu Definition

Let's get right into actual Options Menu design and open up our Eclipse UI project and start to learn exactly how Options Menu objects are defined, created, designed, configured, inflated, handled, evaluated, and tested.

Open up your MainActivity.java tab at the top of your project in Eclipse, showing the code we wrote in the previous chapter, and collapse the three **setOnClickListener()** methods you wrote in the previous chapter by clicking the minus icons in the left margin and then expand the plus icon next to the **onCreateOptionsMenu()** method as shown in Figure 4-1. As you can see, this method has **public** access control, and returns a **boolean** data value. The data value tells the caller of this method whether or not the **Menu** object named **menu** was successfully created (i.e., inflated).

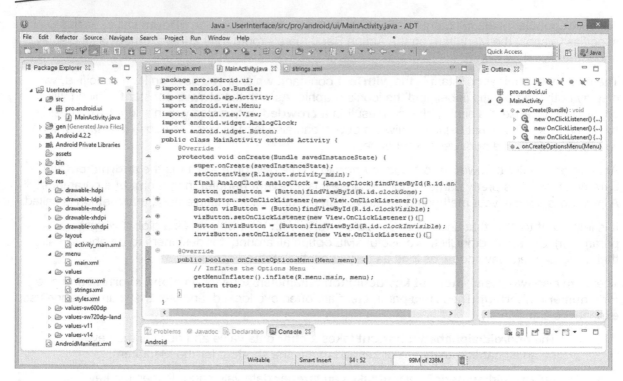

Figure 4-1. *Taking a look at the onCreateOptionsMenu() method that Eclipse ADT created for us in Chapter 2*

Inside the method, we have two Java methods chained together, using dot notation. The **getMenuInflater()** method accesses the **.inflate()** method from the Android **MenuInflater** class, passing it two parameters, a **reference** to the Menu XML Resource and the **Menu** object named **menu**, and then if the Menu object inflates successfully, returns a **true** value via the following code:

```
getMenuInflater().inflate(R.menu.main, menu);
return true;
```

Next, let's take a look at bootstrap Menu XML definition by going into the **/res/menu** folder and right-clicking the **main.xml** XML file and using the **Open** command to open it up inside the Eclipse ADT central editing pane, as is shown in Figure 4-2. As you can see there is one **<menu>** parent tag with the **xmlns:android** parameter correctly defined, along with one **<item>** child tag inside of it with four parameters assigning an **ID**, an **orderInCategory**, a menu label or **title**, and a **showAsAction** constant value setting of **never**.

Figure 4-2. Taking a look at the menu.xml XML Menu definition resource that Eclipse created for us in Chapter 2

Let's get the easy parameters out of the way first. The **android:id** can be anything that you want, so as we expand this example, we may change it to be something other than action_settings. This **android:orderInCategory** can use any order numbering you like, you can use 100, 200, 300, and so on, as is shown here, or 5, 10, 15, 20. I will be using 1, 2, 3, 4, 5 as I expand this menu definition, as we learn how to code an OptionsMenu in this chapter.

The **android:title** parameter gives a title, I like to call it a label, to the MenuItem defined by the <item> child tag, by referencing a <string> tag constant in the **strings.xml** file via this **"@strings/ action_settings"** reference, as shown in Figure 4-2. Soon we open our strings.xml tab and edit (and add) some of these menu titles, or label, text values.

The **android:showAsAction** parameter is set to a constant value of **never** in the screenshot shown in Figure 4.2, and if you use a **Run As ➤ Android Application** and launch the Nexus One emulator, and then hit the hardware **MENU** button on the button panel on the upper-right of the emulator, you will see the pre-3.0 Android Options menu at the bottom of your screen.

The right side of the screenshot in Figure 4-3 shows what happens if we change the constant value from never to **ifRoom**. As you can see, this puts the MenuItem onto the Action Bar at the top-right of the screen shot, and the Menu Panel at the bottom no longer shows up when you click the hardware MENU button on your emulator.

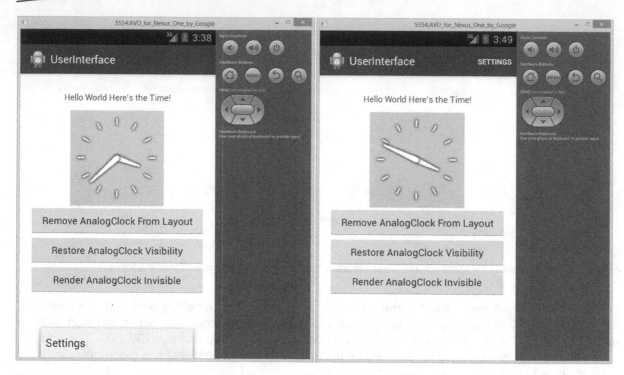

Figure 4-3. OptionsMenu on left with showAsAction="never" OptionsMenu on right with showAsAction"ifRoom"

As you can see, if you have developed your application for Android 2.3 API Level 10 or earlier, then the contents of an OptionsMenu object definition will appear at the bottom of the device display when the user presses the hardware MENU button, as is shown on the left side of Figure 4-3.

When an OptionsMenu object is opened the first visible portion is the icon menu, which holds up to six menu items. If the menu includes more than six items, Android places the sixth item (and any others) into the **overflow menu**, which the user can open by selecting **MORE**. We add more than six <item> child tags to our example code just to see exactly what happens in that use-case scenario.

If you've developed an application for Android 3.0 API level 11 and later, then you would be using an **android:showAsAction="ifRoom"** parameter, so the MenuItem objects from the OptionsMenu are made available in an Action Bar.

By default, the system places all items in the **action overflow icon**, which the user can reveal with the action overflow icon on the right side of the action bar (or by pressing the device hardware MENU button, if available).

To enable easy access only to certain actions, you can promote a few items to appear in the Action Bar by adding android:showAsAction="ifRoom" to the corresponding <item> elements. We will play around with this in our XML as we design an OptionsMenu object and its MenuItem object component objects.

Since the OptionsMenu object appears in the Action Bar Overflow Icon as a menu-like structure, there is a trend toward calling the OptionMenu menu structure the "Overflow Menu" even though it is the OptionsMenu shoehorned into the Action Bar paradigm and ending up in the Overflow Icon drop-down.

It is interesting to note, that if you have developed your application for Android 2.3 and earlier, Android calls onCreateOptionsMenu() to create the OptionsMenu object when your user accesses your menu for the first time.

On the other hand, if you've developed for Android 3.0 API 11 and higher, Android calls onCreateOptionsMenu() when starting your Activity subclass, so that it can show the action menu items on the Action Bar.

Let's add seven MenuItem objects to our existing OptionsMenu object, and change the parameters to suit our own example. The first thing we need to do is to add our seven (fourteen actually, with our condensed menu titles) string constants for our MenuItem options; let's make them colors for now.

Customizing Our OptionsMenu: Adding String Constants

Click the **strings.xml** tab in the central editing pane of Eclipse, and edit the **action_settings** <string> tag, to be named **action_red,** and change the title or menu label value to read "**Blood Red.**" Then, copy and paste this tag underneath itself and remove the underscore character from the name, so it reads **actionred,** and change the "Blood Red" value to "**RED.**"

When you are done, we are going to copy and paste these two <string> tags six more times, to create all the colors in the spectrum. The two tags should look like this, before you copy them, and edit the color portions:

```
<string name=action_red>Blood Red</string>
<string name=actionred>RED</string>
```

Next, select both <string> tags at the same time, and copy them once, and paste them six times underneath themselves. Next, change your tag's **name** parameters, from red to **org, yel, grn, blu, pur**, and **wht**, respectively.

For the action_color named tags, we are going to give a descriptive, or a full length, menu name, so replace the Blood Red value with **Burnt Orange, Banana Yellow, Forest Green, Ocean Blue, Deep Purple**, and **Stark White**, respectively. When you're done the mark-up should look like the following:

```
<string name=action_red>Blood Red</string>
<string name=actionred>RED</string>
<string name=action_org>Burnt Orange</string>
<string name=actionorg>ORG</string>
<string name=action_yel>Banana Yellow</string>
<string name=actionyel>YEL</string>
<string name=action_grn>Forest Green</string>
<string name=actiongrn>GRN</string>
<string name=action_blu>Ocean Blue</string>
<string name=actionblu>BLU</string>
<string name=action_pur>Deep Purple</string>
<string name=actionper>PUR</string>
<string name=action_wht>Stark White</string>
<string name=actionwht>WHT</string>
```

As you can see in Figure 4-4, our XML mark-up is error-free, and we're now ready to add these seven MenuItem tags into our OptionsMenu parent container.

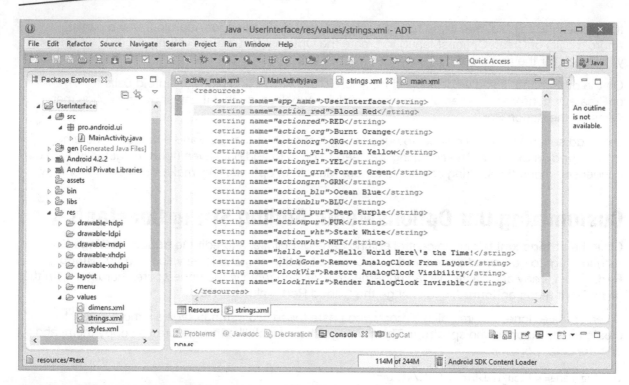

Figure 4-4. Adding seven <string> tags to our strings.xml file, which will be referenced by our ActionBar items

Next, we edit our **main.xml** menu definition file and add in the **android:titleCondensed** tags to give our MenuItem objects alternative shorter menu names, as well as full descriptive menu names using the **android:title** parameter. We'll change some other important parameters as well, such as the android:orderInCategory and android:showAsAction values.

Customizing Our OptionsMenu: Editing the Parameters

Click on the **main.xml** tab at the top of Eclipse and change the **android:id** parameter to reference **@+id/action_red,** and **android:orderInCategory** value from 100 to **1**, and set **android:showAsAction** to the **never** constant value.

Make the same reference change in the **android:title** parameter to reference the **action_red** <string> constant, and then, add the **android:titleCondensed** parameter referencing the **@+id/actionred** <string> constant. As you can see in Figure 4-5 I put two parameters on one line to save some editing space. The XML markup looks like the following block of tags and parameters:

```
<menu xmlns:android=http://schemas.android.com/apk/res/android >
    <item android:id="@+id/action_red" android:title="@string/action_red"
        android:orderInCategory="1"  android:showAsAction="never"
        android:titleCondensed="@+id/actionred" />
```

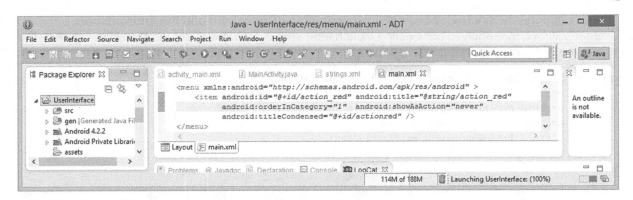

Figure 4-5. Editing the ID, title, titleCondensed tags to reference action_red and showAsAction constant to never

Now we can take a look at the results in the Nexus One emulator by using a **Run As ➤ Android Application** work process. As you can see in Figure 4-6, a Menu Panel with Blood Red appears at the bottom of the display screen when a MENU hardware button is pressed on the upper-right side of the emulator.

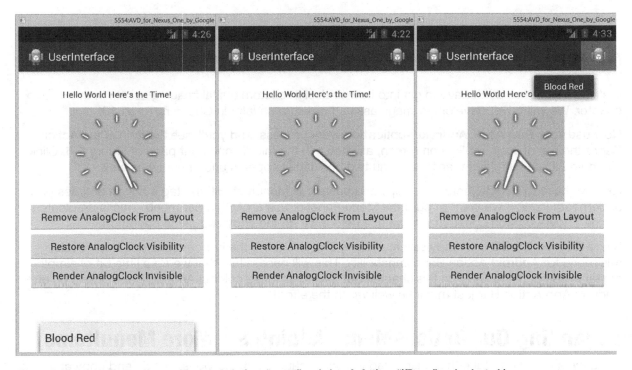

Figure 4-6. Nexus One emulator with showAsAction="never" and showAsAction="ifRoom" and selected icon

Now let's change the android:showAsAction constant to **ifRoom**, and add the **android:icon** parameter with a reference to our existing launch icon image drawable asset, as shown in Figure 4-7. Here is the XML markup that is needed to implement the Android icon:

```
<menu xmlns:android=http://schemas.android.com/apk/res/android >
    <item android:id="@+id/action_red" android:title="@string/action_red"
        android:orderInCategory="1"  android:showAsAction="ifRoom"
        android:icon="@drawable/ic_launcher"
        android:titleCondensed="@+id/actionred" />
```

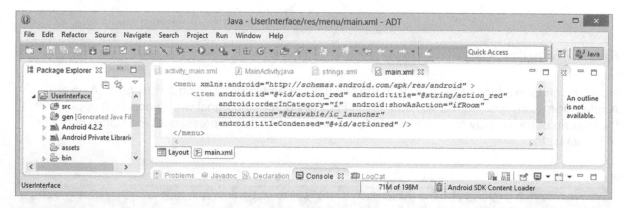

Figure 4-7. Editing the main.xml menu XML definition to change showAsAction to ifRoom and add android:icon

We'll do this so we don't have to get into how to design custom digital imaging assets in this chapter. We will cover developing image assets from scratch later in Chapters 7 and 10.

Now use your **Run As ➤ Android Application** work process, and you'll see the icon in the Action Bar at the top of your application screen, as shown in the middle and right pane of Figure 4-6. Click it and you'll see it highlight, and the menu text title (label) appears underneath it as well.

Now we have to decide, before we copy and paste this MenuItem <item> tag a bunch of times (six) underneath itself, if we want to build the Menu Panel or use an Action Bar menu. This is predicated on the ShowAsAction constant that we use before we do the copy and paste operation.

Since Android 3.0 OS is already seven versions old, let's leave the ifRoom constant, and develop this menu for Android Action Bar compatibility. This will necessitate that we do a little bit of simple digital imaging, using GIMP in this chapter, but having all those colorful Android Robot icons on our Android App Action Bar just might be well worth the effort!

Expanding Our OptionsMenu: Adding Six More MenuItems

Next, we are going to take that <item> tag that we created in the previous section and copy and paste it six more times underneath itself to create a seven options menu so that we can see how showAsAction constants work in the Nexus One emulator.

Select the entire tag, copy it once (Ctrl-C), and paste it six times, using the **Ctrl-V** keystroke combination. Then, change each occurrence of the word **red** to **org, yel, grn, blu, pur,** and **wht,** respectively, as shown in Figure 4-8.

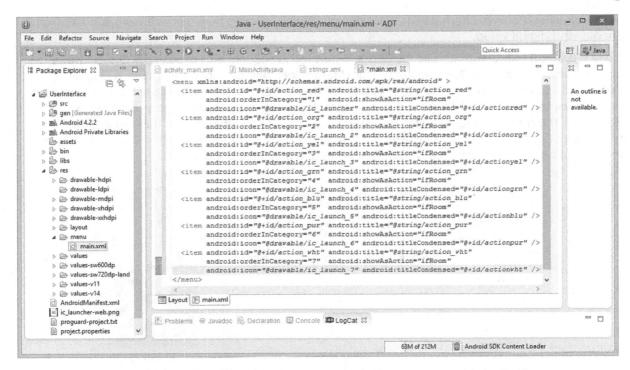

Figure 4-8. Copying and pasting six additional <item> tags to test the Android menu system and Action Bar

Next, be sure your **android:orderInCategory** parameter progresses from **1** through **7**, and also change your **android:icon** tag's drawable asset naming schema to match the orderInCategory numbering, as shown in Figure 4-8.

Once all this is done, you will be ready to create your color-matched icon assets using GIMP in the next section, and then we can test our menu in the Nexus One emulator.

It is important to notice here that we don't have to do any Java coding in order to design and test this menu in the Android emulator. We do have to do some Java coding later on to make these menu items functional, however.

Basic Digital Imaging with GIMP: Creating Our Menu Icons

Since we have inserted the **android:icon** parameter into our <item> tags, we will need to create seven digital image assets to utilize with our menuing items. The easiest way to do this, for now, is to use the **ic_launcher.png** file, which was put into our five **/res/drawable** folders by the New Android Application series of dialogs. Then we use GIMP 2.8 to do some basic color shifting to create Android Bot Icons of every hue of the rainbow.

Launch GIMP 2.8.10 (or later) from your Taskbar quick launch icons and generate six different color shifted variations of your Android launch icon. This icon image asset, named ic_launcher.png, currently lives in our five resolution-specific **/res/drawable** image asset folders.

These include: **/res/drawable-ldpi**, **/res/drawable-mdpi**, **/res/drawable-hdpi**, **/res/drawable-xhdpi**, and **/res/drawable-xxhdpi**. You will be learning about these in greater detail in Chapters 9 and 10 in this book, which covers alternate UI layout design as well as using new media assets such as digital images and digital video.

Once GIMP 2.8 has launched, use the **File ➤ Open** menu sequence to access the **Open Image** dialog, shown in Figure 4-9. Navigate to your **Users** folder, and system name (mine is Default. Default-PC) subfolder. Underneath this, you will find your Eclipse ADT **/workspace** folder, and then your **UserInterface** project folder underneath that. Inside the project folder, as you have seen in Eclipse, is the **/res** (resources) folder and inside that are the drawable folders that I mentioned in the previous paragraph. Let's use **XXHDPI** (extra extra high dots per inch) resolution assets, as they're the largest ones, so we can clearly see what we're doing in the work process.

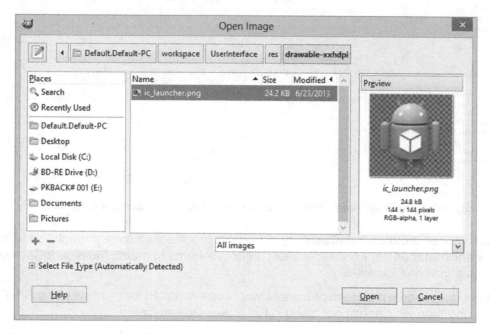

Figure 4-9. Using the File ➤ Open Image dialog to locate our ic_launcher.png

Select the **ic_launcher.png** file as shown in Figure 4-9, and click **Open**. Next, use the **Colors ➤ Hue-Saturation** menu sequence, as shown in Figure 4-10, to access the Hue - Saturation Adjustment Tool in GIMP 2.8. This tool allows us to **color-shift** our robot icon across the spectrum.

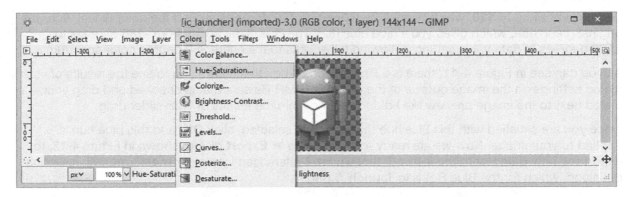

Figure 4-10. Using the Colors ➤ Hue-Saturation menu sequence to access the Hue-Saturation tool in GIMP

As you can see in the **Adjust Hue / Lightness / Saturation** dialog, shown in Figure 4-11, there are **Adjust Selected Color** sliders at the bottom of the dialog that allow you to individually adjust **Hue** (color spectrum position) as well as **Lightness** (black to white values) and **Saturation** (the amount of color versus grayscale, or alternatively known as the color's intensity).

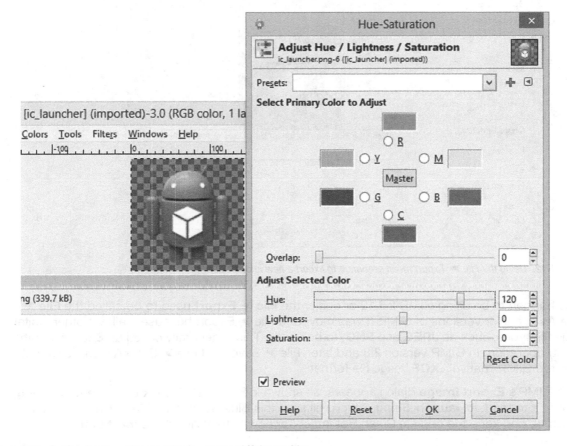

Figure 4-11. Setting the Hue slider to 120 degrees to shift hue to blue

Set the Hue slider to **120**, which represents a **positive 120 degrees** around the color wheel, from the original green hue, which gives you a nice blue hue. The Hue slider spans from **-180** degrees to **+180** degrees in data value settings, allowing full access to the entire 360 degree color spectrum.

As you can see in Figure 4-11, there is a **Preview** checkbox that allows you to see the results of your dialog settings on the image outside of the dialog in GIMP. Be sure that is checked and drag your dialog next to the image preview like I did to see the real-time results of your slider drag.

Once you are satisfied with this blue hue that you have selected, click **OK**, and this blue hue is applied to your image. Now we are ready to use the **File ➤ Export** dialog, shown in Figure 4-12, to export the new Blue Bot to the filename that we have referenced inside our **main.xml** XML file menu definition, which for the Blue Bot is **ic_launch_5.png**.

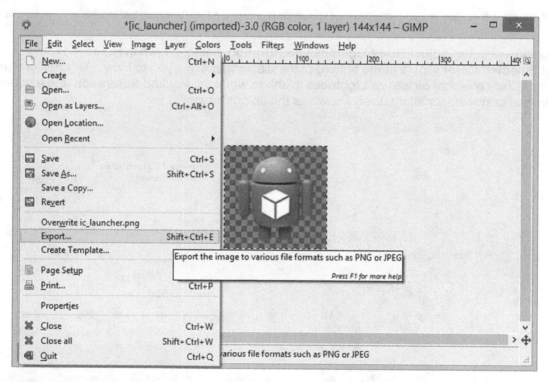

Figure 4-12. Using the File ➤ Export menu sequence to export a new image asset

If you happen to be using GIMP 2.6.12 or earlier the **File ➤ Export** used to be called the **File ➤ Save As** in earlier versions of GIMP. It was moved to File ➤ Export because it allows other digital image file types, such as **JPEG** and **PNG**, to be saved. This is generally called an **Export** (to other format) operation. In GIMP version 2.8 and later, File ➤ Save, and File ➤ Save As, only save out files using the GIMP "native" **.XCF** image file format.

When GIMP's **Export Image** dialog appears, as shown in Figure 4-13, click the **ic_launcher.png**, and edit it to read: **ic_launch_5.png**, which will save this Blue Bot into a different image container (filename), and keep the original Green Bot intact (for now). Then click the **Export** button!

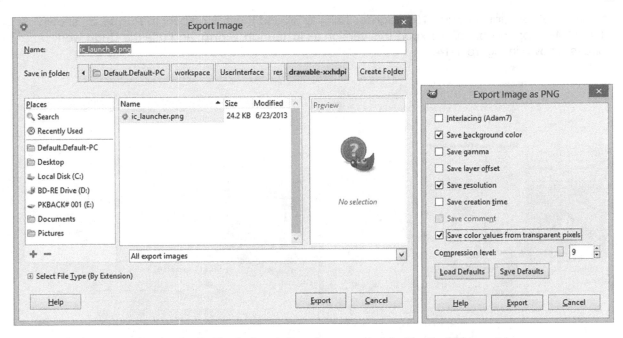

Figure 4-13. Entering our filename for the Blue ic_launch_5.png image asset and setting the PNG parameters

Once you click the **Export** button you'll be presented with the **Export Image as PNG** options dialog, shown on the right side of Figure 4-13. Be sure that the **Save color values from transparent pixels**, as represented by the checkerboard pattern in GIMP, is selected, and click the **Export** button.

The last step in this color-shifting and exporting work process is to **Undo** what you have done for the Blue Bot and do it all over again for the other colors. Use the **Edit ➤ Undo Hue-Saturation** menu sequence, as is shown in Figure 4-14, to return to your original image data and repeat these five steps, shown in Figures 4-10 through 4-14, for the other colors.

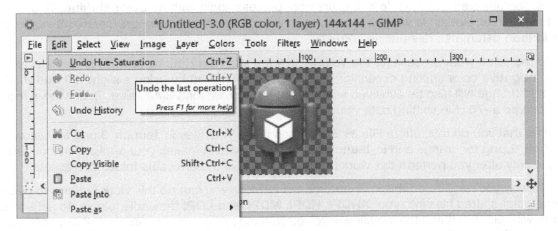

Figure 4-14. Using the Edit ➤ Undo Hue-Saturation menu sequence to start over

Next we'll rotate our Hue value **180 degrees** halfway around the color wheel to **Purple**, as shown in Figure 4-15 on the left side. Export this version as **ic_launch_6.png**, and use the **Undo** work process, shown in Figure 4-14.

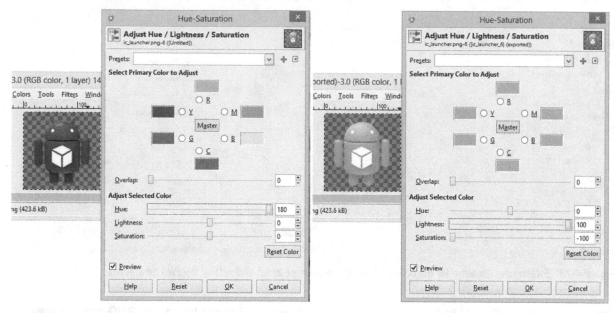

Figure 4-15. Use a Hue-Saturation tool to shift color 180 degrees for purple, and desaturate and lighten to white

To create the White Bot, we can leave the Hue slider alone, and adjust the **Saturation** slider all the way to the left, to **remove all color** and give us a Grayscale Bot. To turn this now Grey Bot white, we then adjust the **Lightness** slider all the way to the right, removing the black values from the image.

Next, **Export** your White Bot to the filename **ic_launch_7.png,** and then use the **Edit ➤ Undo** menu sequence to return to the original Green Bot. Next we need to export this Green Bot into its proper filename container, so use the **File ➤ Export** work process again with **no color shifting**. This exports the Green Bot as: **ic_launch_4.png,** so that it will match our main.xml menu XML mark-up **android:icon** parameter, referencing correctly.

Next do the same work process for the **Yellow**, **Orange** and **Red** Bots by using Hue shifting values into the **negative** color shifting dimension. Yellow can be achieved by using a slight **-20** Hue shifting value, and orange will also be achieved with a slight **-40** Hue shifting data value. To achieve a robust red color, use a **-70** Hue shifting data value.

Each time that you do this, utilize **File ➤ Export** and name your files **ic_launch_3.png** for yellow, **ic_launch_2.png** for orange and **ic_launcher.png** for red, which makes your application icon red as well, but only after you perform this work process for each of the drawable folder icon assets.

I discuss why you need to do this in Chapter 9, but for now, you can do this work process to place all these color-shifted files into your **XHDPI**, **HDPI**, **MDPI,** and **LDPI** drawable folders, to get some practice with GIMP 2.8 and the workflow involved with digital imaging for Android UI development. As you see, Pro Android app development is anything but easy!

If you don't want to color-shift the image two dozen more times, be sure to at least do the **/res/drawable-hdpi** folder image assets, as your Nexus One emulator uses the HDPI image resolution assets. If you don't, you will get a Green Bot where the Red Bot is supposed to be!

Setting a Target Emulator: The Run Configurations Dialog

Before we get into testing the Menu XML definition in an Android Nexus One emulator, I wanted to show you the dialog in Eclipse that allows you to select which one of the emulators which you installed in your AVD Manager will be used when you use the **Run As ➤ Android Application** menu sequence. We learned how to add our new AVD emulators in the previous Chapter 3.

If you right-click your Project folder, inside of the **Run As** menu, you will see a **Run Configurations** menu option. This brings up the dialog shown in Figure 4-16, and is like a **control panel** for choosing options that relate to your AVD emulators, and how they will be launched and used inside your Eclipse ADT application development workspace.

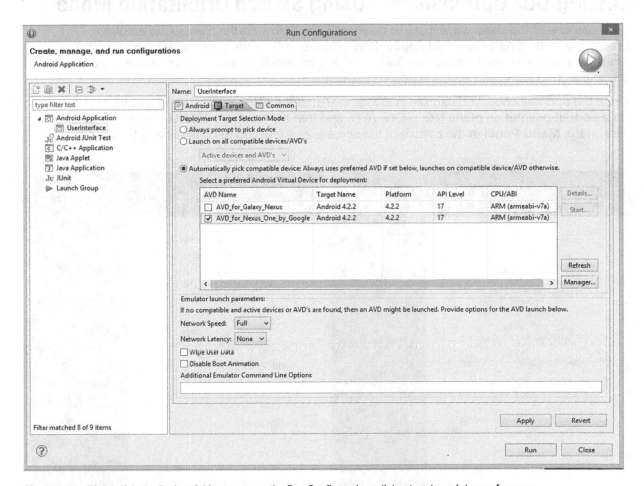

Figure 4-16. Right-click the Project folder to access the Run Configurations dialog to set emulator preferences

In the center of this dialog is the area where you can select a preferred device. I selected the **Nexus One** emulator because it is smaller and works for screenshots for the book better than the massive Galaxy Nexus screen emulator, but you can choose either one or use this dialog shown in Figure 4-16 to switch, as you need to, during your development.

As you can see, there is room to add far more emulators, and easily switch amongst them using this handy **Run Configurations** dialog. Once you choose a new configuration, you can use the **Run** button at the bottom to launch it.

So now you have learned three ways to launch an emulator: the AVD Manager and its **Start** button, the **Run As ➤ Android Application** menu sequence, and the Run Configurations dialog **Run** button.

Next, we will use the Nexus One AVD emulator to test our main.xml Menu XML definition mark-up and learn how to switch emulator orientation modes from Portrait to Landscape and back to see how our Action Bar and Menu renders!

Testing Our OptionsMenu: Using Switch Orientation Mode

Let's use one of the three ways that you now know about to start the Nexus One emulator. I recommend **Run As ➤ Android Application**, because this sends your current project to the emulator and then runs it, rather than just launching the emulator, and then you have to go and find the app icon to launch it.

Once the app launches, you can see in Figure 4-17 that the **ifRoom** constant puts **two** of your icons on a portrait orientation of the Nexus One AVD, and that the hardware **MENU** button brings up the rest on the **Menu Panel** at the bottom of the screen, as shown on the right side of Figure 4-17.

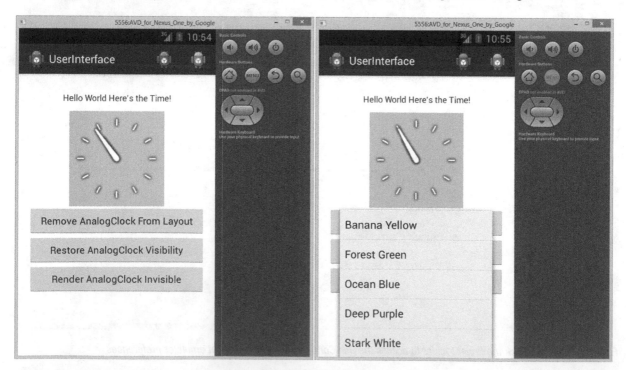

Figure 4-17. Testing the ifRoom constant for the android:showAsAction parameter and clicking the MENU button

Next, we let's see how many icons this **ifRoom** constant allows on to your screen when you **pivot** the Nexus One **90 degrees** into **Landscape** mode. This is done in any AVD emulator by holding down the **left-side Control key** on your keyboard and pressing the **F11** function key (**Ctrl-F11**) to pivot any emulator.

As you can see in Figure 4-18, the Nexus One in Landscape mode allows four icons to display in the Action Bar, with the other three showing up in the Menu Panel, when the hardware MENU key is used. Note that devices that do not support the hardware MENU button or key will display the **three stacked square dots,** and provide Menu Panel access at the top near the Action Bar.

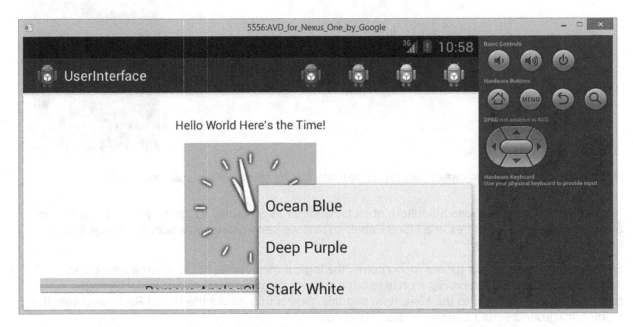

Figure 4-18. Using the Ctrl-F11 keystroke combination to rotate the Nexus One emulator into landscape mode

Now, go into your **main.xml** tab, and change the **ifRoom** constants to **always**. Use your **Run As ➤ Android Application** work process, and as you can see, in Figure 4-19, now all seven of our robot icon drawable assets are displayed comfortably inside of the Android Action Bar!

Figure 4-19. Using an android:showAsAction="always" constant setting to force all the icon image assets to show

Now it is time to make these MenuItem objects, whether they display to the end-user as an icon in an Action bar or as text titles in a Menu Panel, so that we can invoke some sort of change in our application's functionality.

Since we are using colors for our menu items, the logical thing for us to do when a user clicks a Menu Panel item or Action Bar icon is to set a custom color for our AnalogClock UI widget background that is equal to the MenuItem text title. So if a user clicks the Blood Red menu item the clock background would become a Blood Red color.

OptionsMenu Event Handling: onOptionsItemSelected( )

Handling your end-user's clicks on the Menu Panel text title or an Action Bar icon is called event handling, and it's taken care of for menus by the **onOptionsItemSelected()** method, which is a part of the Activity class.

The reason that onOptionsItemSelected() is a part of the Android Activity class, and not a part of the Menu class, is because every activity has, or can have at least, an OptionsMenu object and MenuItem hierarchy structure.

For this reason, the onOptionsItemSelected() part of Menu handling is part of the Activity class, which allows it to become an integral part of your Activity subclasses, and thus it is included with the Activity Class set of Java methods (i.e., Activity-related tools).

When your user selects a text title item from the options menu panel or an icon from your action items in the Action Bar, Android calls your Activity subclass's onOptionsItemSelected() method. This method takes one parameter in the form of a **MenuItem** object named **item** as you can see in Figure 4-20.

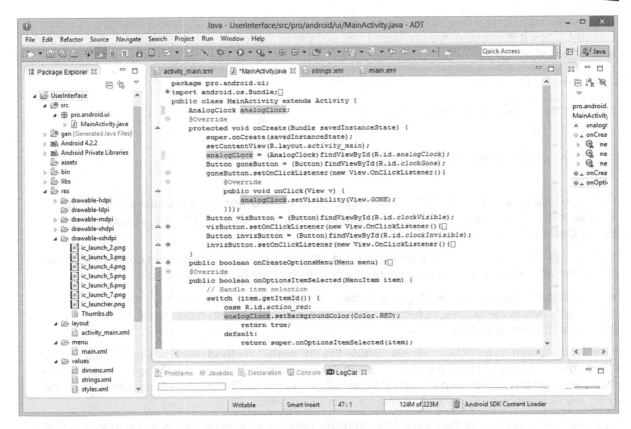

Figure 4-20. Coding our onOptionsItemSelected() method and its switch and case statements to implement items

This MenuItem contains the **ID** value of the MenuItem that the user selected as defined in the **main. xml** menu XML definition. Your Java code will then identify which MenuItem (named item) was clicked by calling a **.getItemId()** method off of the **item** object using dot notation, as shown in Figure 4-20.

This .getItemId() function matches the unique ID that you assigned via XML for each MenuItem object and then matches this ID against known menu items to perform the appropriate programming actions via Java logic which exists inside of the **case statements** inside of this **switch loop**, as is shown in Figure 4-20.

Since the onOptionsItemsSelected() method supports the boolean return data value type, at the end of each case statement we must be sure to include a **return statement** with the **boolean value** of true, indicating to the calling function that the case statement was invoked and the Java program logic inside of it was executed.

This **return true;** statement also serves to drop us out of the switch loop collection of case statements, as the MenuItem named item has successfully been matched to a case statement and processed.

I have implemented only one single case statement, initially, to make sure that everything is working correctly. Once it is working, we can then copy and paste that case statement's block of code, and create the rest of this MenuItem processing logic. Java code for this case statement should read:

```
switch (item.getItemId()) {
   case R.id.action_red:
   analogClock.setbackgroundColor(Color.RED);
      return true;
   default:
      return super.onOptionsItemSelected(item);
}
```

When you type this in, Eclipse ADT will highlight the Android **Color** class with a wavy red underline, because it is not imported for use as yet, so, mouse-over this error highlighting, and select the **import Color** option.

There is one other modification I made to the MainActivity.java class, so that we could more easily access the analogClock object from inside the onOptionsItemsSelected() method.

I **declared** the **AnalogClock analogClock** object for use in the class at the very top of our MainActivity Activity subclass, outside of all our Java methods, which means that we do not have to use a **final** modifier anymore.

Then, I initialized it to the XML definition inside the onCreate() method, very similar to what we did before, but sort of cut in half, if you will, with the declaration on the outside of the method, and the initialization on the inside of the method! I opened one of the OnClickListeners as well so that you could see at least one occurrence of analogClock being called.

Let's test the Java code in the Nexus One emulator now, so we can see if it is working for the first MenuItem, in this case it will be the Red Bot icon on the Action Bar, due to the ifRoom constant which we are currently using in our XML menu definition file named main.xml located in /res/menu.

As you can see in Figure 4-21, when we click the Red Bot icon we get a system-defined **Color.RED** constant value from Android OS behind our clock.

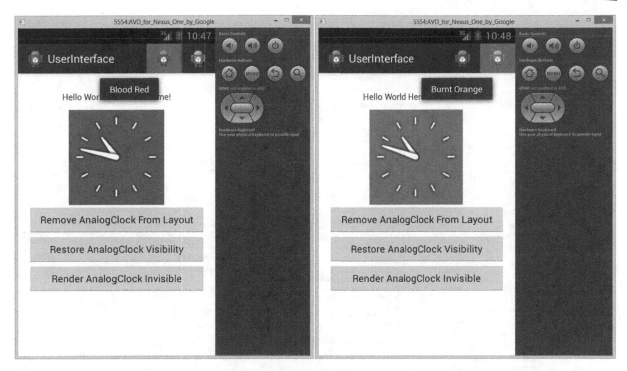

Figure 4-21. Testing the onOptionsItemsSelected() case statements for the action_red and action_org MenuItem

Now let's copy and paste the **action_red** case statement, and create another **action_org** case statement. Change the **Color.RED** constant, to **Color.ORANGE,** and we should be good to go, right? **Wrong.** Eclipse gives us an error code, and on mouse-over, we find that not only does Android **not** have an ORANGE Color constant, but it also does not have a PURPLE Color constant either!

This means that we're going to have to define our own color constants, and so while we're at it, we'll make a good Blood Red and other custom colors.

The first thing we need to do to create our own customized color constants is to create a new **colors.xml** XML file in the **/res/values** folder where XML constant definitions live. Right-click your values folder, as is shown in Figure 4-22, select the **New ➤ Android XML File** menu sequence, and you can then access the **New Android XML File** dialog.

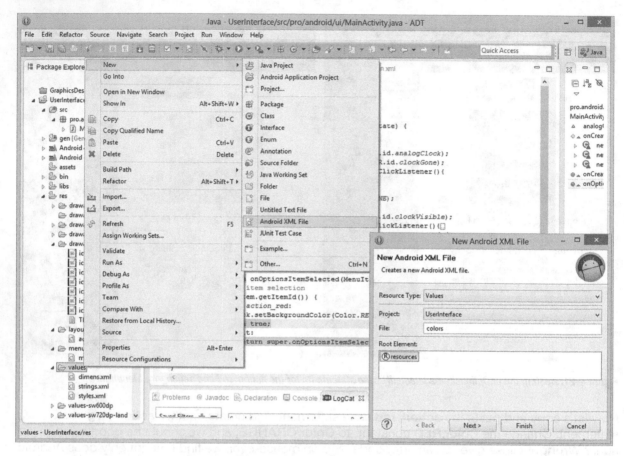

Figure 4-22. Creating a new /res/values folder XML resource file for use in color definition called colors.xml

Enter **colors** into the **File:** name field, and **Values** from the **Resource Type:** drop-down menu selector, and the **resources Root Element:** and then hit the **Finish** button. This creates the **colors.xml** file shown in Figure 4-23.

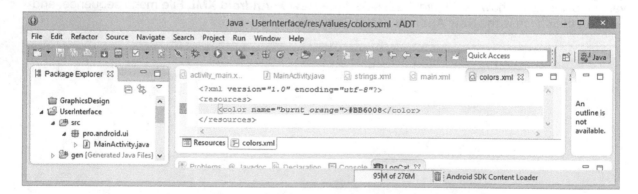

Figure 4-23. Add a <color> child tag to parent <resources> tag with hexidecimal constant value for burnt_orange

You will see a little later in Figure 4-24 that we now have /res/values XML file definitions for quite a few things for our application and we are only in Chapter 4. We have constants defined using XML for Colors as well as Strings, Dimensions, and Styles. Declaring constants in this way is better than doing it at the top of a class as they are more widely accessible.

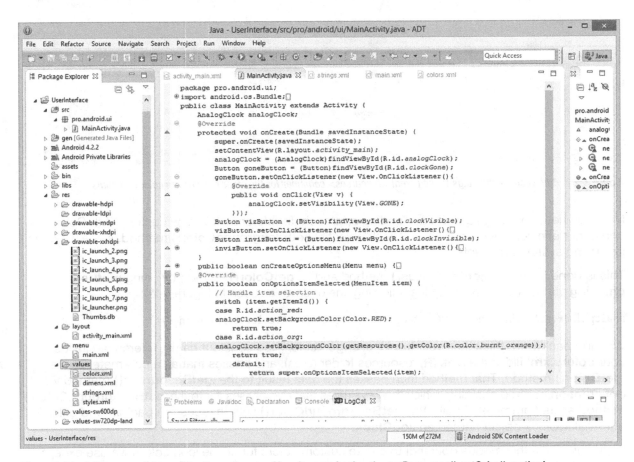

Figure 4-24. Add a case statement for the action_org MenuItem and using the getResources().getColor() method

Enter a color named **burnt_orange** with a hexadecimal color value of **#BB6008** as shown in Figure 4-23 using the following <color> child tag XML mark-up:

```
<color name="burnt_orange">#BB6008</color>
```

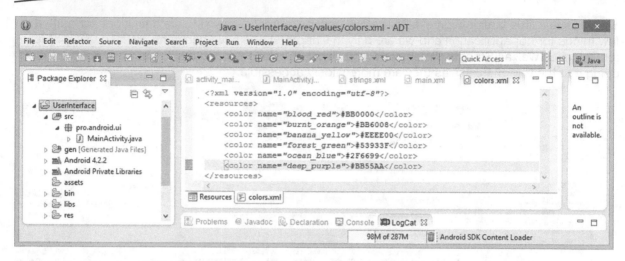

Figure 4-25. Add <color> child tags to the parent <resources> container for the other five custom color constants

Next, we need to design a new Java coding approach, to reference this new custom XML Color constant definition, inside our analogClock object's **.setbackgroundColor()** method, since we're not just using system constants.

This is done using the **getResources()** method and its **getColor()** method by using **method chaining** via dot notation, using the following line of Java, as seen in Figure 4-24:

```
analogClock.setBackgroundColor( getResources().getColor(R.color.burnt_orange) );
```

Working backward, this takes your **burnt_orange** <color> tag constant name, referenced inside your **colors.xml** file in the **/res (R)** resources folder (area), and passes that as a parameter to the **.getColor()** method. That method then passes the data result to the **.getResources()** method via **dot notation method chaining**, which then evaluates that and passes it into the **.setBackgroundColor( )** method as its parameter. Finally, the **.setBackgroundColor()** sets that custom background color for our AnalogClock object named **analogClock**.

We want to use this modus operandi to create custom colors for all the icon colors we use except for White, where we can use a system **Color.WHITE** constant at the bottom of our switch loop's case statement infrastructure as you will see later in Figure 4-26.

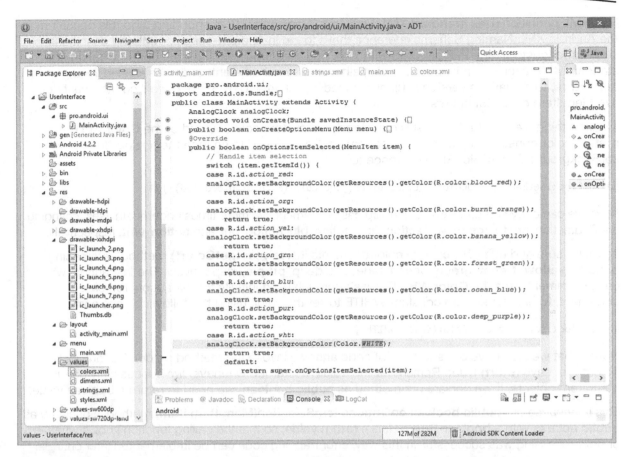

Figure 4-26. Add the remaining case statements referencing the remaining custom color constants in color.xml

Right now, however, let's finish editing our **colors.xml** file, and create the other five custom color values, so that we can then cut and paste the action_org case statement five more times underneath itself and implement a completed seven item menu structure so we can test all this in the Nexus One emulator and see the visual results.

Remember that the hexadecimal color values we are using are 24-bit (6 data slots) and set color channels by #RRGGBB and Zero is fully-off (dark) and FF is fully on (bright, full color for that color) so you can see how we are setting these colors. We will get more into color theory in a future chapter (Chapter 10), but for now, you should be able to see how we're mixing colors!

Here's what the **colors.xml** file mark-up should look like when you're done:

```xml
<? xml version="1.0" encoding="utf-8" ?>
<resources>
    <color name="blood_red">#BB0000</color>
    <color name="burnt_orange">#BB6008</color>
    <color name="banana_yellow">#EEEE00</color>
    <color name="forest_green">#53933F</color>
    <color name="ocean_blue">#2F6699</color>
    <color name="deep_purple">#BB55AA</color>
</resources>
```

This XML definition uses **standard XML** Version 1.0 tags and UTF-8 encoding, and this doesn't need the Android XML Naming Schema reference that's found in Android-specific XML tag definitions, such as for custom tags that are used with View and ViewGroup subclasses. For this reason, the standard XML declaration is much simpler, albeit somewhat different, and uses **<?** and **?>** tag **delimiters,** to declare its version (1.0), and encoding schema (UTF-8). Next we'll cut and paste our five MenuItem case statements for our Menu code.

The first thing we should do is install our **blood_red** custom color instead of the **Color.RED** system color constant in the first case statement. So, we need to change the analogClock. setBackgroundColor(Color.RED) reference to:

```
analogClock.setBackgroundColor( getResources().getColor(R.color.blood_red) );
```

Next, we can copy and paste our action_org case statement five more times underneath itself, changing the R.id.action_org to **action_yel**, **action_grn**, **action_blu**, **action_pur** and **action_wht**, respectively.

Then, be sure and edit your custom color constants inside your **.getColor()** method, referencing **banana_yellow**, **forest_green**, **ocean_blue,** and **deep_purple**, respectively. The last action_wht case statement uses the **Color.WHITE** class approach used initially for the action_red case statement, to use the system constant WHITE to set the color, using the following Java code:

```
analogClock.setBackgroundColor(Color.WHITE);
```

Notice that we also have our short line of code after we invoke the method on our AnalogClock object that says **return true;.** Remember this value is returned whenever we successfully handle any MenuItem objects. If we declare our method as **public boolean**, we need to return a boolean value.

This is because our **public boolean onOptionsItemSelection(MenuItem item)** method is declared as **public access** with a **boolean** (true or false) **return value**, so that the calling function knows whether or not processing was successful. In this way, error trapping code can be implemented later on.

If none of the switch statement cases handle (match up with) the MenuItem value that is passed into the method, there is a special case **default** case statement, which then calls (passes) up to the Superclass implementation of onOptionsItemSelected(), and returns a **false** value, signifying that **none** of the MenuItem objects were handled. The .onOptionsItemsSelected() method is shown in Figure 4-26 in its completed state; now it's time to test it.

It is important to note, that if an application contains multiple Activity subclasses and several of them utilize the same OptionsMenu structure, you can create a custom Activity subclass, which implements these menu related **onCreateOptionsMenu()** and **onOptionsItemSelected()** methods and nothing else and use that as your own custom OptionsMenuing Superclass.

What you would then do is to **extend** this class, for each Activity subclass that needs to share this same Options Menu. In this way, you can manage a single code base for Menu event handling, and each of its code descendants (subclasses) would then **inherit** those MenuItem processing structures.

Also, if you needed to add additional MenuItems to one of these descendant Activity subclasses, you could **@Override** the onCreateOptionsMenu() in that Activity subclass, and add those additional MenuItem objects.

If you do this, then be sure to call **super.onCreateOptionsMenu(menu)** so the original MenuItem objects are created first, and later, you can add in the new MenuItem objects, by using the **menu.add()** method call. You could also **@Override** your Superclass behaviors for individual MenuItem objects.

Let's get to the fun part now, and test our custom colors! Be sure that your MenuItems are set to **always** (constant) for the **showAsAction** parameter and then use the **Run As ➤ Android Application** menu sequence to launch your Nexus One emulator. If it is not in the **landscape** orientation, as shown in Figure 4-27, use your Ctrl+F11 keystroke sequence, and then, click on each of your seven colorful robot icons, to change the background color of your AnalogClock UI widget to Blood Red, Burnt Orange, Forest Green, and so on.

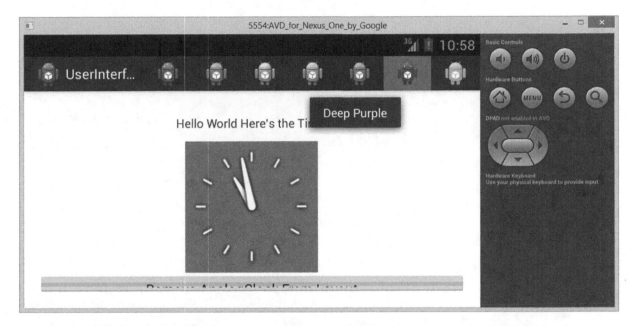

Figure 4-27. Testing the MenuItem icons in a Nexus One in landscape mode with showAsAction constant always

If your users were using a pre-Android 3.0 OS, these icons would instead show up on a Menu Panel, using their text title (label) long-form names.

Summary

In this fourth chapter, we took a look at the foundation for **menus, as well as MenuItems** in Android, the **Menu** Superclass. Then, we overviewed menu types in Android, and looked at how they are defined using XML, using one **<menu>** parent tag, and numerous **<item>** child tags to define MenuItems.

Next we looked at some of the key MenuItem **properties** or attributes as XML parameters. We learned about the **showAsAction constants** and how they allow us to control what displays in an Options **Menu Panel** or in the **Action Bar**. Finally, we took the bootstrap Menu generated for us in Chapter 2, and we customized it via the key menu parameters, to make it do something useful.

In the next chapter, we'll learn how to use the **ContextMenu** and **PopupMenu** classes to implement menus that are **localized** to your View UI widgets.

Chapter 5

Android UI Local Menus: The ContextMenu Class and PopupMenu Class

In this fifth chapter, we will take a look at the other two major types of menu systems in Android: the **context menu** and the **pop-up menu, in the form of the ContextMenu Java interface, and the PopupMenu class**.

I'm calling these two menu structure types "local" menus in this chapter's title because these menus are local to a UI element or View widget itself, and are in fact directly invoked by clicking (PopupMenu), or long-clicking (ContextMenu), on the UI element widget View object that the menu affects.

In fact one of these local menuing types, the PopupMenu class, is actually implemented in Android as a UI widget, as you will learn a little bit later on in this chapter, when we cover pop-up menus in Android in more detail.

Both of these types of menuing structures utilize a similar approach to an OptionsMenu structure– XML definitions, custom event handling methods, and so on. For this reason, most everything that you learned in the previous chapter also applies to menus in this chapter. This is ideal, as we can build on previous knowledge, and not revisit any of that information here.

Since the ContextMenu Java interface is more complicated, and also has the **Action Bar** component to it, which is largely the reason why it is far more complicated, we will cover that first. Android OS wants developers to use ContextMenu objects to invoke operations or functions that relate directly to the View Object (UI widget) that they are attached to and to affect the content that that UI widget contains or to affect the appearance of the UI widget itself. Then we will cover the PopupMenu class and how to implement a pop-up menu on one of the UI widget View objects for noncontextual use.

ContextMenu Overview: The ContextMenu Public Interface

The **ContextMenu** is actually a **public interface** of the **Menu** class and not a direct Menu subclass in and of itself. Thus the import for a ContextMenu implementation in your application would take the form: **import android.view.ContextMenu**, as you will see a bit later on in this chapter.

The ContextMenu has a **nested interface** called **ContextMenu.ContextMenuInfo**, and has **inherited constants** from the **android.view.Menu** class.

As you learned in the Menu overview in the previous chapter, the ContextMenu offers options on a Menu Panel or actions on an Action Bar that can affect a targeted UI element, or a contextual layout container in your UI design.

Developers can provide a ContextMenu for a single UI element View widget, so that they can allow their end-users to long-click on any of their UI elements and get a ContextMenu set of options or actions relating to that UI element, its functionality, and content that it accesses or controls.

ContextMenu objects are also frequently used for MenuItem options in an **array** of UI elements, such as found in the more advanced array-based UI elements such as GridView, ListView, and similar View aggregations where your end-user can perform an action for each item in an array of choices.

There are two ways to provide ContextMenu functionality to your users: via a ContextMenu Panel that pops up and looks much like a dialog would look and contains a set of text (label) options, or via Contextual Actions that are held in an Android Action Bar.

In ContextMenu Panel mode the ContextMenu object appears as a hovering panel containing a number of text-based menu items. When your user invokes a long-click event by pressing and holding on your UI element View widget that has been set up in the Java code to support the ContextMenu, it then appears for use.

In Contextual Actions mode the Android OS implements your ContextMenu MenuItems in its Action Bar interface, usually (or optimally) as icons. A Contextual Action Bar mode is therefore an Android OS user interface area implementation of your ContextMenu object that displays a contextual action set in the Android Action Bar at the top of the user's screen, and contains Action MenuItem objects, which affect the selected MenuItem.

It is important to remember that this contextual action mode is available only after Android 3.0 Honeycomb API Level 11 and has become a preferred technique for displaying ContextMenu MenuItem options when it's available.

Since our next chapter covers more advanced Action Bar UI design, we will cover these contextual actions in that chapter, and focus on the Pop-Up Menu Panel types of menu structures in this chapter. These pop-up type menus are used for ContextMenu Panels and for the PopupMenu class.

ContextMenu Methods: How to Implement a ContextMenu

There are several steps or phases to implementing a ContextMenu object on a View object UI element widget, which we will go over here and implement in your UserInterface application later on in the chapter, as well. Before we start, here's a global view of the code we need to put into place:

1. Instantiate a UI widget object that will be used to access the ContextMenu object

2. Register the ContextMenu object with the UI object via .registerForContextMenu()

3. Implement an onCreateContextMenu() method in that UI object's Activity subclass

4. Inside onCreateContextMenu() method use the getMenuInflater().inflate() method

5. Implement an onContextItemSelected() method in the UI object's Activity subclass

6. Create a switch/case structure inside onContextItemSelected() for each menu item

As you can see in the preceding numbered list, the first thing you need to do, if you haven't done this in your Java code already, is to instantiate the UI widget object that the ContextMenu will be registered to, and then register the ContextMenu object with it, using a **registerForContextMenu()** method call.

The registerForContextMenu() method call takes only one parameter–your UI widget object. You must at least instantiate your UI widget if you want to use it with the ContextMenu, and as I mentioned, it may have already been instantiated for other functional uses in your Activity subclass as well.

Once you have **registered** your View object UI element widget for usage with your ContextMenu, the next step is to implement your **onCreateContextMenu()** method in the Activity subclass which will contain the ContextMenu object.

When the now registered View object processes the long-click system event, Android OS accesses the onCreateContextMenu() method. This method takes three parameters, including the **ContextMenu** object to be created, the **View** object that the developer registered for use with the ContextMenu, and an object that holds your ContextMenuInfo.

This **ContextMenuInfo** object provides additional information about your MenuItem object that has been selected, especially for View object widget UI elements that deal with arrays, such as the ListView or AdapterView class.

If an Activity subclass instantiates more than one UI widget View object, each of which provides its own unique ContextMenu implementation, then you would utilize all three parameters. Three parameters are required for your onCreateContextmenu() method to determine which of your ContextMenu objects you need to inflate, and ultimately create the ContextMenu object structure for any given View widget (object) within your UI design.

Inside your onCreateContextMenu() method is where the MenuItem objects are created. This is done by inflating your XML menu definition resource using the **MenuInflater** class and its **.inflate()** method, as we learned about in a previous chapter. This is similar to a work process that is involved with setting up your OptionsMenu object with its MenuItem definition structure.

The MenuInflater class lets you inflate your ContextMenu object, using its XML menu definition resource, just like it does for an OptionsMenu object. You pass the MenuInflater class the reference to your menu definition file XML, and the ContextMenu object to be inflated, using an **.inflate()** method that is chained off of a **getMenuInflater()** method call using dot notation.

Once all this ContextMenu object registering, creation, inflation, and so on has been accomplished, all you have to do next is to create an event handling hierarchy and structure in your Java code.

You will find that this is very similar to what we did in the previous chapter to implement our OptionsMenu object. I cover this menu event handling process in detail in the next section of this chapter.

ContextMenu Event Handling via onContextItemSelected()

The next step in implementing a ContextMenu for one of your UI elements is to add an **OnContextItemSelected()** method into your Activity subclass. This method contains your event handling hierarchy and structure for processing which MenuItem object was selected by your user. Once this is ascertained, this method then executes your Java code that specifies exactly what logic you want to process associated with the selected MenuItem object.

This works in a similar fashion to the onOptionsItemSelected() method in that the **.getItemId()** method is used inside of a **switch** loop statement, to analyze the **ID** for the selected MenuItem object.

You assigned this ID previously for each of your menu's <item> child tags, using XML in your menu definition file using the **android:id** tag parameter.

Inside the switch statement loop, you have **case** statements for each of these MenuItem ID values. This is so that when the switch function matches one of these ID values, there is a corresponding case statement, with Java programming logic inside that case statement that will be processed. In this way, you can implement whatever you want to happen inside of your app in response to the selection by your user of the ContextMenu Panel option.

Because the onContextItemSelected() method specifies a boolean return value, at the end of each case statement you need to use a return statement to send a boolean value, true or false, back to the calling function.

You return the **true** value when your programming logic was processed, and you return a **false** value if none of your MenuItem objects' ID values matched up with your case statements and no processing occurred.

At the end of the switch loop statement there is a **default** option that is invoked (used) if the switch statement performs no event handling; that is if no MenuItem object ID fields match one of the provided case statements.

In the event (no pun intended) that none of your MenuItem IDs match with a case statement, your switch loop logic will use this default statement at the end (bottom) of the hierarchy to pass that MenuItem object up to the onContextItemSelected() method's Superclass implementation. It then returns the false value to the calling function to indicate that a Context Menu Item function was not executed for the user.

The best way to get an idea of how all this works together is to actually implement a ContextMenu inside our UserInterface application. Let's do that next, and implement a ContextMenu Panel that locally gives our users access to our custom color values so they can customize their AnalogClock.

Creating a ContextMenu for Our UserInterface Application

Now let's fire up Eclipse ADT, if it's not open already, and implement our very own ContextMenu UI design in our UserInterface application. First right-click the Project folder resources subfolder for menu definitions, or **/res/menu** and select the **New ➤ Android XML File** menu sequence, to bring up the dialog shown in Figure 5-1.

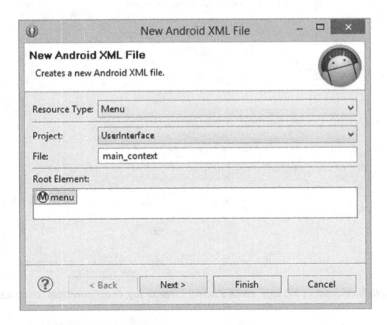

Figure 5-1. Creating our main_context.xml menu resource

Since we right-clicked the **/res/menu** folder the **Resource Type:** of **Menu** is already set for us, as is the **UserInterface Project:** designation, so, just type **main_content** in the **File:** field and select the **Root Element:** of **menu** to add a parent <menu> tag as the menu definition container type.

The reason that we're naming this menu definition file **main_context.xml** is because our MainActivity primary (OptionsMenu) menu is named main.xml, and we want to denote that this menu is also for the MainActivity subclass and is paired with the **main.xml** OptionsMenu. To do this, we add an underscore, and the word **context**, denoting a context menu XML definition file.

Now we're ready to add in the **<item>** child tags that will define our menu contents, which are similar to the OptionsMenu that we created in the previous chapter, only with much more simple parameters.

For a ContextMenu, which pops up a series of menu items in what looks like a dialog, we only really need to specify the **android:id** parameter to label the MenuItem and the **android:title** parameter to give the MenuItem its text labeling. I made the last item an **Invisible** color instead of White so that we could call a couple different kinds of methods in our case statements. The definition takes a couple dozen lines of mark-up, shown in Figure 5-2.

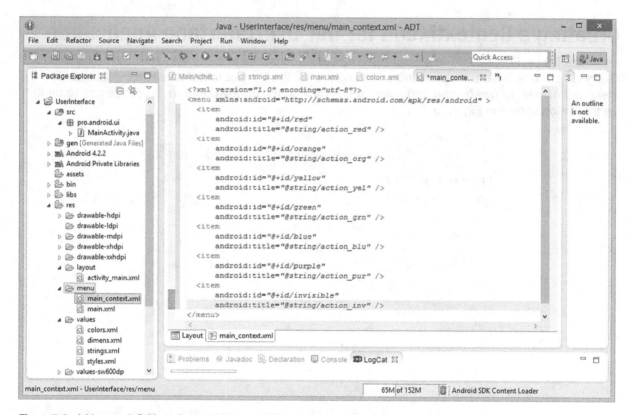

Figure 5-2. *Add menu definition <item> child tags, inside a parent <menu> tag, in our new main_context.xml file*

The XML mark-up to add in these seven MenuItem definitions is as follows:

```
<? xml version="1.0" encoding="uft-8" ?>
<menu xmlns:android=http://schemas.android.com/apk/res/android
    <item android:id="@+id/red" android:title="@string/action_red" />
    <item android:id="@+id/orange" android:title="@string/action_org" />
    <item android:id="@+id/yellow" android:title="@string/action_yel" />
    <item android:id="@+id/green" android:title="@string/action_grn" />
    <item android:id="@+id/blue" android:title="@string/action_blu" />
    <item android:id="@+id/purple" android:title="@string/action_pur" />
    <item android:id="@+id/invisible" android:title="@string/action_inv" />
</menu>
```

I spaced the tags and parameters out a bit in Figure 5-2, since I had the space to make it more readable in the screenshot. If you need more room inside your editing pane, you can add more than one parameter per line.

String Constants for Our ContextMenu: Using a <string> Tag

Next we need to add a <string> constant to support our invisible menu item android:title reference to an **action_inv** named string constant. Click a strings.xml tab at the top of Eclipse ADT and add the <string> constant as shown in Figure 5-3.

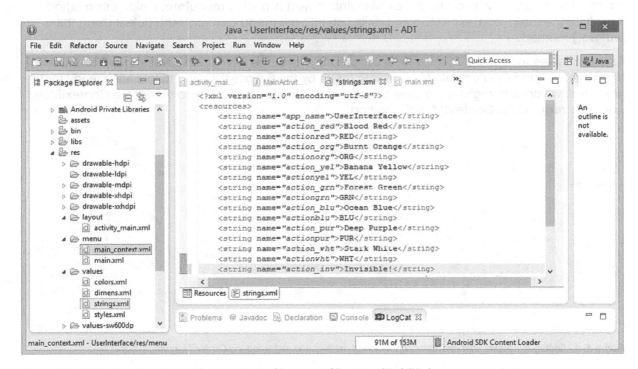

Figure 5-3. Adding an action_inv <string> constant with a menu title value of Invisible for our new context menu

Next we need to get into some Java coding and create the **ContextMenu** object, as well as the **ContextMenuInfo** object, using the onCreateContextMenu() method we reviewed earlier.

Creating an onCreateContextMenu() Method and Inflating the ContextMenu

Inside this method we use the **getMenuInflater().inflate()** work process, which you saw in the previous chapter, to reference our XML **main_context.xml** menu definition, using the Android OS reference path designation **R.menu.main_context.**

This method is fairly straightforward for creating the ContextMenu object and ContextMenuInfo object, and this needs to be put in place, before any of the other code can function. The onCreateContextMenu() method can be easily implemented by using the following Java code:

```java
public void onCreateContextMenu(ContextMenu menu, View v, ContextMenuInfo menuInfo)
{
    getMenuInflater().inflate(R.menu.main_context, menu);
}
```

In the onCreateContextMenu() method the ContextMenu object is named **menu**, the View it is attached to is named **v**, and the ContextMenuInfo object is named **menuInfo**. Inside this method we inflate the **main_context** XML menu definition into the **menu** ContextMenu object using the **.inflate()** method.

As you can see in Figure 5-4, once we enter this Java code we have to do some mouse-overs, and trigger some Import statements to be written for us by the Eclipse IDE, and then we are ready for the next step, which is to register the View object that we are going to utilize to trigger the ContextMenu using the **registerForContextMenu()** method.

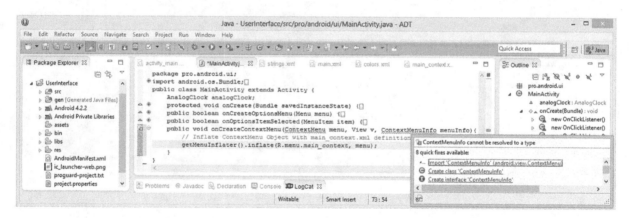

Figure 5-4. Adding our public void onCreateContextMenu() method and importing the ContextMenuInfo class

Registering Our ContextMenu Using registerForContextMenu()

To register our ContextMenu object we must add a line of Java code after we inflate our analogClock AnalogClock object using the **findViewById()** method. Since the line of code that we are adding references this analogClock AnalogClock object, it must be instantiated before we register it for use with a ContextMenu.

As you can see in Figure 5-5, we then add a **registerForContextMenu()** call, which references this **analogClock** named AnalogClock UI widget View as its parameter. This sets the View parameter we saw in the previous paragraph, and is done via a single line of Java code, that looks like the following:

```java
registerForContextMenu(analogClock);
```

Figure 5-5. Using the registerForContextMenu() method to register the analogClock UI for use with ContextMenu

Now we're ready to code an **onContextItemsSelected()** method and case logic.

Just as we did in the previous chapter, let's get our method structure and a case statement (the first one) working and then later on we can copy and paste the other MenuItem case statements, and change their referencing.

Creating an onContextItemSelected() Method to Handle MenuItem Selection

The **onContextItemSelected()** method structure is virtually identical to the onOptionsItemSelected() method that you learned about previously, so utilize the following Java code structure to implement the first red case statement:

```java
@Override
public boolean onContextItemSelected(MenuItem item) {
    switch ( item.getItemId() ) {
        case R.id.red:
        analogClock.setBackgroundColor(getResources().getColor(R.color.blood_red));
            return true;
        default:
            return super.onContextItemSelected(item);
    }
}
```

As you can see in Figure 5-6, our code is error-free and shows both of the Java methods that need to be implemented for our ContextMenu object to be used in the application: **onCreateContextMenu()** and **onContextItemSelected()** that will inflate, then reference, and finally evaluate our XML MenuItem definitions that we created in our **menu_context.xml** file a bit earlier.

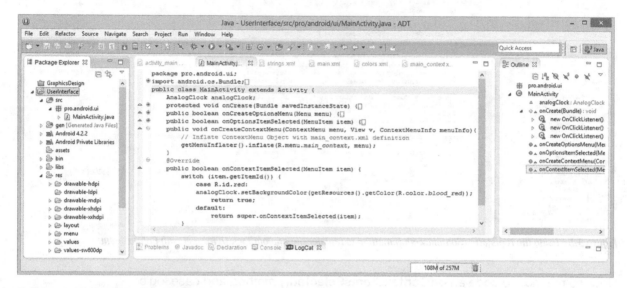

Figure 5-6. Implementing the onContextItemSelected() method and its switch loop and case statement logic

Next, we will test this initial menu code, to be sure that it is working properly, and then we can simply add in the other six of our MenuItem object references once we are sure that we haven't missed anything and that there are no bugs happening once the code is run inside the Nexus One emulator.

As you can see in Figure 5-7, when you long-click (click mouse and hold), the ContextMenu appears as shown on the left side of the screenshot.

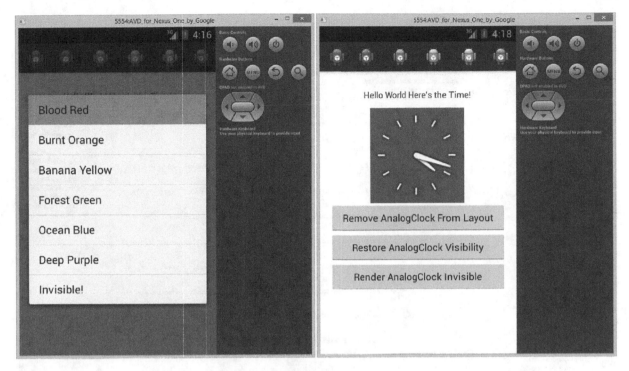

Figure 5-7. Testing our context menu in the Nexus One emulator and showing the seven menu items and result

Since we implemented the first MenuItem case statement, click the Blood Red option at the top of the menu; it turns blue when you click on it as shown in Figure 5-7.

As you can see from the right side of the screenshot the AnalogClock UI widget turned Blood Red, and we know the case statement is working. If you use the Button UI elements we coded in the previous chapters, they now work with the color settings that we set using our ContextMenu object.

Select the case statement, Java method calls, and return true for the red MenuItem evaluation and copy it to the system clipboard. Paste this selection six times underneath itself to create the rest of the case logic statement tree for the onContextItemSelected() method structure.

Now change the R.id.red reference to **R.id.orange**, **R.id.yellow**, **R.id.green**, **R.id.blue**, **R.id.purple**, and **R.id.invisible**, respectively. Next, change your custom color references to read **burnt_orange**, **hanana_yellow, forest_green, oooan_blue,** and **deep_purple** for the five remaining R.color references.

For the **R.id.invisible** case statement, change the method called off the analogClock object to a **.setVisibility(View.INVISIBLE)** method call, and we are ready to **Run As ➤ Android Application** and see the results of our work.

As you can see in Figure 5-8, all our boolean return statements are in place, our Java code is error free, and we're ready to test it thoroughly.

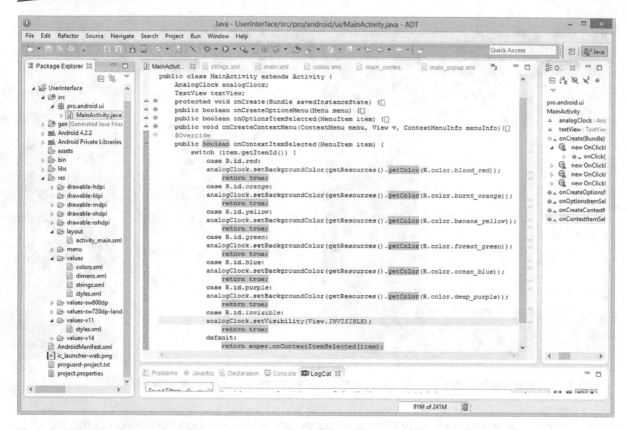

Figure 5-8. *Finish coding the case statements for the onContextItemsSelected() method switch loop structure*

Let's take a look at how everything is working together, and use your **Run As ➤ Android Application** work process to launch the emulator, and when the app appears, **long-click** the AnalogClock UI widget View object, to bring up the ContextMenu and try changing your AnalogClock to show the different color settings. Everything should be working quite well together. Your app should look like it did in Figure 5-7, only with different color values.

The Invisible ContextMenu MenuItem turns off the visibility of the AnalogClock, making it invisible, and the Button UI elements at the bottom of the app allow you to turn the visibility back on or remove an AnalogClock UI widget from the UI layout entirely. These color settings are maintained separately from your visibility settings, so neither of the two parameters will affect each other.

Once you set the color it will remain set until you set a different color, regardless of whether the AnalogClock is GONE or INVISIBLE. It's important to note that if the AnalogClock is GONE or INVISIBLE, that the ContextMenu cannot be invoked, so let's add a PopupMenu UI widget next, which provides localized access to these visibility settings, using a TextView UI widget. Next you'll get a solid knowledge foundation for Android's PopupMenu class.

Android's PopupMenu Class: A UI Widget Localized Menu

A **PopupMenu** is actually a **custom Android menuing UI widget** and is a direct subclass of the **java.lang.Object** master class, and is not a **View** subclass, as most of the other UI widgets in Android are. So, a Java class hierarchy for the PopupMenu class is structured as follows:

```
java.lang.Object
  > android.widget.PopupMenu
```

An import statement for a PopupMenu object implementation in an application takes the following format: **import android.widget.PopupMenu**. You will get some experience with this a little bit later within this chapter.

The PopupMenu has two **nested classes that are actually nested interfaces**. One is the **PopupMenu.OnDismissListener**, which is a callback interface used to notify the application when the PopupMenu Panel has been closed by your user. This is done by clicking (or touching) in your UI layout (ViewGroup) anywhere outside of the PopupMenu Panel area, which "dismisses" it.

The other is the **PopupMenu.OnMenuItemClickListener,** which is the interface that is responsible for receiving MenuItem click events, if the MenuItems themselves haven't implemented individual <item> child tag android:onClick listener parameters, that is. We will get a chance to implement this in an application later in this chapter.

As we learned in the Menu overview in the previous chapter, this PopupMenu UI widget offers options on a Menu Panel but does not offer any actions on the Android Action Bar, so it would be the menu type to use if you don't need to support the new Android Action Bar.

Just like the Action Bar, the PopupMenu UI widget requires that you use a minimum API Level 11 Android 3.0 (Honeycomb) specification (setting) for your application. We will be implementing this later in the chapter when we add a PopupMenu widget to our UserInterface application functionality.

Developers can provide a PopupMenu for a single UI element View widget, so that they can allow their end-users to click on any of their UI elements and get a PopupMenu set of menu options relating to that UI element, its functionality, and the layout that the View object widget is contained in.

The primary difference between the PopupMenu and the ContextMenu is that MenuItem objects in the ContextMenu relate contextually to the UI element, or its contents, that it is attached to, whereas the PopupMenu MenuItem function is not related contextually to the View object widget that the PopupMenu is attached to. Visually, these two types of menus look almost identical, so the only real difference is in how these menus' MenuItem object selection (function) relates to the UI element they're attached to.

Next, let's get our hands dirty, and actually add a PopupMenu that allows us to access our AnalogClock visibility constants as PopupMenu Menu Items.

Creating a PopupMenu UI for the UserInterface Application

Now let's implement a PopupMenu UI widget in our UserInterface application and do something useful with it. The first thing we need to do is create our PopupMenu XML definition. Right-click the Project folder resources subfolder for menu definitions, or **/res/menu** and select the **New ➤ Android XML File** menu sequence for the second time, to bring up your **New Android XML File** dialog, which is shown in Figure 5-9.

Figure 5-9. Creating our main_popup.xml menu resource

Since we right-clicked on the **/res/menu** folder the **Resource Type:** of **Menu** is already set for us, as is the **UserInterface Project:** designation, so, just type **main_popup** in the **File:** field and select the **Root Element:** of **menu** to add a parent <menu> tag as the menu definition container type.

The reason that we are naming this menu definition file **main_popup.xml,** is because our MainActivity primary (OptionsMenu) menu is named main.xml, and we want to denote that this menu is also for the MainActivity subclass and is paired with the **main.xml** OptionsMenu. To do this, we add an underscore, and the word **popup**, denoting the PopupMenu UI widget XML definition file.

Defining Our PopupMenu MenuItem Objects Using XML Markup

Next we need to add in some **<item>** child tags, which define our **PopupMenu MenuItem** contents. This is similar to the Button UI, which we created back in Chapter 3, only with simpler text title (label) values.

For a PopupMenu widget, which pops-up a series of menu items in what looks like a dialog, we need to specify the **android:id** parameter to label the MenuItem, as well as the **android:title** parameter, to give our MenuItem its text titles or menu item labels.

Let's create three MenuItem text titles for our PopupMenu UI widget in the strings.xml file using the <string> child tag, as shown in Figure 5-10. We label our menu items with the View class visibility constants, which are **VISIBLE**, **INVISIBLE,** and **GONE**. The XML mark-up is coded as follows:

```
<string name="popup_viz">VISIBLE</string>
<string name="popup_inviz">INVISIBLE</string>
<string name="popup_gone">GONE</string>
```

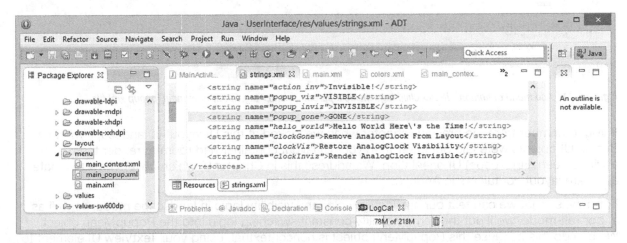

Figure 5-10. Add three <string> constant values to a strings.xml file for VISIBLE, INVISIBLE, and GONE options

Now that we have our string constants in place, we can create our XML pop-up menu definition in the **main_popup.xml** file that is now in our Eclipse IDE.

Click the **main_popup.xml** tab, as shown in Figure 5-11, and add in three <item> child tags for MenuItem objects that reference the visibility states of our AnalogClock UI widget. This should be accomplished using the following menu definition tags and their parameters in your XML mark-up:

```
<? xml version="1.0" encoding="utf-8" ?>
<menu xmlns:android=http://schemas.android.com/apk/res/android >
<item android:id="@=id/viz" android:title="@string/popup_viz" />
<item android:id="@=id/inviz" android:title="@string/popup_inviz" />
<item android:id="@=id/gone" android:title="@string/popup_gone" />
</menu>
```

Figure 5-11. Add menu definition <item> child tags inside a parent <menu> tag, in our new main_popup.xml file

If you remember from the previous chapter when we looked at this UI layout in landscape mode, the Button UI objects were laid out lower than your UI layout container had room to render them using a widescreen (landscape) UI orientation. We address this in Chapter 9, which covers how to create alternate layout containers in Android.

For now, so that we can test our application color and visibility logic in landscape mode, as well as in portrait mode, we'll put the same visibility constant switching logic into the PopupMenu object. We can do this because this PopupMenu object is noncontextual, using your TextView UI element to give you control over your AnalogClock visibility in this Activity screen.

Now click the MainActivity.java tab and let's get into some Java coding so we can instantiate our TextView UI widget, and attach the PopupMenu UI element to it.

Instantiating Our TextView UI Widget Object for Use with a PopupMenu

We do this at the very top of our class, just like we did with an AnalogClock named analogClock in the previous chapter.

First instantiate a TextView and name it **textView**, via the following code:

```
TextView textView;
```

Then, inside the onCreate() method, load this TextView object with its XML definition, using the findViewById() method, with the following code:

```
textView = (TextView)findViewById(R.id.textView);
```

As you can see in the Java code in Figure 5-12, we have several wavy red underline error highlights in the code. Most of these are because we need to **import** the **TextView** widget class to be able to instantiate a TextView object. Mouse-over this TextView class reference in either of these lines of code, and select the **Import TextView** option. The error highlighting will vanish before your very eyes.

Figure 5-12. *Fixing error messages in textView object inflation via a findViewById() method and Import TextView*

Also notice that the findViewById() method is error highlighted because I did not use the proper CamelCase capitalization on the method name. I left this in the screenshot to show that the smallest of oversights can cause an error flag to be thrown in Eclipse ADT, you have to be very careful about what you are doing when programming Android applications.

Once we have imported our android.widget.TextView class and have our Java code error free once more, we can start to implement the code for our PopupMenu UI widget. Remember that the PopupMenu class was introduced in Android 3.0 Honeycomb API Level 11, so there is one more thing that we need to do to our application to make it **API 11** compatible.

Back in Chapter 2, when we created our UserInterface application, by using the New Android Application series of dialogs, we accepted the Eclipse ADT suggestions for setting the default minimum SDK and target SDK options for API Level 8 and API Level 17 support, respectively.

Upgrading Our Application API Level Support to Level 11

Because the PopupMenu class was introduced in API Level 11, we need to edit our **AndroidManifest.xml** file to bring our minimum API support level up to Level 11 from Level 8.

This AndroidManifest.xml file is important to your application, as it contains all the definitions and permissions that allow the Android OS to launch and initialize your application .APK (Android Package) file.

The AndroidManifest uses XML to define everything that lives inside it, which makes it easy enough for us to take a closer look at what is inside it to see what some of the AndroidManifest XML parent and child tags do.

Find your app AndroidManifest.xml at the bottom of your project folder, right-click it, and select the **Open** option, or left-click on it and use the F3 key to open it that way. Inside, you'll see a parent container tag, the **<manifest>** tag, containing the **xmlns:android** schema reference, as well as several other parameters, which define your application's **package** name, its **versionCode**, and its **versionName**.

The first child tag that you see is the one that we need to be concerned with here, the **<uses-sdk>** tag. This tag contains two parameters.

The first parameter, the **android:minSdkVersion** is the one which we need to change, from a value of **8**, to a value of **11**, as shown in Figure 5-13.

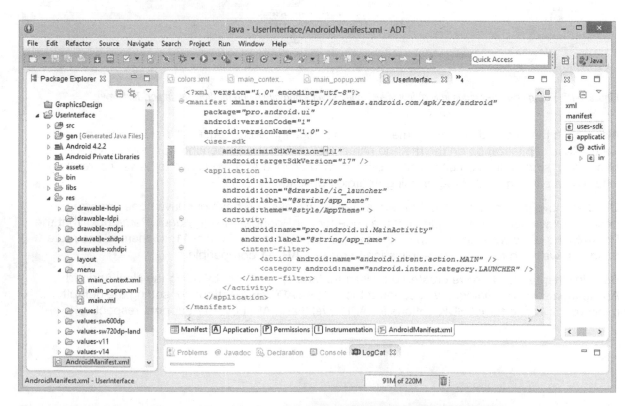

Figure 5-13. Upgrading our Minimum SDK Version from API Level 8 to API Level 11 in the AndroidManifest.xml

Our **android:targetSdkVersion** is already set to the Android 4.2.2 API Level 17, so that can stay the way it is. The next child tag under the <manifest> is an **<application>** child tag and it defines four parameters for our application that set an **allowbackup** flag to true as well as the file reference for an icon drawable image asset and an application label string constant and the **theme** to use for the application. We'll be getting in to all this soon.

The **<application>** child tag has its own child tag called an <activity> tag that defines the name for our MainActivity.java file as well as a label.

The **<activity>** tag also has a child tag called an **<intent-filter>** tag that has an **<action>** child tag, which references our Main Activity, and another **<category>** child tag that references an intent action category constant of LAUNCHER. This Intent serves to launch an Android application by launching the MainActivity top-level Activity subclass to the main display screen.

As you can see by those closing tags at the bottom of the file, there are **five levels of nesting** currently in our Android application Manifest file. Now that we are supporting API Level 11 through 17, or Android 3.0 through 4.2.2, we can go ahead and implement a PopupMenu UI widget in our Java code.

Instantiating a PopupMenu Inside an OnClickListener()

We implement this PopupMenu UI widget object inside of event handling for our TextView UI element, so let's add a **.setOnClickListener()** method to our TextView object, by using the following line of Java code:

```
textView.setOnClickListener( new OnClickListener() { our code will go in here } );
```

Inside the curly braces we code our onClick() handler that contains our PopupMenu instantiation, as well as menu inflation and events handling method calls, and the switch loop and its case statements, all using the following two dozen lines of Java programming logic:

```
textView.setOnClickListener(new OnClickListener() {
@Override
public void onClick(View v) {
    PopupMenu popupMenu = new PopupMenu(MainActivity.this, textView);
    popupMenu.getMenuInflater().inflate(R.menu.main_popup, popupMenu.getMenu());
    popupMenu.setOnMenuItemClickListener(new PopupMenu.OnMenuItemClickListener(){
      public boolean onMenuItemClick(MenuItem item) {
          switch (item.getItemId()) {
          case R.id.viz:
                  analogClock.setVisibility(View.VISIBLE);
                  break;
          case R.id.inviz:
                  analogClock.setVisibility(View.INVISIBLE);
                  break;
          case R.id.gone:
                  analogClock.setVisibility(View.GONE);
                  break;
          }
          return false;
      }
   });
```

```
        popupMenu.show();
    }
});
```

The first thing we do inside our onClick() method is to create our new PopupMenu object, named **popupMenu**, and set two parameters, which serve to reference the context of our MainActivity class and to anchor it to the textView TextView object.

Once we have this popupMenu object created, we call the **.getMenuInflater()** to get the **MenuInflater** class **.inflate()** method, using method chaining and dot notation. We pass the .inflate() method our **R.menu.main_popup** XML menu definition file, and have it inflate the menu settings into this popupMenu object's **.getmenu()** method.

Now that our PopupMenu UI widget is created and inflated, we can then add our .setOnMenuItemClickListener() method structure next that contains the onMenuItemClick() menu event handling for the MenuItem objects and a switch loop and case statements that compare the MenuItem item ID and then execute Java method calls to the analogClock.SetVisibility() method to set the visibility constants for the AnalogClock UI widget View object.

After the menu events processing structure has been set up, all we have to do is finally call the **.show()** method for the **popupMenu** object, and the PopupMenu UI widget displays on the screen since you have created, loaded, and set it up for event handling. The final code can be seen in Figure 5-14.

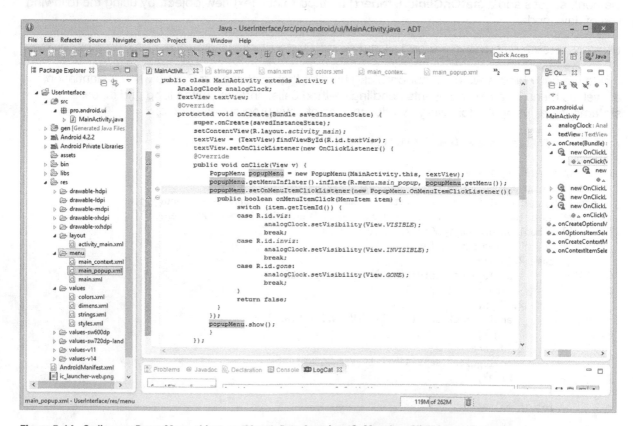

Figure 5-14. Coding our PopupMenu object, .getMenuInflater(), and .setOnMenuItemClickListener() methods

Test a PopupMenu in Android's AVD Nexus One Emulator

Now it is time to test the code in the Nexus One emulator, so use your **Run As ➤ Android Application** work process to launch your application, and when it appears, use the **Ctrl-F11** keystroke sequence to turn your emulator to landscape orientation. We do this so we can see precisely why we added this PopupMenu UI widget functionality to our TextView UI element.

As you can see in Figure 5-15, our Button UI elements are off-screen in the landscape orientation, and so, until we learn about coding alternate UI layouts in a future chapter, we will add our PopupMenu functionality to the top of our UI screen. We will do this using the TextView title for the screen so that the user can redisplay the AnalogClock UI widget when they use the Invisible! option on the context menu that you coded earlier in this chapter.

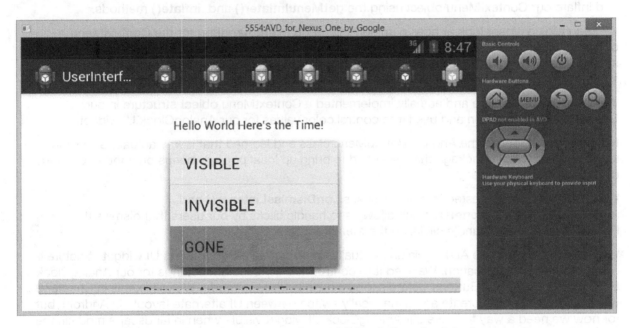

Figure 5-15. Testing PopupMenu object and main_popup.xml menu definition in Nexus One In landscape mode

PopupMenu uses short-click (click) and not long-click as in ContextMenu, so simply click the Hello World Here's the Time! at the top of the screen, and a three bar menu appears allowing access to visibility constants.

Now you can use all three Menu types together to change the color of your AnalogClock UI element, as well as change its visibility constants as you need to to play around with all these different menu types, custom colors, and visibility parameters that we have created thus far.

Summary

In this fifth chapter we took a look at the localized panel-based menus in Android, the ContextMenu interface, and the PopupMenu class, which allow us to attach menu structures to our user interface design elements.

We started out with an overview of the Android ContextMenu interface and took a look at how it works to provide us with our ContextMenu object, invoked via a long-click event on the UI element that it is attached to.

Next, we took a look at the various methods that we need to implement this ContextMenu in our application, and learned about how to register our UI widget for our ContextMenu using **registerForContextMenu()**, create our ContextMenu objects by using **onCreateContextMenu()**, and inflate our ContextMenu object using the **getMenuInflater()** and **.inflate()** methods.

We then took a closer look at how to implement **menu event handling** for the ContextMenu object using the **onContextItemSelected()** method and its **switch** loop and **case** statement Java structure, along with the **.getItemId()** method that evaluates MenuItem objects for this switch loop statement, which then compares those values to the case statements inside its loop structure.

We then fired up Eclipse and actually implemented a ContextMenu object structure in our UserInterface application and used it to control color values for our AnalogClock UI widget.

Next we took a look at the Android PopupMenu class and learned that it was actually a UI widget in the android.widget package that was used to bring up local pop-up menus on another UI widget using a click event.

We looked at the two nested interface classes, **.onDismissListener()** and **.onMenuItemClickListener()**, which allow us to handle clicks by our users that dismiss the PopupMenu and that handle clicks on the MenuItem objects.

We then fired up Eclipse ADT again and actually implemented a PopupMenu UI widget structure in our UserInterface application. We used it to control visibility constant settings for our AnalogClock UI widget because our Buttons were disappearing in landscape mode. We will fix this in Chapter 9 when we cover how to create and dynamically switch between UI alternate layouts in Android, but for now we need a way to make our AnalogClock UI widget visible when in landscape mode in the Nexus One.

In the next chapter, we'll focus primarily on Android's **ActionBar** class, and how it is used to create **actions and contextual actions**, both of which we have touched on in this chapter and in Chapter 4.

Android UI Action Bar: Advanced Action Bar Design and ActionBar Class

Now that we've covered the different types of Android Menu related classes in the previous two chapters, in the sixth chapter, you will begin learning more about the Android **ActionBar** class. The ActionBar was introduced in V3 of Android (**Honeycomb**), also known as API Level 11, or as **Android 3.0**.

An ActionBar approach allows us to free-up more screen real estate for our applications. This is because by using the ActionBar we can keep menu-type operations out of our primary User Interface ViewGroup layout containers.

Android's ActionBar class allows us to create different types of ActionBar structures for our Android application, from **icon-based** ActionBar menus to **tab-based** ActionBar menus to **drop-down-list-based** ActionBar menus.

Since Android's ActionBar is more a part of the Android OS chrome and user interface elements, it will always be at the top of your user's screen, to provide navigation, and other important UI and UX elements, to your apps.

Implementing the ActionBar in Android can range from a simple extension of your Options Menu functionality using icons, as you learned in the previous chapter, all the way to complex fragment-based multi-tab constructs, whose implementation may prove considerably more advanced, as we will code next.

In this chapter, we are going to span this gamut, starting with all the foundational information regarding your ActionBar, and progressing through some fairly robust implementations of navigational interfaces that utilize the ActionBar. We will cover all this so that you will know how to implement ActionBar navigation elements within your Android applications.

ActionBar Components

Let's go over the basic ActionBar components, starting on the left side or "start" of the ActionBar and progressing to the right side or "end" of the ActionBar. If you want to see what an ActionBar looks like there are some screenshots showing this at the end of this chapter (see Figures 6-40 through 6-42).

On the far left of the ActionBar is the **Application Icon**, which is the **branding** for the application. The icon is visible on an application icon launch screen, as well as in the ActionBar area itself, at all times.

Next to the Application Icon, on the left, are the **View Control** user interface elements, which usually include a drop-down menu, or a series of tabs that control switching among the various Views for the application. If your application does not need or support multiple Views, then the area can be used for your application title, providing additional brand impact.

Next on your ActionBar are **Action Buttons**, usually represented using **icons** or text, and providing access to major functionality or "actions" that you provide for your application. These are often defined using a similar work process as that used in creating an Options Menu for pre-3.0 applications.

If there is not enough room on the ActionBar to show both the icon and its text label, users can **long-click** the icon, revealing a text label name.

If you provide more action buttons than will fit in the ActionBar, Android will place them on an **Action Overflow**. This is a **drop-down menu** on the far right of the ActionBar that is represented by **three vertical square dots**.

The ActionBar Navigation Modes

There are three different "modes" that you can use for your ActionBar User Interface Navigation: Standard Mode, List Mode, and Tabs Mode.

The default navigation mode is the easiest to implement and is denoted via the ActionBar class constant: **NAVIGATION_MODE_STANDARD**. Standard ActionBar UI navigation is the default ActionBar behavior that is obtained by using the standard Options Menu approach to implementing ActionBar actions.

You have already had some hands-on experience using the standard ActionBar navigation mode back in Chapter 4 when you implemented an Options Menu in your UserInterface Android application.

If you don't need a lot of ActionBar navigation options for an application (say two or three), then you might want to consider **ActionBar Tabs** as your UI navigation paradigm. This navigation mode is invoked in your Java code, by using the **NAVIGATION_MODE_TABS** constant, from the ActionBar class.

If you have a lot of navigation user interface options for an application, then you will probably want to use an **ActionBar List** as your UI navigation paradigm. This navigation mode is invoked by using a: **NAVIGATION_MODE_LIST** constant, also from the ActionBar class, which we are going to cover next.

The Android ActionBar Class

The Android ActionBar class is a **public abstract** class, and it is a direct subclass of the **java.lang.Object** master class. A direct subclass of Object generally indicates that a functional class is scratch-coded, in this case to implement the ActionBar navigation for apps in the Android environment.

The ActionBar class is a part of the **android.app** package, because it is an application user interface class. The class hierarchy is as follows:

```
java.lang.Object
  > android.app.ActionBar
```

Technically an ActionBar is a **windowing feature** located on the top of your Activity subclass's View (ViewGroup). The ActionBar displays your Activity title, a current navigation mode and other interactive action, contextual, or menu items. Although an ActionBar might appear to be very simple in its nature, its actual implementation can get quite complex "under the hood."

For this reason, when an Activity subclass implements this Android default **Holo** theme, or one of its descendant themes, this ActionBar will appear at the top of your Activity's View window, or, more accurately, on the top of it, or over it, if you will. Thus using the ActionBar class you can access the Android OS "chrome" or OS UI elements, and insert your own UI elements into this generally "restricted" display screen area.

You can add the ActionBar object to your application using the method call **.requestFeature(FEATURE_ACTION_BAR)**, or you can simply instantiate one, as we do later in this chapter, when we create our own tabbed ActionBar user interface design.

You can also implement an ActionBar by declaring it using the custom theme definition by using the **windowActionBar** property. You can also retrieve an instance for your ActionBar object from inside an Activity subclass, by calling the **.getActionBar()** method, which we will also do soon.

Once you have your ActionBar object in place, you will also modify various characteristics for the ActionBar object, via ActionBar class method calls such as **.setText(), .setNavigationMode()**, or any of the three dozen method calls that are a part of the ActionBar class.

Before we can implement a tabbed ActionBar user interface theme in our UI application, we'll need to do some XML and Java set-up before we actually start coding our ActionBar object, its event listener, and use the ActionBar class method calls.

We need to create XML layouts for each tabbed UI area of the app and two Fragment subclasses, for each of the tabs to call. You will learn about Android's **Fragment** class later in this chapter.

Creating an XML Foundation for ActionBar Tabs: Layouts

Fire up Eclipse ADT, and let's create XML layout definitions for an **Analog Clock** and a **Digital Clock**, which will be accessed by each of these UI Tabs that we will add into our custom ActionBar class implementation. We are creating these XML UI layouts to create an ActionBar navigation system that allows our users to choose between an analog clock and a digital clock to show the time on their Android device. To see the final results of this exercise in both portrait and landscape modes, you can take a peek at Figures 6-40 through 6-42.

To create an XML file in your project's **/res/layout** folder, right-click that folder, as shown in Figure 6-1, and select the **New ➤ Android XML File** menu sequence. This opens up a **New Android XML File** helper dialog that guides you through the process of setting the correct parameters for a XML file that contains our Digital Clock Activity subclass UI design.

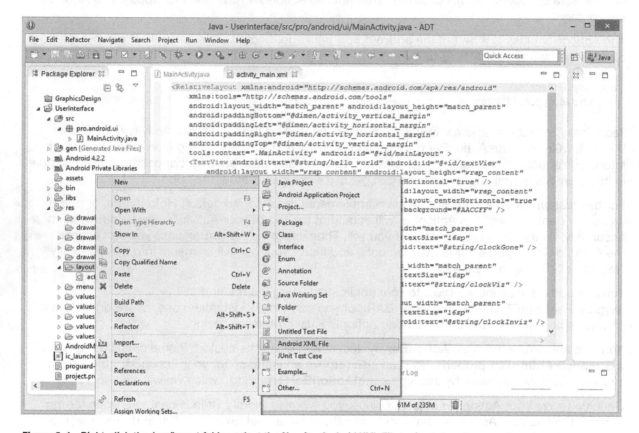

Figure 6-1. *Right-click the /res/layout folder, select the New ➤ Android XML File option to create a new layout*

Since you right-clicked the layout folder in your UserInterface project the first two data fields in the dialog, which is shown in Figure 6-2, are set for you automatically. In the third **File** data field enter the name of the XML UI definition file, let's call it **activity_digital**.

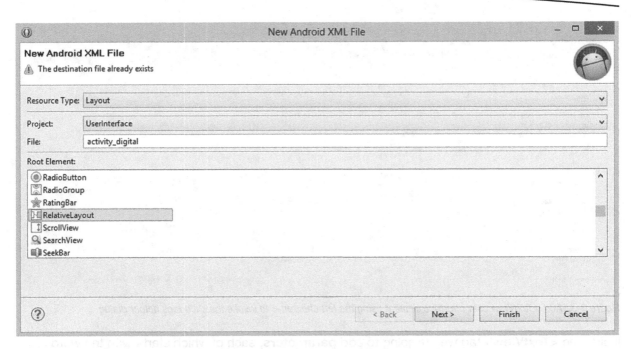

Figure 6-2. Name the file activity_digital and select a Root Element type of RelativeLayout

Finally, in the **Root Element** section of the dialog, find a **RelativeLayout** container parent tag (root element), and select this for our layout type.

We'll be looking at this **RelativeLayout** container type in Chapter 13 in this book, but for now we are using it because it is the most used type of UI layout container within the Android OS. Once you click the **Finish** button, your **activity_digital.xml** tab will open up in Eclipse, as is shown in Figure 6-3. Part of the code that we need to write is already in place, so all we have to do is to add our child UI element tags. To add the first TextView UI element child tag, type the **left chevron <** character under the opening RelativeLayout tag, and the helper dialog appears with all the child tag UI elements that are available for use in a RelativeLayout type of layout container (ViewGroup). Double-click **TextView** to insert it.

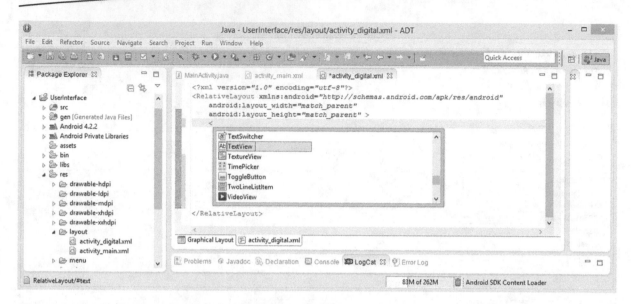

Figure 6-3. Add a TextView user interface element using the left chevron < to invoke the child tags helper dialog

Inside the **<TextView>** tag we are going to add **parameters**, each of which starts with the word **android:** and each of which defines an **attribute** for the TextView UI element object. The first is the message that we already defined earlier in the book, using the **hello_world <string> constant**, and then we will define an **ID**, layout **width** and **height**, **padding,** and **centering** for the TextView, using the following XML markup, as shown in Figure 6-4:

```
<TextView android:text="@string/hello_world"
    android:id="@+id/digitalView"
    android:layout_width="wrap_content"
    android:layout_height="wrap_content"
    android:padding="12dip"
    android:layout_centerHorizontal="true" />
```

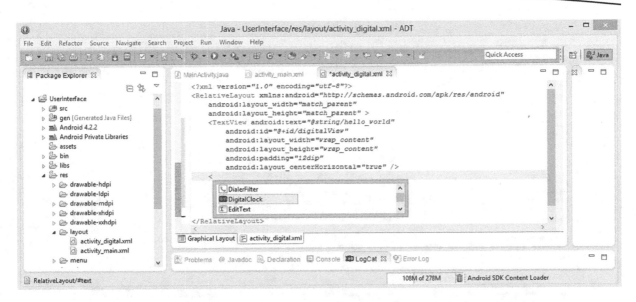

Figure 6-4. Add a DigitalClock user interface element using a left chevron < to invoke the child tags helper dialog

Once this is in place, we can add our next child tag inside (nested in) our RelativeLayout container. Again, utilize a left chevron < work process, and this time find a **<DigitalClock>** UI element child tag, and double-click it, which adds it to your activity_digital.xml layout definition.

Let's give our DigitalClock an ID of **digitalClock**, and use a **wrap_content** constant for the required layout_width and layout_height parameters, and a **32dip** top margin and center the clock horizontally in the ViewGroup. Your XML markup for the DigitalClock UI element should look like the following:

```
<TextView android:id="@+id/digitalClock"
    android:layout_width="wrap_content"
    android:layout_height="wrap_content"
    android:layout_below="@+id/digitalView"
    android:layout_marginTop="32dip"
    android:layout_centerHorizontal="true" />
```

The **android:layout_below** parameter is specific to RelativeLayout container types, and tells the DigitalClock to make sure to lay itself out below the TextView. It specifies this by using a **digitalView** ID parameter reference, as shown in Figure 6-5, halfway down the TextView UI object definition.

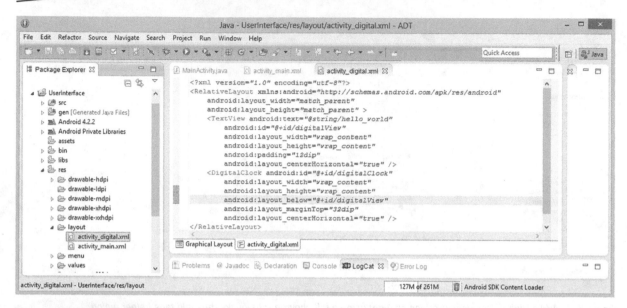

Figure 6-5. Customize the user interface child tags using RelativeLayout parameters and centering parameters

Creating a Java Foundation for ActionBar Tabs: Fragments

Right-click the **/src** folder and create a **New ➤ Class**, shown in Figure 6-6.

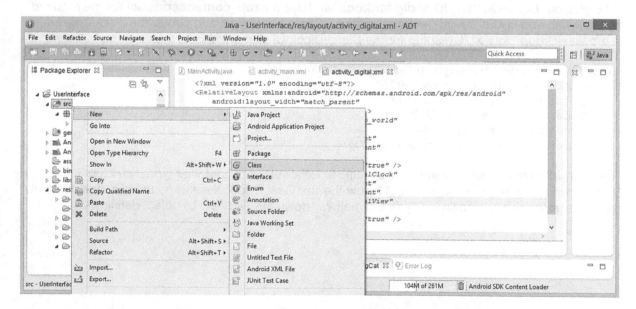

Figure 6-6. Right-click the /UserInterface/src folder and use the New ➤ Class option to create a new Java class

In the New Java Class dialog that appears next, select the **pro.android.ui** package name, using the **Browse** button on the right, and then name your new Java class **digitalClockFragment**. Next, click the **Browse** button next to the **Superclass** data field to open the **Superclass Selection** dialog shown on the right side of Figure 6-7. In the **Choose a type:** data field type "**f**" and then find the **Fragment** class from the **android.app** package after all the "F" classes appear in the **Matching items:** section in the middle of the dialog. Select the Fragment class and click the **OK** button to insert it in the New Java Class dialog and then click the **Finish** button in that dialog.

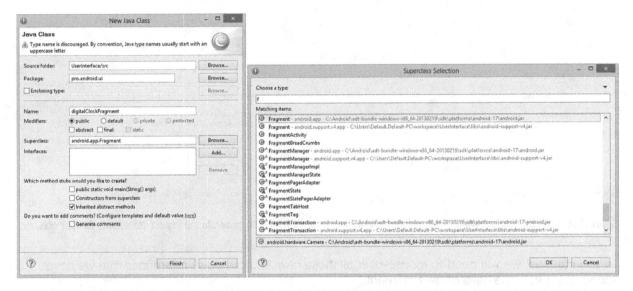

Figure 6-7. Name the class digitalClockFragment, and click the Browse button to select a Fragment Superclass from android.app package

Once you have completed the New Java Class creation process you will see a **digitalClockFragment.java** tab, as shown in Figure 6-8, with **import** statement and the public class digitalClockFragment extends Fragment {. . .} class definition.

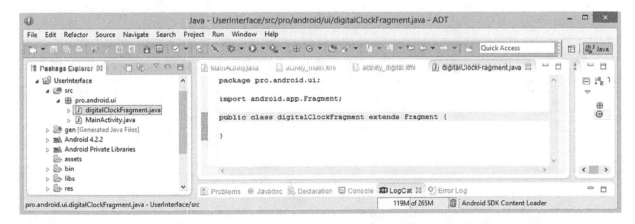

Figure 6-8. Bootstrap digitalClockFragment.java class written by Eclipse with package, import, and extends code

Next we need to add an onCreateView() method call to inflate our UI layout using the Android LayoutInflater class, ViewGroup layout definition and a Bundle object to save our instance of the class state objects, as can be done using the following line of Java code that is shown in Figure 6-9:

```
public View onCreateView( LayoutInflater digitalClock, ViewGroup digClockLayout, Bundle
savedInstanceState ) { Java code for the onCreateView method goes in here }
```

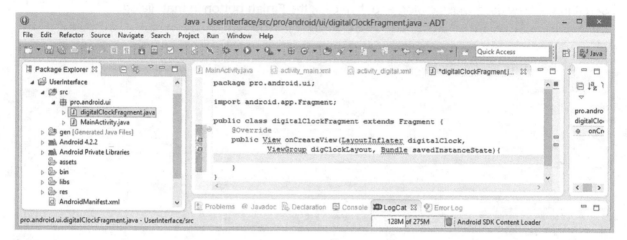

Figure 6-9. *Code the onCreateView() method and mouse-over error highlights to generate the import statements for four classes*

As you can see, we will need to mouse-over all these new Android class references that we have added using this one Java code statement.

Eclipse will write these four import statements for us, as shown in Figure 6-10, where I have invoked three of the Import options, and am about to do the final **Import Bundle (android.os)** option selection so that we can add a **return** statement inside of our onCreateView() to signify its execution. On an invocation of this method, it will return an **inflated UI layout object**.

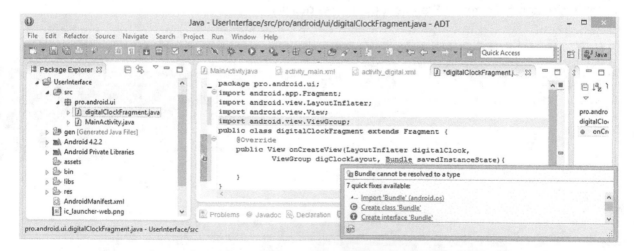

Figure 6-10. *Showing import statements at the top of the digitalClockFragment class and Import Bundle (android.os)*

Once we've imported all four Android class references, we find that we now have even more red ink in our code than we did before! Mouse-over this new error highlighting and breathe a sigh of relief, as all Eclipse wants is a return statement to be implemented, which we were going to do next anyway!

Click the Add return statement option shown in Figure 6-11, and Eclipse writes a return statement for you, free of charge (it's open source).

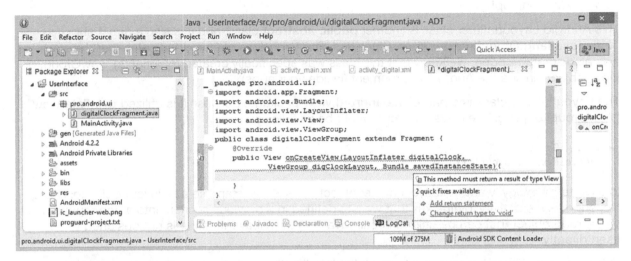

Figure 6-11. *Mouse-over the error highlight and select the Add return statement option to add a return statement*

As you can see in Figure 6-12, when you add the return statement parameter Eclipse will also provide suggestions for that for you as well. Select the digClockLayout ViewGroup object, since we do want to return the UI layout. We will actually be replacing the ViewGroup object reference with a method call which will inflate, and then pass over, this ViewGroup UI definition.

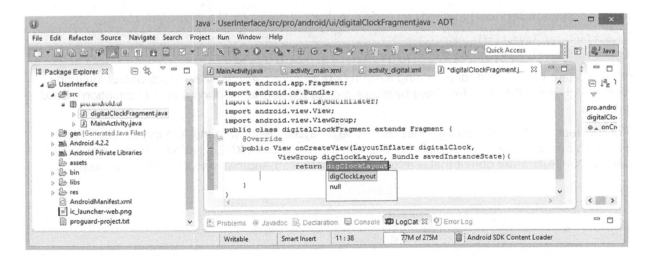

Figure 6-12. *Select the digClockLayout ViewGroup object to complete the return statement (for the time being)*

Android's LayoutInflater Class

This LayoutInflater class or object is exactly what its name belies; it is an inflater of layouts. What exactly does this mean? Inflation is the term that is used in Android to denote the process of taking an XML definition and turning it into a Java object, as if you had coded your Java object in the first place. Android uses XML for design processes to allow non-coders to play in the application design work process without having to learn OOP programming languages such as Java; all they have to learn is XML markup!

This Android LayoutInflater class is another **public abstract** class, and it is also a direct subclass of the **java.lang.Object** master class. Since this direct subclass of Object indicates that the class was also scratch-coded, we know that this class was specifically created for inflating ViewGroup, or View, objects inside the Android environment (inside your apps).

The LayoutInflater class is a part of the **android.view** package, because it is utilized to inflate View (ViewGroup) objects. The class hierarchy would be as follows:

```
java.lang.Object
  > android.view.LayoutInflater
```

In Java terminology, what the LayoutInflater object does is to instantiate a UI layout definition XML file, such as the activity_digital.xml that we just defined in a previous section, into a corresponding ViewGroup object that can be utilized in our Java code. The LayoutInflater is not designed to be used directly.

This means you'll want to use your LayoutInflater indirectly, as part of a more complex Java coding construct, such as you observed in Figures 6-10 through 6-12, where we used it as a parameter inside an **onCreateView()** method call.

You could also use a **.getLayoutInflater()** method call, or alternatively, use the **.getSystemService(String)** method call. These would retrieve a standard LayoutInflater instance that is already wired-up to your current context, and thus would be properly configured for the device the app is running on.

This **.getSystemService()** method call code construct should look like this:

```
LayoutInflater layoutInflaterObject =
(LayoutInflater)context.getSystemService(Context.LAYOUT_INFLATER_SERVICE);
```

It's important to note that for operating system performance reasons, ViewGroup object inflation is performed using XML files that have been pre-processed at (that is, during) your application's build process.

For this reason, it is not currently possible to use a LayoutInflater with the Android XmlPullParser class, so currently you cannot process XML text files at runtime. XML inflation currently only works with an XmlPullParser object that is returned from compiled Android resources (R.resname.file).

Using LayoutInflater

Now that you have learned more about the Android LayoutInflater class, we next call an **.inflate()** method off a **LayoutInflater** object that we named **digitalClock**, and pass the parameters of your layout definition that Android stores in the location **R.layout.activity_digital**, as well as a **ViewGroup** object named **digClockLayout** that we want inflated, along with a **false** boolean value. This false boolean value was for setting the **attachToRoot** parameter value. This third parameter in this method call defines whether or not we want to append or attach to a current View (true value) or replace the current View value with a new View (false value). As you can see in Figure 6-13, our Java code is error-free and our Fragment subclass is complete, and is ready to use with our ActionBar tab UI code.

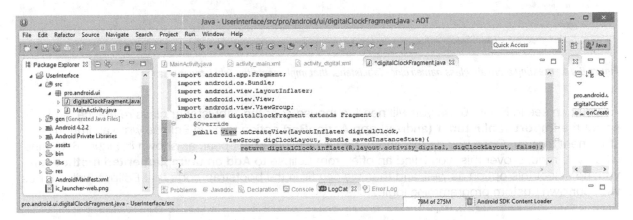

Figure 6-13. Change your return statement to return a digitalClock LayoutInflater after calling an .inflate() method

Now that we've coded the Fragment subclass for our DigitalClock UI, we'll switch gears and create a private inner class inside of MainActivity.java that implements a TabListener to listen for, and act upon, any click on these ActionBar tabs that we are implementing within this chapter.

We will need to code this clockTabListener TabListener subclass before we code the ActionBar object that references it, because the ActionBar code references this clockTabListener class, so this code must be put in place first. A private Java class is a class inside another (public) Java class that can be utilized only within the context of that class, which is why it is allowed to be coded in this fashion.

clockTabListener: A Private Class Implements TabListener

Create a **clockTabListener** class using this Java code shown in Figure 6-14:

```
private class clockTabListener implements TabListener {the class code goes in here}
```

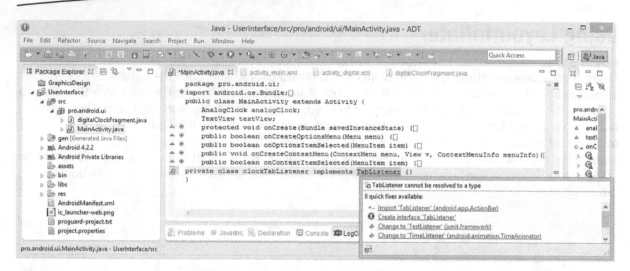

Figure 6-14. *Creating a private class named clockTabListener that implements the TabListener class*

As you can see in Figure 6-14, you will need to mouse-over the TabListener class reference, and select the **Import TabListener (android.app.ActionBar)** option to have Eclipse write an import statement for you. Once you do this another error highlight will appear, as shown in Figure 6-15, and when you mouse-over this, you'll find an offer from Eclipse to **Add** an **unimplemented method** for you, so select this option as well, and then we can fill in the bootstrap code that Eclipse writes for us with our own custom programming logic.

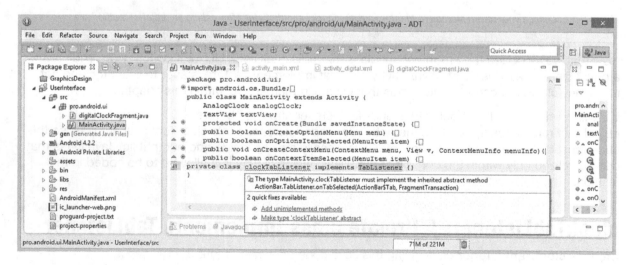

Figure 6-15. *Mouse-over the error highlight under clockTabListener class name and Add unimplemented method*

What Eclipse is going to do for us is make sure all those **@Override** methods that we are going to need to implement to create a valid TabListener subclass are in place and are ready to receive our custom Java code. Then all we will have to do is implement the ones we need and voila we'll have coded an **ActionBar.TabListener** subclass named **clockTabListener**.

As you can see in Figure 6-16, a TabListener subclass needs to implement three custom methods, **onTabReselected()**, **onTabSelected()**, and **onTabUnselected()**.

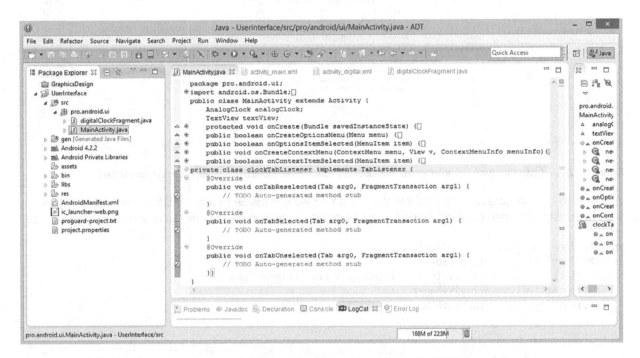

Figure 6-16. *Examining the three unimplemented @Override methods inherited from the TabListener Superclass*

Let's collapse these three methods, using that **minus sign** on the left of each of them, and add our **constructor method** first, as is shown in Figure 6-17.

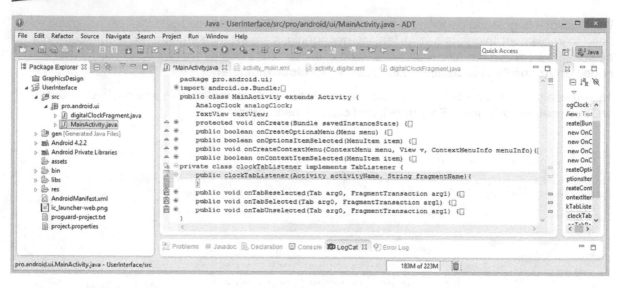

Figure 6-17. *Collapse the three unimplemented methods and add a public clockTabListener() constructor method*

We need to declare two **private final** variables first that we use inside of a constructor method, and then code a constructor method itself, using this following Java programming code, as is shown in Figure 6-18:

```
private final Activity currentActivity;
private final String currentFragment;
public clockTabListener(Activity activityName, String fragmentname){
    currentActivity = activityName;
    currentFragment = fragmentName;
}
```

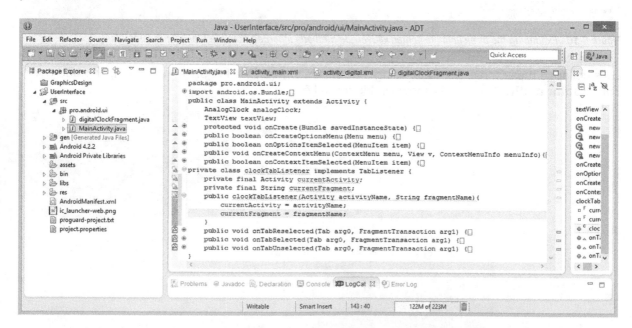

Figure 6-18. *Create variables at top of the clockTabListener class for Activity and FragmentTransaction objects*

This constructor method gets the Activity and Fragment names that we need to utilize later inside the **.instantiate()** method call, which then creates the Fragment object that our ActionBar tab uses to display either our DigitalClock or our AnalogClock UI design on the device screen.

The next thing that we will need to do at the top of this private class is to declare this Fragment object named **launchFragment** that will ultimately hold the result of the .instantiate() method call. We'll do this using the following Java code, as is shown in Figure 6-19:

```
private Fragment launchFragment;
```

Figure 6-19. Declaring a private Fragment object named launchFragment at the top of the clockTabListener class

As you can see in Figure 6-19, you need to mouse-over the initial use of the Fragment class, and select the **Import Fragment (android.app)** option to have Eclipse write this import statement for you. Once this is done, we can use the Fragment object inside the onTabSelected() method, which we are about to code next to launch the Fragment object that we inflated with our activity_digital.xml UI definition earlier in this chapter.

Now that we have declared our Fragment object named launchObject, we can use it inside the onTabSelected() method to instantiate the Fragment and load it with the target Fragment UI definition and the Activity we want to display it in. This is done by using the following line of code:

```
launchFragment = Fragment.instantiate(currentActivity, currentFragment);
```

Before we write any more Fragment-related code, let's take a look at the FragmentTransaction class before we get into using methods from the class.

The FragmentTransaction Class:

The Android **FragmentTransaction** class is another **public abstract** class and it is also another direct subclass of the **java.lang.Object** master class.

Since a direct subclass of Object indicates that a class was scratch-coded we know that the class was essentially created for working with Fragments, or Fragment objects, inside the Android environment (inside your apps).

This FragmentTransaction class is part of the **android.app** package, because it's utilized to work with Fragment objects in apps. A FragmentTransaction class hierarchy would therefore be structured as follows:

```
java.lang.Object
  > android.app.FragmentTransaction
```

This FragmentTransaction class includes **seven** transform constants (Table 6-1), which allow you to control how Fragment objects are **transitioned** onto the View, as well as taken off of a View (screen). These include **TRANSIT_ENTER_MASK, TRANSIT_EXIT_MASK, TRANSIT_NONE, TRANSIT_UNSET, TRANSIT_FRAGMENT_CLOSE, TRANSIT_FRAGMENT_OPEN**, and **TRANSIT_FRAGMENT_FADE**.

Table 6-1. Fragment Transition Constants in Android

Fragment Transition Constant:	Transition Transformation Constant can be Used For:
TRANSIT_ENTER_MASK	Used to Mask a Fragment Entrance Transition
TRANSIT_EXIT_MASK	Used to Mask a Fragment Entrance Transition
TRANSIT_NONE	Used to Remove a Fragment Transition
TRANSIT_UNSET	Used to Unset a Fragment Transition
TRANSIT_FRAGMENT_CLOSE	Used to Close a Fragment Transition
TRANSIT_FRAGMENT_OPEN	Used to Open a Fragment Transition
TRANSIT_FRAGMENT_FADE	Used to Apply a Fragment Transition Fade Special Effect

The FragmentTransaction class also includes **two dozen** methods that can be used to control the display of Fragment objects in your Activity View. We will be using several of these, including **.add()**, **.replace()**, and **.remove()**, a bit later on in this chapter, to control our own Fragment object usage.

Using FragmentTransaction

As you can see in Figure 6-20, our latest line of Java code is error-free, and we can now write the rest of our Java code for this method, which will add this DigitalClock UI Fragment to your Activity View display, using the FragmentTransaction object named arg1 along with the .add() method call.

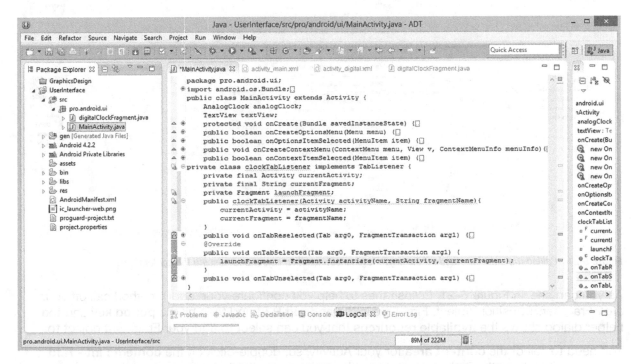

Figure 6-20. *Coding an onTabSelected() method for the clockTabListener private class to instantiate a Fragment*

Now that we've instantiated our **launchFragment** Fragment object, and loaded it up with the Activity we want to launch our UI Fragment in and with what UI Fragment we want to launch, we can use this Fragment object in our next line of code. This code uses an **.add()** method call to add the Fragment information to an arg1 FragmentTransaction object, as shown in Figure 6-21.

Figure 6-21. *Calling the .add() method off the arg1 FragmentTransaction object and passing the content area*

As you can see, in Figure 6-21, Eclipse tries to help you configure your .add() method call off your arg1 FragmentTransition object. First type in the **android.R.id** and then hit the **period** key and the helper dialog shows the **available resources** that you can select to add your Fragment object to.

You need to select the **content area** for your Activity, so, double-click on the **content : int - R.id** option to add this as the first parameter for this .add() method call.

Now that we have defined which area of our application's Activity subclass (the content area) that we want to add our Fragment to, which is the first parameter, we need to specify which Fragment object needs to be added into this content area for the Activity subclass.

The information regarding our DigitalClock Fragment is "passed over" using the second parameter. We'll want to pass over this launchFragment Fragment object, which we just instantiated and loaded with Activity and Fragment related information using the previous line of code.

When we are all done implementing this .add() method call, off the arg1 FragmentTransaction object, the Java programming statement will look like this, as shown in Figure 6-22:

```
arg1.add(android.R.id.content, launchFragment);
```

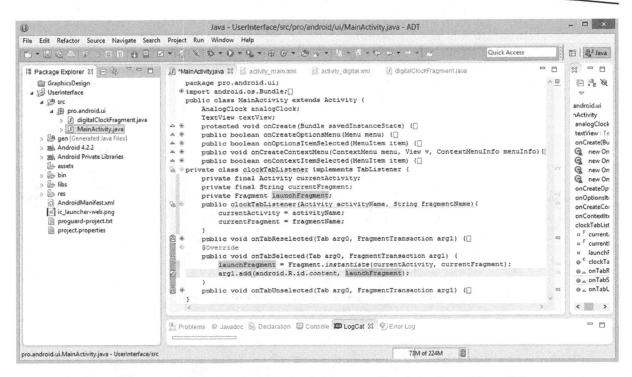

Figure 6-22. Final code for onTabSelected() method, showing the Fragment object declaration and instantiation

Now we have our code in place that launches our Fragment object containing our DigitalClock UI design. This will launch when a user clicks on the DIGITAL tab in your ActionBar tabbed user interface design that you are creating.

However, when we click the ANALOG tab, (which we are going to implement next after we finish coding our clockTabListener class and implementing that class in our MainActivity.java Activity subclass) we need to remove the DigitalClock Fragment from the content area of the display.

So let's implement the **onTabUnselected()** method, which you can see in Figure 6-22 is located right underneath the onTabSelected() method that we just implemented.

As you can see, in Figure 6-22, Eclipse ADT again tries to help configure the **.remove()** method call off an arg1 FragmentTransition object.

This time Eclipse gets it right, as we want to remove this **launchFragment** object from the content area of the application Activity display screen.

So simply select and then double-click the launchFragment object option in the Eclipse helper pop-up dialog that is shown in pale yellow, and your first line of Java code that is needed for the onTabUnselected() method in your clockTabListener class will be (partially, at least) coded for you.

We are almost done implementing our private clockTabListener class, all we have to do now is do some object clean-up (resetting), and we can move on!

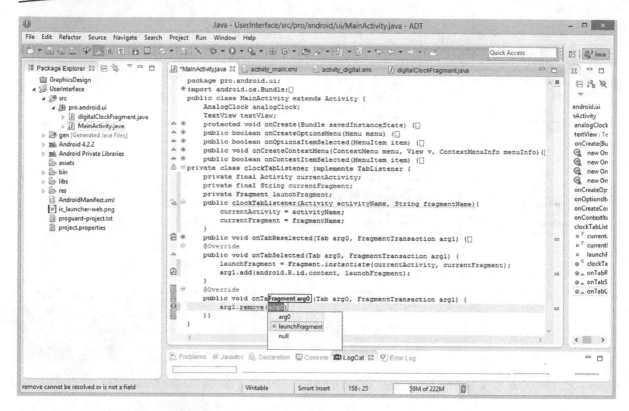

Figure 6-23. *Coding an onTabDeselected() method for the clockTabListener private class to remove the launchFragment Fragment*

The next step in this onTabUnselected() method call—after we remove the Fragment object from the FragmentTransaction object—is to reset the Fragment object so that it is "cleared out" for use again with another tab selection.

By doing this in this fashion in our code, we are only leveraging a single object, which will conserve system memory use, to hold this launchFragment object, which is quite efficient, if you think about it for a millisecond.

The way we reset or clear out the launchFragment Fragment object is by setting it to a value of "null," which generally signifies "declared for use but currently unused" in the Java programming language.

This can be accomplished using the following Java programming statement, as seen at the bottom of the screenshot in Figure 6-24:

```
launchFragment = null;
```

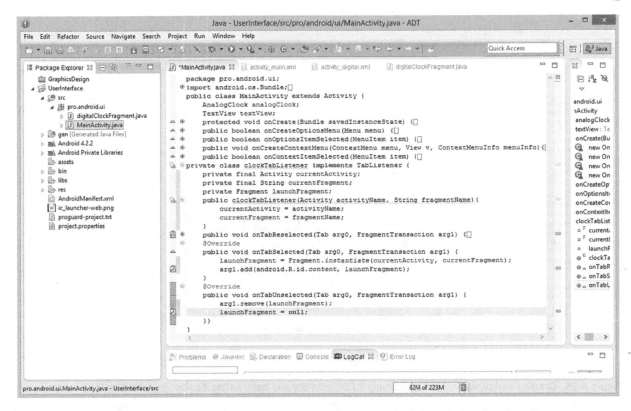

Figure 6-24. Set the launchFragment Fragment object to a null value after removing it from the FragmentTransition

We are now finished implementing this clockTabListener private class, and, we are ready to start working on Java code inside of our MainActivity.java Activity subclass. Notice in Figure 6-24 that we still have yellow warning highlights, under references to the clockTabListener class and constructor method, since we have not yet implemented them in our MainActivity class.

Next we will be working in the MainActivity.java tab, to replace our menu-based user interface with the ActionBar tab navigation user interface, so that you can see how to do this type of UI navigation in your applications as well.

The FragmentTransaction Class

The first thing that we'll want to do at the top of our onCreate() method, after the super. onCreate(savedInstanceState); superclass method call, is to declare, name and instantiate an ActionBar object named tabsActionBar.

This is done using the following line of Java code, shown in Figure 6-25:

```
ActionBar tabsActionBar = getActionBar();
```

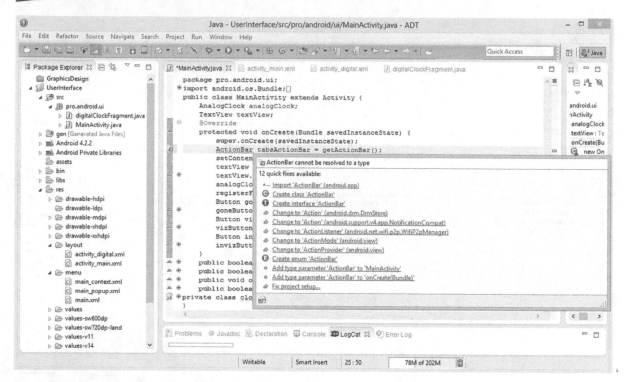

Figure 6-25. Creating an ActionBar object and naming it tabsActionBar and instantiating it using .getActionBar()

This uses the **.getActionBar()** method call, which you learned about earlier in this chapter when we looked at the Android ActionBar class. This is the equivalent of instantiating and loading an ActionBar object so that it can be utilized within your application.

As you can see in Figure 6-25, you'll need to mouse-over this reference to the ActionBar class, and select the **Import ActionBar (android.app)** option.

Now that we have an ActionBar object named tabsActionBar, we will begin to configure it to suit our application's purposes, by declaring it as a tabs navigation mode ActionBar configuration, by using the **NAVIGATION_MODE_TABS** constant from the ActionBar class.

This is accomplished using the ActionBar class **.setNavigationMode()** method call, which you learned about earlier in the chapter, along with one of the navigation mode constants, using the following line of Java code:

```
tabsActionBar.setNavigationMode(ActionBar.NAVIGATION_MODE_TABS);
```

As you can see in Figure 6-26, once you type in this ActionBar class name, and then the **period** character, inside of the parameter area of this method call, the helper dialog will appear, and will be populated with all the supported class constants.

Figure 6-26. Set the navigation mode constant using the .setNavigationMode() method call and the Eclipse helper dialog

Select the NAVIGATION_MODE_TABS constant and double-click it to select and insert it into the parameter area of your method call, as shown in Figure 6-26. Once this is set-up you will be ready to add new Tab objects to your tabsActionBar, which will be used to navigate between your custom UI Fragments and which are created using the **ActionBar.Tab** nested class.

Next we will create a **Tab** object named **tabArray** and instantiate it using the **.newTab()** method called off of the **tabsActionBar** ActionBar object, by using the following single line of Java code, as is shown in Figure 6-27:

```
Tab tabArray = tabsActionBar.newTab();
```

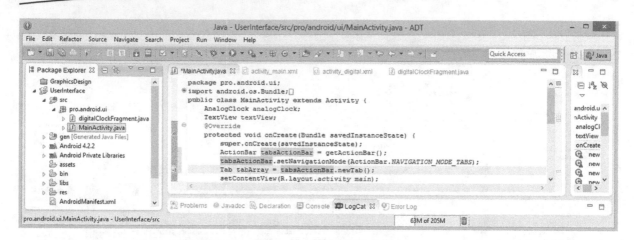

Figure 6-27. Creating a Tab object named tabArray and setting it equal to the tabsActionBar.newTab() method

Once this tabArray Tab object is created we can begin configuring it next.

Before we can use the .setText() method call to begin configuring the Tab object label, we will need to quickly add a couple of **<string>** constants, in our **strings.xml** file in our **/res/values** folder, so that we have string objects to reference in this method call.

Right-click the strings.xml file and select the **Open** option and add two <string> constants at the top of the file, using the following XML markup:

```
<string name="tab_one">DIGITAL</string>
<string name="tab_two">ANALOG</string>
```

These are used as the text labels for our Tab objects in the ActionBar object, and now that they are in place, as can be seen in Figure 6-28, use a Ctrl-S keystroke combination to save the strings.xml file. Now we can reference these two string objects inside of our **.setText()** method calls, one of which we will be coding in our next step.

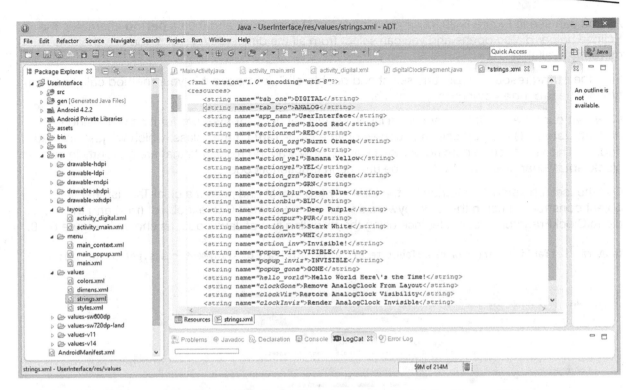

Figure 6-28. Adding the DIGITAL and ANALOG ActionBar tab labels <string> constants to the strings.xml file

Next we will want to call the .setText() method off our tabArray Tab object using the following line of Java code as shown in Figure 6-29:

```
tabArray.setText(R.string.tab_one);
```

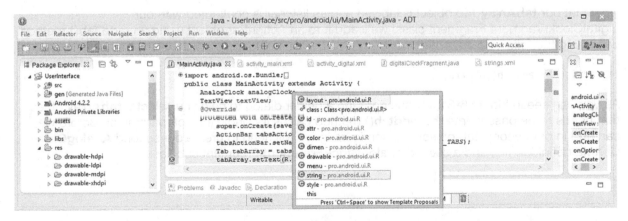

Figure 6-29. Call the .setText() method off the tabArray Tab object and reference the string resource R.string

As you can see in Figure 6-29, once you type in the **R** (resource), and then a **period** character, the Eclipse helper dialog opens and you can select from all the different types of resources that are currently available.

Find the **string** resource type, and select and double-click it to insert it in your method call, and then type in the **tab_one** <string> object name.

Now that our tabArray Tab object has a label, we will set up a **TabListener** for it as well using the **.setTabListener()** method call and our new private **clockTabListener** class, which we just finished coding. This line of code gets rid of those wavy yellow warning highlights that are currently in our clockTabListener class, as it will now be utilized in functional code.

Call the .setTabListener() method off the tabArray tab object and pass it a clockTabListener object constructed using the new keyword as well as the current Context object (this) and the digitalClockFragment class reference using the following line of Java code, as shown in Figure 6-30:

```
tabArray.setTabListener( new clockTabListener( this, digitalClockFragment.class.getname() ) );
```

Figure 6-30. Call a clockTabListener() constructor using the new keyword inside the .setTabListener() method

Now that our **tabArray** Tab object is labeled and its listener is configured with our digitalClockFragment Fragment class, we'll add it to an ActionBar object using an **.addTab()** method call, using the following Java statement:

```
tabsActionBar.addtab(tabArray);
```

As you can see in Figure 6-31, Eclipse pops-up a helper dialog to help you select a **tabArray** object that needs to be passed into the **.addtab()** method call as its single (object) parameter. Before we can add in our second Tab object and configure it, we will need to create our second **AnalogClock** UI XML definition file, and a second **analogClockFragment** Fragment subclass.

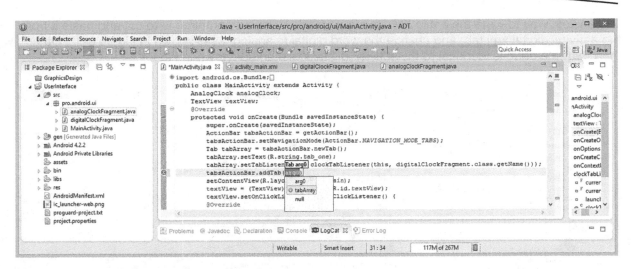

Figure 6-31. *Call the .addTab() method off the tabsActionBar ActionBar object and pass the tabArray Tab object*

Let's create an **activity_analog.xml** AnalogClock UI definition first, using the same work process shown earlier in the chapter in Figure 6-1. Use the same settings, except use an **activity_analog** name as shown in Figure 6-32.

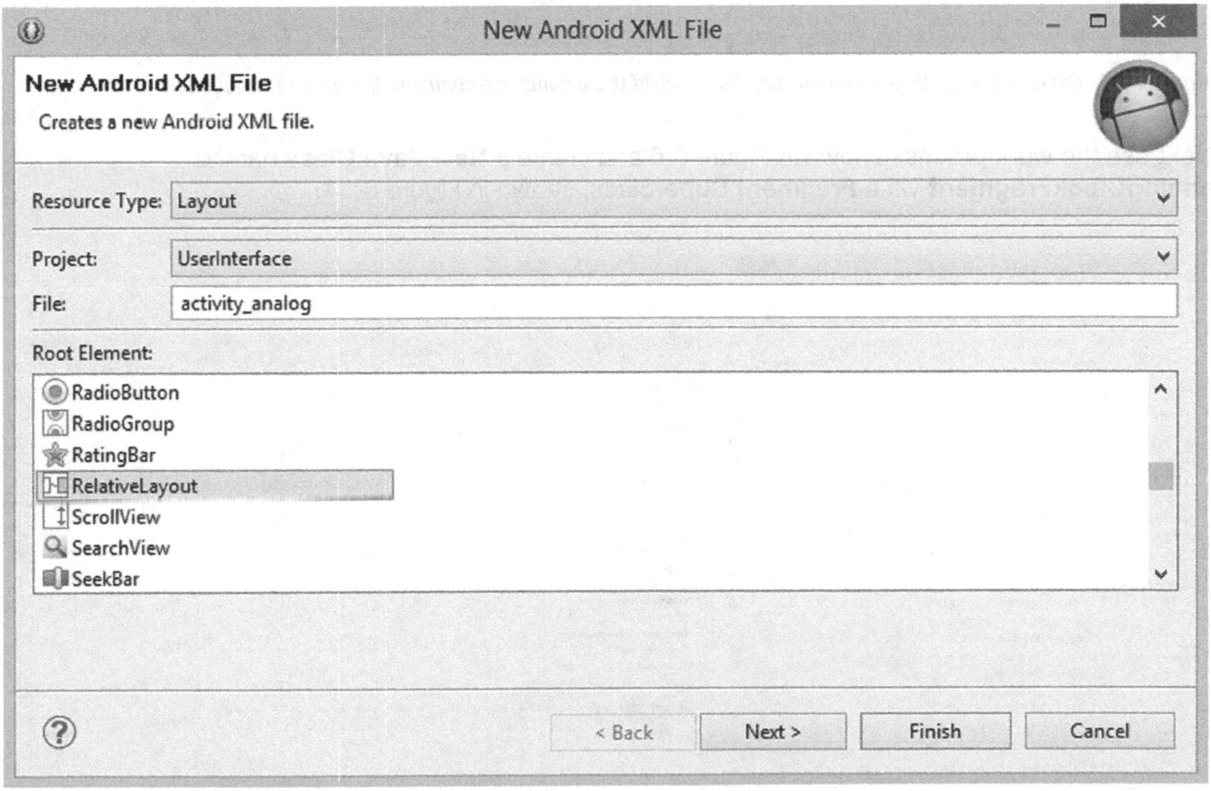

Figure 6-32. *Creating the activity_analog.xml UI definition for the AnalogClock Fragment*

The easiest way to write the entire XML markup for this UI layout container is to cut and paste it from the activity_digital.xml tab, and change the word digital to analog, as is shown in Figure 6-33. Other than that, the code is identical to the activity_digital.xml markup shown in Figure 6-5.

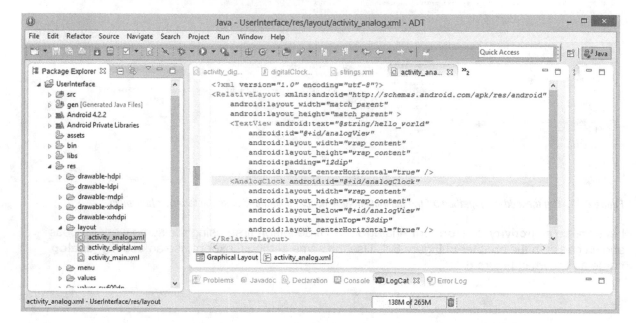

Figure 6-33. Create the <TextView> and <AnalogClock> child UI elements and configure them using parameters

Next use the work process shown in Figure 6-6 and create a **New Java Class** named **analogClockFragment** via a **Fragment Superclass**, shown in Figure 6-34.

Figure 6-34. Create analogClockFragment.java class using the New Java Class and Superclass Selection dialog

The fastest way to create an **analogClockFragment** class is to copy the code for your digitalClockFragment class and change the word **digital** to **analog**, as shown in Figure 6-35. Now we are ready to get back to our ActionBar and Tab object coding and implement our second ActionBar.Tab object so that we can test our code, and make sure that everything is working properly, and finally see the results of all this ActionBar.Tab programming labor.

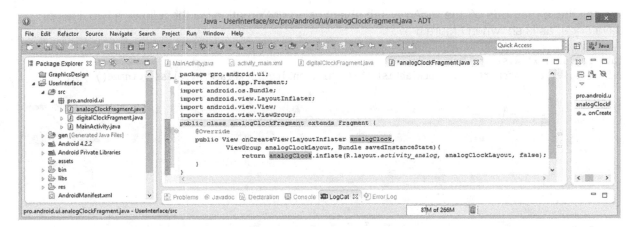

Figure 6-35. Create the onCreateView() method similar to the digitalClockFragment.java class only using analog

Let's use our tabArray Tab object to create another tab for your ActionBar using the **.newTab()** method call off our **tabsActionBar** ActionBar object, using the following line of Java code, as shown in Figure 6-36:

```
tabArray = tabsActionBar.newTab();
```

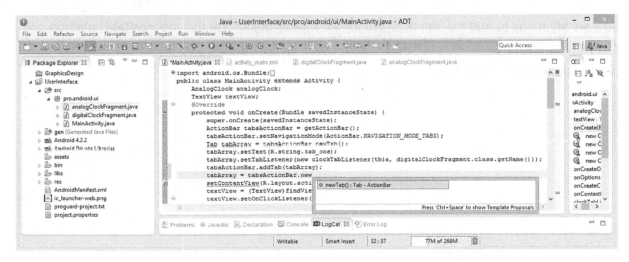

Figure 6-36. The Eclipse helper dialog finishes a .newtab() method invocation off the tabArray object

As you can see in Figure 6-36, Eclipse again helps you finish writing this line of code when you start typing in the new keyword. Select the newTab() method suggested and double-click on it—Eclipse writes the code!

Next we configure the **ANALOG** tab in the same way as the **DIGITAL** tab, using the **.setText()** and the **.setTabListener()** method calls.

We call these methods off the tabArray Tab object using dot notation via the following two lines of Java code, as is shown in Figure 6-37:

```
tabArray.setText(R.string.tab_two);
tabArray.setTabListener( new clockTabListener( this, analogClockFragment.class.getname() ) );
```

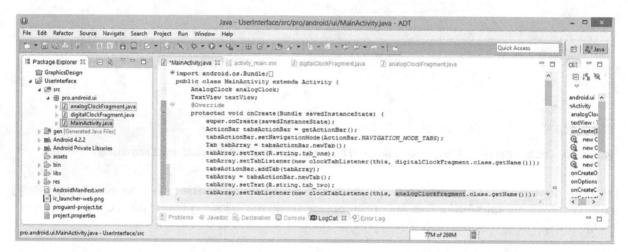

Figure 6-37. Call a clockTabListener() constructor using the new keyword inside the .setTabListener() method

Now we are ready to add the **Tab** object to the **ActionBar** object. We use the **.addTab()** method call using the following Java code, shown in Figure 6-38:

```
tabsActionBar.addTab(tabArray);
```

Figure 6-38. Adding the tabArray object to the tabsActionBar object by using the .addTab() method call

I selected the **Tab object** in the screenshot so you could trace its usage.

Now that our Tabbed ActionBar implementation is coded (and marked-up), all we have to do is to remove the conflicting menuing code, which we wrote in the menu chapters, and we'll be ready to test a new user interface design, for application navigation using ActionBar tabs, which are pretty cool.

You can either comment out all the menu-related code as shown on the first line of the code in Figure 6-39, or you can select it all (it's contiguous fortunately) and either delete it, or right-click on it, and **copy** it, and then paste it into a text editor, such as **Notepad**, and save it to reinsert at some later time. This last option is the best programmer practice, and is what I did. You will see the final code a bit later on in Figure 6-43.

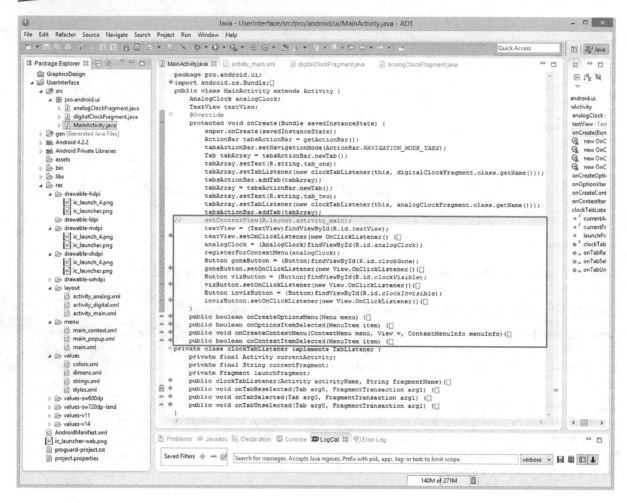

Figure 6-39. *Comment out (as shown on first line of code) or delete all code shown in red box*

Now we can run a tabbed application using the **Run As ➤ Android Application** work process, launching the app in a Nexus One emulator as shown in Figure 6-40. As you can see, you can click on the two tabs to switch clock types.

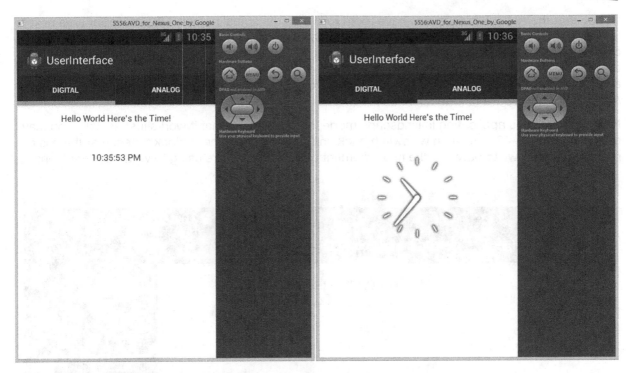

Figure 6-40. Tesing the ActionBar DIGITAL and ANALOG UI Tabs in the Nexus One emulator in portrait mode

Now use **Ctrl-F11** to switch Nexus One into **Landscape**, shown in Figure 6-41.

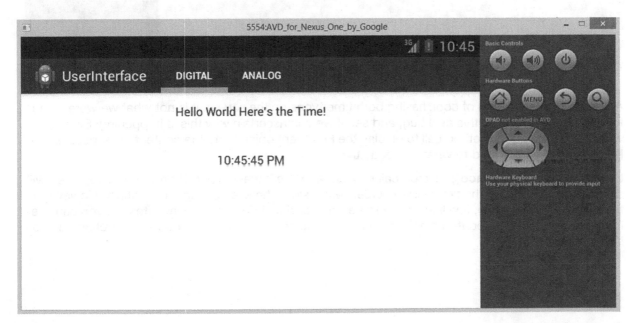

Figure 6-41. Using the Ctrl-F11 keystroke combination to rotate the Nexus One emulator into landscape mode

Notice that the ActionBar tabs now have room to live on the actual primary OS ActionBar area next to your application's icon and title. It you keep a tab label short and concise, you have a better chance of this happening in all orientation modes, not just landscape. Since we used <string> constant values in our programming work process, you could go back to your XML (for practice), and try using **DC** and **AC**, for instance, and see if you could fit your new tabs on the primary OS ActionBar in the portrait mode as well.

Next, let's test this application in landscape mode, and make sure that it works just as well. You may notice in Figure 6-42 that when we switch back and forth between these clock types, that there is a **residual screen write** between the two Fragment objects that we are using to write these screens.

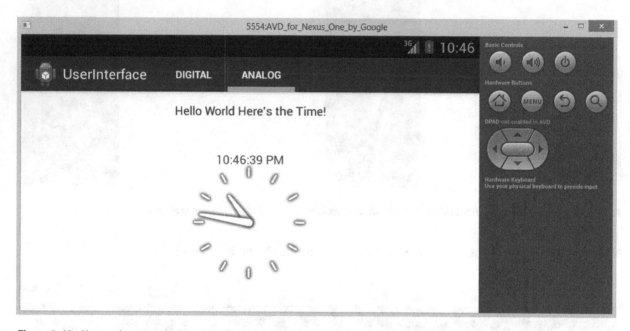

Figure 6-42. Uncovering a bug in the application when switching tabs between the analog and digital fragments

Although this looks kind of cool, having both time types on the screen, it is not what we were going for initially, so let's treat this as a bug, and see if we can ascertain why this is happening. Since we're using an .add() method call to display the Fragment object onto the content area, possibly the Fragment is being added to what is already there.

Let's try using the **.replace()** method call instead, and see if that cures this problem. A .replace() will still perform an add on the first display screen write, since there is nothing there initially. However, if there is something there, it will replace it rather than add to it on later screen writes. As you can see in Figure 6-43, I have updated the Java code, and you can see our final code for this ActionBar Tab implementation as well.

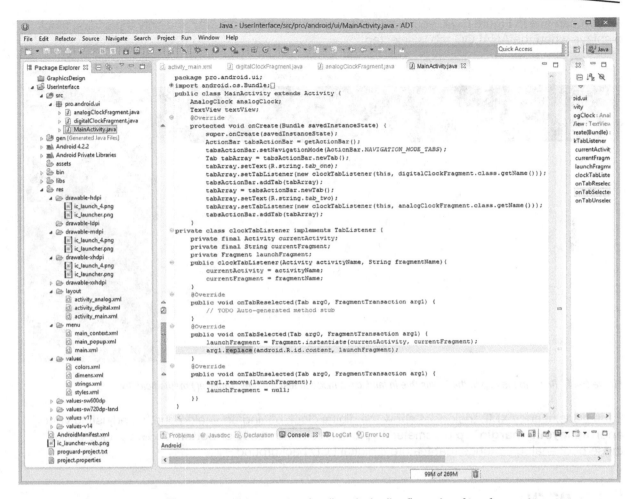

Figure 6-43. Change an arg1.add() method call to an arg1.replace() method call to fix overlay of two fragments

It's important to **learn creatively** from any mistakes, and later use .add() to implement UI elements you want to "build" onto the screen between tabs.

Now it's time to test this new code in landscape mode in the Nexus One, so use the **Run As ➤ Android Application** work process and a **Ctrl-F11** keystroke combination and click the DIGITAL and ANALOG tabs several times back and forth and make sure that you don't experience this dual-time-ghosting any more. You might be wondering why you didn't see this bug while testing in portrait mode, and my speculation is that the spacing of the UI, while in portrait mode, put your digital clock **behind** your analog clock.

If you wanted to ascertain if that is in fact what is happening, define a semitranslucent alpha channel, in your <AnalogClock> **android:background** parameter using a **#AARRGGBB** value of #00000000 or maybe #77FFFFFF for 50% translucent and see whether you see the digital clock behind the analog clock! The XML markup for this parameter would look something like the following:

```
android:background="#00000000" (100% transparent, no background color will be used)
android:background="#77FFFFFF" (50% transparent, and a white background color used)
```

As you can see in Figure 6-44, your application is now working correctly and only the analog clock displays when the ANALOG tab is selected.

Figure 6-44. Running the app in the Nexus One in landscape mode to test the new .replace() method call fix

If the translucency XML trick does show the digital clock behind an analog one, try adjusting your **android:layout_marginTop** parameter, to place it in the top 25% or bottom 25%, so it looks like those cool analog watches that feature a digital LCD background.

Summary

In this chapter, we took a closer look at the **ActionBar** and **Fragment** classes, and at using **ActionBar Tabs** for UI navigation. We learned how to implement the **ActionBar.TabListener** and **ActionBar.Tab** nested classes, and we created an ActionBar tabbed user interface that switched between analog and digital clock user interface designs.

We looked at ActionBar **functional areas** first, then we looked at ActionBar **navigation modes**, and then at the ActionBar class, and nested classes, and methods, some of which we implemented during the remainder of the chapter. We created XML definitions for AnalogClock and DigitalClock screen designs and created Fragment subclasses and a TabListener class to implement those designs. Finally, we implemented a tabbed ActionBar UI in our MainActivity.

In the next chapter, we'll take a close look at the wide number of Android **UI Design Considerations**, including Styles, Themes, Screen Density Targets, and the supported media asset formats for digital images, audio, and video.

Part 3

Android UI Design: UI Layout Considerations, Android OS Design Concepts and Android UI Design Guidelines

Chapter 7

Android UI Design Considerations: Styles, Screen Density Targets and New Media Formats

Now that we've covered the different types of Android UI Navigation using the Menu and ActionBar related classes in the previous three chapters, in this seventh chapter, we will begin learning more about some of the other Android UI Design considerations. Rest assured, there are quite a few!

There are a vast number of different factors that must be considered when developing your Android application, and the majority of them have do with professional Android user interface design, in one way or another.

A primary reason for this is the vast spectrum of Android hardware devices that are available in the markets today, including smartphones and tablets, iTVs and ebook readers, and now, newer consumer electronics verticals have emerged which are powered by Android, such as watches, game consoles, auto dashboards, phablets (phone-tablets), and even eyeglasses (GoogleGlass).

We are going to introduce you to many factors that will influence your Android user interface design's constraints and decisions, from new media formats that are supported for you to use to add imagery, sound effects, video, animation, and special effects to your UI elements, to OS style considerations and Android device display hardware specifics.

I'll also try to implement some of these topics in your UserInterface app, so you can see some of these formats, factors, or considerations in action!

Android Media Formats: Digital Images and Digital Video

I am going to start with new media formats, as most of these standards have been in Android since the early versions of the OS, and unlike some of the other sections of this chapter where considerations change based on the OS version, with a couple of exceptions, new media formats are something that remain pretty straightforward and stable as we move across OS revisions. The primary digital image and digital video formats in Android are shown in Table 7-1.

Table 7-1. Digital Image and Digital Video Formats Supported as of Android 4.4

Format (codec) Name:	Type of Media:	File Extension:	Compression:
Portable Network Graphics	Digital Image	.PNG	Lossless
Joint Photographic Experts Group	Digital Image	.JPG	Lossy
Graphics Interchange Format	Digital Image	.GIF	Lossless
Web Photo (Google/ON2 VP8 WEBP)	Digital Image	.WebP	Lossy
Web Movie (Google/ON2 VP8 WEBM)	Digital Video	.WebM	Lossy
Motion Picture Experts Group	Digital Video	.MP4	Lossy

There are four major image formats that are used in the Android OS, which span from the earliest graphics format known to man, the **Compuserve GIF** or Graphics Information Format, to the more modern-day **PNG** (pronounced PING), which stands for Portable Network Graphics. Both of these formats are what are termed "lossless," as no image data (quality) is lost during compression.

There is also a "lossy" image file format supported in Android called JPEG or Joint Photographic Experts Group. The reason it is a lossy format is it throws away some of the image data to achieve better compression. This can result in reduced quality levels as well as "artifacts" that can easily be seen if you zoom into a JPG compressed image or display it on large screen displays. Android prefers the use of lossless, high-quality image formats.

The preference of Android, or more accurately, the creators of Android, is that you use a high-quality **PNG24** or **PNG32** image, or a well-optimized PNG8 image asset. Those numbers after the PNG tell you the **number of bits** that are used to contain image **color depth** for each pixel (discussed in the next section) in the image. We will get into technical information regarding digital imagery and digital video in the next section in far greater detail, so stay tuned.

The next most preferred image format is the JPEG format because it can get high-quality results, if the **codec** (compressor-decompressor) is applied to the image data optimally. A JPEG format uses 24 bits of data in each pixel so the image always exhibits what's termed "truecolor" colordepth quality.

The least preferred image format is the old Compuserve GIF format, because it only supports using 8-bits of color (256 colors), for the entire image. Additionally, the GIF codec (compression algorithm) is the oldest and least efficient of any of the digital image codecs (formats) in Android.

There are even fewer digital video codec formats supported in the Android OS, with only **MPEG-4** (Motion Picture Experts Group) and **WebM** digital video formats currently supported. The **MPEG4 H.264 AVC** codec is more widely used in the Internet and Television industry currently and ON2's **WebM VP8** codec (format) was recently acquired by Google and was made open source so it is rapidly gaining in popularity and support also, across browsers and OSes.

The quality and compression ratios are very similar between these two file formats (codecs) as can be seen in my *Pro Android Graphics* book (Apress, 2013), so I will utilize both formats and see which one does a better job with any given DV content. It is important to note that these are the two primary formats in HTML5 browsers and HTML5 apps (and HTML5 OSes) currently as well.

The Terminology of Digital Image and Digital Video Color

I need to make sure that you have a solid foundation with the terminology and concepts that underlie digital imaging and digital video compositing, so that when I talk about the concepts within this book, you will know how each concept we're covering fits into an overall application of new media.

The foundational building block for both digital imaging and digital video is called a "**pixel**." This stands for **picture** (pix) **element** (el) and as one single dot in an **array** of pixels in a digital image or a frame of video it carries **color** information, **transparency** information, as well as a **position** coordinate. So pixels will have a color value, a translucency value, which we will be talking about soon, and a position (X and Y coordinate) value.

Each pixel will have its **color depth**, which is the depth (amount) of color information that each pixel can "carry." This is traditionally one of four levels, based on file format (codec). **Eight-bit** color has up to **256** colors, whereas **16-bit** color has **65,536** colors and is available in the Targa (TGA) file format, which is not currently supported in Android. Next, there is a **truecolor** or **24-bit** color depth, which can hold **16,777,216** colors, as well as a **truecolor with alpha** or **32-bit** color depth, which holds these 24-bits of color, plus 8-bits of **alpha channel** (translucency level) information.

For truecolor images, which are the highest quality, and the most commonly used in digital imaging, website design and application development, each pixel color is defined using **three 8-bit** "planes," or **channels**, or layers, if you need a way to visualize this concept in 3D in your mind. One of these is **Red (R)**, one of them is **Green (G)**, and one of them is **Blue (B)**. This is where the digital imaging term "**RGB**" comes from. There's also an **ARGB** (or **RGBA**) term, which includes an **alpha channel** (A) as a fourth bit-plane. We are going to discuss how the alpha channel is utilized next.

The concept of **alpha** applies to the **transparency level** of any given pixel, so that when we combine images in a process known as **compositing**, we can control the **blending** of pixel color between each of the **image plate** layers in the **composite image**. Software, such as Photoshop or GIMP, is used to create composite images. Image compositing and blending using Java code is covered in my *Pro Android Graphics* title, but we'll cover these concepts here, so we can used them in our user interface designs later on.

Since the **alpha channel** contains **8-bits** of data, each of the pixels in the image can have **256** different levels of transparency, allowing precise image compositing to be done from one image layer to the next. Often alpha channels are used to isolate or mask parts of an image to extract them for overlay, or compositing, onto a background image plate. If you're familiar with bluescreen or greenscreen real-time compositing technology, which was made popular by weather forecasters, you know that placing one subject in another scenario is a common objective in both digital imaging and digital video. All these types of compositing operations use alpha channel data.

Digital Image Compression: Concepts and Terminology

You may have noticed that I am using this term "**codec**" interchangeably with the term "file format," thus far in this chapter. This is because in order to implement a file format in an operating system or a browser, that OS or browser must have the decoder side of the codec (**CO**der**DEC**oder) in place so that the data for that format (codec algorithm) type can be decrypted.

As a developer, you will be working with both sides of the codec coin, the **encoder**, which you will utilize in software packages, such as Photoshop or GIMP (imaging), or Lightworks or Squeeze (video), and a **decoder**, which you will pass the digital image or video assets over to inside the Android OS.

Each of these digital image and digital video formats that we discussed in the first section of this chapter employ a **different codec algorithm**. This is why they have different features, such as lossy (JPEG, MPEG, or WebM) or lossless (PNG or GIF) compression quality, different color depth support, and different data footprint optimization (resulting file size) results.

So Android OS contains all these decoding algorithms for the digital video and digital imaging formats that we have discussed, as well as all the digital audio formats that we are going to be discussing next. You need to realize as a developer that this also means the Android OS must use system resources, such as memory and processor cycles to implement these decoding algorithms, and thus to play back, or display, your new media assets.

Some of the codecs, such as **PNG24** or **PNG32**, simply apply the **maximum** level of compression possible without losing any of the original image data, and obviously these provide the best results, but at the cost of a **larger data footprint** (resulting file size). Other codecs, such as JPEG and MPEG, allow you to select a **quality level**, usually ranging from **0% to 100%**, that controls how much of your original image data will be thrown away (yes, trashed) by the codec in its attempts to greatly reduce the data footprint of your resulting data file. This is why Android OS (creators) prefer that you use PNG24 or PNG32 image format, as PNG provides the most optimal user experience, and thus makes the Android platform look the best, relative to other competing platforms. If you look at market share percentages, this seems to have worked, as Android has the majority market share currently.

The GIF codec uses a reduced color depth of 8-bit color (up to 256 colors) to achieve its data compression results. It does this by using a "palette" or an "index" of up to 256 colors, which the codec pulls from the original 16,777,216 colors in the image. This is the reason that 8-bit color images are called indexed color images in the digital imaging industry.

For some images that use few colors, such as white puffy clouds in a deep blue sky, this approach can work fairly effectively, but for other images, using indexed color can cause an ugly effect called **color banding**.

There is a **dithering** option for indexed color images that can reduce this banding effect, in many cases, quite effectively. This dithering algorithm uses **dot patterns** between any two adjacent color values that are close to each other in their color value. The algorithm does this to trick the eye into thinking the banding is not really there. Thus, dithering can simulate as many as 512 colors in 256 color images, but only if all the colors in that image are located next to each other. Dithering will not be applied between vastly different colors, and the reason for this is a need to maintain **sharp edge quality** at all times within an indexed color image.

It is important to note that the **PNG8** image format also uses indexed color and also achieves better image compression results. This is because it utilizes a more advanced indexed image compression algorithm.

Now that we have covered those primary characteristics of visual new media elements for an Android application, let's take a look at aural, or audio, new media codecs, and formats that are available to us in the Android OS.

Sound for Android: Digital Audio Codecs and Formats

There are more digital audio codecs in Android OS than digital imaging and digital video codecs combined. This is because there are far more uses for digital audio in Android devices, such as making phone calls, using Skype, listening to music, and using an Android device as your personal digital voice recorder.

Android supports the popular .MP3 (MPEG3) file format, Wave (PCM or Pulse Code Modulated) .WAV files made famous by the Windows OS, MPEG4 audio .MP4 (or .M4A) files, OGG Vorbis (.OGG) audio files, Matroska (.MKS) WebM audio files, FLAC (.FLAC) open source audio, and even MIDI (.MID, MXMF and .XMF) data files, which technically aren't really even digital audio data at all.

Let's start with the most common digital audio format supported by Android, which is the **MPEG3** digital audio file format. Most of us are familiar with MP3 files, due to music download websites such as Napster, and most of us collect songs in this format to use on popular MP3 players and via CD-ROM and DVD-ROM based music collections. The reason an MP3 digital audio format is so popular is because it has excellent compression to quality ratio and because the codec needed to play MP3s can be found anywhere, including the Android OS.

MP3 would be the format to utilize in an Android application if your audio source audio files are already encoded using this format, and as long as whoever compressed these MP3 files got the best quality level out of them, by using an optimal encoding work process.

It is important to note that MP3 is a lossy audio file format, like JPEG is for imaging, where some of the audio data (and thus quality) is thrown away during the compression process, and thus cannot later be recovered.

Android also has the **lossless** audio compression decoder called **FLAC**, which stands for: **Free Lossless Audio Codec**. FLAC is an open source audio codec, and its support is almost as widespread as MP3s, due to the free nature of its software decoder. Thus it would be possible to use completely lossless new media assets in an Android application by using PNG24, PNG32, and FLAC.

FLAC is supported in **Android 3.1** and later, so if your end-users are using modern Android devices, you should be able to safely utilize a FLAC codec.

The FLAC codec is very fast (tightly coded) and supports **HD (24-bit) audio** and there are no patent concerns for using it. This is a great audio codec to use if you need high-quality audio using a fairly small data footprint.

FLAC supports a wide range of sampling resolutions, from 4-bits per sample up to 32-bits per sample. It supports a wider range of sampling frequency, from 1Hz to 655350Hz (65 kHz), in 1Hz increments, so it is very flexible.

From an audio playback hardware standpoint I'd suggest using 16-bit sample resolution, and either a 44.1 kHz or 48 kHz sample frequency. If you are developing for the new Android devices that use 24-bit HD audio hardware, then you can use a 24-bit sample resolution and 48 KHz sample frequency. I will go over some of the audio technology terms in the next section.

Another open source digital audio codec supported by the Android OS is the **Vorbis** codec, a **lossy** audio codec from the **Xiph.Org** Foundation. The Vorbis codec audio data is most often held inside of an **.OGG** data file container, and thus Vorbis audio is commonly called **Ogg Vorbis** digital audio format.

Ogg Vorbis supports sampling rates from **8 kHz up to 192 kHz**, and up to **255** discrete channels of digital audio (as we now know, this represents 8-bits worth of audio channels). Ogg Vorbis is supported in all Android versions.

Recently Vorbis is approaching the quality of HE-AAC or WMA (Windows Media Audio) Professional, and is superior in quality to an MP3, AAC-LC, or WMA. It is a lossy format, so FLAC would still have a higher quality level than Ogg Vorbis, as FLAC contains all the original digital audio sampling data.

Android supports most popular **MPEG-4 AAC**, or **Advanced Audio Coding** codecs, including **AAC-LC**, **HE-AAC**, or **AAC-ELD**. These codecs can all be contained in MPEG4 containers (**.3gp, .mp4, .m4a**) and can be played back in all versions of Android, except for AAC-ELD, which is only supported after Android 4.1.

In case you are wondering, the **ELD** stands for **Enhanced Low Delay**, and this particular codec is intended for use in a **real-time two-way communications** application, such as those popular **digital walkie-talkie** implementations.

The basic MPEG-4 AAC codec is an **AAC-LC**, or **Low Complexity** codec, which is widely utilized and should be sufficient for most applications. The AAC-LC should yield a high-quality result, with a lower data footprint, than MP3!

The most complicated AAC codec is the **HE-AAC** or **High Efficiency AAC** codec. This codec supports sample rates from **8 kHz to 48 kHz** and supports both **Stereo** and **Dolby 5.1** channel encoding, allowing pro audio new media.

Android supports decoding both the V1 and V2 levels for this HE-AAC codec, and Android also encodes audio using the HE-AAC v1 codec, but only in Android devices that support Android OS Version 4.1 or later (Jelly Bean).

For encoding human speech, which usually features different types of sound waves than encoding music does, there are two other **AMR** or **Adaptive Multi-Rate** audio codecs. These are highly optimized toward encoding things such as speech or even short-burst sound effects which do not require high-quality sound reproduction (such as, for instance, a laser beam sound effect).

There is also an **AMR-WB**, or **Adaptive Multi-Rate Wide-Band** codec in Android, which supports **9** discrete settings, from **6.6 to 23.85 kbps** audio bit-rates sampled at **16 kHz,** which is a premium sample rate where voice is concerned.

The AMR-WB would be the codec to use for your Narrator vocal track, if you were creating interactive children's storybook applications, for instance.

There is the **AMR-NB**, or **Adaptive Multi-Rate Narrow-Band**, codec in Android, which supports **8** discrete settings from **4.75 to 12.2 kbps** audio bit-rates, sampled at **8 kHz**, which is an adequate sample rate if the data going into the codec is high quality, or if a resulting audio sample does not require high quality due to its noisy nature, such as for a bomb blast effect.

Finally, we have a **PCM** or **Pulse Code Modulated** audio, commonly known as the **WAVE** or **.WAV** digital audio format. You may be familiar with the format, as it is the original audio format utilized for the Windows operating system.

PCM audio is also commonly used for CD-ROM and DVD-ROM content, as well as for telephony applications. This is because PCM Wave audio is uncompressed digital audio, and has no computationally intensive compression algorithms applied to its data stream. For this reason decoding (CPU overhead) is not a performance issue for telephone equipment or CD-ROM or DVD-ROM players.

For this reason, as you will see, when we start compressing digital audio assets into the various formats using Audacity 2.0.5, we can use PCM as a baseline digital audio format to measure our other compression ratios with to get an idea of which is giving us the best compression result.

Because PCM has no compression, we probably won't be putting it into our .APK file, because there are other formats, like FLAC and AAC, which will give us the same perceived audio quality, but using an order of magnitude less data footprint.

Ultimately, the only way to really find out which audio formats in Android have the best digital audio codec for a given audio data asset or instance is to actually encode your digital audio using the primary codecs which we know are well supported and are efficient. Then you would observe the data footprint results, and then finally listen to your audio playback quality, and then make your final decision regarding which audio asset to utilize.

Next, we should take a look at some of the audio concepts and terminology that is commonly utilized in digital audio, just like we took a look at the digital imaging terminology and concepts.

The Terminology Behind Digital Audio and Sound Design

Those of you who are pro "audiophiles" know that sound is created by sound waves pulsing through the air, which is why a sub-woofer needs Its massive 18-inch (or 24-inch) cone, which rapidly pushes air around, using magnetic pulses. This throws huge invisible sound waves into an audience of fans at major rock concerts, for instance, or even in your home's living room.

Just as sound is generated by various size speaker cones, which are simply membranes made out of some flexible material that generates sound waves by pulsing them into existence, so too are our ears sound receptors that can receive and then hear these sound waves. Our ears do this by receiving the pulses of air or vibrations and turning them back into data that our brain can then process and decipher using a life of experience processing them.

Sound waves generate different tones (notes) depending on the frequency of the sound wave. A wide or long wave produces a low bass tone, and a narrow or short wavelength will produce a higher, more treble tonality.

It's important to note a correlation between audio and images that exists, as different wavelengths of light also produce different colors in exactly the same way as different wavelengths of sound produce different tones.

The volume for a sound wave will be defined by the amplitude of that sound wave, which is the height of the sound wave if you happen to be looking at it on an oscilloscope. Thus the frequency or tone is defined by how narrow a sound wave is in the X (width) dimension, and the amplitude or volume is defined by how tall the wave is as measured along the Y axis or dimension.

Those of you who have engaged in audio synthesis and sound design might be aware that there are other types of core sound waves used in sound design, such as a saw wave, which looks like the edge of a saw (hence its name), or the rectangular shaped pulse wave that is shaped by using right angles (resulting in an immediate on or off sound, which translate into pulses).

Sampling Sound

Next we will take a closer look at how analog audio sound waves are turned into digital audio data. This is done via a process called **sampling**, which is a fundamental tool of sound design and of music synthesis. You may have heard about a type of keyboard called a **"sampler"** if you are familiar with the music industry. Sampling is a process of digitizing an audio wave into segments, which allows the wave to be stored using its basic shape and any other wave perturbations (such as noise) in a digital format, using binary data (zeroes and ones).

The digital segments or slices of the audio sound wave are called **samples**, as they take a sampling of your sound wave at any given point in time. The precision of this sample is determined by how much datum is used to define each wave slice. Just like in digital imaging this precision is termed the resolution, in this case it's the sampling resolution, and again this will be defined using 8-bit, 16-bit, 24-bit, or 32-bit.

Audio also uses a 12-bit sampling resolution when sampling voice and sound effects. In digital imaging (or video) the resulting quality is quantified in the amount of color (colordepth), whereas in digital audio, the quality can be quantified using the sample resolution, that is, how many "bits" of data are used (in the Y dimension) to define each of your audio samples.

As you may have surmised, a higher sampling resolution, or more data taken to reproduce a given sound wave sample, will yield a higher audio playback quality. This is the reason why 16-bit audio which is also widely known as "CD quality" will sound far better than 8-bit audio. This is just like the 24-bit truecolor image, which will look better than an 8-bit indexed color image. In digital audio, you now have a 24-bit data sampling, known in the digital audio industry as HD digital audio. HD digital broadcast radio has a 24-bit sampling resolution; each audio sample, or slice of a sound wave, contains 16,777,216 bits of sample resolution.

Some of the newer Android devices may also support HD audio, such as those HD audio smartphones you see advertised, which means there is 24-bit audio hardware codecs on the motherboard inside of that smartphone or tablet.

Besides the digital audio sampling resolution we also have a digital audio **sampling frequency**. This determines **how many** samples are taken (X axis) at a particular (Y axis) resolution during one second of time.

In digital imaging terms, the sampling frequency would be analogous to the number of pixels used within the image. A sampling frequency could also be called a **sample rate**, and you may be familiar with CD quality audio, which is defined as using a 16-bit sample resolution and a 44.1 kHz sample rate.

A 44.1 kHz sample rate will take 44,100 samples each of which will contain 16-bits of data, or 65,536 bits of X-axis data, within each Y-axis sample.

You can find out how many bits of data are used to provide one second of raw (uncompressed) digital audio data by multiplying 16-bit (65,536 bits) by 44,100 samples. This gives you a data value of 2,890,137,600 bits used to represent one second of CD quality audio. Bytes can be obtained by dividing this by 8, giving a value of 361,267,200 bytes and when you divide this by 1024 it will give you a value of 352,800KB or kilobytes. Divide by 1024 again and you get 344MB or megabytes.

So to figure out raw data in an audio file, you will multiply the sampling bit-rate by the sampling frequency, by the number of seconds in that audio snippet. Rest assured it will be a large number! Fortunately, audio codecs are great at optimizing the data down to a small data footprint, with very little loss in audio quality.

Common sample rates in the digital audio industry include: 22 kHz, 32 kHz, 44.1 kHz, 48 kHz, 96 kHz, 192 kHz, and recently, 384 kHz. A lower sampling rate, such as 22 kHz or 32 kHz, would be adequate for sampling voice-based digital audio, such as dialog or narrator track for an ebook for instance.

Next let's take a look at the concepts and terminology of digital video.

Digital Video Compression: 4D Concepts and Terminology

Digital video combines both digital audio and digital imagery, introducing the **fourth dimension** (time) to the digital imagery, to create the illusion of motion. A digital video file contains multiple types of new media data, with moving image data and one or more tracks of digital audio data, which is usually a left and right audio track, and sometimes a narration track.

The image data in your digital video file is contained in something called a **frame**, which is essentially one image in a series of images, which, when played together, create an illusion of motion. All the concepts we covered in the earlier section of this chapter, where we covered imaging concepts, such as codecs, pixel, colordepth, alpha channel and so on, can be applied to digital video for this very reason: because digital video is simply a collection of digital image frames.

So digital video takes digital imaging to the next level of complexity by using frames, to add motion, and the way to optimize the data footprint for digital video is to store fewer frames. This is done by reducing the **frame rate** for the digital video file which is represented by a number of **frames per second** or FPS. The **raw data footprint** for a digital video clip is found by multiplying this FPS by the number of seconds in the digital video **clip**, which gives a number of total frames that need to be compressed by the digital video codec.

Typical frame rates used in real world applications include 24 FPS for motion pictures (film) and 30 FPS for television and 60 FPS for game consoles. These frame rates are quite high and generate a lot of data footprint, so I must also advise you that you can use lower frame rates, such as 20 FPS or even 15 FPS and as low as 12 FPS and still achieve a smooth illusion of motion for your digital video asset. These lower frame rates will reduce the data footprint.

The other factor used to reduce the data footprint during the compression process is the bit-rate, which is one of the key parameters that you give to the codec to tell it the target data pipe size that you want the video to be able to stream through and still have a decent quality level. A low number, such as 256 Kbps, gives a smaller data footprint for the digital video file but also results in a lower level of quality. A higher bit-rate setting such as 1024 Kbps (or 1 Mbps) will result in higher quality.

Remember that factors that affect digital imagery compression and quality also apply to digital video compression and quality. The most important of these is physical resolution, so the more pixels that are in the video the higher quality it will have. This also increases the data footprint of the resulting file size, because there is more data in each video frame.

Thus optimizing digital video assets comes down to determining the minimum amount of pixels that will provide the maximum visual quality, the minimum amount of frames that will provide a smooth playback, and the minimum bit-rate that will provide both of these, using the smallest data footprint.

Define a UI Screen Look and Feel: An Introduction to Styles

Those of you who are familiar with HTML5 UI design might also be familiar with the concept of cascading **styles**, which allow a developer to develop a look and feel for their application which is consistent and uniform across their webpage or HTML5 app. By using Cascading Style Sheets, also known as CSS, developers can "extract" their UI design "style" definitions into a separate CSS file, which every HTML5 page can access and use.

This is done to keep the UI design consistent across the entire website or HTML5 application mark-up. The Android OS features its own application styling feature, which is essentially the exact same thing as the CSS that we have with HTML5, and calls it a **style**.

It is important to note that Android OS also supports CSS as well, so make sure not to get these two different types of style applications confused!

Like CSS, Android Styles allow you to specify UI design parameters such as fonts, padding, colors, and similar things that affect the "look and feel" for your applications. These are the same exact parameters that you apply in your UI design process, by using your XML definition files.

Thus, just like you would do in your CSS document, the styling definitions are **extracted** to an external style document and referenced globally by all application components, to use to style or define the look and feel across the application, to keep it consistent and professional in its appearance.

The way that this is done in Android is by using XML style **resources** that are kept in the **/res/values** folder in your application project that uses them. The parent XML tag that is used is the **<resources>** tag and the child tag that is used to define the style resource is the **<style>** tag.

There is a default **styles.xml** file that is defined within this folder in which you can define all your application styles. However as styles can be referenced using any filename, you can make up your own file names to classify your styles in any way that you like. We will create styles in this way in the next section of this chapter, and make sure you understand that you don't have to "lump" all the style definitions together in one styles.xml file.

Although the approach of consolidating all your styles in one single styles.xml file works great as well, as long as you make sure that you name each of your <style> tags uniquely. We will create a couple of style XML files in the next section, including a txtClock.xml style XML file to define our TextView styles, which we use with our DigitalClock and AnalogClock UI designs, and the clockStyle. xml file, to use to define your styles for your digital and analog clock tags and their parameters.

To do this, we will have to use the **New ➤ Android XML File** work process to create new XML files for these resource definitions from scratch, which we will do in the next section, where we'll implement our own custom styles.

Creating a Style for Our UserInterface Application Clocks

Fire up Eclipse, if it isn't open on your desktop already, and open up the **/res** (resources) folder, and select your **/values** subfolder, as is shown in Figure 7-1. Right-click the /res/values folder and select the New menu, and then the Android XML File sub-menu, which allows you to open a New Android XML File dialog, which we will use to name and populate our style.

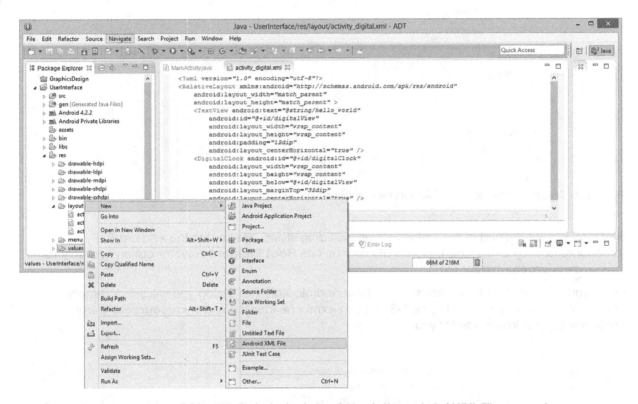

Figure 7-1. Create a new style definition XML file in the /res/values folder via New ➤ Android XML File command

When this dialog opens up, you will notice that your **Resource Type** data field is already set to **Values** because you have right-clicked the **/res/values** folder. Additionally, the **Project** data field is also set correctly to your **UserInterface** project, which this dialog got from your master project folder's name value.

Since this style definition XML file is going to configure your <TextView> portion of the analog and digital clock UI designs, let's name this file **txtClock** by using the **File** data field, as is shown in Figure 7-2.

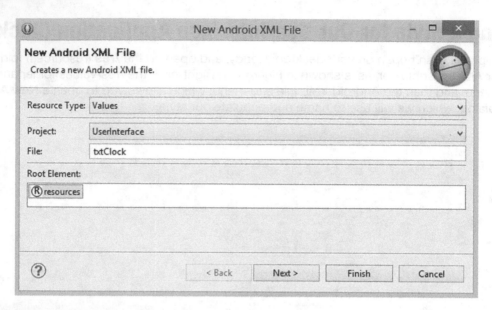

Figure 7-2. *Configuring the txtClock.xml file with the <resources> root element*

Since constants defined in the /values folder, including styles, are kept in the Android **R** (or resources) area of the OS, there should only be one **Root Element** selector option available to you, a **<resources>** parent tag.

Once you click on the **Finish** button in the New Android XML File dialog you will see an empty bootstrap file, as is shown in Figure 7-3, with an **<xml>** header tag and a **<resources>** parent container tag put into place for you.

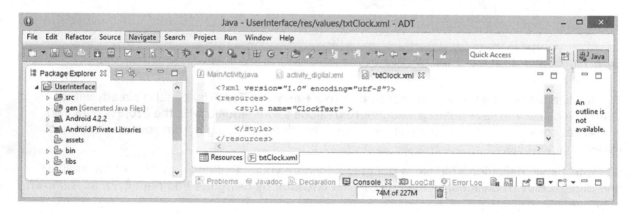

Figure 7-3. *Add a <style> child tag to a parent <resources> tag and name it ClockText and close it using </style>*

To prepare our **txtClock.xml** style definition to hold our parameter <item> child tags, we need to add a **<style>** child tag under the <resources> tag. If you type in a left chevron < you will get a pop-up dialog where you can select the <style> tag if you wish, or, you can simply type that in. Next, add your name parameter, and set it equal to a value of "**ClockText**." Once you type in the right-facing chevron > character, Eclipse will also add a closing </style> tag for you, as shown in the following markup:

```
<style name="ClockText"></style>
```

Add a line of space in between these parent <style> tags to hold your nested <item> tags that will hold each parameter that you will be adding to your style definition.

The styling parameters that we are going to define in your txtClock.xml style definition can be seen in Figure 7-4, and include everything except for the **ID**, which must always be unique, and the **android:text** value, which is what will be styled using the style application we are about to create.

Figure 7-4. Select the <TextView> tag parameters that we are going to transfer to the style definition and delete

Let's add these four TextView styling parameters, using **<item>** tags, along with a **name** parameter and a **data value** (the style parameter setting), in a format that is shown in Figure 7-5 as well as in the following XML markup:

```
<item name="android:layout_width">wrap_content</item>
<item name="android:layout_height">wrap content</item>
<item name="android:padding">12dip</item>
<item name="android:layout_centerHorizontal">true</item>
```

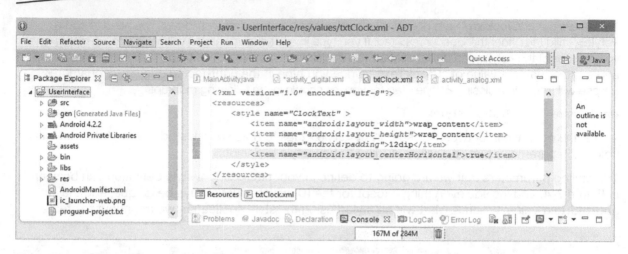

Figure 7-5. *Install the <item> child tags inside the <style> tag to define the layout and padding parameter styles*

Once the styles are in place, delete the parameters selected in Figure 7-4.

Once you have deleted the parameters which we have styled, drop the ID and text parameters down a line and add the **style=** parameter, and you will see that Eclipse will pop-up the helper dialog with all the different types of value constant definition files that you could reference. Next, select the **@style/** option, as shown in Figure 7-6, and double-click it, to insert it in your markup, and then finally type in **ClockText** to complete it.

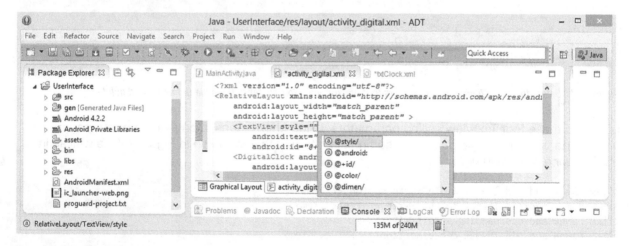

Figure 7-6. *Add a style reference parameter in the activity_digital.xml file and select a @style/ value folder option*

Now we need to do the same work process in our activity_analog.xml file, as shown in Figure 7-7, where you can see the completed style parameter, implemented using the following XML markup:

```
<TextView style="@style/ClockText"
        android:text="@string/hello_world"
        android:id="@+id/analogView"
```

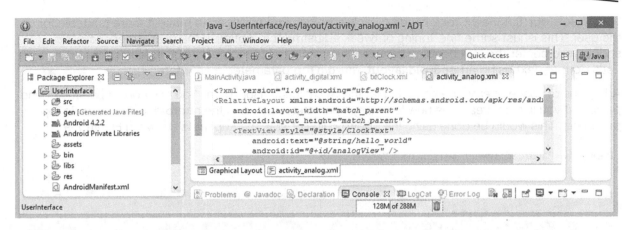

Figure 7-7. *Add a style reference parameter in activity_analog.xml file, referencing the @style/ClockText <style>*

Now if you run the app using **Run As ➤ Android Application,** you'll see that it runs exactly the same as it did before, only using fewer lines of XML.

Now we can style both of our Clock UI designs in one location, so let's adjust the strength (boldness) of the text, and space it out more evenly at the top of our Clock UI design(s). To do this we would add a new <item> tag in our txtClock.xml style definition, rather than in the source UI XML definition files as we would have done before we created our style.

As you can see in Figure 7-8, the **android:** work process to pop-up a helper dialog works from inside of the <item> tag name definition, which I didn't expect. You need to be careful as it lists all parameters, because it can't see what container you are in! Find the android:textStyle parameter and double-click it to add it as your <item> tag name parameter, and then add the bold parameter setting as the <item> tag data definition, as shown in the following XML markup:

```
<item name="android:textStyle">bold</item>
```

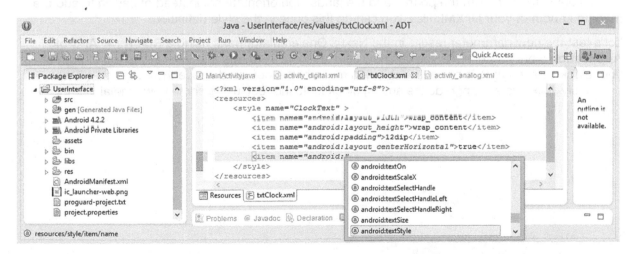

Figure 7-8. *Add an <item> style definition parameter and inside the name type android: to access helper dialog*

This makes our TextView Clock heading thicker, bolder, and stronger, to make it more readable for the user. This is just some fine-tuning or tweak adjustment to optimize the user experience. We should also center the text heading between the Clock and the top of the UI screen or container. Let's do that next using an **android:layout_marginTop** parameter in an **<item>** tag.

Add a line of space after your <item> tag for the layout_centerHorizontal. You can copy a parameter and paste it, if you like, to create the new top margin parameter, by using the **android:layout_marginTop** parameter. This would be done using the following line of XML markup, as is shown in Figure 7-9:

```
<item name="android:layout_marginTop">25dip</item>
```

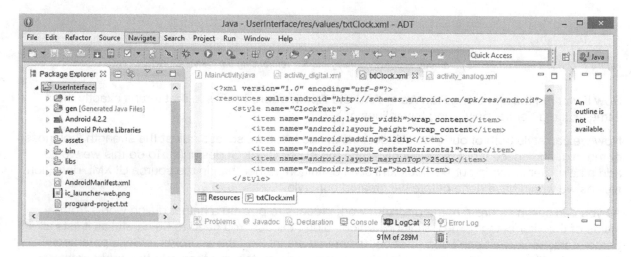

Figure 7-9. Add <item> style definition parameter to push <TextView> style down from the top of the screen 25dp

This pushes down your Clock title's text element, centering it between the clock UI element and the top of your screen, in both the portrait and the landscape orientations. Instead of having to add the markup in both of your UI XML files, you can do this once in the style definition.

Let's test the new parameter results in the Nexus One emulator next, using a **Run As ➤ Android Application** work process. As you can now see, in Figure 7-10, the text label at the top of both of your clock screen types is more readable and much better centered above the clocks that it was previously. Next we will upgrade the analog clock look and feel, using some new media!

Figure 7-10. Testing the new ClockText style definition in the Nexus One emulator with both ActionBar clock tabs

Using Digital Images and Alpha Channels: A New Media UI

The Android AnalogClock UI widget is one of the best examples of combining new media assets with your Android UI elements, which is what this book is all about, so let's give our AnalogClock UI element a little personality!

Since I also want to show you how alpha channels in PNG32 image assets can be utilized within Android, we will use **PNG32 ARGB** image assets which have alpha channels included. We will composite these together, both in Android as well as in GIMP 2.8.10, so that you will see how alpha channels are used in both work processes. You know what they say: "there's more than one way to skin a clock!"

First you need to copy an **analogclock480** pixel PNG asset into your project folder's **/res/drawable-xhdpi** subfolder, as is shown in Figure 7-11. This installs your **extra-high density** (480 dpi) version of your image asset into your project hierarchy, and later Android can scale that asset up or down for any other screen densities, as needed.

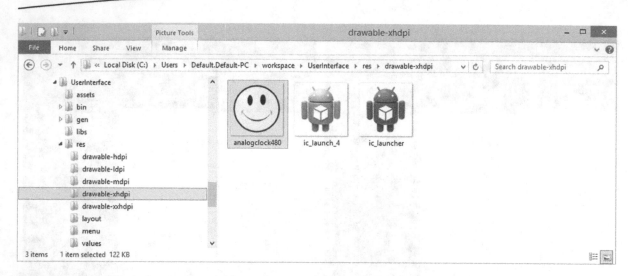

Figure 7-11. Copy 480 pixel analog clock background image to UserInterface project's /res/drawable-xhdpi folder

When you add any asset into the **/res** folder or any of its subfolders, and you do this external to Eclipse, in this case we used the **Windows Explorer** file manager, you need to right-click the project folder and invoke the **Refresh** command.

What the Refresh command will instruct Eclipse to do is to go out into the project folder hierarchy, and to reload everything that it finds there, as it did on launch of the software. What this does is to refresh the project in the Eclipse software memory space. If you do not do this, your XML code will not "see" the new digital image asset that you have added. As you can see in Figure 7-12 on the left side of the screen, the PNG is now visible.

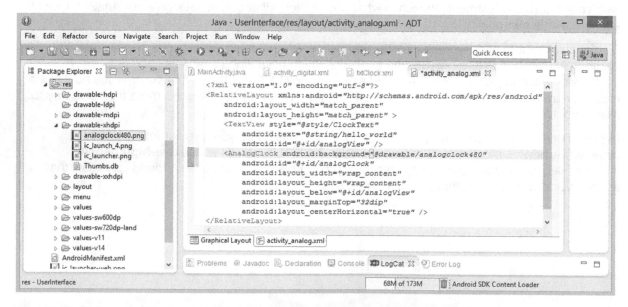

Figure 7-12. Add an android:background parameter which references this analogclock480 digital image asset

Now we can add the **android:background** parameter, which references this PNG file using the **@drawable** resource area, using the following XML mark-up:

```
android:background="@drawable/analogclock480"
```

Now that we have a background image we are going to add a foreground image as well, so Android OS will composite those together for us into one final image result. What allows your results to be seamless and professional are transparent alpha channels in each of these images. Copy your **clockhoop480** PNG32 file into your project **/res/drawable-xhdpi,** as shown in Figure 7-13.

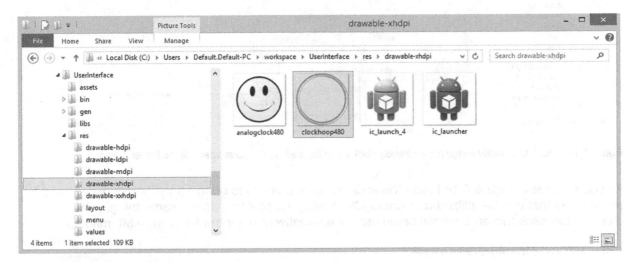

Figure 7-13. *Copy 480 pixel clock hoop background image to UserInterface project's /res/drawable-xhdpi folder*

Adding a foreground image element in the AnalogClock image can be done via an **android:dial** parameter, which allows you to specify your own customized perimeter for the outside of your AnalogClock. Notice in Figure 7-14, that there are also **android:hand_hour** and **android:hand_minute** parameters if you want to customize your AnalogClock UI element even further.

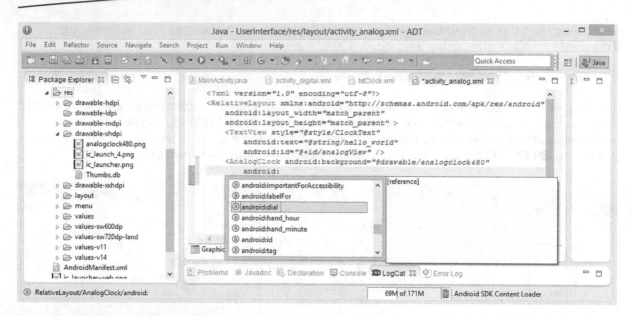

Figure 7-14. *Add a foreground image for the analog clock using the android:dial parameter using a helper dialog*

As you can see in Figure 7-14 I used the android: work process to bring up the helper dialog of all parameters that can be utilized with AnalogClock widgets, so if you do the same thing, select and then double-click this android:dial parameter, or alternatively, enter the following XML markup:

```
android:dial="@drawable/clockhoop480"
```

This references the **clockhoop480.png** image asset that you copied into the /res/drawable-xhdpi folder in the previous step, and sets it as your image plate to utilize for your AnalogClock dial perimeter image detail element.

To preview the results of these XML parameters, which essentially instruct the Android OS to do an **image compositing operation**, involving your analog clock UI element, click the **Graphical Layout Editor** tab, at the bottom-left of your Eclipse central editing pane, which you can see at least part of in Figure 7-14.

As you can see in Figure 7-15, the clockhoop480 image, using alpha channel transparency, both inside and outside of the hoop perimeter, is overlaying the happy face background image perfectly, as if it were one single image. This result is really what image compositing is all about; the illusion of a single image, using more than one image plate or layer. Doing this gives you more control as programmers as you can apply code to each image plate.

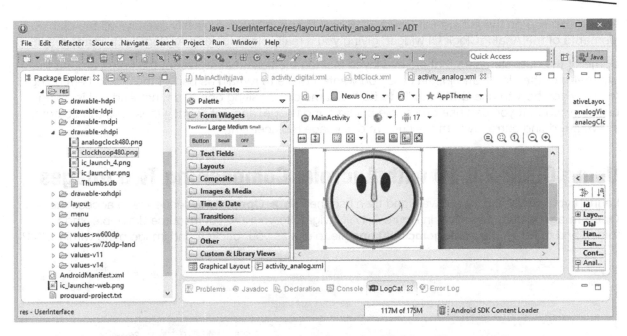

Figure 7-15. Use the Graphical Layout Editor tab to preview the foreground and background images together

Now use a **Run As ➤ Android Application** work process, shown in Figure 7-16.

Figure 7-16. Testing the android:dial parameter (left), and using only the android:background parameter (right)

As you can see on the left side of Figure 7-16, your hoop image seamlessly overlays all the dial elements of the AnalogClock UI widget, giving you a really clean looking AnalogClock image result.

Some of the dual elements that are overlayed include the ticks that represent the hours around the perimeter of the clock, and just in case you wanted these to remain as part of the clock, I am going to show you how to use GIMP 2.8.10 to do the same compositing operation that Android is doing currently, so that you can use one single background image, and not overlay these hour indicators, as we are doing currently with the custom dial image replacement.

Using GIMP 2.8.10 with Android: Compositing Two Images

Launch your **GIMP 2.8.10** software and then use the **File ➤ Open** menu sequence to access the **Open Image** dialog, as shown in Figure 7-17. Navigate to your project resource drawable-xhdpi folder, and open up the **analogclock480.png** file to use as your background image plate within GIMP.

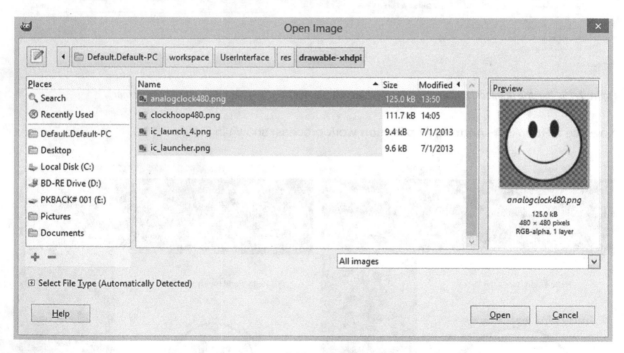

Figure 7-17. Open the analogclock480.png truecolor PNG32 file with alpha channel in GIMP using File ➤ Open

Once your background image is visible in the central editing area of GIMP, you can use the **File ➤ Open as Layers** menu sequence, shown in Figure 7-18, to insert the **clockhoop480.png** image into the **compositing layer** above this background image. Transparent (alpha channel) areas of your images in GIMP are represented via a **checkerboard pattern**, as you can see in Figure 7-18.

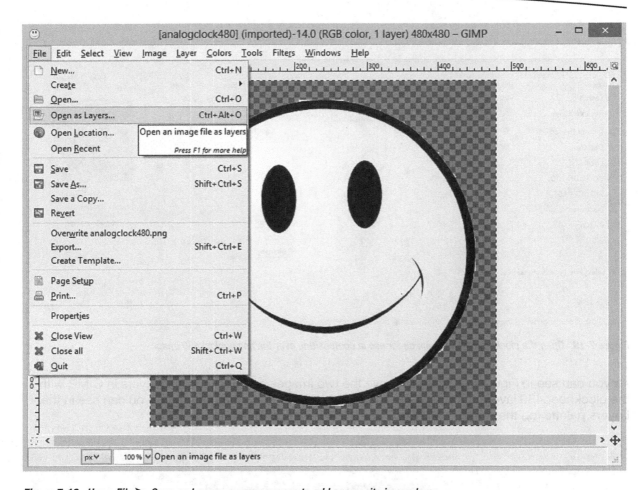

Figure 7-18. *Use a File ➤ Open as Layers menu sequence to add composite image layer*

Find the **clockhoop480.png** image file and open it, as shown in Figure 7-19.

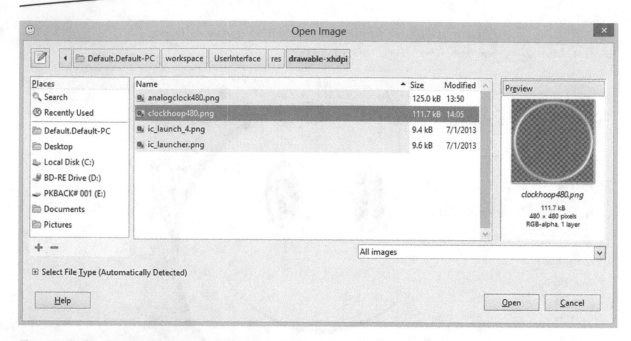

Figure 7-19. Open the clockhoop480.png image for use in compositing over the analogclock480 image

As you can see in Figure 7-20, we now have the two images composited using layers in GIMP, with the clockhoop480 layer on top, and the analogclock480 layer on the bottom, as you can see in the Layers palette (on the right).

Figure 7-20. Image composite shows clockhoop480 layer on top of the analogclock480 layer to create one image

Now we can use the **File ➤ Export** menu sequence, to **export** our composite as one single image, as is shown in Figure 7-21. Let's name the composite PNG image analogclockhoop.png and export it to (save it in) the same drawable-xhdpi folder as our other assets are currently stored in. The PNG settings which I used are also shown on the right side of the screenshot.

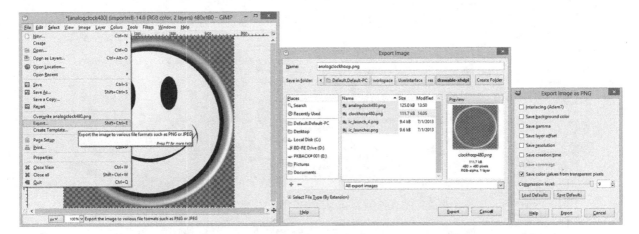

Figure 7-21. *Use File ➤ Export menu sequence to export new, composited file to analogclockhoop PNG32 format*

As you can see in Figure 7-22, in the Windows Explorer, a composited image is now present, along with two source image plates, in your drawable-xhdpi folder. Now we are ready to style our AnalogClock UI using only one image!

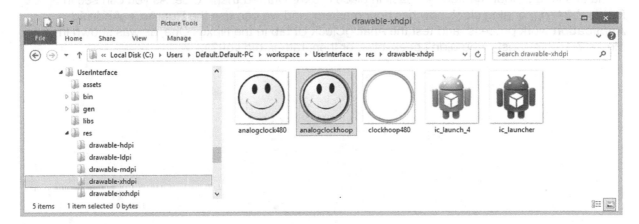

Figure 7-22. *Showing a new analogclockhoop.png PNG32 file saved into the /res/drawable-dpi folder for app use*

To get the **hour markers** back onto your AnalogClock face, we need to remove the **android:dial** parameter that allows us to replace these with an image. Then we need to change your **android:background** image reference to point to the image composite that you created in GIMP which has both the background image and the hoop (rim) foreground image for the clock in a single image.

This new XML markup, for our background parameter, is seen in Figure 7-23:

```
android:background="@drawable/analogclockhoop"
```

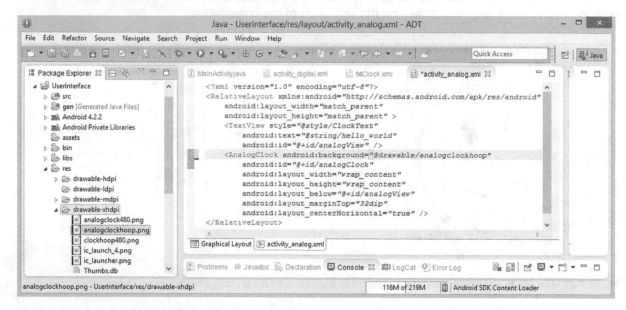

Figure 7-23. *Edit the activity_analog.xml file to use one single background image to get hour markings on clock*

Next, we can click the Graphical Layout Editor tab, and preview the new AnalogClock configuration, to make sure our hour markers are back in place like we wanted them to be. As you can see in Figure 7-24, our analog clock now has hour markers, and we can use the **Run As ➤ Android Application** work process, and test the AnalogClock UI tab in the Nexus One, as was shown in Figure 7-16 previously (you didn't peek, now, or then, rather, did you?!).

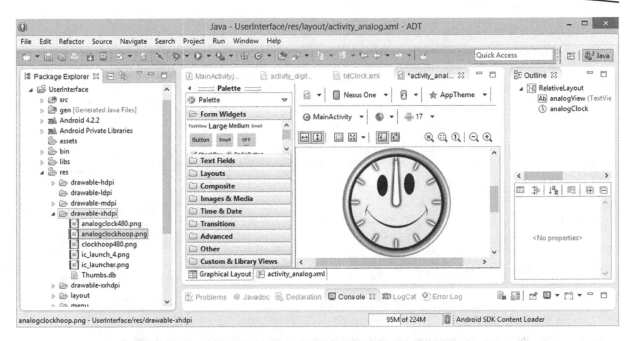

Figure 7-24. Use the Graphical Layout Editor tab to preview the background image composite and hour markings

Now all we have left to do to really cover our bases (or change the b to an s and re-arrange to suit) is to create a range of analogclockhoop.png image assets that will fit everything from a Google watch to an iTV set!

Creating Resolution Density Image Assets for All Devices

One of the most perplexing things regarding Android development, something which has absolutely nothing to do with Java programming or XML markup, is providing a wide range of new media assets that will fit different device display screen resolutions, densities, shapes, sizes, and orientations.

If you are not a multimedia producer, this may well prove more daunting to you than complex algorithm programming! Providing a range of digital image assets is so important in Android that when you create the new project, as we did in Chapter 2, a half-a-dozen resolution-density-specific drawable folders are created for you automatically. The Android OS selects your resolution density assets at runtime, based on user device hardware. This is to reduce the amount of image scaling that needs to be done at runtime.

To show you the work process for doing this, launch GIMP and use a **File ➤ Open** menu sequence to open the **Open Image** dialog, as shown in Figure 7-25.

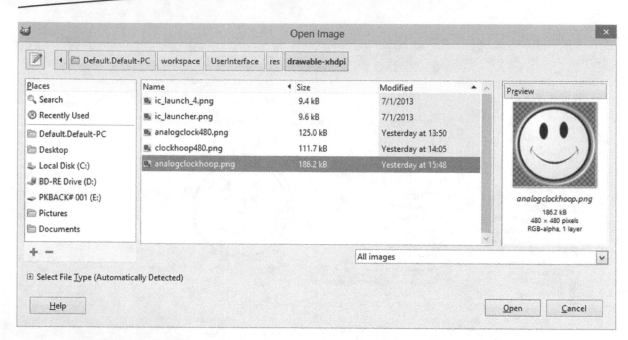

Figure 7-25. Open the analogclockhoop.png 480 pixel asset in drawable-xhdpi folder to use to create dpi assets

Once open, use the **Image ➤ Scale Image** menu sequence shown in Figure 7-26.

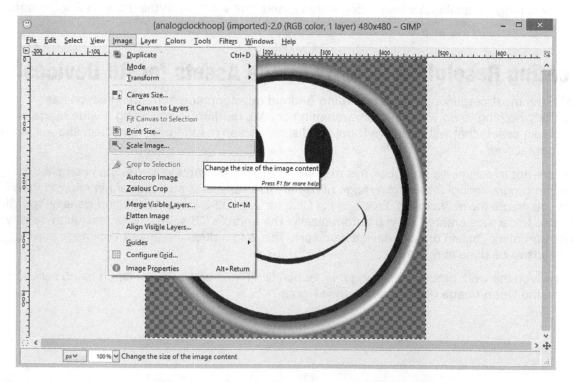

Figure 7-26. Using the Image ➤ Scale Image… menu sequence to invoke the Scale Image dialog to downsample

This invokes the **Scale Image** dialog, seen in Figure 7-27, which we'll be using three times during this work process, to create **240**, **160** and **120** DPI resolution assets for the **HDPI**, **MDPI** and **LDPI** drawable asset folders, respectively. Enter the **240** pixel value in the **Width** and **Height** fields and make sure the **Cubic Interpolation** is selected, and click the **Scale** button.

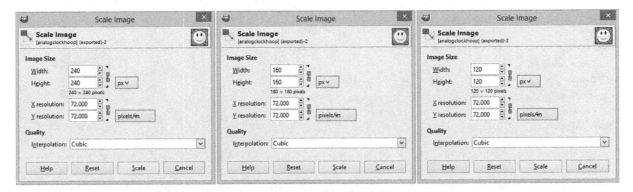

Figure 7-27. Showing the Scale Image dialogs for the HDPI (240), MDPI (160), LDPI (120) resolution densities

As you can see in Figure 7-28, the image has been scaled down, also known as a "downsampling" of its data, to half of its original size, in both the X and Y axis. Now, we can use the **File ➤ Export** menu sequence, to open the **Export Image** dialog, which we'll use to save our asset in another folder.

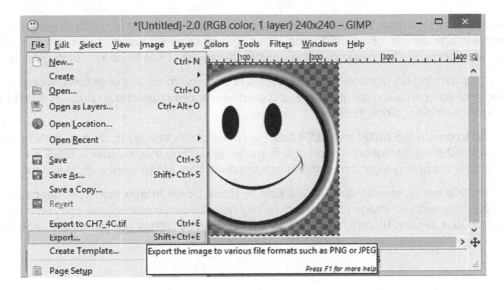

Figure 7-28. Using File ➤ Export menu sequence to invoke the Export Image dialog to save out dpi asset version

Once you're in the **Export Image** dialog, as shown in Figure 7-29, find your project's **/res/drawable-hdpi** folder, and make sure your file has the same name, which should be **analogclockhoop.png**, and then use the **Export** button to save the new image asset into this different folder using the same filename. As long as you put this PNG32 asset into a different folder, it will not replace the original 480 pixel digital image asset.

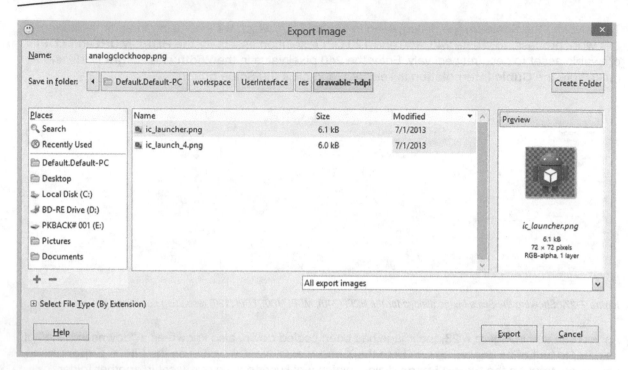

Figure 7-29. Using the Export Image dialog to save each dpi resolution density version into the appropriate folder

This is one of the many things that can be confusing about the provision of multiple resolution density digital image assets for Android apps. The name must be the same, and is referenced in your application Java code or XML markup, using only the **first part** of the filename (analogclockhoop).

Additionally, the naming convention for these assets is that you must use **only lowercase characters**, and you can also use **numbers** and an **underscore** character to provide spacing if you wish (for instance analog_clock_hoop).

Next, we need to create the **MDPI** and **LDPI** asset versions of this image. To do this, we'll need to go back to the 480 pixel resolution version of this image. We will do this to provide GIMP's Cubic Interpolation downsampling algorithm with the most optimal data set to work with (downsample from).

To accomplish this easily, we can use GIMP's **Edit ➤ Undo Scale Image** menu sequence, shown in Figure 7-30, to revert our image to its 480 pixel high resolution version. Since you have already saved the 240 pixel version to your hard disk drive, this does not affect our prior work process.

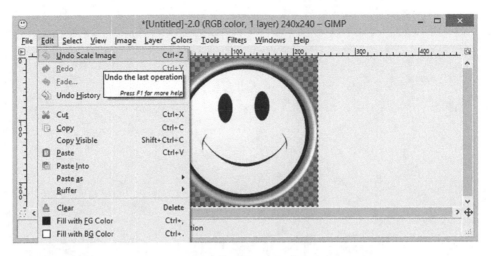

Figure 7-30. Showing an HDPI 240 pixel image asset in GIMP 2.8.6, and the Edit ➤ Undo Scale Image menu path

Once you have undone your 480 to 240 pixel downsampling, redo the steps of the work process shown in Figures 7-26 through 7-30 to create image assets of 160 pixels and 120 pixels, as is shown in Figure 7-27 in the center and right sides of the screenshot. Save these in your **/res/drawable-mdpi**, and **/res/drawable-ldpi** folders, respectively, via the work process that's shown in Figure 7-28 and 7-29. Now you have a nice range of image assets for use with the analog clock. Notice that they're all even multiples of the XHDPI asset (120x4, 160x3, and 240x2 all equal 480 which is why they scale well).

Summary

In this seventh chapter, we took a close look at Android Styles as well as supported New Media assets and some of the concepts which underlie them. We also looked at how to utilize new media assets in an app, how to composite two images using alpha channels together, using both GIMP and Android, and finally we learned how to create four resolution-density targets targeting all popular Android device screen sizes, resolutions and densities.

We created a txtClock.xml style definition for our application which made it easier to apply multiple styling parameters across all our clock UI elements. We then implemented a background and foreground image plate for our AnalogClock UI, and then combined those, using GIMP, into one image.

In the next chapter, we take a look at the UI Prototyping **Pencil software**, and how to use this application to prototype Android UIs using wireframes.

Summary

8

Android UI Design Concepts: Wire-framing & UI Layout Design Patterns

Now that we've covered the different types of new media in Android as well as how to use styles, and also have an understanding of the View, ActionBar, and ViewGroup containers that all Android user interface designs are built on top of, in this eighth chapter, we will take a look at some of the popular Android UI design patterns that are currently in use for Android devices.

We will also take a closer look at how to use the open source **Pencil 2.0.5** Wire-framing tool that we downloaded and installed along with some of the other leading open source new media development software back in Chapter 1. Also we take a look at the myriad of design scenarios that can be utilized for providing flexible, seamless UI Layout Design for your Android application across the currently available types of consumer electronics devices that host the Android OS.

The reason the UI design is becoming so much more critical in your Android application development is because an app must run across many widely disparate types of Android-based hardware products. Soon you will have the Android OS on your wrist in Android watches, Android on your face in GoogleGlass, Android on your living room wall in GoogleTV, or Android on your car dashboard. Also Android will be on your game consoles, ebook reader, tablet, Android PC, and of course across hundreds of smartphones.

To do something a bit different for a change, we'll first learn how to use Pencil 2.0.5 to replicate some of the UI designs we've put together in the past. After that, we'll go over several types of **UI layout design patterns** that are found in Android and the widgets that are used to implement them.

Prototyping the UI Design: Wire-framing Using Pencil 2.0.5

Let's get right into learning a cool UI wire-framing application, the open source Pencil 2.0.5, which you can use to prototype UI layouts and designs for your applications. You could also use Pencil to generate visual design prototypes, so that your client can see your design vision and approve your designs more quickly and with peace of mind. If you haven't downloaded Pencil as yet, you can find it at the following URL:

http://pencil.evolus.vn/

Setting Up a Pencil Working Environment for Android OS

Launch Pencil by clicking the Pencil icon on your OS TaskBar. After the software launches, collapse the unused platform tools using the minus icon on the left of the toolgroup titlebar. When you have done this for all the UI element collections except for the Android ICS group, the Pencil screen will look like it does in Figure 8-1. Resize the primary panes so that you have two-thirds of the screen for UI elements and a third for your design.

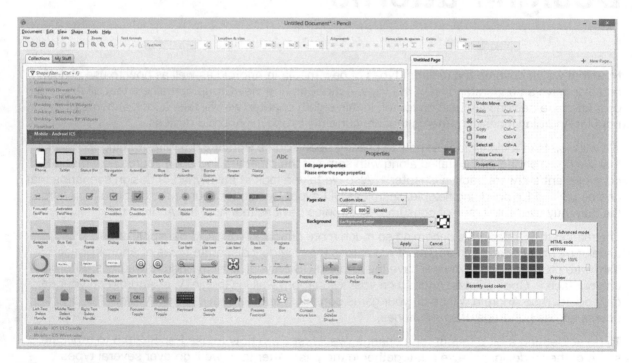

Figure 8-1. Setting the properties of the layout we are designing to match the Nexus One 480 by 800 pixels

The first thing that we need to do to replicate our AnalogClock UI design is to set the preview to conform to the Nexus One emulator specifications, so right-click in that white area, under the **Untitled Page** tab, and select the **Properties** menu item at the bottom. When this Properties dialog opens up, name the **Page title Android_480x800_UI** and set the **Page size** to **Custom size** and then enter the **480** by **800** resolution. Finally, set the **Background** color to white by clicking on the icon to open up a color picker, as shown in Figure 8-1 on the bottom-right corner. Select **#FFFFFF**, and click **Apply**.

The next thing we want to do is to configure your Pencil environment to be the way that you want it to work, which is done using the **Tools ➤ Options** menu sequence, as shown in Figure 8-2. Select (check) the second option of "**Snap objects to grid,**" so that UI elements will align themselves a little bit better when you drop them into place, and then click the **Apply** button.

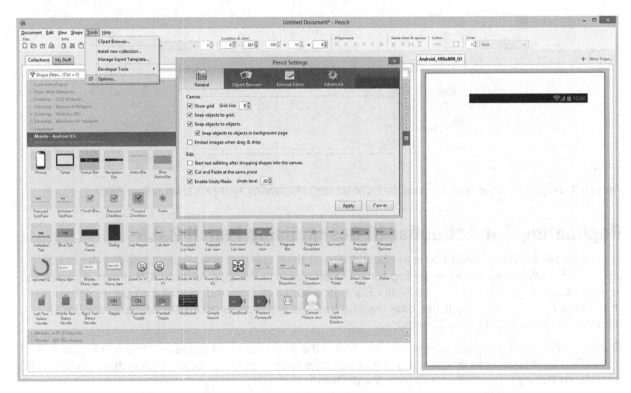

Figure 0-£. Using the Tools ➤ Options menu to set the Pencil options and dragging out the Status Bar UI element

Now that you've set up your Pencil environment, drag your first UI element onto the top of your virgin UI screen, and start to build your UI design. This would be the Android Status Bar, which is the third UI element on the top row. This is selected in light blue in Figure 8-2 as and is also shown as dropped into your UI design on the right side of the screenshot.

Once you drop this into your new blank UI design, you can drag it into any placement you like; in this case, this would be your upper-right corner of the UI design, as is shown in Figure 8-3.

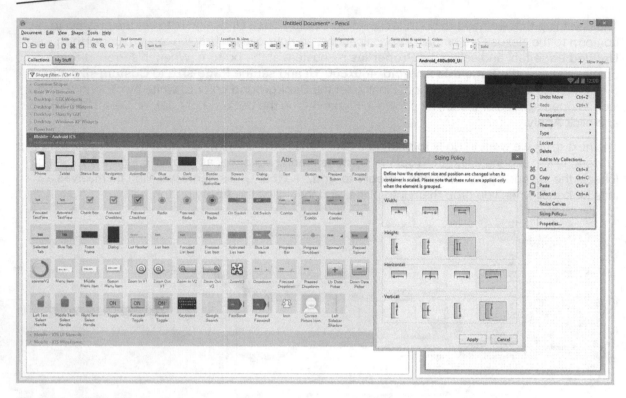

Figure 8-3. Drag an ActionBar UI element onto design, resize using blue handles, right-click to set a Sizing Policy

Replicating Our ActionBar UI Design Using Pencil 2.0.5

Now that the Android Status Bar is in place, the next thing down in the UI would be the ActionBar, which is the fifth UI element on the top row of UI elements in Pencil's Android ICS group, as selected in light blue in Figure 8-3. Drag the ActionBar onto your UI design and snap it into place, right under the Status Bar. You can use those blue resizing handles around the perimeter of the ActionBar UI element to resize it to fit your design.

Once you have used the resizing handles to resize the ActionBar into place as shown in Figure 8-3, right-click on it to access all the actions you can take regarding the ActionBar UI element, and select the **Sizing Policy** menu command near the bottom.

Since the ActionBar scales to fit its environment in Android, we'll select the sizing options that will resize the ActionBar UI element for both the **Width** and **Height**, as well as for your **Horizontal** and **Vertical** positioning, as is shown in the **Sizing Policy** dialog in Figure 8-3.

The next thing down on the UI screen in your AnalogClock UI design is your Tab UI element, which is your first UI element icon in the third row down, as shown in light blue in Figure 8-4.

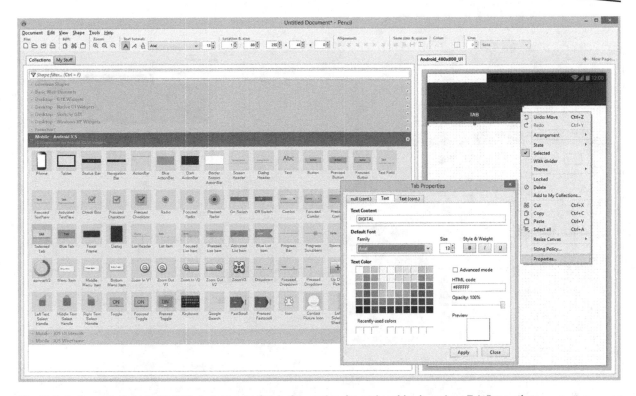

Figure 8-4. *Drag the Selected Tab UI element onto the design, and resize and position it, and set Tab Properties*

Drag this Selected Tab UI element onto the screen, and resize it using the resizing handles to be half of the screen width, and also drag and snap it into position on the right side of the UI screen under the ActionBar.

To access the Selected Tab options and properties, right-click on the Tab, and notice that the **Selected** option is checked. If you wanted to turn this into an Unselected Tab UI element, all that you have to do is uncheck this option. Select the **Properties** menu option, at the bottom of the menu, and open up the **Tab Properties** dialog, as is shown in Figure 8-4.

Let's set our **Text Content** field to the **DIGITAL** text value, for your first tab, and also make sure we are using the most commonly used **Arial** font.

Click on the **Bold** icon in the **Style & Weight** area, and select a **White** text value of **#FFFFFF**, and a **Size** value of **13**, then click on the **Apply** button.

Next, drag and drop another **Selected Tab** UI element into place, right next to the DIGITAL Tab, and resize it into place, and use this same exact work process to name it **ANALOG**, and set it to a **White** color, and **13** pixel **Arial** font with a **Bold** font setting.

Since the ANALOG Tab needs to be selected, right-click the DIGITAL Tab, and **uncheck** the **Selected** option, so that it becomes the Deselected Tab UI element, as is shown in Figure 8-5.

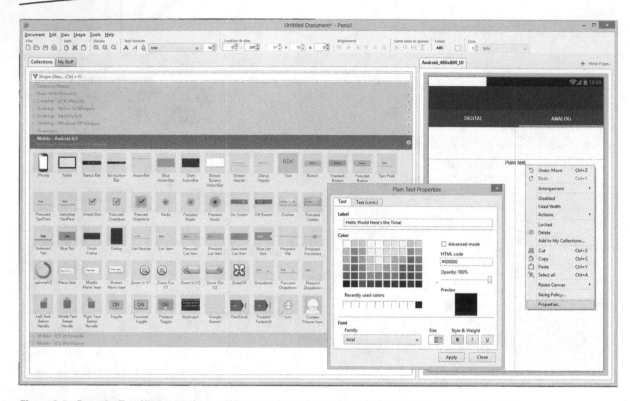

Figure 8-5. Drag the Text UI element into position, and right-click it, and open the Plain Text Properties dialog

Now we are ready to add our TextView UI element, so drag the **Text** element, as shown in Figure 8-5 as selected in light blue, and located on the first row of UI elements in the eleventh position, in position on the UI design.

As you can see, there are some **centering** and **positioning** "**guidelines**" that appear to help you with your positioning of the TextView UI element. These guidelines can also be useful in helping you fine-tune your positioning of your Tab UI elements, which as you can now see are not perfectly centered. Select your DIGITAL and ANALOG Tab UI elements, and resize them to adjust!

Let's right-click on your Text UI element, and select the **Properties** menu option, and open up the **Plain Text Properties** dialog, so we can set up our Text UI element parameters. Set the Label data field to **Hello World Here's the Time!** Next, select the color of **Black** or **#000000**, and a **Font Family** of **Arial** and a **Size** value of **16**. Finally, click the **Bold** button, under the **Style & Weight** area of the dialog, and when you are done setting up all these TextView parameters, click the **Apply** button.

The next UI element that we need to add is the **AnalogClock** UI element, and since Pencil 2.0.5 doesn't have this UI element icon option, we'll have to create one. Always remember if there's a will there's a way.

Fire up GIMP 2.8.10 and open the **analogclockwidget4pencil.png** file from the Chapter 8 folder of the resources for this book available on the Apress.com website, and then select the **Edit ➤ Copy Visible** menu option in GIMP to copy this data into your workstation's clipboard. Since we're going to do this for an Android application icon as well, you can look at Figure 8-8, if you want to see a visual of what this will look like in GIMP. Once you have the AnalogClock in clipboard memory, go back into Pencil and use an **Edit ➤ Paste** menu command sequence to paste it underneath your TextView UI element, as shown in Figure 8-6. Notice the positioning guidelines are provided for the pasted UI element graphic, and you can see that our adjusted Tab UI positions are now perfectly centered.

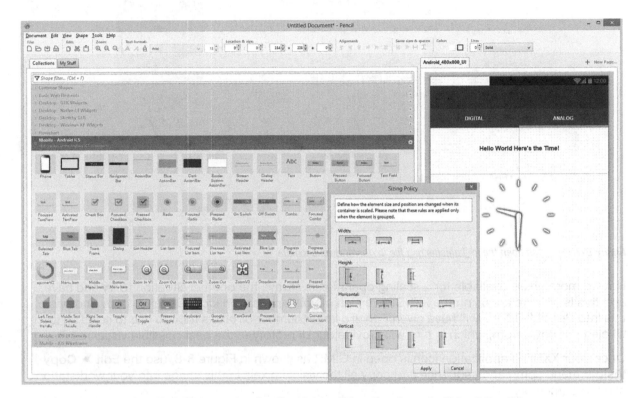

Figure 8-6. Paste an AnalogClock UI element into Pencil, and right-click on it, and open its Sizing Policy dialog

Next, right-click on your AnalogClock graphic, and open up a Sizing Policy dialog. Here you can specify that the AnalogClock UI element not be scaled but rather centered within your UI design. This is done by using the icons showing the **fixed Width** and **Height** and showing the **centered Horizontal** and **Vertical** UI element placement.

Adding the Application Icon and Title to the ActionBar

Now that all the major UI elements are in place and configured, we can add the detail UI elements of the App Icon and Title up in the ActionBar.

We will do this in a similar fashion to what we did with the AnalogClock, so open up GIMP, and use the **File ➤ Open** menu sequence to access the **Open Image** dialog, as shown in Figure 8-7. Navigate to your **/workspace** folder, and your **/UserInterface** subfolder, and finally into your **/res/drawable-xxhdpi** folder and click the **Open** button to open the highest resolution version of your application icon which you have available to work with.

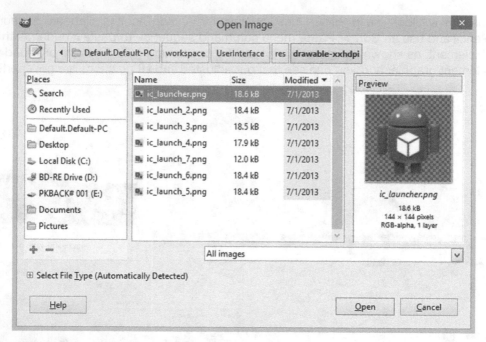

Figure 8-7. Find and open the ic_launcher.png file in /res/drawable-xxhdpi

Having more pixels available for a scaling operation is always the optimal situation to try and have, and this is why we are using the XXHDPI version of your application icon. Once we copy and paste this into Pencil 2.0.5 we will have given Pencil a larger number of pixels for it to use to scale an icon UI element down from, which in turn will provide our UI prototype the best possible visual result.

Once your XXHDPI application icon is open in GIMP, as shown in Figure 8-8, use the **Edit ➤ Copy Visible** menu command sequence and copy all the visible pixels in this image into your workstation's clipboard (memory).

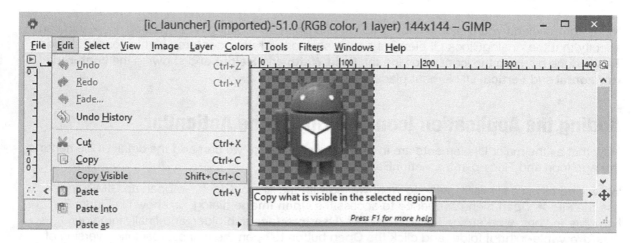

Figure 8-8. Use the Edit ➤ Copy Visible menu command sequence to copy the icon to the workstation's clipboard

This command in GIMP takes the alpha channel data which is present in your image into account when it copies your image into your clipboard memory, so that only the masked image itself is actually copied into the clipboard.

When we paste the application icon into Pencil, only the application icon pixels will be there, which is the end-result that we want to achieve. Now you have a work process to be able to provide (using GIMP) any UI element, or icon, which is not provided for you inside of Pencil in your UI design!

Now, switch over into Pencil 2.0.5, and use the **Edit ➤ Paste** menu sequence to paste your application icon into your UI design prototype, as is shown in Figure 8-9. Use the blue resizing handles to scale the application icon down to fit in the ActionBar, and drag it into place on the left side, to match the screen that you designed in the previous chapter.

Once you have done this, right-click your application icon UI element, and open the **Sizing Policy** dialog, and use the icons that fix the icon in place in the Width and Height dimensions, and which align it on the left and top in the Horizontal and Vertical dimensions, as shown in Figure 8-9.

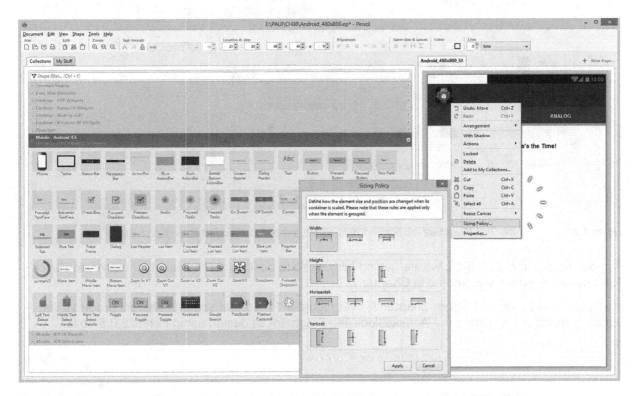

Figure 8-9. Paste an Application Icon UI element into Pencil and right-click it, and open its Sizing Policy dialog

Next we need to add a Text UI element to create the application title, and finish off our UI design prototype. Drag your Text UI element, as shown in Figure 8-10, onto the UI design prototype, and then drag it into position, next to your application icon, on top of your ActionBar UI element, and on the left side of your UI design prototype.

Right-click on the Text UI element, and select the **Properties...** menu option to open up the **Plain Text Properties** dialog, and this time, you select the **White** color value of **#FFFFFF**, and an **Arial Font Family** and **Size** of **21**, and click the **Apply** button to configure your application title UI element, as is shown in the dialog that is pictured in Figure 8-10.

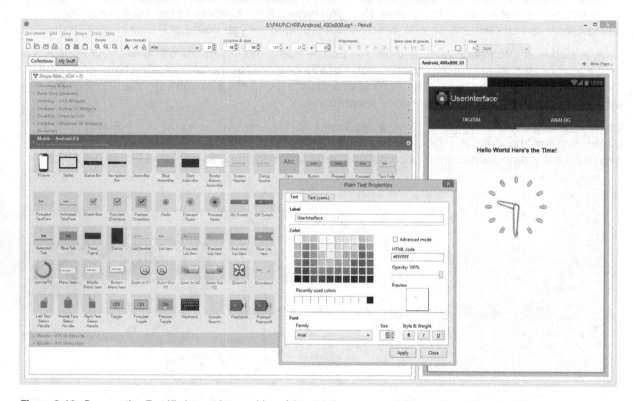

Figure 8-10. *Drag another Text UI element into position, right-click it, and open a Plain Text Properties dialog*

As you can see in Figure 8-10, we are getting fairly close to our original UI design for our AnalogClock Tab Fragment, which we created in Chapter 7.

I will place the Figure 7-10 from Chapter 7, over Figure 8-11, so that you can see the progress that we have made in simulating our AnalogClock Tab Fragment UI design using Pencil 2.0.5 so far.

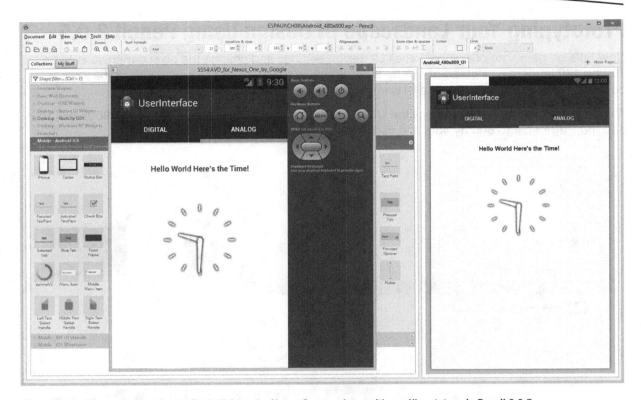

Figure 8-11. Comparing our AnalogClock UI from the Nexus One emulator with our UI prototype in Pencil 2.0.5

As you can see in Figure 8-11, you probably will need to tweak your sizing and positioning for your ActionBar UI elements, and your Tab UI elements a little bit more to get to an exact pixel for pixel replication of what you will see in your Nexus One emulator for this particular Android UI design.

However, as you can see, the Pencil software does a reasonably good job in prototyping an Android UI design, and so you can use this tool reliably in your UI design prototyping work process if you want to play around with UI design for Android.

What is really cool about Pencil Is it allows you to photo-realistically prototype Android UI designs without having to write any of the Java code and XML markup that you would have to put in place to prototype UI designs using the Eclipse ADT AVD emulators. This is why I took the first half of the chapter to get you up to speed on how to utilize the tool, as it can be an important Android UI design tool.

Make sure to use the **File ➤ Save** work process to save all your hard work, so that you don't have to redo all this tedious positioning! Next, let's change the orientation of the UI layout to match the landscape version of the UI which we created in Chapter 6 and see how Pencil handles the changes.

Prototyping Your Landscape UI Design Using Pencil 2.0.5

Now let's go back into our global Pencil UI design settings and change the pixel dimensions to be 800 by 480 landscape instead of 480 by 800 portrait so that we can see how much of the Android code that resizes and rescales the UI is implemented inside of Pencil.

To change UI orientation, right-click the UI tab, and change the **Page title** to **Android_800x480_UI,** and the **Page size** to **800** by **480,** and click the **Apply** button, as is shown in Figure 8-12.

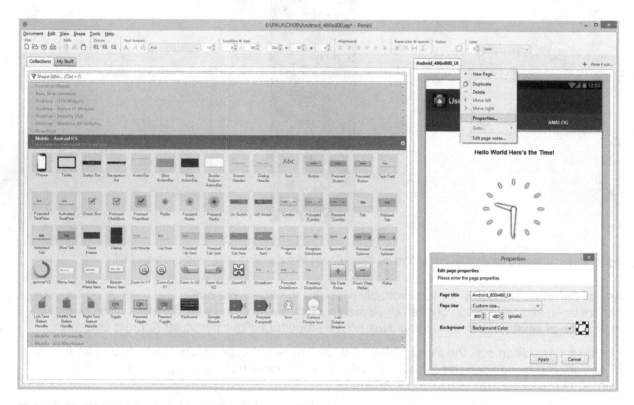

Figure 8-12. *Right-click the Android_480x800_UI tab, select the Properties dialog, and change the orientation*

Make sure that you have first saved the Android_480x800_UI prototype using the Pencil file format, and then you can save the Android_800x480_UI file, once you have created the landscape orientation UI design prototype.

We are going to simulate our landscape orientation AnalogClock UI design next, using the various tools in Pencil 2.0.5, to see how this is done.

Now that we've rotated our UI design canvas into its landscape orientation as is shown in Figure 8-13, we need to reposition our UI elements, since Pencil's Sizing Policy dialog information settings, which we set in the previous section of this chapter, clearly is not yet implemented in the Pencil programming logic, as you can see from this screenshot.

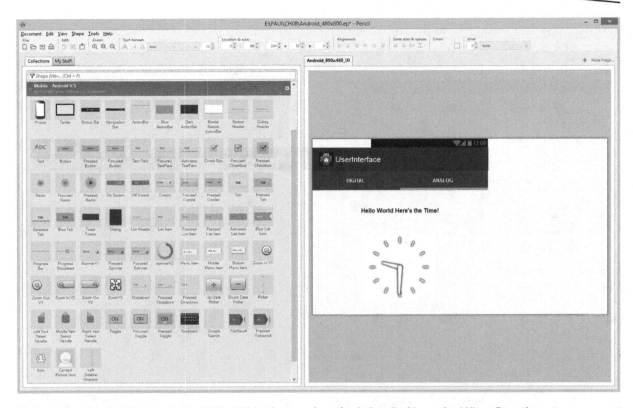

Figure 8-13. *Showing UI design in the 800 by 480 landscape orientation in Pencil with a resized UI configuration*

If the Sizing Policy settings had been implemented in the code, when we reset the UI document to the landscape orientation, the UI elements would have repositioned themselves as we had specified via this dialog. We can still use this dialog as designers, to "remember" (or tell others on the design team) how we want these elements to position and scale relative to the UI design that we are prototyping.

Since we are using Pencil as a UI prototyping and wire-framing tool, that is okay, as we can still use this tool to play around with different design ideas, and get approval for those designs from clients, so the tool still has value to us, especially because it is free!

The only UI components which we will not need to adjust are our ActionBar application icon, and application title, and if the StatusBar was scalable that would probably be positioned correctly as well.

We clearly have some more work to do, to rescale all these UI elements into their proper landscape positioning, which we are going to do next to get some more practice in how to utilize Pencil for our UI design prototyping workflow.

Rescaling the UI Design in Pencil to Landscape

First, let's drag our StatusBar UI element, to the top-right corner of the new landscape UI design, as is shown in Figure 8-14. This UI element does not resize for some reason; next, let's resize the ActionBar UI element by selecting it and dragging the right-middle handle to the right until it fills the new landscape screen's 800 pixel width.

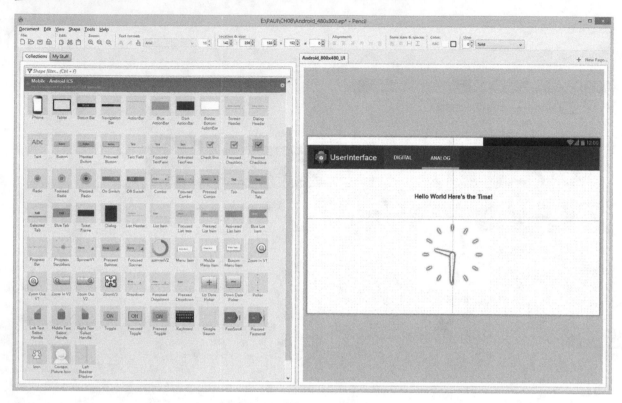

Figure 8-14. *Reconfigure the Pencil UI element landscape layout to match the Nexus One landscape orientation*

Since our application icon and application title are in the correct place the next thing that we need to do is to select, resize, and reposition the DIGITAL Tab UI element to be smaller and on top of the ActionBar, as it would be in a landscape UI orientation in Android.

Once this is in place you can select, resize, and reposition the ANALOG Tab UI element to match the DIGITAL Tab UI element, as shown in Figure 8-14.

Now we are ready to position the TextView UI element, using the centering guidelines that Pencil provides for this purpose. Center your TextView UI element; then perform the same operation on the AnalogClock UI element, as is shown in Figure 8-14, which shows the AnalogClock centering guidelines.

Now that we have prototyped our two primary UI designs in Pencil, let's take a look at some of the various design considerations that we have to deal with in Android and that we will be learning about during the course of this book.

Android UI Design Is Complex: The Many Considerations

The reason that Pro Android UI design is more difficult for the Android OS platform is primarily due to its affordability, as well as its popularity.

Whereas competing OS platforms, such as the RIM Blackberry, Apple iOS, and Microsoft WinOS each have a few smartphone and tablet consumer electronics product offerings, nearly one hundred manufacturers, such as Amazon, Sony, Dell, Samsung, nVidia, Qualcomm, LG, Casio, and similar big brand consumer electronics giants, have chosen to use Android OS to power their products.

This is probably in fact the foundational reason that you are reading this Pro Android UI book right now, as creating an application for this Android OS will span offerings from dozens of major manufacturers, so applications will also function with hundreds of popular consumer electronics products.

These Android products span across a dozen different consumer electronics device "genres," including: smartphones, tablets, e-readers, iTVs, 4K iTV, game consoles, car stereos (and even car dashboards), smartwatches, and even the GoogleGlass eyewear.

This causes UI design to become complicated because your UI design must be able to fit a wide variety of screen shapes–from square smartwatches to super-wide iTVs–as well as a wide variety of screen resolutions, from a 240 pixel smartwatch and flip-phone screens to 4096 pixel 4K iTV screens. One might conceptualize this as 2D UI design as it spans the X and Y dimension only, but Android also supports 3D technology via OpenGL ES 3.0, so if the app supports 3D, then you must also consider the third dimension (Z axis).

The fourth dimension is time, and this 4D aspect can also serve to make UI design for Android OS more challenging. This is because the Android OS supports time-based new media such as motion videos, and 2D and 3D animation. Interestingly, the Android OS itself also spans over time, because it changes every few months by releasing different OS revisions.

These OS versions, also called API Levels, add new features and hardware support for new types of Android product genres. Most recently, Android 4.3 and 4.4 added "under the hood" upgrades that made performance faster, so the Android 3D game consoles from manufacturers such as nVidia could be supported. Android 4.3 added an XXXHDPI resolution constant to support the new 4K iTV products which are coming out from major display manufacturers, such as LG, Sony, and Samsung.

This adds yet another layer of design complexity to UI design, which is termed "backward compatibility" in the software development industry. There are popular Android 2.x devices, such as the Amazon Kindle Fire, which runs Android 2.3.7, as well as popular Android 3.x devices and Android 4.x devices. In this chapter we will take a look at backward compatibility considerations along with other UI design factors.

With major OS version changes come "look and feel" changes, which, in the Android OS, are controlled using "themes," which we will be looking at in detail in Chapter 10. This adds another layer of UI design look and feel considerations which, although not as important as the screen aspect ratio, resolution, orientation, or backward compatibility are, is still an important consideration in a highly competitive Android app marketplace.

There are other UI design considerations that are also important no matter what version, theme, or hardware you are using. These relate to user experience and UI design intuitiveness and usability, and we'll take a look at those in this chapter as well.

These UI design considerations involve gesture support, checking with your user before you make a change to their Android environment or file system, icon design and usage, application help system design, multi-pane layouts, fonts and typography, writing style, and keeping the way your application functions consistent with the way that the Android OS itself functions.

Basic Android UI Design Rules: Conforming to Android UI

The Android OS has its own custom UI look and feel, which can change based on what theme you are using. The Android UI look and feel is significantly different when compared to the other major competitors in the marketplace, namely the Windows 8 OS and the Apple iOS. Google prefers their developers not create UI elements, or a look and feel, that emulates or mimics one of these other OSes. This is not surprising given the level of competition in the marketplace currently, so I will outline some UI design caveats here.

- **Use "chrome" UI elements:** Standard UI elements, such as buttons, text fields, checkboxes, and radio buttons should be used to develop your UI designs unless you are using custom image-based elements with some of the tricks we will be looking at during this book. The important thing to realize here, is that you should not use these "digital image assets as UI elements substitution" tricks to simply make an app look like it is an iOS or WinOS app, as this would provide a confusing user experience (UX).

- **Use standard icons:** The same principles apply to the standard icons which are used in the OS; if you are going to use a search, back, trash, refresh, bookmark, home, or menu icon, be sure and use one of the icons that is standard for Android, and thus familiar to your Android users.

- **Use top-mounted ActionBar:** Because Android uses the top-mounted ActionBar and iOS uses the bottom-mounted ActionBar, be sure to put your ActionBar Tabs, which you learned how to create in Chapter 6, on the top of your UI design, and not on the bottom. This will keep your app consistent with other Android app design.

- **Use standard Back button:** Other platforms "label" their Back buttons with information regarding what the user is going back to. Android does not do this due to the rapid and real-time nature of app use, and so make sure not to artificially add text to your back button in the ActionBar to simulate other platform UI design.

- **Do not use chevron > character:** Another competing platform UI convention is to use a right-facing chevron > character on menus that have sub-menus. Make sure not to "artificially" implement this into your design, as Android implements a different design for this in the Android OS and developers need to respect that UI design.

- **Use Intent class (and object) and API:** Android frowns on hard-coding links, as well as launching other apps, from inside of the application Java code. This is because one of the many UI design principles that we'll be talking about in this chapter is giving the Android user base the maximum latitude to choose application software that they want to use to accomplish any given objective. The proper way to implement interapplication communication and data-share operations in Android is by using the Intent class (and object) and API to launch an Activity. This offers an application selection UI paradigm that allows the user to select an application they want to process that type of data, so that they can work on the data in a familiar working environment.

Android UI Screen Navigation: Primary Gestures Used in Android

There are some standard ways to use the Android OS UI via a touchscreen, and these are termed "**gestures**" within the Android OS (and other OSes). These are summarized in Table 8-1.

Table 8-1. *Primary Gestures Used in Android and Their Mouse-click Equivalents*

Gesture Name	Mouse Equivalent	Used in Android OS For
Touch	Left mouse button click	Selection or activation of UI elements or content objects
Long Touch	Right mouse button click	Context-sensitive menus
Double Touch	Double-click	Zoom
Drag	Click, hold and move	Moving elements on the screen
Swipe	NA	Multi-page navigation
Pinch Open	NA	Zoom in
Pinch Closed	NA	Zoom out

The most basic of the gestures is the "**Touch**" gesture, where a UI element is touched to select and activate a given UI element feature. This is the equivalent of a **left mouse-click**, or **left mouse-up**, operation in computer OS programming terminology.

The next most often-used gesture is the "**Long Touch**," also known as a **long press**, and this is the equivalent of the **right mouse-click** operation in PC OS programming. This type of gesture gives a UI element two different ways to be utilized, and prior to Android 3.0 was used to bring up the context-sensitive menu, just like a right-click operation does in Linux and WinOS.

The next most often used gesture is the "**Double Touch**." The gesture is the equivalent of the left mouse button double-click operation in PC OS terms. The double touch is usually used to zoom into visual content or as a third way to access TextView related UI widgets, to allow easier textual content selection.

The next most often used gesture is the "**Drag**" gesture, which is the PC OS equivalent of a left mouse-down and mouse movement with a left mouse-up at the end of that movement. This drag gesture and operation is used to move elements around the screen, or to "drag and drop" elements on top of other elements to complete some sort of visual operation. This is often utilized in game applications such as checkers, backgammon or chess, for instance.

There are other gestures that involve movement of the user's finger across the touchscreen display, such as the "**Swipe**" gesture or operation, which can be used to bring offscreen UI elements onscreen, like navigating to different pages or panes of information. There is no standard equivalent for this operation in PC-based OSes, at least until they all standardize on touchscreen displays, which will probably never happen. Long live the mouse! Ever tried 3D modeling using a touchscreen?

There are also a couple dual-touch gestures that utilize two points of touch on the touchscreen to process their gesture. These require a multitouch display, which can process more than a single point of contact or touch at the same time, which is considerably more advanced processing.

To zoom into the visual content on a screen, Android users use the "**Pinch Open**" gesture, where the user's thumb and forefinger are placed close to each other on the touchscreen, and then dragged apart from each other.

To zoom away from visual content on a screen, Android users use the "**Pinch Closed**" gesture, where the thumb and forefinger are placed far apart from each other on the touchscreen, and then dragged together, or toward each other. These standard gestures should not be replaced in an app UI design.

Advanced UI Navigation Classes: Navigation Drawer or Swipe View

Thanks to the swipe gesture, the Android UI has a way to make your display screen seem wider than it is in reality, using either a **Navigation Drawer,** or a **Swipe View** UI design paradigms. These allow additional content and UI design elements to be placed (stored) off-screen and then brought into the central display screen area by users (when needed), using a swipe gesture.

We will be taking a closer look at the Android **DrawerLayout** class which is used to create the **sliding drawer** user interface designs a bit later on in this book in Chapter 15, so I'll cover the UI design concepts behind it in this chapter.

This sliding drawer UI element container, which is also referred to as the navigation drawer, always extends itself from the **left side** of the Android user's screen, so make absolutely sure to design the navigation drawers in your application in this fashion (sliding out from the left to the right).

The navigation drawer UI design paradigm should never be used for the top-level application functions. You would want to use your ActionBar Tabs for that navigational level. You could use a sliding drawer full of menu items or navigational icons to access lower-level user interface functions or to switch between different "cross-level" functional screens, via any of your high-level (those accessed using your ActionBar UI Tabs) Activity screens.

We will be taking a closer look at the Android **ViewPager** class, as well as the **PagerAdapter** class later on in the book in Chapter 17. These Android classes are used to implement the **swipe view** user interface designs, so I'll cover the UI design concepts behind the swipe view UI design pattern within this chapter, and we will implement one in detail later in the last section of this book.

Swipe views can be used when you want to "flatten" a vertical (nested) UI design or hierarchy, into a horizontal (side-by-side) access methodology.

This UI design pattern allows users to swipe the screen from side to side, to more quickly and fluidly access their application content. If your apps use a previous-next button UI navigation paradigm, consider upgrading them to use this swipe view design paradigm, especially if you are planning to deliver your app on more modern Android OS versions and via touchscreens.

Your swipe views UI design can be "wired up" with your ActionBar Tabs, so that when your user selects an ActionBar Tab the correct swipe view shows, and when your user decides to access those views using swipe gestures, the ActionBar Tabs update themselves, to show your users where they are in the application UI structure. This is done by using a **.setCurrentItem()** method from the **ViewPager** class, to navigate into the correct view when a tab is selected, and by using the **ViewPager.OnPageChangeListener()** public interface to update UIs to display the correct tab, when the swipe gesture is used to navigate between views.

Android Intra-Application Navigation: The Difference Between Up and Back

Android provides some "hard-coded" UI navigation in its OS and even on the hardware that runs the Android OS. Prior to Android 3.0 the OS offered the system **Back** button, now implemented as a U-turn-arrow (faces left or back) on the bottom-left of the bottom Android navigation bar or controls.

With the addition of ActionBar navigation in Android 3.0 and later came an **Up** button. The Up button is comprised of your **application icon** and a left-facing chevron or **caret** symbol.

The Up button is used to navigate back up your application **UI hierarchy,** and will reverse the UI navigation that your user has used to get to a certain place inside of your Android application structure.

The Back button represents a **chronological** or **temporal order** for a display screen's access in Android, and can include screens from the Android OS or from other apps. This means that your Back button can go "outside of" your apps, whereas the Up button will always keep users inside of your apps.

As you might imagine, the Back button will often simulate the same results as using the Up button will. Thus, in many instances, the two buttons will produce the same results for the users of your application, which is fine.

For this reason, your application's Home Screen should not feature this Up button, but will always support a Back button. The Back button can perform a number of Android OS user interface features that the Up button cannot.

These Back button functions include dismissing pop-up windows and dialogs, closing contextual ActionBars, removing the highlighting from selected UI elements, and hiding the Android onscreen virtual keyboard utility.

Certain changes in your UI View objects will not be considered navigation, and thus will not be entered into the **navigation history** that is accessed by the Up and Back buttons. These include sorting, or filtering, a list of UI elements, changing display characteristics via zooming or swiping, and even changing views using ActionBar Tabs or Drop-Down Menus.

In the case where an Android widget on your Android device's Home Screen takes you to a screen that is deep inside of your application (i.e. not your app's Home Screen) the Up button should take you to your application Home Screen.

When navigating between apps in the Android OS, which is done when one app uses the facilities of another app, such as a browser or an e-mail client, the Back button, being temporal in nature, will take the user back to the calling application from within the called application. If the user wishes to remain in (and utilize) the features of the called application they can use the Up button to access other levels of that application, rather than use the Back button to return along the temporal navigation history path.

Allowing Users to Configure Your Apps: Settings and Help

One of the legacies of software in general—on any platform and hardware—is customizing the way the software application works to each user's taste, as well as getting Help or instruction regarding the features of your software app, and how to best utilize features.

This should be no different for Android applications, and part of your UI design should be implementing the Help System and Application Settings for your application.

Settings have their own area in the UI design because they are usually set once by the user, and then left configured in one way thereafter. Settings can control the look and feel of your application and how your application handles certain usage scenarios when those scenarios arise during usage.

Since settings are not accessed frequently, your Settings menu item should be kept near the bottom of the ActionBar OverFlow menu, as should the Help menu item, for similar reasons. Android convention specifies that the **Help** menu should be last and your **Settings** menu should be second to last.

Be sure to only make features into settings for your application that need to be settings! Don't make actions (such as Refresh Screen) or information such as disclaimers part of your application Settings Dialog.

If you have more than nine or ten settings, consider grouping the settings together using setting genres, so that users do not have to process dozens of settings all at one time. Don't include any settings that all users are going to set in the same way; simply make them fixed application features.

Settings dialog design patterns include using a **checkbox** (checkmark) for a toggled (on or off) setting, and using a **multiple choice list** for settings that have more than one option. For settings that have a **range** of numeric or ordinal values use a **slider** UI widget, and for those settings that can be enabled or disabled completely, use an **ON/OFF switch** UI widget.

The Help area for your application should be "hidden away in plain sight," just like your Settings area. This is because you certainly would not want to show unsolicited help when you think your users need it, as it might be perceived as insulting, especially to experienced (and intuitive) users.

To make your Help menu more streamlined and allow your users to access the Help topics that they need help with more quickly, consider implementing submenu structures with the different help subject matter areas, as well as other areas that are needed to contain legal disclaimers and copyright information, for instance, or a Privacy Policy or your Terms of Service.

You can also use these Help submenu functional areas to ask for feedback regarding your application, or to provide a connection with your Customer Service Department, if your company has one.

Feedback in UI Design: Notification and Confirmation

It is important to keep your users "in the loop" regarding what your app is doing to their Android device hardware, especially where their screen and data storage (SD Card) is concerned. This is similar to what you are familiar with on PC operating systems using dialogs, messages, and things such as UI elements that are dimmed or ghosted when they are not available.

When a user invokes an operation in your application that could be either destructive (delete data) or take up limited hardware resources (save data to an SD Card), it is important to use one of the Android confirmation UI tools (dialog or message) to allow the user to acknowledge that they want to perform that function and then confirm that they actually want to have that operation performed. This provides the user with a second chance to pull out of the operation, as well as a follow-up that the operation has been performed.

Confirming operations is usually done using one of the Android Dialog classes, and an acknowledgement is usually done using one of the messaging classes, such as the Android Toast class. Confirming progress during an operation is usually done using one of the Android Progress Dialog classes. We cover these classes in detail in this book where it is appropriate.

The Android Dialog or Toast classes usually use text UI elements to convey their message, although the Dialog class and subclasses support visual UI elements as well. There is also a convention in Android for implementing a visual representation of UI elements, especially Button class based widget derivatives, within their various "**states**" of usage, which we will review. These states are also used on the PC platform, so they should be familiar.

- The **Normal** state of a UI button will be its default look, with no color added and no translucency (dimming) applied to its appearance. This is the Button (or other UI element) when it's not being used or has not just been used. This would be the equivalent of a mouse-out state in PC programming.

- The **Pressed** state of a UI Button in Android adds a blue color to your UI Button, and is the equivalent of a mouse-down event in PC programming. The intent of this state is to give the user feedback that the Button has been pressed, and when released, a Button goes into a Focused mode or state.

- The **Focused** state in Android adds both color and translucency to your UI Button, with **50% transparency** or alpha value being used to achieve this. You can also use a 2dip border of blue around the edge if you want.

- A **Disabled** state in Android uses 30% of the UI widget's appearance, or a **70% transparency** or alpha value. This makes your UI element appear ghosted or disabled. This shows your user that the function that is invoked using this UI element is not currently available to them for use.

- The Android **Focused and Disabled** state is the rarest use-case. The state uses a **70% transparency**, plus the coloration used for the Focused state.

Branding in UI Design: Writing Style, Fonts, and Icons

The visual branding for the application is a part of the UI Design process and involves the writing style that is used within the application UI design and content, the font that you use, and the icons that you use.

Your writing style should be informative and affable, never condescending, and address the most important information first and less important issues last. Keep the written content concise and relevant to the section of your application that the user is engaged in, and avoid repeating information.

Make sure that you keep your written content as simple as possible, while still conveying the information that needs to be transferred to your user. Only include information that is absolutely necessary for your application and set limits on your text similar to the social media or texting engines so that your screen is not overflowing with text. Try and minimize the "tech jargon" used so that as many users as possible are able to understand what you are trying to convey.

Users will visually assess the amount of text that they'll have to read on the screen before they'll read it. For this reason, an overwhelming amount of text will be less likely to be read by your users (than concise prose).

Using the correct **typography**, or fonts and font styles, can also make your text content more palatable to users. This is because using the right font makes text easier to read. Ever seen a font, or combination of fonts, that gives you a headache when you look at it? It is important to use the right fonts with your Android application UI design, for this very reason.

Android Ice Cream Sandwich introduced a new font named **Roboto**, named after an Android Robot, and it's a simple sans-serif font that scales well and is very elegant and easy to read on any size or density screen.

The Roboto font has two members of its font family, so you can select from Roboto or **Roboto Condensed**, which has much tighter **kerning**. Font kerning determines how closely together the characters in your font are spaced, and so Roboto Condensed is more compact, whereas Roboto is more spaced out (no pun intended).

Roboto has several different styles, including regular, thin, light, medium, and bold. There's also a super-thick **Roboto Black**, which is reminiscent of Arial Black, so a fontographer or type designer has a lot to work with.

Finally, the icons for the app represent a visual shortcut to application functions (action icons), messages and alerts (status icons), and your app branding (the application launch icon). Since icons are small image assets and contain very few pixels, they must be provided in a range of optimized sizes from 48 pixels (MDPI), to 96 pixels (XHDPI), to recently 192 pixels (XXXHDPI) for the new 4K iTVs and mega-tablets for your app **launcher icon**.

You can design smaller (24 to 32 pixels) icons for use in your application status bar, menus, ActionBar, ActionBar Tabs, and Dialog implementations.

UI Design Patterns: Grouping Devices by Product Genres

Different genres of Android OS products exhibit different display screen shapes, default orientations, screen sizes, and pixel densities.

- **Smartwatches**, for instance, tend to be square in aspect ratio, and feature Low Density Pixel Per Inch (LDPI) screens that are 2 to 3 inches in size. Smartwatches' screen resolutions range from 160 to 320 pixels, with 360 and 400 pixel screens featuring Medium Density (MDPI) just around the corner. Since smartwatches are primarily square, there is no default orientation.

- **Smartphones** have a 16:9 (widescreen) aspect ratio and feature High Density Pixel (HDPI) screens, which range from 4 to 6.5 inches in size and are held in the (default) portrait orientation. Smartphone screens that are 5.5 inches or larger have also been recently been called **Phablets**.

- **Tablets** use the 16:10 (tall-widescreen) aspect ratio, and feature Medium Density Pixel (MDPI) screens, because of their lower WSVGA 1024 by 600 and WVGA 800 by 480 resolutions on larger screens that range from 7 to 12 inches in size. Tablets are held in landscape default orientations as they are a recent replacement for netbooks and notebooks.

- **E-readers**, such as the Kindle Fire HD (and new HDX), are similar to tablets, except that they feature an Extra High Density (XHDPI) screen, as they are more compact than tablets, but feature a Super HD 1920 by 1200 resolution. E-readers tend to range from 8 inches to 10 inches in display screen size.

- **Interactive television sets**, or **iTVs** tend to have 16:9 (HDTV) 1920 by 1080 resolution displays that feature Low Density Pixel (LDPI) screens because the screen sizes range from 32 inches to 60 inches. Landscape orientation is used as a default for the iTV, which is also often called GoogleTV.

- **4K iTV** a recent new IMAX-resolution device type became available, which uses Ultra High Density (XXHDPI or XXXHDPI) screens featuring 4096 by 2160 pixels. The 4K iTV products have recently been termed **UHDTV**, which stands for **Ultra High Definition Television**.

- **Game consoles** are another new genre of Android devices, such as the new nVidia Shield that features a 1280 by 720 pseudo HD touchscreen, which can play Blu-ray movies, and defaults to landscape mode for iTV-like gameplay.

- **Automotive products** such as auto stereos and even automobile dashboards are also Android-based. These utilize Android OS as their platform, which drives their feature set. Watch for Android appliances too!

The Android OS is providing developers and UI designers with opportunities that span almost every type of consumer electronic device, appliance, and automotive market vertical. This is why developers worldwide are flocking to Android to create User Interfaces, User Experiences, and Applications on the widest range of hardware products to ever share the same OS platform.

UI Design Patterns: Why Different Layouts Are Necessary

The reason different UI designs become necessary, both for Android and for HTML5 App (or website) development has primarily to do with display screen shape. If display screens were square, like most new Android smartwatches, then we would have a lot less work to do for our UI design prototyping.

The fact is most screens these days are what one would call widescreen and use aspect ratios ranging from 16:10 or 1920 by 1200 resolution, such as the Kindle Fire HD, to 16:9 used in 1920 by 1080 HDTV and iTV resolutions specification, to 16:8, which is also 2:1 aspect ratio, meaning two square 1:1 screens right next to each other.

The problem with the widescreen aspect ratio when it comes to UI design is that you don't know in which orientation a user is using their widescreen!

What this wide aspect leads to is a need to provide user interface designs that fit well in a vertical or **portrait** screen declination (orientation), as well as a user interface design that fits well in the horizontal or the **landscape** screen declination. This is not generally an easy task, although it can be, it just depends on what your application is and what it does.

The different user interface design orientations require vastly different UI layout approaches, and this will necessitate that we design and create two completely different UI design "patterns" or UI design approaches for the same exact Android application.

Not only are there two different screen orientations, (three, if you count the new square screen orientation made popular by smartwatches), but there are also **different sizes** of display screens, and different **pixel densities** (pixel sizes, expressed as pixel pitch), as well.

For this reason, developing across a plethora of different Android devices and screens, as well as across different product types and genres can make Android development more difficult than simply programming Java software. This will ultimately require that Pro Android UI designers and Pro Android Graphics designers become involved in the application design process.

For this reason I'm going to spend the next chapter talking about the many different technical UI layout factors that go into determining, designing, and developing different UI layout design patterns for a different screen shape, size, and orientation.

This will include looking at, in depth, the concept of single-pane versus multi-pane layouts, configuration qualifiers to support multiple different screen sizes and densities, providing alternate layouts to support these differing screens, and providing a range of drawable assets to fit these different screen characteristics. But before we end this chapter, let's cover the concept of backward compatibility, and Android's design principles.

UI Design for Backward Compatibility: Android 2, 3, and 4

The Android OS tends to evolve rather quickly, adding features such as new fonts, themes, classes, methods, and capabilities. Creating an application that spans across all versions of Android is challenging to say the least.

A reason for this rapid change is because many major manufacturers support Android, and are requesting features to be added to Android so that it can support their unique hardware product (Android device) capabilities.

Major OS changes come from new hardware genres being supported by Android. For example, Android Version 3.0 moved to support touchscreen smartphones, by deprecating (which means discontinuing, but continuing OS support for) hardware-based (external on the device) navigation keys such as Home, Back, and Menu. These were replaced with virtual navigation such as the Up, Back, and Overflow menu, as well as ActionBar and Tabs, which you learned about in Chapter 6.

Android Version 4.0 moved to support tablets and iTVs by continuing this virtual navigation support trend, and adding new themes (a look and feel). We will cover themes in Chapter 10. Version 4.x also added new higher density screen support via an XXHDPI and XXXHDPI constant as well as a new font, Roboto, which we discussed earlier in this chapter.

Backward compatibility between Version 3.0 and Version 4.0 is thus easier than between Version 2.0 and Version 4.0–as might be expected. ActionBar items that don't fit in 4.0 will be placed on the ActionBar Overflow Menu so make sure your most important menu items are implemented first.

There are still a significant number of Android devices being manufactured with physical navigation hardware components (keys or buttons) included as part of the hardware design, including some smartphones and tablets with a bottom-mounted external hardware key groups, or iTVs, with remote controls that also feature these keys, or Android PCs, with keyboards which feature these keys.

In these cases, an Android virtual navigation key bar won't display at the bottom of the Android OS. Additionally, the ActionBar Overflow Menu will be triggered using the hardware Menu key, and will appear from the bottom of the display screen, much like menus did in Android 1.x or 2.x versions.

If you design an Android application using an Options Menu UI design style that supports Version 2.x and earlier, when that application is run using Android Version 3 or Version 4.x, those Options Menu items are going to be displayed using an ActionBar Overflow Menu (three vertical square dots on the right end of the ActionBar).

Thus if you are going to support Android 1.x or 2.x devices, you will have to use Options Menu code and settle for your navigation being accessed via the ActionBar Overflow Menu instead of using ActionBar Tabs (or Icons).

Android UI Design Principles: Exciting, Simple, and Personal

There are about a dozen and a half design principles that are outlined on the Android developer website, which Android feels are important enough to be stated overtly, and so I'll cover these here, so you can be sure to try and follow these as you try to conform to the technical side of UI design.

- **"Delight me in surprising ways"** is an indication that Android wants you to develop a visually intoxicating, powerful, moving, joyous user experience.

- **"Real objects are more fun than buttons and menus"** shows Android wants you to use custom graphics and interactive objects within the app's UI design.

- **"Let me make it mine"** shows Android wants you to make an app customizable, using graphics, and the Settings Menu we discussed earlier in the chapter.

- **"Get to know me"** indicates Android wants your app to learn from your users as they use your app over time, remembering previous choices and settings.

- **"Keep it brief"** covers what we learned about keeping text short and sweet.

- **"Pictures are faster than words"** shows Android would prefer you use visual means for conveying information and settings in your app rather than text.

- **"Decide for me, but let me have the final say"** means that you should offer your user a suggestion for each action, but also allow them to change it.

- **"Only show me what I need when I need it"** indicates that Android wants you to keep your UI design compact, concise, and organized into logical levels.

- **"I should always know where I am"** covers the navigational principles which we covered earlier regarding Up or Back, and labeling UI screens properly.

- **"Never lose my stuff"** simply means that developers should save the user's settings, data, images, video, audio recordings. and similar to an SD card.

- **"If it looks the same, it should act the same"** indicates Android wants app design to be consistent and non-modal, so users are not confused by modes.

- **"Only interrupt me if it's important"** tells us Android wants us to shield our users from unimportant information that distracts from your app.

- ■ **"Give me tricks that work everywhere"** shows Android wants apps to utilize conventions, such as swipe view navigation that users can use across apps.

- ■ **"It's not my fault"** prompts developers to treat their user with kid gloves when something goes wrong; give clear recovery instructions or auto-fixes.

- ■ **"Sprinkle Encouragement"** by designing your app to use easily accomplished stages. Be sure to give visual feedback as to where a user is in your app.

- ■ **"Do the heavy lifting for me"** hints that developers need to code apps to multitask.

- ■ **"Make important things fast"** prompts developers to streamline (optimize) apps.

Summary

In this eighth chapter, we took a closer look at UI prototyping, using the open source **Pencil 2.0.5** software package, and learned how to use primary features of the software to put together UI designs for Android OS.

We also looked at what makes UI design in Android so complex, and at some of the design rules that Android developers need to follow. We looked at the presses and gestures that are used in Android, and some of the more complex design patterns such as swipe views and navigation drawers. We looked at the difference between using the Up and Back buttons as well as how to best implement application settings and help menu areas. We learned how to notify users and provide operation confirmation, and took a look at the use of fonts, including the new Roboto font, and how to best write content for apps. We took a look at application icons and how to best provide a range of icons across devices, and then looked at device genres, which allow us to group design patterns according to device-type characteristics.

Finally, we looked at backward compatibility issues and considerations and went over the 17 stated design principles that Android considers important for Android developers to conform their application designs to. In the next chapter, we will take a more advanced look at how to create UI layout designs for Android OS, which work across different devices, screen orientations, screen sizes, and pixel densities.

Chapter 9

Android UI Layout Conventions, Differences and Approaches

Now that we've covered basic user interface design patterns and principles for Android and how to use the Pencil user interface prototyping software, we can get into UI layout theory and practice. We will explore some of the UI layout-specific concepts, differences and approaches that will arise in Android development across the different types of hardware devices, screen sizes, pixel densities, screen orientations, and Android application types.

We'll take a close look at the 48 DIP UI layout convention in this chapter as well as multi-pane layouts and types of compound view expansions that a developer can harness when a user changes their device orientation.

We'll also take a look at some of the most often used UI design parameters that allow Android OS to scale and position our UI designs for us, without us having to do anything other than harnessing these parameters correctly, and possibly testing our UI design in different orientations, to make sure that the results are acceptable and professional across different devices.

We will also take a look at the popular RelativeLayout UI design container and the special parameters that it offers that allow a precise UI element position to be achieved even when a user changes their device orientation.

For more advanced UI design control, we'll then take a look at the concept of resource qualifiers, which allow us to create user interface designs in every popular screen resolution, density, orientation and even wide aspect ratio. We'll learn how to use layout aliases and then implement UI designs which span across different size and orientation screens to get some real-world experience with all these advanced Android UI design concepts.

UI Layout Spacing: The 48 DIP User Interface Layout Rule

User Interface components in Android are usually designed to utilize **48 DP** (Density Independent Pixels, abbreviated as DIP or DP) spacing, either for the UI element itself, such as a Button or EditText UI widget, or for your spacing between UI elements. Android List items are also laid out in 48 DP increments, as are section headings and similar content dividers.

The Android ActionBar is 48 pixels tall for instance, as is the Navigation Bar at the bottom of Android touchscreens on those devices that feature no hardware keys or buttons. The one exception to this is the Status Bar that is located at the very top of the Android screen, which is usually 24 DIP, or half of the 48 DIP UI element and spacing convention.

Spacing between the UI elements should generally be either 4 DP or 8 DP on each side, or on top and at the bottom, to provide an even visual result. The reason for this is that 48 DP equates to about a centimeter on display screen hardware, which is a size that most user's fingers can touch easily but which doesn't take up an inordinate amount of touchscreen real estate.

Android UI spacing layout conventions state that UI elements should be **7mm** to **10mm** in size on an actual physical display screen, regardless of actual screen size or pixel density. This maximizes the ability of the tip of the user's finger to accurately select (or touch) the UI element, a term which Android OS calls "targetability."

UI Layout Panes: Single Pane Versus Multi-Pane Layouts

Since Android devices have many disparate sizes, shapes, and orientations, we must design and code our Android applications to accommodate these many different screen sizes and orientations by providing different UI layouts. This means that we must provide more than one design so our UI elements fit the different screen sizes, densities, and orientations.

One of the ways to achieve this UI design flexibility is to utilize **panes**, or **panels**, which group UI elements in such a way that they can be reformed based on screen orientation. You can assemble these UI panes into **compound views** across a wide screen, or stack them vertically on a portrait screen.

Whereas on a portrait display, you may expand views, when a master UI list or element is selected, or use the swipe view approach to achieve the same end result. On landscape displays, such as on tablets, all the elements can be combined into one compound view, where everything is visible all at once. When using compound views that show your UI and content at the same time, the UI design convention is to use panes on the left for UI selector elements, and panes on the right for your selected and displayed content.

UI Layout Compound View Types: Orientation Changes

Obviously your UI design should maintain its usage theme and functionality in both a portrait display mode as well as in a landscape display mode. So the name of the UI design game with compound (multi-pane) views is to have the UI design look and function in a similar fashion even when the Android user rotates their device.

There are a number of different UI design approaches to accomplish this in your application, and I'll cover many of those in this section.

If your multi-pane compound view UI design consists of two vertical panes, one on the left for UI control for the other on the right, for the content display, then you can **stretch** (or compress down) the UI panes by expanding the right pane (to a much greater degree or percentage) to fill this extra space. You can also adjust the left pane to some extent to achieve a resulting visual balance in your UI design.

If a multi-pane compound view UI design consists of horizontal panes, then you can **stack** the UI panes for the portrait mode, and arrange them side by side for the landscape view.

If your multi-pane compound view UI design consists of two vertical panes, one on the left for controlling your content on the right, then you could **expand** (for landscape, or collapse for portrait) your UI pane by expanding the left UI pane to fill up extra space afforded in landscape mode, adding additional UI element "perks" such as a picture of the user, for instance, when a left UI pane contains user information, such as name, address, etc.

As a last resort, if rotation from landscape mode into portrait mode can't accommodate both of your UI design panes in a multi-pane design, show only the content pane and **hide** the UI control pane, and allow access to that UI pane using the Up icon in the ActionBar or provide a UI element for access of that pane in the content pane. You could also use swipe views or drawer UI design to handle this situation; as you'll see in this chapter, as well as in the rest of the book, Android provides tons of classes and constants which allow you to control, customize, and even morph your UI designs into different device orientations and densities.

At the end of the day, determining your multi-pane compound view UI design approach, and then its implementation, is largely what this book is about.

Once you are exposed to everything in this chapter regarding how UI layout design can be controlled and morphed between Android devices, you will get a much better feel as to how to create morphing UI designs, as well as the many issues involved regarding this complicated design and coding process.

The complicated part, from a UI design perspective, is discovering the way to make the UI design for your apps morph between different devices, while remaining functional, attractive, accessible, enjoyable, and organized.

Auto-Scaling and Positioning UI Design: Layout Constants

The two primary UI element or layout constants, which are used in your XML UI design parameters, are the **wrap_content** and the **match_parent** constants. These are used with the **android:layout_width** and the **android:layout_height** parameter options inside of the UI element (View widget), or the UI layout (ViewGroup layout container) XML definition tags.

These two constants are utilized (and required) for both Android ViewGroup (layout container) XML definitions, as well as in Android View (UI widget) XML definitions, because UI elements and layouts must be defined as being either fixed (using wrap_content) or morphable (using match_parent).

What these do, especially in the case of this match_parent constant, is to stretch or expand your layout (ViewGroup) or UI element (View) to fill its parent container. This match_parent constant can thus be used to design UI panes and UI elements that will scale to fit changes in device screen sizes, density, or orientation.

The wrap_content constant does the exact opposite of the match_parent, so it is not as useful for the purpose of creating UI designs that can morph between different screen sizes and orientations. The wrap_content constant makes sure your user interface element does not scale (or distort) at all.

The wrap_content constant instructs the View (or ViewGroup) to conform its UI element (or layout container) boundaries to the content which is inside of it. For instance, to keep your ImageView from scaling the digital image content contained inside of it, you would use this constant for both the X and Y (width and height) dimensions so that the ImageView remains fixed.

The wrap_content constant is also what you would want to utilize to create a fixed pane for the UI layout, as using this constant will keep an entire layout and everything defined inside of it from scaling to fit your parent UI layout container. Remember that at the top-level, a UI layout container is a "child" of your display screen, so all this applies to scaling (or not scaling) the UI Design to fit the available screen area when these are applied at the top-most level of your XML UI definition markup.

To implement **variable positioning** within a UI layout design, whether it is fixed, using wrap_content, or dynamic, using match_parent, there's also an **android:layout_gravity** parameter that will automatically place UI elements on the screen if the screen size or orientation changes. This also applies to child UI layout containers, so it can also be used nested underneath to accomplish extremely useful centering (or alternate alignment) objectives.

Although **layout gravity** doesn't scale a UI element to fit a design, it can allow your UI design to **dynamically conform** to screen size and orientation changes. This allows Android OS to do much of the UI layout placement work that otherwise would have to be "hard-coded" using DP values. For instance you could center a UI element (View widget) or entire UI layout ViewGroup, or right-align or left-align a UI layout pane using one simple parameter.

Design UI Elements Relative to Each Other: RelativeLayout

The default layout container ViewGroup subclass implemented using the New Android Application dialog is the RelativeLayout container. You discovered this earlier in the book when we created our UserInterface Android app.

This container is here because Android developers sometimes fall into the bad habit of nesting LinearLayout containers, which uses system memory and processing cycles, when they can achieve the same exact design using a single RelativeLayout container.

Additionally, this RelativeLayout class has significantly more parameters, and a number of these fall into the Android layout scaling and positioning category. This means that these parameters could be used to design layouts that automatically accommodate differing screen sizes and orientations.

The RelativeLayout class has many positioning parameters that allow you to specify the position of each UI element in your design relative to all the other UI elements as well as to the parent layout container itself. This allows far more complex user interfaces to be designed using a single layout container with nested UI element widgets inside it, and each of these UI widgets can be configured with parameters that allow dynamic and relative positioning at the same time, allowing you to craft a UI design that will morph between all different screen sizes and orientations while maintaining your UI design look and feel as well as its design objectives.

Since we have an entire chapter on RelativeLayout in this book, Chapter 13, I will not go into the parameters in detail here, as we will be using them soon.

Using Multiple UI Layout Definitions: Resource Qualifiers

Since it is not always possible to develop a single design that will scale to fit every screen size, density, and orientation, Android OS provides us with the ability to create our own resource folder (/res) layout subfolder names, so that we can provide custom UI designs for different screen sizes and orientations. Android looks at our user's screen characteristics at run-time, and selects the correct UI design, based on layout folder naming.

These /layout subfolder naming conventions are called **resource qualifiers**, and they are one of the key things that we'll be learning about in detail during this chapter. There are resource qualifiers that cover **orientation** (port and land), **size** (small, normal, large, and xlarge), **densities** (ldpi, mdpi, hdpi, xhdpi, xxhdpi, xxxhdpi, tvdpi, nodpi), and **aspect ratio** (long, and notlong). These can also be used in conjunction with each other, as long as they are specified in the following order: size then density then orientation then aspect ratio. For example, a large, MDPI portrait layout definition for widescreens would go in **/res/layout-large-mdpi-port-long**.

Defining the Same Layout More Than Once: Layout Aliases

Android has two types of size resource qualifiers, both of which should be implemented if you are going to create designs for differing screen sizes.

The original type, which was used prior to Android 3.2, is called **abstract size resource qualifiers**. These include small, normal, large, and xlarge.

The other type could be called the **DIP dimension resource qualifiers**, and these were implemented after Android 3.2. We will be looking at these in the next section of this chapter covering DIP-specific width and height screen resource qualifiers.

To really do things right, you will have to put the same UI layout design into two different /res/layout-qualifier folders. Instead of putting this same file into two different folders, you can utilize something called a **layout alias** to store the file (data) once in your /res/layout folder and reference it from the appropriate /res/layout-resource folders.

So what you would want to do is to put the dual-pane wide screen layout in the /res/layout folder, and name it **dual_pane.xml**. Then, in a **/res/values-large** folder you would have a file named **layout. xml** that would contain the following XML markup:

```
<resources>
    <item name="main" type="layout">@layout/dual_pane</item>
</resources>
```

What this does is allow Android to find your dual_pane.xml UI definition file in the /res/values-large folder under the standard filename layout.xml and then reference the dual_pane.xml UI definition in your /res/layout folder.

Now that your dual-pane wide screen layout is in your /res/layout folder, and named dual_pane.xml, you can again reference it using the post 3.2 version of Android DIP qualifier, using a **/res/values-sw720dp** folder.

Again, in that folder, you would also have an XML file, named **layout.xml,** which would contain the exact same XML markup:

```
<resources>
   <item name="main" type="layout">@layout/dual_pane</item>
</resources>
```

This points Android OS versions after Android 3.2 to the same XML UI definition, dual_pane.xml, if the user were using a screen whose smallest width value was 720 (or greater). When you use layout aliases to set this up in this fashion, both Pre-3.2 OSes (for large screens) as well as Post-3.2 OSes (for smallestWidth of 720 DIP screens or larger) will reference the same dual_pane.xml UI definition markup. If you are only developing for Android 3.2 and later revisions, you can simply use the qualifiers we are going to be covering in the next section of this chapter.

Pre-Android 3.2 Resource Qualifiers: Small, Large, XLarge

If you are developing for Android 3.2 and earlier and don't need a precise DIP screen resolution control qualifier, which we will be covering in the next section, you can utilize the **/res/layout-small** (folder name) resource qualifier for your small screen layouts and the **/res/layout-large** resource qualifier for your large screen layouts. There's also a **/res/layout-xlarge** resource qualifier folder name that you can use, for extra large screen UI layouts, for instance on iTV sets, large tablets, PCs, netbooks, or notebooks.

If you wanted to specify a portrait UI layout for any of these non-normal-size resource qualifier names, you would then add **-port** to the end of your folder name. Thus, if you had a small screen portrait UI design, you would have that design in a specially named **/res/layout-small-port** folder. It is important to note that the -port must always come after the size modifier.

If you wanted to specify landscape UI layouts for any of these non-normal–sized resource qualifier names, you would then add **-land** to the end of your folder name. Thus if you had a large screen landscape UI design, you would have that design in a specially named **/res/layout-large-land** folder. It is important to note that the -land must always come after the size modifier.

Normal, also known as medium-sized screen layout designs, do not require a resource qualifier. These UI designs would be kept in the "root" UI layout folder, or the /res/layout folder, and this "primary" or default UI design would also define the name use for the other files in the other folders.

So if you named your XML UI definition file **gui_design.xml** in your project /res/layout folder, you would also name the file in the /res/layout-large-land folder gui_design.xml as well. That goes for any other designs in any other resource qualifier folder names, such as /res/layout-small-port. The normal (or medium) screen size portrait UI definition would thus be in the /res/layout-port resource qualifier folder and a normal (medium) landscape UI definition would be in the /res/layout-land resource qualifier folder.

Imagery (drawable) assets use a different resource qualifier folder naming schema, under the **/res/drawable** folder, and use the **-ldpi** and **-hdpi** naming extensions, instead of those -small and -large naming extensions that the layout folder resource qualifier naming schema utilizes.

Thus for **120 DPI low resolution** assets you would have a **/res/drawable-ldpi** folder, and for your **240 DPI high resolution** assets, you would then have a **/res/drawable-hdpi** folder. There is also a

/res/drawable-xhdpi folder, for **320 DPI extra high resolution** assets, and as of Android 4.2, there is also a **480 DPI extra extra high resolution** asset folder /res/drawable-xxhdpi. A recent Android 4.3 version added 4K iTV support with a **640 DPI extra extra extra high resolution** asset folder, which is named **/res/drawable-xxxhdpi**.

Next you'll learn about DIP screen size qualifiers; make sure not to use different size qualifier types together (res/layout-large-sw600dp).

Post-Android 3.2 Resource Qualifiers: Screen Size in DIP

Android 3.2 changed how screen size resource qualifiers were defined, by adding three different DIP size based resource qualifiers: **SmallestWidth**, which is written as **-sw#dp**, or -sw480dp, for instance, **AvailableWidth**, as indicated using a **-w#dp**, or -w600dp for instance, and **AvailableHeight**, as indicated using a **-h#dp**, or -h720dp for instance.

What these do is to give the developer a much finer numeric control over a given UI design to screen characteristics pairing. With the small, medium, large, and xlarge resource qualifiers, developers had to rely on Android to determine what screen resolutions qualify for these general categories. A screen size specific resource qualifier allows for a pixel-precision value to be set by the developer, so there is zero guesswork as to what design will be used with any given physical screen resolution characteristics.

The SmallestWidth or -sw modifier looks at the smallest possible dimension of the screen, regardless of its orientation, which makes it significantly different from an AvailableWidth or -w modifier, which will change numeric value evaluation within the OS every time that a user changes their device orientation. The same goes for the AvailableHeight, or -h modifier.

SmallestWidth is used to determine whether enough DIP width is available for your UI design regardless of the orientation of the device.

The most common dimension for an Android screen is 480 pixels, which is -sw480dp and is found in devices with 320x480, 480x800, and 480x854 resolution screens. The next most common is 800 pixels, common in 480x800 and 800x1280 screen size devices, such as smartphones and tablets. Now that smartwatches such as the Samsung Galaxy Gear are becoming popular, 320 pixel devices like a 320x320 Galaxy Gear or 320x480 entry-level touchscreen smartphone will also become a popular resolution, so a **-sw320dp**, **-sw480dp**, and **-sw800dp** qualifier will also be used quite frequently by Android developers.

Some popular resolutions have only one resolution out there, such as the 1024x600 netbook resolutions, which use a **-sw600dp** qualifier, and the Pcoudo HD 1200x720 resolution, which uses a **-sw720dp** qualifier.

It is important to note that the SmallestWidth calculation algorithm that is implemented by the Android OS takes into account any system chrome, that is, any Android OS UI elements such as status bars and bottom mounted virtual control button bars. This means the SmallestWidth algorithm won't match the physical screen resolution, but rather the available resolution that can be used to contain your parent UI ViewGroup layout container.

The SmallestWidth -sw#dp qualifier can be used in conjunction with a -port and a -land qualifier, such as /res/layout-sw480dp-land to allow developer control over UI design for any screen size and orientation. This allows a developer precise control over not only how their UI fits any device, but also over how digital image or digital video content is displayed.

The other two **-w#dp** and **-h#dp** resource qualifiers **re-evaluate for any orientation change** for a user's Android device, so the resource qualifiers can be used to replace Java code that detects device orientation changes, and then implements a different UI design or even content design paradigm.

If you have already worked through the recent *Pro Android Graphics* title, also from Apress, you have already experienced how complex Java code that deals with screen orientation can become. Thus by using these two resource qualifiers, you can implement a clever way to handle this objective, using only custom /res/layout folder names and UI design definition XML markup.

Since these -w#dp and -h#dp qualifiers can be used to determine one screen axis resolution, and since this changes with device orientation, you could use them with a -port and -land qualifier to match any popular resolution.

For instance -w480dp on its own would call both a 320x480 resolution entry level smartphone, when it is in landscape orientation, and also an 480x800 or 854x480 smartphone or tablet when it's in portrait orientation. To also control which of these device scenarios you are matching your UI design to you can add -port and -land, so to fit a 320x480 entry-level (inexpensive) smartphone use -w320dp-port and use -w480dp-port to fit 800x480 or 854x480 smartphones or tablets when they are being used in portrait mode. It would be cool to be able to use these two together to specify a complete display screen resolution, but because they are in the same category this can't be done currently. Luckily, it is just as effective, that is, you can achieve the same result, by using the size and orientation qualifiers together.

Table 9-1 shows some of the different types of Android devices and the DIP (or DP) screen size ranges, typical resolution and smallest width normally associated with each type of device.

Table 9-1. Android-based Consumer Electronics Device, Typical Screen Size Range, smallestWidth, and Resolution

Consumer Electronics Device	Size (Inches)	Smallest Width DP	Common Resolutions
Smartwatch and flip phone	1 to 2 inches	160dp to 320dp	160x240, 320x320
Small touchscreen smartphone	3 to 4 inches	320dp to 480dp	320x480, 480x800
HD smartphone and phablet	4 to 6 inches	600dp to 720dp	600x1024, 720x1280
Tablet	6 to 11 inches	600dp to 800dp	600x1024, 800x1280
eBook Reader (Kindle Fire HD)	7 to 9 inches	1080dp to 1200dp	1920x1080, 1920x1200
Game console	5 to 10 inches	720dp to 1080dp	1280x720, 1920x1080
iTV set	24 to 72 inches	1080dp	1920x1080
4K iTV set	32 to 96 inches	2160dp	4096x2160

App Screen Size Support: Declaring Via AndroidManifest

It is also possible to restrict your applications to only run on devices that support certain screen size, density, and resolution characteristics. This is done by using an "analog" or equivalent of the resource qualifier that you just learned about (Smallest Width). This XML parameter is used inside the **<supports-screens>** tag, which is a child tag of your parent **<manifest>** tag for your application manifest.

The parameter is the **android:requiresSmallestWidthDp** parameter, which does the same thing as the -sw#dp resource qualifier, so it looks at the smaller of the two X:Y or W:H screen dimensions, and uses the tag format:

```
<supports-screens android:requiresSmallestWidthDp="720" />
```

This makes sure that the Android device supported at least Pseudo HD resolution (1280x720). If this tag were present in the AndroidManifest.xml file, the GooglePlay store would not permit your Android application to be purchased and downloaded by potential customers with incompatible devices.

This isn't really a good XML parameter to use, especially if you have this resolution value set at a higher number, as millions (if not billions) of Android devices have 240, 320, 480, or 600 SmallestWidth characteristics.

If you were to implement this in your application manifest file, you would be restricting your potential app sales (customer pool) significantly, and since this book is ultimately about increasing app revenues, I am going to strongly recommend against using it.

What I recommend that you do instead is to take the time to implement your UI design for each of the major physical hardware screen width resolutions (320, 480, 600, 720, and 1080) using the concepts we have covered in the prior couple of sections regarding screen size DP resource qualifiers, and using custom drawable (image) assets for each of the LDPI, MDPI, HDPI, XHDPI, and XXHDPI screen density drawable asset folders.

This is not easy to do by any stretch of the imagination, and, in fact, is why this chapter is in this book. It is difficult due to the determination of the proper resolutions to "break" your UI designs (and content) into as well as the proper pixel resolutions, and densities, to optimize the image assets into. Even more difficult is doing this across five different break points, because it means developing five times more assets and UI designs.

Even more interesting is the fact that, according to the Android Developer website, Google Play does not even support an android:requiresSmallestWidth screen size parameter for filtering out incompatible application purchases and downloads. I'm not certain for the reason for this—having a parameter that is not implemented (supported) and thus is not really usable (useful) to developers to harness for their applications seems somewhat pointless.

Creating Morphable UI Designs: Using Resource Qualifiers

Now it's time to expand upon our AnalogClock user interface design that we created over the previous chapters and add in some user interface controls that will allow our users to customize their AnalogClock graphic design to select between a happy face, planet graphic, or just a 3D decorative hoop.

The first thing that we will need to do is to add some Button UI elements, which will allow our users to select different background images for their AnalogClock UI element. We will initially expand our current design, so we can create a portrait standard UI design orientation.

After that, we will test this design in the Nexus One AVD emulator in both portrait and landscape modes, and then if it is needed, we will create the landscape version of the design, and implement a resource qualifier folder to show you how Android will automatically select the correct UI design as long as we set everything up correctly. Finally, we will test this dual UI design set-up, and will see firsthand if resource qualifiers really work!

AnalogClock Graphics: Adding a Button to Our UI Design

Go into your UserInterface project and open the activity_analog.xml file, or if it's already open, click on the tab at the top of your IDE to view the XML markup.

The first thing that we want to do is to pull the AnalogClock UI widget up a bit, to make room for the Button UI elements, which we are about to add.

In the <AnalogClock> tag change the android:layout_marginTop parameter to a value of 2, which brings the AnalogClock UI element up another 30 DIP on the screen, giving us some more room for our three Button UI elements.

Next add a <Button> UI element tag, and then configure it using parameters to have an ID of simpleClock and make sure to set the layout_width as well as the layout_height to the wrap_content constant. We'll use a top margin setting of 16dip to push the Button UI element away from the AnalogClock a bit, and we will use a text string reference of @string/simpleClockLabel.

We will also use a RelativeLayout specific parameter called **layout_below** to specify that our Button UI element be laid out below the AnalogClock UI element, and we will keep everything centered nicely in the screen UI design by using the same **layout_centerHorizontal** parameter that we use for the AnalogClock UI widget. This is all done via the following XML markup:

```
<Button android:text="@string/simpleClockLabel" android:id="@+id/simpleClock"
    android:layout_width="wrap_content" android:layout_height="wrap_content"
    android:layout_below="@+id/analogClock" android:layout_centerHorizontal="true"
    android:layout_marginTop="16dip" />
```

As you can see in Figure 9-1, once you type this in, you will have one error highlight, because you have not yet created your Button label string constant. Since we are going to do this next, you can ignore the error highlighting for now. It is interesting to note that a small error such as this can "percolate" throughout your entire project, creating more than six error flags (or more if you open the /src sub-folder hierarchy), so do not become alarmed, as these will vanish when you add in your string constant!

Figure 9-1. Adding a Button UI element child tag to the activity_analog.xml file, and configuring it with parameters

At this point we should take a look at how the UI design is laying out, by using the Graphical Layout Editor tab, which is located at the bottom-left of the Eclipse central editing pane as shown in Figure 9-1. Click this tab and take a look at your new UI design, with the AnalogClock UI element nicely centered between your TextView screen header and the new Button UI element that we just added.

As you can see in Figure 9-2, your UI design looks centered, evenly spaced, and professional, and so now we can proceed to create all our Button label string constants (three of them), and after that, we can copy and paste this completed Button tag to create two more UI Button elements.

Figure 9-2. Using a Graphical Layout Editor tab in Eclipse to preview the UI design after the first Button is added

Notice in Figure 9-2 that the Graphical Layout Editor will tell us, in the light yellow error and warning area underneath the preview, that we have a resource error. Underneath this error message the GLE also actually tells us what this error is (the absence of the @string/simpleClockLabel string resource).

Because I don't like errors and warning highlighting in my IDE, in the next section we will create all three of the Button UI element's label string constants, and then we will return to the XML file editing to add the final two Button UI elements (this time, they will all be error free).

To prepare for adding your three new <string> tags to create label string constants, open the **/res/ values** sub-folder, and right-click and **Open** your **strings.xml** file, or left-click it and hit the **F3** key on your keyboard.

Creating Multiple Button Labels: Adding String Constants

At the top of your strings.xml string constant values XML file, add in the following three <string> tag constants to set-up labels for your Button UI elements, using the following XML markup:

```
<string name="simpleClockLabel">Simple 3D Clock</string>
<string name="worldClockLabel">World 3D Clock</string>
<string name="happyClockLabel">Happy 3D Clock</string>
```

As you can see in Figure 9-3, after you hit your **Ctrl-S** to **Save** your XML markup for the strings.xml file, all the error flags in your IDE will disappear, and your IDE will be clean as a whistle once again.

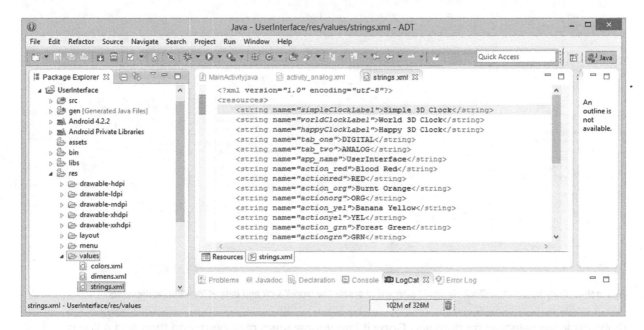

Figure 9-3. Adding three Button UI element caption <string> constants in the strings.xml file in the /res/values folder

Next, you go back into your activity_analog.xml tab at the top of the Eclipse central editing pane, and you copy and paste your now error-free Button UI element, to create additional AnalogClock settings Button UI elements, to fill up your portrait orientation UI layout design.

Creating Multiple Button Elements: Using RelativeLayout

Select (I like to say "stripe out"), in its entirety, your first Button UI element tag, and all its parameters, as is shown in blue (or dark gray) reverse selected in Figure 9-4.

Figure 9-4. *Copying a simpleClock Button UI element to create the worldClock and happyClock Button elements*

Right-click the selected markup and **Copy** it into your system clipboard, and then add a line of space under the <Button> tag and before the closing </RelativeLayout> tag, and right-click again, and select the **Paste** option, or alternatively, you could also use a **Ctrl-V** (Paste) keystroke shortcut.

Do this process twice, so that you end up with a total of three Button UI elements at the bottom of your markup. Make sure that you paste these into your RelativeLayout parent tag before the </RelativeLayout> closing tag.

This process pastes the <Button> tag markup two more times beneath itself, and once you do this, you can edit these new Button tags, adjusting their spacing and adding in the correct referencing for relative layout parameters.

This allows you to fine-tune your portrait UI layout design. Make sure that you use your Graphical Layout Editor during this process, so that you can see as you edit your parameters how exactly the UI design is evolving.

The primary changes that you will need to make to the second two Button UI elements is to change the **layout_marginTop** parameters to use **8dip** spacing, instead of 16dip as the first button does, which brings your Button UI element a bit closer together. Also make sure to change the **ID** and **text** or string references to reflect the correct Button type (world or happy), and edit **layout_below** parameters to reference the Button ID for the UI element which is directly above them. This is done using the following XML markup:

```
<Button android:text="@string/simpleClockLabel" android:id="@+id/simpleClock"
    android:layout_width="wrap_content" android:layout_height="wrap_content"
    android:layout_below="@+id/analogClock" android:layout_centerHorizontal="true"
    android:layout_marginTop="16dip" />
```

```
<Button android:text="@string/worldClockLabel" android:id="@+id/worldClock"
    android:layout_width="wrap_content" android:layout_height="wrap_content"
    android:layout_below="@+id/simpleClock" android:layout_centerHorizontal="true"
    android:layout_marginTop="8dip" />
<Button android:text="@string/happyClockLabel" android:id="@+id/happyClock"
    android:layout_width="wrap_content" android:layout_height="wrap_content"
    android:layout_below="@+id/worldClock" android:layout_centerHorizontal="true"
    android:layout_marginTop="8dip" />
```

Once this is all in place we can use the **Run As ➤ Android Application** menu sequence, which can be accessed off a right-click on your UserInterface project folder. We'll do this at this point in time to visualize what this final portrait UI design layout will look like in the Nexus One emulator. The resulting portrait UI layout can be seen in Figure 9-5.

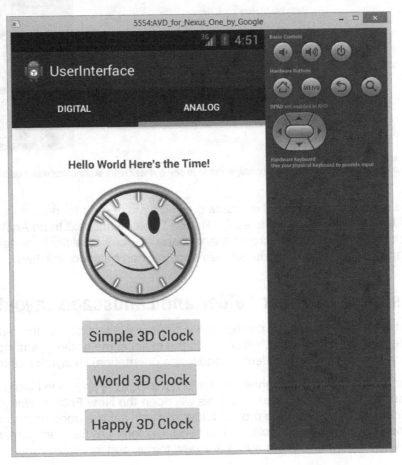

Figure 9-5. Viewing our portrait UI layout design in the Nexus One emulator

Since this looks good in the portrait orientation, the next thing that we will need to do is to see what this UI layout markup looks like when it is viewed in landscape mode.

To do this in the Nexus One emulator, in fact, in any Android emulator, we need to hit the **Ctrl-F11** keystroke combination. This switches the Nexus One emulator into a landscape mode, just as if we had turned our Nexus One phone onto its side.

As you can see in Figure 9-6, this UI layout XML definition when viewed in landscape mode is not at all desirable or professional, and although the top UI elements look fine, the bottom half of the design is not visible.

Figure 9-6. *Testing a portrait UI layout design in landscape mode to see if it will work without resource qualifiers*

This is exactly the situation that Android resource qualifiers are perfect for resolving, as we can create a second UI layout design that places the Button UI elements next to an AnalogClock UI element instead of underneath it. Let's create a landscape resource qualifier folder and a custom layout for landscape use next, so that you can see how this can be accomplished.

Create a Resource Qualifier Folder and Landscape Layout

The first thing that we need to do in our project folder hierarchy is to create a subfolder under the resource /res folder called **/layout-land**, which holds the exact same **activity_analog.xml** XML filename, but which contains a vastly different (landscape orientation) UI layout design.

The first step to accomplish this is to right-click the /res folder, as is shown in Figure 9-7, and select the **New ➤ Folder** menu command sequence. This will open the **New Folder** dialog, which is used to create a subfolder within your Eclipse project folder hierarchy. It is a good idea to do this within the Eclipse IDE (instead of external to Eclipse using your Explorer OS file management tool) so the Eclipse project "view" in memory knows about any new folder, and its place within your project folder hierarchy.

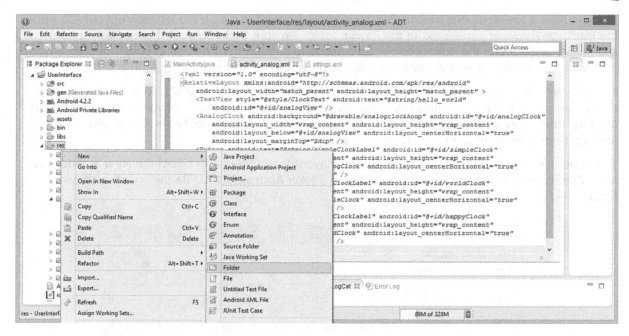

Figure 9-7. Right-click the /res folder and select New ➤ Folder menu command sequence to create new folder

If you create folders external to Eclipse, you will have to right-click on your UnderInterface project's master folder, and use the **Refresh** option on the menu that appears, or exit and relaunch the Eclipse IDE so it can load the correct project folder hierarchy into your system's memory.

Enter **layout-land** Into the **Folder name** field, and click the **Finish** button.

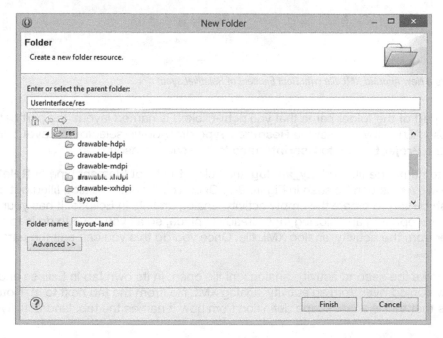

Figure 9-8. Create a new folder named layout-land under the /res parent folder

Once you have created your **/res/layout-land** folder, you will see it on the left side of your IDE under the Package Explorer pane, next to the /layout folder. Be sure that you do not put a /layout-land sub-folder underneath the /layout folder, as it needs to be next to or beside it, under the /res folder. You will see what this is supposed to look like, a bit later on in this section, in Figure 9-10.

Now that you have a /res/layout-land sub-folder, you need to create an XML file to live inside of this folder, and this file must have the same name as the file that is inside of your /res/layout folder: **activity_analog.xml** so that the filename matches up with the filename that is referenced in your **analogClockFragment.java** Fragment subclass.

To create this XML file, right-click your new /res/layout-land folder, and select the **New ➤ Android XML File** menu command sequence to bring up a **New Android XML File** dialog, as is shown in Figure 9-9.

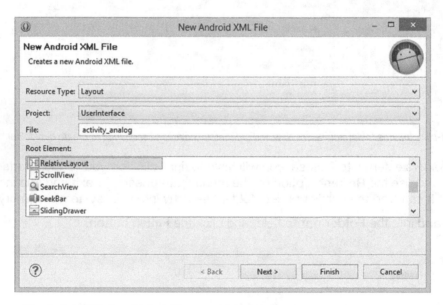

Figure 9-9. Create a New Android XML file with Root Element of RelativeLayout

Since the first part of the folder name that you right-clicked is named layout (the part before the hyphen), Eclipse ADT knows to set the **Resource Type** drop-down selector to **Layout** and also knows to set the **Project** folder to **UserInterface** for the same reason.

You will need to name the file **activity_analog** and select the Root Element type of **RelativeLayout** by yourself, however, as can be seen in Figure 9-9. Once you have this dialog filled out correctly, click the **Finish** button to create the empty activity_analog.xml file in Eclipse. It has your <RelativeLayout> opening and closing tags already in place, so all you have to do is to copy the child tags over from the activity_analog XML file. Once you do this you can edit the parameters to create a new UI.

Figure 9-10 shows the second activity_analog.xml file open, in its own tab in Eclipse and with the child tags now copied over from an activity_analog XML file (from the tab next to it). Notice that Eclipse knows that this is a landscape definition from how it names the tab: land/activity_analog.xml and so we have seen Eclipse intelligently take both the first part as well as the second part of the /res/layout-land resource qualifier folder name, and implement those correctly in the IDE dialog and tab work processes.

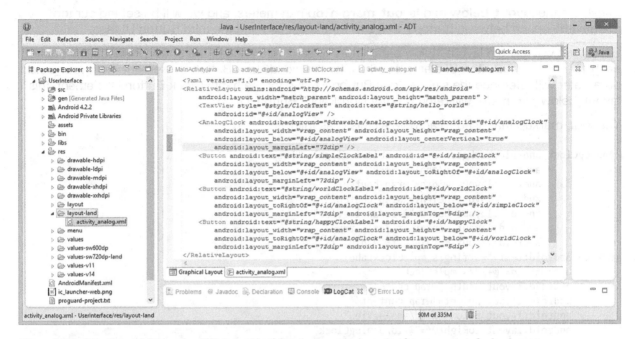

Figure 9-10. Copy the activity_analog XML to land/activity_analog.xml tab; customize parameters for landscape

Next, we need to morph our portrait UI layout design into the landscape UI layout design by modifying the parameters inside each of the child UI tags starting with the AnalogClock UI element, because we're going to leave the TextView screen caption at the top of the screen the same in both designs.

The most important change we need to make is to change the centering of an AnalogClock UI element from horizontal to vertical, as we will need the UI element to be on the left side of the screen and not in the center. We'll use a layout_marginLeft parameter to put some space between the left side of the AnalogClock and the edge of the screen by using a value of 72 DIP.

Next, we need to make some more significant modifications to our Button UI elements, so that they live on the right side of the UI design, instead of underneath the AnalogClock, as they did in the portrait UI layout design.

Let's start with the first simpleClock (ID) Button UI element, since in a RelativeLayout, everything is laid out relative to each other. We need to add an **android:layout_toRightOf** parameter that references the AnalogClock UI element ID **@+id/analogClock**, so the Button will live beside your clock.

We will also need to add an **android:layout_marginLeft** parameter set to **72 DIP** so that there is a similar amount of spacing on the right side of the display as is on the left side of the display for the UI layout design.

Your second and third Button UI elements will also feature both of these new parameters with the same settings, as well as two additional parameter changes, which will ensure that these other two Button UI elements will be positioned correctly, relative to the first and second Button UI elements.

These are the **layout_below** and **layout_marginTop** parameters, and we will be setting our top margin (the space between buttons) to **5 DIP** for the second and the third Button UI tags.

Finally, we will use the layout_below parameters to set a reference to the button immediately above each of the current Button UI elements. Thus, for the worldClock Button UI element the layout_below parameter will reference the simpleClock Button ID, and for the happyClock Button UI element, this layout_below parameter will reference the worldClock Button ID.

The XML markup that used to achieve all this is as follows:

```
<AnalogClock android:background="@drawable/analogclockhoop"
             android:id="@+id/analogClock"
             android:layout_width="wrap_content"
             android:layout_height="wrap_content"
             android:layout_below="@+id/analogView"
             android:layout_centerVertical="true"
             android:layout_marginLeft="72dip" />
<Button android:text="@string/simpleClockLabel"
        android:id="@+id/simpleClock"
        android:layout_width="wrap_content"
        android:layout_height="wrap_content"
        android:layout_below="@+id/analogView"
        android:layout_toRightOf="@+id/analogClock"
        android:layout_marginLeft="72dip" />
<Button android:text="@string/worldClockLabel"
        android:id="@+id/worldClock"
        android:layout_width="wrap_content"
        android:layout_height="wrap_content"
        android:layout_toRightOf="@+id/analogClock"
        android:layout_below="@+id/simpleClock"
        android:layout_marginTop="5dip" />
<Button android:text="@string/happyClockLabel"
        android:id="@+id/happyClock"
        android:layout_width="wrap_content"
        android:layout_height="wrap_content"
        android:layout_toRightOf="@+id/analogClock"
        android:layout_below="@+id/worldClock"
        android:layout_marginTop="5dip" />
```

Now that we have designed our landscape UI layout, we can go ahead and see if the /res/layout-land resource qualifier folder that we created actually works in our real life application (or at least in the Nexus One emulator, which is pretty close at this point to actual real world device testing).

It is time to use the **Run As ➤ Android Application** work process, and test our new resource qualifier savvy application in the Nexus One emulator.

As you can see in Figure 9-11, now that you have put this new landscape UI resource qualifier in place, when you hit a Ctrl-F11 keystroke combination you will access your landscape UI layout design, which fits the new screen orientation correctly.

Figure 9-11. Running the application in the Nexus One emulator in landscape mode to see whether /layout-land UI used

So here we are using the stack UI layout reorganization approach, which we looked at earlier in the chapter, and stacked the Button "bank" underneath the AnalogClock in portrait mode, and stacked the Button "bank" or "pane" next to the AnalogClock in landscape mode.

In the next chapter, we will continue to expand this UI design by taking a look at different Android themes, as well as learning about digital media assets, such as digital images and digital video, and their attributes. We will also take a closer look at how to implement the different resolution density UI assets and size-specific layout design and resource qualifiers.

Summary

In this chapter, we took a closer look at UI layout considerations, especially as they relate to the myriad of different Android device screen sizes, pixel densities, as well as potential device orientation changes. Orientation changes to an Android device may well be invoked by your user base as they utilize your application by turning the device onto its side.

I wanted to get into all these "foundational" UI design guidelines and information before we started learning about all Android's different UI layout container classes. It is better if all these concepts are understood first, so that I can reference them, as you learn about core UI layout containers (ViewGroup subclasses) during the second half of this book. UI design is a tricky proposition in Android for a myriad of reasons.

First, we looked at the **48 DIP** UI element and spacing sizing principle, or rule, in Android UI design. This has been implemented in Android to keep a UI design attractively spaced, as well as making the screen layout easy to use with the touch of your fingertip, and so that users do not have to use a stylus to touch any small or thin area of your screen designs.

Next, we looked at the popular UI design conventions in Android, of having both a single-pane and a multi-pane UI layout design, to help when a user's device changes orientation, from portrait to landscape, or, to use if the device has a lot of display screen real estate to leverage for UI design elements (such as a tablet, notebook, e-reader or iTV set). We looked at the different ways to change these compound (multi-pane) views when the user changes your app's screen orientation from portrait to landscape. We looked at several screen re-organization concepts, including **stretch**, **stack**, and **expand**, as well as **show** and **hide**.

We then took a look at XML layout parameters and constants that allow the Android OS to scale your UI design to fit almost any screen size or orientation, including the **MATCH_PARENT** and **WRAP_CONTENT** constants and the **android:layout_gravity** and **android:gravity** parameters. We learned about the **RelativeLayout** container type and how it allows complex UI designs to be created that are relative to each other and thus can scale properly.

We took a look at the concept of layout aliases and how they are set up for spanning support from Pre-3.2 to Post-3.2 resource qualifier usage. We took a look at the generic size (**-small, -large, and -xlarge**) resource qualifiers that were used prior to Android 3.2 and the screen size in DP resource qualifiers (**-sw#dp, -w#dp, and -h#dp**), which were implemented in Android 3.2 (and later).

Finally, we looked at how to specify a screen size for your application at the Google Play (store) level by using the **android:requiresSmallestWidthDp** parameter, and discussed why this was not a good idea to utilize as it can reduce your potential app revenue stream. We also learned that this is not yet implemented, and discussed how spending the work to design your UI for many different Android device characteristics would be a much better idea. We implemented some of this newfound knowledge in our AnalogClock application, so that we can design both a portrait and a landscape version of our existing app and set it up with some UI Buttons so that in the next chapter, we can add digital media elements and size qualifiers to the mix.

In the next chapter, we will take a more advanced look at how to harness a given Android UI theme within Android so that you'll have complete control over how your standard UI elements will look on any given device screen. An in-depth discussion of digital media asset format support and concepts will also take place in the next chapter so that we can start implementing new media assets in our Pro Android UI designs.

Chapter 10

Android UI Theme Design and Digital Media Concepts

Now that we've covered how user interface designs for Android are laid out in 2D space (spacially), we can get more into how these look (and feel) by starting to look at **UI themes**, or different UI element "looks" or designs. Since we're getting into UI element color and detailing and 3D effects and the like, this is also a logical chapter to cover how to integrate **digital new media elements**, such as images, audio, animation, and videos, into a UI design workflow or screen layout "look and feel" UI design work process.

To do this we must first understand the **foundational principles** behind the new media assets themselves, such as **pixels** in images, **samples** in audio, or **frames** in video and animation. This knowledge will allow you to understand why Android does things certain ways regarding new media, as well as why it supports certain new media formats and capabilities.

First, we'll cover Android **themes**, and how they can be created and applied to our entire Android application, or alternatively to individual Activity subclasses within our applications. We will look at some of these standard Android themes, and how they can be specified in our **AndroidManifest** XML file.

We'll also look at how to set-up different themes for different API levels in Android, again using **resource qualifier** folder names in the **/res/values** project folder. This is similar to what we did for UI layout design in our /res/layout folders, and what we are going to do with **/res/drawable** folders for UI layout designs which incorporate graphics design (termed: drawable) assets.

We will learn about Android drawable graphics assets and the theory behind them, as well as how to implement these correctly in Android. We will take a look at digital images, digital video, digital audio, and 2D animation in Android, and we will see how Android OS handles the use of these different types of new media elements within our **Pro Android UI** design work process.

Introduction to Themes: Styling an Entire App or Activity

Android OS leverages something called a **"theme"** to allow app developers to globally apply a **universal set of UI element styling parameters** to Android applications as a whole, or, alternatively, to a single Activity subclass. As you will see during the chapter, this is done using the **AndroidManifest** XML file and either your **<application>** or the **<activity>** tag, if not both.

If you are familiar with programming HTML5 apps or websites, this is the equivalent of using a Cascading Style Sheet (CSS), which defines a theme for your HTML5 app or website. This CSS file holds the stylistic settings for how your HTML5 app or website looks, which keeps it uniform across all the pages as well as helping to reduce redundant code and markup on each individual page.

As you learned in previous chapters, the Android style definition specifies the visual characteristics of those user interface elements that comprise your UI design or display screen layout. These may include padding values, font characteristics, standard UI colors, widget heights, and so forth.

To guarantee the identical Android look and feel between all the different applications from all the different developers on the Android platform, an Android OS standard exists that provides developers with three mainstream Android OS "system themes," which you can specify in your Android Manifest XML file when you are developing apps for Version 3.0 and later versions.

These "canned" Android UI themes include the Android **Holo Light Theme,** as well as the **Holo Dark Theme**, and there is also a hybrid between these two Holo Themes that features the **Holo Light Theme with the Darker ActionBar**.

Whereas the themes for Android Honeycomb and later are called **Holo**, themes prior to Honeycomb are simply called **Theme**, the name of Android's original theme. There are light and dark variations of Theme as well, called **Theme**, which is the default OS theme (if no theme is specified) and is dark, and **Theme.Light,** which needs to be specified in the AndroidManifest.xml file if you want to use it. **Theme.Holo** is the default, dark theme, for Android 3.0 Honeycomb and later. You could also specify the **Theme.Holo.Light** theme for an Android 3.x application. There is also a **Theme.Holo.Light. DarkActionBar** that is standard for Android 4.0 (API Level 14) and later, as you will see in the next section, where we'll set different themes for our application.

Developers are strongly encouraged to utilize these Holo themes as they're building their apps, so that the resulting look and feel will fit nicely within the general "visual language" that is used for the Android OS. You should select a system UI theme that is best optimized for your needs and design aesthetic for the Android application-specific UI design objective.

If the desire is to have a more unique look and feel for the app, then try to design that custom theme by using one of the Android OS UI themes as a starting point. This is how you're going to learn how to develop the custom themes that we create in this chapter, so you will learn the most optimal way to implement your own theme "tweaks" to the standard Android UI theme.

These standard system themes provide developers with a solid foundation on top of which they can selectively implement their own visual UI style, and looking at how a theme is put together is one of the best ways of learning how to develop your own custom UI theme, besides tweaking existing themes.

Applying Application-wide Theme: The <application> Tag

To start out on the "top level" with the Android Holo themes, let's take a look at how to change the look and feel for your application using various Holo themes at an **<application>** tag level in the **AndroidManifest.xml file**.

Open your UserInterface project in Eclipse, and right-click the Android Manifest XML file located at the bottom of the project folder, as is shown in Figure 10-1. Select the **Open** option to view the current manifest in the tab, which you can see Eclipse labels as **UserInterface Manifest**, since that is exactly what it is. Notice that the New Android Application series of dialogs has already defined your <application> tag and added parameters for you, one of which is the **android:theme** parameter, which is referencing a <style> tag definition named **AppTheme** using a **@style/AppTheme reference**.

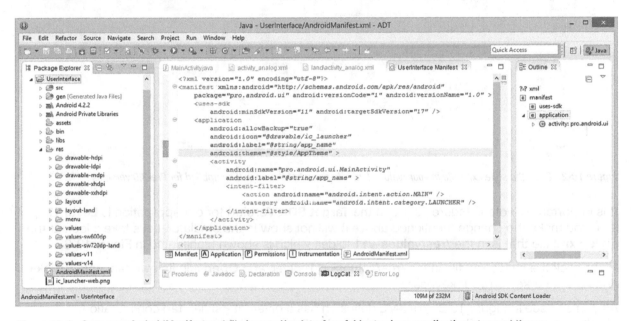

***Figure 10-1.** Open your AndroidManifest.xml file in your UserInterface folder to view <application> tag and theme*

Thus it looks like Eclipse ADT (Android) has set-up the application theme XML markup files, resource qualifier folders, and defaults for us already, so let's investigate this now. Later on in the chapter we can add to this infrastructure that has been set-up for us and learn how to create our own custom theme. For now, let's focus on learning how to change amongst Holo themes, and get a feel for how everything is set-up and works together to allow us to specify custom themes for Android 2.x, 3.x, and 4.x level OSes.

First, right-click the styles.xml file in the /res/values folder and take a look at the markup that specifies the theme for Android OSes prior to API Level 11 Honeycomb Version 3.0.

As you can see in Figure 10-2, your <resources> parent tag has been set-up for you, and <style> child tags have been set up to create an **AppBaseTheme** style, which takes its default settings from the parent **android:Theme.Light** style definition. Then a second <style> tag creates an AppTheme style that is referenced in the AndroidManifest.xml using the AppBaseTheme style as a parent style. Thus if you want to change the theme for the application you will need to go to the top of this parenting chain or tree, and change the android:Theme.Light to instead be android:Theme if you want to use a black UI theme for versions of your application previous to Version 3.0, such as the popular 2.3.7 version used on the original Amazon Kindle Fire.

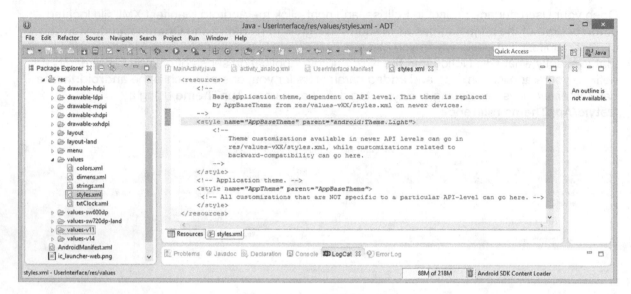

Figure 10-2. Open the styles.xml file in your /values folder to see what theme will be applied for Pre-3.0 versions

It is important to note in Figure 10-1 that the **Target SDK Version** for our application is **Level 17**, so if you make the change mentioned above it will not show in the emulator. Let's take a look at the **styles.xml** file that is in the **/res/values-v11** folder, which is shown highlighted in Figure 10-2.

Right-click the styles.xml file in the **/res/values-v11** folder, and **Open** it in its own tab, or left-click it, and hit the **F3** key on your keyboard.

As you can see in Figure 10-3, this XML definition has a different <style> tag configuration, which replaced the AppBaseTheme style in version 3.0 or later of Android, as you can read in the comments in this file.

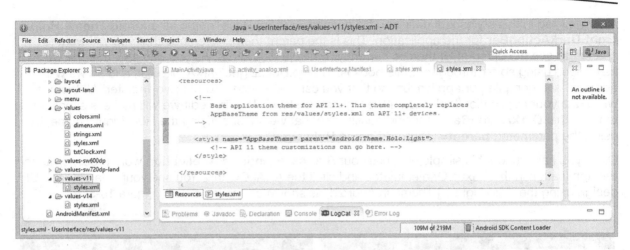

Figure 10-3. Open the styles.xml file in your /values-v11 folder to see what theme will be applied for 3.x versions

As you can see, the **android:Theme.Holo.Light** is the parent theme that is referenced for use with Android 3.0 Honeycomb API Level 11, and if we were to change this to **android:Theme.Holo** in an attempt to get the dark (black) theme, we would still not get the results that we are looking for (or are expecting) in the emulator, because as you'll notice in Figure 10-3, there is also a **/res/values-v14** folder as well. Since we are targeting API Level 17, we'll also need to take a look at the styles.xml file in this folder.

Right-click the styles.xml file that is in the **/res/values-v14** folder, and as you can see in Figure 10-4, there is an even more refined UI theme in place in this file, which is used when Android 4.0, 4.1.2, 4.2.2, 4.3.1 or 4.4.2 OS versions are being utilized on the Android hardware device.

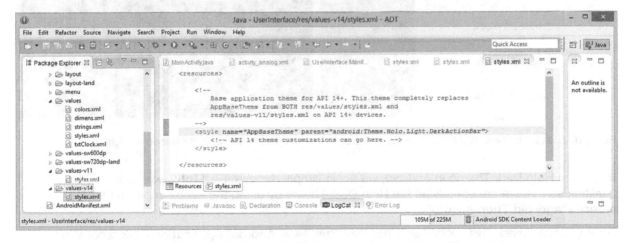

Figure 10-4. Open the styles.xml file in your /values-v14 folder to see what theme will be applied for 4.x versions

A <style> tag in this styles.xml definition file defines your AppBaseTheme as **android:Theme.Holo. Light.DarkActionBar** for the application. This is the parent theme reference that you will want to change to see the different UI themes currently available in Android. As you can see, the one we have been using so far throughout this book is: Theme.Holo.Light.DarkActionBar, and so we will edit this, and compile our application, so that you can see what the other two "master" UI themes will make your application look like on the highest use level. The first edit we will make is simply to remove the **.DarkActionBar** extension qualifier, so that we are specifying the Holo Light Theme, by using the parameter: **parent="android:Theme.Holo.Light"**

Once you have made this simple edit, use your **Run As ➤ Android Application** work process, launch the application in the Nexus One emulator, and click the ANALOG tab. You see your AnalogClock UI design using the Holo Light UI Theme in Android, as shown on the left side of Figure 10-5.

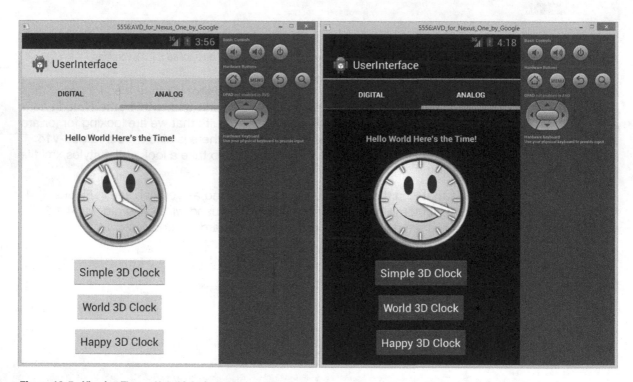

Figure 10-5. Viewing Theme.Holo.Light in the Nexus One on the left, and Theme.Holo in Nexus One on the right

To get the Holo Dark Theme in Android, we again simply remove the **.Light** extension qualifier, so that we are specifying the Holo Dark Theme by using the even simpler parameter: **parent="android:Theme.Holo"**

Once you have made this second edit, use your **Run As ➤ Android Application** work process and launch the application in the Nexus One emulator. Click the ANALOG tab and you see your AnalogClock UI design using the Holo Dark UI Theme in Android, as shown on the right side of Figure 10-5.

As you can see, the Theme.Holo, or Holo Dark Theme, looks very impressive, especially with our AnalogClock portrait UI design. Since the button color is translucent, the buttons take on a percentage of the background color.

It is important to note that the Holo.Dark theme uses less power on an Android device over time, as the black pixel values on an LED, LCD, or OLED display represent all color channels being turned off (#000000), and thus, each black pixel is using zero power. We'll be covering RGB color channels later in this chapter, after we finish covering custom UI theme design. If you want to see the older UI themes in the Nexus One emulator, you can just change the **targetSdkVersion** parameter to **10** (Pre-11) or **13** (Pre-14).

Customizing the Theme: Creating a Grey Color ActionBar

Let's customize the Holo Dark theme, since that UI looks the best with our AnalogClock UI design. The one thing that is bugging me about the UI theme as seen in Figure 10-5 is that both the ActionBar, as well as the UI Tabs, use the same color (black) value, which looks less than professional.

I want this ActionBar to use a **75% grey** (75% black and 25% white) color to differentiate it a little bit, while still keeping it generally dark.

To do this we need to create an **AppBaseTheme.ActionBar** style with a parent reference to the **android:style/Widget.Holo.ActionBar** that holds the style characteristics for the Android ActionBar UI element. Inside this style container will be an <item> child tag that defines a 75% grey hexadecimal color value for the android:background parameter, as shown in Figure 10-6.

Figure 10-6. Create custom ActionBar background color with 75% grey color value using Widget.Holo.ActionBar

Once this AppBaseTheme.ActionBar style has been defined, it can then be referenced from inside of the AppBaseTheme style using an <item> child tag named **android:actionBarStyle**, and referencing this AppBaseTheme.Actionbar style using the **@style/AppBaseTheme.ActionBar value**, as shown in the first <style> definition in Figure 10-6.

Also notice that I have added the xmlns:android parameter to the parent <resources> container tag, since the ADT New Android Application series of dialogs forgot to do so when our project was created. The XML markup to define the custom theme so far would look like the following:

```
<resources xmlns:android="http://schemas.android.com/apk/res/android">
 <style name="AppBaseTheme" parent="android:style/Theme.Holo">
    <item name="android:actionBarStyle">@style/AppBaseTheme.ActionBar</item>
```

```
</style>
<style name="AppBaseTheme.ActionBar" parent="android:style/Widget.Holo.ActionBar">
    <item name="android:background">#FF333333</item>
</style>
</resources>
```

Next let's take a look at the results of our new system UI theme design by using the **Run As ➤ Android Application** work process. As you can see here, in Figure 10-7, there's now enough of a visual offset (difference) between the Tabs UI elements and the ActionBar to give the top of your application a much more professional appearance.

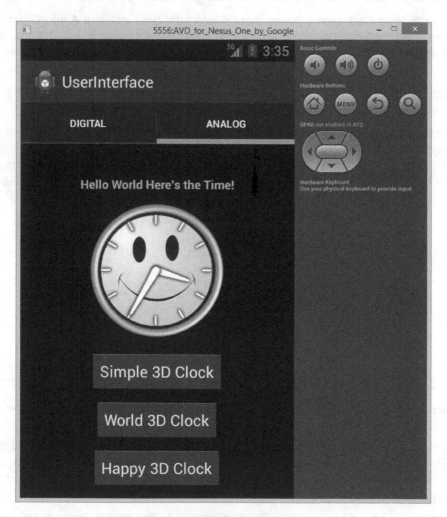

Figure 10-7. Testing the new custom Holo Dark Theme ActionBar in the Nexus One

Next, let's test the application theme and UI design in landscape mode, to make sure that the resource qualifier that we put in place in the previous chapter is still working, and see how our new Holo Dark and Grey ActionBar theme looks (and functions) in landscape mode. Use your **Ctrl-F11** keystroke combination to rotate the Nexus One emulator 90 degrees, which will put it into landscape mode.

As you can see in Figure 10-8, when in landscape mode, the Tab UI elements actually become a part of the ActionBar, which actually looks quite good.

Figure 10-8. Testing the custom Holo Dark Theme ActionBar in the Nexus One using the landscape orientation

Thus, our first custom UI theme modification looks good, and works well in both portrait and landscape orientations. Next I want to change the Title Text for the ActionBar to match the color of the application icon, maybe a bit lighter and a bit more orange or peach colored, which will look great against the dark grey color of the ActionBar. Let's add that to the theme in the next section, so you can see how to go one more style level deeper.

Customizing the Theme: Creating Red Title Text

Now I am going to add some detail refinement by changing the Title Text for the ActionBar to match the red application icon, so the two elements are "married" together a bit more. This is done using the **TextAppearance** style characteristic.

It is important to note that we're using these custom theme style upgrades to style Android system UI elements, such as the ActionBar and Title Text, which we cannot more easily style by using parameters in our XML UI layout container definitions

It is possible to define all your UI designs using this top level theme definition approach, however most Android developers will simply use theme modifications, such as you are learning about here to tweak the Holo themes for synergies between the application UI design and the Android OS design.

Let's add a style named **AppBaseStyle.ActionBar.TitleTextStyle**, and use the parent parameter to set its parent android:style referencing to point to: **android:style/TextAppearance.Holo.Widget .ActionBar.Title** which will set-up the style definition to allow us to add an <item> tag for our **textColor** UI modification, as seen in Figure 10-9, and in the following XML markup:

```
<style name="AppBaseTheme.ActionBar.TitleTextStyle" parent="android:style/TextAppearance.Holo.
Widget.ActionBar.Title">
    <item name="android:textColor">#FFEECCAA</item>
</style>
```

Figure 10-9. Create a TextTitleStyle with red textColor value using TextAppearance.Holo.Widget.ActionBar.Title

We'll reference this style definition inside the **AppBaseTheme.ActionBar** style definition, since the **TitleTextStyle** modification is a child element of an ActionBar parent OS UI element. This is done using the following XML markup, which adds a second <item> tag to the AppBaseTheme.ActionBar style:

```
<style name="AppBaseTheme.ActionBar" parent="android:style/Widget.Holo.Actionbar"
    <item name="android:background">#FF333333</item>
    <item name="android:titleTextStyle">@style/AppBaseTheme.ActionBar.TitleTextStyle</item>
</style>
```

Now we are ready to test our latest Holo Dark Theme UI modification in the Nexus One emulator, and see how the new ActionBar TitleText renders in conjunction with our current application UI design.

Use your **Run As ➤ Android Application** work process to launch your emulator and test the new modified theme definition in portrait and landscape modes by using the **Ctrl-F11** (landscape), and **Ctrl-F12** (portrait) keys, respectively.

As you can see in Figure 10-10, this new ActionBar TitleText UI element is easy to read and matches up well with the application icon on its left.

Figure 10-10. Testing the Holo Dark Theme ActionBar TextTitle in the Nexus One using a landscape orientation

Next we will take a look at how easy it is to define these custom themes for an individual activity in your application rather than applying them application-wide.

Applying an Activity-wide Theme: Using <activity> Tags

You can apply these same theme design principles from these previous two sections to your **<activity>** tag in your AndroidManifest XML file instead of, or even in addition to, the <application> tag in your AndroidManifest XML file.

The way that you would move this theme definition that you created in this chapter from the <application> level to the <activity> level, is simply to remove the **android:theme="@style/ AppTheme"** from the <application> tag, and put it inside of your <activity> tag after the android:label parameter. You can see this fairly clearly by looking at Figure 10-1, even though the android:theme parameter is inside the <application> tag.

This should be done if you have one Activity (section) of your application that needs to have a different theme than a standard Android OS UI theme. Otherwise, it would be wiser (and use less memory) to just have one high-level theme that is defined in the <application> level AndroidManifest XML file. Not only would this be more memory-efficient, but it also provides a more standard look and feel across your Android application.

Android Digital Image Formats: PNG8, PNG24, PNG32, JPEG, GIF, WebP

The Android OS supports a number of popular digital image formats, which I covered in Chapter 7 at an introductory or basic level and which I discuss in more detail here, as I wanted to cover digital imaging thoroughly in this chapter before we get into specific layout container classes in the rest of the book.

Some of these have been around forever, such as CompuServe's Graphics Information Format (GIF), or the Joint Photographic Experts Group (JPEG) format. Some of Android's graphics file formats are more modern, such as Portable Network Graphics (PNG, pronounced "ping") and WebP (Web Photo) developed by ON2 as part of VP8, and acquired, and then made open source by Google.

The oldest format, **CompuServe's GIF,** is partially supported by the Android OS, but is not recommended for use. A GIF is a **lossless** digital image file format, as it does not throw away image data to achieve better compression results like the JPEG format does. I say partially supported because aGIF, or animatedGIF format, is not supported in the Android OS currently.

This GIF compression algorithm is not as refined (not as powerful) as the PNG format, and it only supports **indexed** color, which we will be learning about in detail later in the chapter. However, if all your image assets are already created using GIF format, you can use them with no problems (other than less efficient compression) within your Android apps.

The next most popular digital image file format that Android will support is **JPEG**, which uses the **truecolor** color depth, instead of an indexed color depth. We'll be covering color theory and color depth in a future section.

JPEG is what is termed a **lossy** digital image file format. This is because it throws away image data in order to achieve a smaller file size, so that data is lost forever–unless you were smart and saved your original image!

If you magnify the JPEG image after compression, you will see a discolored area (effect) which clearly was not present in your original imagery. This degraded area or areas in the image are termed **compression artifacts** in the digital imaging industry. This only occurs in lossy image compression.

The recommended image format to use in Android is called a **PNG** or Portable Network Graphics file format. PNG has both an indexed color version, called **PNG8**, and a truecolor version, called **PNG24 or PNG32**. The PNG8, PNG24, and PNG32 (extensions) represent the **bit depth** of color support, which we will be getting into later on in this chapter when we talk about color theory.

The reason that PNG is the recommended format to use in Android is because it has good compression and because it's lossless. Thus PNG has both great image quality as well as reasonable levels of data compression efficiency.

The most recent image format added to Android OS is the **WebP** image format. This format is supported under Android 2.3.8 for image read, or playback, support, and in Android 4.0 or later for image write, or file saving support for use with camera hardware. WebP is the static version of the **WebM** video file format, also known in the industry as ON2's **VP8** codec. We'll be learning about **codecs** and **compression** in a future section.

Digital Image Resolution: Pixel Arrays and Aspect Ratios

A digital image is made up of a **2D**, or two-dimensional, array of **pixels**. The number of pixels in an image is expressed by its **resolution**, which is the number of pixels in an image's Width (W, also sometimes referred to as the X axis) and Height (H, also sometimes referred to as the Y axis) dimension.

To find the total number of image pixels, multiply the Width pixels by the Height pixels. For instance, a Wide VGA 800 by 480 image contains 384,000 pixels, which is 3/8ths of 1 megabyte.

The more pixels an image has, the higher its resolution. This is similar to how digital cameras work. The more megapixels in an image capture, the higher quality level that can be achieved.

Android supports resolutions ranging from low resolution 320 by 320 pixel smartwatch display screens or 320 by 480 entry-level smartphones to medium resolution 854 by 480 pixel display screens (mini-tablets, and mainstream smartphones), up to high resolution 1280 by 720 pixel display screens (HD smartphones and mid-level tablets), and extra high resolution 1920 by 1080 pixel display screens (large tablets and iTV sets). Recently 4K iTVs were introduced, which feature an amazing 4096 by 2160 wide IMAX resolution.

A more complicated specification of image resolution is the image's **aspect ratio**, a concept which also applies to Android device display screens.

Aspect ratio is a ratio of **width:height** or **W:H**, and will define how square or rectangular (also known as "widescreen") images or display screens are.

A 1:1 aspect ratio display (or image) is perfectly square, as is a 2:2, or a 3:3 aspect ratio image. It is the ratio between these two variables that defines a shape of the image or screen, not the actual numbers themselves.

Most Android screens have an **HDTV** aspect ratio, which is **16:9** and some are a little less wide, being a **16:10** (or 8:5 if you prefer) aspect ratio. Wider screens will also surely appear, so look for 16:8 (or 2:1, if you prefer) Ultra-Wide HDTV screens which have a 2160 by 1080 resolution LCD or OLED display.

An aspect ratio can also be expressed as the smallest pair of numbers that can be achieved (reduced) on either side of the aspect ratio colon. If you paid attention in math class, while you were learning about the lowest common denominator, then an aspect ratio will be very easy for you to calculate.

I usually do an aspect ratio calculation by continuing to divide each side of the colon by two. Thus, if you take the SXGA 1280x1024 resolution as an example, half of 1280x1024 is 640x512 and half of 640x512 is 320x256. Half of 320x256 is 160x128, half of that again is 80x64, half of that is 40x32, half of that is 20x16, half of that is 10x8, and half of that is 5x4. Thus, the 1280x1024 resolution uses a 5:4 aspect ratio.

Digital Image Color Values: Color Theory and Color Depth

Your color values for digital image pixels can be defined by the amount of three different colors, **red**, **green,** and **blue** (or **RGB**), which are present in different amounts in each pixel. Android display screens leverage **additive colors**, which is where wavelengths of light for each RGB **color channel** are summed together to create 16.8 million different color values.

Additive color utilized in LCD or OLED displays is the opposite of subtractive color used in printing. To show you the different results, under a subtractive color model, mixing red with green (inks) will yield a purplish color, whereas in an additive color model, mixing red with green (light) creates a vibrant yellow color.

There are **256 levels** of each RGB color for each pixel. This allows **8 bits** of brightness variation for each of these red, green, and blue values–from a minimum of zero (off, or dark, or black) to a maximum of 255 (full on or maximum color contributed). The number of bits that are used to represent color in the digital image is referred to as the **color depth** of the image.

Common color depths used in the digital imaging industry include 8-bit, 16-bit, 24-bit, 32-bit, 48-bit, and 64-bit. See Table 10-1 for the most common ones, along with their formats.

Table 10-1. Popular Digital Image Color Depths, their Terminology, and Popular Formats that Use Them

Bit-Depth	Terminology	Number of Colors	Used in these Digital Image File Formats
8-bit	Indexed Color	256	PNG8, GIF, BMP, TGA, TIFF
16-bit	HighColor	65,536	TGA, BMP
24-bit	TrueColor	16,777,216	PNG24, BMP, TIFF, TGA, PSD, JPEG, RAW
32-bit	Truecolor+Alpha	16M + 256 Alpha	PNG32, BMP, TIFF, TGA, PSD
64-bit	HDRI	16-bits per Channel	PSD, RAW

The lowest color depth exists in **8-bit indexed color** images, which feature **256** color values, and use the GIF and the PNG8 image formats to hold this indexed color type of digital image data.

A medium color depth image features a **16-bit** color depth and thus contains **65,536** colors (calculated as 256 times 256), and is supported in the TARGA (TGA) and Tagged Image File Format (TIFF) digital image formats.

It is important to note the Android OS does not support any of the 16-bit color depth digital image file formats (BMP, TGA, or TIFF) which I consider an oversight. Indeed, 16-bit color depth support would greatly enhance the developer's potential image data footprint optimization. Data optimization is a subject that we'll be covering a little bit later in the chapter.

A **truecolor** depth image features the **24-bit** color depth, and thus contains over 16 million colors. This is calculated as 256 times 256 times 256, and equals **16,777,216 colors**. File formats that support 24-bit color include JPEG (or JPG), PNG, BMP, XCF, PSD, TGA, TIFF, and WebP. Android OS supports four of these, JPG, PNG24 (24-bit) and PNG32 (32-bit), and WebP.

Using 24-bit color depth gives you the highest quality level, which is why Android prefers the use of a PNG24, PNG32, or a JPEG image file format.

Since PNG24 is lossless, it features a high-quality compression result, or in other terms, the lowest amount of original data lost. PNG24 also has the highest quality (truecolor) color depth and so PNG24 or PNG32 is Android's preferred digital image format to use, as it produces the highest quality. Next, let's take a look at how we represent transparency in a digital image!

Image Compositing: Alpha Channels and Blending Modes

In this section we'll take a look at image transparency via alpha channels and how they are used for **compositing** digital imagery. Compositing is the process of **blending** more than one **layer** of digital imagery.

Compositing is useful when you want to create an image on the display that appears as though it is one image, but is actually the seamless collection of more than one **composited** image **layer**. One of the principal reasons you would want to set up your image composite is to allow programmatic control over various elements in those images, by having them on different layers.

To accomplish this, we need to have an **alpha channel** (transparency) value that we can utilize to precisely control the **blending** of that pixel with the pixel (in that same location) on the other layers above and below it.

Like the other RGB channels, an alpha channel has **256 transparency levels**. In Java and XML programming, the alpha channel is represented by the first two slots in a hexadecimal representation for an **ARGB** data value, which we cover in detail in the next section. Alpha channel ARGB values feature **8 slots (32-bits)** of data, rather than the 6 slots used in a 24-bit image, which is really a 32-bit image with zero alpha channel data.

If there's no alpha channel data, make sure not to waste an 8-bit channel of data storage, even if it's filled with Fs (fully opaque pixel values, which essentially equate to saving unused alpha transparency values).

Thus, a 24-bit PNG24 image has no alpha channel, and will not be used for compositing, unless it's the **bottom plate** in your compositing layer stack. On the other hand, PNG32 images are used as **compositing layers** on top of something else, which need the ability to show through (via alpha channel transparency values) in some of your pixel locations in your image composite. We saw this in Chapter 7 when we created our AnalogClock.

How do image alpha channels and the concept of image compositing factor in to Pro Android UI Design? The primary advantage is the ability to break the UI design, and the graphics elements it includes, into a number of component layers. This is to apply Java programming logic to individual UI or graphic image elements to control parts of your UI designs that you could not otherwise individually control, were it one single UI design (and image).

There is another part of image compositing called **blending modes** that also factors heavily in professional image compositing capabilities. A blending mode in Android is applied by using the **Porter-Duff** class. The class gives Android developers most of those same compositing modes that Photoshop or GIMP may afford to digital imaging artisans. This makes Android a powerful image compositing engine, just as Photoshop CS is, and controllable at a fine level, using custom Java code. Some of Android's Porter-Duff blending modes include: ADD, SCREEN, OVERLAY, DARKEN, XOR, LIGHTEN, and MULTIPLY. Next, let's take a look at how we represent image color and alpha data in our code!

Represent Color or Alpha in Code: Hexadecimal Notation

So now we know what color depth and alpha channels are, and that color and transparency are represented by using a combination of four different red, green, blue, and alpha **image channels** within any given digital image. It is also important to understand how as programmers we're supposed to represent the four ARGB image color and transparency channel values in Java and in XML.

In the Android OS, color and alpha is not only used in 2D digital imagery, called **bitmap** imagery, but is also used in 2D illustration, termed **vector** imagery. Color and alpha values are also often used in **color settings,** for instance, for background color for the UI screen, or other color settings.

In Android different levels of ARGB color intensity values are represented using **hexadecimal notation**, which is based on the original **Base16** computer notation used long ago to represent 16 bits of data values. Unlike **Base10**, which counts from zero through 9, Base16 counts from zero through F, where F would represent a Base10 value of 15 (0-15 yields 16 data values).

A hexadecimal value in Android always starts with a **pound sign**, like this: **#FFFFFF.** This hexadecimal color value represents the color **White**, using no alpha channel. Each slot in a 24-bit hexadecimal representation represents one Base16 value, so to get the 256 values we need for each RGB color will take 2 slots, as 16 times 16 equals 256. Thus, for a 24-bit image we would need six slots after the pound sign to hold each of the six hexadecimal data values.

The hexadecimal data slots represent the RGB values in the following format: **#RRGGBB**; so, for the color White, all red, green, and blue **channels** in this hexadecimal color data value representation are at the maximum **luminosity**.

If you additively sum all these colors you'll get white light. As I have mentioned before, the color **Yellow** is represented by the red and green channels being on and the blue channel being off, so the hexadecimal representation would be **#FFFF00,** where both red and green channel slots are on (FF or 255), and blue channel slots are fully off (00 or a zero value).

The eight hexadecimal data slots for an **ARGB** value will thus hold data in the following format: **#AARRGGBB**. Thus for the color White, all alpha, red, green and blue **channels** in the hexadecimal color data value representation would be at their maximum **luminosity** (or opacity) and the alpha channel is fully opaque, that is, not transparent, as represented by an FF value, so, its hexadecimal value would be: **#FFFFFFFF**.

A 100% transparent alpha channel can be represented by an alpha slot being set to zero, thus, a fully transparent image pixel would be **#00FFFFFF**, or, **#00000000**. It is important to note that if the alpha channel values equate to full transparency, then color values in the other six (RGB) hexadecimal data value slots will not matter, because that pixel will be evaluated as not being there (composited in a final image or UI composite) whatsoever.

Digital Image and UI Masking: Alpha Channel UI Compositing

One of the primary applications for alpha channels in UI design is to **mask** out areas of an image or UI element so that it can be utilized in an image or UI design compositing scenario. **Masking** is a process of cutting subject matter out of an image, or making a portion of the UI element transparent, so that these can be placed onto their own virtual layer via alpha values.

This allows us to seamlessly meld our digital image assets and UI elements using virtual digital layering that is not detectable by our user base. This also extends to include digital media elements such as video or animation, which we'll be covering in greater detail later on in the book.

Digital image compositing software such as Photoshop and GIMP have many tools and features, which are specifically included for use in masking and image compositing. You can't really do effective image compositing without doing effective masking, so this is an important area to master for UI designers who want to integrate graphic elements, such as images and animation, into their UI designs. The art of masking has been around for a very long time!

Masking can be done for you automatically, using bluescreen or greenscreen backdrops and computer software that can automatically extract those exact color values to create a mask or an alpha channel (transparency). This can also be done manually (by hand) in digital imaging software using the **Selection** tool in conjunction with the **sharpening** and **blur** algorithms.

You'll learn a lot about this work process during this book, using popular open source software packages such as GIMP 2 and EditShare Lightworks 11. It is a complex and involved process, and thus must span a number of chapters instead of trying to fit it all in a single chapter in the book.

A key consideration in the masking process is getting smooth, sharp edges around the masked object, so that when you place it into a new background image, it looks like it was photographed there in the first place. The key to doing this lies in your **selection** work process, and using digital image software selection tools, such as the Scissors tool in GIMP, or the Magic Wand tool in Photoshop, in the proper way (a correct work process) is critical.

For instance, if there are areas of **uniform color** around your object that you want to mask (maybe you shot it against a bluescreen or a greenscreen) you could use a **magic wand tool** with a proper **threshold** setting to select everything except your object, and then **invert** that **selection set** to obtain a selection set containing the object. Oftentimes a correct work process involves approaching something in reverse.

Other selection tools contain complex algorithms, which can look at color changes between pixels. These can be very useful in **edge detection**, which we can use other types of selection tools to do. These tools allow us to drag our cursor along the edge of an object which we wish to mask while the tool's algorithm lays down a precise pixel-perfect placement of a selection edge.

Achieving Smooth Edges in a Design: Using Anti-Aliasing

Anti-aliasing is a popular digital image compositing technique, where two adjacent colors in a digital image that are on an **edge** between two areas of different color are blended together along that edge. This serves to make this edge look smoother (less jagged) when an image is zoomed out.

This "tricks" the viewer's eye into seeing a smoother edge, and gets rid of what has come to be called "image jaggies." Anti-aliasing provides an impressive result by using averaged color values between two different colors and using only a few colored pixels along those edges that need to be made smoother.

By averaged color values I mean some color range that is a portion of the way between the two colors that are colliding at an image's jagged edge.

Here is an example of this to show you what I am talking about. Look at Figure 10-11 and you will see that I created what appears to be a razor-sharp red circle on a yellow background. I zoomed into that circle's edge, and took another screenshot and placed this to the right of the zoomed out circle. This reveals a range of 7 orange anti-aliasing color values, between the red and yellow colors bordering each other at the edge of this circle.

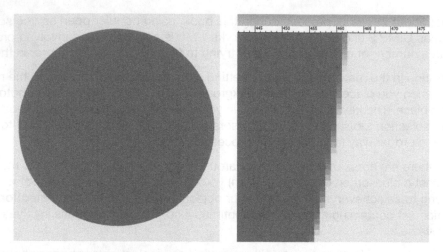

Figure 10-11. A red circle on a yellow background (left), and a zoomed in view (right) showing anti-aliasing

It is important to note that Android will anti-alias UI elements against your background colors and background imagery, but you'll be responsible for correctly compositing (and anti-aliasing) your multi-layered imagery!

Digital Image Optimization: Compression and Dithering

There are a number of factors that affect your **image compression**, and some basic techniques that you can use to achieve a better quality result with a smaller **data footprint**. This is a primary objective in optimized digital imagery; obtaining the smallest possible data footprint, while at the same time achieving the highest quality visual result.

We'll start with the aspects that most significantly affect data footprint—**resolution, color depth, dithering,** and **alpha channel**—and examine how each of them contributes to data footprint optimization of any given digital image. Interestingly, these are similar to the order of the digital imaging concepts that we have covered so far in the chapter.

Digital Image Resolution and Color Depth

The most critical contributor to a resulting file size, or data footprint, is the **number of pixels**, or the **resolution** of a digital image. This is logical because each of these pixels need to be stored, along with the color and alpha values for each of their channels. The smaller you can get the image resolution while still having it look sharp, the smaller its resulting file size will ultimately be.

Raw or uncompressed image size is calculated by **Width times Height times 3** for 24-bit **RBG** images, or possibly **Width times Height times 4** for a 32-bit **ARGB** image. Thus, an uncompressed truecolor 24-bit VGA image will have 640 times 480 times 3, equaling **921,600** bytes, of original uncompressed data.

To determine the number of **kilobytes** in this raw VGA image, you divide 921,600 by 1024, the number of bytes that are in a kilobyte, and this gives you an even **900KB of data in a truecolor VGA image**.

As you can see, image **color depth** is the next most critical contributor to the data footprint of an image, because the number of pixels in that image is multiplied by 1 (8-bit), or 2 (16-bit), or 3 (24-bit), or 4 (32-bit) color data channels. This is one of the reasons indexed color (8-bit) images are still widely used, especially using a **PNG8** image format, which features a superior lossless compression algorithm over what the GIF format utilizes.

Indexed color images can simulate truecolor images, if the colors that are used to make up the image do not vary too widely. Indexed color images use only 8-bits of data (256 colors) to define the image pixel colors, using a **palette** of 256 optimally selected colors instead of 3 RGB color channels.

Dithering

Depending on how many colors are used in any given image, using 256 colors to represent an image originally containing 16,777,216 colors can cause an effect called **banding**. This is where the transfer between adjoining colors isn't gradual (and thus doesn't look smooth). Indexed color images usually have an option to correct for this visually, called **dithering**.

Dithering is the algorithmic process of creating dot-patterns along those edges between any adjoining colors within an image, to trick the eye into thinking there is a third color used.

Dithering gives us a maximum perceptual amount of colors of 65,536 colors (256x256), but this will only happen if each of the 256 colors borders on one of the other (different) 256 colors. Still, you can see the potential for creating additional colors, and you would be amazed at the results an indexed color image can achieve in some scenarios (with certain imagery).

Let's take a truecolor image, such as the one that's shown in Figure 10-12, and save it as a PNG8 indexed color image to show you the dithering effect. We will take a look at this dithering effect, on the driver's side rear fender on the Audi 3D image, as it contains a gradient of gray color.

Figure 10-12. A truecolor image source which uses 16.8 million colors that we are going to optimize to PNG5

It is interesting to note that you can use less than the 256 maximum colors that can be used in an 8-bit indexed color image. This is often done to further reduce the image's data footprint. For instance, an image that can attain good results by using only 32 colors is actually a 5-bit image and would technically be called a **PNG5**, even though the format itself is generally called PNG8 for the indexed color usage level.

We will set the PNG8 image, shown in Figure 10-13, to use 5-bit color (32 colors), so that we can see this dithering effect clearly. As you can see, **dot patterns** are made between adjacent colors to create additional (perceived) colors.

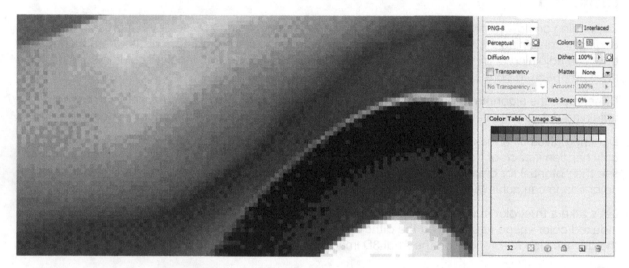

Figure 10-13. Showing the effect of dithering with an indexed color image compression setting of 32 colors (5-bit)

Also notice that you can set the **percentage of dithering** which is used. I often select either a 0% or 100% setting, but you can **fine-tune** dithering effects anywhere in between these two extreme values. You can also choose between dithering algorithms. I use **diffusion** dithering; it gives a smooth effect along irregularly shaped gradients, as is seen in the car fender.

Dithering, as you might imagine, adds **data patterns** that are more difficult to compress. Thus, dithering increases data footprint, by a few percentage points. Be sure to check on resulting file size with and without dithering applied, to see if it's worth the improved visual result which it affords.

Alpha Channel

The final concept that can increase the data footprint of your image is the alpha channel, as adding an alpha adds another 8-bit color channel (used to define the image's transparency) to the image being compressed.

However, if you need the alpha channel to define transparency to support future compositing needs using the image, there is not much choice but to include this alpha channel data. Just make sure not to use a 32-bit image format to contain a 24-bit image which has an empty alpha channel.

If an alpha channel contains all zeroes, which would define your image as being completely transparent, or contains all Fs, which would define your image as being completely opaque, you would essentially in practical use be defining an alpha which does not contain any useful alpha data values.

Finally, most alpha channels that are used to mask objects in your images should compress very well, as they are largely areas of white (opaque) and black (transparency), with some grey values along the edge between the two colors to **anti-alias** your mask. This provides the visually smooth edge transition between the object and any image that might be used behind it.

Since in an alpha channel image mask the 8-bit transparency gradient from white to black defines transparency, the grey values on the edges of each object in the mask will essentially average the colors of the object edge and its target background. This provides **real-time anti-aliasing** with any target background that might be used, including animated backgrounds.

Creating Our World Clock Image Asset: GIMP Compositing

Let's fire up our GIMP 2.8.10 software and create our other two AnalogClock image assets so that we can finish up what we started over the past couple of chapters and get it all working. Then we'll take a look at implementing size qualifier folders by compositing some different starfield backgrounds behind our AnalogClock UI design.

After GIMP launches, use the **File ➤ Open** menu to access the **planetclock480** PNG32 image asset, as shown in Figure 10-14 (look in the titlebar area).

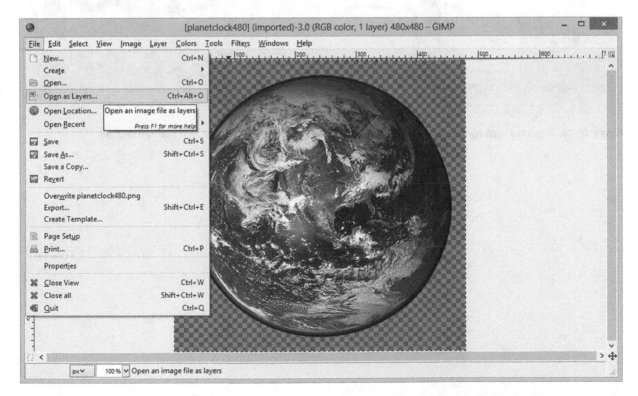

Figure 10-14. Open the planetclock480.png file, and use a File ➤ Open as Layers command to composite a hoop

To composite your 3D outer clock ring on top of this planet Earth image, use the **File ➤ Open as Layers** menu sequence, also shown in Figure 10-14. This adds a new layer on top of your planet Earth image. Use an Import dialog, which will appear once you select this menu option, to load the 32-bit **clockhoop480** PNG file into this second image compositing layer.

The resulting image composite can be seen on the left side of Figure 10-14 and needs to be changed to match the Earth image's primary coloration, so that it will be different from your Happy Face Clock UI design treatment.

Drop down the **Colors** menu, and click the **Hue-Saturation** menu item, to open the Hue-Saturation dialog shown in the center of Figure 10-14. Apply a **120** degree color shift using the Hue slider, and check the **Preview** checkbox so you can see the new purple hoop color as shown on the right side of Figure 10-15. Export this file as **worldclockhoop.png**, as shown in Figure 10-16.

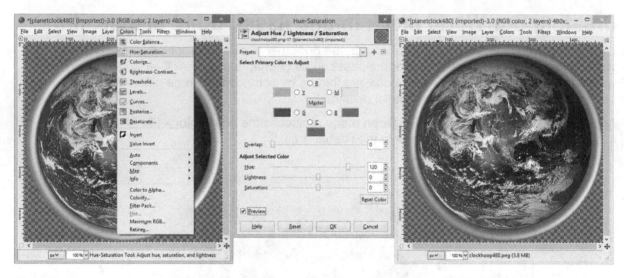

Figure 10-15. Imported hoop composite layer on left and using the Hue-Saturation to color shift hue 120 degrees

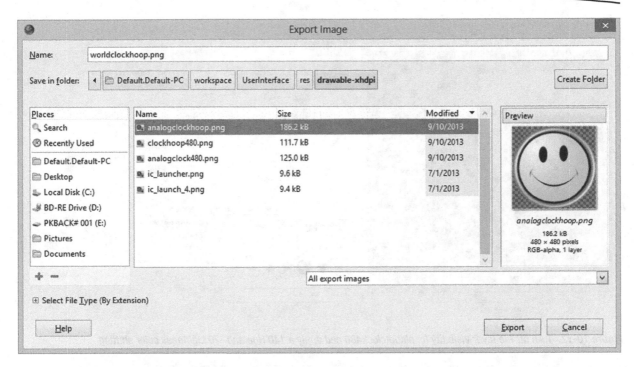

Figure 10-16. Use an Export ➤ Image menu sequence to access an Export Image dialog to save worldclockhoop.png

Next all we have to do is to create our third **SimpleClock** UI design, which will use a golden version of our hoop image asset, which we will create in the next section to craft a simple but effective third AnalogClock design.

Creating Our Golden Hoop Clock: Shifting the Hue in GIMP

To work just with the metal hoop composite layer, click the **eye icon** on the left side of your **planetclock480** layer, as is shown in Figure 10-17. This turns that layer's visibility off, leaving only the hoop image element visible.

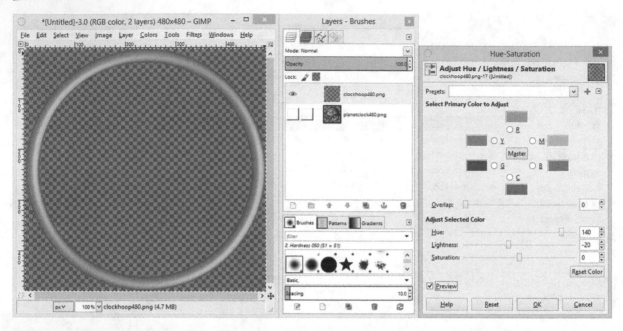

Figure 10-17. *Turn off the layer visibility for planetclock480 and apply a 140 Hue and -20 Lightness color shifting*

Again we need to use the **Colors ➤ Hue-Saturation** menu sequence to open the Hue-Saturation dialog, and shift the Hue slider **140** degrees further around the Hue circle, so that you have a nice bronze color. I also darkened this metal look a bit by using a **-20** value on the second **Lightness** slider.

It's important to note before we export our file to a new name placeholder (a new filename is needed, so we do not overwrite our worldclockhoop.png) that if you leave the visibility of the worldclock480 image layer off, you prevent that data from being saved into any file that you might export.

Let's use this fact to our advantage, and create two image assets, using a single work process here, by invoking the **File ➤ Export** menu sequence, and naming the PNG32 image asset **goldclockhoop. png** in the Export Image dialog, as shown in Figure 10-18. To save some typing in the dialog you can select the **worldclockhoop.png** (seen in blue) and replace the "world" with "gold."

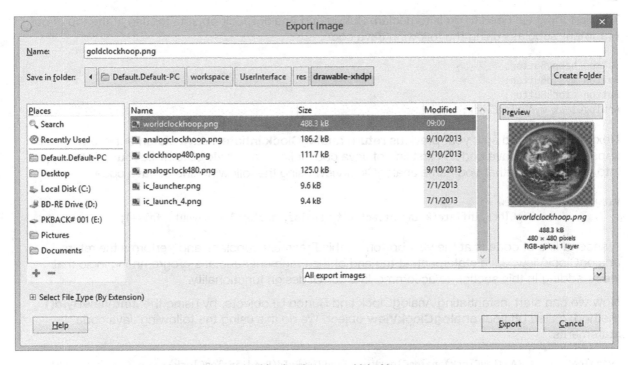

Figure 10-18. Selecting worldclockhoop.png and editing it to become goldclockhoop.png

Finally, if you wanted to be meticulous you could perform the work process that you learned in Chapter 7 and create an LDPI, MDPI, and HDPI resolution asset, so that Android OS does not have to scale down your 480 pixel XHDPI asset. If you want to skip all the extra work, that is fine as well, as these 480 pixel image assets we are using seem to scale quite effectively.

Next, we need to write the Java code which changes our AnalogClock UI look and feel (image background) with these different clock treatments when the user clicks on the appropriate button in the UI design.

Implementing AnalogClock UI in Java Code: Finishing Up!

To get all this work that we have done over the last couple of chapters to come together into something really useful, we will need to go into our analogClockFragment class and implement three Button UI elements, as well as the AnalogClock UI element. We need to do this so that we can use the Button UI elements to change our AnalogClock UI element's **background resource**, so that it points to all the different images that we created in the previous section of the chapter.

We will do this using the **.setBackgroundResource()** method call off our AnalogClock object, which we'll name **myAnalogClock** in our Java code.

Since you saved your images directly into your **/res/drawable-xhdpi** folder, you do not need to go into your file management utility and do any copying or pasting. Just make sure to right-click the project folder and select the **Refresh** tool if Eclipse was open while you performed the imaging work.

The first thing we need to do is to declare Button and AnalogClock objects for use at the top of our Fragment subclass using the following Java code:

```
Button happyButton;
Button worldButton;
Button clockButton;
AnalogClock myAnalogClock;
```

Next, you'll need to split your previous **return analogClock.inflate()** Java statement into two separate lines of Java code. A first line of Java code inflates an **analogClock LayoutInflater** object into a **View** object that you name analogClockView using the following line of Java code:

```
View analogClockView =
        analogClock.inflate(R.layout.activity_analog, analogClockLayout, false);
```

A second line of code is at the very bottom of this Fragment subclass and performs the return analogClockView; Java statement, at the end of the Fragment subclass programming logic that we're adding in this section to accommodate our UI design functionality.

Now we can start instantiating AnalogClock and Button UI objects, by using the **.findViewById()** method, called off your **analogClockView** object. We do this using the following Java code statements:

```
myAnalogClock = (AnalogClock)analogClockView.findViewById(R.id.analogClock);
happyButton = (Button)analogClockView.findViewById(R.id.happyClock);
```

Next add the event handling code to the happyButton UI element so that when it is clicked it will call the .setBackgroundResource() method off the myAnalogClock UI element, and then we can copy this structure two more times and create a worldButton and clockButton UI element Java code.

Event handling code for a happyButton UI element looks like the following:

```
happyButton.setOnClickListener(new View.OnClickListener() {
@Override
  public void onClick(View v) {
    myAnalogClock.setBackgroundResource(R.drawable.analogclockhoop);
  }
});
```

I clicked the myAnalogClock object in the code shown in Figure 10-19 to show the progression of the AnalogClock UI object from its declaration to its instantiation to its modification inside of the event handler code.

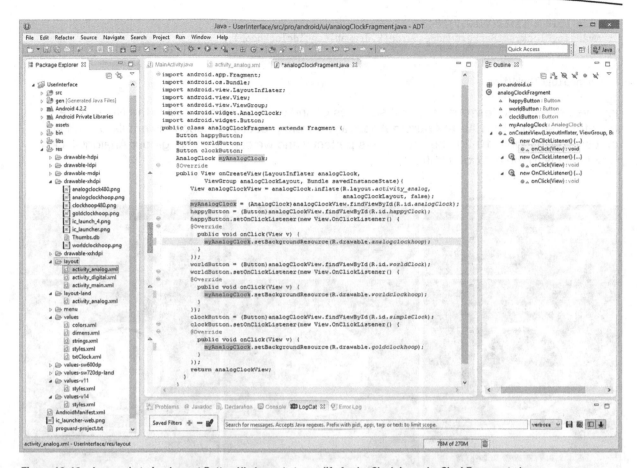

Figure 10-19. *Java code to implement Button UI elements to modify AnalogClock in analogClockFragment class*

To create your next two Button UI element Java constructs, copy and paste these happyButton instantiation and event handling code blocks two more times underneath the happyButton code, as is shown in Figure 10-19, and edit the "happyButton" to change it to "worldButton" and "clockButton."

Be sure to change your **R.id** references to **worldClock** and **simpleClock**, respectively, and your **R.drawawble** references to point to **worldClockHoop** and **goldClockHoop**, respectively. Your final code should look like this:

```
worldButton = (Button)analogClockView.findViewById(R.id.worldClock);
worldButton.setOnClickListener(new View.OnClickListener() {
@Override
  public void onClick(View v) {
    myAnalogClock.setBackgroundResource(R.drawable.worldclockhoop);
  }
});
clockButton = (Button)analogClockView.findViewById(R.id.simpleClock);
clockButton.setOnClickListener(new View.OnClickListener() {
@Override
```

```
public void onClick(View v) {
    myAnalogClock.setBackgroundResource(R.drawable.goldclockhoop);
  }
});
return analogClockView;
```

Now we are ready to test our Fragment subclass UI and event handling code in the Nexus One emulator. Use your **Run As ➤ Android Application** work process to launch the emulator, and as you can see in Figure 10-20, the code works perfectly and we can now change our AnalogClock's personality with the click of a button!

Figure 10-20. Testing all three AnalogClock UI Button elements in the Nexus One emulator using portrait mode

Next let's add a layout container background element and get into some UI compositing and use the smallestWidth resource qualifier to use different NASA space background images for some different resolution displays.

Screen Size Resource Qualifiers: An AnalogClock in Space

I have prepared three NASA public domain space images, which are legal for us to use for educational purposes. I saved these at three of the most popular smallestWidth device screen sizes: 480, 720, and 1080.

They include the three most popular resolutions across all Android devices, which include WVGA (Wide VGA or 800x480), Pseudo HD (1280x720), and True HD (1920x1080). These all scale down (or up, in the case of True HD on a 1920x1080 or an Ultra HD 4096x2160 screen) with great results based on the smallestWidth qualifiers, which we are about to implement in this section.

The first thing that we need to do is to copy the three plasma files into your project's **/res/drawable-xhdpi** folder, as is shown in Figure 10-21.

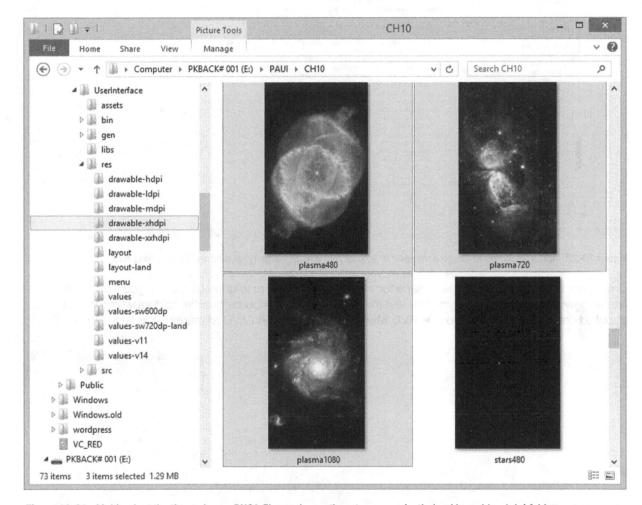

Figure 10-21. Multi-select the three plasma PNG8 files and copy them to your project's /res/drawable-xhdpi folder

Once you have done this, right-click your project folder, if Eclipse is open already, and use the **Refresh** menu option to let the IDE know that you have added image assets to your project folder hierarchy.

The first thing we need to do in the XML UI definitions in the **/res/layout** and **/res/layout-land** folders is to edit the <RelativeLayout> parent tag in each.

UI definition and add an **android:background** parameter that references the **plasma480** image asset, as shown in Figure 10-22.

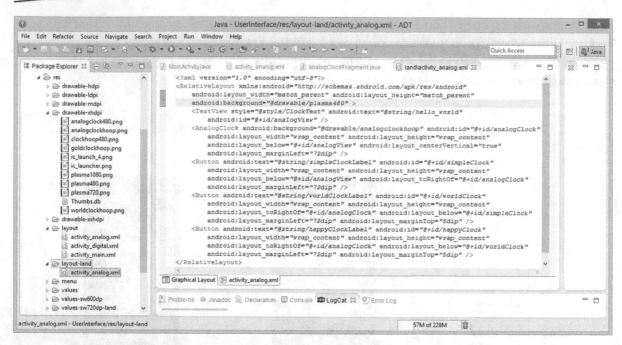

Figure 10-22. Add a background image parameter to both of your existing activity_analog.xml UI definition files

Once your background image is in place for your default (lower) resolution UI design, you'll be ready to create new AVD emulators so you can test the smallestWidth resource qualifier folders which we are about to create. Use the **Window ➤ AVD Manager** menu to open AVD Manager as seen in Figure 10-23.

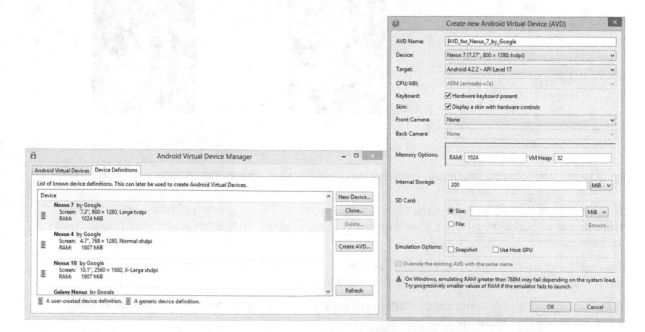

Figure 10-23. Use the Window ➤ AVD Manager menu to open an Android Virtual Device Manager to add devices

Click the **Create AVD** button, on the right of the AVD Manager dialog, which allows you to then create a **Nexus 7** AVD, once you click the **OK** button.

While you are in this dialog, create a number of AVDs for your UI testing. I created the Galaxy Nexus, Nexus 7 and 10, and 7-inch WSVGA tablet to add to my Nexus One AVD that I use as a default testing AVD, as you can see in Figure 10-24.

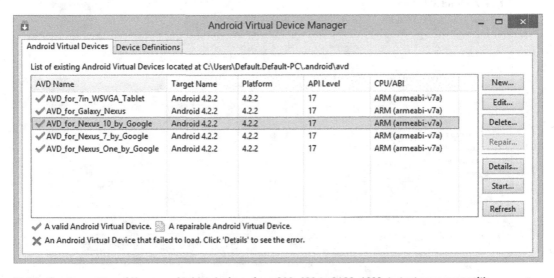

Figure 10-24.   Create a range of Nexus and tablet devices–from 800x480 to 2160x1200–to test your apps with

Next, we'll need to create the **/res/layout-sw720dp** and **/res/layout-sw600dp** folders to hold UI designs which feature higher resolution images. Use a **New ➤ Folder** menu command to access the dialog seen in Figure 10-25.

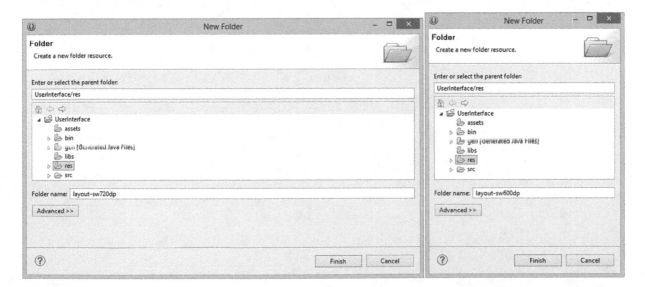

Figure 10-25.   Create a /res/layout-sw720dp and /res/layout-sw600dp folder using New ➤ Folder menu sequence

Next we need to populate these two folders with the activity_analog.xml UI definition files, so use your **New ➤ Android XML File** menu sequence to open the dialog shown in Figure 10-26 and create the files in both -sw folders.

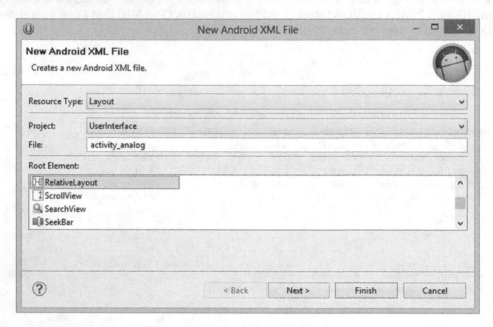

Figure 10-26. Create activity_analog.xml files for your two new layout folders

Now you can copy UI layout definitions into the new activity_analog files, editing resource referencing **720** and **1080** files, as shown in Figure 10-27.

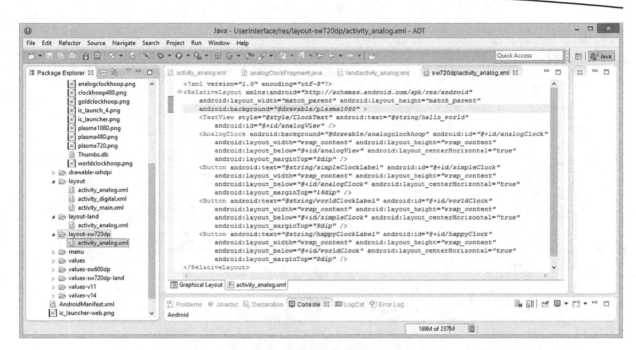

Figure 10-27. Add a plasma1080 image reference to sw720dp UI definition and plasma720 image to sw600dp UI

Notice that Figure 10-28 shows the **/res/layout-sw600dp/activity_analog.xml** file (and editing tab), and its **@drawable/plasma720** reference. Figure 10-28 also shows the **Run As ➤ Run Configurations** menu sequence that we will need to use next to change among all the different AVD emulators that we have installed previously.

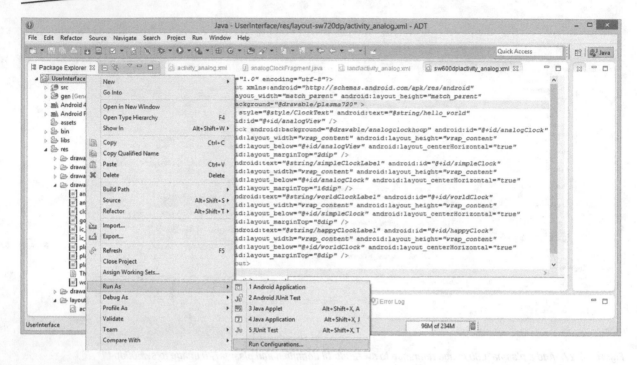

Figure 10-28. Use a Run As ➤ Run Configurations menu sequence to change your current AVD emulator setting

Before you switch AVD emulators you might want to use the **Run As ➤ Android Application** work process to make sure that the **plasma480.png** image file is being used for the default **/res/layout** UI definition's background imagery.

I included the Nexus One AVD emulator screenshot in Figure 10-30, so that you could see the comparison between these different AVD emulators and how different Android device screen sizes now utilize different plasma images!

As you can see in Figure 10-29, the **Run Configurations** dialog provides you with a complete control panel to use for controlling which AVD emulator is used in the Eclipse IDE at any given time during your development process.

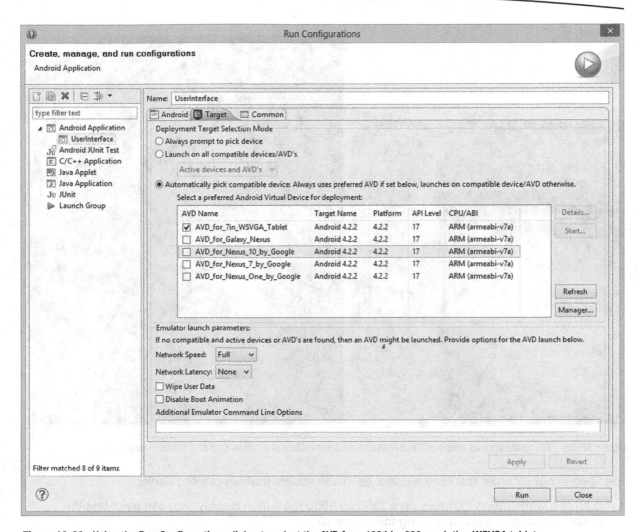

Figure 10-29. Using the Run Configurations dialog to select the AVD for a 1024 by 600 resolution WSVGA tablet

To select any of the installed AVD emulators simply place a check mark next to the emulator that you want to switch over to and click the **Apply** button at the bottom of the dialog to apply that new emulator selection.

The current emulator you are using is shown as checked until you apply a different emulator. There is also a convenient **Run** button that can be used to launch the new emulator from the dialog so that you do not have to exit the dialog and then use the **Run As ➤ Android Application** sequence.

Now we can select the **Nexus 7** AVD emulator, **Apply** it, and **Run** it using this dialog, and see how the smallestWidth resource qualifiers will choose your XML definition that uses a different space image for higher resolution UI screen design.

As you can see in Figure 10-30, when we run this application in the Nexus One emulator our application uses the background image with the 800x480 resolution, and when we run this application in the Nexus 7 emulator the application uses the background image with the 1280x720 resolution, as

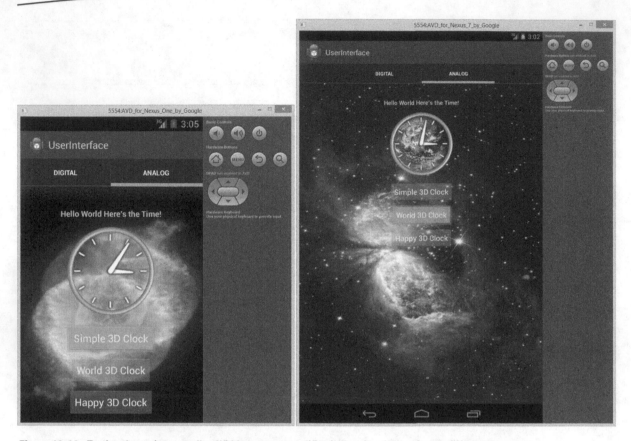

Figure 10-30. Testing the various smallestWidth resource qualifier folders in a Nexus One and Nexus 7 emulator

specified in our different resource qualifier definition folders that we created earlier.

If you have a workstation that runs on a 2560 by 1600 resolution display, you can even test the smallestWidth resource qualifier using the Nexus 10.

Summary

In this chapter, we took a closer look at Android UI **themes**, digital **imaging concepts**, and actually implemented **size-based resource qualifiers**.

I wanted to get all these foundational UI design concepts regarding themes and digital imaging covered before we started learning about the different UI layout container classes in Android. I also wanted to finish coding the AnalogClock Fragment subclass we've been coding, so that it's working, has an attractive look and feel, and implements an image compositing pipeline.

In the next chapter we will start learning about the different ViewGroup layout container subclasses, starting with the most basic UI container, the **FrameLayout** container. We will also delve into digital video.

Part 4

Basic Android UI Design: Basic Layout Containers: FrameLayout, LinearLayout, RelativeLayout and GridLayout

Android's FrameLayout Class: Using Digital Video in Your UI Design

Now that we've covered all the foundational Android UI classes such as View (widgets), ViewGroup (layout containers), and ActionBar (System UI), we can commence covering core Android layout container classes for the rest of the book. These provide the foundation for Pro Android UI design.

The most basic layout container in Android is the **FrameLayout** container class, which is usually used to contain one UI element. This could be a digital image, using the ImageView class, or more likely a digital video, using the VideoView class, which we will be learning about in this chapter.

A FrameLayout can also be used to hold more advanced graphics-related code constructs, such as Android's Canvas class. A Canvas object could possibly be used to hold real-time interactive gameplay action, or OpenGL ES 3.0 real-time interactive 3D, or i3D, rendering pipeline results.

Since we covered Digital Image concepts in depth in your previous chapter, it's also logical for us to build upon this knowledge and take it into the fourth dimension (time). Since that material is fresh in your minds, we'll immediately cover advanced digital video concepts in depth in this chapter.

We will learn how Android scales both imagery and videos, and how to keep your aspect ratio locked for that scaling operation, and how to scale asymmetrically, or with image aspect ratio unlocked. Since this can distort some visual elements, it is important to cover, and since a FrameLayout UI container keeps aspect ratio locked when scaling the content that's inside it, this is a good chapter to cover those topics in as well. We will learn about the FrameLayout and its nested classes first, and then we'll create one!

Android's FrameLayout Class: Framing Individual Content

The Android **FrameLayout** class is the most basic layout container class of all the Android UI layout classes. The FrameLayout is usually utilized to contain one single UI widget containing some sort of new media content.

An example of this would be a **VideoView**, containing MPEG-4 digital video, or some sort of interactive **SurfaceView**, such as a **Canvas** holding a game.

This FrameLayout class is a **public class** that extends the **ViewGroup** super class, which is the master "blueprint" class that is used to create layout container subclasses in Android. These layout container subclasses are the UI layout classes that we are going to be covering in detail over the next eight chapters in this book, so you're going to be well-versed in layouts!

The FrameLayout class hierarchy, starting with the Java language's Object "master class" and progressing down from View to ViewGroup to FrameLayout, would be structured like this:

```
java.lang.Object
 > android.view.View
   > android.view.ViewGroup
     > android.widget.FrameLayout
```

The FrameLayout class was designed by Android OS developers to specify the area on a display screen that is intended to display one single item. This is why it's named using "frame" as typically a frame holds a single image.

For this reason the FrameLayout should be used to hold a single child View object, because it is the simplest of the Android layout classes, and does not have a lot of methods defined that give it a lot of layout positioning attributes or parameters. This also makes the class very memory efficient.

Using multiple "child" View objects inside a FrameLayout container makes it difficult to accurately position these child View UI objects, that is, the nested UI layout containers or widgets, in a way that is correctly scalable across many different screen sizes, shapes, and orientations.

What happens when you attempt to use the FrameLayout to organize multiple UI elements is that you see a high occurrence of UI elements overlapping each other, which is not the professional result that you seek for your UI design. The only way, in fact, to control positioning of child View object instances within a FrameLayout UI container is by assigning a "**gravity**" to each child View object. This is done by utilizing an **android:layout_gravity** parameter, or attribute, inside each View in your XML UI definition file.

The **gravity** UI design feature does not allow developers to do any of their own (pixel-precise) positioning, and basically allows the Android OS to do all your UI design positioning, so that your UI design can be scaled to fit all the different Android device screen sizes and orientations. The gravity parameter is supplied by a nested class **FrameLayout.LayoutParams**.

We cover this nested class in the next section of this chapter.

If any child View objects overlap, they will be drawn using a specified **z-order**, onto a virtual layer "**stack**," with the most recently added child on top. So the first UI elements added to the FrameLayout container have a z-order value starting with zero and are on the bottom of the stack, and subsequently added child elements will add one to the previous element z-order value for each UI element added to the FrameLayout container.

The physical size in pixels of your FrameLayout UI design on a screen will be the size of your largest child View object, plus any **padding**. This is true whether your View objects are set to be **VISIBLE** or **INVISIBLE**. If a View is set using the **GONE** visibility constant, it will not be calculated, unless the **ConsiderGoneChildrenWhenMeasuring** constant is set to true.

Since it is such a basic class, the FrameLayout class can also be utilized for creating other more specialized UI-related classes. The classes that you create by subclassing the FrameLayout class would be known as **direct subclasses**. of the FrameLayout. If you use this FrameLayout class to create another subclass, the FrameLayout class becomes a superclass.

Some of the already known direct subclasses of FrameLayout, that is, the FrameLayout subclasses which have already been coded for you and added as permanent members of the official Android API, include: MediaController, CalendarView, DatePicker, TabHost, ScrollView, TimePicker, ViewAnimator, HorizontalScrollView, GestureOverlayView, and the AppWidgetHostView classes.

> **Note** This FrameLayout class also has several known **indirect subclasses**, which are part of the Android UI API as well. These include the FragmentTabHost, ImageSwitcher, TextSwitcher, ViewFlipper, and the ViewSwitcher classes. Although not discussed in this chapter, I mention these in case you happen to encounter them at a later time.

The FrameLayout.LayoutParams Nested Class: Gravity

The FrameLayout.LayoutParams class is actually a **nested class** that extends the **ViewGroup. MarginLayoutParams** nested class, which, in turn, extends the **ViewGroup.LayoutParams** nested class, which was originally coded (using the Object class) to create layout parameters for all ViewGroup subclasses.

These layout parameter nested classes are what provide layout parameters for your UI designs, which are often created using XML, as we will see a bit later in this chapter when we create a FrameLayout, containing our VideoView UI element and its MediaController transport UI control element.

The FrameLayout.LayoutParams class hierarchy, which starts out with a Java Object and progresses down the class hierarchy from ViewGroup.LayoutParams to FrameLayout.MarginLayoutParams, would thus be structured like this:

```
java.lang.Object
  > android.view.ViewGroup.LayoutParams
    > android.view.ViewGroup.MarginLayoutParams
      > android.widget.FrameLayout.LayoutParams
```

A FrameLayout.LayoutParams class inherits all ViewGroup.LayoutParams, as well as all ViewGroup. MarginLayoutParams (margin parameters). This class also adds in the **layout_gravity** parameter and its **constants**, which we are going to cover in detail in this section, since these constants are specifically intended to be used with the FrameLayout UI container and layout_gravity. The gravity constants are shown in Table 11-1, along with their intended functionality.

Table 11-1. The android:layout_gravity Constants Defined by the Nested Class FrameLayout.LayoutParams

Gravity Constant	Functionality Specified by Using Gravity Constant
top	Aligns UI element to or at the TOP of a FrameLayout container
bottom	Aligns UI element to or at the BOTTOM of a FrameLayout container
left	Aligns UI element to or at the LEFT of a FrameLayout container
right	Aligns UI element to or at the RIGHT of a FrameLayout container
center_vertical	Centers the UI element (or UI layout container) vertically
center_horizontal	Centers the UI element (or UI layout container) horizontally
center	Aligns UI element to or at the CENTER of a FrameLayout container
fill_vertical	Scales UI element (or layout container) to fill Frame vertically
fill_horizontal	Scale UI element (or layout container) to fill Frame horizontally
fill	Scales UI element to FILL the FrameLayout container
clip_vertical	Clips the top and bottom edges of the UI element for FrameLayout
clip_horizontal	Clips the left and right edges of the UI element for FrameLayout
start	Aligns UI element to or at the START of the FrameLayout container
end	Aligns UI element to or at the END of the FrameLayout container

The most commonly seen gravity constant used with a FrameLayout container is **fill**, as one usually wants content or UI elements, such as a VideoView, to be displayed "full screen." Your second most often used constant would be **center**, which is similar to fill but does not scale the content; rather centers the content or UI element (the child View object) in the display.

There are also constants provided to fill or center your UI widget(s) or a nested UI layout container in only the **horizontal (X)** or the **vertical (Y)** dimensions. These are fill_vertical and fill_horizontal and the center_vertical and center_horizontal constants, which allow you to fine-tune how Android positions the UI design in the FrameLayout container.

There are also two advanced constants, **clip_horizontal** and **clip_vertical**, which clip, that is, remove a portion of your UI element or content, in either the vertical (Y) or the horizontal (X) axis.

In digital imaging, this operation is known as "cropping," and instead of scaling your content or UI design to fit any given screen dimension, these clipping constants instead remove (clip away) parts of the content or design to make it fit the new screen size and dimensions.

The **start** and **end** constants can be used to accommodate both **RTL** and **LTR** UI layouts, and would be used when there are more than one child View object (multiple UI widgets or nested ViewGroup layout containers), similar to the way you would use the top, bottom, left, and right constants to pin UI elements or layout containers to the sides of the FrameLayout (display).

These RTL (Right To Left) and LTR (Left To Right) layout constants were recently added in Android 4.2 to allow languages which are read starting on the right side of the screen and moving to the left.

UI designs must also be able to accommodate this directional change, and thus the start and end constants were added to allow UI design constants that will work under both the LTR and RTL screen design directions. The value of the start and end constants will reverse depending on whether a RTL or a LTR screen direction is being used by the user (language).

Before we get into Java coding and XML markup to implement a FrameLayout and Video Player in our UserInterface Android application, I want to discuss the VideoView and MediaPlayer related classes in detail so that you have the foundational knowledge about how all these classes work.

After that, we can implement this knowledge and code a UI design that features a FrameLayout and VideoView, and then we will take some time to learn about digital video concepts, and create video using the Terragen 3.0 virtual world creation software package.

Android's VideoView Class: Using Digital Video in a Frame

The Android **VideoView** layout container class is a direct subclass of the Android **SurfaceView** class, which is a direct subclass of the Android **View** class, which is the direct subclass of the **java. lang.Object master** class.

The SurfaceView superclass (View subclass) is similar to the FrameLayout (ViewGroup subclass) in as much as it is intended to provide a class for creating View widgets that are used for one purpose. In the case of the VideoView subclass this is usually playing digital video content. The Android VideoView class hierarchy is therefore structured as follows:

```
java.lang.Object
  > android.view.View
    > android.view.SurfaceView
      > android.widget.VideoView
```

Android's VideoView class is stored in the **android.widget** package, making a VideoView a user interface element, also known as a UI widget. For this reason, your **import statement** for using the VideoView class in an Android application would reference **android.widget.VideoView** as its package path.

This VideoView class is a **public** class and has some two dozen method calls and callbacks that one might think of as being part of a MediaPlayer class but which are actually coded as methods in the VideoView class. Ultimately these two classes are inexorably bound together, and we will see precisely how these two important Android classes intertwine during this chapter.

We'll take a quick look here at some of these more useful method calls for video playback, so that you are familiar with them, in case that you need to implement any of the extended digital video features in your own video playback applications. Then in the next section we'll go over the Android VideoView digital video playback lifecycle, and see just how all these different video playback **states** fit together.

The simplest VideoView method calls include: **.pause()**, **.resume()**, **.stop()**, **.start()**, **.suspend()**, and **.stopPlayback()**. There's a **.setVideoURI()** and a **.setMediaController()** method call, as well as a **.setVideoPath()** method call that accomplishes much of the same end-result as the .setVideoURI() call.

There are four .get() method calls, **.getDuration()**, **.getCurrentPosition()**, **.getBufferPercentage()**, and **.getAudioSessionId()**, as well as an **.isPlaying()** method call to see whether the video is playing back currently. There are also three .can() method calls that ascertain what the VideoView can do via the MediaPlayer class: **.canPause()**, **.canSeekBackward()**, and **.canSeekForward()**.

There are also standard event handler method calls that are inherited from Android's View superclass. These include the **.onTouchEvent()**, **onKeyDown()**, and the **onTrackballEvent()** method calls.

Finally, there are specialized method calls, such as **.resolveAdjustedSize()** or **.onInitializeAccessibilityEvent()**, that are included to allow developers to implement accessibility standards if needed for their video playback code.

An Android Video Lifecycle: Eight Video Playback Stages

Before you start working with all the digital video classes in Android, or learn about digital video concepts and create digital video assets, you really should first understand the different stages that a digital video asset goes through inside the Android operating system. Playing digital video might seem simple from an end-user perspective: Play, Pause, Rewind, Stop, and similar basic transport functions. All these are involved in the overall video playback process or lifecycle; however, there are additional "under the hood" stages that allow the Android OS to load the video asset into memory, or to set parameters for playback, or other more system-level considerations. These unseen stages allow a developer to create an optimal user experience, and give a developer a wider variety of playback options.

When you implement your VideoView UI element, you are also instantiating a MediaPlayer object, even though you don't have to explicitly write any XML markup, or Java code, to create this MediaPlayer object. This MediaPlayer object, essentially the video playback engine, plays the digital video asset associated with your VideoView UI element using a **URI** object and the digital video asset (location) reference which the URI object contains. We will cover the URI class and the MediaPlayer class in the next sections of this chapter. The eight video playback states can be seen in Table 11-2.

Table 11-2. Video Playback States and How these Affect the Android MediaPlayer Object and Its Video Playback

Video Playback State	What is happening with the MediaPlayer object (video playback)
Idle State	MediaPlayer object is instantiated and ready for configuration
Initialized State	MediaPlayer object is initialized with data path, using a URI
Prepared State	MediaPlayer object is configured, or "prepared," for playback
Started State	MediaPlayer object is started and is decoding the video stream
Paused State	MediaPlayer object is paused and stops decoding video frames
Stopped State	MediaPlayer object is stopped and stops decoding video frames
Playback Completed	MediaPlayer object is finished decoding the video data stream
Ended State	MediaPlayer object is ended and removed from system memory

When a MediaPlayer object is first instantiated, it's not doing anything; thus, the MediaPlayer object would be in what is termed its **Idle state**.

Once you load your MediaPlayer object with a data reference using the **URI** object, via the **Uri. parse()** method call or **.setDataSource()** method call, the MediaPlayer object will enter what is termed its **Initialized state**.

There is an intermediary state, between the **Initialized** MediaPlayer object state and a **Started** MediaPlayer object state called a **Prepared** MediaPlayer object state. This state is accessed using **MediaPlayer.OnPreparedListener**, a **nested class** that we will be learning about in the next section of this chapter, and that we will be using inside our application's Java code.

Once a MediaPlayer object has been Initialized and loaded with video data, it can be **prepared** or **configured** for use, and then it can then be Started.

Once **Started** and playing, it can be **Stopped** using the **.stop()** method call, or **Paused** using the **.pause()** method call. These three video states should be the most familiar to users of digital video as they are the three major buttons that are found on the **video transport bar**, which in the Android OS is provided by the **MediaController** class. We will also be taking a look at this video-related UI class a little bit later on in this chapter as well.

Your final MediaPlayer object video playback state is a **Playback Completed** state. When you reach this state it means that the video asset has stopped playing, unless you have invoked a **.setLooping(true)** method, called off the MediaPlayer object. In this use-case, your digital video continues to loop seamlessly forever, until you call the **.stop()** method to stop it.

There are **.start()** and **.reset()** method calls available for the MediaPlayer object that can **start** and **reset** the MediaPlayer object at any time, based on any needs in your Java programming logic. Finally, there's a **.release()** method call, which invokes the **End state** for the MediaPlayer object, which will terminate your MediaPlayer object, **removing it from system memory**.

As you will see in the next section, there are other **nested classes** that also allow you to "listen" for errors (**MediaPlayer.OnErrorListener**), as well as for other states of the MediaPlayer, such as when it reaches a **Playback Completed** state (**MediaPlayer.OnCompletionListener**).

Android's MediaPlayer Class: The Video Playback Engine

The Android **MediaPlayer** class is a direct subclass of the **java.lang.Object** master class. This indicates that Android's MediaPlayer class was designed for creating **MediaPlayer** objects. MediaPlayer is a part of the VideoView widget, as the MediaPlayer class provides a **playback engine**.

Android's MediaPlayer class hierarchy is therefore structured as follows:

```
java.lang.Object
  > android.media.MediaPlayer
```

The MediaPlayer class belongs to the **android.media** package. Therefore, the **import statement** for using a MediaPlayer class in your app would reference the **android.media.MediaPlayer** package, as you will soon see in this book.

The MediaPlayer class is a **public** class, and features **nine nested classes**. Eight of these nested classes offer **callbacks**, for determining information regarding how a MediaPlayer video playback engine is currently operating.

A ninth nested class, the **MediaPlayer.TrackInfo** nested class, is utilized to return video, audio, or sub-title **track metadata** information.

A callback that we'll be implementing later on in the chapter will be the **MediaPlayer. OnPreparedListener,** which allows us to configure a MediaPlayer object before playback starts the first time. Other often called callbacks include the **MediaPlayer.OnErrorListener,** which can respond to or handle error messages, and the **MediaPlayer.OnCompletionListener**, which can be used to run other Java statements once your video asset playback is completed.

There's also a **MediaPlayer.OnSeekCompletedListener**, which can be called on when a **seek operation** is detected, and a **MediaPlayer.OnBufferingUpdateListener**, which is called to obtain **data buffering status** for a video asset that is being streamed over a network.

There are also a couple of more obscure MediaPlayer nested classes, such as the **MediaPlayer. OnTimedTextListener,** which is used when **timed text** becomes available for display on-screen, and **MediaPlayer.OnInfoListener**, which can be used when **information** or **warnings** regarding your video media being used become available for display. These nested classes aren't used very often, as far as I can tell, but they are available if they're ever needed.

Before we start implementing our FrameLayout UI container with a VideoView widget and MediaPlayer and MediaController object instances, I want to give an overview of the MediaController class, so you know how it fits into the equation of VideoView + MediaPlayer = DigitalVideo! Let's look at this now.

The MediaController Class: Controlling Video Playback

The Android **MediaController** class is a direct subclass of the **FrameLayout** class, which is why it is important to cover it in this chapter. This is also why we use a VideoView as our UI element of choice in showing how a FrameLayout can be utilized to do something impressive for your UI apps.

The Android MediaPlayer class was designed to create the UI that displays **transport controls** for the **MediaPlayer** object that powers the VideoView UI widget.

The Android MediaController class hierarchy is thus structured as follows:

```
java.lang.Object
  > android.view.View
    > android.view.ViewGroup
      > android.widget.FrameLayout
        > android.widget.MediaController
```

This MediaController class belongs in the **android.widget** package; for this reason, the **import statement** for using a MediaController class in your app should reference the **android.widget. MediaController** package.

The MediaController object is a UI element (View widget) that contains the digital video transport controls for controlling the playback cycle of the VideoView object's MediaPlayer object. The MediaController UI element contains buttons with symbols on them indicating features such as Rewind, Play, Pause, and Seek Forward, as well as a progress slider.

A MediaController object handles the synchronization with the transport UI controls that appear on top of a VideoView. These transport controls will ultimately control the states of the MediaPlayer object that we learned about earlier in this chapter.

The MediaController class is a **public** class and features **one nested class**. The nested class is an interface called MediaController.MediaPlayerControl and provides the MediaController class's video transport control methods, which are listed in Table 11-3 for your convenience.

Table 11-3. MediaController.MediaPlayerControl Nested Class Method Names and their Corresponding Functions

Method Name	Method Function
.start()	Starts digital video asset Playback
.isPlaying()	Determines whether digital video is currently playing
.pause()	Pauses digital video asset Playback
.canPause()	Determines whether digital video can be paused
.seekTo()	Allows video to be shuttled to a certain point in the video
.getCurrentPosition()	Determines the current location point in the digital video
.getDuration()	Determines the total length of the digital video asset
.getBufferPercentage()	Determines the percentage of the video that has been streamed
.getAudioSessionId()	Determines an Audio Session Id for the MediaPlayer being used
.canSeekForward()	Determines whether the video is capable of forward seek shuttling
.canSeekBackward()	Determines whether the video is capable of backward seek shuttling

The way to implement this class in your application is to use Java code to instantiate a MediaController object programmatically. A MediaController UI element can currently be created using XML markup, in a UI definition, but if you create it this way, functions such as .show() and .hide() will have no effect, so I am going to show you how to create a MediaController using Java code, which is the more advanced and comprehensive way to create it.

This MediaController object creates a standard Android video transport control set that matches the current OS UI Theme, and puts it in a window (a floating bar UI element) below your VideoView and its video content.

You have control (by using your Java code) over where these transport controls are located. Developers can specify a View object that these transport controls will appear below by using the **.setAnchorView()** method.

The video transport control bar UI will vanish if it's left unutilized for more than **three seconds**, and will reappear after the user touches the View object that has been defined using the .setAnchorView() method call.

The MediaController object will hide and show transport buttons according to the following Java programming rules:

- The **previous** and **next** buttons will remain hidden until the **.setPrevNextListeners()** method is called

- The **previous** and **next** buttons remain visible but disabled if the **.setPrevNextListeners()** method was called with null listeners

- The **rewind** and **seek forward** buttons will always be shown, unless the **MediaController(Context, boolean)** constructor uses a boolean set to false

Now that we've reviewed all the various classes that we will be utilizing in the chapter, it's time to start coding and learning about digital video concepts and software. We've lots to do to achieve this; let's get to it!

A UserInterface App SplashScreen: Using a FrameLayout

Let's take your UserInterface Android application back to "square one" for the remainder of the book, so that we can rebuild our UserInterface app so it has one Activity subclass for each of the Android ViewGroup layout container classes that we are going to cover from here on out in this book (one ViewGroup subclass per chapter).

We'll implement the OptionsMenu class in Chapter 12, which will access our different layout container Activity subclasses during the remainder of the book. We'll use a FrameLayout container and a VideoView UI widget for your homescreen, splashscreen, or app intro screen, so there's a cool intro!

The first thing that we will want to do in our MainActivity.java code base is to delete the ActionBar and Fragment related code so that we're back to a basic bootstrap application shell, using the **onCreate()** method.

Inside the standard onCreate() method we will call the superclass using the **super.onCreate()** method call. Then we'll use a **setContentView()** method call, referencing your new **activity_main. xml** user interface XML definition file. This UI definition file currently defines the AnalogClock UI design, which we are going to modify (or transmute) into a digital video asset UI. We'll do this next, after we finish modifying our Java programming logic.

In case you are wondering why you are reverting your MainActivity.java code to the minimum bootstrap of code that is required to get an Activity subclass to run, it is because I wanted you all to focus solely on how to define the FrameLayout, VideoView, and MediaController structure.

We'll start this process inside the main_activity.xml UI definition and build the support for digital video on the application's splashscreen from the ground up. This allows you to focus solely on the complexities of using the VideoView and MediaController classes.

As you can see in Figure 11-1, this is the minimum Java code needed to be able to place a UI design on the application homescreen or splashscreen. We will add the OptionsMenu code in Chapter 12 when we need to access the other UI layout container design Activity subclasses.

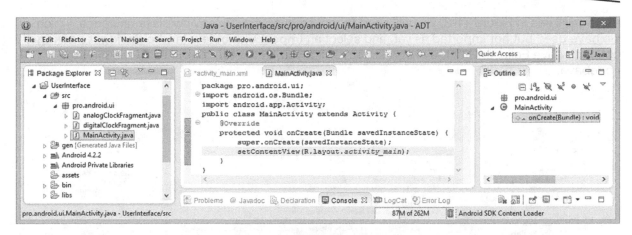

Figure 11-1. Reverting the MainActivity.java file to the minimum bootstrap Java code to build our intro video

Next, we need to open your activity_main.xml XML UI definition, and change the <RelativeLayout> parent tag to be a <FrameLayout> parent tag, as well as change the first <TextView> child UI element to be a <VideoView> child UI element. Delete the <AnalogClock> and <Button> child tags as they are not needed. Change your **android:id** parameter for the <FrameLayout> tag to **frameLayout,** and your android:id parameter for your <VideoView> tag to **videoView**, as is shown in Figure 11-2.

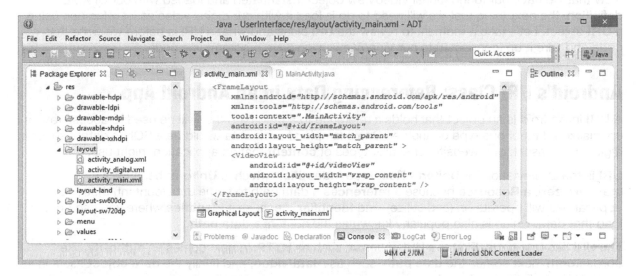

Figure 11-2. Change the activity_main.xml <RelativeLayout> container into a <FrameLayout> and <VideoView>

Now we can go back into our Java code and instantiate our VideoView object and name it **introVideo** and reference it to the VideoView XML UI definition with the findViewById method using the following single line of Java code:

```
VideoView introVideo = (VideoView) findViewById(R.id.videoView);
```

As you will see in Figure 11-3, you will need to mouse-over your VideoView class reference, which we have used but not imported as yet, and select an **Import VideoView (android.widget package)** option to have Eclipse write the Import statement for you, at the top of your Activity subclass codebase.

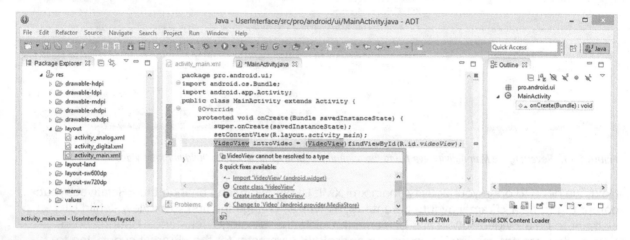

Figure 11-3. *Instantiate a VideoView object named introVideo and reference the videoView ID from activity_main*

Now that we have our foundational VideoView object instantiated and loaded with our UI XML definition, the next thing that we will need to do is load it with our digital video asset reference using a **URI** object. Let's take a moment to review the URI class and what a URI is before we write that code and wire it up (connect it) to our VideoView using Java programming code.

Android's URI Class: Referencing Data in an Android App

A **URI** in Android is an object that holds a reference to a data path that will be used to access raw or specialized data of one type or another. One example of such data would be a SQLite database, or a digital video asset, or a website, or similar types of **content** that an application might use.

URI is the abbreviation for **Uniform Resource Indentifier**, which is **Uniform** because it's **standardized**, a **Resource** because it **references** a data path to some data (content) that your applications will operate on (and utilize), and **Identifier**, because it **identifies** where you can go and load that data, which is also popularly known as the content's **data path**.

The URI has four parts. First is a URI **schema**, such as **HTTP://**, next comes an **authority**, like **apress.com**, next comes the **data path**, such as **/data/video**, and finally the **data object** itself, in its file format, such as **asset.mp4**.

This Android **Uri** class is a direct subclass of the **java.lang.Object** master class. There's also a Uri class in the core Java programming language, but as we're using Android here, we'll utilize the Android-specific Uri class. Just so you don't get confused when you look at the Android developer site documentation, note that this **java.net.Uri** class also exists alongside the **android.net.Uri** class. However, I suggest that you use an Android specific version of the URI class, as it's optimized for use within the Android OS.

The Uri class is a **public abstract** class, and has over three dozen methods that allow developers to work with URI objects (and data path references).

The Android Uri class hierarchy is structured as follows:

```
java.lang.Object
  > android.net.Uri
```

The Android Uri class belongs in the **android.net** package, making it a tool for accessing data across a **network**. For this reason, the **import statement** for using the Uri class inside your Android application would reference a package path of **android.net.Uri**, as you will see in the next section.

The Android Uri class allows developers to create **URI objects** that provide an **immutable** URI reference. In Android, you make your objects immutable by placing them into system memory for use, and we'll need to do this for our URI data path reference, by using Android's Uri class.

Your URI object reference includes a **URI specifier**, as well as a **data path** reference, which is the component of your URI following the '**://**'. The Uri class takes care of **building** and **parsing** a URI object that references data in a manner that will conform to a **RFC 2396** technical specification.

To optimize Android operating system and application performance, the Uri class performs very little data path validation. What this means is that a behavior is not defined for handling an invalid data input. This means the Uri class is very forgiving in the face of an invalid input specification.

As a developer you have to be careful in what you are doing, as URI objects will return garbage, rather than throw an exception, unless you specify otherwise using your Java code. Thus **error trapping** and **data path validation** are left up to the developer to do inside their code.

Now we can use this Uri class and configure our VideoView UI element so we can access our digital video asset. Let's do that next.

Using the Uri.Parse() Method: Feeding Our VideoView Data

You will instantiate the URI object in much the same way that you did with your VideoView object, by declaring it, then naming it and then setting it equal to the result of the **Uri.parse()** method call, by using the following single line of Java code (shown here split onto two lines):

```
Uri introVideoUri =
Uri.parse( "android.resource" + getPackagename() + "/" + R.raw.intro );
```

As you can see in Figure 11-4, we have written this code using one line of text. There is a wavy red error highlight in the Java code, underneath the word **raw** in the R.raw.intro digital video asset reference. This is because there is currently no /res/raw folder to hold digital video assets in your project as yet, so right-click the /res folder and use the **New ➤ Folder** work process as you've done previously in the book and create a **raw** folder to use for your digital video assets, which are kept in this folder. We'll get into digital video formats, folders, and concepts in the next section.

Figure 11-4. *Instantiate a Uri object and name it introVideoUri and use the .parse() method to load reference*

As you can see in Figure 11-5, our **/res/raw/** folder is now in place, shown highlighted on the left, but the wavy red error highlighting is still not gone. This is because we still need to create and place the **intro.mp4** file into this folder, and once we do this the error under the reference to the file will disappear.

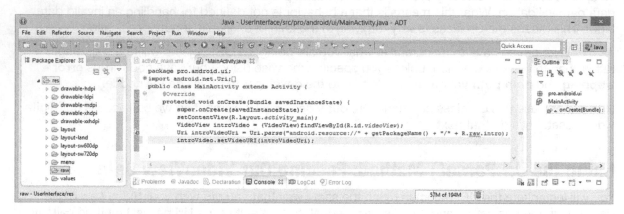

Figure 11-5. *Wire the introVideo VideoView object to an introVideoUri Uri object using the .setVideoURI() method*

Before we can create this digital video asset we will need to obtain some foundational knowledge regarding digital video concepts, formats, and even some software that can be used to create digital video assets for Android applications. Let's do this next, and once we have learned about video and created our intro.mp4 asset, we can finish implementing it in Java code.

Core Digital Video Concepts: Frames, Frame Rate, or FPS

Digital video extends digital imaging into the fourth dimension (time), by using frames. Video is comprised of an ordered sequence of frames displayed rapidly over time. The term frame comes from the film industry, where even today frames of film are run via film projectors at a rate of 24 frames per second (FPS) creating an illusion of **motion**.

As every frame of digital video actually contains a digital image, all the concepts that we learned about in Chapter 10 can be applied to video, and all these imaging concepts can be readily applied to work in video content development, as you will soon see, as well as implemented in a UI design.

Since digital video is made up of this collection of digital image frames, the concept of a digital video **frame rate**, expressed as **frames per second**, or more commonly referred to as **FPS**, is also very important when it comes to our digital video data footprint optimization work process.

The optimization concept with frames in a digital video is very similar to the one regarding pixels in an image (the resolution of the digital image) because video frames multiply the data footprint with each frame used. In digital video, not only does the frame's (image) resolution greatly impact the file size, but so does the number of frames per second, or frame rate.

In Chapter 10, we learned that if we multiply the number of pixels in the image by its number of color channels we'll get the **raw data footprint** for the image. With digital video, we will now multiply that number again with the number of **frames per second** at which our digital video is playing, and again by the **number of total seconds** that are contained in our video file.

To continue the VGA example from Chapter 10, we know a 24-bit VGA image is **900KB**. This makes your calculation to take this to the next level easy for this example. Digital video traditionally runs at **30 FPS**, so one second of **Standard Definition** (SD) or VGA raw uncompressed digital video would be 30 image frames, each of which is 900KB, yielding a data footprint of **27000KB**.

To find out how many Megabytes (MB) this will be, you need to divide 27000 by 1024, which gives us a result of **26.37MB** of data for **a second** of video.

You can see why having video file formats that can compress this raw data footprint that digital video creates is extremely important. Therefore in the next section of the chapter, we'll review all the different digital video codecs that the Android OS currently supports.

You will be amazed (later on in this chapter) at some of the digital video data compression ratios that we will achieve using the MPEG-4 video file format, once we know exactly how to best optimize a digital video compression work process by using the correct bit-rate, frame rate and frame resolution for our digital video content. We'll also get into the concept of bit-rates as well as video optimization during the next few sections of this chapter.

Digital Video in Android: MPEG4 H.264 and WebM Format

Android supports the same **open source** digital video formats as **HTML5** does, namely the **MPEG-4** (Motion Picture Experts Group) **H.264** and the **VP8** format, which was acquired by Google from ON2 Technologies and renamed **WebM.**

This is quite optimal from the **content production** standpoint, as the video content that developers produce and optimize can be used in HTML5 engines such as HTML5 apps, browsers, and devices, as well as in the Android OS.

The open source digital video format cross-platform support will afford us content developers with the "produce once, deliver everywhere," production scenario. This reduces content development cost, increasing your revenues, as long as "economies of scale" are taken advantage of by the professional Android application developer.

Since most Android devices these days have displays that are using medium (854 by 480) to high (1280 by 720) resolution, if you are going to use the MPEG4 file format, you should utilize the **MPEG4 H.264 AVC** format, which is currently the digital video format most often used in the world today.

The **MPEG-4 H.264 AVC** (**Advanced Video Coding**) digital video file format is supported across all Android OS versions for video playback, and under the **Android 3.0** and later OS versions for **video recording**. Recording video is only supported if the Android device has video camera hardware capability.

If you are a Pro Android UI content producer, you'll find that this MPEG-4 H.264 format has the best compression results, especially if you are using one of the more advanced encoding suites, like **Sorenson Squeeze Pro 9** software, which we'll be using a bit later on in this chapter.

File extension support for MPEG4 video files includes **.3GP** (MPEG4 SP) and **.MP4 (MPEG4 H.264 AVC)**. I suggest using the latter (.MP4 AVC), as that is what I use for HTML5 apps and MP4 is more common to use in an AVC format, but either type of file extension should work just fine in the Android OS.

A more recent digital video format that Android now supports is called the **WebM (VP8)** digital video format. This format also provides a great quality result with a **small data footprint**. This is probably the reason why Google acquired ON2, the company that developed the VP8 codec. We'll learn about codecs a bit later on in this chapter. Playback of WebM videos is natively supported in (and after) Android **2.3**. The term native support is used with code that has become **natively a part of the operating system** OS software.

WebM also supports something called **video streaming**, which we will also be learning about in a later section of the chapter. The WebM video streaming playback capability is supported only if users have Android OS version **4.0** (and later, such as all 4.x revisions). For this reason, I would recommend using WebM for captive (non-stream) video assets (2.3 through 4.4 support) and MPEG4 H.264 AVC if you are going to be streaming video (all versions).

Digital Video Compression: Bit-Rate, Streams, SD and HD

Let's start out covering the primary resolutions used in commercial video. Before **HDTV** or **High Definition** came along, video was called **SD** or **Standard Definition**, and used a standard pixel vertical resolution of **480 pixels**.

HD video comes in two resolutions, **1280 by 720**, which I call "**Pseudo HD**," and **1920 by 1080** which the industry calls "**True HD**." Both are 16:9 aspect ratio, and are now used not only in TVs and iTVs, but also in smartphones (Razor HD is 1280 by 720), and tablets (a Kindle Fire HD is 1920 by 1200, which is, by the way, a less wide, or taller, **16:10** pixel aspect ratio).

There's also **16:10 Pseudo HD** resolution that features **1280 by 800** pixels. In fact, this is a common laptop, netbook, and mid-size tablet resolution. Generally, most developers try to match their video content resolutions to the resolution of each Android device that the video will be viewed on.

Regardless of the resolution you use for your digital video content, video can be accessed by your application in a couple of different ways. The way I do it, because I'm a data optimization nut, is **captive** to an application, which means the data is **inside** of the Android application **APK** file itself, inside the **raw data resource** folder.

The other way to access video inside your Android app is by using a remote **video data server**, and in this case, the video is **streamed** from the remote server, over the Internet and into your user's Android device as the video is playing back, in real-time. Let's hope this video server doesn't crash.

Video streaming is more complicated than playing captive video data files, because the Android device is communicating in real-time with remote data servers, receiving **video data packets** as the video plays. Video streaming is supported via WebM on Android 4.0 and later devices, using WebM format.

The last concept that we need to cover in this section is the concept of bit-rate. **Bit-rate** is a key setting used in the video compression process, as bit-rates represent a **target bandwidth**, or **data pipe size**, which can accommodate a certain number of bits streaming through it every second. Bit-rate must also take into consideration **CPU processing power** within any given Android phone, making video data optimization even more challenging.

This is because once bits travel through a data-pipe, they also need to be processed and displayed on the device screen. In fact **captive video assets** that are included in Android application APK files only need optimization for processing power. This is because if you use captive video files there is no data pipe for the video asset to travel through and no data transfer overhead. Thus bit-rates for digital video assets need to be optimized not only for bandwidth, but also in anticipation of variances in CPU processor power. Single-core CPUs may not be able to decode high resolution bit-rate digital video assets without dropping frames, so make sure to optimize low bit-rate video assets if you are going to target older or cheaper devices.

Digital Video Compression: Using Codecs and Settings

Digital video is compressed using software utilities called **codecs**, which stands for **code-decode**. There are two "sides" to the video codec; one that **encodes** the video data stream, and the other which **decodes** this video data stream. A video decoder will be part of the OS, or browser, which uses it.

The **decoder** is primarily optimized for speed, as smoothness of playback is a key issue, and the **encoder** is optimized to reduce data footprint for the digital video asset it is generating. For this reason the encoding process can take a long time, depending on how many processing cores a workstation contains. Most content production workstations should support eight cores.

Codecs (the encoder side) are like plug-ins, in the sense that they can be installed into different digital video editing software packages, to enable them to encode many different digital video asset file formats.

Since Android supports H.263 and H.264 MPEG4 formats, and the ON2 VP8 WebM format for video, you need to make sure that you're using one of the video codecs that encodes video data into these digital video file formats.

More than one software manufacturer makes MPEG encoding software, so there will be different MPEG codecs (encoder software) that will yield different (better or worse) results, as far as encoding speed and file size goes.

The professional solution, which I highly recommend that you secure if you want to produce video professionally, is called **Sorenson Squeeze**, which is currently at version 9. Squeeze has a professional-level version that I use in this book, which costs less than a thousand dollars.

There is also an open source solution called **EditShare Lightworks 11.5** that is scheduled to natively support output to the MPEG4 and WebM VP8 codec by 2014. So for now I will have to use **Squeeze Pro 9** for this book, until the codec support for Android is added to EditShare Lightworks 11.5 in 2014.

When optimizing (setting compression settings) for digital video data file size, there are a large number of **variables** that directly affect the video data footprint. I'll cover these in the order in which they affect a video file size from the most impact to the least impact, so that you know which parameters to **tweak** to obtain the result that you're looking for.

Like in digital image compression, the **resolution**, or number of pixels, in each frame of video is an optimal place to start the optimization process. If a target user is using 854x480 or 1280x720 smartphones or tablets, then you don't need to use **True HD** 1920 by 1080 resolution to get good visual results for your digital video assets.

With super-fine density (dot pitch) displays out there, you can scale 1280 video up 33% and it will look reasonably good. The exception to this might be iTV apps for GoogleTV, where you would want to use True HD 1920x1080.

The next level of optimization would come in the **number of frames** used for each second of video (FPS) assuming the actual seconds of the video itself can't be shortened. This is known as the **frame rate** and instead of setting the **video standard 30 FPS** frame rate, consider using a **film standard** frame rate of **24 FPS**, or the **multimedia standard** frame rate of **20 FPS**. You might even be able to use a low **15 FPS** frame rate, depending on your content.

Note that 15 FPS is half as much data as 30 FPS (or 100% reduction in data going into the codec) and for some video content this will playback (look) the same as 30 FPS content! The only real way to test this is to try these framerate settings during the content optimization encoding work process.

The next most optimal setting in obtaining a small data footprint would be the **bit-rate** that you set for a codec to try and achieve. Bit-rate equates to the **amount of compression** applied and thus sets a **quality level** for the video data. It is important to note that you could simply use 30 FPS, 1920-resolution HD video and specify a low bit-rate ceiling. If you do this the results would not be as good looking as if you first experimented with low frame rates and resolutions, using the higher (quality) bit-rate settings.

The next most effective setting in obtaining a small data footprint is the number of **keyframes** that a codec uses to **sample** your digital video. Video codecs apply compression by looking at a frame, and then encoding only the changes, or **offsets**, over the next few frames, so that it does not have to encode every single frame in your video data stream. This is why a talking head video can encode better than a video where every pixel moves on every frame (such as video using fast panning, or rapid zooming, for instance).

A keyframe is a setting in a codec that forces that codec to take a fresh sampling of your video data asset every so often. There is usually an **auto** setting for keyframes that allows a codec to decide how many keyframes to sample, as well as a **manual** setting that allows you to specify a keyframe sampling every so often, usually a certain number of times per second or a certain number of times over the duration of the video (total frames).

Most codecs usually have a **quality** or a **sharpness** setting (a slider) that controls the amount of blur applied to a video before compression. In case you don't know this trick, applying a slight blur to your images or video, which is usually not desirable, can allow for better compression as sharp transitions (sharp edges) in an image are harder to encode (take more data to reproduce) than soft transitions do. That said, I'd keep the quality or sharpness slider between an 85% and 100% quality, and try to get your data footprint reduction using the other variables that we have discussed here.

Ultimately there are a number of different variables that you will need to fine-tune in order to achieve the best data footprint optimization for any given video data asset, and each will be different (mathematically) to the codec. Thus, there can be no "standard" settings that can be developed to achieve any given results. That said, experience tweaking various settings will eventually allow you to get a feel, over time, as to the settings you need to change as far as all the parameters go to get your desired result.

Creating Digital Video Content: Using Terragen3 Software

The next thing that we need to do is to create some digital video content that we can use to show the various concepts, such as seamless looping, in our Android application's FrameLayout container.

I'm going to use **Terragen3**, a world creation 3D animation software package from Planetside Software, because it is not only an impressive 3D software package, but is also a professional-level, 3D production software package.

Fortunately there is a free version as well as a paid Pro version, which I suggest that you purchase, if you are serious about having all the primary production tools in your quiver. Go to the Planetside. co.uk website, shown in Figure 11-6, and download the latest version of Terragen3.

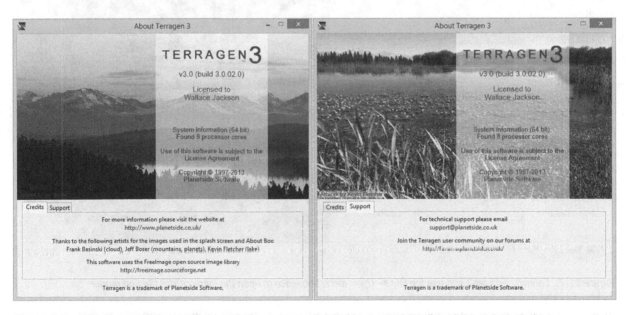

Figure 11-6. Using Terragen3 world building software to create digital video content (credit and support screens)

After you download and install this software, launch it using its shortcut icon. You will see the Credits and Support tabs, shown in Figure 11-6, in the various rendered start-up screens for the software. You'll soon see exactly what this software is capable of by viewing these startup screens, which will change as you use different start-up tabs. As you can see, this software package rocks in the hands of a seasoned user!

Next, we will open a basic seamless looping camera fly-through, around the basic world that you will find in your Pro Android UI assets folder called **loopingOrbit_v03.tgd** (tgd stands for **TerraGen Data**). Use your **File ➤ Open** menu sequence to open this in the software, as shown in Figure 11-7. Click the **Renderers** tab, on the right, to access the **render settings** panes.

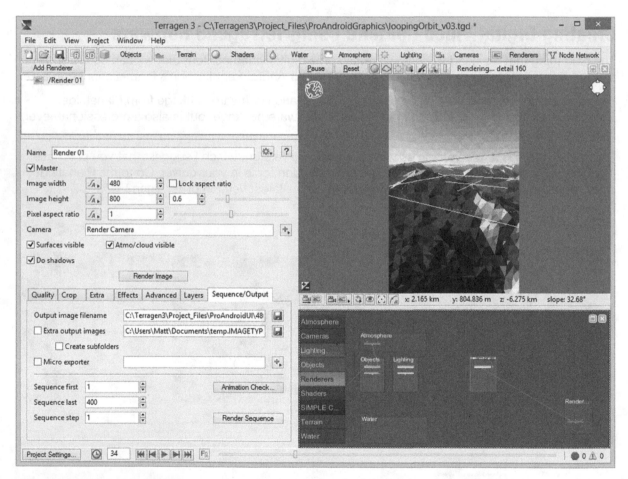

***Figure 11-7.** Launch Terragen3 and use the File ➤ Open menu sequence to open the loopingOrbit file and render*

In the top part of the render dialog shown on the left, set an image width of 480 pixels and an image height of 800 pixels, which is one of the most popular Android screen resolutions, and a resolution that will scale down or up with good results. Leave all the other settings at their defaults.

If you just want to render one frame, you can use the Render Image button, which is in the middle of this dialog, but this will not create a sequence of frames, which we'll need to create motion video data. At the bottom of the dialog you will see seven tabs that control advanced settings. Click the seventh (rightmost) tab labeled **Sequence/Output**, to set our output file specifications and image sequence settings.

Enter your project files directory in the **Output image filename** field, as shown in Figure 11-7. Mine is C:\Terragen3\Project_Files\ProAndroidUI and make sure that your **Sequence first** field is set to a value of **1**, and set a value of **400** in the **Sequence last** field. Set the **Sequence step** to **1** frame. Click the **Render Sequence** button once you're done and generate 400 frames!

Creating an Uncompressed AVI Format: Using VirtualDub

The next software package we will need to use is VirtualDub 1.9, which takes the 400 frames we created in Terragen3 and loads them into an AVI file format, which we can then import into Sorenson Squeeze for our compression work process. Download and install VirtualDub, and launch it and you will see the empty screen, shown in Figure 11-8. Use a **Video ➤ Compression** menu sequence to set the compression for the resulting file to **Uncompressed**.

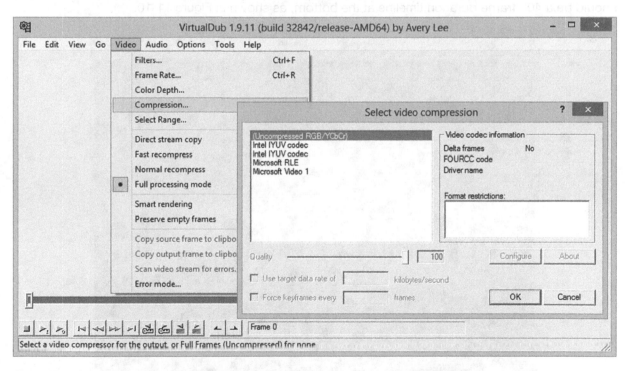

Figure 11-8. Launch VirtualDub and use the Video ➤ Compression menu to set to be Uncompressed

Use the **Frame Rate, Color Depth,** and **Select Range** menu items to set these parameters to **10 FPS**, **24-bit color**, and **0 to 400**, as shown in Figure 11-9.

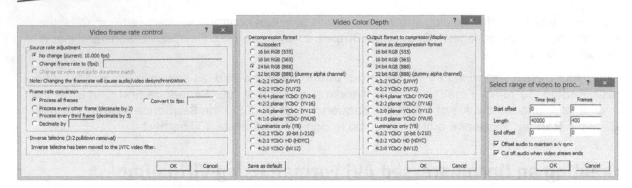

Figure 11-9. Setting the frame rate, video color depth, and frame range for our intro.avi uncompressed video file

Now you are ready to load your 400 frames using the **File ➤ Open** video file menu sequence. Select the first file in your 400 frame sequence, and click the **Open** button to open all 400 frames in VirtualDub. You will see Frame 1 displayed in the software when all 400 frames are loaded, and there should be a 400 frame duration timeline at the bottom, as shown in Figure 11-10.

Figure 11-10. Use File ➤ Open menu to open the first frame of your 400 frame rendering sequence in VirtualDub

Use the **File ➤ Save AVI 2.0 File** menu sequence to open the dialog shown in Figure 11-11. Name the file **intro** and use the **Save** button to save the AVI.

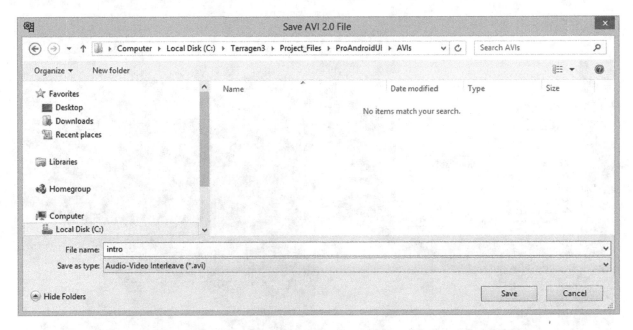

Figure 11-11. Use the File ➤ Save AVI 2.0 File and save an uncompressed AVI in your Terragen3 Project folder

After you click **Save** you'll see the progress dialog shown in Figure 11-12.

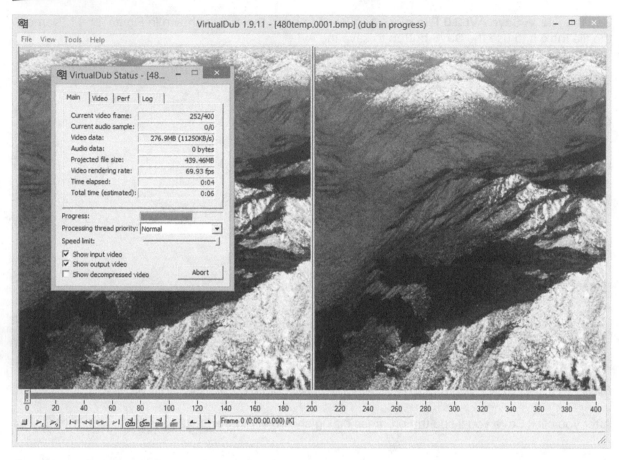

Figure 11-12. VirtualDub inserting 400 frames into uncompressed AVI showing progress stats

Now that you have your 400 frames of digital video data in your AVI format that Sorenson Squeeze can import, you can go into Squeeze and proceed with the video compression (data footprint optimization) work process.

Applying Video Compression: Using Sorenson Squeeze

Next we're going to use Sorenson Squeeze Pro to compress our digital video asset. Install Squeeze 9, launch it, and then click on the Import File icon on the upper-right, as shown in Figure 11-13. Notice Squeeze software has left panels for holding different codec and folder settings, as well as a top preview area and a bottom application timeline area, which we will be using soon to apply our codec presets to our intro.avi file.

Figure 11-13. Launch Sorenson Squeeze and click on the Import File icon on the upper-left to import intro.avi file

Once you click the Import File icon you will see the Select one or more source media files to open dialog, shown in Figure 11-14. Navigate to your Terragen3 Project_Files folder and ProAndroidUI subfolder and click on the **intro** AVI file, and then on the **Open** button, to load your uncompressed AVI data into Squeeze. We are using uncompressed data to give Squeeze the best high-quality source data to work with, going into the compression process.

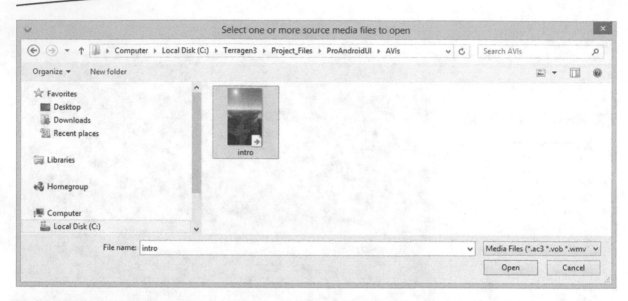

Figure 11-14. Sorenson Squeeze Import File dialog showing intro.avi file and path to Terragen3 project directory

As you can see in Figure 11-15 on the left side, the video data loads into Squeeze, and displays the intro.avi file in a bottom area of the software, where we will apply presets once we create them. Click the right-facing arrow next to the MPEG-4 codecs, and open up the MPEG-4 codecs, so you can right-click the **768Kbps_360p** preset that comes with Squeeze. Select the Edit menu option, so that we can edit these presets to create our own data compression settings for our 480x800 intro.mp4 file we are creating here.

Figure 11-15. Squeeze showing AVI file loaded and codecs (left) and right-click on MPEG4 codec to Edit settings

Editing Your Squeeze Pro Presets

This Edit menu option opens the Presets dialog, shown in Figure 11-16, where you can set all the different options we've been learning about.

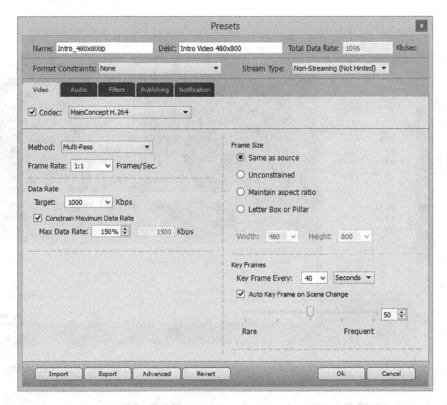

Figure 11-16. Codec setting for intro.mp4 at 480x800 1000Kbps

Name the preset **Intro_480x800p** and then enter a description of **Intro Video 480x800** at the top of the dialog, as shown in Figure 11-16. Make sure that **Stream Type** is set to **Non-Streaming** and **Format Constraints** is set to **None**.

Select the **MainConcept H.264 MPEG-4** codec in the **Codec** drop-down menu, and in the **Method** drop-down, select the **Multi-Pass** option, which will take the longest time to compress your content, but will yield the best compression to quality results.

Leave the Frame Rate drop-down at 1:1, and set your **Target Data Rate** to **1000 Kbps**. Select the **Constrain Maximum Date Rate** checkbox and set a **Max Data Rate** of **150%** which will give you a bit-rate ceiling of **1500 Kbps**.

On the right side of the Presets dialog, set your **Frame Size** to match your source .AVI resolution of 480x800, by selecting the **Same as source** option.

In the **Key Frames** area of the dialog, set a single keyframe by setting the **Key Frame Every** drop-down to **40 seconds**, as this is your duration for your 400 frame video that is compressed in VirtualDub at 10 FPS, yielding a 40 second duration. Also, be sure to check the **Auto Key Frame on Scene Change** option, which will allow this codec to determine when to take a new sample (that is, a key frame) of your digital video frame data.

We are doing this to allow this MainConcepts codec to decide algorithmically the optimal number of key frame samples to take during the video compression process. When everything is set, click the **OK** button. As you can see in Figure 11-17, the preset is now added and you can right-click it, and select the **Apply Preset** option to add it to your project.

Figure 11-17. Right-click to Apply Preset (left) and show applied preset and generated AVI after Squeezelt (right)

Compressing the MPEG4 File Using Squeeze It! Button

Once you have applied the preset to your intro.avi file as shown in Figure 11-17, you can click the **Squeeze It!** button and create your **intro.mp4** file using the codec preset that you just designed. This creates your video asset, and as you can see, on the right-side of Figure 11-17, you can also preview it by using the translucent play button on top of the video icon.

Open your operating system's file management software, on Windows 8.1 it's Explorer, and find your Terragen3 projects folder, and a ProAndroidUI sub-folder and rename the MPEG-4 file that Squeeze saved out for you **intro.mp4** as is shown in Figure 11-18. Then right-click it and **Copy** it to your OS clipboard, so in the next step, you can **Paste** it into your **/res/raw** folder.

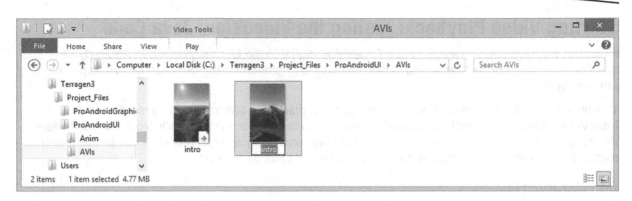

Figure 11-18.   Go into ProAndroidUI/AVIs folder and rename MP4 file to intro.mp4 and right-click and select Copy

Now find your **/workspace/UserInterface/res/raw** folder, and right-click and **Paste** the intro.mp4 file into this folder. This /res/raw folder in Android is where assets that you have already optimized, and which you do not want Android to optimize (or try to optimize) anymore for you, will be placed.

Figure 11-19 shows your intro.mp4 in your /res/raw folder, and now, we can get back into our Java code, and testing our application and continuing to look at how to implement cool things like seamlessly looping intro videos, and digital video streaming and the like in the remainder of this chapter.

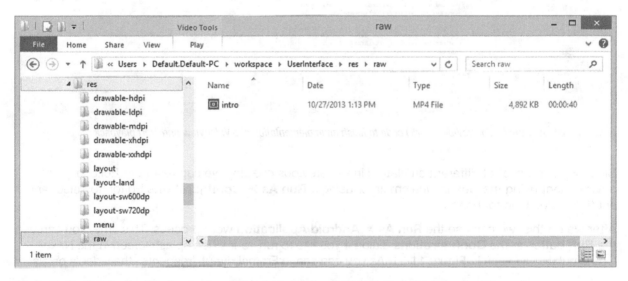

Figure 11-19.   Find the UserInterface/res/raw folder, right-click it, and select Paste, to finish copying intro.mp4

Now let's go back into Eclipse and test our minimum XML and Java code that is needed to implement video assets in a FrameLayout container in Android.

Starting Video Playback: Testing the VideoView Java Code

Now that we have a video asset to use to develop digital video UI designs with in Android, we can finish the Java code that we have been writing to implement a digital video on our application splashscreen.

The only line of Java code that we have not put into place is a call to a **.start()** method off the **introView** VideoView object, which we've already loaded with our **/res/raw/intro.mp4** video asset. We accomplished this using the Uri.parse() Uri class and the .parse() method. A call to this .start() method, off the introVideo VideoView object is done via this Java code:

```
introView.start();
```

As you can see in Figure 11-20, our Java code is now error-free, and ready for to test. Notice that the red error underline under the **R.raw.intro** reference is now gone as well, since we have put a video asset into place.

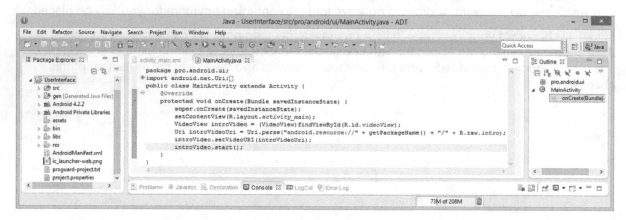

Figure 11-20. Add the final introVideo.start() code to finish an implementation of a VideoView and start playback

Since we used a lot of different emulators in the previous chapter, we can reset our Eclipse environment using the Nexus One emulator using a **Run As ➤ Configurations** Editor, to select and set the Nexus One for usage.

After we do this, we can use the **Run As ➤ Android Application** work process. This time, you can use the **Run** button in the **Configurations** dialog if you like to run your video splashscreen in the Nexus One emulator, as seen in Figure 11-21. As you can see, a FrameLayout "respects" the video's pixels.

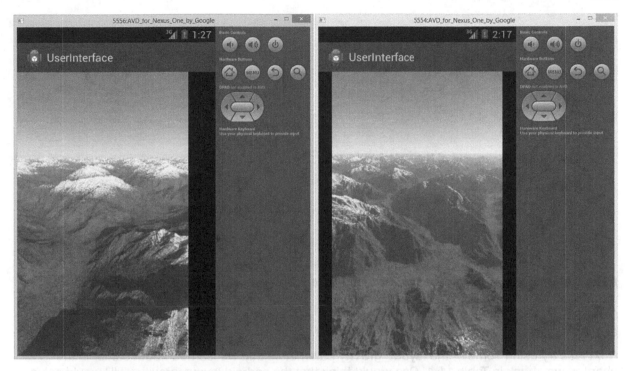

Figure 11-21. Testing our VideoView and FrameLayout in the Nexus One emulator, using layout_gravity constant

What this means is that a FrameLayout container doesn't scale or otherwise alter what is inside its container, which stands to reason, as it's the intent of this UI container type to display a fixed result on your screen.

Scaling Video to Fit Screen Aspect using a FrameLayout UI Container

Let's see if there is any method that we can use to force this FrameLayout class to scale our video to fit the display screen. The first thing that I would try, starting at the core, bottom-line level of the scale processing chain, is to change the **layout_width** and **layout_height** parameters. We will change these from **wrap_content**, to use the **match_parent** constant, as shown in Figure 11-22. The results are shown on the left side of Figure 11-21.

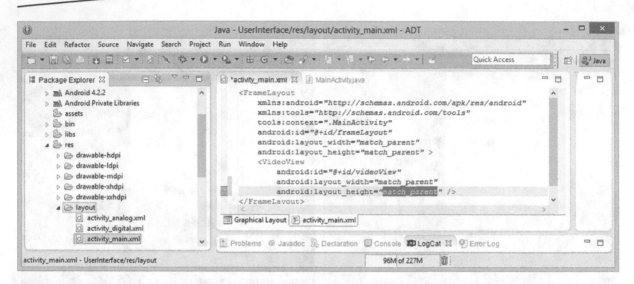

Figure 11-22. Changing the wrap_content constants to be match_parent constants to try and fill layout container

So far our FrameLayout refuses to scale our video asset to fit the screen, which could be construed as a good thing, and a reason to use FrameLayout, if our video aspect ratio needs to remain fixed.

Next let's try using some of the **layout_gravity** parameters that we learned about earlier in the chapter, way back in Table 11-1. One would think that the android:layout_gravity="fill" would solve this problem, so try adding that to the FrameLayout, and (or) the VideoView UI definitions, and again use your **Run As ➤ Android Application** work process to see if you can scale your video up to fill the screen. The results are shown in Figure 11-21 on the left side. Again, FrameLayout will not scale video asymmetrically.

It's important to note the FrameLayout scales a video asset up or down to fit different resolutions, however, it won't change its shape or aspect ratio. This is actually something very important to note as Pro Android UI developers, because we need to have control over our User Experience. In Chapter 13, we will learn how to make your video scale to fit any screen shape, or aspect ratio. Since we can't "fill" the video, let's try using the **android:layout_gravity="center"** parameter to center your video. This will make your UI design (video) look more attractive on your screen.

Add a line of space under the last parameter in your <VideoView>, by using the Return key, and then type in the word *android* and a colon (:) to bring up the parameter helper dialog, as shown in Figure 11-23. This shows a list of all parameters that are available for use in a FrameLayout class.

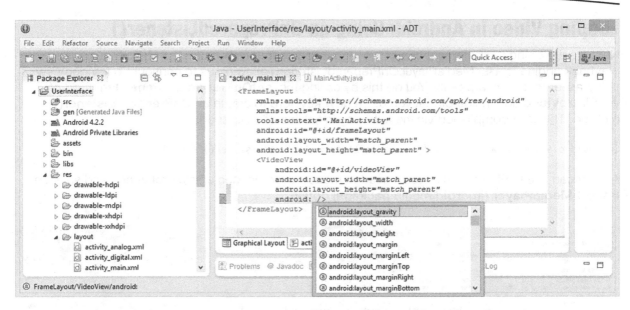

Figure 11-23. *Using an android: work process to access all of the possible parameters for the FrameLayout class*

Double-click this layout_gravity parameter and insert it, and then edit it and add in the **center** constant, which can be seen in Figure 11-24. This centers the VideoView in the FrameLayout container and on the screen.

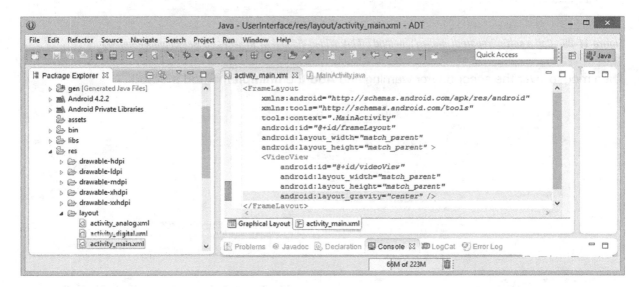

Figure 11-24. *Implementing an android:layout_gravity="center" parameter to center the video in the FrameLayout*

Finally, use the **Run As ➤ Android Application** and test the XML markup. The centered video result can be seen on the right side of Figure 11-21.

Looping Video in Android: Using an OnPreparedListener()

Next we are going to implement one of the most used nested classes for the MediaPlayer video playback engine (class) MediaPlayer.OnPreparedListener() allowing us to configure our VideoView video asset to loop seamlessly. You do this by calling the **.setOnPreparedListener()** method off your **introVideo** and inside of that you use a **new** keyword to create an **OnPreparedListener()** method. This is accomplished via the following initial line of Java code:

```
introVideo.setOnPreparedListener(new MediaPlayer.OnPreparedListener() {   });
```

As you can see in Figure 11-25, you'll need to mouse-over the MediaPlayer reference and select an **Import MediaPlayer (android.media package)** option.

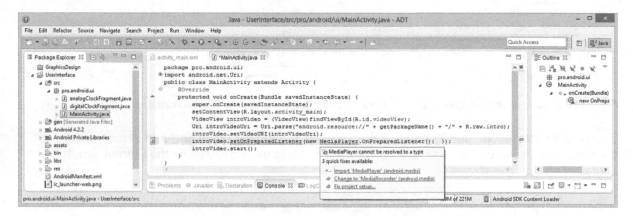

Figure 11-25.   Call a setOnPreparedListener() method off introVideo VideoView to access a .setLooping() method

Then mouse-over the second error warning and **Add the unimplemented method**.

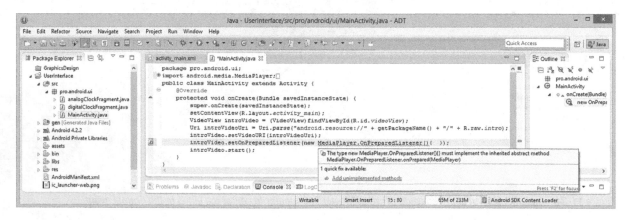

Figure 11-26.   Adding the unimplemented method to our new MediaPlayer.OnPreparedListener() method call

Now all we have to do is to add a .setLooping() method call and parameter to the public void onPrepared() method inside the OnPreparedListener() method, called off the MediaPlayer object named arg0 that Eclipse has created for us. This is all done using the following Java program logic:

```
introVideo.setOnPreparedListener(new MediaPlayer.OnPreparedListener(){
    @Override
    public void onPrepared(MediaPlayer arg0){
        arg0.setLooping(true);
    }
});
```

As you can see in Figure 11-27, our code is error-free and we are ready to use a **Run As ➤ Android Application** work process, and watch our intro video loop seamlessly on the screen. We have implemented a digital video intro in our UserInterface application using only a dozen or so lines of Java code!

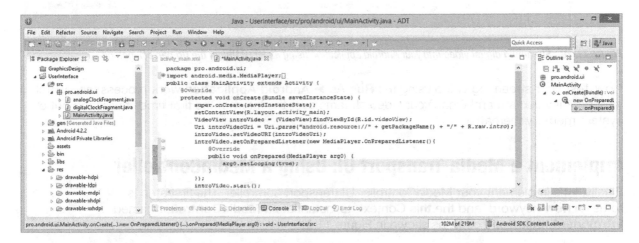

Figure 11-27. Calling a .setLooping(true); method off the arg0 MediaPlayer object in the onPrepared() method

Next I'm going to show you how easy it is to stream video instead of using captive video assets in Android. All we have to do is change a URI object!

Stream Digital Video in Android: Use an HTTP URL in URI

Since Android handles most of the logistics regarding streaming video from the Internet into the hardware device, all we as developers really have to do is to provide an HTTP:// **URL**, or **Uniform Resource Locator**, in the place of the R.raw.intro resource locator that we have been using up until now.

This is done by replacing the **android.resource://UserInterface/R.raw.intro** with an **HTTP://www.e-bookclub/intro.mp4** reference to an external server, a server that I own in this particular case.

As you can see in Figure 11-28, a Uri.parse() method call accommodates an HTTP:// URL reference as easily as it does the android.resource:// URI.

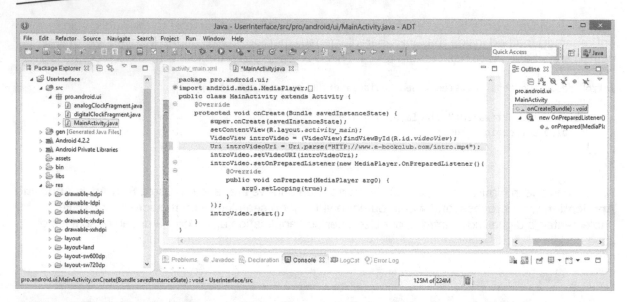

Figure 11-28. *Streaming digital video into your Android application using an HTTP URL in the Uri.parse() method*

Now, test your streaming video using the **Run As ➤ Android Application** work process, and watch your digital video stream! Once your video streams over the Internet the first time, it will loop out of system memory thereafter.

Implement a Media Transport UI: Using a MediaController

Finally, let's implement your MediaController UI transport controller. The first step is to use a **new** keyword, and the **this** Context, to instantiate a **MediaController** named **introVideoMediaController**, as shown in Figure 11-29.

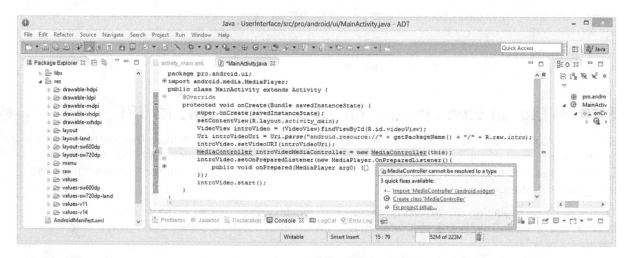

Figure 11-29. *Instantiating a MediaController object named introVideoMediaController using the new keyword*

Next use the **.setAnchorView()** method to wire the **introVideoMediaController** and the **introVideo** objects together, as can be seen in Figure 11-30.

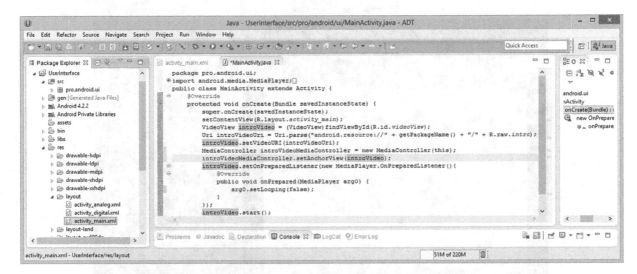

Figure 11-30. Use a .setAnchorView() method to wire the introVideoMediaController to the introVideo VideoView

Finally, use your **.setMediaController()** method, and wire these two objects together, this time going in the other direction, as seen in Figure 11-31.

Figure 11-31. Using the .setMediaController() method to set the introVideoMediaController up for the VideoView

As you can see in Figure 11-32, a MediaController UI transport works well!

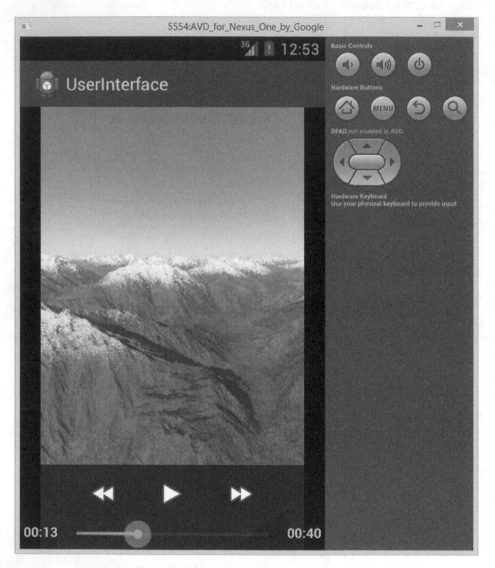

Figure 11-32. Testing the MediaController UI transport in the Nexus One emulator

Summary

In this chapter, we took a closer look at the Android FrameLayout class, as well as at the VideoView UI widget commonly used in this class. We looked at the MediaPlayer and MediaController classes, as well as video concepts needed to work with these classes. We created video assets using popular 3D and digital video software packages, and then implemented intro video in our UserInterface application, made it loop and stream, and then created a MediaController UI transport. Let's look at Android's LinearLayout class next!

Chapter 12

Android's LinearLayout Class: Horizontal and Vertical UI Design

Android's **LinearLayout** class has become one of the most often used layout container classes, and for very good reasons. Like the FrameLayout, it is memory efficient, simple to implement, and efficiently provides the basic user interface layout designs that are so popular on the Internet today.

These designs generally feature either a row of buttons or icons along the top of the webpage (or in this case the application screen) or alternatively down the side of the webpage or app. As we learned previously, the Android OS guidelines prefer that we use the left side of the screen for UI design elements, however, with the advent of **LTR** and **RTL** designations (in Android 4.2) even that can change depending on the language that's being utilized.

Since many website and application designs use icons for their GUI buttons and navigation, we will also cover the Android **ImageButton** class in detail in this chapter, as this is the class which would be used to create the UI design approach that features this visual type of navigation, rather than simply using text UI elements for the UI buttons, which would be done with the **Button** UI class, which we have already covered previously in the book.

As you may have already noticed with the layout container classes that we are embarking on, I am going to cover the most logical UI widget class for use with each of these layout containers, so that we are not just covering the layout container (ViewGroup) subclasses, but also the UI widget (View) subclasses during the remainder of this book. Fortunately, we have already covered digital media asset concepts, as well as styles, themes, and design concepts that we'll need, so from here on out, we can focus on UI classes.

LinearLayout Class: Android's Most Used UI Class

One of the most frequently used Android User Interface (UI) classes is the LinearLayout class. This class is simple, memory efficient, and effective, and for applications that do not require complex UI layout this is the perfect class to utilize. After all, there is no reason to use a more complex GridLayout or RelativeLayout when all you need is the basic LinearLayout for your Button panel. Let's learn all about this class now!

The LinearLayout Class: Horizontal or Vertical UI Design

The Android **LinearLayout** class is the most basic UI layout container class of all the remaining Android ViewGroup subclassed user interface layout classes. It can be nested inside of another UI layout subclass, however, I am going to show you how to avoid nesting layout classes during this book, so that you can minimize your app's system memory usage whenever possible.

The LinearLayout class hierarchy, starting with the Java language's Object master class, and progressing down from View to ViewGroup to LinearLayout, would be structured something like this:

```
java.lang.Object
 > android.view.View
  > android.view.ViewGroup
   > android.widget.LinearLayout
```

The LinearLayout class is a **public class** that extends the **ViewGroup** super class and is generally used for creating user interface designs that need to have the UI elements (View widgets) arranged in a single **horizontal row** or in a **vertical column**, as far as the UI design orientation is concerned.

The LinearLayout UI orientation, vertical or portrait versus horizontal or landscape can be set using the **.setOrientation()** method in your Java code, or by using XML via the **android:orientation** parameter. The constants that can be specified for the orientation parameter are **vertical** or **horizontal**.

In addition to the orientation of your UI widgets within a LinearLayout UI container, you can also specify their **alignment** within the orientation, by using those same **layout_gravity** parameters that we covered during the previous chapter when we learned about the Android FrameLayout container.

The way to achieve specifying a layout gravity (dynamically, in real-time) would be by using Java code, by calling your **.setGravity()** method. Layout gravity can also be specified **statically**, that is, at design-time, rather than at runtime, by using the XML parameter that you implemented in the previous chapter called **android:layout_gravity**.

Besides specifying the general alignment or the direction that UI elements within the Linear Layout are going to gravitate toward, Android developers can additionally specify the general **percentage** of the screen that each UI element will take up initially, and scale up or scale down to fit when display screen resolution or orientation changes.

This feature is implemented using an **android:layout_weight** parameter that we will be covering in detail during the next section of this chapter.

Some of the commonly known direct subclasses of LinearLayout, that is, the ones which have already been coded for you and are a permanent part of the Android API, include: **TableLayout**, **NumberPicker**, **ZoomControls**, **RadioGroup**, **TableRow**, **SearchView**, and the **TabWidget** class.

The LinearLayout class has **one nested class**, the **LinearLayout.LayoutParams** class, which we cover right after we take a more detailed look at the LinearLayout's unique concept of layout weight, and how weights are implemented by using ordinal (rather than cardinal) integer values.

UI Element Spacing in LinearLayout: Using Layout Weight

The LinearLayout class is one of the only UI layout classes that supports assigning a **weight** to an individual user interface child element in the layout container. This is done by using the **android:layout_weight** attribute along with a floating point (also known in Java as a **float**) numeric value.

This weight attribute or parameter serves to assign an "importance" value to the child View UI element, in terms of what percentage of screen space the View should occupy within your screen's overall UI design.

A relatively larger weight value allows that UI element to garner more of the total screen real estate in the direction (dimension) that has been defined for that UI element. The default setting for the weight parameter, if none is specified, is zero or the lowest priority. If other UI elements have been assigned a higher weight value, then this would be an equivalent of the wrap_content layout constant setting being applied to a UI element.

If all child View UI elements specify weight values, then the screen space in the parent LinearLayout ViewGroup is allocated to children according to the relative proportion between all of their declared weights. Since float values are allowed, a logical way to approach this is to use percentage of one values, such as 0.25, for 25% of the screen real estate, and then make sure that all your weight values add up to 1.0.

As an example, if you have three Button UI elements, within a LinearLayout container, and you set the weight to 1 in two of these, while the other is given no weight parameter, that is, set to zero, then your third Button UI element without any weight will not expand to fill any UI design space and will only occupy the area required by its content. This is why I made that **zero weight is an equivalent to wrap_content** analogy earlier.

Under this scenario, other two Button UI elements will expand equally, and fill the remaining screen space. If the third UI Button element were to be given a weight of 2, instead of zero, that UI Button would be specified as being more important (or having more weight) than your other two UI Button elements. Under this scenario, that UI Button would get half of your total screen real estate, while the first two UI Buttons share the rest equally, that is, each would get one-quarter, or 25%, of the total UI design space.

The way that this would be calculated is **1+1+2=4** and 2/4 is 50% and 1/4 is 25%. As I mentioned before an easier way to set weight would be to use 0.5 instead of 2 and 0.25 instead of 1 in this particular example, which would allow you to numerically conceptualize the screen weight as percentages of the screen width (or height), rather than numbers relative to each other.

LinearLayout.LayoutParams Nested Class: Layout Weight

This **LinearLayout.LayoutParams** class is another **nested class** that extends the **ViewGroup.MarginLayoutParams** nested class, which, in turn, extends the **ViewGroup.LayoutParams** nested class, which was originally coded using Java Object class to create layout parameters for all the ViewGroup subclasses.

The LinearLayout.LayoutParams class hierarchy, which starts with your Java Object and progresses down the class hierarchy from ViewGroup.LayoutParams through ViewGroup.MarginLayoutParams, would thus be structured like this:

```
java.lang.Object
  > android.view.ViewGroup.LayoutParams
    > android.view.ViewGroup.MarginLayoutParams
      > android.widget.LinearLayout.LayoutParams
```

A LinearLayout.LayoutParams class inherits the ViewGroup.LayoutParams, as well as ViewGroup. MarginLayoutParams or margin layout parameters, and then adds in **layout_weight** and **layout_gravity** parameters and the layout gravity **constants** which we covered in detail in the previous FrameLayout chapter.

It is important to note that although the LinearLayout container type also implements the same layout_gravity constants, it does not accomplish this by subclassing the FrameLayout class. It implements the gravity constants in parallel, making it easy on us developers by using the same constants.

That being said, Table 11-1 in the previous chapter, plus all the information regarding layout_gravity still holds true for LinearLayout container usage as well, as so I will not repeat that content again here.

ImageButton Class: Create Custom Button Graphics

Before we code the LinearLayout Activity subclass, I wanted to give you an overview of the ImageButton UI widget class before we use that inside of our LinearLayout UI container. We'll get all these class reviews over at the beginning of the chapter before we code!

The ImageButton is a widget UI element class used inside of a UI layout class, and although this book focuses on UI layout container classes at its top-most level, I am also going to strive to cover the major widget classes as well.

Android ImageButton Class: Multi-State Graphical Buttons

The Android **ImageButton** class is a **direct subclass** of the **ImageView** class, which is itself a subclass of the **View** superclass, which, as we learned in Chapter 3, is a subclass of the **java.lang. Object** master class and used for creating UI widgets.

The class hierarchy for the ImageButton class is structured as follows:

```
java.lang.Object
  > android.view.View
    > android.widget.ImageView
      > android.widget.ImageButton
```

The ImageButton, like its parent class ImageView, is stored in a separate Android package for UI widgets called the **android.widget** package. This is because ImageButton is an often-used UI widget that can be leveraged for custom Button UI elements that can be created using digital images.

The ImageButton UI widget is used when a developer needs to create a custom UI Button element that displays a Button as an image instead of as a standard text label on a square background, such as a standard UI Button element. We implemented these in the chapters covering ActionBar.

Just like the Android Button class UI widget, an ImageButton UI widget can be pressed (by using a click or a touch event) by the user, and could have Button focus characteristics defined as well, by using multi-state images.

If you don't utilize any of its custom parameters, your ImageButton widget will have a visual appearance of a standard Android Button, with that gray transparent button background, which changes color to blue when the button is pressed. That being said, don't use an ImageButton unless you are going to implement the digital image assets and the multi-state features that we are going to cover within this chapter; use a Button UI element instead!

The ImageButton can have up to four different ImageButton "states" defined using XML markup, which we will be doing a bit later on in the chapter. I will cover these ImageButton states in detail, in the next section of this chapter, after I cover a couple of the key XML parameters and Java methods here in this section on the ImageButton class member methods and features.

The **default image** for your ImageButton UI widget, which defines its **normal state**, can be defined statically by using the **android:src** XML parameter in a **<ImageButton>** child tag inside your XML layout container UI definition.

The **default image** for your ImageButton UI widget, which defines its **normal state**, can be defined dynamically (at runtime) as well in your Java code, and this can be implemented by using the **.setImageResource()** method.

We will be using XML to define our UI designs, as Android prefers that we do, in this book. If you use the android:src parameter to reference image assets, this will replace your standard ImageButton background image.

It's important to note that developers can use both the android:background parameter, which allows you to install a background image plate, or layer, in the ImageButton UI element, as well as the android:src parameter, which allows you to install the foreground image plate (layer) asset at the same time. Be sure to use every parameter that you can with your UI widgets!

You want to define both a foreground image plate and a background image plate (asset) at the same time in the same UI element so that you could take advantage of the awesome power of digital image **compositing** that Android affords via these multiple image plates.

You can also set the ImageButton background color value to be **transparent** (#00000000), if you want to composite with other image layers behind your ImageButton, such as the background image asset for your LinearLayout!

ImageButton States: Normal, Pressed, Focused, and Hovered

An ImageButton class allows the definition of custom image assets for each of the states of a UI Button. States include **normal** (the default or not in use), **pressed** (a user's touching, or pressing down on, the click selection hardware), **focused** (recently touched and released or clicked and released) and **hovered** (user is over an ImageButton with the mouse or navigation key, but has not touched it or clicked on it yet).

This hovered state was added recently in Android 4, API Level 14, possibly in anticipation of using the Android OS for the Google Chromebook products or in anticipation of the Dell Project Ophelia Android USB PC products.

I've summarized the primary ImageButton states, along with the mouse event equivalents, which would be used on non-Touchscreen devices, in Table 12-1.

Table 12-1. The Android ImageButton Class Primary Image Asset State Constants and Mouse Usage Equivalents

ImageButton State	Description of State along with the Mouse Event Equivalent
NORMAL	Default ImageButton State when not in use. Equivalent: Mouse Out
PRESSED	ImageButton State when touched or clicked. Equivalent: Mouse Down
FOCUSED	ImageButton State when touched and released. Equivalent: Mouse Up
HOVERED (API 14)	ImageButton State if focused (not touched) Equivalent: Mouse Over

ImageButton UI elements are difficult to implement, because you want to create a unique digital image asset, for each ImageButton state. Different images visually indicate to a user your different ImageButton states, as we will soon see later in the chapter. The reason this can be difficult is not because of the XML markup involved but rather the extensive digital imaging work that will need to be done, across several resolution levels.

We'll be using GIMP 2.8.10 later on in this chapter to create these digital ImageButton UI states for each of these ImageButtons that we are going to implement in each of the resolution densities required by Android to span across different device types and screen sizes and resolutions.

A standard work process to define an ImageButton state is to utilize a XML drawable definition file that lives in the **/res/drawable** folder and uses a parent **<selector>** tag and child **<item>** tag that define each of the ImageButton states, using custom digital image asset references. Once this XML definition is set-up Android will automatically change the image asset based on the state of your ImageButton. The order of the state definitions is important, as they are evaluated in order. This is why the normal image asset comes last, because it will be displayed after **android:state_pressed** and **android:state_focused** states have both been evaluated (and are false).

Creating a UserInterface Menu Structure: UI Layouts Menu

Next let's put in place the OptionsMenu structure that we are going to use for the remainder of the book, and add our first LinearLayout menu item to it. I am doing this so that we will have a different Activity subclass for each of the UI layout container classes (ViewGroup subclasses) that we'll implement during the remainder of this book. Edit your **/res/menu/main.xml** menu XML file in Eclipse, reverting it to a single menu item, with an **ID** of **linear_layout**, and a string reference to a string constant named **linear_layout** with the data value "**LinearLayout**," as shown in Figure 12-1.

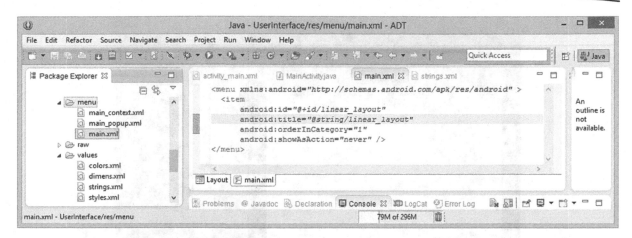

Figure 12-1. *Creating a LinearLayout menu entry in our new /res/menu/main.xml menu definition XML file*

Next add a standard onCreateOptionsMenu() method, as shown in Figure 12-2.

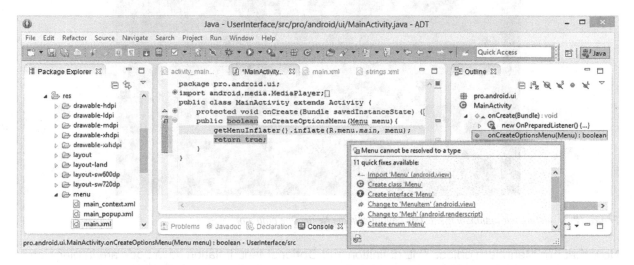

Figure 12-2. *Create the onCreateOptionsMenu() method to inflate our new layouts menu using getMenuInflater()*

This creates a Menu object named menu inflated with your main.xml menu definition by using the getMenuInflater() method using the following code:

```
public boolean onCreateOptionsMenu(Menu menu) {
    getMenuInflater().inflate(R.menu.main, menu);
    return true;
}
```

As you can see in Figure 12-2, you will need to mouse-over the reference to the Menu class, and select the **Import Menu (android.view)** option. Now you are ready to test the Menu object in the Nexus One, using **Run As ➤ Android Application** work process, and test your MenuItem, as shown in Figure 12-3. As you can see, the Linear Layout menu item appears as expected, and looks attractive and professional, with a nice gray background provided by Android.

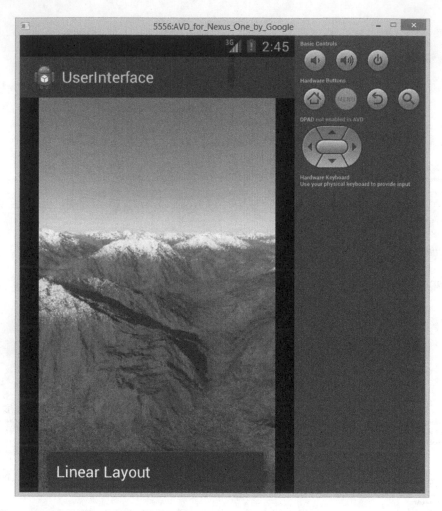

Figure 12-3. Testing our main.xml menu XML definition in the Nexus One emulator

Now that our MenuItem object XML definition and OptionsMenu inflation Java code are in place and working, the next thing we'll need to put into place is the onOptionsItemSelected() method, which holds our switch case logic.

The Java for this method and its switch case logic should look like this:

```
@Override
public boolean onOptionsItemSelected(MenuItem item){
    switch (item.getItemId()){
    }
    return true;
}
```

As you can see in Figure 12-4, you'll need to mouse-over your reference to the MenuItem class, and select the **Import MenuItem (android.view)** option.

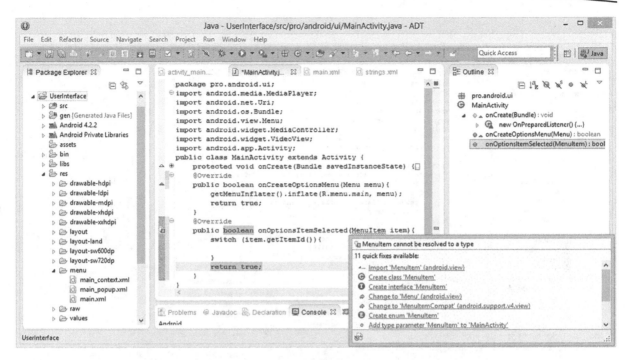

Figure 12-4. Create an onOptionsItemSelected() method to process MenuItem objects; import MenuItem class

Next, you need to add in the case statement for your LinearLayout Activity subclass. This detects your MenuItem object using its ID reference of **R.id.linear_layout** and then creates an Intent object named **intent_ll** using the new keyword and referencing the LinearActivity.class using the following two lines of Java code, as are shown in Figure 12-5:

```
case R.id.linear_layout:
    Intent intent_ll = new Intent(this, LinearActivity.class);
```

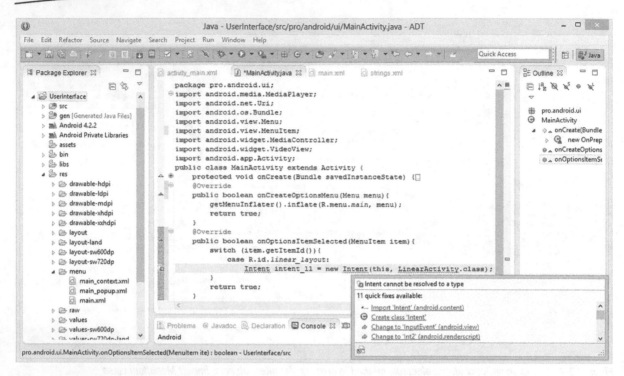

Figure 12-5. Create a switch case structure with an Intent object named intent_ll and then Import Intent class

You'll need to mouse-over the reference to the Intent class and select the **Import Intent (android.content)** option, to generate your Import statement.

Once you import your Intent class, you will notice that there is still an error underline under your **LinearActivity.class** reference, as can be seen in Figure 12-6 on the lower-right side of the screenshot. This is because the LinearActivity.java Activity subclass has not yet been created, and you are referencing it inside the Intent object instantiation Java code, so Eclipse throws an error highlighting to alert you to this.

Figure 12-6. Mouse-over the LinearActivity.class reference and select the Create class 'LinearActivity' option

Mouse-over this error highlighting and you see an option to create this class for you, which is the easiest way at this point to get this done, so click this first option, **Create class 'LinearActivity'** and have Eclipse create this Java class for you.

This brings up the **New Java Class** dialog, which should be filled out with the **LinearActivity** class name, as well as your package name, and every other piece of information that is needed, except for the superclass from which you want to subclass this Activity class. Chances are that the default Java.lang.Object superclass specified in this dialog is not the superclass that you wish to use, so let's select our own custom Android class that we wish to superclass next.

Click on the **Browse** button next to the **Superclass** field (see Figure 12-7), and type in a few characters of the word "activity," to bring up all the Activity classes in Android inside of the **Superclass Selection** dialog, which can be seen on the right side of Figure 12-7. Find an **android.app.Activity** superclass, and select it, and click the **OK** button at the bottom of the dialog. This sets Android's Activity Superclass as the class from which you want to subclass. Once you do this, the Superclass Selection dialog disappears.

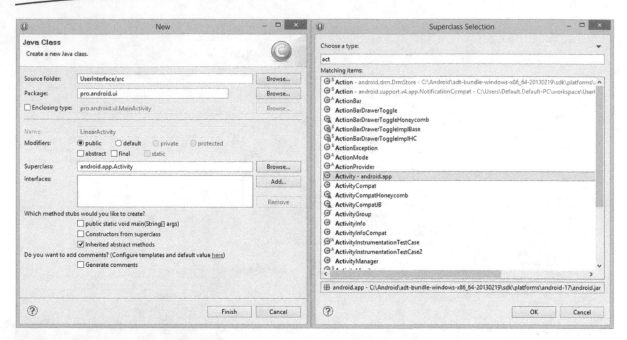

Figure 12-7. *A New Java Class dialog (on left); select the android.app.Activity Superclass via Superclass Selection dialog (on right)*

Once everything has been filled out correctly, click the **Finish** button.

After you click Finish, Eclipse opens up the **LinearActivity.java** tab as you can see in Figure 12-8. We will fill out this class in the next section of the chapter with our LinearLayout UI design.

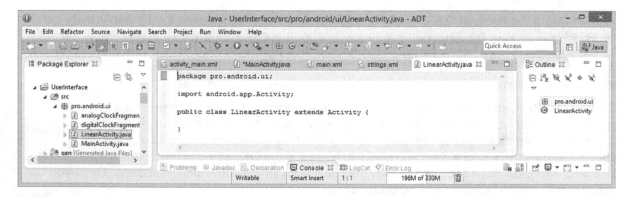

Figure 12-8. *The LinearLayout.java Activity subclass created by the New Java Class dialogs launched by Eclipse*

Now let's finish our case statement for the linear_layout Intent object by using a **.startActivity()** method to call our **Intent** object named **intent_ll**, so that when this MenuItem object is selected our Activity is launched via the following line of Java code, which can be seen shaded in Figure 12-9:

```
this.startActivity(intent_ll);
```

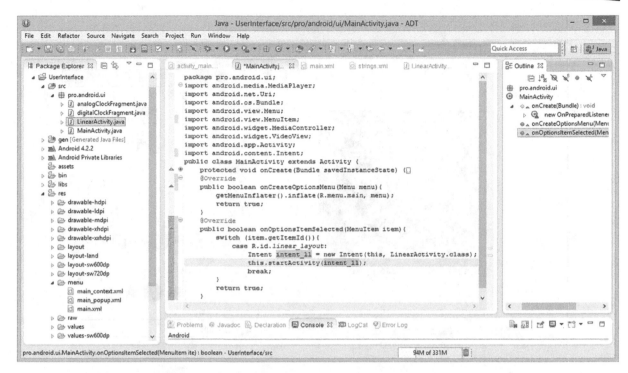

Figure 12-9. *Use a .startActivity( ) method called off a Context object (this) to launch LinearActivity class via an Intent object named intent_ll*

Now we have the infrastructure in place to add layout container menu items for each of the remaining chapters, and we can go ahead and create digital image assets for your ImageButton UI elements. After that we will create a LinearLayout UI design using a LinearLayout XML parent tag, and child tags for ImageButton UI elements and some supporting TextView UI elements.

Using GIMP Digital Imaging Software for UI Design

Let's use one of the most popular open source digital image editing and compositing software packages to add our own style and flair to the UI Button elements, and expand our content production workflow outside of simply using Eclipse ADT, Java coding, and XML markup.

Creating Multi-State ImageButton Assets: Using GIMP 2.8.10

The first thing you'll need to do—before you can create your LinearLayout and ImageButton based UI design—is to create a dozen digital image assets, to provide the four ImageButton states for MDPI, HDPI, and XHDPI resolution densities. Let's do that now. Launch GIMP and use the **File ➤ Open** command, and open the **earth_256.png** image asset to set that as the background layer (plate) in GIMP. Next, use the **File ➤ Open as Layers** command to import the **button_styling.png** button UI styling element into a second layer on top of the earth_256.png background layer, as shown in Figure 12-10 on the right.

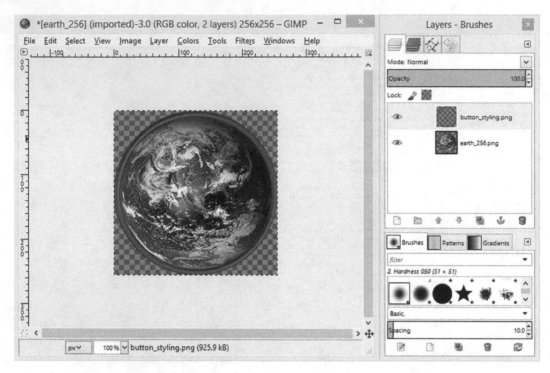

Figure 12-10.   Use File ➤ Open to open earth_256.png and File ➤ Open as Layers to import button_styling.png

This creates our **hover** image button state, which would be a red ring appearing around the Earth button when the mouse was hovered over it.

We need to export this ImageButton hover state to our **/res/drawable-xhdpi** folder, using the **File ➤ Export** menu command sequence, as is shown in Figure 12-11. Name the file **ib_earth_hover.png** for ImageButton Earth Hover State, and click the **Export** button once you have navigated to the **/Users/YourName/workspace/UserInterface/res/drawable-xhdpi** folder as shown in Figure 12-11 at the top next to the **Save in folder:** label. The **Name:** field should have the **ib_earth_hover.png** file name using lowercase.

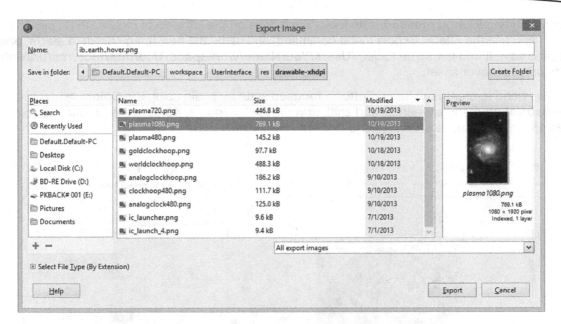

Figure 12-11. Export hover button state as ib-earth-hover.png into the /res/drawable-xhdpi folder

Next, click the **button_styling** layer to select it for modification, pull down the **Colors** menu, and select the **Hue-Saturation** menu command. The Hue-Saturation dialog opens, where you can adjust your **Hue 60 degrees** and increase the **Lightness 15%,** as shown in the middle of Figure 12-12.

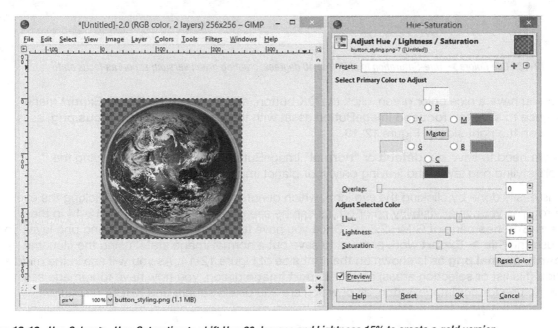

Figure 12-12. Use Colors ➤ Hue-Saturation to shift Hue 60 degrees and Lightness 15% to create a gold version

Once your ImageButton **pressed** state looks like it does on the left side of Figure 12-12, click the **OK** button, and use the **File ➤ Export** menu command, and name the new image asset **ib_earth_press. png**, and save it into the same folder, **/Users/YourName/workspace/UserInterface/res/drawable-xhdpi** as your hover asset.

Next, we need to create our ImageButton's **focused** state by again using the **Colors ➤ Hue-Saturation** menu sequence, and shifting your Hue by another **40 degrees** around the color wheel to a green hue, as shown in Figure 12-13.

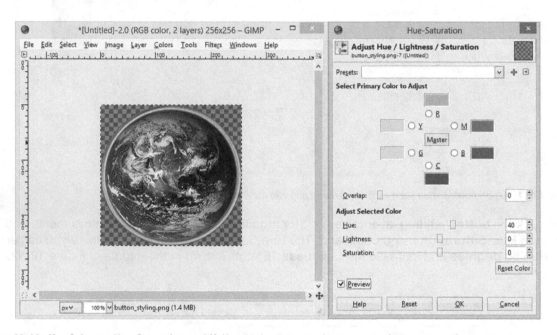

Figure 12-13. Use Colors ➤ Hue-Saturation to shift Hue 40 degrees, creating green version; export as focus state

Once you have a nice color green, click the **OK** button, and then use the **File ➤ Export** menu sequence to save the **focused** ImageButton asset with the filename **ib_earth_focus.png**, as is shown on the right side of Figure 12-13.

Now we need to save our **default** or "**normal**" ImageButton initial state, by removing the button_styling.png layer, and leaving only your planet image.

This is easily done by clicking the eye icon, which denotes the layer's visibility. Clicking the eye icon toggles your layer visibility on or off, as can be seen in the middle of Figure 12-14 in the **Layers-Brushes** pane of GIMP 2.8.10. Once you have turned off the button_styling.png layer, you can use the **File ➤ Export** work process to save out a normal image state, using the filename **ib_earth_normal.png** as is shown on the right side of Figure 12-14. As you will see in the middle portion (file list or selection areas) of your **Export Image** dialog, you now have four image asset states to use for our ImageButton, all of which are 256 pixels square and XHDPI resolution.

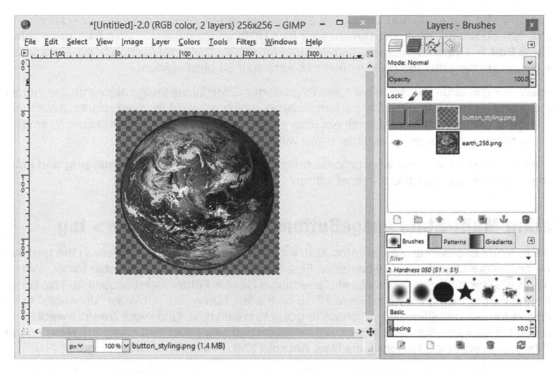

Figure 12-14. Deselect eye (visibility) icon in button_styling.png layer, creating default version; export as normal state

Next perform this same work process shown in Figures 12-11 through 12-14 to create HDPI (128 pixel) and MDPI (64 pixel) image assets. Use the **Image ➤ Scale Image** menu sequence in GIMP, the dialogs for which are shown in Figure 12-15.

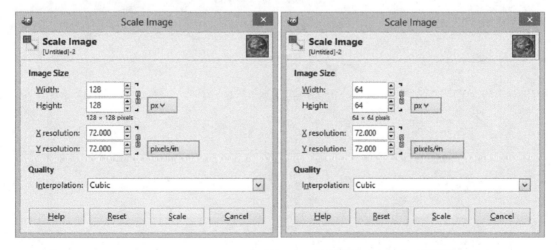

Figure 12-15. Use Image ➤ Scale Image to scale image, creating 128 pixel (HDPI) and 64 pixel (MDPI) versions

It's important that you scale from an original 256 pixel image for both of the scale operations. After you do a 128 pixel work process to create your four **HDPI** image assets, in your **/res/drawable-hdpi** folder, use **Edit ➤ Undo** as the menu sequence to return to a 256 pixel version of your image assets before downsampling the 256 pixel version to create your 64 pixel version.

The reason for this is because you will need to give your GIMP Scale Image algorithm the largest amount of source data with which to perform scaling, which will yield the best results. Always scale from a large asset to each smaller level, not from largest to medium, and then medium to small. This is to avoid rescaling the scaling artifacts, if you will.

You'll need to repeat the entire work process outlined in this section for the **venus.png** and **jupiter. png** image assets to create those ImageButtons!

Creating Multi-State ImageButtons: Using a <selector> tag

Now we're ready to create an ImageButton XML infrastructure, which we will access in the next section, after we create our LinearLayout UI container. First create the generic **/res/drawable** folder, right-clicking on the /res folder work process and selecting a **New ➤ Folder** menu sequence. This brings up the **New Folder** dialog shown in Figure 12-16 on the left. Name your subfolder "drawable" to hold your XML drawable definition files, which we're going to create next. Once your **/res/drawable** folder appears within your UserInterface project, right-click on that new folder, and select the **New ➤ Android XML File** menu sequence, launching the **New Android XML File** dialog shown in Figure 12-16.

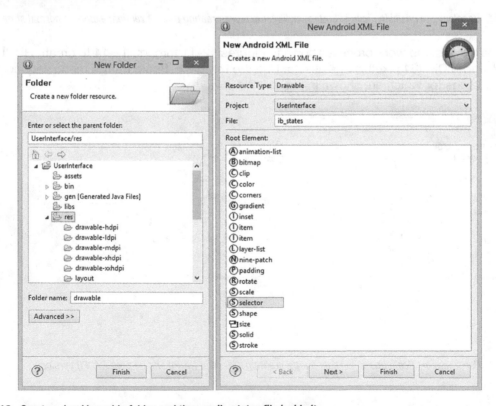

Figure 12-16. Create a /res/drawable folder, and then an ib_states file inside it

Name the file **ib_states** and select the **<selector>** root element parent tag, and then click **Finish** and create the **ib_states.xml** file. This open up for editing automatically in Eclipse, and is shown (with child tags, which we are going to add in next) in Figure 12-17.

Figure 12-17. Add a parent <selector> tag and child <item> tags to access four ImageButton state image assets

We need to add in four child <item> tags that will represent our different ImageButton states. We accomplish this using the following XML markup:

```
<?xml version="1.0" encoding="utf-8"?>
<selector xmlns:android="http://schemas.android.com/apk/res/android >
    <item android:state_hovered="true"
          android:drawable="@drawable/ib_earth_hover" />
    <item android:state_pressed="true"
          android:drawable="@drawable/ib_earth_press" />
    <item android:state_focused="true"
          android:drawable="@drawable/ib_earth_focus" />
    <item android:drawable="@drawable/ib_earth_normal" />
</selector>
```

The order that you put the ImageButton states inside the parent <selector> container is important, because this is the order in which the Android OS processes them.

Interestingly, this also happens to be the same order that you (as a user) will approach a UI element in with your mouse! First you **hover** over the UI element, then you **press** (click) down on it, once that has been done the UI element has the **focus**, and once you move on to use another UI element this returns to the unused or **normal** (which is the default) state.

The last thing that you'll need to do, before you create your LinearLayout UI definition in XML, is to use the same exact work process as outlined in this section to create your **ib2_states.xml** file, referencing your **ib_venus** ImageButton image assets and an **ib3_states.xml** file referencing **ib_jupiter** ImageButton image assets.

Remember that you created these two dozen ImageButton image assets, in the previous section of this chapter, using the same work process that you used to create your original dozen ib_earth ImageButton image assets.

As you can see here, your work process for implementing new media based UI elements in Android can get very involved indeed, as you have created four states for each ImageButton element, in each of three resolution densities (12 assets) and for three ImageButton UI elements. This means that you had to create 36 completely different digital imaging assets, and then reference them via 3 different XML definition files! This equated to creating close to 40 different PNG and XML files to implement three ImageButton UI elements across every Android device.

Creating a LinearLayout UI Design: Using <LinearLayout>

The first thing that you need to do is to create your **activity_linear** XML UI definition file that matches up with the **LinearActivity** Java class.

Right-click your **/res/layout** folder, and select the **New ➤ Android XML File** menu sequence, which brings up the New Android XML File dialog.

Name your file **activity_linear**, and select the Root Element **<LinearLayout>** parent tag for this UI Layout XML definition file that you are creating here, as shown in Figure 12-18. Then click the **Finish** button to create the file.

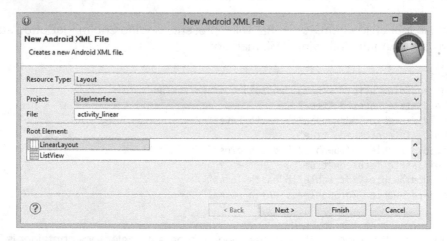

Figure 12-18. Creating the activity_linear.xml UI Layout definition file

After you create this file, Eclipse opens the file in its own tab in the IDE and sets the preview tab mode to Graphical Layout, as shown in Figure 12-19. Also shown in this screenshot are your three ib_states XML files, and the dozen ImageButton image asset states in your drawable-hdpi folder, which I have opened to show you that these assets have been added.

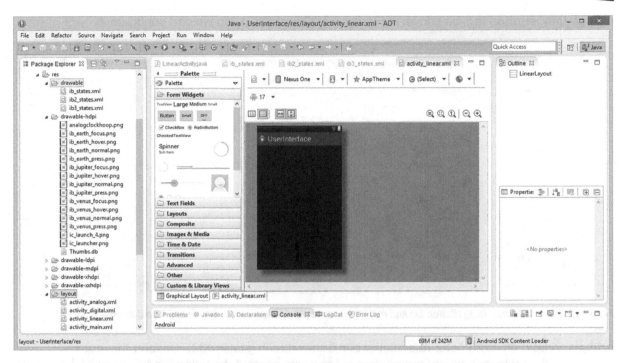

Figure 12-19. *Viewing LinearLayout container in Graphical Layout tab opened for you by a New XML File dialog*

Since we're learning how to write code and markup in this book and not how to use drag-and-drop tools (GLE), click the **activity_linear.xml** tab at the bottom of the editing pane shown in Figure 12-20, and switch the GL Editor into XML editing mode. Once you do this, you will see the XML markup for a LinearLayout container, including the required width and height parameters and the orientation parameter set to the vertical constant. In the line of space after the parent tag, type in a **<** left chevron to bring up a helper dialog with all the child tags that can be utilized with LinearLayout.

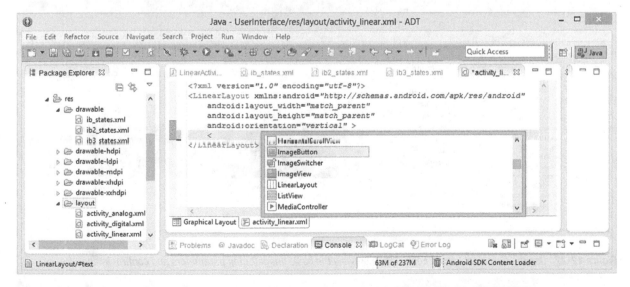

Figure 12-20. *Using the left-chevron to open the helper dialog containing all the available LinearLayout child tags*

Add an ImageButton tag, as shown in Figures 12-20 and 12-21, so we can configure it.

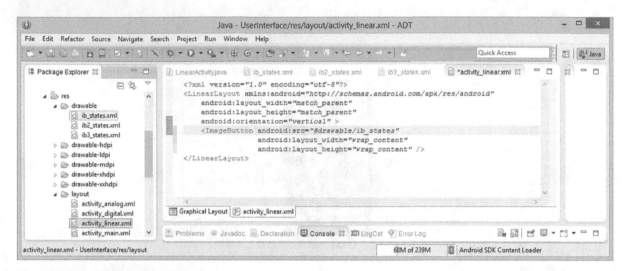

Figure 12-21.   Insert basic ImageButton tag and required parameters defining source image and layout constants

Add an android:src parameter referencing our @drawable/ib_states XML file, and the required layout_width and layout_height parameters set to wrap_content, by using the following XML markup:

```
<ImageButton android:src="@drawable/ib_states"
    android:layout_width="wrap_content" android:layout_height="wrap_content" />
```

Once this markup is in place, click the Graphical Layout tab at the bottom of the IDE, shown in Figure 12-22, and preview your UI design so far.

Figure 12-22.   Use the Graphical Layout Editor tab to preview the basic ImageButton parameters and confirm image

As you can see we need to get rid of a gray area behind the ImageButton so we can take advantage of your ImageButton asset's alpha channel data. Type **android:** to invoke the dialog shown in Figure 12-23, and add a **background**.

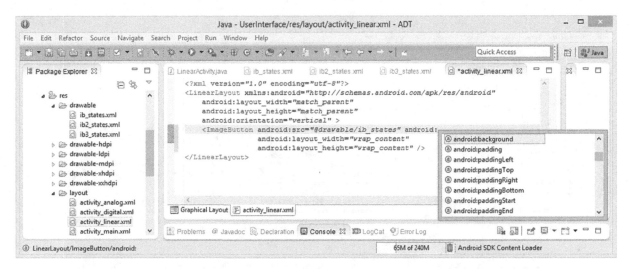

Figure 12-23.   Add a transparent background, using the android: work process to access parameter helper dialog

Set the **android:background** value to **transparent** using the **#00000000** value, and add the required **android:contentDescription** parameter for the impaired, and reference it to the **ib_earth**, **ib_venus** and **ib_jupiter** <string> values, which you need to add to your **strings.xml** file, as shown in Figure 12-24.

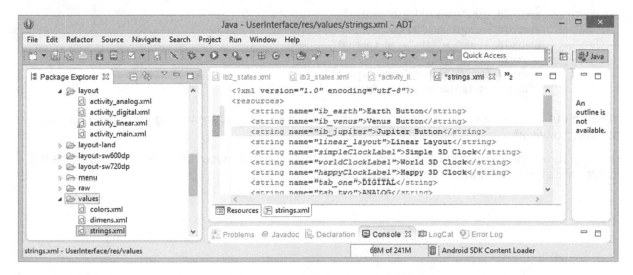

Figure 12-24.   Add three <string> constants in the strings.xml file for the contentDescription parameters to access

Finally, before you copy and paste this first ImageButton UI definition to create the next two, add the **android:id** parameter, so we can reference the ImageButton UI element inside of your Java code, as shown in Figure 12-25.

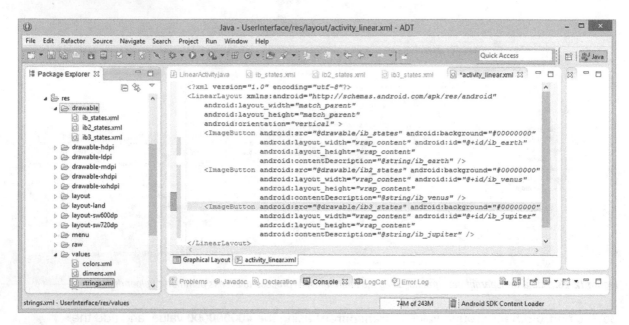

Figure 12-25. Copy and paste the first ImageButton tag to create the second and third ImageButton UI elements

The final XML markup for the ImageButton UI element should look like this:

```
<ImageButton android:src="@drawable/ib_states"
             android:background="#00000000"
             android:layout_width="wrap_content"
             android:id="@+id/ib_earth"
             android:layout_height="wrap_content"
             android:contentDescription="@string/ib_earth" />
```

You can cut and paste this if you wish; I would type it in to get practice writing your own mark-up directly, however!

Once all three ImageButton tags are in place, use the Graphical Layout tab at the bottom of the IDE to preview your UI design, shown in Figure 12-26.

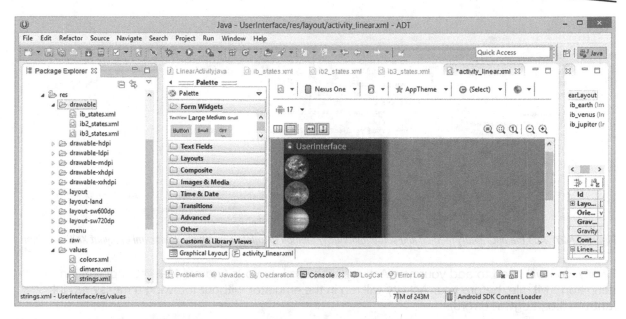

Figure 12-26. *Using the Graphical Layout Editor tab to preview the ImageButton UI elements using transparency*

Unfortunately, the Graphical Layout Editor tool in Eclipse cannot simulate the states of the ImageButtons, so we will have to implement the UI layout design in Java to test these UI elements thoroughly in the Nexus One emulator, which we will do in the next section.

Inflating the LinearLayout UI Design: Coding LinearActivity

Before we can see our LinearLayout UI layout and ImageButton UI widgets in the Nexus One emulator, we will need to put some Java code in place in our virgin LinearActivity class. This includes the **onCreate()** method to create the Activity, and the **setContentView()** to inflate the **activity_linear.xml** UI definition. The Java code, also seen in Figure 12-27, looks like the following:

```
protected void onCreate(Bundle savedInstanceState) {
    super.onCreate(savedInstanceState);
    setContentView(R.layout.activity_linear);
}
```

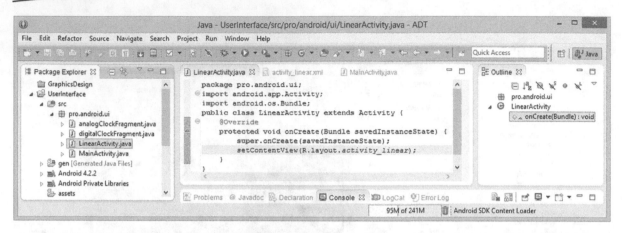

Figure 12-27. *Add the onCreate() method and setContentView() method to inflate our activity_linear.xml UI layout XML definition*

Finally, you will need to add your new Activity subclass into your Android Manifest application definition XML file, before your Activity will run in the emulator without throwing a messy red ink tantrum (i.e., LogCat errors).

Right-click your UserInterface **AndroidManifest.xml** file, at the bottom of your project folder, and **open** it in the Eclipse IDE. Add an **<activity>** tag underneath the MainActivity <activity> tag structure, and add **android:name** and **android:label** tags, using the following markup, also shown in Figure 12-28:

```
<activity android:name="pro.android.ui.LinearActivity"
          android:label="@string/linear_layout" />
```

Figure 12-28. *Adding an <activity> tag in the AndroidManifest.xml file for the LinearActivity class*

We're using the same <string> constant as we used for our MenuItem object.

Now you can use your **Run As ➤ Android Application** work process to test the ImageButton and LinearLayout XML markup that you have in place so far with the Nexus One emulator. As you can see in Figure 12-29, the button styling element that we added to alert the user that the ImageButton is being used appears when we click (or touch) these ImageButton UI elements.

Figure 12-29. Testing the ImageButton states using the Nexus One

I am not showing the red and green versions of your ImageButton styling states because when you test your LinearLayout user interface design using the Nexus One emulator, the hovered and focused image states will not show a hovered ImageButton state or a focused ImageButton state. This is because this Nexus One Android device that we are emulating using this AVD is a consumer electronics product that features a touchscreen only, and thus hover and focus states are not represented.

If you test this app on a device that supports hover (mouse) and focus, you will find that the code that we put in place works as expected. It is always advisable to include all four ImageButton states when you develop, as that way your application will support every type of hardware device!

Nesting UI Layout Containers for Advanced Design

You can also "nest" UI containers, to create more complex user interface designs, although this can take up more system memory, which is something that we will look at a bit later on in the book. Let's take a look at this next, just so that you are exposed to this UI layout container nesting concept and option.

Complex LinearLayouts: Nesting LinearLayout Containers

Next, let's add a TextView UI element that adds a label to the right side of the ImageButton and tells our user what the planet name is. We'll do this using a nested horizontal LinearLayout construct, to show you how to use a nested LinearLayout structure, which is often done in Android development.

Add a line of space after your vertical (parent) LinearLayout tag, and add a LinearLayout tag with a **horizontal** orientation, as seen in Figure 12-30. Make sure that you also add in the required **layout_width** and **layout_height** parameters set to a **wrap_content** constant, using the following XML markup:

```
<LinearLayout android:orientation="horizontal"
    android:layout_width="wrap_content" android:layout_height="wrap_content" >
```

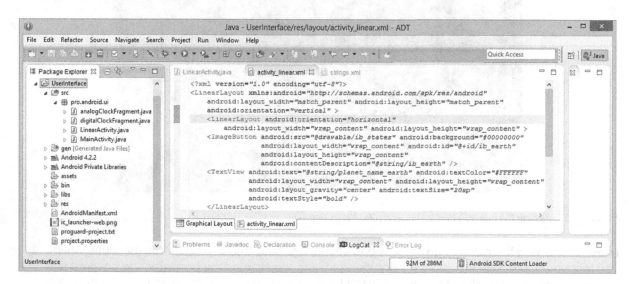

Figure 12-30. *Add a nested horizontal <LinearLayout> and a <TextView> UI element to enhance your UI design*

Add a **<TextView>** UI element tag after your ImageButton UI element tag, and configure it via text and layout parameters with the following XML markup:

```
<TextView android:text="@string/planet_name_earth" android:textColor="#FFFFFF"
        android:layout_width="wrap_content" android:layout_height="wrap_content"
        android:layout_gravity="center" android:textSize="20sp"
        android:textStyle="bold" />
</LinearLayout>
```

The **android:text** parameter references a <string> constant you will create, named **planet_name_earth** that contains the text "**Planet Name: Earth**" and an **android:textColor** parameter referencing an **#FFFFFF** hexadecimal color value for White. Then add your required wrap_content constants for layout_height and layout_width, and let's use the **layout_gravity** parameter, with a value of **center** to automatically center our TextView UI element.

To make your Text UI element stand out a bit more, let's also use a couple of text styling parameters, the **android:textSize** parameter set to **20sp**, or standard pixels, and the **android:textStyle** parameter set to the **bold** value (constant). Finally we have the **</LinearLayout>** closing tag for our nested LinearLayout UI container.

Be sure that you duplicate the nested LinearLayout construct for the other two ImageButton UI elements, changing the word earth to venus and jupiter, respectively, of course.

When you are all done, you can use your **Run As ➤ Android Application** work process, and test your new UI design, which should look like what you see on the left side of Figure 12-31. Let's add some additional parameters to the current UI definition to space this UI design out more professionally.

Figure 12-31. Testing the nested LinearLayout in the Nexus One emulator and making parameter additions to it

To center each horizontal LinearLayout let's add an **android:layout_gravity** parameter set to **center** in each nested <LinearLayout> tag, and to push the TextView away from the ImageButton let's add an **android:layout_marginRight** parameter to the ImageButton, set to a value of **8dp**. Your final XML markup for each planet's UI layout construct should look like the following:

```
<LinearLayout android:orientation="horizontal"
    android:layout_width="wrap_content" android:layout_height="wrap_content" >
    <ImageButton android:src="@drawable/ib_states" android:background="#00000000"
            android:layout_width="wrap_content" android:id="@+id/ib_earth"
            android:layout_height="wrap_content"
            android:contentDescription="@string/ib_earth" />
    <TextView android:text="@string/planet_name_earth" android:textColor="#FFFFFF"
            android:layout_width="wrap_content" android:layout_height="wrap_content"
            android:layout_gravity="center" android:textSize="20sp"
            android:textStyle="bold" />
</LinearLayout>
```

This XML markup renders a result shown on the right side of Figure 12-31.

Three Deep LinearLayouts: Nesting Nested LinearLayouts

It's important to note that you can nest LinearLayout containers as deeply as you wish, although I would not recommend this, as it is not very memory efficient. It is fairly common to find Android apps that nest LinearLayout containers three levels deep, however, which we are going to do next, to add planet information to this UI design to make it more functional and interesting.

In Chapter 13 we'll be learning how to use one single UI layout container to achieve a similar design to what we are going to create here, where we add some more information regarding the planet mass and gravity.

It is important to note that every time you add a nested LinearLayout class it adds an instance of that class in system memory, so if you go two levels deep you already have at least three or more LinearLayout instances used in memory. Going three or more levels deep could result in dozens of LinearLayout instances in memory. In this case it's better to use a single RelativeLayout, which we will be learning about very soon.

Since we need to add more information about these planets that are used in your ImageButton designs, we will add a LinearLayout container around your TextView UI elements. To do this, you will add a line of space, after your ImageButton tag, and add a <LinearLayout> tag, with a vertical orientation and centering gravity, using the following markup, also shown in Figure 12-32:

```
<LinearLayout android:orientation="vertical" android:layout_gravity="center"
    android:layout_width="wrap_content" android:layout_height="wrap_content" >
```

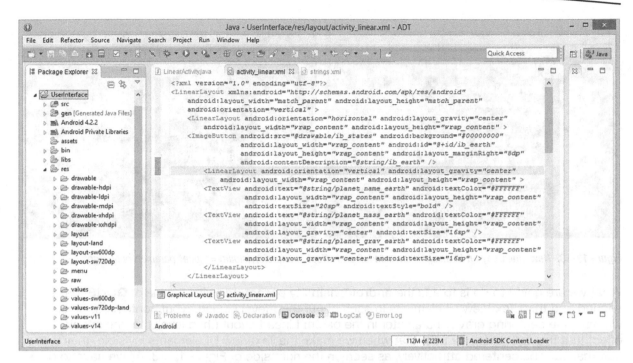

Figure 12-32. Add a third level of nested LinearLayout containers to align planet information elements vertically

We are using this vertical orientation because we want the text to stack on top of each other, and a center constant for the layout_gravity because we want any content within this LinearLayout container to center itself.

It's more efficient to apply the centering gravity at a LinearLayout level instead of inside of each TextView UI element, plus we're going to do some tricky parameter usage next which is going to allow us to make a UI design interactive, based on our ImageButton use. We're going to add Java code to make our ImageButton UI elements function in the next chapter section.

Now to see our three-deep LinearLayout UI construct in the Nexus One AVD, use the **Run As ➤ Android Application** work process and click on the MENU UI button in the emulator and launch your LinearLayout Activity subclass and as you can see on the left side of Figure 12-33, we now have an attractive and professional planet information panel on the right side of each planet in our user interface. Since this information should only appear when each planet ImageButton UI element is clicked, we will get some practice using the **android:visibility** parameter next, and see what it can do for our UI!

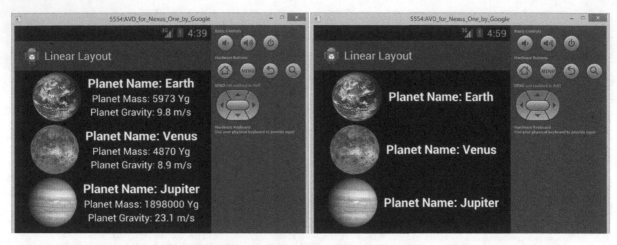

Figure 12-33. New LinearLayout UI design shown on left and effect of android:visibility="gone" parameters on right

What we are going to do is to add the **android:visibility parameter** with a value of **GONE** to the second and third TextView UI elements in each of our third-level LinearLayout containers. Since we have the centering gravity parameter in the parent LinearLayout (third level) tag, the special effect that this will create for us is that when we make the TextView UI elements invisible, they will automatically be centered attractively, as seen on the right side of Figure 12-33. All we have to do is add the **android:visibility** parameter and an **android:id** parameter to the second and third TextView UI elements, so that we can control them from our Java event handling code.

The markup for the TextView UI element will look similar to the following:

```
<TextView android:text="@string/planet_name_earth" android:textColor="#FFFFFF"
          android:layout_width="wrap_content" android:layout_height="wrap_content"
          android:layout_gravity="center" android:textSize="16sp"
          android:visibility="gone" android:id="@+id/tv2_earth" />
```

As you can see in Figure 12-34, the information TextView UI elements are now configured and are ready to access via the LinearActivity.java class.

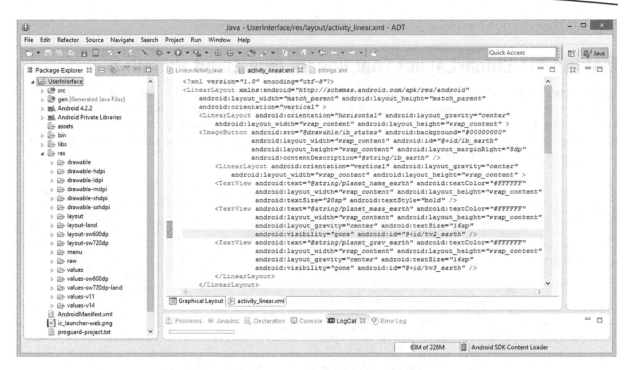

Figure 12-34. Add android:visibility="gone" parameter to the non-title TextView UI elements to set-up interactivity

Make sure that you've added the <string> constants that are referenced in your UI design, in the strings.xml file in the /res/values project folder. These nine constants, three for each planet, can be seen in Figure 12-35.

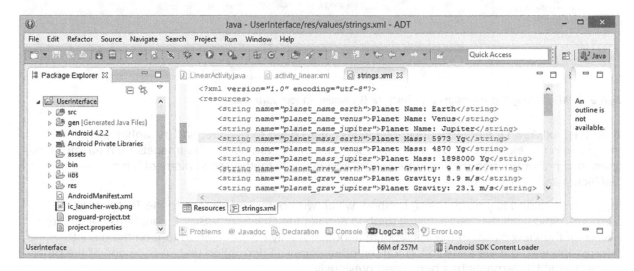

Figure 12-35. Nine <string> constants defining all the planet names, masses and gravity information for your UI

Now it is time to code the LinearActivity.java class to make this UI work!

Making the LinearLayout Functional: Java Event Handling

To implement the TextView UI elements, which we are going to access in our Java code inside of two different methods, onCreate() and onClick(), we'll need to declare these at the top of our Activity, and give them a name, as shown in Figure 12-36. Then inside the onCreate() method we'll instantiate them when our Activity is created, inflating them with your XML definition file reference using the ID you assigned in your XML file.

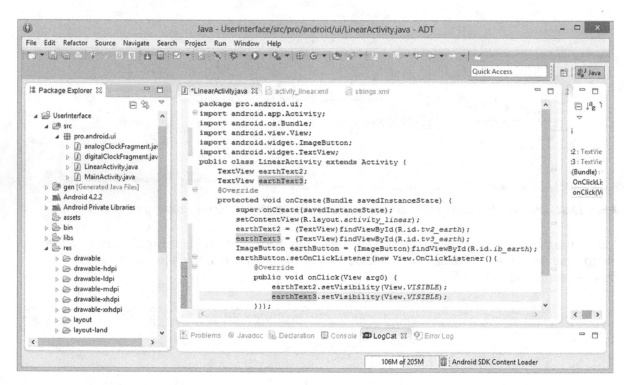

Figure 12-36. Creating and instantiating the TextView UI elements in your Java code

After the TextView UI elements are implemented, we'll need to declare, and instantiate, the ImageButton UI element inside of the onCreate() method. I am calling the ImageButton **earthButton** (planetNameButton) and then using a setOnClickListener() method to implement a new OnClickListener() method.

Inside this method is your onClick() method, which will contain references to the TextView UI elements which call the .setVisibility() method and set the GONE or VISIBLE constants, which are called off the View class. In the onClick() methods, not only do we need to turn on the planet's Information text, but we need to turn off the other planet's information text, in case one of the other ImageButton UI elements has been used previously.

In Figure 12-37, you can see your Java code construct for all six TextView UI elements, and one onClick() construct, which controls the visibility of all six TextViews. You will need to replicate this earthButton ImageButton declaration, instantiation, and event handling code for your other two planet buttons, changing the GONE and VISIBLE constants to match each planet's info.

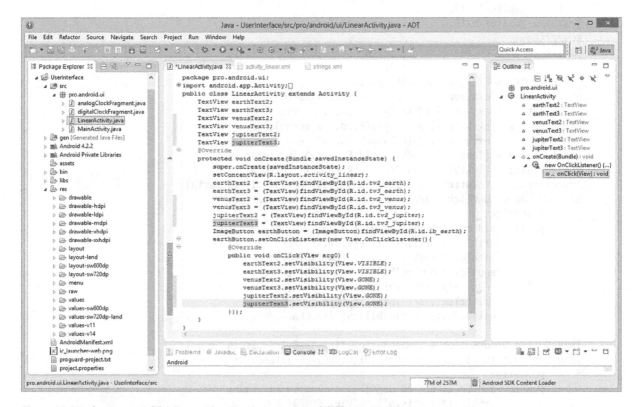

Figure 12-37. Create an onClick() event handler that sets your visibility constants

Once you have one ImageButton construct completed and working, you can cut and paste these 11 lines of Java code twice again underneath the first construct, and change the variable earth to venus or jupiter, respectively. Be sure to remember to change the R.id.ib_earth to R.id.ib_venus, and then to R.id.ib_jupiter in the findViewById() method in addition to the name of the ImageButton object (earthButton to venusButton then to jupiterButton).

Next you need to change the visibility constants so that the VISIBLE constants match the planet ImageButton that the onClick() event handler is servicing, and set the other four planet information TextView objects to a GONE constant value, so that your UI design can reconfigure how they look.

We are using GONE rather than an **INVISIBLE** constant to take advantage of the android:layout_gravity parameter that we're learning more about in this chapter. By using GONE, we are forcing Android to reposition our UI design for us using OS code, rather than having to write our own!

```java
public class LinearActivity extends Activity {
    TextView earthText2;
    TextView earthText3;
    TextView venusText2;
    TextView venusText3;
    TextView jupiterText2;
    TextView jupiterText3;
    @Override
    protected void onCreate(Bundle savedInstanceState) {
    super.onCreate(savedInstanceState);
    setContentView(R.layout.activity_linear);
    earthText2 = (TextView)findViewById(R.id.tv2_earth);
    earthText3 = (TextView)findViewById(R.id.tv3_earth);
    venusText2 = (TextView)findViewById(R.id.tv2_venus);
    venusText3 = (TextView)findViewById(R.id.tv3_venus);
    jupiterText2 = (TextView)findViewById(R.id.tv2_jupiter);
    jupiterText3 = (TextView)findViewById(R.id.tv3_jupiter);
    ImageButton earthButton = (ImageButton)findViewById(R.id.ib_earth);
    earthButton.setOnClickListener(new View.OnClickListener(){
        @Override
        public void onClick(View arg0) {
                earthText2.setVisibility(View.VISIBLE);
                earthText3.setVisibility(View.VISIBLE);
                venusText2.setVisibility(View.GONE);
                venusText3.setVisibility(View.GONE);
                jupiterText2.setVisibility(View.GONE);
                jupiterText3.setVisibility(View.GONE);
        }});
    ImageButton venusButton = (ImageButton)findViewById(R.id.ib_venus);
    venusButton.setOnClickListener(new View.OnClickListener(){
        @Override
        public void onClick(View arg0) {
                earthText2.setVisibility(View.GONE);
                earthText3.setVisibility(View.GONE);
                venusText2.setVisibility(View.VISIBLE);
                venusText3.setVisibility(View.VISIBLE);
                jupiterText2.setVisibility(View.GONE);
                jupiterText3.setVisibility(View.GONE);
        }});
    ImageButton jupiterButton = (ImageButton)findViewById(R.id.ib_jupiter);
    jupiterButton.setOnClickListener(new View.OnClickListener(){
        @Override
        public void onClick(View arg0) {
                earthText2.setVisibility(View.GONE);
                earthText3.setVisibility(View.GONE);
                venusText2.setVisibility(View.GONE);
                venusText3.setVisibility(View.GONE);
                jupiterText2.setVisibility(View.VISIBLE);
                jupiterText3.setVisibility(View.VISIBLE);
        }});
    }
}
```

Figure 12-38 shows the result of the **Run As ➤ Android Application** process.

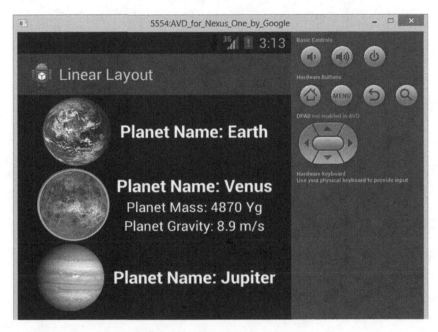

Figure 12-38. *Testing the final LinearLayout ImageButton UI design in the Nexus One*

As you can see in Figure 12-38, your application now works perfectly, with each planet's information appearing when its button is clicked, and hiding the other planet info at the same time to achieve a professional result.

Summary

In this chapter, we took a closer look at the Android **LinearLayout** class, as well as at the **ImageButton** UI widget often used with this class. We looked at the LinearLayout and ImageButton classes, and at ImageButton states, which we need to understand to be able to work with these classes.

We created **multi-state** ImageButton assets, using the popular GIMP 2.8.10 digital image editing software, and then implemented these multi-state ImageButton UI elements in our UserInterface application, in a LinearLayout container.

We also looked at **nesting** LinearLayout containers, to achieve more complex UI designs that will scale correctly using different screen densities and orientation. We got some experience implementing an **android:layout_gravity** parameter and we learned how to implement the **android:visibility** parameter in conjunction with UI layout and gravity parameters, to achieve some cool auto-formatting end-results in our LinearActivity.java Activity subclass.

In Chapter 13, we will take a closer look at **RelativeLayout**, and see how we can use one single layout container to create a complex UI design!

Android's RelativeLayout Class: UI Design Using One Layout Container

The Android **RelativeLayout** class is another one of those often used layout container classes. In fact, it is the layout container that was generated when you used Eclipse's New Android Application sequence of dialogs, as we did initially to create your UserInterface application infrastructure.

This tells us that it is one of Android's recommended UI layout container classes. Like the LinearLayout, it is fairly **memory efficient**, especially because it allows a complex UI design to be executed using one single layout container. Unless you have a specialized UI design, which would use one of the UI layout container classes covered during the remainder of this book, you should consider using the RelativeLayout UI container for your UI design.

What we're going to do in this chapter is show you how a complex UI design such as the one in the previous chapter, which utilized three LinearLayout containers nested three levels deep, can be achieved using a single layout container. The RelativeLayout container has considerably more parameters, and allows UI elements to be laid out and aligned relative to each other, which as you will soon see can provide a lot of power to the UI designer.

The first thing that we will do is to take a look at the RelativeLayout class and its related classes and methods, and then we will create our second RelativeLayout MenuItem and use (largely) the same Java code that we used in Chapter 12, only referencing a RelativeLayout UI definition.

This will allow us to focus this entire chapter on the RelativeLayout and its parameters and capabilities, since our ImageButtons, TextViews, event handling, and visibility constants were already developed in Chapter 12.

The RelativeLayout Class: UI Design Using Your Relatives

Android's **RelativeLayout** class is a more complex UI layout container class than the ones we have covered thus far, given the large number of parameters that it supports. It's named Relative Layout because it allows you to design your UI layouts by structuring your UI widgets relative to the other UI widgets in the UI design, using a number of powerful alignment parameters.

These parameters take another UI element's ID value and align your current UI element to the specified UI element, based on that ID value, along with an alignment characteristic. Alignment characteristics include: **above, below, left, right, start, end, top, bottom, centerHorizontal, centerVertical**, and **baseline**, to name a few.

You can also align UI elements relative to the parent layout container, in addition to aligning UI elements relative to other UI elements within that parent container, so this class features dozens of ways to align your UI design's component objects.

If you do not define any alignment for a UI element in your RelativeLayout container, the default alignment is at **0,0** (or the upper-left corner of the layout container).

The RelativeLayout class hierarchy begins at the Java Object master class, progressing from the View class to the ViewGroup class to the RelativeLayout class, and is structured like the following:

```
java.lang.Object
 > android.view.View
   > android.view.ViewGroup
     > android.widget.RelativeLayout
```

Android's RelativeLayout class is a **public class**, extending the **ViewGroup** superclass. It is referenced using an **import android.widget.RelativeLayout** statement at the top of your Java Activity subclass, as you will soon see.

The Android RelativeLayout class has only two known direct subclasses, the **DialerFilter** class and the **TwoLineListItem** class. It has one nested class, the **RelativeLayout.LayoutParams** class, which we will take a look at in the next section of this chapter, as it contains the parameters that we'll be learning about during the course of this chapter.

> **Note**   In case you are wondering what a "known" class in Android is, it is a class which has been added to the Android API officially. An "unknown" class is a custom class that you have written that has not been made public (known) by adding it permanently to the Android OS in one of the official Android package libraries.

The RelativeLayout class has two inherited XML attributes that we should cover here, before the specific relative layout parameters we are going to cover in the next section. These are **android:gravity** and **android:ignoreGravity**.

Gravity differs from layout_gravity, in as much as it aligns the UI widget content along the X and Y axes, relative to the boundaries of its own View container. The ignoreGravity parameter specifies that your View object is not affected by android:gravity settings, which, as we did in the previous chapter, allows us to design-in (specify) UI parameters in XML that can be switched on and off (or changed) using Java code. In essence, UI design using XML is called **static** UI design, and is established at "**design-time**," whereas a UI design using Java can be **dynamic**, and changed during an application's **runtime**.

The RelativeLayout.LayoutParams Nested Class: UI Design

The RelativeLayout.LayoutParams class hierarchy begins at the Java Object master class, and progresses from the ViewGroup.LayoutParams class to the ViewGroup.MarginLayoutParams class to the RelativeLayout.LayoutParams class, and is structured like the following:

```
java.lang.Object
 > android.view.ViewGroup.LayoutParams
   > android.view.ViewGroup.MarginLayoutParams
     > android.widget.RelativeLayout.LayoutParams
```

Android's RelativeLayout class is a **public static class,** extending the **ViewGroup.MarginLayoutParams** superclass. This class provides the constants that are used in your XML UI definition file, to create RelativeLayout UI designs. We discuss these in blocks of five to seven parameters, from the most often used through the least often used.

General Layout Positioning Parameters: Above, Below, and Center

The most commonly used RelativeLayout parameters are the **layout_above** and **layout_below** parameters, especially where portrait UI layout is concerned. These make sure that the UI element is in the correct order on the screen, but do not provide alignment, just general positioning. Layout "centering" parameters are also commonly used, and provide general positioning, as far as **XY** (parent container) centering using **layout_centerInParent**, as well as **Y** (horizontal) centering, using **layout_centerHorizontal**, and **X** (vertical) centering, using the **layout_centerVertical** parameter, seen in Table 13-1.

Table 13-1. Five of the Most Common RelativeLayout Attributes or Parameters, Along with Primary Functionality

RelativeLayout Attribute	Parameter Function Description (anchor view specified via android:id parameter)
layout_above	Bottom-edge of View is positioned above anchor View location
layout_below	Top-edge of View positioned below the anchor View location
layout_centerInParent	Centers the child View in X and Y dimensions within parent
Layout_centerHorizontal	Centers the child View horizontally within parent ViewGroup
Layout_centerVertical	Centers the child View vertically within a parent ViewGroup

The next most commonly used parameters allow you to align your UI elements using their outer container edges as well as baseline alignment, which are commonly used with TextView UI elements and in the Fontography profession.

Layout Alignment Parameters: Top, Bottom, Left, Right, Start, End

The layout_alignBaseline parameter aligns View UI widgets with an "anchor" View UI widget or element provided using an ID parameter reference. This works best with text-based UI elements and works with other UI elements, once you determine where the baseline is assigned within those elements.

The next four layout_align parameters align your View to the top, bottom, left, and right sides of the anchor View (ID) UI element, and are used to achieve razor-sharp positioning within your UI design, especially when the display changes its size or orientation. If your app supports changing RTL to LTR orientations, there are also **layout_alignStart** and **layout_alignEnd** parameters that allow you to design alignment that changes with RTL and LTR screen direction changes, used to support all types of languages. These seven precision alignment parameters can be seen in Table 13-2.

Table 13-2. RelativeLayout Alignment Attributes or Parameters, Along with their Primary Functionality

RelativeLayout Attribute	Parameter Function Description (anchor view specified via android:id parameter)
layout_alignBaseline	Aligns View and its anchor View on the anchor View baseline
layout_alignTop	Aligns the Top Edge of View with Top Edge of the anchor View
layout_alignBottom	Aligns Bottom Edge of View with Bottom Edge of anchor View
layout_alignLeft	Aligns the Left Edge of View with Left Edge of anchor View
layout_alignRight	Aligns the Right Edge of View with Right Edge of anchor View
layout_alignStart	Aligns the Start Edge of View with Start Edge of anchor View
layout_alignEnd	Aligns the End Edge of View with the End Edge of anchor View

Localized Layout Positioning Parameters: toLeftOf and toRightOf

There are also **positional** alignment parameters for left, right, start, and end UI design positioning shown in Table 13-3. However instead of aligning based on View sides, they position the UI elements relative to these designations. These are analogous to your above and below layout parameters, seen in Table 13-1, as they define a relative positioning, rather than an alignment, as the parameters in Table 13-2 do.

Table 13-3. RelativeLayout Positioning Attributes or Parameters, along with their primary functionality

RelativeLayout Attribute	Parameter Function Description (anchor view specified via android:id parameter)
layout_toLeftOf	Positions right-edge of View to left-edge of anchor View
layout_toRightOf	Positions left-edge of View to right-edge of anchor View
layout_toStartOf	Positions end-edge of View to the start-edge of anchor View
Layout_toEndOf	Positions start-edge of View to the end-edge of anchor View

Finally, there are six layout_alignParent parameters which align your View UI widgets (elements) inside a parent container with that parent container itself. These parameters can be very useful, especially if a parent layout uses the **MATCH_PARENT** constant to conform to the Android device's display.

Align Parent Layout Positioning Parameters: AlignParentTop et. al.

To get a visualization in your mind of what these do, imagine a UI design where you want the UI elements to "ring" or surround the top, bottom and sides of the display as a screen size increases. To achieve this particular UI design, you would use the parameters shown in Table 13-4 to align your UI elements to a ParentTop, ParentBottom, and ParentStart and ParentEnd (or ParentLeft and ParentRight if you are only supporting the LTR screen direction) UI alignment.

Table 13-4. RelativeLayout Parent Container Alignment Attributes or Parameters, Along with Primary Functionality

RelativeLayout Attribute	Parameter Function Description (anchor view specified via android:id parameter)
layout_alignParentTop	Align the Top Edge of the View with Top Edge of the parent
layout_alignParentBottom	Align Bottom Edge of View with Bottom Edge of the parent
layout_alignParentLeft	Align the Left Edge of View with Left Edge of the parent
layout_alignParentRight	Align the Right Edge of View with Right Edge of the parent
layout_alignParentStart	Align the Start Edge of View with Start Edge of the parent
layout_alignParentEnd	Align the End Edge of View with the End Edge of the parent

There is also one "flag" (allows a true or false setting) parameter called **layout_alignWithParentIfMissing** that allows you to specify that if a View has been set to GONE (missing), as we did in a previous chapter to achieve some cool UI design effects, your other positioning and alignment settings will still be calculated as if that parent UI element or container were in the VISIBLE or INVISIBLE mode setting. This parameter clearly allows a lot of advanced UI design "tricks" to be applied and achieved in Android.

Now that you have a handle on 23 RelativeLayout positioning and alignment parameters, it is time to create our **RelativeActivity.java** Activity class and **activity_relative.xml** UI XML definition file so that we can replicate the three nested LinearLayout UI design, using a single RelativeLayout UI container. We'll put this infrastructure in place quickly and efficiently so that we can focus on UI design using the RelativeLayout container type for the remainder of the chapter.

Adding RelativeLayout to the UserInterface Menu Structure

Let's follow the same work process that we did to create our LinearLayout Activity subclass and XML UI definition file:

1. Install a MenuItem object in our menu.xml file.

2. Add a case statement and Intent object, to launch the Activity.

3. Create the RelativeActivity.java class.

4. Create the XML for the activity_relative and AndroidManifest XML files that will be needed to hold our UI design and add the new Activity.

First copy an <item> tag for the linear_layout <item> seen in Figure 13-1, pasting it underneath itself, and change linear_layout to relative_layout. Add a **<string>** constant named **relative_layout** with the data value "**Relative Layout.**"

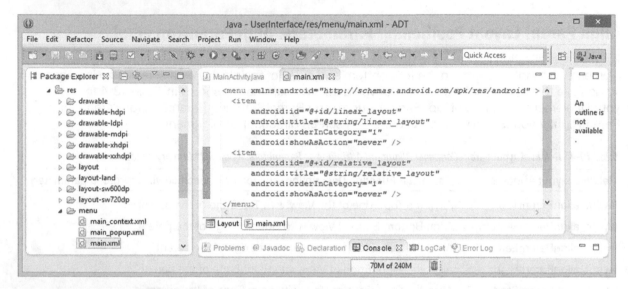

Figure 13-1. Adding the second <item> MenuItem object to our Menu object for the RelativeLayout UI design

Next, add a second case statement in your MainActivity.java file using the same work process, as shown in Figure 13-2. Copy and paste the first case statement; change the word **Linear** to **Relative**, and **intent_ll** to **intent_rl**.

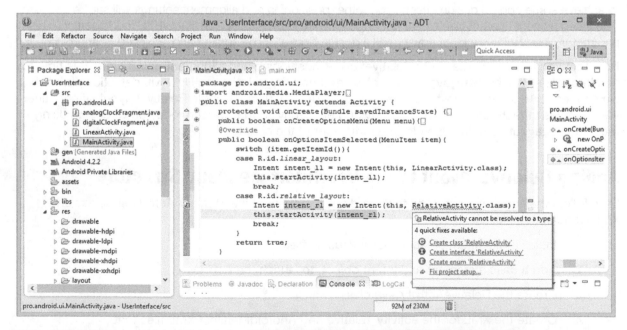

Figure 13-2. Adding a second case statement and Intent object to start a RelativeActivity.class Activity subclass

Next mouse-over the wavy red error highlighting under the RelativeActivity class reference, and select the **Create class RelativeActivity** option. This will bring up a **New Class** dialog shown in Figure 13-3, where you'll select the **android.app.Activity** superclass using the **Superclass Selection** dialog.

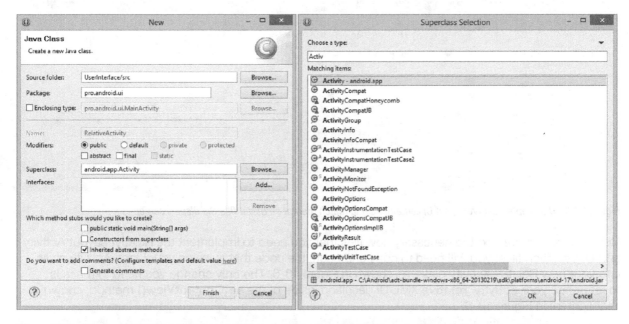

Figure 13-3.   Creating a RelativeActivity.java Activity subclass and specifying the android.app.Activity superclass

Now that you have created your Java class, you will need to create your UI XML definition file. Right-click on your /res/layout folder and select the **New ➤ Android XML File** menu sequence and name your file **activity_relative**, as shown in Figure 13-4, and then click on the **Finish** button to create it.

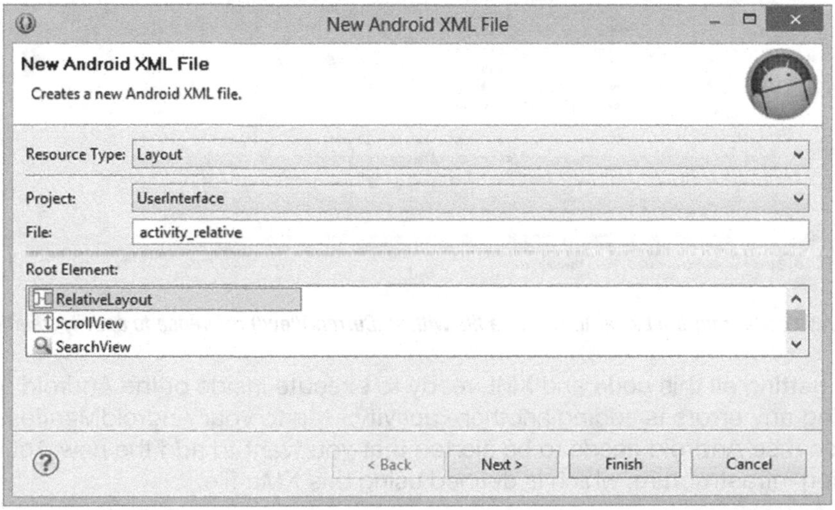

Figure 13-4.   Creating a New Android XML RelativeLayout UI

This opens up your activity_relative.xml file, as seen in Figure 13-5.

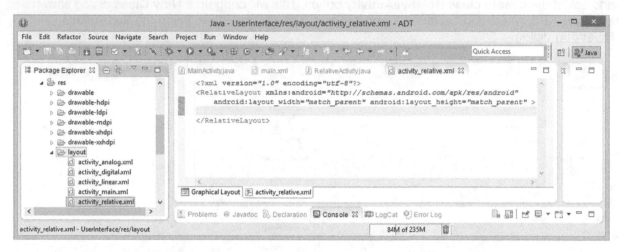

Figure 13-5. *Our empty RelativeLayout UI container set to match_parent so that it fills the display screen*

Now that you've created the necessary new files that you need to implement the RelativeLayout Activity and UI definition files, you will need to copy and paste the code that is inside your LinearActivity class into your new RelativeActivity class, as shown in Figure 13-6. The only change you need to make is to reference your **activity_relative** XML UI definition inside of the **setContentView()** method, shown (highlighted) in Figure 13-6.

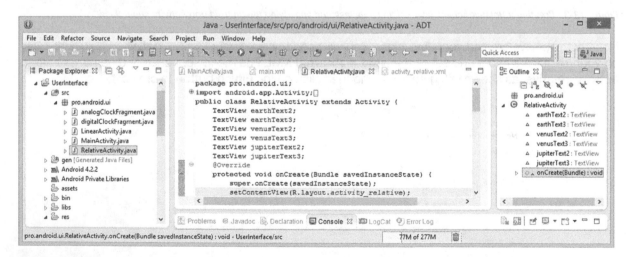

Figure 13-6. *Using Java code from the LinearActivity.java file with setCurrentView() reference to activity_relative*

The final step in getting all this code and XML ready to execute inside of the Android application without generating any errors is adding another <activity> tag to your AndroidManifest.xml file. You must add this because Android needs to be alerted that you want to add the new Activity subclass to your application infrastructure, which is defined using this XML file.

Your new RelativeActivity <activity> XML tag can be seen in Figure 13-7.

Figure 13-7. Adding an <activity> tag for our RelativeActivity Activity subclass to the AndroidManifest.xml file

Now we can focus on building our UI design from scratch, using parameters from the RelativeLayout class, and do it using one single UI container! The reason that we want to use one single UI layout container, which we will address in detail a bit later on in the chapter, is to maximize system memory usage and code a more elegant application using a **flat layout design** hierarchy.

Porting a LinearLayout Design to a RelativeLayout Design

First, let's copy your three <ImageButton> UI element child tags from your LinearLayout XML UI definition file (activity_linear.xml tab, seen ghosted on the right side of the editing page in Figure 13-8), and paste them into your new **activity_relative.xml** file as shown in Figure 13-8. Remove the **android:layout_marginRight** parameters, as we are going to be using only RelativeLayout alignment parameters, at least initially, to position and then align our UI design again, from scratch. Replicating the 70 line LinearLayout UI design from scratch would be a lot of work, so we are going to use a copy and paste process to get non-alignment parameters (ID, font, source, background, etc.) into the RelativeLayout, so we don't have to type them all in again. The result of copying three ImageButton UI elements and removing layout_margin parameters can be seen in Figure 13-8.

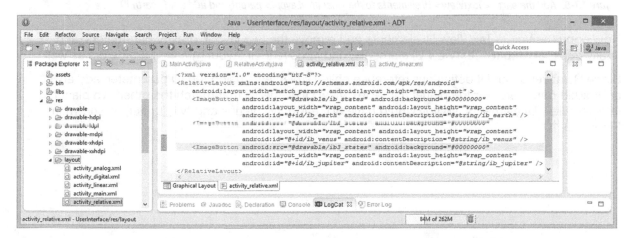

Figure 13-8. Adding the child <ImageButton> UI elements to the <RelativeLayout> parent layout container

The next thing we'll want to do is to copy your three TextView UI elements for planet Earth from your LinearLayout UI container XML definition and paste them under your three ImageButton UI elements.

It's interesting to note that in a RelativeLayout UI design, you can group logical UI elements together in this way. This is because UI elements in a RelativeLayout container are referenced to each other using **android:id** parameters, so the child tags don't have to be physically located (nested) next to each other in the same way they need to be in a nested LinearLayout UI design XML definition.

Your planet buttons and names are shown in Figure 13-9, and are using only 20 lines of XML markup thus far, to create a basic planet names UI design. Make sure to remove the **android:layout_gravity** parameter in the second and third "info" TextView UI elements.

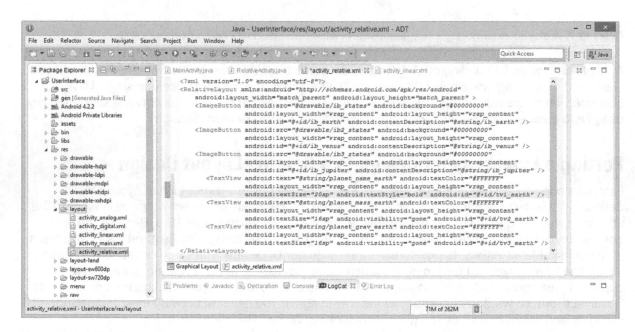

Figure 13-9. Add the earth <TextView> UI elements to the <RelativeLayout> parent, and add a tv1_earth ID

Now copy the Venus TextView UI elements and remove the two layout_gravity parameters, and finally copy the Jupiter TextView UI elements, and remove their layout_gravity parameters as well.

Since RelativeLayout UI definitions reference child UI elements using the ID parameter, add an android:id parameter for the planet name TextView UI elements that match the other two planet info TextView UI elements, so you would have tv1_earth, tv1_venus and tv1_jupiter, as shown in Figure 13-10.

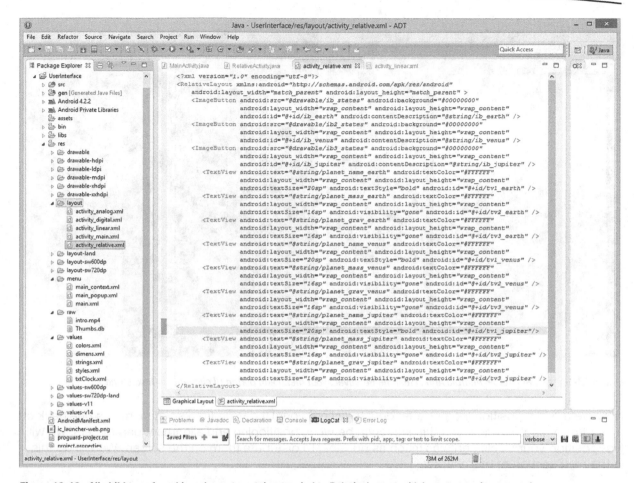

Figure 13-10. All child tags from LinearLayout container copied to RelativeLayout with layout_margin removed

We now have about three dozen lines of XML defining your RelativeLayout UI design, approximately half of what we had with our LinearLayout, and using one single UI layout container class (ViewGroup) in system memory, instead of using three, so our UI definition XML is significantly more efficient! This is why Android OS uses RelativeLayout as its default (recommended) UI layout container (ViewGroup) class when creating a New Android Application using the series of dialogs which we used to create our UserInterface app.

As you can see in Figure 13-10, we are defining a dozen UI elements using one block of XML markup, including IDs, source data, background settings, content descriptions for the impaired, font size, font color, font style, and visibility parameters.

Next, let's use the **Run As ➤ Android Application** work process to see what these parameters (minus the margin parameters from the ViewGroup.MarginLayoutParams superclass we learned about,) would look like, if we do not add any of the RelativeLayout.LayoutParams nested class attributes that we learned about earlier in the chapter.

As you can see in Figure 13-11, as expected, all the UI elements are in place, but located at X,Y location **0,0** or the upper-left corner of the UI.

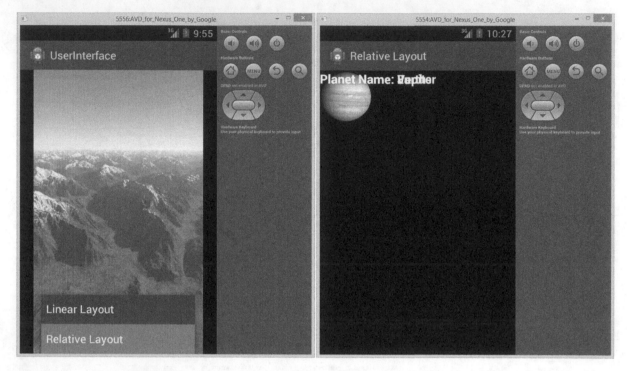

Figure 13-11. Use Run As ➤ Android App to test the RelativeLayout menu and ported UI elements in Nexus One

Now we are in a position (no pun intended) to lay out your UI design from scratch, minus one heck of a lot of re-typing! To show you the difference between positioning and alignment parameters, we will first position your UI elements as much as possible to distribute them on the screen. We will do this in the next section of this chapter.

After that, in the following section, we'll then utilize the alignment UI parameters to fine-tune the UI positioning relative to the other elements.

Finally, we'll re-introduce some of your margin parameters in order to fine-tune the global positioning of your UI design.

Positioning UI Designs Using RelativeLayout Position Tags

Let's position your ImageButton UI elements first, because they are at the top-left corner of your design. Since everything is laid-out relative to each other, our ib_earth UI element will ultimately anchor (top of the UI "tree") each View object inside of this entire ViewGroup layout container.

The ib_venus lays out under the ib_earth, and the ib_jupiter under the ib_venus. The tv1_earth lays out to the right of ib_earth, and the tv2 and tv3 TextView lays out relative to that. Once we add in all these relative layout definitions, we move ib_earth and the entire UI will move!

Add an android:layout_below="@+id/ib_earth" parameter to the ib_venus tag, as shown in Figure 13-12, and an android:layout_below="@+id/ib_venus" tag parameter to the ib_jupiter tag, to position the ImageButton UI elements.

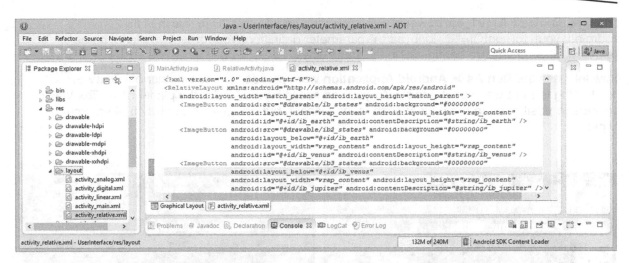

Figure 13-12. Using the android:layout_below parameter to position the venus and jupiter ImageButtons

Next add **android:layout_toRightOf** parameters that reference the ib_planet ImageButtons to the planet name TextView elements as seen in Figure 13-13.

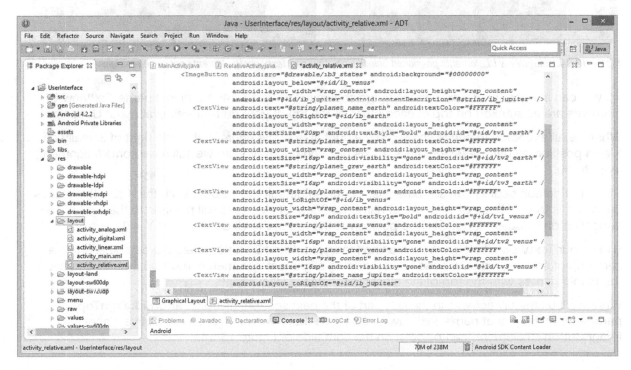

Figure 13-13. Using the android:layout_toRightOf parameter to position the planet name TextView UI elements

Thus the TextView ID **tv1_earth** would reference the ImageButton ID **ib_earth** in its android:layout_toRightOf="@+id/ib_earth" parameter definition. Your other two planet name TextView UI elements are configured in the same way.

Now let's use the **Run As ➤ Android Application** work process to see whether our TextView positioning is what we expect it to be. As you can see in Figure 13-14, the planet name TextViews are indeed positioned to the right of each of the planets, but not quite in the way that you may expect!

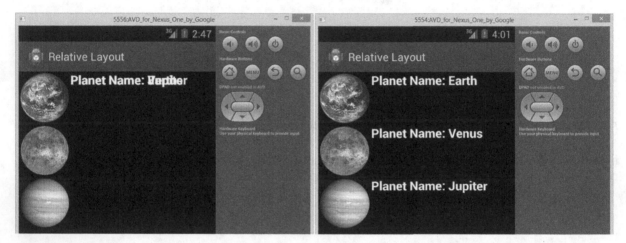

Figure 13-14. ImageView UI elements positioned below each other and TextView UI elements positioned to right

As you can see, on the left side of the figure shown in Figure 13-14, our planet name TextView UI elements are all stacked on top of each other, at the top of your current RelativeLayout UI design.

What we all expected to see is shown on the right side of the figure, but to the right of is really an X axis positioning parameter, not an X-Y axis position parameter, so we still have some (alignment) work to do.

Since the default position unless otherwise specified defaults to zero for both the X and the Y axes, the result is that all three of your planet name TextView UI elements will position to the right of the ImageButton UI objects, but will also position at the top of the UI definition, at **Y = 0**.

Since your TextView UI element positioning (android:toRightOf) parameters are default aligning at zero (top of screen), we now need to start adding alignment parameters next, so that we can align the planet names with the top of the planet (ImageView) UI elements.

What we'll ultimately achieve in the first part of the next section, using an **android:alignTop** parameter in the planet name TextView UI elements that references each respective planet's ImageButton UI element, can be seen on the right side of Figure 13-14.

Aligning the UI Design Using RelativeLayout Alignment

Next, we will start adding alignment parameters to further refine our UI layout to be more attractive and professional, as our LinearLayout was.

We need to add an alignment parameter to align the planet name TextView UI elements with the top of each of your ImageView UI elements. Next to your android:layout_toRightOf parameters in each of your planet name TextView UI definitions, add an android:layout_alignTop parameter that references the same ID as the toRightOf parameter references (ib_earth, ib_venus and ib_jupiter), using the following XML markup, as shown in Figure 13-15:

```
android:layout_alignTop="@+id/ib_earth"
```

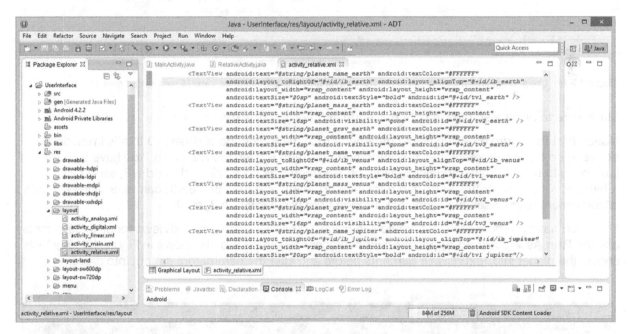

Figure 13-15. Use an android:alignTop to align planetname TextView UI elements with ImageButton UI elements

Next you will need to align your planet information TextView UI elements, with their tv2_planetname and tv3_planetname ID designations, to the tv1 planet name TextView UI elements.

You'll do this by using **android:layout_below** and **android:layout_alignLeft** parameters, the first will position your TextViews, under your planet name TextVlews, and the second will align your TextViews using your planet name TextViews. This is done using the following markup, shown in Figure 13-16:

```
android:layout_below="@+id/tv1_earth"
android:layout_alignLeft="@+id/tv1_earth"
```

Figure 13-16. Use android:layout_below and android:layout_alignLeft to align info TextView UI with planet name

Make sure to add these tags in both tv2_earth and tv3_earth TextView tags.

Notice that the android:layout_below parameter must reference the textView ID that is immediately above it, so tv2_earth references tv1_earth and tv3_earth references tv2_earth. You have a bit more latitude with the next android:layout_alignLeft parameter, as both tv2_earth and tv3_earth can reference tv1_earth, or tv2_earth can reference tv1_earth and then tv3_earth can reference tv2_earth which essentially passes the alignment through from tv1_earth to tv3_earth.

Once you have put both of the parameters in place, for all six planet info TextViews for all three planets, use the **Run As ➤ Android Application** work process to see the results shown in Figure 13-17, which shows the planet info TextView UI elements before and after the parameters are put into place.

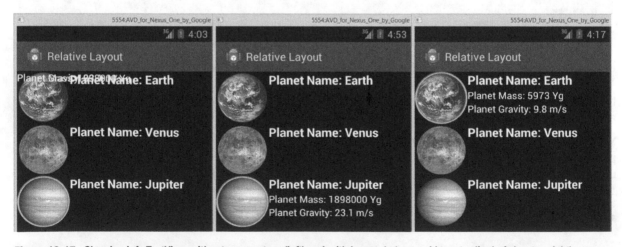

Figure 13-17. Showing info TextView without parameters (left) and with layout_below and layout_alignLeft (center, right)

Margin Aligning a UI Design Using the Anchor UI Element

Next, we will use a single pair of marginLeft and marginTop parameters, in the ib_earth "master" anchor View for this RelativeLayout container, which will push the entire UI design away from the sides of the display. This works because all your UI elements are positioned (and aligned) relative to each other, and thus moving the Anchor ib_earth View to the right and down from the top of the screen will percolate down through the rest of your UI design alignment parameters, and thereby reposition the entire UI design.

Add a line of space after the ib_earth ImageButton's source and background parameters and add the layout_marginLeft and layout_marginTop parameters.

This is done using the following XML markup, shown in Figure 13-18:

```
android:layout_marginLeft="10dip"
android:layout_marginTop="10dip"
```

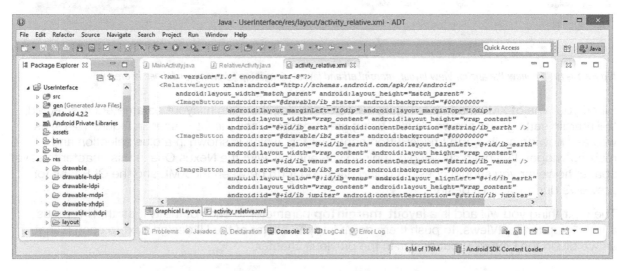

Figure 13-18. Add a layout_marginLeft and layout_marginTop parameter set to a value of 10 DIP to anchor View

It is important to note, that using the Graphical Layout Editor works well for previewing RelativeLayout designs, as can be seen in Figure 13-19, and as you can see it also shows **alignment guidelines** based on the selected or active line of XML markup in the XML editing pane.

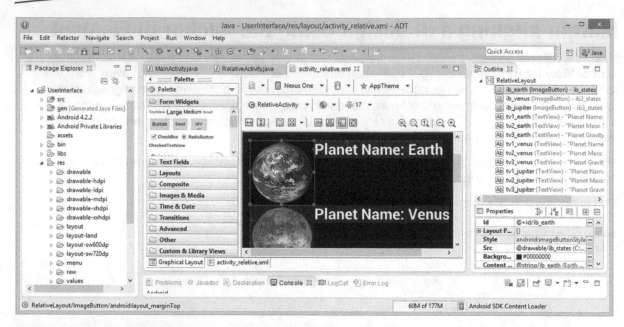

Figure 13-19.   Preview the anchor View layout_marginLeft and layout_marginTop (showing guidelines in green)

Since your line of XML markup in Figure 13-18 containing the margin layout parameters is selected, the margin settings are shown visually using green dashed lines the GLE, seen in Figure 13-19, as well as showing an ib_earth ImageButton container tag, which is shown in a blue selection and resizing widget. I've been showing combined screenshots with the Nexus One in this chapter to save space; however you should consider going back and forth between the XML and the GLE tabs for previews during your UI design.

The next thing you will add is a **layout_marginTop** parameter to each of the tv1_earth, tv1_venus and tv1_jupiter TextViews, to push them down into the center of the UI design next to each planet, as we did in the LinearLayout design in the previous chapter.

Using a MarginTop Parameter to Center Your Planet Names

Just like you did with the ib_earth anchor View ImageButton UI element, add the new line of space, this time after your android:text and android:textColor parameters, and add an android:layout_marginTop="30dip" parameter.

This serves to push your planet name TextView down, so it is next to the planet ImageButton UI element. You need to do this for all the TextView UI elements, tv1_earth, tv1_venus and tv1_jupiter, as is shown in Figure 13-20.

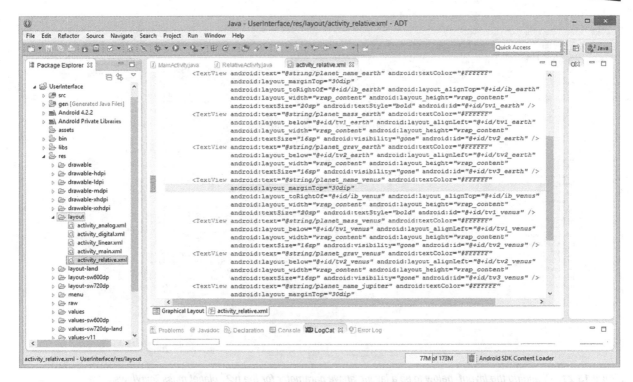

Figure 13-20. *Adding an android:layout_marginTop="30dip" parameter to push the planet name TextView down*

Since our tv2_ and tv3_ TextView UI elements that specify planet mass and planet gravity are "anchored" to this tv1_ TextView, this will also serve to push these down with that TextView UI element.

To observe this effect, use the **Run As ➤ Android Application** work process and take a look at your UI design in your UserInterface application, after using the MENU button to access the RelativeLayout Activity and clicking on a couple of the planet ImageButtons to reveal the subtext UI elements.

We will need to alter our UI design slightly to correct this and to make it more professional, and we will do that next so you can get some more experience regarding how relative layout positioning functions and how it gives you to tools to achieve any type of UI design that you may need to implement.

Next let's add a little more symmetry to your design and split your planet information so that it surrounds the planet name central TextView. We will do this because the planet information TextView UI elements currently look significantly different than the planet name UI elements.

Balancing Your RelativeLayout UI Design by Tweaking Parameters

Thus, putting your mass information above the planet name, and the gravity information below the planet name, should look more balanced when the user clicks each of the planet ImageButtons.

With a RelativeLayout this turns out to be quite easy to achieve, you will simply change the android:layout_below="tv1_earth" parameter to instead be an android:layout_above="tv1_earth" parameter, as shown in Figure 13-21. This changes position of your planet mass information, relative to the planet name. Make sure you do this for all three planet_mass TextViews.

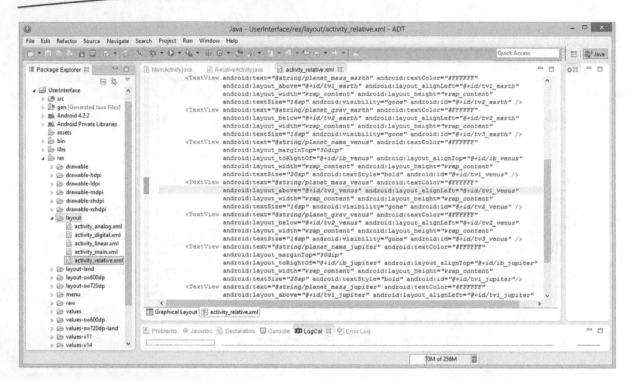

Figure 13-21. Changing the layout_below to be a layout_above parameter for the tv2_ planet mass TextViews

If you use your **Run As ➤ Android Application** work process, and click the ImageView UI buttons, you will see that both of your planet information TextView UI elements are now located above the planet name TextView.

This is because your tv3_ TextView references your tv2_ TextView using the layout_below parameter, and needs to reference the tv1_ TextView utilizing this parameter, to ensure the planet gravity information TextView is located symmetrically underneath your tv1_ planet name TextView.

To fix this problem, go into all three of your planet_grav TextViews and change the android:layout_below reference to the tv1_planet IDs, so that your planet gravity information is now be underneath your planet name.

This change is shown highlighted in Figure 13-22, and we are now ready to test our UI design by using the **Run As ➤ Android Application** work process.

Figure 13-22. Changing your relative ID reference for the tv3_ TextViews to layout_below the tv1_ TextViews

As you can see on the left side of Figure 13-23 we still have a minor kink that needs to be worked out of our RelativeLayout UI design. This is being caused by the android:layout_marginTop="30dip" that is attached to your tv1 TextView UI element to push it down (center it) next to the ImageButton UI element. This top margin parameter is keeping the tv2 TextView at bay, and we need to find a way to overcome this problem using a margin setting that counters this phenomenon for the tv2 TextView. We will fix this problem next, as can be seen in the middle and right screens in Figure 13-23.

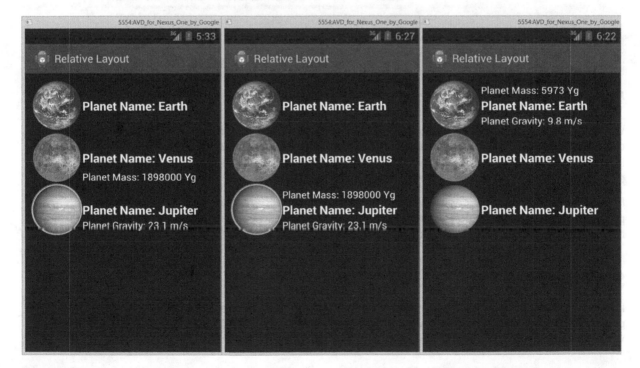

Figure 13-23. Testing your RelativeLayout UI design in the Nexus One emulator (broken left, fixed middle/right)

It is also interesting to note that you can use a negative numeric value for your margin or padding value. This can often be used to significant UI advantage in certain situations, and I will show you one of these here.

This is one of your scenarios where you could use a negative numeric value with your **android:layout_marginBottom** parameter. Using a negative value with this parameter serves to "pull the TextView down" over the top of the layout_marginTop parameter ,which is keeping your tv2_ planet_mass TextView pushed away from where we ultimately wish to see it positioned.

Similarly, using a negative parameter with a layout_marginTop pulls it up, and a negative parameter with a layout_marginLeft will pull it to the left, and a negative parameter with a layout_marginRight will push that to the right. There is no rule in Android that says don't use negative values for your margin or padding parameters that I am aware of, so use this new knowledge to expand what you can achieve in your Pro Android UI design.

Figure 13-24. Using an android:layout_marginBottom="-30" parameter to pull your planet mass TextView down

We've created a RelativeLayout UI design that works with our existing Java code that we created for our LinearLayout UI design, which points out how the division of XML markup UI design and Java logic programming in Android allows UI designers who cannot code and programmers who cannot design to work side-by-side without getting in each other's way.

Pro Android UI designers can try vastly new approaches without the need to ask the Java programming staff to change one character of code, as we have demonstrated here in this chapter, by creating this cool RelativeLayout UI design through the use of an existing LinearLayout UI design.

Summary

In this chapter you learned all about the Android **RelativeLayout** class and its layout parameters, provided by a **RelativeLayout.LayoutParams** nested class, which is subclassed from the ViewGroup.MarginLayoutParams as well as the ViewGroup.LayoutParams class.

You looked at the RelativeLayout.LayoutParams nested class and at its many (nearly two dozen) positioning parameters, which we covered grouped by the effect which they have. You looked at positioning and alignment parameters as well as parent alignment parameters that allow you to align your child UI design to its parent UI layout container.

You created a RelativeActivity Activity subclass, to hold this chapter's GUI design, and designed the RelativeLayout version of the LinearLayout design to show how similar UI designs can be achieved by using a vastly different XML markup structure and within a single UI layout container, which can be called a "flat" UI design in Android terminology.

You first positioned the ImageButton and TextView UI elements, through the use of positioning parameters, and then you aligned them to other "anchor" UI elements by using alignment parameters. You then utilized layout_margin parameters to position the entire RelativeLayout UI design "tree" to fine-tune a design, and observe how UI elements will all move together relative to their anchor UI elements.

In the next chapter, we will take a closer look at **GridLayout**, and see how we can use a slightly more complicated single layout container to create a complex UI design that has even more auto-alignment features than Relative Layout features.

14

Android's GridLayout Class: UI Design Using a Grid-based Layout

The Android **GridLayout** class is a fairly recent addition to the Android OS in the Ice Cream Sandwich Version 4.0 release. Although RelativeLayout can be used to create grid-like UI designs, enough developers were using grid-like UI designs that Android developers decided to go ahead and create the GridLayout (ViewGroup subclass) user interface layout container class.

The GridLayout class is optimized specifically for creating grid UI design using a minimal amount of system memory, and can render both horizontal UI element and vertical UI element alignment at the same time in the same UI.

Although Android's GridLayout has half the number of parameters (12 versus 24) that the RelativeLayout container class has, it is more complicated as it is actually more of a "Grid Layout Engine," and thus is more complex in the sense that you have to understand how it will process your parameters for you to saliently design UI layouts using its many attributes.

There are more ethereal concepts to be covered within this chapter, such as grid flexibility, grid spanning, multiple constant gravity settings (also available with other UI container classes that support gravity, but useful with GridLayout containers, so we cover this concept within this chapter), and for once, a layout container (ViewGroup subclass) class featuring more parent (global) parameters used to set layout engine attributes than child UI element parameters, which is fairly unique within Android OS UI design.

What we're going to do in this chapter is to create a GridLayout UI design, which will be a significant improvement upon (expansion of) your multiple planet UI design, which you created during the last couple of chapters.

The GridLayout Class: UI Design Using a Grid

The Android **GridLayout** class is a recent UI layout container class that is optimized to allow arrangement of the child UI widgets using a "grid-like" rectangular layout design, hence its name. The grid layout defined by this GridLayout class is comprised of a collection or array of "infinitely thin" grid lines. These grid lines separate the viewing area into "**cells**."

The GridLayout class hierarchy begins with your Java Object master class, progressing from the View class to the ViewGroup class to GridLayout, and is structured using the following class hierarchy:

```
java.lang.Object
  > android.view.View
     > android.view.ViewGroup
        > android.widget.GridLayout
```

The Android GridLayout class is a **public class**, extending the **ViewGroup** superclass. It is referenced by using the **import android.widget.GridLayout** statement at the top of your Java Activity subclass, as you will soon see.

Within the GridLayout class, grid lines are referenced using **grid indices**. A grid with a Y number of columns will have Y+1 grid indices that will be numbered starting at 0 and running through Y as the last column index.

Regardless of how your GridLayout container may be constructed, grid index 0 will be fixed to the leading edge of the layout container and grid index Y will be fixed to the trailing edge, after padding is taken into account.

Using the RowSpec and ColumnSpec Parameters

Your GridLayout child UI widgets (View objects) can span one or more cells as defined by their **rowSpec** and **columnSpec** layout parameters. We will soon learn all about the grid layout parameters, when we cover the nested class that contains these called **GridLayout.LayoutParams**.

Each of these parameters can be used to define a set of rows (rowSpec), or columns (columnSpec), which are to be occupied by your child View objects. You can also specify how these child UI Views are to be aligned within the resulting group of grid cells.

It is important to note that while grid cells do not normally overlap in a GridLayout, the GridLayout class doesn't prevent child UI Views from being defined in such a way that they will occupy the same cell, or span a group of cells. This affords a UI designer a great deal of flexibility, in using the GridLayout container to create creating grid-based scalable UI design.

If you design with more than one child UI element per grid cell, however, or with more than one grid cell per child UI element (spanning) note that there is no guarantee that children will not themselves overlap after the layout operation completes. For this reason, make sure that you test well!

About GridLayout Locations, Flexibility, Space, and Gravity

If a child UI element tag does not include any parameters specifying a row and column index of the grid cell which it needs to occupy, the GridLayout class will assign its cell locations automatically. This is done by the GridLayout class algorithmically, and is based on your GridLayout container definition, along with its orientation, rowCount, and columnCount attributes or property (parameter) settings.

White (unused) space between child UI elements must be specified either by using an instance (an object) of the Android SpaceView class that we will take a look at in this chapter as well. Space between View objects in a GridLayout can also be specified using the margin parameters layout_leftMargin, layout_topMargin, layout_rightMargin, and layout_bottomMargin from the ViewGroup.MarginLayoutParams nested class if you want to use inherited parameters rather than SpaceView objects.

When the GridLayout class **android:useDefaultMargins** XML property is set to true, default margins around child UI elements are automatically allocated based on the UI style guide for the Android platform running on the device at that time. To access this particular GridLayout parameter via your Java code, implement the **.setUseDefaultMargins()** method call with a true value.

It is important to note that each of these margins, automatically defined using the **useDefaultMargins=true** specification, may each be independently overridden via the assignment of one of the four layout_margin parameters. Automatically generated margin values will generally produce a reasonable spacing result between your child UI elements, however, keep in mind that any given margin value could change depending on what version release of the Android platform your application is being rendered with.

It is also important to note that a GridLayout class child UI distribution of excess space is based on a **priority principle** and not on a principle of weight, which is currently unique to the LinearLayout container type. For this reason a child UI element's ability to "stretch" is inferred from the alignment properties for its row and column groupings. These alignment characteristics are set by specifying a **gravity** property for each child UI element's **layout_gravity** parameter. If alignment was defined along a given X or Y axis, then the UI element is considered **flexible** in that direction. If zero alignment characteristics have been specified, then the GridLayout class will consider the UI element to be fixed, and thus to be **inflexible**.

If you have multiple UI elements inside the same row or column grouping, these UI elements will be considered to be acting together or in parallel. Such a grouping will be considered to be flexible, but only if all your child UI elements inside of it are also configured to be deemed flexible.

If you wanted to make one of your GridLayout columns **dynamic** (stretchable), you would simply make sure you define a layout_gravity parameter for each of the UI elements that are contained within that particular column.

Conversely, if you wanted to prevent any of the GridLayout UI columns from stretching, or in other words make them **fixed** or **static**, you would need to ensure that one of the UI elements in that column doesn't define a setting for the layout_gravity parameter.

When this layout_gravity parameter specified principle of **grid flexibility** is defined in a way that can be interpreted by the GridLayout algorithm in more than one way (i.e., ambiguously), the GridLayout class algorithms will prioritize flexibility for rows and columns which are closer to your right and bottom sides of your UI design (the ViewGroup layout container).

Conversely, any GridLayout row and column groups that exist on either side of a common fixed (or static) boundary are considered to act in a **series**. Thus, any grid composite group, made up of two or more elements, will be deemed to be flexible if any one of its component elements is flexible.

Using Visibility with the GridLayout Class: Using GONE

We have already created some cool UI effects using the visibility constant GONE with the android:visibility parameter, and this is also possible with the GridLayout container. In fact, using GONE with a GridLayout allows you to "collapse" the grid cell down to a single infinitely small point, which essentially disappears the grid cell.

This is because for UI layout purposes the GridLayout class evaluates View objects whose visibility parameter has been set to GONE as having a zero width and a zero height. Or even better, either a zero width (column collapse) or zero height (row collapse). You can imagine the cool effects that can be achieved with the GONE constant, which is why we are covering it in its own section here.

It's important to note this is different from your usual Android OS policy of simply not evaluating a View UI element whose visibility is set to GONE in the UI layout calculations at all. We have looked at this in particular in the LinearLayout and RelativeLayout chapters, so you are familiar with what GONE can do, and how Android will normally evaluate it.

If you designate a View object as GONE and it is alone in its column, that column would then collapse to a zero width, if no layout_gravity parameter were to be defined on that View. If a layout_gravity was defined, then the View object designated GONE would have no effect on the UI layout, and the GridLayout container would be laid out as if the View had never been added to it, thus achieving normal GONE behavior. This principle applies in the same fashion to rows as well as columns, and also to groupings of rows and columns. This usage of GONE with layout_gravity makes GridLayout powerful!

Shortcomings of GridLayout Class: No Weight Parameter

One of the major shortcomings, or limitations, of this GridLayout class is that it does not yet support the **android:weight** parameter. This capability, which is found in the LinearLayout class, would be a great feature for this GridLayout class.

Unfortunately, it is therefore not currently possible to configure your UI GridLayout container to distribute a precise percentage of spacing between multiple UI element View objects. I suspect that this was left out because it increased the memory usage footprint for the layout container too much.

Some of the more common UI design scenarios that might have utilized this grid cell weighting feature may still be able to be accommodated, however, through the application of clever use of the native GridLayout attributes, which are available in the GridLayout class, and which we will be covering during this chapter. For instance, if you wanted to designate an equal amount of space around a UI element that was in a cell grouping you could use the CENTER alignment, via the application of an android:layout_gravity="center" parameter.

Another trick to simulate evenly divided weights is to use the alignment constants together using the vertical bar "|" character. Many developers are not aware that this is possible, and later on in the chapter we will be using this technique to "corner align" our grid design using constant combinations within the android:layout_gravity parameter. For instance, if you wanted to align your UI element in your GridLayout in the top-left corner, you would use the android:layout_ gravity="top|left" parameter, inside of the grid cell whose indices were both zero. Remember, the upper-left corner of your screen (and its grid) will always be at 0,0.

Combining alignment parameters can come close to simulating almost all the standard weight distributions normally or typically used in UI design, and this may have been another reason the GridLayout favors using gravity constants (parameter) and a concept of flexibility over weight parameters. However, if you absolutely needed complete control over the percentage of the space distribution in a given row or column, you could nest the LinearLayout and use its android:weight capability. This would serve to distribute UI elements within any given cell grouping. Keep in mind that nesting various GUI layout containers will probably take up more of your user's valuable system memory than using a flat UI design.

When using either of these work-around techniques remember to keep in mind that cell groupings can be defined to overlap, so you need to practice the GridLayout UI design process quite a bit before you get it working the way that you expect it to every single time that you design a Pro Android UI.

Layout Parameters in GridLayout: Nested Classes

Before we actually implement a GridLayout UI container in our app, let's take a look at some of the **nested classes** under GridLayout that are used to define grid layout parameters and the like. You will be using some of these with your GridLayout UI designs later on in this chapter.

The GridLayout.LayoutParams Nested Class: Layout Parameters

The GridLayout.LayoutParams class hierarchy also begins at the Java Object master class, and progresses from the ViewGroup.LayoutParams class, to the VlewGroup.MarginLayoutParams class, to a GridLayout.LayoutParams class and is structured in the following fashion:

```
java.lang.Object
  > android.view.ViewGroup.LayoutParams
    > android.view.ViewGroup.MarginLayoutParams
      > android.widget.GridLayout.LayoutParams
```

The Android GridLayout.LayoutParams class is a **public static class,** and it extends the **ViewGroup.MarginLayoutParams** superclass.

This class provides the constants used in your XML UI definition file to create your GridLayout UI designs. We will go over these five GridLayout parameters here, as seen in Table 14-1, and we'll use most of them in the GridLayout UI we create during the chapter.

Table 14-1. Five GridLayout Attributes or Parameters, Along with their Primary Functionality

RelativeLayout Attribute	Parameter Function Description (anchor view specified via android:id parameter)
layout_column	Column boundary indicating left group of cells occupied by View
layout_row	Row boundary indicating top group of cells occupied by the View
layout_gravity	Gravity specifying how View UI widgets are to be placed in cells
layout_columnSpan	Difference between left and right boundary delimiting cell span
layout_rowSpan	Difference between top and bottom boundary delimiting cell span

The GridLayout.LayoutParams class contains only four **static** XML parameters shown in Table 14-1. These include: **column**, **row**, **columnSpan**, and **rowSpan**.

There is also one **dynamic** Java method, **.setGravity()** which can also be set or configured using your GridLayout XML definition file using the familiar **android:layout_gravity** parameter.

You may be thinking, hey, this is a small number of configuration options, for what's considered to be a very complex or powerful UI layout container class! This is because there are another **seven** XML attributes (parameters) in the GridLayout class itself, which specify **global** (parent class) **values** that can be set to configure the "**grid alignment engine**," which this class creates for you. These parent parameters can be seen in Table 14-2 and are included in this section so that we can keep these XML parameters together in one place. There are also two other nested classes, which deal with XML parameters, which we'll cover during the next two sections of the chapter.

Table 14-2. GridLayout Parent Layout Container Attributes or Parameters Along with their Primary Functionality

GridLayout Parent Container Attribute	Parameter Function Description
layout_columnCount	A maximum column count to use when auto-positioning Views
layout_rowCount	A maximum row count to use when auto-positioning Views
layout_useDefaultMargins	Uses auto-margin algorithm when no margins specified
layout_alignmentMode	Sets how to align the grid, relative to View's margins
layout_columnOrderPreserved	Forces column boundaries to be in same order as indices
layout_rowOrderPreserved	Forces row boundaries to be in same order as indices
layout_orientation	Sets orientation for grid (unused in layout algorithm)

The most commonly used parent attributes are the **rowCount** and **columnCount** parameters, which allow you to define your GridLayout in a static fashion, which is more memory efficient, and how we'll be defining our grid design. There are also three flag (true or false) parameters for turning on or off margins, and preserving row and column order, and two constant parameters, which are used for specifying alignment modes and the UI grid orientation.

GridLayout.Alignment Nested Class: Alignment Constants

The **GridLayout.Alignment** class hierarchy begins at the Java Object master class, and directly creates this GridLayout.Alignment nested class, which you could think of as the "alignment constants" for the GridLayout class.

This nested class's hierarchy is structured using the following hierarchy:

```
java.lang.Object
  > android.widget.GridLayout.Alignment
```

This Android GridLayout.Alignment nested class is a **public static abstract class**, and it extends the **java.lang.Object** superclass. This class provides the **nine** grid row and column **alignment constants** that are used to set the GridLayout **rowSpec** and **columnSpec** objects, which hold grid definition data.

The rowSpec and columnSpec objects are utilized to define the GridLayout's overall layout algorithm functionality for your UI design, and are defined internally to the GridLayout class using the **GridLayout.Spec** nested class, which we will be covering briefly in the next section of the chapter.

These nine rowSpec and columnSpec **alignment constants** can be seen in Table 14-3. It is important to note that one of these constants can be utilized, that is, defined, for each direction or axis, X and Y, for the GridLayout.

Table 14-3. RelativeLayout Parent Container Alignment Attributes or Parameters, Along with their Primary Functionality

GridLayout.Alignment Constant	Alignment Constant Function Description
TOP	Align the top edge of the View with top edge of other Views
BOTTOM	Align bottom edge of View with bottom edge of other Views
LEFT	Align the left edge of View with left edge of other Views
RIGHT	Align the right edge of View with right edge of other Views
START	Align the start edge of View with start edge of other Views
END	Align the end edge of View with the end edge of other Views
CENTER	Center all the Views contained within a given cell group
FILL	View should be expanded to fill the entire cell group area
BASELINE	Views in cell group (rows only) should be baseline aligned

This alignment constant specifies how your View UI elements will be placed within the cell grouping or how they should be scaled (resized) to fit the cell. Each X and Y alignment constant operates independently of the other. As I mentioned before, these can also be combined, using the vertical bar.

GridLayout.Spec Nested Class: Horizontal or Vertical Spec

A **GridLayout.Spec** nested class hierarchy begins with a Java Object master class, and directly creates this GridLayout.Spec nested class, that you could think of as specifying and containing the "row and column alignment objects," which are used at the core of the Android GridLayout UI class. A Spec object is used to define each of the horizontal or vertical attribute settings (parameters or characteristics) of a given group of grid cells.

This GridLayout.Spec nested class hierarchy is structured as follows:

```
java.lang.Object
  > android.widget.GridLayout.Spec
```

The Android GridLayout class is a **public static class,** and it extends the **java.lang.Object** superclass. This class provides the two objects that are used to define the core definition and functionality for the GridLayout algorithm, which is used to create the scalable Grid Layout UI designs.

Since these Spec objects are used internally, inside the GridLayout class, we will focus in this chapter on your design of the GridLayout UI, and its parameters rather than get into the inner algorithm workings of the class.

The Many GridLayout Class Parameters: Default Settings

The GridLayout class has a dozen primary parameters, which are used in the grid layout engine algorithm contained in the GridLayout class. These need to have a default setting defined for a grid algorithm to work correctly.

These parameters should all be considered, and set, in your UI design, and have default values, shown in Tables 14-4 and 14-5, assigned in case any of these settings are overlooked, or are left with their default settings. In this way the class (algorithm) throws no errors or exceptions, and thus we need to learn what the default values in the class are set to in the code.

Table 14-4. GridLayout Row and Column Specification Parameter Default Data Values

XML Parameter Used to Set:	Object Data Field Name:	Default Value:
android:layout_width	PARAMETER IS LEFT UNSPECIFIED	WRAP_CONTENT
android:layout_height	PARAMETER IS LEFT UNSPECIFIED	WRAP_CONTENT
android:layout_row	rowSpec.row	UNDEFINED
android:layout_column	columnSpec.column	UNDEFINED
android:layout_rowSpan	rowSpec.rowSpan	1
android:layout_columnSpan	columnSpec.columnSpan	1
android:layout_gravity	rowSpec.alignment	BASELINE
android:layout_gravity	columnSpec.alignment	START

Table 14-5. GridLayout Margin Specification Parameters Default Data Values (Based on useDefaultMargins Flag)

Margin XML Parameter	useDefaultMargins=false	useDefaultMargins=true
android:layout_topMargin	0	UNDEFINED
android:layout_bottomMargin	0	UNDEFINED
android:layout_leftMargin	0	UNDEFINED
android:layout_rightMargin	0	UNDEFINED

As you can see, you do not have to specify a layout_width or layout_height for child View objects in a GridLayout. Your WRAP_CONTENT and MATCH_PARENT constants are evaluated the same way (considered to be the same thing in a GridLayout), and thus these are hard-coded in the GridLayout's algorithms.

Row and column specifications are left as undefined by default, and are automatically calculated by the GridLayout algorithm when they aren't specified. These can be specified, if you know the grid dimensions that you are designing for, and this is more memory and processor efficient as you might well imagine.

RowSpan and ColumnSpan variables default to one, which essentially equates to "do not span." We will implement a span in our example later in this chapter, so that you can see exactly how this span functionality works.

Default **alignment** for rows is **BASELINE**, which is very logical if you think about it, and the default alignment for columns is **START**, which is also the alignment constant that I would have guessed would be used as the default. RowSpan and ColumnSpan define the rows and columns spanning behavior, but do not specify how they will be aligned (left, right, center, etc.).

Margins default to zero, if you set the android:useDefaultMargins="false" parameter in your parent <GridLayout> tag, and remain undefined, that is, they will be controlled by the GridLayout algorithm, if set to "true."

We will use the true setting so that margins are automatically set for us by the GridLayout, although, if we decide to use margin parameters, these will be "respected" by the GridLayout algorithm as well, as you will see.

Implementing GridLayout in the UserInterface App

Now it's time to implement the GridLayout UI design in your UserInterface application, using the information covered in the first part of the chapter.

Adding GridLayout to the UserInterface Menu Structure

To create our GridActivity.java Activity subclass we need to follow that same work process that we did to create a RelativeLayout Activity subclass and XML UI definition file in Chapter 13. If you need complete visuals for this, refer to the figures from the previous chapter. The work process is the same; first you will install a MenuItem object in your menu.xml file; then you'll add a case statement and Intent object to launch the Activity; you'll next create the GridActivity.java class; and finally, you'll create your XML for the activity_grid.xml and AndroidManifest.xml files, which will be needed to hold your GridLayout UI design and to add your new GridActivity, respectively.

First copy the <item> tag for your relative_layout <item> (refer to Figure 13-1 in the previous chapter), and then you paste that underneath itself, and change relative_layout to grid_layout.

Next add your **<string>** constant named **grid_layout** with data "**Grid Layout**."

Next, add a third case statement in your MainActivity.java file, using the same work process, (please refer to Figure 13-2). Copy and paste your second case statement and change the word **Relative** to **Grid**, and **intent_rl** to read **intent_gl**. The Java code for this case structure looks like the following:

```
case R.id.grid_layout:
Intent intent_gl = new Intent(this, GridActivity.class);
this.startActivity(intent_gl);
break;
```

Mouse-over the wavy red error highlighting under the GridActivity class reference, and select the **Create class 'GridActivity'** dialog option.

This brings up the **New Class** dialog (refer to Figure 13-3), where you'll select the **android.app.Activity** superclass, using the **Superclass Selection** dialog.

Now that you have created your Java class, you will need to create your UI XML definition file. Right-click your /res/layout folder and select the **New ➤ Android XML File** menu sequence and name your file **activity_grid**, and then click the **Finish** button to create an XML definition file. I did a combined screenshot showing these last two steps in Figure 14-1.

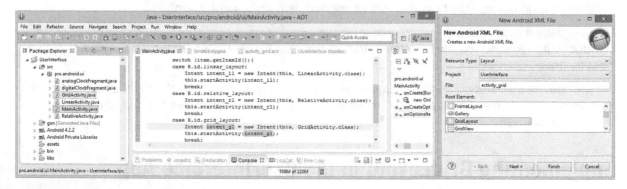

Figure 14-1. Add a third case statement for the GridActivity class and create a new GridLayout activity_grid.xml

Clicking the **Finish** button opens up your **activity_grid.xml** file for editing in Eclipse ADT, where you can start to configure your GridLayout UI parent parameters.

If you have your **Minimum API Level** for your app set to less than Level 14, you will also get a warning dialog (you may have it set to API Level 11 currently). This dialog advises you to change this setting in your AndroidManifest.xml file, which you will do in the next step. After you add the third GridActivity <activity> tag into your application's Manifest XML definition file, upgrade the minimum SDK version support from Level 11 to Level 14 as shown in Figure 14-2.

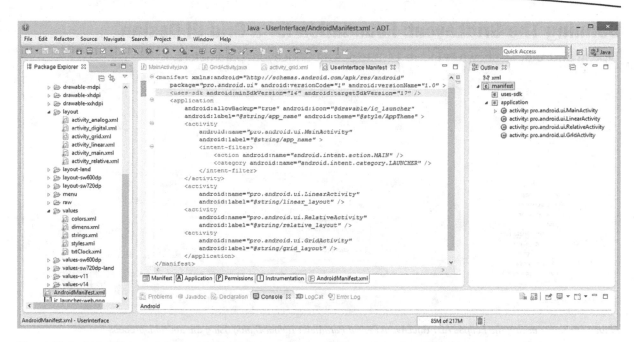

Figure 14-2. Add a third <activity> tag for GridActivity and upgrade your <uses-sdk> minSdkVersion to Level 14

After you have created these necessary new files that you will need to put in place to implement your GridLayout Activity, Manifest, and UI definition files, we can get down to business and spend the rest of the chapter in an XML UI definition file defining your <GridLayout> parent container and its UI element (View widget) children objects.

Let's add the GridLayout to your UserInterface app by adding your third <activity> tag to your AndroidManifest.xml file as well as upgrading your minimum SDK version. The XML markup to upgrade the minimum SDK version is found inside of the <uses-sdk> tag definition, and should look like the following markup, and can also be seen at the top of Figure 14-2:

```
<uses-sdk android:minSdkVersion="14" android:targetSdkVersion="17" />
```

The XML markup to add the third <activity> definition should look like the following, and can be seen near the bottom of Figure 14-2:

```
<activity
    android:name="pro.android.ui.GridActivity
    android:label="@string/grid_layout" />
```

Now we can focus on building your GridLayout UI design from scratch, using both parent tag and child tag parameters, from the GridLayout (parent tag parameters) and GridLayout.LayoutParams (child tag parameters) classes.

Defining The GridLayout: Foundation for a Grid UI Design

Type in **android:** as shown in Figure 14-3 to see all GridLayout parameters.

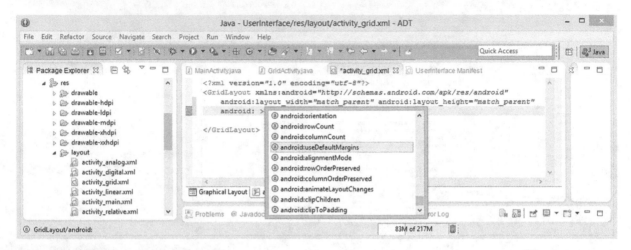

Figure 14-3. *Accessing the Eclipse ADT GridLayout Parent Parameter Helper Dialog using the android: process*

We'll add your **global configuration parameters** to your <GridLayout> parent tag first, by adding in a line of space and using the **android + colon** work process to get your GridLayout **parent parameter helper dialog**, as is shown in Figure 14-3. As you can see, those GridLayout specific parameters that have been added at the bottom of the parameter list include the seven that we learned about earlier in the chapter, as listed in Table 14-2. Notice we have already added the **useDefaultMargins="true"** and a **gridLayout** ID value (see Figure 14-4).

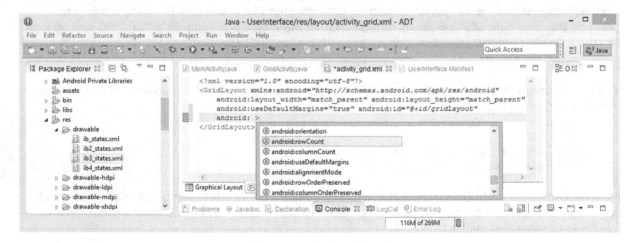

Figure 14-4. *Adding an android:id for the GridLayout named gridLayout and adding five more parent parameters*

First, let's create the basic 2x2 grid to hold four planets, Earth, Venus, Jupiter, and soon Neptune. We will also define the alignment mode, and set flags that preserve row and column order, to keep your GridLayout as fixed as possible, and thus to use as little system memory as possible. We'll do this by using the following parameters in XML markup, seen in Figure 14-5:

```
android:rowCount="2"
android:columnCount="2"
android:alignmentMode="alignMargins"
android:rowOrderPreserved="true
android:columnOrderPreserved="true"
```

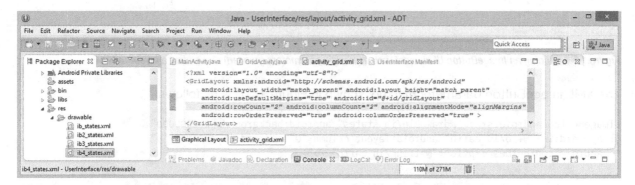

Figure 14-5. Final GridLayout parent tag & parameters setting rows, columns, ID, and various GridLayout settings

As you can see, you set your rowCount and columnCount to a value of **2**, and turn on your rowOrderPreserve and columnOrderPreserve options, using a **true** value. Next, set the alignment mode to the **alignMargins** constant, and then you are ready to add your ImageButton child tags to each grid cell.

Since GridLayout child tags don't need margin parameters, we can configure the <ImageButton> UI element child tag using only a half-dozen parameters.

Copy the ib_earth <ImageButton> tag from the <LinearLayout> UI definition and delete all the layout_margin parameters. Next type in the **android:** character sequence to get your parameter helper dialog, which is shown in Figure 14-6, and now contains the five GridLayout.LayoutParams attributes we covered in Table 14-1. Add the layout_row and layout_column parameters.

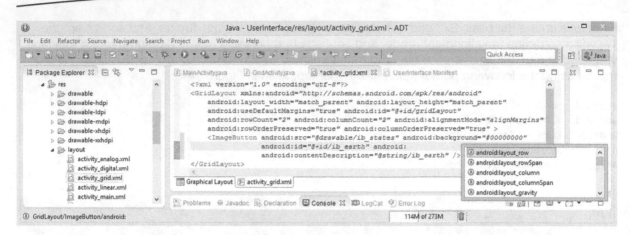

Figure 14-6. *Adding an ImageButton UI element with no margin parameters (needed) and adding a layout_row*

The XML ImageButton parameter markup, shown in Figure 14-7, is as follows:

```
<ImageButton android:src:="@drawable/ib_states" android:background="#00000000"
    android:id="@+id/ib_earth" android:layout_column="0" android:layout_row="0"
    android:contentDescription="@string/ib_earth" />
```

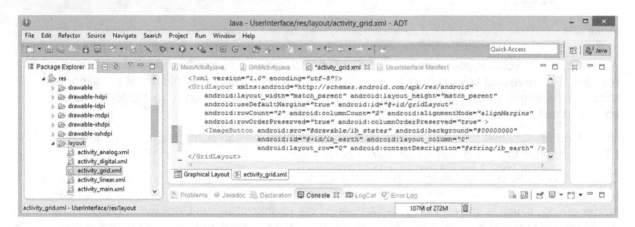

Figure 14-7. *Final parameter configuration for your initial ImageButton UI element in the upper-left corner of grid*

Once your first <ImageButton> child tag is configured, copy (and paste) it underneath itself three more times, since we'll need four planets for your four grid cells, and change the IDs to ib_venus, ib_jupiter and ib_neptune and your android:src references to: ib_states, ib1_states, ib2_states, and ib3_states, respectively.

Now match your contentDescription <string> references with the appropriate planet names. Next put planet Venus in **Row Zero Column One** (top-right) and put planet Jupiter in **Row One Column Zero** (bottom-left) and planet Neptune in **Row One Column One** (bottom-right) using the GridLayout parameters. Your XML markup, shown in Figure 14-8, should look just like the following XML:

```
<ImageButton android:src:="@drawable/ib_states" android:background="#00000000"
    android:id="@+id/ib_earth" android:layout_column="0" android:layout_row="0"
    android:contentDescription="@string/ib_earth" />
<ImageButton android:src:="@drawable/ib2_states" android:background="#00000000"
    android:id="@+id/ib_venus" android:layout_column="1" android:layout_row="0"
    android:contentDescription="@string/ib_venus" />
<ImageButton android:src:="@drawable/ib3_states" android:background="#00000000"
    android:id="@+id/ib_jupiter" android:layout_column="0" android:layout_row="1"
    android:contentDescription="@string/ib_jupiter" />
<ImageButton android:src:="@drawable/ib4_states" android:background="#00000000"
    android:id="@+id/ib_neptune" android:layout_column="1" android:layout_row="1"
    android:contentDescription="@string/ib_neptune" />
```

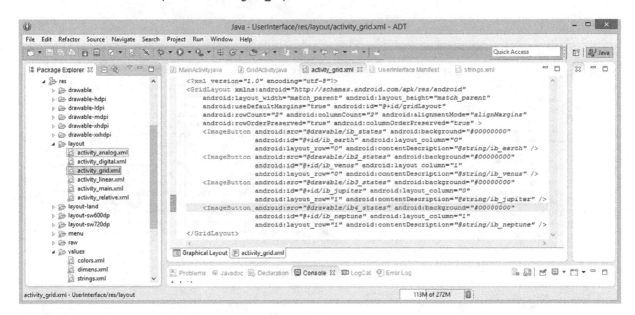

Figure 14-8. Add four ImageButton UI elements to a GridLayout and configure their grid row and column location

Next we need to create the digital image assets for a Neptune ImageButton, and while we're at it, we will add in <string> constants for a planet size info TextView UI element, in order to make our application more complete.

Adding More Planets and Information: Upgrading strings.xml

Next, you will need to create your ImageButton digital image assets, using the neptune256.png image file, which is provided with the book assets, which can be found on the *Pro Android UI* page on the Apress.com website. Use the work process outlined in Chapter 12, to create your fourth ImageButton asset's normal, hovered, pressed and focused state image files.

After that is completed for each of the major MDPI, HDPI and XHDPI density resolution targets, you will need to create the ib4_states.xml multi-state ImageButton <selector> XML definition file, following the work process you used in Chapter 12 in the "Using GIMP Digital Imaging Software for UI Design" section.

Once this is finished, the fourth ImageButton UI definition will have image assets and XML to reference, and all you'll have left to do is to add your <string> constants for the Neptune ImageButton, TextViews, and new <string> constants for the planet size information that we are going to add to your GridLayout UI design during the remainder of this chapter.

Your new <string> constant XML is as follows, and is shown in Figure 14-9:

```
<string name="planet_name_neptune">Planet Name: Neptune</string>
<string name="planet_size_earth">Planet Diameter: 12,756 KM</string>
<string name="planet_size_venus">Planet Diameter: 12,104 KM</string>
<string name="planet_size_jupiter">Planet Diameter: 132,984 KM</string>
<string name="planet_size_neptune">Planet Diameter: 49,528 KM</string>
```

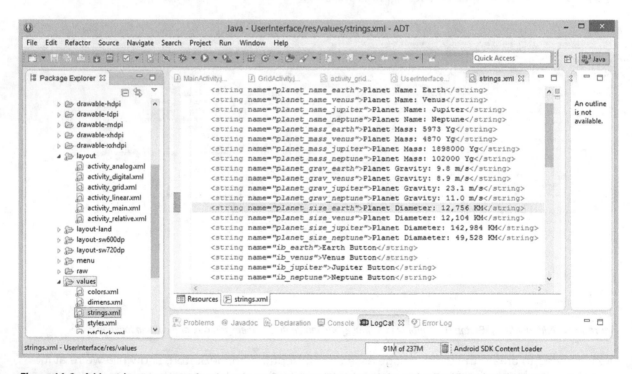

Figure 14-9. Add <string> constants for planet ImageButtons and the planet information TextViews in strings.xml

Now we're ready to get into the Java programming for our GridActivity.java Activity subclass, where we will initially explore using the GONE constant with a GridLayout, which will collapse a grid cell down to zero (nothing), and thus allow us to "disappear" the grid cells, which can be very useful.

Interacting with GridLayout UI via Java in GridActivity.java

Next add in **final** ImageButton instantiation and referencing for your four ImageButton UI elements, after the setContentView() method call, and then, add .setOnClickListener() constructs for each like you did in the Chapter 12 and set each planet to GONE, and the others to VISIBLE, as shown in Figure 14-10, so that when you click each ImageButton it disappears.

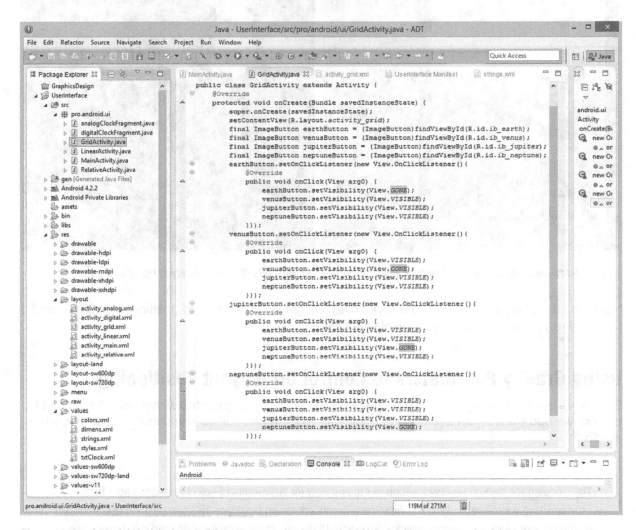

Figure 14-10. Code GridActivity.java Activity subclass to implement the GONE visibility parameter for GridLayout

Once you have the Java code in place, use the **Run As ➤ Android Application** and test the Grid Layout menu and GridLayout in the Nexus One, as shown in Figure 14-11. When you first run your GridLayout, you see all four planets in a grid, and when you click each planet, it disappears, and reappears when one of the other planets is clicked to collapse its grid cell down to zero.

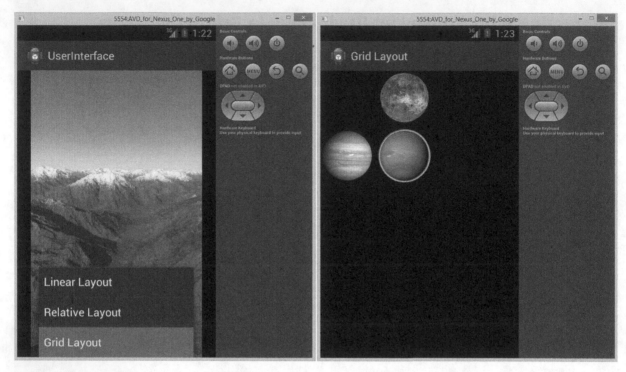

Figure 14-11. Show the GridLayout MenuItem, and testing the GridLayout and GONE functionality in Nexus One

Next, you are going to implement the android:layout_gravity parameter, to position your GridLayout cells where you want them on your display screen.

Using Gravity Parameters to Control GridLayout Positioning

Before we use the layout_gravity parameter to practice positioning control within your GridLayout UI design, we add the android:background parameter to each grid cell, to completely visualize it, while we do this.

> **Tip**   Adding the background color parameter to any View (or ViewGroup) UI object is a useful little trick, for visualizing your View (widget) and ViewGroup (layout container) boundary. This can be quite useful to do during your UI design process (as you create your UI design), to visualize what Android is actually doing with your design, and so I will do it here, to show you how this technique helps during the fine-tuning of UI designs.

At the end of this chapter, we will change these background values back to transparent, and add a space background image or two to your GridLayout UI container. We will do this to take our grid UI design to the next level, and to implement some advanced image compositing workflow into your GridLayout design process. After all, this book is about Pro Android UI!

Now it's time to add the android:layout_gravity parameter I talked about earlier in the chapter combined with an ability to use two alignment constants via the vertical bar separator. Let's put our planet ImageButton UI elements into the four corners of your screen, by using four different combinations of left, right, top, and bottom.

As you can see in Figure 14-12, we are going to put your Earth ImageButton grid cell in the left|top corner of your UI design, your Venus ImageButton grid cell in the right|top corner of your design, your Jupiter ImageButton grid cell in the left|bottom corner of your UI design, and finally, your Neptune ImageButton grid cell in the right|bottom corner of the UI design.

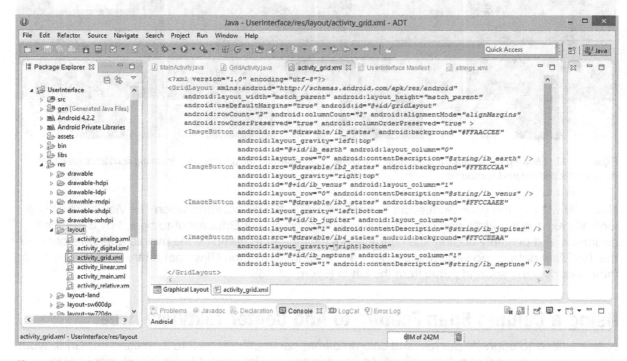

Figure 14-12. Adding a fourth planet ImageButton for Neptune so that we can have a planet in every grid corner

Also notice that I've added an android:background parameter to each of the ImageButton UI definitions. I am using four different combinations of the hexadecimal values AA, CC, and EE, to produce different pastel background coloration. The leading #FF makes sure the color is fully opaque, and thus Earth uses #FFAACCEE or light blue, Venus uses #FFEECCAA or light orange, Jupiter uses #FFCCAAEE or lilac, and Neptune uses #FFCCEEAA or lime green.

Now you are ready to use the **Run As ➤ Android Application** work process and test your new GridLayout configuration. As you can see on the left side of Figure 14-13, the layout_gravity parameters and combined alignment setting constants work perfectly, pegging your grid cells into the corners of your display screen. We can now visualize this UI design, due to the background color we installed, allowing you to see the size and shape of a grid cell.

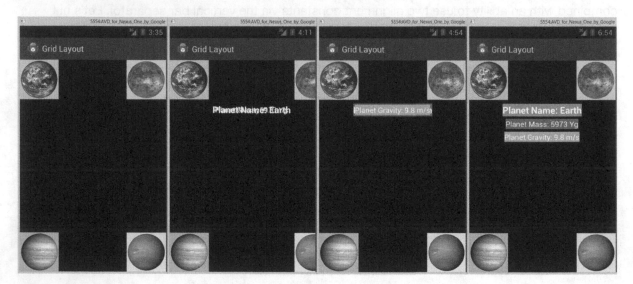

Figure 14-13. Showing the Neptune ImageButton, grid corner alignment, and the progression for adding TextViews which we cover in this and the next section

Next, we will expand your GridLayout to accommodate the planet information TextViews, which will logically exist in a middle grid cell. This involves expanding our GridLayout to be a 3 by 3 grid cell structure, and possibly adding span parameters if we need to combine the middle grid cells because the TextView data is too large and pushes our planet ImageButton UI widget off the screen (hint: examine the second panel from the left in Figure 14-13).

Using a Column Span Feature to Add Center TextView Area

First we need to upgrade our row and column parent parameters from 2 to 3, making our GridLayout a 9 cell layout instead of a 4 cell layout. As you can see, in Figure 14-14, this is fairly easy to do, and you can now copy over the three existing TextView UI elements from one of your other XML definitions, and remove any layout_margin parameters, so that you can start configuring your TextView alignment 100% from scratch.

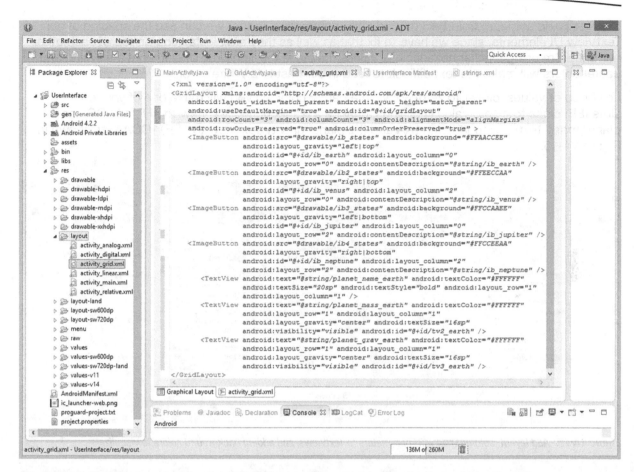

Figure 14-14. Changing the columnCount and rowCount parameter to 3 and adding the three existing TextViews

Add your android:layout_row and android:layout_column parameters, each set to a value of 1, to initially place the TextView UI elements in the center of the screen, which is where you want them to be in your UI design.

Next test your result using the **Run As ➤ Android Application** work process, and as you have seen in Figure 14-13, in the second pane from the left, your TextViews currently overlap.

There are a number of things that we need to do at this point and each can be accomplished using parameters. The most important is to allow your text to span the middle cells of the GridLayout, which we will accomplish using an android:layout_columnSpan="3" parameter, added to each of your TextView UI containers.

Notice that you'll also need to change the android:layout_column parameter for each of the TextView UI elements, forcing them to originate (start) in column 0, rather than column 1. When combined with your columnSpan setting of 3, this makes the entire middle of your GridLayout into one huge row!

Next let's add some android:background color parameters so that we can see the spacing of our TextView UI elements, since we have to fix that as well as they are all stacking on top of each other currently. I'm using smaller hexadecimal values, because the TextView UI elements are White, and pastel colors will make the text difficult to read in contrast to a White color.

Lower color values (closer to zero) will yield a darker color, so you will make one of your color slots (EE) close to a zero value (11). Thus, change a planet name TextView to #FF11AACC, the planet mass TextView to #FFCC11AA and the planet gravity TextView to #FF11CCAA, as shown in Figure 14-15.

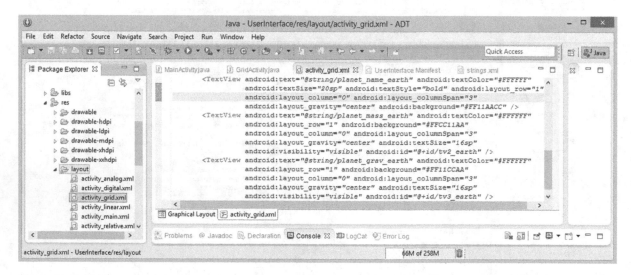

Figure 14-15. Add layout_columnSpan="3" parameters to TextViews, and adding background colors to visualize

Next use your **Run As ➤ Android Application** work process, which should show the results seen in the third pane of Figure 14-13. Next, we'll use margin parameters in each of the first two TextView UI elements, to push TextView UI elements away from each other, by using the android:layout_marginBottom parameter with 60dp increments, as can be seen in Figure 14-16.

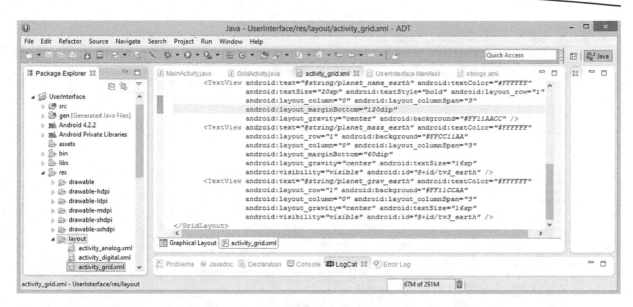

Figure 14-16. Adding layout_marginBottom parameters to push TextViews apart, and adding background colors

Now let's add in the fourth planet size TextView UI element by copying the third planet gravity TextView UI element and pasting it underneath itself. The last TextView does not need a margin parameter, as it is "pushed down" at the bottom of this TextView "stack." However, you will need to change the layout_marginBottom parameter for the first three TextView UI elements to be 180, 120 and 60dp respectively, as shown in Figure 14-17, as well as in the following markup, which now shows all four completed TextViews:

```
<TextView android:text="@string/planet_name_earth" android:textColor="#FFFFFF"
          android:textSize="20sp" android:textStyle="bold" android:layout_row="1"
          android:layout_column="0" android:layout_columnSpan="3"
          android:layout_marginBottom="180dip" android:id="@+id/tv1_earth"
          android:layout_gravity="center" android:background="#00000000" />
<TextView android:text="@string/planet_mass_earth" android:textColor="#FFFFFF"
          android:layout_row="1" android:background="#00000000"
          android:layout_column="0" android:layout_columnSpan="3"
          android:layout_marginBottom="120dip"
          android:layout_gravity="center" android:textSize="16sp"
          android:visibility="visible" android:id="@+id/tv2_earth" />
<TextView android:text="@string/planet_grav_earth" android:textColor="#FFFFFF"
          android:layout_row="1" android:background="#00000000"
          android:layout_column="0" android:layout_columnSpan="3"
          android:layout_marginBottom="60dip"
          android:layout_gravity="center" android:textSize="16sp"
          android:visibility="visible" android:id="@+id/tv3_earth" />
<TextView android:text="@string/planet_size_earth" android:textColor="#FFFFFF"
          android:layout_row="1" android:background="#00000000"
          android:layout_column="0" android:layout_columnSpan="3"
          android:layout_gravity="center" android:textSize="16sp"
          android:visibility="visible" android:id="@+id/tv4_earth" />
```

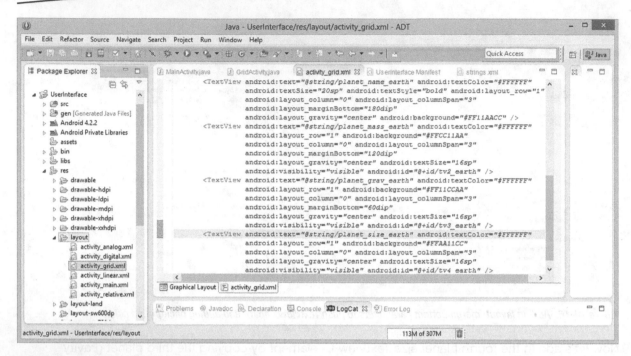

*Figure 14-17. Add a fourth tv4_earth TextView UI element for planet size information using an android:id of tv4_*

If you use the **Run As ➤ Android Application** work process, you will see that the TextView UI elements now line up the way you want them to, and you can now remove the background color parameters from your TextView UI elements, (but not from your ImageButton UI elements, as we are going to use these a bit later) to get ready to do some digital image compositing, which we are going to do later, after we implement your Java code in the next section. Figure 14-18 shows the elements aligned before and after the background colors are removed, as well as the planet information that is shown with the Venus ImageButton is clicked.

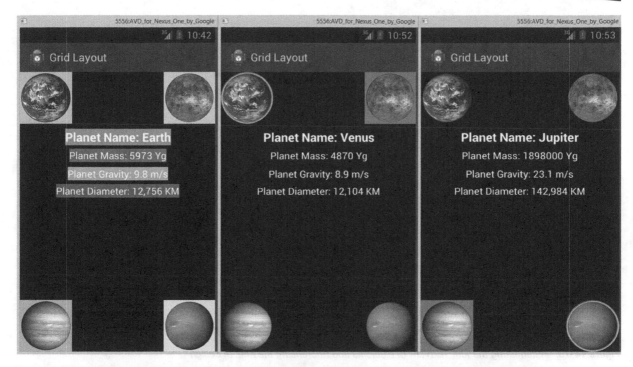

Figure 14-18. Showing our complete UI design and positioning and removing color and using translucency value

Next we will instantiate our TextView and ImageButton UI elements in the Java code in the GridActivity.java Activity subclass, so that we can make your GridLayout UI design interactive, and ultimately, fully functional.

Adding the Java Code to Make Your GridLayout Interactive

Add the same TextView declarations at the top of your class that you did in the LinearLayout and RelativeLayout chapters, and instantiate TextView and ImageButton UI objects in the onCreate() method. In fact, if you want to, you can copy the Java code structures over from either of these class codebases, which are in your project already, and simply modify the code, to fit what we need to do in this GridActivity class.

As you can see in Figure 14-19, everything we need to use is now in place—object declarations, instantiations, XML referencing, and OnClickListener() methods—and we're ready to add Java code inside of our onClick() methods.

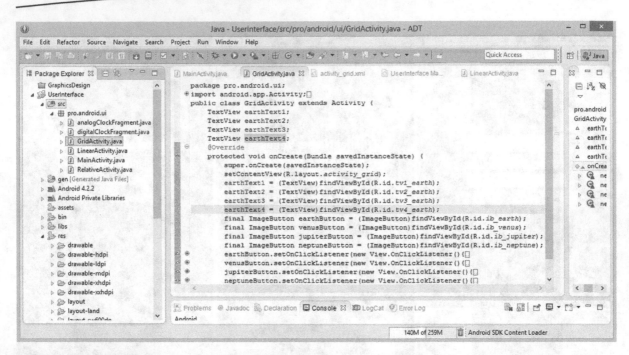

Figure 14-19. Instantiating the four TextView UI elements and referencing the XML UI design

The Java code inside your onClick() listener methods needs to "set" the background of the currently active ImageButton UI element to be 50% transparent with White color. This highlights the selected ImageButton for the user as being currently in use, and also still reveals part of the background image for your UI design, which we are going to add in the next section.

To set this translucency effect dynamically in Java code, utilize the **.setBackgroundColor()** method, along with the **.argb()** method, for each of the ImageButton UI elements. The currently active ImageButton sets a value of **#77FFFFFF** (50% alpha White) or in integer terms **128,255,255,255**, which is what the .argb() method takes (four integer parameters separated by commas). The Java code for the Earth ImageButton is

```
public void onClick(View arg0) {
    earthButton.setBackgroundColor(Color.argb(128, 255, 255, 255));
    venusButton.setBackgroundColor(Color.argb(255, 255, 255, 255));
    jupiterButton.setBackgroundColor(Color.argb(255, 255, 255, 255));
    neptuneButton.setBackgroundColor(Color.argb(255, 255, 255, 255));
}
```

As you can see in Figure 14-20, the preceding Java code is error-free, and you are ready to call the **.setText()** method, to set your TextView's data values. Also shown in Figure 14-20 is how Eclipse helps you add your String reference, and once you do the error highlight disappears.

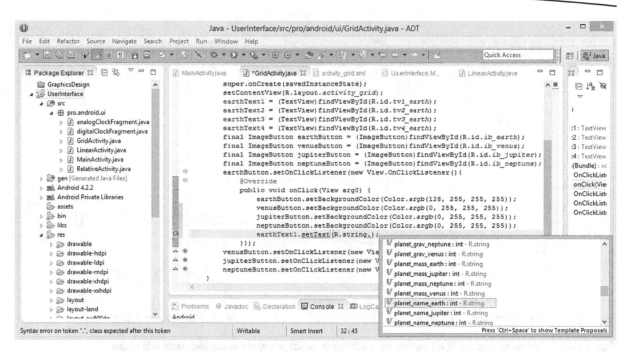

Figure 14-20. Using the .setText(R.string.planet_name_earth) method call to load the string data into a TextView

Once you type in the first earthText.setText() method call and an **R.string** resource path, which will tell Android where to look, Eclipse will open up the helper dialog, shown in Figure 14-20, which lists all your <string> constant definitions.

Locate the **planet_name_earth:int - R.string** about 60% of the way down this list and double-click it. This completes this Java statement and loads the **earthText1** object, which we're using in this Activity subclass to hold each of your planet text data values (you may change this to planetText if you want to be more generic or precise in your TextView variable naming).

You need to replicate this line of code for each of your four earthText objects, and reference earthText1 to the planet_name_earth, earthText2 to the planet_mass_earth, earthText3 to the planet_grav_earth, and earthText4 to the new planet_size_earth <string> constants, as shown in Figure 14-21.

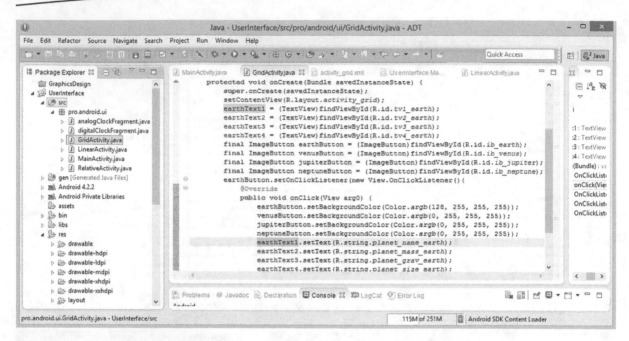

Figure 14-21. The completed onClick() method for earthButton, which you now can cut and paste into others

Next do this for the Venus, Jupiter and Neptune onClick() listener methods and be sure to use planet_name_venus, planet_mass_venus, planet_grav_venus, and planet_size_venus (or jupiter or neptune, respectively), to have each listener method load the correct string data into these earthText objects.

Once you have done this, use the **Run As ➤ Android Application** work process and test your code. When I first tested this copied and modified code, the emulator crashed because I didn't have an android:id="tv1_earth" parameter in my first TextView object, which I'm going to add next to allow the Java code and XML markup to work together seamlessly, with zero runtime errors.

Add an android:id="@+id/tv1_earth" parameter, as shown in Figure 14-22.

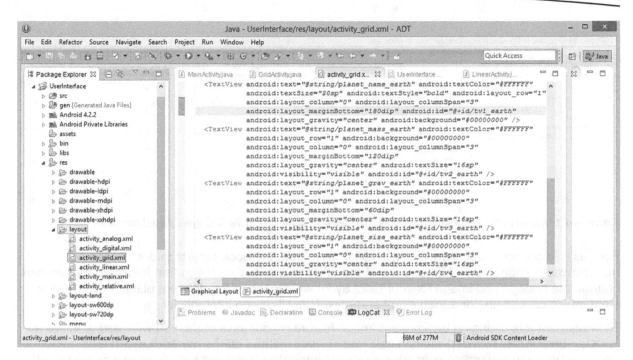

Figure 14-22. Adding an android:id= +@+id/tv1_earth" so that we can access (change) the planet name info

Now test your application again in the Nexus One, and make sure that it is working correctly, and that the ImageButton UI elements are highlighted in transparent white (which looks medium grey on a black background) and that the TextView data changes to match up with each respective planet's button UI element, and then we will be ready to add some wow-factor to the design in the next section of the chapter.

Adding New Media Elements and Compositing to Your Grid UI

To install a background image into your GridLayout container, you need to add an android:background parameter that references an image file that is in your /res/drawable folder hierarchy. This is done using an android:background="@drawable/stars480" XML parameter, as seen highlighted in Figure 14-23.

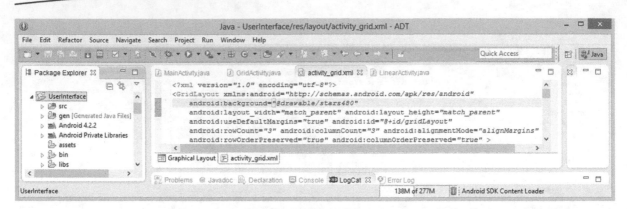

Figure 14-23. Add an android:background="@drawable/stars480" parameter to the GridLayout parent container

For this to work you must copy the stars480.png file from the book project folder into the /res/drawable-xhdpi folder. Make sure that the other image files are still in that folder, so that we can change the background image for your GridLayout when each of the different planet ImageButton elements is clicked on, for added effect and maximum UI design interactivity.

To implement this changing background image feature in your Java code, you will need to utilize a **.setBackgroundResource()** method call. You call this method off the **myGridLayout** GridLayout object, which you instantiate right after your setContentView() method call, as shown at the top of Figure 14-24, using the following single line of Java code:

```java
final GridLayout myGridLayout = (GridLayout)findViewById(R.id.gridLayout);
```

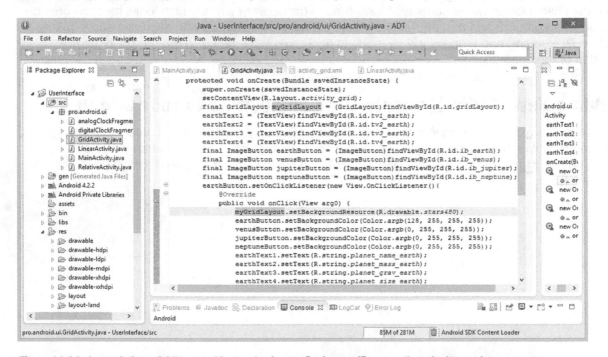

Figure 14-24. Instantiating a GridLayout object and using .setBackgroundResource() method to set image asset

If you wanted to omit the **final** access modifier before the ImageButton and GridLayout objects, you can declare the ImageButton and GridLayout objects at the top of your class, and later instantiate and reference them, within the onCreate() method, in exactly the same way that you did with your four TextView objects.

Once your GridLayout is instantiated, and inflated with the XML definition reference to the XML **gridLayout** (ID) GridLayout UI definition, you will be able to add a **.setBackgroundResource()** method call off of the **myGridLayout** object, shown in Figure 14-24, into each of the four event listening methods next.

The .setBackgroundResource() method call references a different digital image asset in your /res/drawable-xhdpi folder for each of the planet ImageButton .onClick() event handling method structures. This Java statement should take the following format, as shown in Figure 14-24, highlighted in the middle of the screenshot:

```
myGridlayout.setBackgroundResource(R.drawable.stars480);
```

I used the plasma480.png image asset for Venus, a plasma720.png image for Jupiter, and the plasma1080.png image for Neptune, but you can use any of these for any of your onClick() event listeners that you wish, and Android OS will scale them to fit the Nexus One emulator's resolution density.

Once you have added the myGridLayout.setBackgroundResource() method call to each of your four onClick() event handling method structures, you can use the **Run As ➤ Android Application** work process to test the application and I think you'll find the results are pretty darned cool, as can be seen in Figure 14-25. If you really want to fine-tune your GridLayout UI design more, go back into your activity_grid.xml file, and play around with using the **android:shadow** parameters (there are four of them) and use a **#77000000** 50% Alpha Black **android:shadowColor** value, to make the text more readable.

Figure 14-25. *Use a Nexus One emulator to test and preview the planet ImageButtons and different backgrounds*

Summary

In this chapter, you learned about a new Android **GridLayout** class and its layout parameters, which are provided in both the GridLayout class and its **GridLayout.LayoutParams** nested class.

You looked at the GridLayout.LayoutParams nested class and at its child UI element positioning parameters used within the child UI element tags. You looked at the seven GridLayout parent tag parameters, which are part of the GridLayout class and allow a GridLayout "engine" to be configured for use.

You looked at the GridLayout concepts of rows, columns, cells, gravity, and flexibility, as well as at how to use the GONE parameter to collapse your grid cell to zero. You learned how to use a layout_gravity parameter to align grid cells and their child View content, as well as how to use more than one alignment constant, by using the vertical bar | delimiter. Then you implemented a GridLayout of your own, using XML markup and Java code.

In the next chapter, we will take a closer look at the **DrawerLayout** class, and see how you can use another UI class to fabricate "interactive drawer" UI designs that allow you to save display real estate, and store your UI designs off-screen and access them using a swipe motion to bring them on-screen.

Part 5

Advanced Android UI Design: Advanced Layout Containers: DrawerLayout, SlidingPane, ViewPager, PagerTitleStrip and PagerTabStrip

15

Android's DrawerLayout Class: Using a UI Drawer in Your UI Design

The Android **DrawerLayout** class is also a recent addition to the Android OS as of the Android 4.0 Ice Cream Sandwich release. It was developed to permit developers to put their UI elements into a drawer that can slide on-screen when needed and then slide out of the way, off-screen, allowing more screen real estate to be available for the application's primary content and use. If you want to take a quick peek at what your DrawerLayout is going to look like, you can take a look at Figure 15-22.

This DrawerLayout class is often used with the **ListView** UI class, so we'll learn about ListView objects as well in the chapter, since we have not yet covered ListView UI objects in the book, and they're useful for UI design.

This Android ListView class is based on the **AbsListView** class, and its XML parameters, one of which we will be utilizing in our DrawerLayout Activity subclass within this chapter. Thus, we will also be covering this class in this chapter, and using it in conjunction with the DrawerLayout UI class.

The Android AbsListView class is based on the Android **AdapterView** class as well as the Android **Adapter** interface, so we'll also be covering these two classes in this chapter, so that you have an overview of each API that is involved in the Java code hierarchy from a Java Object down to a ListView.

What we're going to do with your UserInterface application in this chapter is to create a DrawerLayout "Drawer UI" design. This will be a significant improvement on (another expansion of) the current multi-planet UI design which you've been creating during the last several chapters. You'll create the **DrawerLayout.java** Activity subclass and the MenuItem selection for the MainActivity. java Activity, and create an **activity_drawer** UI design using XML, which you'll later make interactive, using Java and **onListItem()** event handling.

The DrawerLayout Class: Designing Using a Retractable UI

The Android **DrawerLayout** class is another UI layout container class that was introduced in Android Version 4.0. The DrawerLayout class provides the developer with an interactive layout container for user interface content that can be stored off-screen to save screen real estate (space).

A DrawerLayout UI definition provides the Android user with an interactive UI element drawer (ViewGroup), which can be "flicked" out from the edge of the Android device's display. This is accomplished by using a rapid swipe gesture, usually from left to right.

The Android design convention for a DrawerLayout is similar to all the other design conventions that we have covered thus far in this book, and you should thus make your UI drawer emerge from left to right, unless your app is in RTL mode, in which case the UI drawer would emerge from right to left. For this reason we will be using the start and end constants in this chapter rather than the left and right constants. In this way, whether RTL or LTR is in place, the design will work correctly according to the design guidelines that we need to follow for our Android application development.

The DrawerLayout class hierarchy begins with the Java Object master class, progressing from the View class to the ViewGroup class to the DrawerLayout class, which is part of a special **android.support.v4.widget** package and is structured using the following class hierarchy:

```
java.lang.Object
 > android.view.View
   > android.view.ViewGroup
     > android.support.v4.widget.DrawerLayout
```

The Android GridLayout class is a **public class**, and extends the **ViewGroup** superclass. It is referenced by using this specialized support.v4 package, using an **import android.support. v4.widget.DrawerLayout** statement, located at the top of your Java Activity subclass, as you will soon see.

The UI Drawer position and layout in your design is controlled by using an **android:layout_gravity** attribute on the child View object XML definition, which is most cases is the ListView UI widget, which we are going to learn about in this chapter as well. This android:layout_gravity parameter's constant will correspond with the side of the ViewGroup UI layout container which you wish your UI drawer to telescope out from. Suggested use is the start constant, or left, in a LTR user mode, or right for the RTL mode. If you are developing for platforms which don't support RTL user mode, you can use a left (or right) constant.

As we learned earlier in this book, Android's OS Design guidelines specify that any UI element, in this case a UI drawer, should be designed to be on the left (or start) and should always contain UI content that is earmarked for navigating around the application. If you wanted to position your UI drawers on the right of your UI design, you need to make sure that these UI elements contain "actions" that your user can take on the content currently displayed on your screen. This is so this approach conforms to the same navigation on the left, actions on the right user interface design approach that is currently used in the Android ActionBar, and similar "fixed" OS UI areas.

Next we're going to dive right in and learn how to implement DrawerLayout, along with a ListView UI widget inside of it, to hold your UI selections. To do this you will position your primary content View, in this case we'll use a LinearLayout containing your UI elements, as the initial child View. You will use the MATCH_PARENT constant for your required layout_width and layout_height parameters, so the LinearLayout will fill your first layer. The DrawerLayout class implements the concept of z-order, so, the first UI elements placed in the container will be on the bottom, and the ones after that, in this case a ListView UI, will slide out over the top of these. This is why you will be using a LinearLayout as your UI container, for the "bottom" layer of your DrawerLayout UI design in this chapter, and a then a ListView UI widget, which you will define in your XML, after you define the LinearLayout. In this way you will be taking advantage of the z-order, to slide your UI drawer's planet selections over (on top of) the UI design contained within the LinearLayout.

Although we are actually going to configure our ListView first, since that is what is inside our DrawerLayout's UI drawer, as far as an XML tag order goes, your UI Drawer will eventually contain child TextView UI objects inside a LinearLayout View. We will configure your ListView first, so that I can show you exactly how to set the android:layout_gravity and android:choiceMode correctly as well as some other parameters for configuring the selection items and divider lines. UI elements in a UI drawer usually use the MATCH_PARENT constant for the layout_height parameter and some fixed DIP value for layout_width.

Before we start coding our DrawerActivity Activity subclass, I want to go over the ListView class, as well as a couple of other classes that it is tied to, so that we can look at some of the constants and methods that we will be utilizing in our Java code and XML markup within this chapter.

Android Classes Used with DrawerLayout

There are a number of classes that are used in conjunction with the DrawerLayout class that I feel we should take an overview of first, so that you have some background in place before we start using these classes in your Java code.

The Android ListView Class: UI Design with Selection Lists

The Android **ListView** class creates a View object that displays items for a user to select, using a vertical list. If there are enough items on the list, the list will implement the scrollbar function automatically. These items come from the ListAdapter associated with your View; in our example, we will be using an Array of String[] to hold the planet name selections. As you will see in the class hierarchy, an AdapterView is used in a ListView.

The ListView class hierarchy also begins with the Java Object master class and progresses from a View class, to a ViewGroup class, to the **AdapterView** class, which is used to create the **AbsListView** class, which is subclassed in order to create the ListView class. We will take a closer look at both of these classes next, before we get into writing code to implement our UI design which leverages the DrawerLayout and ListView classes.

These half-dozen classes that are utilized to create the Android ListView class are ultimately structured by using the following class hierarchy:

```
java.lang.Object
  > android.view.View
    > android.view.ViewGroup
      > android.widget.AdapterView<T extends android.widget.Adapter>
        > android.widget.AbsListView
          > android.widget.ListView
```

The Android ListView class is a **public class**, and extends the **AbsListView** superclass. It is referenced by using the android.widget package, using the **import android.widget.ListView** statement, located at the top of your Java Activity subclass, as you will soon see.

The ListView class has one known direct subclass, the ExpandableListView, and most of what we are going to utilize for the ListView comes from the AbsListView class, which we are going to cover next.

Android's AbsListView Class: Base Class for Virtual Lists

The Android **AbsListView** class is a "base class," which can be utilized to create custom classes that implement a "virtualized" list of UI elements or even contain content items, such as in a GridView.

An AbsListView list does not have a spatial definition at this base class level, because it will be used to create different types of View objects. These objects will list objects in some fashion, either linear (ListView), or matrix based (GridView). For instance, subclasses of the AbsListView class could display content in the list using a grid, or a carousel, or possibly an expanding stack.

The AbsListView class hierarchy begins with the Java Object master class, and progresses from a View class, to a ViewGroup class, to the **AdapterView** class that is used to create the **AbsListView** class. The four classes utilized to create the AbsListView class hierarchy are

```
java.lang.Object
 > android.view.View
  > android.view.ViewGroup
   > android.widget.AdapterView<T extends android.widget.Adapter>
    > android.widget.AbsListView
```

The Android AbsListView class is a **public class**, extending the **AdapterView** superclass. It is referenced by using the android.widget package, using the **import android.widget.AbsListView** statement, if you're going to create a custom subclass of your own similar to the ListView or GridView classes.

Most of the XML parameters that you use with the ListView class come from the AbsListView class, which is why I included it in this chapter. Parameters you can use with ListView and GridView are shown in Table 15-1.

Table 15-1. AbsListView Class and XML Parameters Inherited by the ListView or GridView Subclasses

XML Parameter Name:	Description of this Parameter's or Attribute's Function:
android:choiceMode	Defines the choice mode or behavior for the View object
android:cacheColorHint	Indicates list will be drawn on a solid color background
android:fastScrollEnabled	Enables fast scroll thumb, allowing quickly scrolling mode
android:scrollingCache	If true, the list uses the drawing cache during scrolling
android:stackFromBottom	Used by ListView or GridView to stack content from bottom
android:smoothScrollbar	If true, list will use a more refined calculation method
android:listSelector	Drawable used to indicate a currently selected list item
android:drawSelectorOnTop	If true, the selector will be drawn over the selected item
android:textFilterEnabled	If true, the list will filter results, as the user types
android:transcriptMode	If true, sets the transcript mode as active for the list

The XML parameter that we are going to leverage is the **android:choiceMode** as it allows us to put our ListView in single choice mode, so it functions like a menu would. This is accomplished by using a **singleChoice** constant.

The Android AdapterView Class: Using Array-based Views

The Android **AdapterView** class is a "View Adapter class," which extends the Android **Adapter Interface**, to create custom View objects which implement an Array object to manage large collections or "lists" of UI elements or even content elements, such as digital images. We discuss this in the next section of this chapter. Simply stated, the AdapterView object is a type of View object whose child objects are determined and managed using an Android Adapter object. We use an Array of **String** objects with our <TextView> UI elements.

The AdapterView class hierarchy begins with your Java Object master class, and progresses from a View class, to a ViewGroup class, to the **AdapterView** class. The three classes that are utilized to create the AdapterView class hierarchy are structured as follows:

```
java.lang.Object
  > android.view.View
    > android.view.ViewGroup
      > android.widget.AdapterView<T extends android.widget.Adapter>
```

The Android AdapterView class is a **public abstract class**, and extends the **ViewGroup** superclass. It's referenced using the **android.widget.AdapterView** package by using an **import android.widget.AdapterView** statement, if you're going to create a custom subclass of your own similar to an AbsListView or AbsSpinner classes.

Note that because this class is an abstract class, it is thus designed to be used to subclass other classes for use, and not to be used directly itself, for any direct programming implementations, other than subclassing AdapterView direct subclasses, such as the AbsListView, or indirect subclasses such as the ListView, which we will be implementing later on during this chapter.

AdapterView-based classes are fairly common in Android, which is why we're covering the class here. Direct subclasses include the AbsListView, as well as the AbsSpinner and AdapterViewAnimator classes. The indirect subclasses include the ListView, which we are going to implement later on in the chapter in your Java code, and GridView, StackView, Spinner, Gallery, ExpandableListView, and AdapterViewFlipper.

Before we get into coding the UserInterface application, let's get a brief overview of the Android Adapter Interface.

The Android Adapter Interface: Using Array-based Views

The Android **Adapter** Interface is used by the Android **AdapterView Class** and when an Adapter object is created, it will serve as a "bridge" between the AdapterView and the underlying data array defined for that View object.

The Adapter Interface provides access to any data items that are defined and contained in your data array. In this chapter's example, we'll be creating a String[] array of data containing the planet names, which we will then utilize inside your ListView construct to provide some selection options for your drawer UI design.

The Android Adapter Interface is also responsible for constructing a View object in memory for each of the items contained in your data array.

The Android Adapter Interface is a **public interface**, and it is referenced using the **android.widget. Adapter** package. Indirect subclasses include the BaseAdapter, CursorAdapter, ListAdapter, SimpleAdapter, ArrayAdapter, ResourceCursorAdapter, WrapperListAdapter, SimpleCursorAdapter, and the HeaderViewListAdapter. We will be using the Adapter Interface with the AdapterView class.

Creating a DrawerLayout Activity for Your UserInterface App

Let's get down to business and actually implement a DrawerLayout UI container in its own Activity subclass and MenuItem in your UserInterface Android application.

Defining DrawerLayout: Creating a UI Drawer XML Definition

The first thing that we will do is to create our activity_drawer.xml file, using the **New ➤ Android XML File** work process shown in Figure 15-1 (on the left). Notice that there's no <DrawerLayout> parent layout container in the Root Element selector area of the dialog. This is most likely because this DrawerLayout class is contained in the android.support.v4.widgets special package, and so you will have to get creative and have Eclipse ADT create a <ListView> UI container instead, and then modify it in the XML text editor, as shown on the right in Figure 15-1. Change <ListView to <android.support.v4.widget. DrawerLayout, and add an android:id="@+id/drawerLayout" parameter so it has an ID value.

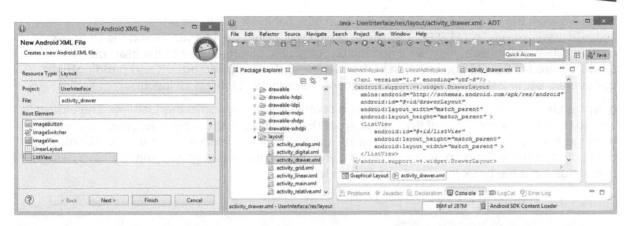

Figure 15-1. Create your activity_drawer.xml layout container, and edit it to contain a DrawerLayout and ListView

The closing </ListView> and </android.support.v4.widget.Drawerlayout> tags should be nested in the proper order (in the reverse order from the top). If you copied the initial <ListView> structure inside of itself to create the nested ListView (before you changed the parent tag to a DrawerLayout), then you should add an android:id="@+id/listView" parameter to the default layout parameters currently set to MATCH_PARENT.

Next you'll edit your <ListView> parameters; first change the layout_width to be **200dip** and add an android:choiceMode="singleChoice" parameter after your ID parameter. Since your user will click on a single choice to change the content area to access that planet information, we will want to use a **singleChoice** constant for this example. To decorate your ListView to make it look more like a selection menu, use an **android:divider="#77FFFFFF"** and an **android:dividerHeight="2dip"** parameter, as can be seen in Figure 15-2.

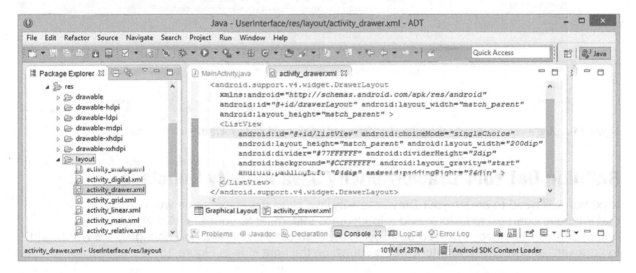

Figure 15-2. Configure the <ListView> using ten parameters; specify: ID, size, choiceMode, gravity, padding, etc

Since we want the UI drawer to partially show what is behind it, we'll use an
android:background="#CCFFFFFF" parameter, which will lighten the images behind the UI drawer
using a White color value. Next we'll add the layout gravity parameter set to the **start** constant,
as we covered in the previous section of the chapter, and add a **paddingLeft** and **paddingRight**
parameters set to **24DIP**, to center your selection items in this ListView UI layout.

Now we are ready to add your <LinearLayout> content container, above this ListView. The easiest
way to do this is to copy one of the LinearLayout UI containers that contains TextView UI elements
from the activity_linear.xml file, as is shown in Figure 15-3. We will leave these TextView UI elements
configured to show Earth content as a default, and use the same parameters that we have been
using thus far in the book for planet information text.

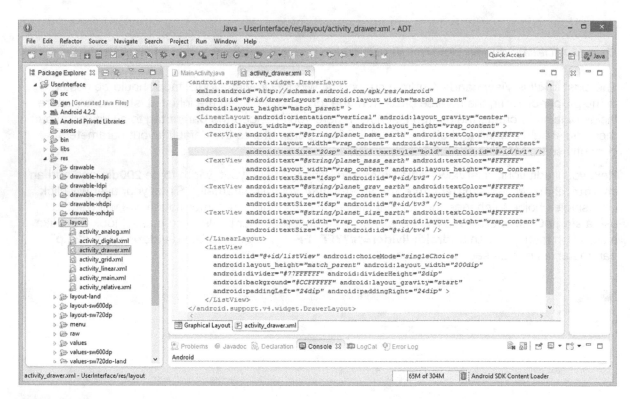

Figure 15-3. Add a <LinearLayout> above the <ListView> and inside it add the four <TextView> UI elements

Building Out Your DrawerActivity Java Activity Subclass

Next you will need to create your DrawerActivity.java class using the same work process
that we have been using before. Add a fourth case statement to your MainActivity.java
onOptionsItemSelected() method by copying the third case statement and changing the word "grid"
to "drawer," and intent_gl to intent_dl, as shown on the right side in Figure 15-4.

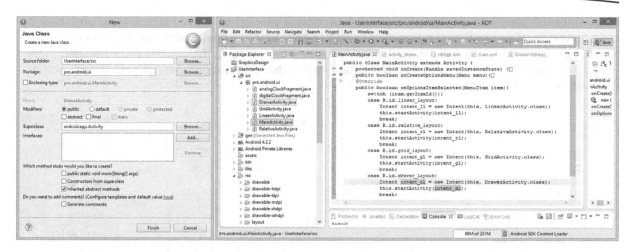

Figure 15-4. Add a fourth case statement to the MainActivity; Eclipse creates New Java Class for DrawerActivity

Mouse-over the wavy red error highlighting that's under the DrawerActivity reference and select the "add new class" option to open the **New Java Class** dialog, which is shown on the left side of Figure 15-4.

Click the Superclass **Browse** button and find the android.app.Activity class and then click the **Finish** button to create the DrawerActivity.java class.

The first thing you will do is to add two **private** object declarations to hold your **String[] Array** object and your **ListView** object, which will access this String[]Array. This is done at the top of the class, using the following code:

```
private String[] drawerLayoutListItem;
private ListView drawerLayoutListView;
```

As you can see in Figure 15-5, you need to mouse-over your reference to the ListView class, and select the **Import 'ListView' (android.widget)** option. Once this is done, you can add your **onCreate()** method and start to add in the functionality that allows you to make the DrawerLayout and its ListView UI widget fully operational.

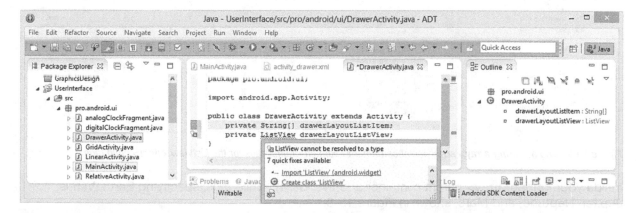

Figure 15-5. Declare two private variables to hold the String Array object and the ListView object for the Activity

Copy the protected void onCreate() method from one of your other Activity subclasses, and then change your setContentView() method's parameter, to **R.layout.activity_drawer**, to reference your XML UI definition you created earlier. As you can see in Figure 15-6, the code is error-free and there is only warning highlighting, referring to the fact your object declarations are not yet utilized, which they will be, after our next few steps.

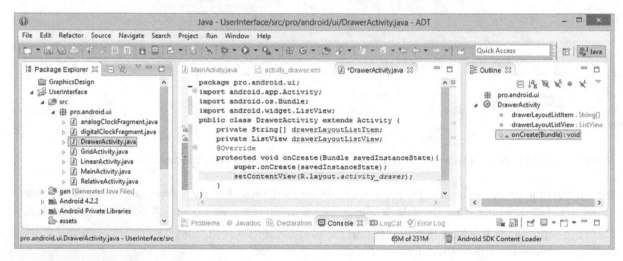

Figure 15-6. Adding the onCreate() method and setContentView() method referencing the new activity_drawer UI

The next thing that you want to do is to create your **<string-array>** XML definition, which lives in your strings.xml file, in your /res/values folder, as you may have guessed. Add a line of space after the <resources> parent container and type in a left chevron < character to access the help dialog, and select the **string-array** option, as is shown in Figure 15-7.

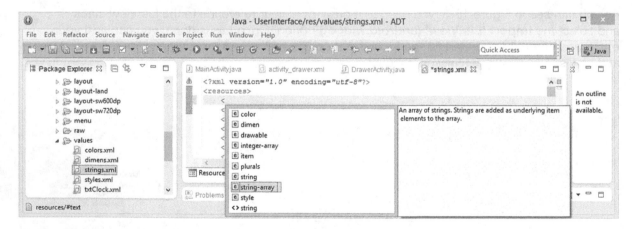

Figure 15-7. Add a <string-array> array parent container to contain <item> tags for the ListView <item> child tags

Inside your <string-array> parent container add five **<item>** child tags, specifying Earth, Venus, Jupiter, Neptune, and Mars, shown in Figure 15-8.

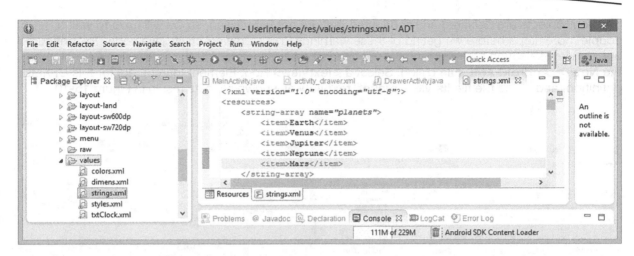

Figure 15-8. *Add five <item> child tags to the <string-array> parent container for the five planets in the ListView*

Now that your String[] Array object has been defined using XML you can go back into your DrawerActivity.java editing tab and add the instantiation for the two objects that you declared at the top of the Activity subclass. This is done using a **.getResources().getStringArray()** method chain for the String[] Array object and using the **findViewById()** method for the ListView object, using the following two Java statements:

```
drawerLayoutListItem = getResources().getStringArray(R.array.planets);
drawerLayoutListView = (ListView)findViewById(R.id.listView);
```

As you can see in Figure 15-9, your warning highlighting is still present on these two object declarations. This is because instantiating an object, and inflating it using a reference to an XML object definition does not constitute object use!

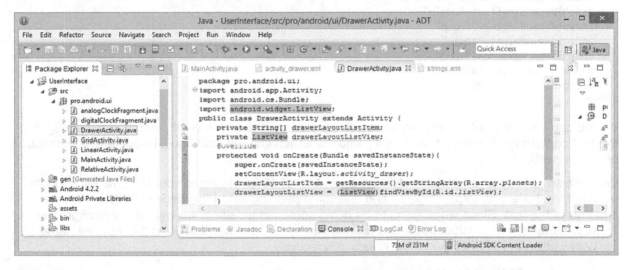

Figure 15-9. *Instantiate drawerLayoutListItem using getResources().getStringArray() and drawerLayoutListView using findViewById()*

Thus our objects are declared and configured, but are not yet utilized, so we will have to wait a couple more steps before we get rid of these warnings in our DrawerActivity.java code. To configure our ListView selection item element, we will need to create one more XML UI definition file, using the **New ➤ Android XML File** dialog. Select a <TextView> Root Element (parent tag) for this UI XML definition, and name the file **listview_planet_textview** as shown (with its result) in Figure 15-10.

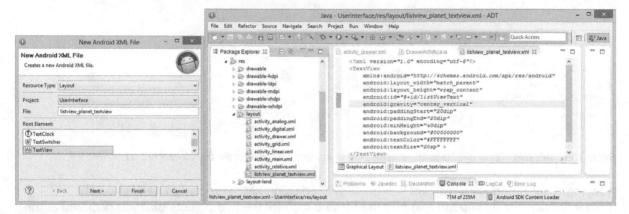

Figure 15-10. *Create and configure a TextView layout resource named listview_planet_textview.xml in /res/layout*

Add the following parameters to this <TextView> parent container, using the following XML markup:

```
<?xml version="1.0" encoding="utf-8"?>
<TextView
    xmlns:android="http://schemas.android.com/apk/res/android"
    android:layout_width="match_parent"
    android:layout_height="wrap_content"
    android:id="@+id/listViewText"
    android:gravity="center_vertical"
    android:paddingStart="20dip"
    android:paddingEnd="20dip"
    android:minHeight="40dip"
    android:background="#00000000"
    android:textColor="#FFFFFFFF"
    android:textSize="20sp" >
</TextView>
```

As you can see we want our content to match the parent container in width, and match the height of the text content itself in height, and we'll name the ID listViewText, and use a layout_gravity constant of center_vertical.

We will also specify an **android:minHeight** parameter of **40dp**—to make your UI items tall enough to touch for those with larger fingers—and use some padding set to the value of **20dp** on the start and end of the text. Since we're going to be doing some compositing, we will set our background to be transparent using **#00000000**, and use the same textColor and textSize as our planet name TextView, using #FFFFFFFF and 20sp values, respectively.

Now we are ready to implement the **.setAdapter()** method call, called off of the ListView object named **drawerLayoutListView**, and pass over the context, ListView item UI definition that we just created, and the String[] Array object, using the following line of Java code:

```
drawerLayoutListView.setAdapter(new ArrayAdapter<String>(this,
R.layout.listview_planet_textview, drawerLayoutListItem));
```

As you can see in Figure 15-11, this Java statement removes all error and warning highlighting, and our Java code is ready to test in the Nexus One.

Figure 15-11. Use a setAdapter() method on drawerLayoutListView object to configure ListView with String Array

Use the **Run As ➤ Android Application** work process to launch your Nexus One emulator and use the cursor to swipe from the left side of the screen into the center of the screen, which will open up your DrawerLayout ListView UI element, as you can see in Figure 15-12.

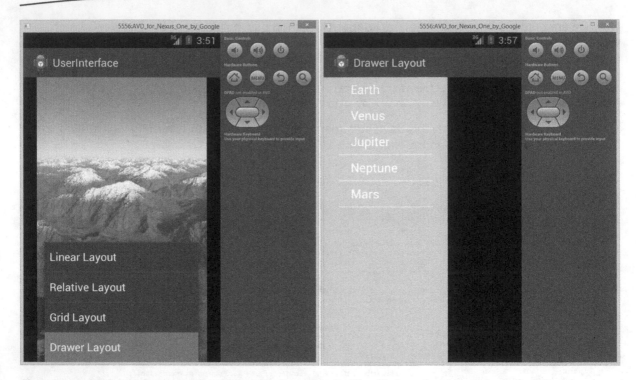

Figure 15-12. Testing the DrawerActivity thus far using Nexus One; TextView UI elements not appearing in the UI Design

Note that even though the ListView UI element and UI drawer functionality are working correctly, that something is wrong with the <LinearLayout> and <TextView> UI elements. Go into your activity_drawer.xml UI definition tab and look at the parameters that are in your <LinearLayout> and <TextView> UI element definitions, to try and ascertain which of these parameters might be causing this problem.

The only parameter that I can see that could be causing the problem is the **android:layout_ gravity="center"** parameter, which was copied over from the LinearLayout example, but which may not be supported inside of a DrawerLayout UI container. Let's try removing that parameter next, and replace it with something else with a similar functionality.

Remove the android:layout_gravity parameter, and then type in **android:** as shown in Figure 15-13 to see what parameters are supported. Notice that layout_gravity is not one of them, so this probably was your (my) problem. We will use a **layout:padding** parameter, at least for now, to see if we can get the LinearLayout to display its content in the content layer of your DrawerLayout UI design. Once you use the **Run As ➤ Android Application** work process, you will see that this indeed does solve the problem and we can make our UI functional.

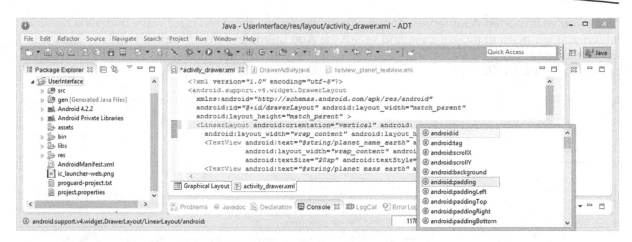

Figure 15-13. *Remove the android:layout_gravity parameter causing the TextView to not render and add padding*

Adding ListView Event Handling: Making the UI Functional

To make the ListView that is in our UI drawer functional, you must add an event handling method to your ListView using the .setOnItemClickListener() method call and a new OnItemClickListener() method basic structure, using the following Java code:

```
drawerLayoutListView.setOnItemClickListener(new OnItemClickListener() {code here});
```

As you can see in Figure 15-14, you will then need to select the **Import 'OnItemClickListener' (android.widget.AdapterView)** option, and import the AdapterView class for use in your DrawerActivity Activity subclass.

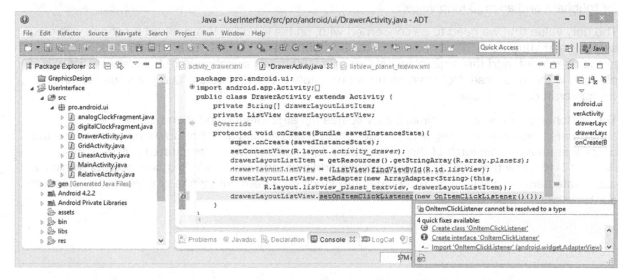

Figure 15-14. *Adding event handling to the ListView using the setOnItemClickListener() new OnItemClickListener*

Once you've imported AdapterView for use, there will be one more red error wavy underline highlight which you will need to mouse-over, and select the **Add unimplemented method** option. Once you do this, Eclipse will write your bootstrap Java code for your **.onItemClick()** method for you, which is shown in Figure 15-15.

Figure 15-15. Invoke Add unimplemented method option, and have Eclipse write this empty onItemClick() method

The onItemClick() method takes an arg0 AdapterView<?> parameter, an arg1 View parameter, an arg2 integer which we will use to determine which String[] object in the Array was clicked on (or touched) and an arg3 long value.

The only value that we need to be concerned with, on the inside of this method functions within our switch-case statement. This construct determines what your ListView UI element does in response to the user input, and this arg2 integer represents your user's selection from the ListView list of our planets, in this use-case. Now that we have our empty method structure and parameter list in place, we can craft our case logic.

The switch statement is quite simple, it evaluates the arg2 integer, and then has five case statements, each with an integer value, starting at 0 and ending at 4. For now I will just include the break statement within each of these, to make a functionally empty case statement, as shown in Figure 15-16. Now that this is in place, we can add method calls to our TextView objects within each case statement, to call your correct planet info string data from our strings.xml file that defines all our text data.

Figure 15-16. Adding an empty switch-case structure for the five planet ListView items based on integer arg2

As you know from doing this in previous chapters, this takes the format of TextView object name, dot notation and the .setText() method call, which references the appropriate string constant, using the following Java code:

```java
switch (arg2){
case 0:
planetText1.setText(R.string.planet_name_earth);
planetText2.setText(R.string.planet_mass_earth);
planetText3.setText(R.string.planet_grav_earth);
planetText4.setText(R.string.planet_size_earth);
case 1:
planetText1.setText(R.string.planet_name_venus);
planetText2.setText(R.string.planet_mass_venus);
planetText3.setText(R.string.planet_grav_venus);
planetText4.setText(R.string.planet_size_venus);
}
```

I have shown the first two case statements, in Figure 15-17, and your code is error-free. Before we add the final case statements, we need to add the string data for the planet Mars, inside your /res/values/strings.xml file.

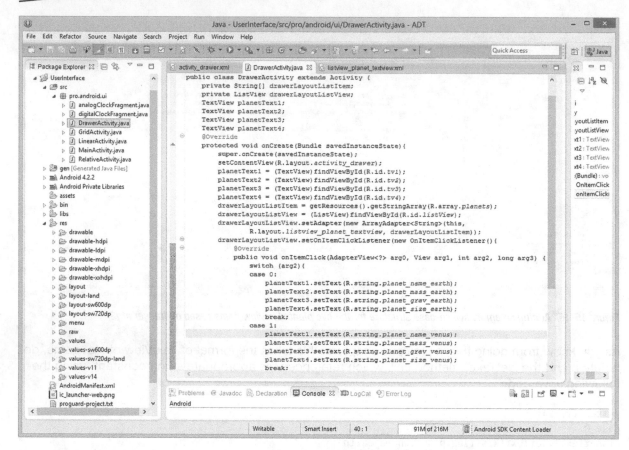

Figure 15-17. Add the first two case statements to call the .setText() method to configure Earth and Venus info

Adding <string> Constants for Planet Mars: More Planet Info

As you can see in Figure 15-18, we have added these following XML <string> constants for the Mars planet information data using the following markup:

```
<string name="planet_name_mars>Planet Name: Mars</string>
<string name="planet_mass_mars>Planet Mass: 642 Yg</string>
<string name="planet_grav_mars>Planet Gravity: 3.7 m/s</string>
<string name="planet_size_mars>Planet Diameter: 6,972 KM</string>
```

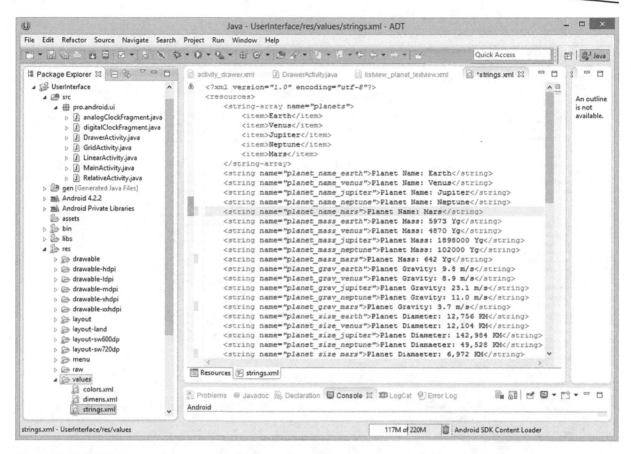

Figure 15-18. Adding new <string> constants for Mars; planet name, planet mass, planet size, and planet gravity

As you can see in Figure 15-18, our application is getting quite robust, and we now have more than two dozen planet-related <string> constants to educate our users regarding the most popular planets in our solar system.

Now you can finish coding all the case statements in your onItemClick() method, so you can test your DrawerLayout, ListView, and TextView objects, to see whether they are all working together seamlessly. As you can see here in Figure 15-19, all our planet information TextView objects are configured!

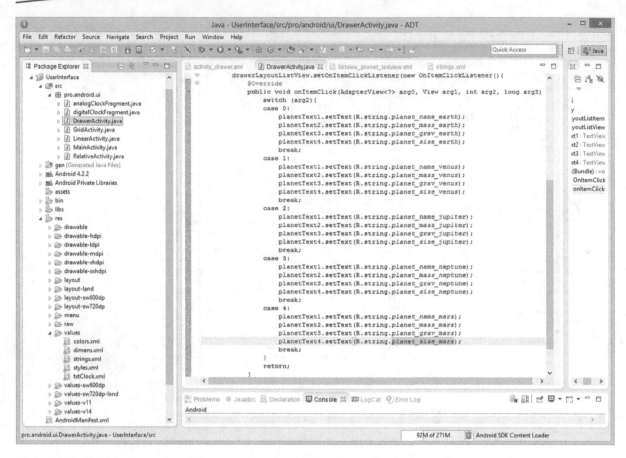

Figure 15-19. Finish implementing all five case statements for planets Earth, Venus, Jupiter, Neptune and Mars

Use a **Run As ➤ Android Application** work process to test the DrawerActivity class, and swipe out your ListView UI drawer, and click on your different planet selections, to change the planet information text.

Since the ListView is translucent, you can see the planet info text change or alternatively you can swipe your ListView UI drawer back into place to view the planet info data.

This looks like what you see in the next section in Figure 15-22. The next section covers automating the retraction of the drawer when your user clicks on their planet selections, and then in the section after that, you will start to fine-tune the look and feel of your ListView UI element, adding image elements for wow factor and compositing pipeline.

Adding Auto-Drawer Retraction: The closeDrawer() Method

Next, we are going to implement a **.closeDrawer()** method, and to do this we must declare and instantiate a DrawerLayout object, which we can call this method off of. The declaration of the DrawerLayout named **myDrawerLayout** is shown in Figure 15-20 as is instantiation by using a findViewById() method referencing the **drawerLayout** ID for your <DrawerLayout> XML definition.

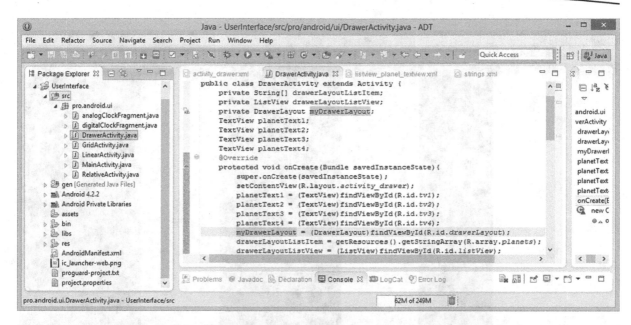

Figure 15-20. *Declare and instantiate a DrawerLayout object named myDrawerLayout, so it can be used in Java*

Now all you have to do at the bottom of your switch statement is to call a `myDrawerLayout.closeDrawer(drawerLayoutListView);` as seen in Figure 15-21.

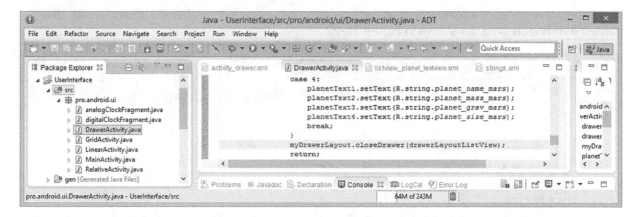

Figure 15-21. *Calling the .closeDrawer() method on the myDrawerLayout object using the drawerLayoutListView*

Next, use your **Run As ➤ Android Application** work process and test the app, and you will see that after you select the planet, the drawer animates back into the left side of the display screen.

Refining the DrawerLayout in Your DrawerActivity Class

Next, let's add some chrome bars as separators, rather than just two pixel lines, as shown in Figure 15-22.

Figure 15-22. *Testing the ListView DrawerLayout and adding different digital image divider UI element thickness settings*

To do this, change your **android:divider** parameter, to reference a drawable file (image asset) that's named **listviewdiv.png**, as shown in Figure 15-23.

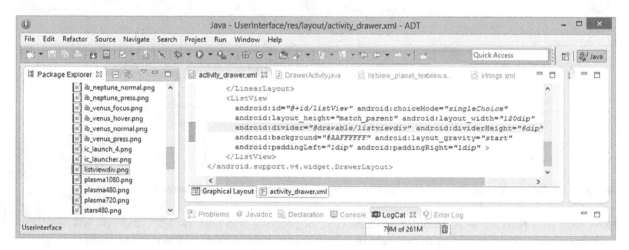

Figure 15-23. *Changing the android:divider from a hexadecimal color value to a /res/drawable asset reference*

This XHDPI image can be found in your book assets ZIP file on the Apress website. The XML markup for this new android:divider parameter would look like the following:

```
android:divider="@drawable/listviewdiv"
```

Next let's add planet images into your UI design using an <ImageView> tag. As you can see in Figure 15-24, I added two <ImageView> tags inside of the LinearLayout, one at the top using your **ib_earth_normal** image asset, and another under the planet name TextView that uses the **listviewdiv.png** asset that we're using in the ListView as a divider albeit with different visual results.

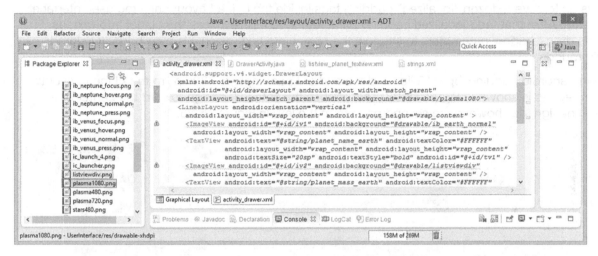

Figure 15-24. Add a background image to <DrawerLayout> and <ImageView> UI widgets to the <LinearLayout>

Using image assets for more than one use is an impressive design trick, if you can manage to achieve varied but impressive results, as you are doing here. Notice in Figure 15-24 that Android wants you to add in an **android:contentDescription** tag to support your sight impaired users, so do that as well to get rid of the pesky yellow warning underline highlights.

Now use your **Run As ➤ Android Application** work process and test the new UI design in the Nexus One. As you can see on the left side of Figure 15-25, the new design looks more professional, but is pegged to a top-left (0,0) corner location on your display screen.

Figure 15-25. Adding android:padding and android:shadow parameters to our UI design to refine and clarify it

Let's add parameters into your <LinearLayout> and <TextView> UI elements, to refine (tweak) the UI design a bit, so it looks even more professional.

First add android:paddingTop and android:paddingLeft parameters to the <LinearLayout> tag, which moves your entire design out and down on the screen. Adding these tags at this "global" level allows us to save a dozen "localized" padding tags inside the LinearLayout child tag user interface elements. After that, add localized padding parameters, to further tweak the planet info text, as well as drop-shadow parameters to shadow the planet info text, when it is over brightly colored backgrounds.

Add the android:paddingTop="16dip" and the android:paddingLeft="30dip" to the <LinearLayout> parent tag, as is shown in Figure 15-26. This pushes the entire UI design toward the center of the screen design, as shown in the second pane from the left, in Figure 15-25.

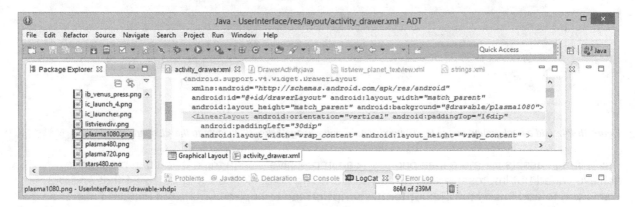

Figure 15-26. Add an android:paddingTop and android:paddingLeft parameter to a <LinearLayout> UI container

Next, let's add an android:paddingTop and android:paddingLeft parameter to your TextView UI elements, to position them underneath your chrome UI bar. Use a paddingTop value of 12dip and a paddingLeft value of 30dip at first.

These padding parameters have a cumulative effect, that is, they are added onto your global padding values in the LinearLayout UI container.

Next we need to add android:shadow parameters to drop-shadow the TextView UI elements when they appear over brightly colored background imagery, and there are four parameters we will add, as is shown in Figure 15-27.

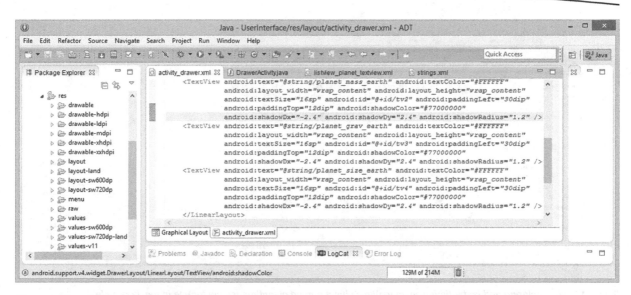

Figure 15-27. Adding android:padding and android:shadow parameters to the planet info <TextView> UI widgets

The **android:shadowColor** parameter sets the shadow transparency (50%) and a color of Black using the hexadecimal value of **#77000000** for all three text UI elements for the last three TextView widgets that hold the planet info.

The **android:shadowDx** and **android:shadowDy** hold "delta" (D) or offset values, a negative value will be needed for your android:shadowDx parameter, to pull the shadow to the left, and a positive android:shadowDy value will be used to pull the shadow down.

Finally, the **android:shadowRadius** parameter is used to define an amount of shadow realism (blur radius). These last three parameters take float, or floating point values; we'll use **1.2** for the shadowRadius, and **2.4** for the Dx and Dy offsets, as you can see in the XML markup shown in Figure 15-27.

Next you will go back into your DrawerActivity Java code and you'll finish implementing these UI design elements, so that they are interactive within your ListView UI drawer implementation.

Changing ImageView and Backgrounds for Each ListView

Now that we have added in ImageView and Background Images for compositing our special effects, we should change them to match each of our switch-case UI designs, using the **.setBackgroundResource()** method call in our Java code.

To do this we must declare an ImageView named **planetImageView** at the top of our Activity subclass along with the other ListView, TextView, DrawerLayout and String[] objects, as well as instantiating the ImageView object in the onCreate() method using the findViewById method along with a reference to the iv1 ID, as can be seen highlighted here in Figure 15-28.

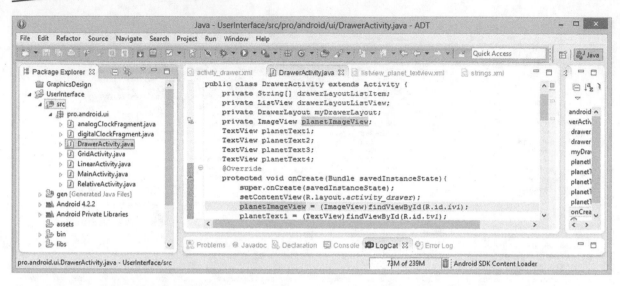

Figure 15-28. Declaring and instantiating an ImageView object named planetImageView for use in the Java code

To make our DrawerActivity.java really leverage all these UI design assets, we can add in .setBackgroundResource() method calls on the planetImageView ImageView object and myDrawerLayout DrawerLayout object.

For the Earth case section, this would involve the following Java code:

```
planetImageView.setBackgroundResource(R.drawable.ib_earth_normal);
myDrawerLayout.setBackgroundResource(R.drawable.plasma1080);
```

As you can see, we are using our ImageButton normal state (no decoration, planet image only) image asset, except for planet Mars where we are using the mars256.png asset, which you should get from the book project assets repository and install (copy into) in the /res/drawable-xhdpi folder.

For the DrawerLayout background image asset, we are using one of the space backgrounds named with stars or plasma prefixes, so that we have different image backgrounds for each of the ListView selections once it is selected.

After we put all this new Java code into place, our switch-case statements will have a half-dozen method calls each to set all our UI elements based on what planet has been selected, and our **.closeDrawer()** method call at the end will close the UI drawer automatically once the user has made a selection of a planet to explore.

Additionally, your ListView UI element itself has now been decorated using translucent backgrounds, and a chrome bar separator UI element, which you have also leveraged in your LinearLayout UI design to maximize your use of your digital image assets, since they will be in your project file anyway.

As you can see in Figure 15-29, your Java code is error-free, and you are ready to use your **Run As ➤ Android Application** work process, so that you can test your ListView, DrawerLayout, LinearLayout, and TextView objects.

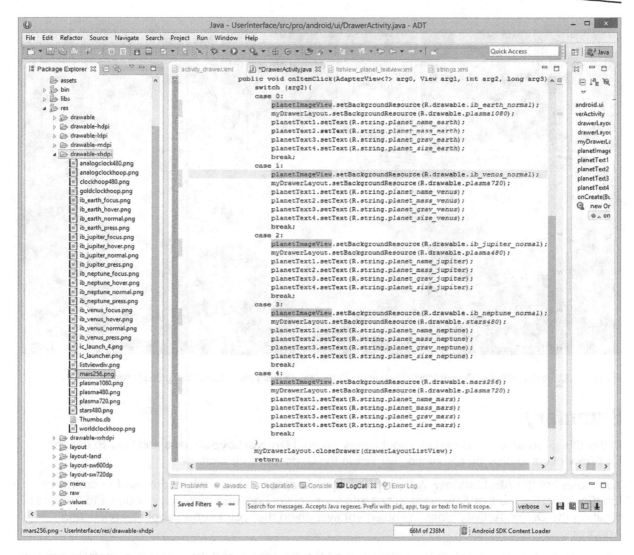

Figure 15-29. Adding .setBackgroundResource() methods to the planetImageView and myDrawerLayout objects

Once the Nexus One emulator launches, test the five planet selection items thoroughly, making sure the planet information text is correct and matches up with each planet's image.

Make sure each planet has a different background image, and your TextView shadow parameters make this planet information text more readable over the brightly colored areas of the DrawerLayout background image.

As you can see in Figure 15-30, your application UI design has a balanced and attractive visual appearance, and your planets really look like they are floating in space. Your information is professionally separated using UI elements, such as an attractive rounded chrome bar UI detail element.

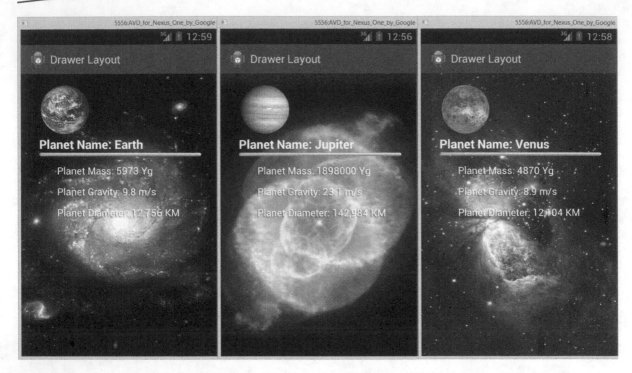

Figure 15-30. Testing the final DrawerActivity class in the Nexus One, showing the different background imagery

Summary

In the this chapter, you learned all about a new Android **DrawerLayout** class and how to use the **ListView** class to provide a selection list inside the UI drawer that it creates.

You looked at the **AbsListView**, **AdapterView**, and **Adapter** classes, which are used to create the functionality that the ListView class brings into your application, and then you got down to business creating the DrawerActivity class to implement everything that you learned about ListView and Adapter.

You created your DrawerActivity.java class and a MenuItem for it, and then created an activity_drawer. xml UI definition file where you defined your <DrawerLayout> UI container as well as a <ListView> for your sliding UI drawer and a <LinearLayout> to contain your <TextView> and <ImageView> content outlining five popular planets and their imagery and information. You also implemented image compositing, using galaxy background imagery.

In the next chapter, we will take a closer look at the **SlidingPaneLayout** class, and see how you can use another UI class to fabricate "interactive sliding pane" UI designs that allow you to save display real-estate, and store your UI designs off-screen and access them using a handle to bring them on-screen.

Android's SlidingPaneLayout Class: Using SlidingPanes in Your UI Design

The Android **SlidingPaneLayout** class was also a recent addition to Android OS, as of the Android 4.0 Ice Cream Sandwich release. This UI layout class was developed to help developers design a two panel, side-by-side UI that can morph between different screen sizes, shapes, and orientations.

The SlidingPaneLayout class was utilized to create the UI foundation for the Google Hangouts application. If you want to see SlidingPaneLayout in action on an Android device, it is utilized in at least one of your Android OS-supplied applications.

What we're going to do with your UserInterface application in this chapter is to create an Android SlidingPaneLayout "Sliding UI" design that allows your users to slide the main content pane to the right and reveal planet selection ImageButton UI elements that they can click to access planet information about each of the five planets that we have installed in the UserInterface application thus far.

You'll first create an **activity_slidingpane.xml** UI definition and the Menu and String and Manifest XML markup logic that you would need to implement your new Activity subclass, and then create your **SlidingPaneActivity.java** Activity subclass along with the MenuItem selection for your MainActivity Activity subclass. Last, you'll tweak the **activity_slidingpane** UI design, which you will later make interactive, using Java and **onClick()** event handling.

SlidingPaneLayout Class: UI Design Across Device Types

The Android **SlidingPaneLayout** class is another UI layout container class that was introduced in Android Version 4.0. The SlidingPaneLayout class is designed to provide a **horizontal, dual-pane**

user interface layout for use at the top level of your application UI design. These two panes morph to fit different screen characteristics, using a sliding motion paradigm. If you want to take a peek at what the SlidingPaneLayout is going to look like in your application, check out Figure 16-12.

Because of the nature of its sliding functional operation, this UI layout container is your perfect solution for creating UI layouts which smoothly adapt across many different screen sizes. In fact, this is the very reason the Android developers designed this ViewGroup subclass so that developers could easily implement a UI design that expands to its full extent on larger (tablet and iTV) screens, but which will also contract inward on a smaller screen (smartwatch and smartphone) and remain usable for the user.

The SlidingPaneLayout Class Hierarchy

A SlidingPaneLayout class hierarchy starts at the Java Object master class and progresses from the Android View class, to the Android ViewGroup class to the SlidingPaneLayout class. The SlidingPaneLayout is part of a special **android.support.v4.widget** package, and is structured using this following class hierarchy:

```
java.lang.Object
 > android.view.View
   > android.view.ViewGroup
     > android.support.v4.widget.SlidingPaneLayout
```

This Android SlidingPaneLayout class is a **public class,** and it extends the **ViewGroup** superclass. It is referenced by using the specialized support.v4 package by using the **import android.support. v4.widget.SlidingPaneLayout** statement, located at the top of your Java Activity subclass.

The left pane, which is the first pane to be defined in your XML UI layout definition file, is treated as the **content list** or as the content browser. This pane is designed to be subordinate to, or of a lower priority than, a **primary detail view**, which is the right pane, used for displaying content.

The SlidingPaneLayout class may sound quite similar to the DrawerLayout class that we covered in the previous chapter; however, it is actually used for different UI design objectives than the navigation drawer, which is implemented using the DrawerLayout class.

Optimal UI Design Usage for a SlidingPaneLayout Class

Your optimal usage of the SlidingPaneLayout class would involve UI element "pairings", which required two panes of UI and content or information which you the developer wanted persistent (visible) on the display screen at all times. An example of this would be your phone contact list and subordinate interactions with those contacts, or a recent e-mail list with the content pane displaying the text contents of the selected e-mail, or, in your app, a visual list of planets in our solar system and their planet information. An objective of the class is having UI and content simultaneously visible.

The SlidingPaneLayout should not be utilized to implement screen switching UI designs, which allow your user to navigate between different functional Activity subclasses within your app, such as navigating from the VideoView content viewer Activity where one watches digital video to an Activity the user uses to add data to their contacts database or favorites database.

Task-switching use cases such as these should use a DrawerLayout UI drawer design approach instead, or one of the other more general layout container classes which we have covered during the second half of this book.

The use of a SlidingPaneLayout should be for an app or Activity that keeps the user in one task mode and then optimizes the UI design to maximize the functionality between your UI and the content parts of the screen, as well as to provide a UI design layout that will morph between different screen densities, sizes, aspect ratios, and orientations.

Thus the SlidingPaneLayout UI design is a more "niche" UI layout container that could be considered as a memory-efficient approach to implementing a dual-pane UI layout that targets primary usage via larger display screens (tablets, notebooks, and iTVs), but that can adapt its usability to small screens (smartphones or smartwatches) in a user-empathetic fashion.

Within the SlidingPaneLayout parent container (tag) the child (tag) View objects are allowed to overlap, but only if their combined width exceeds the available width specified for the SlidingPaneLayout parent container, which is usually a MATCH_PARENT constant, and thus defined to fit all the available screen real estate.

When an overlap UI layout happens, your users can slide the UI (first or top z-order View child object) away from obscuring your content View. The user accomplishes this by dragging the UI pane, and this can also be achieved using a keyboard, by navigating in the direction of the overlapped View. If the UI (or content) for the child view is horizontally scrollable, then your user may also grab this content, using the edge of this content.

Using a Weight Parameter with Your SlidingPaneLayout

It is important to note that we are finally covering another UI container that supports the **android:weight** parameter just like a LinearLayout does!

The SlidingPaneLayout class implements this use of weight layout parameter constants by using the nested class **SlidingDrawerLayout.LayoutParams**. This nested class only contains a single **layout_weight** attribute (or parameter) so I won't add an entire section on it in the chapter–I'll cover it here!

This weight parameter will be used by the SlidingPaneLayout "engine" (algorithm) to determine how Android divides leftover space between the two pane child View objects, after a changed screen size or orientation has been detected by Android and the new screen measurement data has been assessed.

The **android:layout_weight** parameter for a SlidingPaneLayout class will be considered as relevant by the SlidingPane algorithm (engine) only for the **width** dimension. When the two pane View objects involved in the UI design do not overlap at all, your weight behaves as it would in a LinearLayout.

This allows developers to define the percentage of the screen that is used by each of these two panes, and remember that these two weight values need to add up to 1 or 10 or 100, so the best approach is to use floating point values that add up to one, such as 0.35, for 35% of your screen width, and 0.65 for the other 65% of your screen width. This allows precise dual pane dividing values to be assigned by the Pro Android UI developer.

If View objects are more constrained by device screen width, such as in a portrait display orientation, the panes will overlap, and a slightly more complex weight assessment algorithm will be utilized. As you might imagine in this circumstance, your weight specification is not as closely followed by the

SlidingPaneLayout engine algorithm, and it instead will favor your content View object, allowing the UI View object to slide over the content only when it is needed by the user.

The weight assigned to your slideable UI pane is evaluated so the content pane is sized to fill all available screen space when the UI pane is in its closed state.

The weight assigned to the fixed (not slideable) content pane that becomes covered by a UI pane will be evaluated in such a way that the content pane is sized to fill most of the available screen space. However, a small (minimal) strip of the UI pane is left visible, which allows the user to grab the slideable view and pull (swipe) it back over the content view, if it is needed by the user for the application's intended functionality.

Exploring the Three SlidingPaneLayout Nested Classes

Besides SlidingPaneLayout.LayoutParams and its weight parameter, there are two other nested classes for the SlidingPaneLayout class. They include the **SlidingPaneLayout.PanelSlideListener** interface, which is an event listener interface designed specifically to be used in monitoring events associated with your SlidingPaneLayout UI design implementation.

You would utilize an interface for subclassing your own PanelSlideListener subclass, to create your own customized MyPanelSlideListener class, for instance, as that is what interfaces are utilized to provide.

There is also the **SlidingPaneLayout.SimplePanelSlideListener** nested class, which provides a **simple listener class**, which does just this; it sublasses the SlidingPaneLayout.PanelSlideListener interface and implements it as a class with the minimum amount of functionality. That is, it adds zero additional features, containing only basic event listening functionality.

Since we already covered the android:layout_weight parameter and constants in detail back in Chapter 12 when we covered Android's LinearLayout class, I am going to dive right into a real world example detailing how to create a SlidingPaneActivity subclass.

Adding a SlidingPaneLayout to Your UserInterface App

In this section, you will create an **activity_slidingPane.xml** UI definition file, as well as a **SlidingPaneActivity.java** class, and then define the SlidingPaneLayout UI design, and implement some digital image compositing techniques to make it look professional and exciting to the end-user. After that, you'll test the UI design across different screen sizes and orientations to see it work!

Defining a SlidingPaneLayout: Code a SlidingPane UI in XML

Let's start with your XML UI definition file creation, and right-click on the /res/layout folder and use the **New ➤ Android XML File** menu sequence to create your **activity_slidingpane.xml** file. Similar to what you encountered in the previous chapter, there is no SlidingPaneLayout root element in the dialog, so let's get as close as we can, and select a SlidingDrawer option and edit that (after you click Finish) in the XML editing pane which opens up, as shown in Figure 16-1. Add an android:id="@+id/spl" so we can access the SlidingPaneLayout later on in your Java code. Next use the left-facing chevron (<) work process to bring up the child tag dialog. Find a LinearLayout option to add a LinearLayout container, to hold your ImageButton elements.

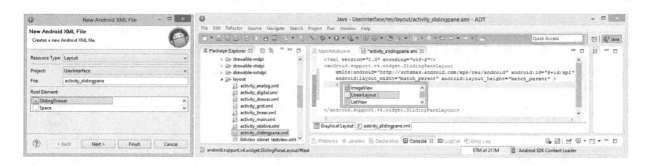

Figure 16-1. *Use New ➤ Android XML File to create activity_slidingpane.xml, and add a <LinearLayout> child tag*

Copy your ib_earth ImageButton XML markup from your activity_linear.xml UI definition file and paste it under the <LinearLayout> parent tag, as shown in Figure 16-2. You'll be copying and pasting the <ImageButton> tag four more times underneath itself, changing the ib_earth to be ib_venus, ib_jupiter, ib_neptune, and ib_mars, and your ib_states to be: ib2_states, ib3_states, ib4_states, and ib5_states after we create our Mars ImageButton XML assets.

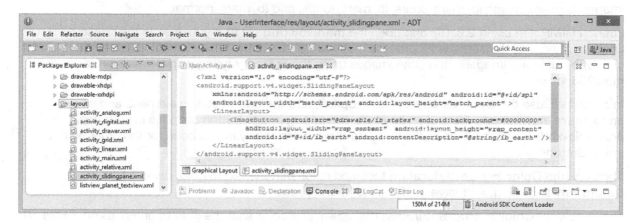

Figure 16-2. *Add an <ImageButton> child tag in the parent <LinearLayout> tag; reference ib_earth and ib_states*

Before we add in four ImageButton tags we need to create an ib5_states.xml multi-state Mars ImageButton definition as well as the dozen image assets (four button states in the three MDPI, HDPI, and XHDPI resolution densities) that this XML definition file will eventually access.

Creating a Mars ImageButton: Using GIMP and XML

Right-click the /res/drawable folder and select the **New ➤ Android XML File** menu sequence to create a drawable XML definition with a <selector> tag root element, as is shown in Figure 16-3. Copy the four items from the ib_states.xml file and change the word "earth" to "mars" and save the file.

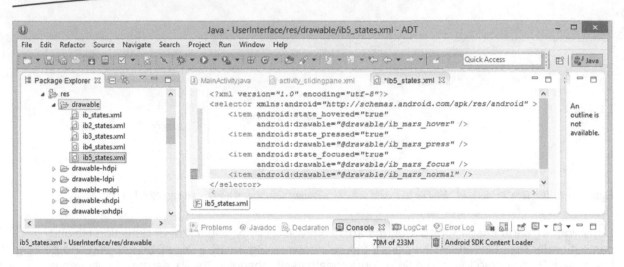

Figure 16-3. *Create an ib5_states.xml file to hold Mars ImageButton multi-state XML definition image references*

Next, we need to create the image assets that will be referenced in this new XML file using the PNG images ib_mars_hover, ib_mars_press, ib_mars_focus, and ib_mars_normal.

Launch GIMP (I'm using 2.8.10), and open the **mars256.png** file that you used in the previous chapter. Then, use the same work process that you learned in the LinearLayouts Chapter 12 and create the different ImageButton state images using the **button_styling.png** in the layer above the mars256 image.

In a nutshell, use the **Open as Layers** menu option, add the button styling element, and save an **ib_mars_normal.png** file and an **ib_mars_hover.png** image button state file in your /res/ drawable-xhdpi project folder, just like you have done previously in this book for the other planet ImageButtons.

Then use the **Color ➤ Hue-Saturation** tool, and color shift the red to gold, using a **Hue 60**, **Saturation 15** setting, and save the file as **ib_mars_press**.

Then use your **Color ➤ Hue-Saturation** tool again, and color shift the gold to green, using a **Hue 40** setting, and save the file as **ib_mars_focus**.

Repeat this same work process after resizing the 256 pixel image to 128 pixels and save these same four files into the **/res/drawable-hdpi** folder. Finally, go back to the 256 pixel source mars256.png image and repeat the entire process again, this time scaling 256 pixels down to 64 pixels, and save the files into your **/res/drawable-mdpi** folder. The first part of this process can be seen in Figure 16-4, exporting the ib_mars_hover.png file.

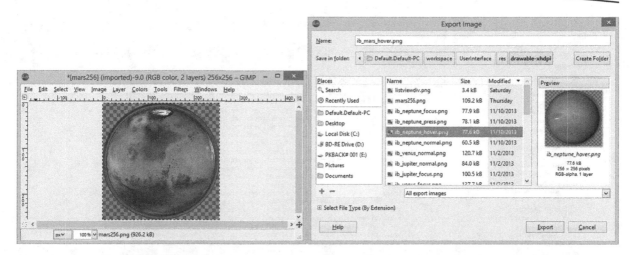

Figure 16-4. Use GIMP to open the mars256.png and button_styling.png and export ib_mars ImageButton states

Once you have completed this entire 12 image file creation work process in GIMP, you can use your OS's File Management Utility (for Windows 8.1 it is called File Explorer), shown in Figure 16-5, to make sure that you have 20 image files in each of the /res/drawable-xhdpi, /res/drawable-hdpi and /res/drawable-mdpi folders. As you can see, you now have a handful of ImageButton assets that you can use in your application's UI design endeavors to create your visual UI design.

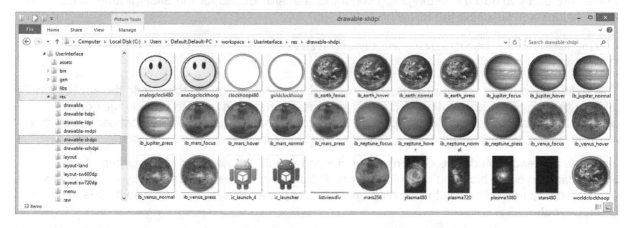

Figure 16-5. Showing /res/drawable-xhdpi folder with 20 ImageButton image assets and the galaxy backgrounds

Now you are ready to finish adding all five <ImageButton> tags to your UI.

Finishing the Planet UI Pane Definition: Adding Four ImageButtons

Now you are ready to copy and paste the first <ImageButton> tag underneath itself four more times, and change the **android:src** parameters to ib2, ib3, ib4, and 1b5, and your **android:id** and **android:contentDescription** parameters to reference the proper planet names venus, jupiter, neptune, and mars, as seen in Figure 16-6. Change your **android:layout_width** parameter, to use a value of **200dip** for now, to give your UI pane a **fixed width** value.

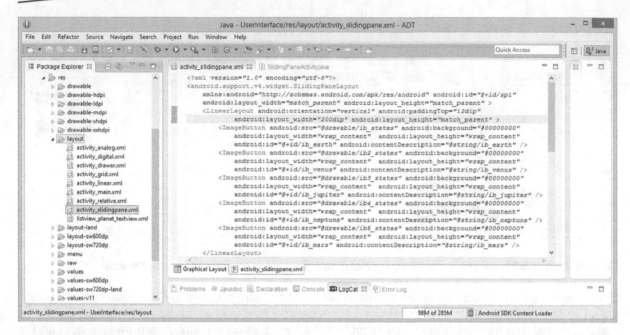

Figure 16-6. Copy and paste the first ImageButton to create four more and name them for each planet and states

Make sure that you add the <string> tag constants that are needed for the SlidingPaneActivity class in the strings.xml file using the following XML:

```
<string name=sliding_layout>SlidingPane Layout</string>
<string name=ib_mars>Planet Mars</string>
```

The sliding_layout text constant is used in your AndroidManifest.xml file to provide the application label at the top of the application, and the ib_mars text constant is used to provide the content description data for the sight impaired when they access that ImageButton. In most use cases, the Android device synthesizes the words "Planet Mars" by using the speech synthesis feature.

Now you are ready to add the **content pane** <LinearLayout> UI definition XML markup to your SlidingPaneLayout, which you are going to "steal" from your DrawerLayout Activity example, since you've already tricked that out using a chrome bar and planet image, and because it already uses a LinearLayout.

Defining a Planet Information Pane: Adding Five TextViews

Open your activity_drawer.xml file for editing, by right-clicking it in the /res/layout folder, and selecting the markup construct that includes your <LinearLayout> with your <ImageView> and <TextView> child tags inside it, and paste this entire construct into your activity_slidingpane.xml as your second <LinearLayout> construct, for your planet information content pane (see Figure 16-7).

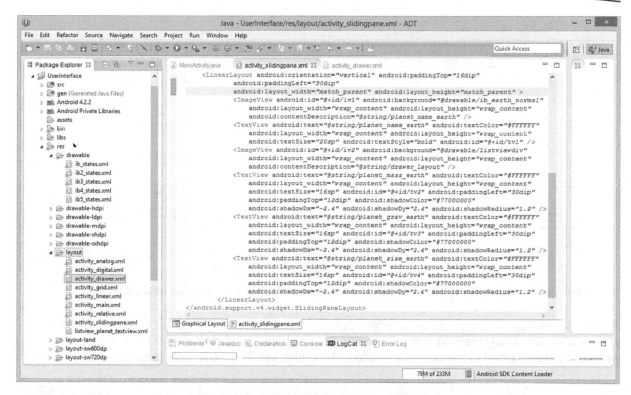

Figure 16-7. Copy a second planet information content <LinearLayout> from the activity_drawer.xml UI definition

Be sure your second <LinearLayout> construct uses the MATCH_PARENT constant for its layout_width and layout_height parameters, as we want the content area of the SlidingPaneLayout UI design to fill the display screen area when it is not being "slid" out of view by users to reveal the planet selection pane, which will be utilized to change your planet info content.

Other than changing your WRAP_CONTENT constant to a MATCH_PARENT constant, it is probably okay to leave the other child tags configured as they are. If you are super meticulous, you can change the android:contentDescription in your second <ImageView> from drawer_layout to sliding_layout. Since these UI designs function so similarly to each other, I just left it as is, as a SlidingPaneLayout UI to an end-user is quite similar to a DrawerLayout UI. Now you are ready to create your SlidingPaneActivity Activity subclass.

Creating a SlidingPaneActivity Subclass to Launch Your UI

Let's follow the most optimal work process and have Eclipse create the new Activity subclass for you, by adding your **sliding_layout** case statement to your MainActivity.java class, and once it is in place, using a **Create class 'SlidingPaneActivity'** option in the helper dialog, as seen in Figure 16-8.

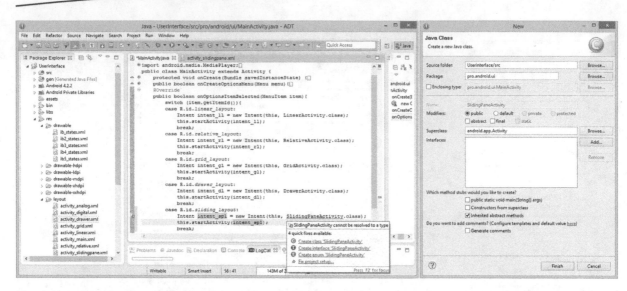

Figure 16-8. Add the case statement and Intent objects in the MainActivity class, and create SlidingPaneActivity

In your SlidingPaneActivity.java pane, which opens up in Eclipse, add your onCreate() method and your setContentView() method call, referencing your **activity_slidingpane.xml** UI definition file, which you just created in the previous section of the chapter. The Java code is shown in Figure 16-9.

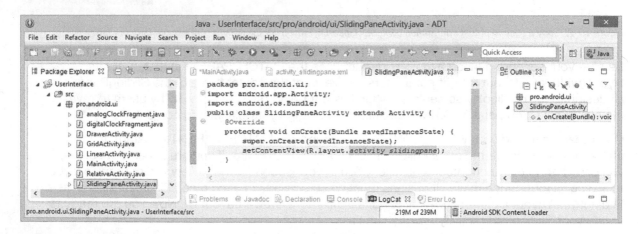

Figure 16-9. Add the onCreate() method and setContentView() method and reference the activity_slidingpane UI

Now that your Java and XML is in place for your SlidingPaneActivity class, all you have to do is to add a declaration for this <activity> to the AndroidManifest.xml file, and test the initial UI design and code by using the Nexus One emulator, which we are going to do in the next section.

Adding Your SlidingPaneActivity Class to the Android Manifest

Before you can test this Activity, you will need to add the <activity> tag to your Android Manifest file. Right-click the AndroidManifest.xml file in the root of your UserInterface project folder, and open it for editing, as shown in Figure 16-10. The easiest way to do this is to copy the drawer <activity> tag and change the android:name and android:label parameters to reference a SlidingPaneActivity class and sliding_layout <string> constant by using the following XML markup:

```
<activity android:name="pro.android.ui.SlidingPaneActivity"
          android:label="@string/sliding_layout" />
```

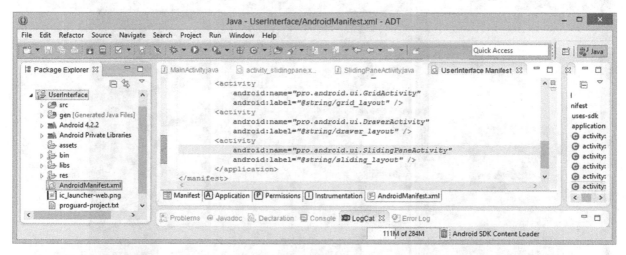

Figure 16-10. Adding a fifth <activity> tag to the AndroidManifest.xml file to enable your SlidingPaneActivity class

Finally, you will need to make sure that you have added the sliding_layout <item> to your existing MenuItem <item> XML definitions. These can be seen in your main.xml file, which is contained in the /res/menu folder. The XML markup looks like the following, and can be seen in Figure 16-11:

```
<item android:id="@+id/sliding_layout"
android:title="@string/sliding_layout"
android:orderInCategory="1"
android:showAsAction="never" />
```

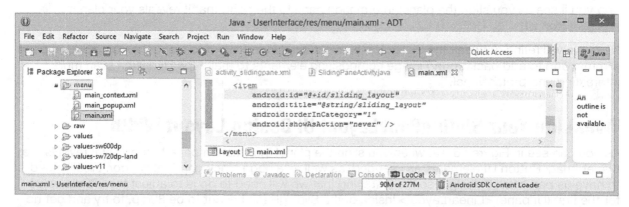

Figure 16-11. Add an <item> tag for the sliding_layout MenuItem in the main.xml file in the /res/menu folder

If you forget to add this MenuItem, the application may still compile and run, however there will not be a SlidingPane Layout menu selection at the bottom of the OptionsMenu (see Figure 16-12).

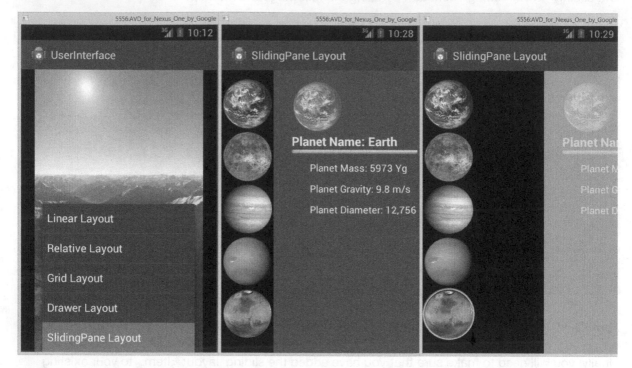

Figure 16-12. Testing the SlidingPaneActivityand the Mars ImageButton (far right) UI element in the Nexus One

Once your MenuItem definition has been put into place in the XML menu file you can use your **Run As ➤ Android Application** work process to test your UI definition thus far. One of the cool things about Android is that you can test your UI design and its layout container, without having to add in any functional Java code, which we are going to do later, after we tweak our UI design and add in image compositing elements for some wow factor. Your results can be seen in Figure 16-12 and you'll see as you slide the planet information pane to the right, that it reveals your planet ImageButton UI.

Next, we will refine or tweak the SlidingPaneLayout and LinearLayout to make the ImageButton pane slimmer and to add background image compositing elements to make the UI design even more interesting and professional.

Tweaking Your SlidingPaneLayout UI Design Layout Width

As you can see in Figure 16-12, when you slide the planet information pane to the right it reveals the planet ImageButton UI elements as intended, as well as a huge black gap that we don't really need to have as part of a UI design, so the first thing that we will need to do is to adjust the 200dip value for the first (UI pane) <LinearLayout> inside of the SlidingPane Layout to be 80dip, to try and get rid of all the additional space, as shown in Figure 16-13.

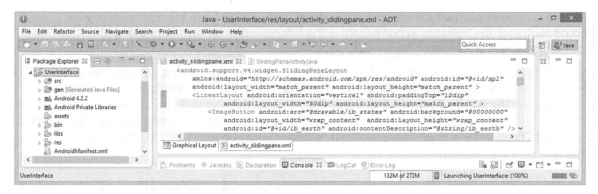

Figure 16-13. Adjusting the android:layout_width parameter to 80dp to more closely match the width of the UI

Now use your **Run As ➤ Android Application** work process, and slide the info content pane to the right, and as you can see in Figure 16-14 on the right side, only your planets are revealed behind your starfield image and the rest of your UI design shows all your planet information.

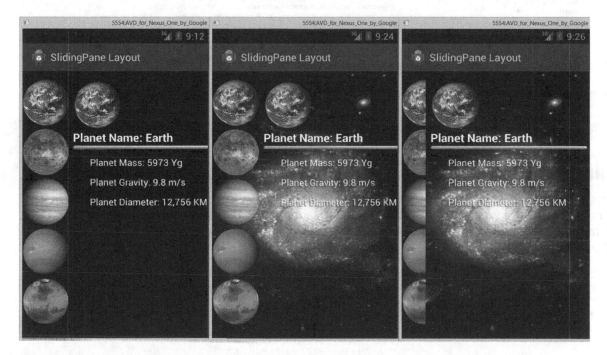

Figure 16-14. Testing the SlidingPaneLayout UI tweaks in Nexus One, and addition of plasma background image

Compositing Imagery in Your SlidingPaneLayout UI Design

The next thing we want to take a look at is how the SlidingPaneLayout container handles digital image compositing, especially as one pane slides over another. It should be interesting to see how an image asset in the parent <SlidingPaneLayout> tag parameters is treated between your two panes. You can actually see your answer to this question in the center and the right side panels in Figure 16-14, which shows that the image asset is used for both panes.

This gives a unique special effect opportunity to developers if they have the transparency defined correctly for the content, in our case it is the ImageButton UI elements using an `android:background="#00000000"` parameter.

After you add your `android:background="@drawable/plasma1080"` parameter, as is shown in Figure 16-15, referencing a **plasma1080.png** digital image asset in your /res/drawable-xhdpi folder, you can use your **Run As ➤ Android Application** work process, and pull your content pane over your UI pane and see your planet ImageButtons magically disappear, and also reveal a plasma cloud in their place! This can be a useful special effect, which is why I covered it here first, so you can leverage it in your UI designs.

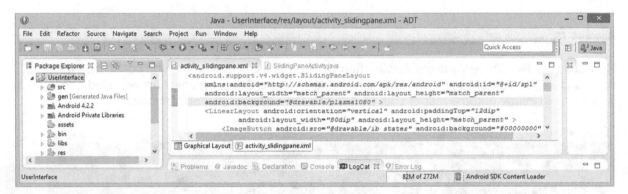

Figure 16-15. *Adding an android:background parameter to the SlidingPaneLayout parent tag referencing a plasma1080 image*

Next, let's move this UI background parameter to your second LinearLayout.

Using Multiple Images in the SlidingPaneLayout UI Design

As you can see in Figure 16-16 an `android:background="@drawable/plasma1080"` parameter has been removed from your <SlidingPaneLayout> tag, and placed into your second <LinearLayout> container. If you want to look ahead, the results from doing this can be seen in Figure 16-17, in the left panel.

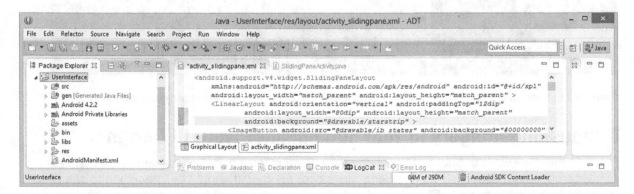

Figure 16-16. *Adding android:background parameters to <LinearLayout> child tags instead of SlidingPaneLayout parent tag*

Figure 16-17. Installing background images in LinearLayout tags, and centering a planet image over the plane name

You'll need to provide a second digital image asset for your first UI pane <LinearLayout> container, so I have provided the **starstrip.png** image asset in the book file repository. First, copy the file into the **/res/drawable-xhdpi** folder. Next, right-click your project folder, and use the **Refresh** menu option, to show Eclipse the file is now present in your project hierarchy.

Now use your **Run As ➤ Android Application** work process to launch the Nexus One emulator, and as you can see in Figure 16-17 in the center panel, your SlidingPaneLayout UI design now features two different background images.

The content pane background image now replaces both the ImageButton and the UI pane background image when sliding over, so to use different backgrounds or images for your SlidingPaneLayout UI design, use the LinearLayout containers (or other child UI layout containers or UI widgets) to contain the background parameter. To use a single background image, place the parameter in the parent <SlidingPaneLayout> tag.

The final adjustment or tweak that I would like to perform on this UI design is to move the planet <ImageView> over the planet name, rather than having it on the left next to the planet <ImageButton> UI elements.

This is because when the content pane slides over to the right revealing the UI pane, it looks less than professional to have the two planet images so close together, so let's add an **android:layout_marginLeft** parameter to the first <ImageView> tag to move the planet over the actual name of that planet in the first planet name information text UI element.

As you can see in Figure 16-17, in the right panel, this is going to look great!

To finish the UI design, add an android:layout_marginLeft="100dp" parameter after your layout_ height parameter, as is shown in Figure 16-18. This pushes your planet <ImageView> over the name of the planet and in the center of the content pane, which looks better when your content pane is both open as well as closed, as you can see on the right side of Figure 16-17.

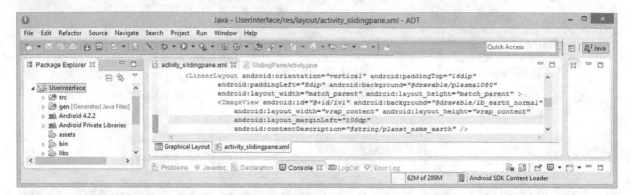

Figure 16-18. Adding an android:layout_marginLeft parameter and its 100dp value to the <ImageView> tag

Now we can add in the Java code to make your UI design functional, so that when you click the planet ImageButton UI element in the UI pane it changes the imagery and information text in your SlidingPaneLayout content pane.

Making the SlidingPaneLayout Design Interactive Using Java

The first thing that we need to do before we make our SlidingPaneLayout UI design interactive using Java code, is to add the android:id="@+id/uiPane" parameter to your second <LinearLayout> container, so that we can change a background image reference for the content pane, which we will do with the **.setBackgroundResource()** method call.

This parameter addition to your XML markup is shown in Figure 16-19, as is a slight tweak to your **android:layout_marginLeft** parameter for the UI pane <LinearLayout>, setting that to **85dip** instead of 80dip. I am doing this so that there is a bit more room in the UI pane to hold the button decoration hoop, which will appear when the user clicks or touches the ImageButton UI element, and which I will be sure to show you in a subsequent Nexus One screenshot.

Figure 16-19. *Add an android:id="@+id/uiPane" to the content pane <LinearLayout> tag, and adjust the layout_width to 85dip*

Now it's time to open up the **SlidingPaneActivity.java** class in Eclipse, if it is not open already, and add your LinearLayout, ImageView, and TextView object declarations at the top of your class, as is shown in Figure 16-20.

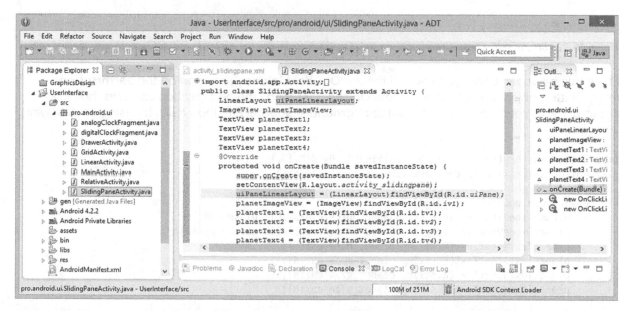

Figure 16-20. *Add LinearLayout, ImageView, and TextView declarations, and instantiations, to the SlidingPaneActivity subclass*

Next, inside the **onCreate()** method add instantiations for these objects using the **findViewById()** method, with references to the XML UI definitions for each of these, using their android:id parameter IDs that you assigned. Once this has been done, you will be ready to add event handling, to make the UI pane ImageButton UI elements interactive.

Next, you will need to instantiate the **earthButton** ImageButton object, and use your **.findViewById()** method, to configure it with your **ib_earth** ID XML definition, as shown in Figure 16-21.

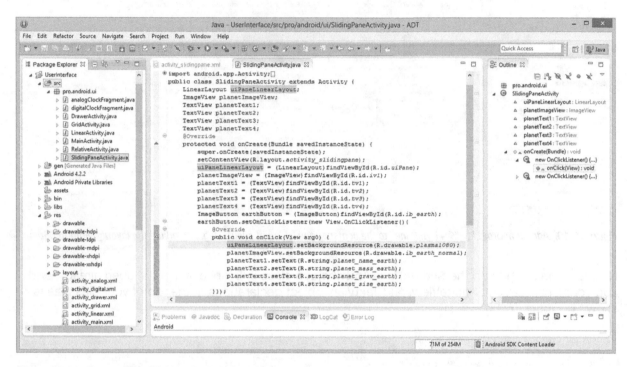

Figure 16-21. *Create .setOnClickListener() and .onClick() methods containing the .setText() and .setBackground() method calls*

Once this has been done, you can call the **.setOnClickListener()** method off the **earthButton** ImageButton object and use a **new View.OnClickListener()** method creation call, and then load the construct with your **.setText()** and **.setBackgroundResource()** method calls, by using the following Java code:

```
ImageButton earthButton = (ImageButton)findViewById(R.id.ib_earth);
earthButton.setOnClickListener(new View.OnClickListener() {
    @Override
    public void onClick(View arg0) {
        uiPaneLinearLayout.setBackgroundResource(R.drawable.plasma1080);
        planetImageView.setBackgroundResource(R.drawable.ib_earth_normal);
        planetText1.setText(R.string.planet_name_earth);
        planetText2.setText(R.string.planet_mass_earth);
        planetText3.setText(R.string.planet_grav_earth);
        planetText4.setText(R.string.planet_size_earth);
    }
});
```

As you can see in Figure 16-21, the Java code is error-free, and you can copy this entire 12 line Java code construct, four more times underneath itself, changing earth to venus, jupiter, neptune, and mars, respectively.

Be sure to also change the ImageView planet image asset reference to the correct planet image asset, for Venus it would be **ib_venus_normal.png**, for instance, and select a different background stars or plasma image for your second LinearLayout UI container (content pane) compositing background.

Since this SlidingPaneActivity.java Activity subclass is getting close to a hundred lines of code, I've collapsed some of the (similar) code blocks in Figure 16-22, and I am just showing the declarations, instantiations, and the event handling for the Mars planet code block, because you can get this code from this book's code repository if you want to.

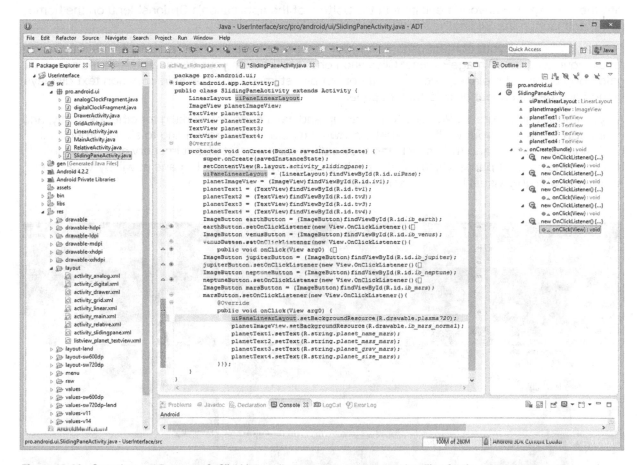

Figure 16-22. Copy the earthButton.setOnClickListener() structure to create event handling for the other planets

I suggest that you write it from scratch, as that is the best way to learn how. Eclipse points out your mistakes and that ends up being great for learning, because we all know that the most memorable way to learn is to fail!

Don't be afraid to play around with the SlidingPaneLayout UI design and to experiment with your XML markup, and your Java programming logic as well.

For instance, you could try placing the android:layout_marginLeft="85dip" parameter in the second LinearLayout container, and attempt to set up the SlidingPaneLayout in an already open position, by using only XML markup.

This opens up the SlidingPane, but it cannot be closed over the UI pane if you use this approach. This would not be a UI parameter configuration that you will want to use with this layout container class.

Of course, the only way for you to actually ascertain this, and to learn what to do, and more importantly, what not to do, with a given UI container class, is to actually try out different things in your XML markup and Java code!

Our next task is to test your SlidingPaneActivity.java class thoroughly in the Nexus One emulator, so let's use our **Run As ➤ Android Application** work process and launch the Nexus One emulator, go into the SlidingPane Layout menu item at the bottom of the application's OptionsMenu on the home page, and launch the SlidingPaneActivity Activity subclass.

Pull (slide or swipe) your content pane using your mouse (or finger on touchscreen) to the right, and reveal your five planet ImageButtons. Click each one, and be sure your pressed state reveals your gold hoop around the planet, and that your correct planet image and planet information text displays in the SlidingPaneLayout class's content pane.

As you can see in Figure 16-23, your XML markup and Java code are working together perfectly, and your 85dp UI Pane Layout Width parameter allows the gold UI decoration ring to show through the UI design completely, and the ImageButtons all call up their correct planet imagery and planet info text onto the content pane, which can be slid back and forth over your UI pane at will by your users. Another cool highly visual UI design achieved!

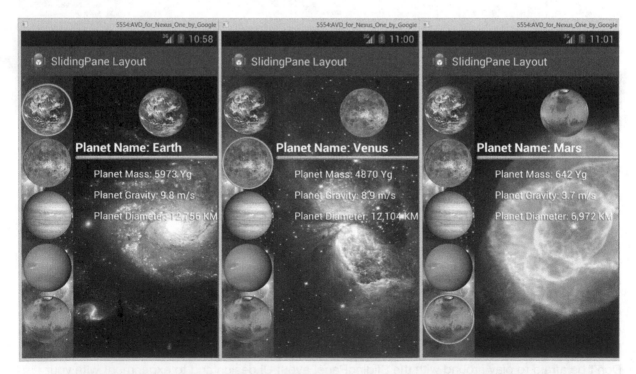

Figure 16-23. Test SlidingPaneLayout in the Nexus One emulator, showing three planet screens and showing the ImageButton pressed state (gold hoop)

Next we need to test the SlidingPaneActivity using a different emulator to see how your UI design and composited imagery will scale up with different screen sizes and orientations.

Testing the SlidingPaneLayout Using a Different Emulator

Let's use the HD resolution (1280 by 720) **Nexus 7** tablet AVD next to test your SlidingPaneLayout class. Right-click your UserInterface project folder and select the **Run As ➤ Configurations** menu sequence to open up the **Run Configurations** dialog, which is shown in Figure 16-24.

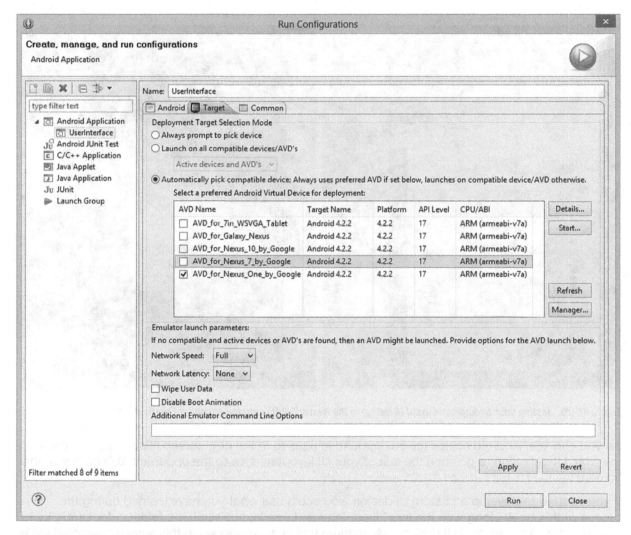

Figure 16-24. Selecting the Nexus 7 AVD for testing the Apply and Run buttons

Find the **AVD_for_Nexus_7_by_Google** emulator, and place a check in the select checkbox to the left of it, and then click the **Apply** button to apply this new AVD emulator to your Eclipse ADT development environment.

Once you've applied this new AVD emulator to your Eclipse ADT installation you can use the **Run** button to launch the Nexus 7 emulator, and you can now test your SlidingPaneActivity.java Activity subclass to see how the design will be rendered using a different resolution. After that, we'll place the Nexus 7 in landscape mode, so that we can see exactly how that affects our UI design, as it will be rendered by the Android SlidingPaneLayout class.

As you can see in Figure 16-25, the Nexus 7 AVD uses an ActionBar Overflow Menu (three square dots) to display the OptionsMenu. You use this to select the SlidingPane Layout option and launch the SlidingPaneActivity class, as is shown on the left and right sides of the screenshot.

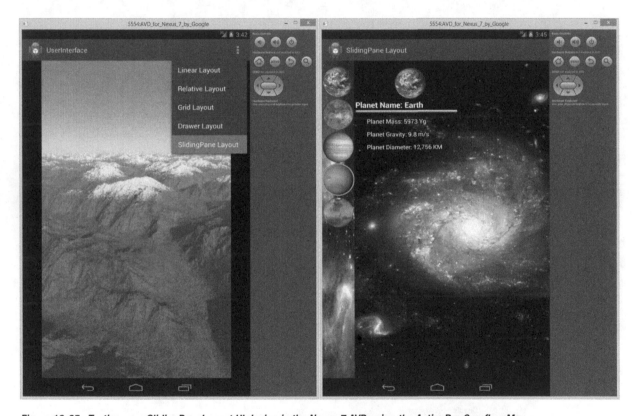

Figure 16-25. Testing your SlidingPaneLayout UI design in the Nexus 7 AVD using the ActionBar Overflow Menu

As you can see, Android scales the background images to fit the new screen resolution, and uses the XML UI definition to position the rest of your UI layout relative to the upper-left (0,0) corner of the screen.

If you wanted to develop a custom UI design, you could use what you have learned during the course of this book along with the /res/layout-land and /res/layout-sw600dp folders;. for example, to place custom imagery and UI design XML markup that is accessed when this screen characteristic is utilized, as it is here with the Nexus 7 AVD emulator.

This is a great exercise (or practice) to implement what you have been learning about over the course of this book, so take some time and copy your activity_slidingpane.xml file into these folders and customize the UI design so that it will be even more refined in high-resolution and landscape modes.

Next, you are going to take a look at your SlidingPaneActivity class, this time in landscape mode. This can be accomplished by using the **Ctrl-F11** keystroke combination, which rotates the emulator 90 degrees clockwise.

If you wanted to rotate the AVD emulator back into portrait mode, use the **Ctrl-F12** keystroke combination, or, optionally, you could use this Ctrl-F11 keystroke combination as a toggle mode, if you wanted to.

As you can see in Figure 16-26, your background image resizes to fit the new aspect ratio. When you create your **/layout-land** UI definition, be sure to go into GIMP 2.8.10 and create an alternate image that has been rotated 90 degrees to use in the landscape UI definition for an alternate background image asset reference (galaxy480land.png, for instance).

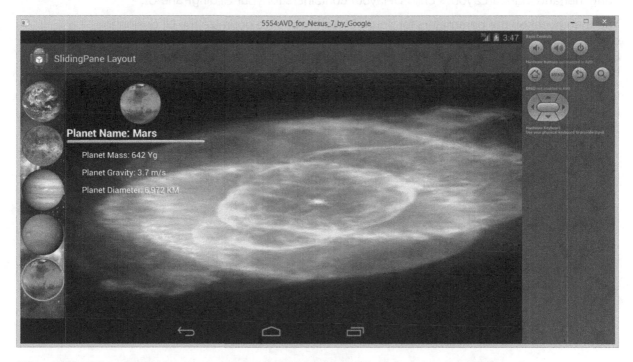

Figure 16-26. Using a Ctrl-F11 key sequence to test the SlidingPaneLayout in landscape mode in the Nexus 7

It would also be a good exercise to develop a /res/layout-land UI design XML definition file specifically for landscape mode that adjusted the positioning of the TextView and ImageView UI elements to refine the design for each type of device, resolution, aspect ratio, and orientation.

As you can see, this SlidingPaneLayout class gives developers some fairly impressive functionality, but like any of the Android UI container classes it will need to be customized for different screen sizes, densities, aspect ratios and orientations.

Summary

In this chapter, you learned about the Android **SlidingPaneLayout** class and how to set-up an XML UI design definition for this unique class.

You looked at the SlidingPaneLayout and related classes, which are used to create the functionality that the SlidingPanelayout class brings into your application, and then got down to business, creating a SlidingPaneActivity class to implement everything that you learned about this unique UI class.

You created your SlidingPaneActivity.java Activity subclass and a MenuItem for it, and then created your activity_slidingpane.xml UI definition file, where you defined your <SlidingPaneLayout> UI container and <LinearLayout> child UI layout containers for your SlidingPane UI.

You then tweaked the parameters for your <LinearLayout> to optimize the UI design to display the five popular planets in the UI pane and the planet information in a content pane of SlidingPaneLayout parent UI container. You also implemented image compositing, using galaxy background imagery.

In the next chapter, we will take a closer look at the Android **ViewPager** class, and see how you can use this UI class to allow your users to flip through pages on your application display screen using horizontal swipes.

Android's ViewPager Class: Using ViewPager to Navigate Horizontally

Android's **ViewPager** class is another recent addition to the Android 4.0 OS, and is the most complicated of the new UI layout container classes added in the android.support.v4 libraries.

This is because ViewPager class uses the **PagerAdapter** (Array) class (object) to manage the View object pages, which is why it is called a ViewPager in the first place.

The ViewPager UI layout class was developed to help developers to design a multi-panel side-to-side swipeable horizontal UI that allows users to flip between different View objects. In this chapter, you will use ImageView UI widgets to hold your images of space (your stars and galaxy image assets).

The ViewPager class is utilized to create the UI foundation for a number of Android applications, and, at least on my Galaxy Note II, it is used to flip between different application icon repositories.

It's important to note, however, that according to the developer documents the ViewPager class is still under development and could change at any time.

To quote the current ViewPager Class page from the Android Developer site:

"Note this class is currently under early design and development. The API will likely change in later updates of the compatibility library, requiring changes to the source code of apps when they are compiled against the newer version."

I am still going to cover this class in this book because I cannot see the API being pulled out of the Android OS, although, I usually do not include classes that are "currently under early design and development." Because I speculate that readers will want to know more about this class and how it functions, I'm going to include the chapter in the book and go over how to set up a basic ViewPager Activity class, which I will name as the ViewPagingActivity.

We are going to add this class to your UserInterface application to create an Android ViewPager "paging UI" design that allows users to swipe UI screens back and forth across a their content pane. In this chapter you'll utilize ImageView UI elements to allow users to flip through space imagery assets. This chapter shows you how to use ViewPager in your app to page through View (image) objects.

As usual, I will go over the foundational classes, methods, constants, interfaces, nested classes, and the like, to provide the foundation for what we will be doing in the remainder of the chapter.

After that you will create your ViewPager <string> and <menu> XML assets, and then add your case statement for a **paging_activity** MenuItem object. As you know, this then prompts you to have Eclipse create your **ViewPagingActivity.java** Activity subclass.

This is the class that you'll eventually implement your ViewPager, and PagerAdapter, Java objects inside of. After you create this ViewPagingActivity.java class, you will add an <activity> tag to your AndroidManifest.xml file so that the class is declared for use in Android.

After that you will create your **activity_viewpaging.xml** UI definition and its <ViewPager> parent class (and parameters) which you'll eventually need to reference in your ViewPagingActivity subclass. You will then create the eight methods which are required to implement the ViewPager object in your Activity subclass. After that, we'll test the class and see the impressive results that the class can add to your Pro Android UI design work process!

The ViewPager Class: Horizontal Sliding Screen UI Design

The Android **ViewPager** class is another UI layout container class that was introduced in Android Version 4.0. What is interesting about the ViewPager class is that it is in fact a layout container (ViewGroup subclass) class, but it does not have a Layout as part of the class name (ViewPagerLayout)! If you want to see a screenshot of what ViewPager does, you can take an advance peek at Figure 17-12.

The ViewPager layout class is designed to provide a **horizontally scrolling multi-pane user interface layout** for use at any level of the application's UI design. The multiple panes of a ViewPager UI design are connected (side to side), and can be flicked back and forth across the display screen. You may be familiar with this on the home screen of your Android devices–mine has five app icon "reservoir" screens that I use to store my launch icons.

The ViewPager could be thought of as a "Layout Manager," that is more than just a UI layout container. This class allows your users to swipe left and right through pages of UI design data, contained in View (ViewGroup) data structures. These ViewPage structures are referenced using an Array object.

You supply an implementation of a **PagerAdapter** to generate your pages that each ViewPage shows. You will be taking a look at several of the ViewPager nested classes, which are utilized in conjunction with a ViewPager, during this first part of the chapter.

This ViewPager implementation is far more complicated than other "static" UI layout design containers, such as the often used FrameLayout, GridLayout, RelativeLayout, LinearLayout, DrawerLayout, and so on.

These are primarily implemented "statically," using XML, while ViewPager is primarily implemented "dynamically," using Java code.

The ViewPager class hierarchy starts at the Java Object master class, and progresses from the Android View class, to the Android ViewGroup class to the ViewPager class. The ViewPager is part of the **android.support.v4.view** package, and is structured using this class hierarchy:

```
java.lang.Object
  > android.view.View
    > android.view.ViewGroup
      > android.support.v4.view.ViewPager
```

The Android ViewPager class is a **public class** and it extends the **ViewGroup** superclass. It's referenced by using a specialized **support.v4.view** package by using the **import android.support. v4.view.ViewPager** statement.

This import statement reference should also indicate to you that ViewPager is indeed a layout container, and not a UI widget. If it were a UI widget, it would be included as a part of the support. v4.widget package.

A ViewPager UI layout design is most commonly used in conjunction with the **PagerAdapter** class, which we will learn about after we cover the ViewPager class, constants, and layout parameters or attributes.

There are three constants in the ViewPager class, a **SCROLL_STATE_DRAGGING**, **SCROLL_ STATE_SETTLING** (coming to rest), and a **SCROLL_STATE_IDLE** (not being used), which the developer can poll to find out what the user is doing as far as using the ViewPaging engine provided by the ViewPager class.

There are also a couple of attributes that we should cover that are part of the ViewPager. LayoutParams nested class. These provide an indication to the ViewPager "engine" which does the ViewPaging as to whether certain View objects are part of the paging Views. Paging Views would be the Views that move in or with the ViewPages in the ViewPager class's "ViewPaging engine."

Developers can flag other View objects in their UI designs as being "decoration" Views. **Decoration Views** are View objects that are not part of the ViewPages themselves, but have been included in your UI design as decoration or detail elements for the UI design and are not earmarked for the Viewpager's "horizontal movement between pages" feature.

We cover the **ViewPager.LayoutParams** nested layout class next, and then we get into the PagerAdapter class, which manages the ViewPager content.

ViewPager.LayoutParams Nested Class: Layout Attributes

Android's **ViewPager.LayoutParams** nested class defines the layout parameter attributes for your ViewPager UI layout container class, and is subclassed from the ViewGroup.LayoutParams class, so it inherits the layout parameter attributes that can be used with any of the ViewGroup layout containers I have covered in this book.

The ViewPager.LayoutParams class hierarchy starts out with the Java Object master class, and progresses from the Android ViewGroup.LayoutParams class to the ViewPager.LayoutParams class. The ViewPager.LayoutParams is part of the **android.support.v4.view** package, and is structured using the following class hierarchy:

```
java.lang.Object
  > android.view.ViewGroup.LayoutParams
    > android.support.v4.view.ViewPager.LayoutParams
```

The Android ViewPager.LayoutParams nested class is a **public static class**, and it extends the **ViewGroup.LayoutParams** superclass. It's referenced by using XML parameters in the UI design definitions for your View objects.

The ViewGroup.LayoutParams nested class defines two parameters and their implementation for the ViewPager viewpaging engine. These user interface layout parameters only need to be supplied for Views added to a ViewPager or used on the same UI design (screen) as a ViewPager is used.

The one layout parameter from this nested class that is already familiar to you is the **gravity** parameter. This parameter will not evaluate when it is utilized in a View object that is controlled, managed, and manipulated using a ViewPager viewpaging engine.

The gravity parameter uses the constants that you have learned all about during this book, and supports the usage of multiple values, by using the horizontal | bar element to combine these constants.

At this point you are probably wondering why would the gravity parameter even be included at all in the nested class?

This is because of a second layout parameter included in this nested class called the **isDecor** parameter. This parameter is short for "is decoration," and uses a true or false setting value, which is a "flag," setting.

This Decor parameter is used to indicate if your View object, which this parameter will be contained within, is intended by Pro Android UI designers to be used for "decoration" for your ViewPager UI layout design.

What decoration indicates is UI design elements that are not contained in the ViewPager UI elements that are being horizontally paged (controlled) by the ViewPager's viewpaging engine. So if a View UI element has this set to true, then the gravity parameter can be included as well, and will work.

The PagerAdapter Class: Manage an Array of ViewPages

This Android **PagerAdapter** class was designed specifically for utilization with the ViewPager View paging engine. This class provides an Adapter object to hold an Array of objects, which ultimately are used for inflating or populating ViewPages that are used by the ViewPager class.

The Android PagerAdapter class is a **public abstract class**, and it extends the Java **Object** superclass, which means that it was created (coded) specifically to provide an Array of ViewPages to the ViewPager viewpaging engine.

The PagerAdapter class is referenced using a specialized **support.v4.view** package by using an **import android.support.v4.view.PagerAdapter** statement.

A PagerAdapter class hierarchy starts at the Java Object master class, and directly subclasses the class to create the PagerAdapter class and object.

The PagerAdapter class is part of the **android.support.v4.view** package, and it is structured using the following class hierarchy:

```
java.lang.Object
  > android.support.v4.view.PagerAdapter
```

PagerAdapter Methods: Overriding Methods to Implement a PagerAdapter

As you will see during the remainder of this chapter, when you implement a PagerAdapter class, you will need to "override" (@Override) at least these following PagerAdapter class methods at the very minimum:

- The **.instantiateItem(ViewGroup, int)** method instantiates (or creates) your ViewPage UI design elements. These are then used by your ViewPager object, which you will "wire up" to your PagerAdapter using a **.setAdapter()** method call. We will be implementing all this a bit later in this chapter.

- The **.destroyItem(ViewGroup, int, Object)** method does the opposite of this .instantiateItem() method, and destroys (removes from system memory) the ViewPage UI design elements.

- The **.getCount()** method is used as a "counter," to keep track of which ViewPage object is currently being viewed (on the display) by your end-users.

- The **.isViewFromObject(View, Object)** method is used by the ViewPager object to determine whether a ViewPage is associated with any specific key object as returned by the .instantiateItem() method call.

You will be overriding these four methods, as well as four others, in your Java implementation of the ViewPager and PagerAdapter classes during the second half of this chapter. Later in this section I will also include a table with all 15 of the PagerAdapter method calls, more than half of which we will be implementing in the **private ViewPagerAdapter** class you will be creating later in the chapter for use with your **ViewPagingActivity** class. For now, let's focus on learning about the PagerAdapter class, and how it works to provide ViewPages to the ViewPager viewpaging engine. This makes the complex code we are about to write much more comprehensible!

ViewPager Indexing Using the Key Object

The ViewPager class associates each of the pages in the PagerAdapter using a "**key**" Object instead of working with the View objects directly, much as a pointer object is used in C++ programming to reference items in memory.

This key Object can then be used to locate and uniquely identify any given ViewPage independent of its position in the PagerAdapter Array. A call to the PagerAdapter method **.startUpdate()** indicates that the contents of your ViewPager object are about to change.

One or more calls to **.instantiateItem()** and **.destroyItem()**then occur and at the end of the Viewpager update process there is a method call to the **.finishUpdate()** method, all of which we implement in our code later on in this chapter.

By the time the .finishUpdate() method returns the View objects associated with the key object returned by the .instantiateItem() method, they should be added to the parent ViewGroup passed into these methods. Similarly your View objects associated with the key passed into the .destroyItem() method are removed by that method.

The method **.isViewFromObject()** can be used to identify whether a ViewPage is associated with any given key object, so you can keep track of where UI design components are at any given time in the active ViewPager screen.

The PagerAdapter class is capable of supporting dataset changes. This will allows for more complicated ViewPager applications to be created using the .notifyDataSetChanged() method call.

It is important to note that dataset changes need to occur on the main app thread, and also need to end with a method call to **.notifyDataSetChanged(),** much like one would do using an AdapterView Adapter that was derived from the Android BaseAdapter class.

A dataset change involves ViewPages being added, removed, or changing their position. The ViewPager keeps your current page active, provided that your ViewPagerAdapter implements the method **.getItemPosition()**, which you will see in a little bit here that it does.

A simple PagerAdapter, such as is used in the basic ViewPager example we will be using in this chapter, may choose to use the ViewPage itself as the key object, returning it from the .instantiateItem() method call after creating and adding it to the parent ViewGroup.

Your matching **.destroyItem()** method implementation should then remove this View from the parent ViewGroup, using a **.removeView()** method. Additionally your **.isViewFromObject()** method call should implement a **return** statement that sets your View == Object as you'll see a bit later on in the chapter.

Table 17-1 is a compilation of the currently active, that is, not deprecated method calls that can be utilized with the PagerAdapter class. You will implement the first eight of these in this chapter to create a basic ViewPager and PagerAdapter marriage that allows digital images of space to be swiped (paged) through, using the ViewPager UI for your UserInterface application.

Table 17-1. PagerAdapter Method Call, Access, Type, and Data or Object Type Along with What Each Method Call Is Used For

Method Access, Type, and Name:	Method Description:
abstract int getCount()	Returns a Number of View Objects that are available
Object instantiateItem()	Create ViewPage for a given position in your Adapter
void destroyItem()	Remove ViewPage for a given position in your Adapter
abstract boolean isViewFromObject()	Determines whether a ViewPage is associated with a specific key object returned by .instantiateItem()
Parcelable saveState()	Save the instance state associated with the Adapter
void restoreState()	Restore instance state associated with Adapter
void startUpdate()	Called when a change in a ViewPage is going to start
void finishUpdate()	Called after the change in a ViewPage is completed
int getItemPosition()	Called if attempting to determine item position
float getPageWidth()	Returns proportional width of a ViewPage as percent
CharSequence getPageTitle()	Called by a ViewPager to obtain a title string
void setPrimaryItem()	Informs Adapter which item considered to be primary
void notifyDataSetChanged()	Data for Adapter has changed and Views should update
void registerDataSetObserver()	Register observer to receive data changed callbacks
unregisterDataSetObserver()	Unregister the observer for data changed callbacks

It is important to note that this PagerAdapter class (object) is much more generalized than other Adapter objects that are typically used in Android for implementing AdapterView subclasses, such as ListView, GridView, Gallery, Spinner, and StackView. If you remember, we recently looked at these Adapter and AdapterView classes back in Chapter 15, regarding Android DrawerLayout.

Instead of providing the View recycling mechanism directly, your ViewPager object uses callbacks to indicate the steps taken during its updates.

The PagerAdapter object may implement a form of View recycling if need be, or, it could utilize more sophisticated methods for controlling ViewPages.

For instance, Fragment transactions could be utilized instead of View and ViewGroups, where each ViewPage could be represented by its own Fragment object. This adds an additional level of complexity to the ViewPager.

These are two known subclasses of the PagerAdapter class that can be used to implement Fragment objects, instead of View objects, with the ViewPager class viewpaging engine.

These **FragmentPagerAdapter** and **FragmentStatePagerAdapter** subclasses, along with each of their related methods, could be used to build Fragment-based user interfaces in conjunction with the ViewPager class.

These are the standard PagerAdapter subclasses, or objects, which you will use to implement the use of a Fragment object with a ViewPager object, in case you wanted to use Fragment subclasses instead of Activity subclasses in your UI design.

Define a ViewPaging Layout: Coding Multi-Pane UIs in XML

Let's start implementing our ViewPagingActivity class by creating the Menu object and MenuItem for our application home screen. Right-click on your /res/values folder and open the strings.xml file, and add a <string> tag constant named **paging_layout** with the text value "ViewPager Layout" using the following single line of XML markup as shown in Figure 17-1:

```
<string name="paging_layout">ViewPager Layout</string>
```

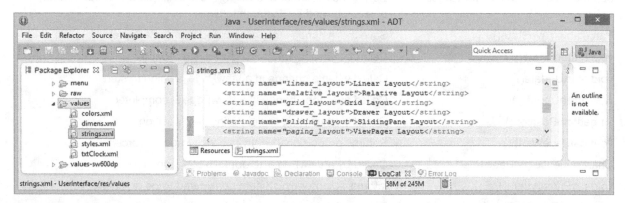

Figure 17-1. Open the strings.xml file, add a <string> constant named paging_layout with the text value "ViewPager Layout"

Now we have what we need in place to create our MenuItem object in XML, so open the /res/menu folder, and right-click the main.xml file, and add an <item> structure at the end of the file referencing the paging_layout string and ID, using the following XML markup, as shown in Figure 17-2:

```
<item android:id="@+id/paging_layout"
      android:title="@string/paging_layout"
      android:orderInCategory="1"
      android:showAsAction="never" />
```

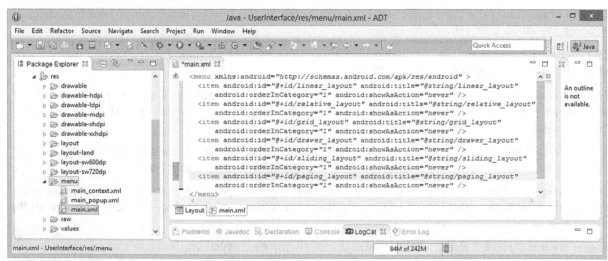

Figure 17-2. Add a paging_layout <item> child tag in the parent <menu> tag, referencing the paging_layout <string>

Now you are ready to add the paging_layout case statement to your home screen in your MainActivity.java Activity subclass.

Add a ViewPagingActivity Class to Your MainActivity Menu

Open your /src/pro.android.ui folder, and then right-click your MainActivity.java file to open it in a tab in Eclipse for editIng.

Add your case statement at the end of your onOptionsItemSelected() method, which will access the paging_activity MenuItem object in a case evaluation statement, and then create an Intent object named **intent_vpl** and use it to launch your **ViewPagingActivity.class** by using the .startActivity() method call, using the following block of Java code shown in Figure 17-3:

```
case R.id.paging_layout:
    Intent intent_vpl = new Intent(this, ViewPagingActivity.class);
    this.startActivity(intent_vpl);

break;
```

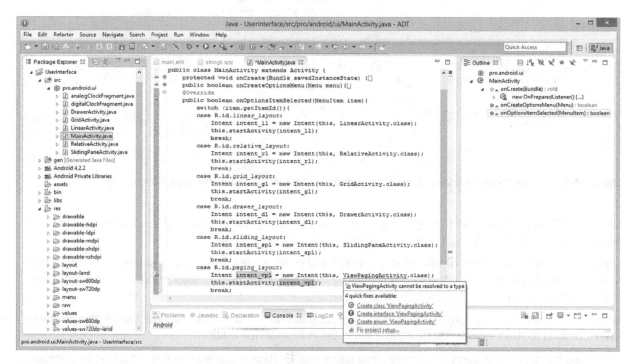

Figure 17-3. Create a case statement for the paging_layout MenuItem referencing the ViewPagingActivity class

As you can see in Figure 17-3 there's a wavy red error underline highlight under your ViewPagingActivity.class reference, because this class has not yet been created, so mouse-over this red error highlighting and pop-up the helper dialog, and select the **Create class 'ViewPagingActivity'** option, so that Eclipse creates this class for you.

Once you click this option Eclipse opens up the **New Java Class** dialog, shown in Figure 17-4, already populated with the source folder, Package name, Class name, modifiers, and even abstract method inheritance settings.

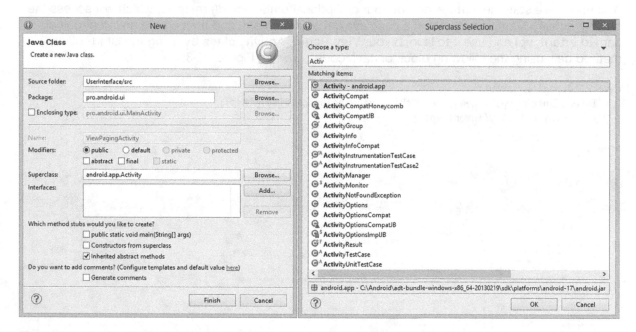

Figure 17-4. *Click the Create class ViewPagingActivity option so Eclipse opens a New Java Class dialog for you*

Click the Browse button on the right end of the Superclass specification field, and open up the Superclass Selection dialog, shown on the right side of Figure 17-4.

Type in the first few letters of the word "Activity" and double-click the Activity superclass option to select it, which will enter it into the Superclass field in the New Java Class dialog, shown on the left side of Figure 17-4.

Next, click the Finish button, at the bottom right of this dialog, to create the new ViewPagingActivity. java class. This then opens the new Java class up in Eclipse for editing.

Since we have already seen the empty Java class that Eclipse generates in this situation in previous chapters, I will forgo this screenshot, and we will get right into configuring your AndroidManifest.xml file for your app to add support for this Activity subclass using the <activity> tag.

Configuring AndroidManifest.xml

Once your ViewPagingActivity.java class is created and open in Eclipse, it can be seen on the left side of the four open tabs)shown in Figure 17-5). Find your AndroidManifest.xml file, at the bottom of your UserInterface root project folder, and right-click it and select Open to open it for editing in Eclipse. Add an <activity> tag using the following XML markup:

```
<activity
    android:name="pro.android.ui.ViewpagingActivity"
    android:label="@string/paging_layout" />
```

Figure 17-5.   Open AndroidManifest.xml and add an <activity> tag defining the ViewPagingActivity class for use

This enables you to test the application later using the Nexus One.

Now you are ready to create the **activity_viewpaging.xml** ViewPager UI file.

Finish Defining Planet UI Pane: Adding Four ImageButtons

Let's create our ViewPager XML UI definition file now by right-clicking the UserInterface /res/layout folder and selecting the **New ➤ Android XML File** menu sequence. This opens the **New Android XML File** dialog, as shown in Figure 17-6, where you can name the file and select a root element tag.

Figure 17-6. Use a New Android XML File dialog to create activity_viewpaging.xml

Name the file **activity_viewpaging** and select the Resource Type: Layout and Project: UserInterface, and try and find the Root Element of: <ViewPager>.

If you can't locate the ViewPager root element, you still need to add a tag for it to your XML UI definition. Much like the other V4 support library UI layout containers we have been covering in recent chapters, you will find that it is not listed, so you will have to find a close analog, such as the <ViewFlipper> UI layout container, and then click on the **Finish** button.

Edit the <ViewFlipper> parent tag and change it to be a ViewPager parent tag, or **<android. support.v4.view.ViewPager>** as shown in Figure 17-7. Add an android:id parameter and name the ViewPager **planetViewPager** and leave the other default parameters in place, using the following XML markup:

```
<?xml version="1.0" encoding="utf-8"?>
<android.support.v4.view.ViewPager
    xmlns:android=http://schemas.android.com/apk/res/android
    android:id="@+id/planetViewPager"
    android:layout_width="match_parent"
    android:layout_height="match_parent" />
```

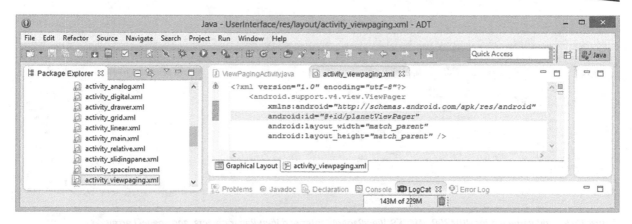

Figure 17-7. Edit the <ViewFlipper> parent tag to make it into a <android.support.v4.view.ViewPager> parent tag

Now you have a ViewPager XML UI definition, which your ViewPagingActivity can reference in a setContentView() method and use for the ViewPager engine.

Now you have everything in place to be able to go back into your bootstrap **ViewPagingActivity. java** class that Eclipse created for you, and start to build out your ViewPager implementation with its PagerAdapter subclass.

Create a ViewPagingActivity Class to Swipe Space Images

Let's set-up our public ViewPagerActivity class, which extends Activity, by adding a half-dozen import statements and a handful of variables at the top of the class, using the following Java code, as shown in Figure 17-8:

```java
import android.app.Activity;
import android.os.Bundle;
import android.os.Parcelable;
import android.support.v4.view.pagerAdapter;
import android.support.v4.view.ViewPager;
import android.view.View;
import android.view.ViewGroup;
import android.widget.ImageView;
public class ViewPagingActivity extends Activity {
    private static int NUMBER_IMAGES = 4;
    private ViewPagerAdapter viewPagerAdapter;
    private ViewPager viewPager;
    private int[] space = { R.drawable.stars480, R.drawable.plasma480,
                            R.drawable.plasma720, R.drawable.plasma1080 };
}
```

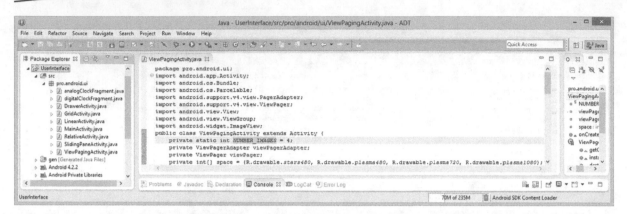

Figure 17-8. *Add variables for NUMBER_IMAGES, ViewPagerAdapter and ViewPager objects, and space[] array*

This sets up everything that we will need to for the onCreate() method and the ViewPagerAdapter class, including all the classes we will be using, and an array count variable named **NUMBER_IMAGES**, your digital image assets array named **space**, your ViewPager object named **viewPager**, and finally a ViewPagerAdapter object named **viewPagerAdapter**.

As you can see in Figure 17-8, your Java code is error-free, and you are ready to create your onCreate() method, where you will set your content view and instantiate the viewPagerAdapter object and the viewPager object.

Create your **public void onCreate()** method, which will call the Superclass .onCreate() method with the saveInstanceState Bundle, as well as using the setContentView() method referencing your new **activity_viewpaging.xml** file in the /res/layout folder.

You'll also create a new **viewPagerAdapter** ViewPagerAdapter object, as well as a **viewPager** ViewPager object that references the ViewPager object XML definition, using the **R.id. planetViewPager** ID.

Finally, to make everything you have set up so far "see" each other, you will wire or connect the viewPager object to the viewPagerAdapter using the **.setAdapter()** method call.

This is accomplished by using the following onCreate() block of Java code inside of your public void onCreate() method, as is shown in Figure 17-9:

```java
public void onCreate(Bundle savedInstanceState){
    super.onCreate(savedInstanceState);
    setContentView(R.layout.activity_viewpaging);
    viewPagerAdapter = new ViewPagerAdapter();
    viewPager = (ViewPager) findViewById(R.id.planetViewPager);

 viewPager.setAdapter(viewPagerAdapter);
}
```

Figure 17-9. Add the onCreate() method and setContentView() method and reference the activity_viewpaging UI

The last line of code is the linchpin here, as it wires or connects your ViewPager object named viewPager to the PagerAdapter object that is named viewPagerAdapter. This is done using the .setAdapter() method call.

This short but important Java statement allows your ViewPager "engine" to talk back and forth with your PagerAdapter object that you have loaded and configured with your space image array and its ImageView UI elements, which you want to page through.

As you can see in Figure 17-9, the code is error-free, and we can proceed!

Next you are going to create a private ViewPagerAdapter class, which contains the methods that we covered earlier in the chapter. These serve to keep track of what ViewPage your user is on and instantiate, destroy, and track your ViewPager objects for the ViewPager viewpaging engine.

Adding ViewPagerAdapter Class to the ViewPagingActivity

The next thing that you need to do is to create a custom class that extends the PagerAdapter class. This is a private class–internal to your ViewPagingActivity Activity subclass–and contains the methods we learned about earlier in the chapter that control the ViewPager engine.

Adding the getCount() Method

The first method we will write is the simplest and the most important, as it tells the ViewPager the boundaries of the ViewPages, that is, first through last, so that when you get to the last page (or back to the first) the ViewPager stops advancing pages.

It's important to note that if you set your getCount() Array to the wrong value, your ViewPager will work until you get to the last page, and then crash. If you want to see this in action, set your NUMBER_IMAGES initial value to 5 instead of 4, and run your application. The Java code to create your ViewPagerAdapter private class and the getCount method is as follows:.

```
private class ViewPagerAdapter extends PagerAdapter {
    @Override
    public int getCount() {
        return NUMBER_IMAGES;
    }
}
```

Adding the .instantiateItem() Method

The next method that you code is the public Object .instantiateItem() method, which is the most complex of the methods we implement.

This method instantiates an ImageView object named **spaceView** and sets it equal to a new (keyword) instance of the ImageView class object and sets its Context object to the ViewPagingActivity class Context using the this keyword (ViewPagingActivity.this).

The method then loads the spaceView ImageView object with the current image asset from the **space[]** Array object using the **.setImageResource()** method and a reference to the space[galaxy] array location.

Finally, the method adds the View to the ViewPager using the **.addView()** method call referencing the spaceView ImageView object, and returns the spaceView ImageView object to the calling function via a **return** statement.

This is all done using seven lines of Java code, as shown in Figure 17-10:

```
@Override
public Object instantiateItem(ViewGroup imageArray, int galaxy) {
    ImageView spaceView = new ImageView(ViewPagingActivity.this);
    spaceView.setImageResource(space[galaxy]);
    ((ViewPager) imageArray).addView(spaceView, 0);
    return spaceView;
}
```

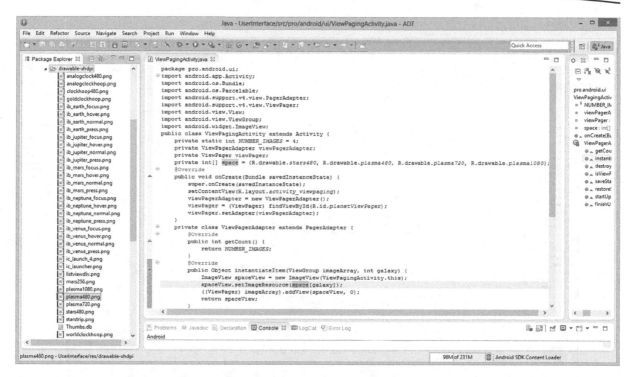

Figure 17-10. *Add a private class named ViewPagerAdapter extending PagerAdapter to your ViewPagingActivity*

Adding the .destroyItem() Method

The next method that you need to write is the **.destroyItem()** method, which essentially does the opposite of the .instantiateItem() method, and removes the View object from the ViewPager object using the **.removeView()** method call. This is done by using the following Java code block for your **public void .destroyItem()** method, as is shown in Figure 17-11:

```
@Override
public void destroyItem(ViewGroup imageArray, int galaxy, Object spaceView) {
    ((ViewPager) imageArray).removeView((ImageView spaceView);
}
```

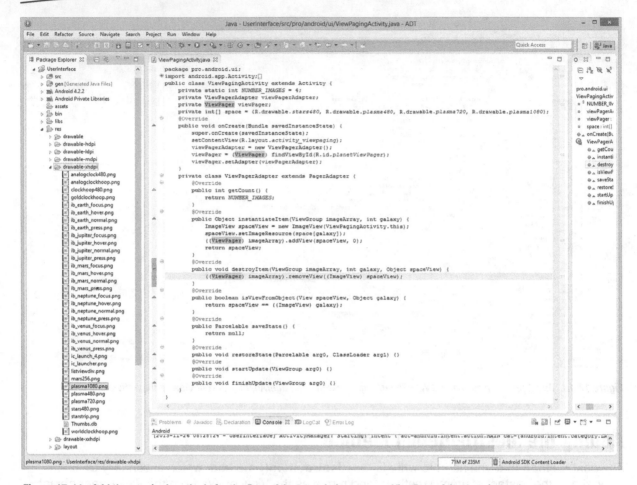

Figure 17-11. Add the required methods for the PagerAdapter subclass to your ViewPagerAdapter private class

Adding the .isViewFromObject() Method

Next, we need to add the **.isViewFromObject()** method, as well as four other methods which all need to be implemented in the PagerAdapter subclass, but which are either shell or "empty" methods, or which return a **null** value.

The .isViewFromObject() method sets the current View, which is an ImageView named spaceView, equal to the galaxy Object and returns it to the caller.

This is accomplished by using the following line of Java code inside of an .isViewFromObject() method structure, as is shown in Figure 17-11:

```
@Override
public boolean isViewFromObject(View spaceView, Object galaxy) {
    return spaceView == ((ImageView) galaxy);
}
```

Adding the public Parcelable .saveState() Method

Next, we will implement your **public Parcelable .saveState()** method, which simply returns a **null** value to the calling entity, as we do not currently need to save any state information regarding our space galaxy image asset.

This is accomplished by using the following Java statement, inside your .saveState() method structure, as is shown in Figure 17-11:

```java
@Override
public Parcelable saveState() {
    return null;
}
```

Adding .restoreState(), .startUpdate(), and .finishUpdate()

The .restoreState(), as well as the .startUpdate() and .finishUpdate() methods, are all added next, and all are empty, so they will simply refer to the same methods implemented in the PagerActivity Superclass.

These classes are implemented using the following Java code, as shown in Figure 17-11:

```java
@Override
public void restoreState(Parcelable arg0, ClassLoader arg1) {

}
@Override
public void startUpdate(ViewGroup arg0) {
}
@Override
public void finishUpdate(ViewGroup arg0) {
}
```

As you can see, if you allow Eclipse to create your ViewPagerAdapter PagerAdapter subclass for you by mousing over the wavy red underline highlighting that appears when you write your viewPagerAdapter = new ViewPagerAdapter(); line of code, and select the **Create private class ViewPagerAdapter** option, Eclipse writes all these empty methods for you using these arg0, arg1, arg2, arg3, and so on variables. You can rename these later, as you wish, as I have done in this private class example code.

Testing Your Galaxy Digital Image Asset Paging UI Interface

Now it is time to test your galaxy digital image asset paging UI interface using the Nexus One emulator, and see how well it works. Use your **Run As > Android Application** work process and

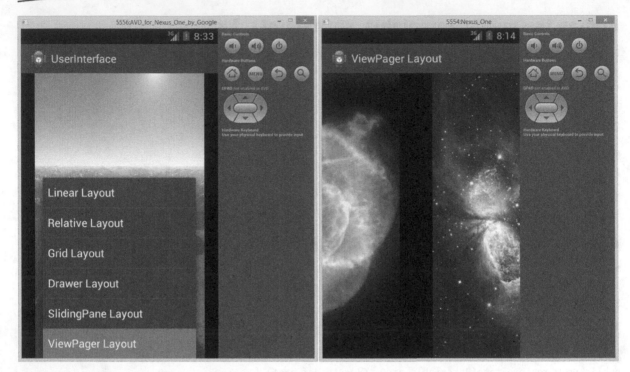

Figure 17-12. Testing the ViewPagingActivityand the space ImageView objects (swipe at right) in the Nexus One

launch the emulator and click the **MENU** button at the top left of the emulator panel and open the app's menu and select the **ViewPager Layout** menu item as shown on the left side of Figure 17-12.

When the first stars480.png ViewPage image appears, drag the ViewPager to the right and you will see that the other three galaxy images appear, and that once you get to the end (fourth) image, your ViewPager will no longer drag to the right, but will drag back through the four images to the left, until it stops at the first stars480 space image.

Summary

In this chapter, you learned about the Android **ViewPager** class and how to set-up an XML UI design definition using this viewpaging class.

You looked at the **PagerAdapter** class, which was designed specifically to provide the functionality that the ViewPager class requires to manage View Pages for your application, and the 15 methods that can be used to manage ViewPager content, eight of which we implemented in your UI app.

Next, we created the **ViewPagingActivity** class and a **ViewPagerAdapter** class to implement everything that you learned about in the chapter, and then created a space images ViewPager UI design within your UserInterface application.

In the next chapter, we'll take a closer look at the Android **PagerTabStrip and PagerTitleStrip** classes, and see how you can use these UI classes to allow your users to flip through pages on your application's TitleBar UI.

18

Android's PagerTitleStrip and PagerTabStrip: ViewPager Navigation UI

Android has two additional classes that can be used to enhance **ViewPager** UI designs. These are **PagerTitleStrip** and **PagerTabStrip**, which are used to provide Tab or Title UI elements to the Viewpager, as you may have guessed from the names of these classes.

I will cover both of these classes in this chapter, so that you will have a full understanding of what is available for use with your ViewPager apps UI design. I will discuss the PagerTitleStrip class first, as it is fairly straightforward to add to your existing ViewPager application you created in the previous Chapter 17. We will look at the PagerTitleStrip class, and then add the PagerTitleStrip functionality to your ViewPagerAdapter class.

After that I cover using the PagerTabStrip class, which can be more complicated to implement, especially using ActionBar Tab objects, which we will also get into in this chapter. In that way, by the time you get to the end of this book (the end of this chapter) you'll have experience implementing a ViewPager engine and its related classes using both the Activity and the ActionBar Tab UI design approach.

We are going to add a PagerTitleStrip onto your current ViewPagingActivity class to add text labels at the top (or bottom) of your ViewPager screens.

After that we're going to add a PagerTabStrip to your implementation, to show you how all that is done using the classes that we have covered over the past two chapters. So we will start with the simple PagerTitleStrip addition to the current ViewPager, and then create the more complex PagerTabStrip UI.

The PagerTitleStrip Class: Horizontal Sliding Screen Titles

The Android **PagerTitleStrip** class is a UI layout container class that was also introduced in Android Version 4.0, to provide support and enhancement for enhancing UI designs targeting the new V4 ViewPager viewpaging engine.

The PagerTitleStrip class provides developers with a text-based, static or non-interactive indicator of your current, next, and previous ViewPages in your ViewPager UI design and implementation.

A PagerTitleStrip class hierarchy starts with a Java Object master class, and progresses from the Android View class to the Android ViewGroup class to the PagerTitleStrip class. The Android PagerTitleStrip class is part of an **android.support.v4.view** package, and is structured via the following class hierarchy:

```
java.lang.Object
 > android.view.View
   > android.view.ViewGroup
     > android.support.v4.view.PagerTitleStrip
```

This Android PagerTitleStrip class is a **public class,** and it extends the **ViewGroup** superclass. It is referenced using a specialized **support.v4.view** package, using an **import android.support. v4.view.PagerTitleStrip** statement.

The import statement reference also indicates that a PagerTitleStrip class is indeed a layout container, and not a UI widget. If it were a UI widget, it would be included as a part of the support. v4.widget package.

This PagerTitleStrip UI layout design is also commonly used in conjunction with the **PagerAdapter** class, which we learned about in Chapter 17 where we covered the ViewPager class, constants, and layout parameters.

The PagerTitleStrip UI container is specified using XML as a child view of the ViewPager widget, thus it is intended to be used "underneath" or under the control of your ViewPager viewpaging engine implementation.

To implement a PagerTitleStrip object for your ViewPager, simply add it as the child UI element inside your ViewPager. This is done using your XML layout container file definition, as you will see in the next section.

To locate your PagerTitleStrip UI element at the top or the bottom of your ViewPager UI design, you would set its android:layout_gravity to a TOP or a BOTTOM constant, respectively.

The titles for your ViewPages are supplied by using the method call to a **.getPageTitle()** method located in your custom PagerAdapter object. For a private ViewPagerAdapter class, such as the one that you supplied to your ViewPager object, this represents adding the additional method to the ones that you created in Chapter 17.

If you want to provide an interactive ViewPage indicator, you will want to implement a **PagerTabStrip**, which is why we'll also be discussing this class in the second half of this chapter.

It's important to note that these two classes can also be used at the same time, so if you want to be extremely thorough, you could use this fact to provide a longer PagerTitleStrip UI text value for each of your more concise PagerTabStrip UI text values.

Table 18-1 provides a list of the method calls that can be utilized with the PagerTitleStrip class. You will implement most of them in this chapter to create your PagerTitleStrip and ViewPager marriage.

Table 18-1. PagerTitleStrip Public Method Calls and their Return Data Type, Along with What Each One Is Used For

Method Type and Name	Method Used For
void setGravity()	Sets Gravity used to position text within TitleStrip
void setTextSize()	Sets the default text size to a given unit and value
void setTextColor()	Sets a color value used for all displayed page titles
void setTextSpacing()	Sets the required spacing between the title segments
void getTextSpacing()	Returns the current spacing between the title segments
Void setNonPrimaryAlpha()	Sets the alpha value to use in non-primary page title
Void requestLayout()	Called when something changes which invalidates layout

You'll set gravity in your XML UI file using an **android:gravity** parameter, and use the next three (and sixth) method calls listed using Java. There are four **protected methods** for this class, which are shown in Table 18-2.

Table 18-2. PagerTitleStrip Protected Method Calls and their Return Types, Along with What Each One Is Used For

Method Type and Name	Method Used For
void onAttachedToWindow()	Method is called when the View is attached to a window
void onDetachedFromWindow()	Method is called when a View is detached from a window
void onMeasure()	Measure View to determine its measured width and height
void onLayout()	Call from Layout for View to assign a size and position

These methods are used to run custom code for your PagerTitleStrip object, when it's added or removed, or when you need to determine width and height measurements for it, or when you need to adjust child UI element position.

Loading the PagerTitleStrip Data: Create a String[ ] Array

The best way to learn about all the parameters and methods is to get right down to business using them, so open your UserInterface project in Eclipse and right-click the ViewPagingActivity.java class shown in Figure 18-1, and use the **Open** command to open it for editing in a tab in Eclipse ADT.

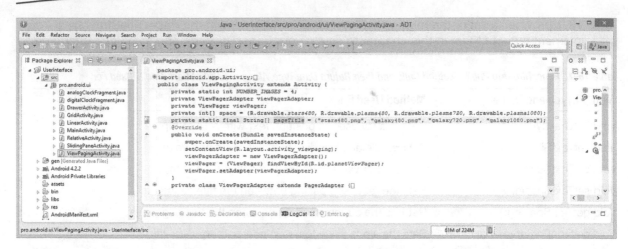

Figure 18-1. Open the ViewPagingActivity.java file, add a String[ ] Array named pageTitle with filename values

The foundation for your PagerTitleStrip implemention is a database of page title values, held in an Array object of type String[ ] that you will name **pageTitle**, and which you'll load with the filenames of the galaxy and star images currently displayed using your ViewPager UI design.

Make this array **private**, so only this class can access it, as well as both **static** and **final**, so it remains fixed (immutable) in system memory and cannot be altered by any other function within your UserInterface app.

The Java code to achieve this can be implemented using a single statement:

```
private static final String[] pageTitle = { "stars480.png", "galaxy480.png",
                                            "stars720.png", "galaxy1080.png" };
```

Now that you have your two arrays, one integer and one String, which reference your space images and their text titles, you will need to make sure they match up as far as their data array order is concerned.

As you can see in Figure 18-1, this is quite easy to do, as the filenames used in your R.drawable reference path in the space array and in the pageTitle array are the same, as you are using the filenames to label each of your digital image assets which your are using for this example.

Now that your pageTitle PagerTitleStrip text title values are in place and in the correct order, we can add the **.getPageTitle()** method to the private ViewPagerAdapter class pagerAdapter subclass so the ViewPager can use it.

Calling the PagerTitleStrip Layout: .getPageTitle() Method

Click the + icon that is next to your private ViewPagerAdapter class shown in Figure 18-1, and open up the class for editing as shown in Figure 18-2.

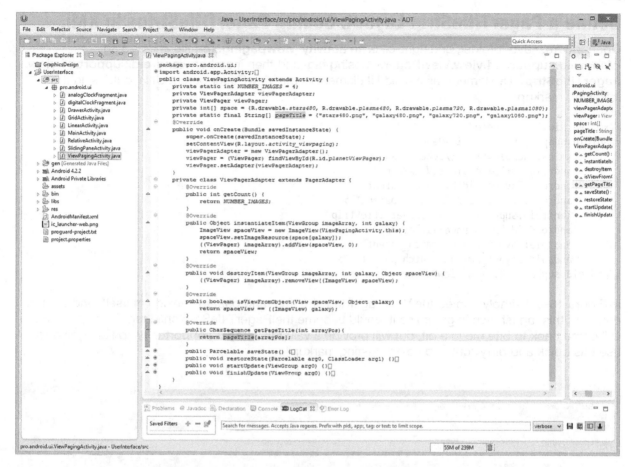

Figure 18-2. *Add a .getPageTitle() method that returns the current arrayPos (position) in the pageTitle Array*

Add the **public CharSequence getPageTitle()** method, I added one right after the **.isViewFromObject()** method structure, using the following Java code:

```java
@Override
public CharSequence getPageTitle(int arrayPos){
    return pageTitle[arrayPos];
}
```

This returns the array position (an integer) for the current title in the pageTitle (String) array, matching the current ViewPage with its title.

Next, you will need to define your <PagerTitleStrip> in an XML definition.

Define a PagerTitleStrip Layout: Coding PagerTitleStrips in XML

Open the /res/layout folder, and right-click an **activity_viewpaging.xml** file and add an **</android.support.v4.view.ViewPager>** closing tag, and then insert an **<android.support.v4.view. PagerTitleStrip>** UI element, as a child UI element of the ViewPager parent UI layout, using the following markup:

```xml
<?xml version="1.0" encoding="utf-8"?>
<android.support.v4.view.ViewPager
        xmlns:android=http://schemas.android.com/apk/res/android
        android:id="@+id/planetViewPager"
        android:layout_width="match_parent"
        android:layout_height="match_parent" >
        <android.support.v4.view.PagerTitleStrip
        android:id="@+id/pagerTitleStrip"
        android:layout_width="match_parent"
        android:layout_height="match_parent" />
</android.support.v4.view.ViewPager>
```

In Figure 18-3, I simply copied the ViewPager tag structure and pasted it inside of itself, and then changed this tag (shown in green) so it would become the PagerTitleStrip child tag. This approach will come back to bite me in a bit, but will provide a valuable learning opportunity so I am going to use this quick and dirty "cut and paste existing markup".

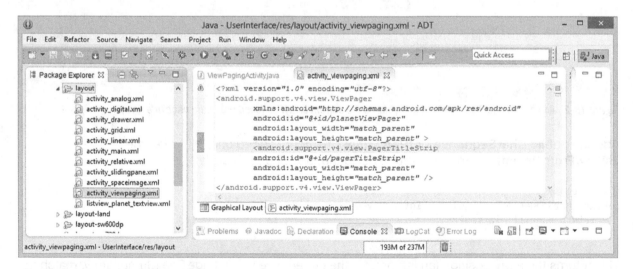

Figure 18-3.   Create a <android.support.v4.view.PagerTitleStrip> child tag inside of the ViewPager parent tag

The <android.support.v4.view.PagerTitleStrip> tag needs to be a child tag inside your <android. support.v4.view.ViewPager> parent tag because the PagerTitleStrip UI is part of your ViewPager UI definition.

This is because the PagerTitleStrip UI is "attached" to the ViewPager engine, and becomes a part of your seamless Pro Android UI design.

Testing Your ViewPagingActivity Class with PagerTitleStrip

Right-click the project folder and use the **Run As ➤ Android Application** work process to launch the Nexus One emulator. Click the **MENU** UI button and select the **ViewPager Layout** MenuItem located at the bottom of the menu, which then launches your ViewPager UI design, as shown in Figure 18-4.

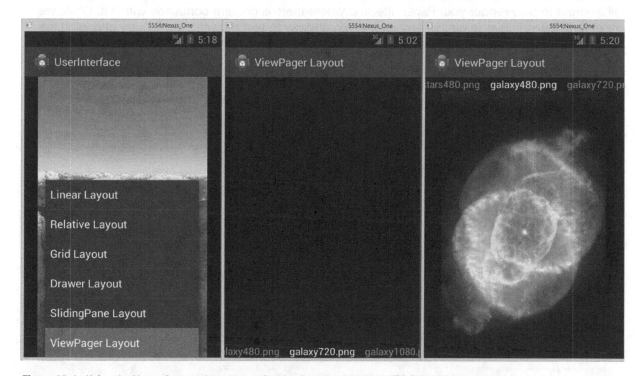

Figure 18-4. Using the Nexus One emulator to test the ViewPager and its PagerTitleStrip UI implementation

Notice that in the center pane of the screenshot, your PagerTitleStrip is now in place, but the space images in your ViewPager have disappeared!

Either something's wrong in the Java code that is preventing the ViewPager from displaying, or something is wrong in your PagerTitleStrip definition, in your activity_viewpaging.xml UI definition XML file.

Since you haven't changed your Java code for the ViewPager, take a look at your XML definition for the new PagerTitleStrip child tag UI element that you added, since the problem started happening after you added the markup.

As you copied the ViewPager tag and changed the tag name and an android:ID parameter, which must be correct as the PagerTitleStrip is displaying, the problem must be with the android:layout_width or android:layout_height.

We know that the android:layout_width is correct, as we want the UI design to fill your screen from side to side, which it is, so the problem must be with your android:layout_height parameter. This parameter is currently set to MATCH_PARENT, which tells the PagerTitleStrip to fill the height of the display, which may well be the problem that we are seeing right now.

So the question becomes: Does the PagerTitleStrip UI have a higher z-order than the ViewPager UI? If so, it would be rendered on top of, or over, the ViewPager, and thus a MATCH_PARENT layout_height parameter would draw your PagerTitleStrip over the ViewPager image assets, like closing the venetian blinds at night would obscure your view of all the beautiful night stars.

The solution here, of course, is to use the **WRAP_CONTENT** constant instead. This constant will tell Android to only render your PagerTitleStrip where there is content contained within it. While we are at it, since we have to run our emulator again anyway to test the solution, let's try changing the **android:gravity** parameter to a value of **top**, and put our titles on the top of the screen for a change.

As you can observe in Figure 18-4, this fixes your problem and lets your stars and galaxy images shine (glow?) through. The PagerTitleStrip is now at the top of your UI design, and everything is working together very well, using only a dozen lines of XML markup, as shown in Figure 18-5.

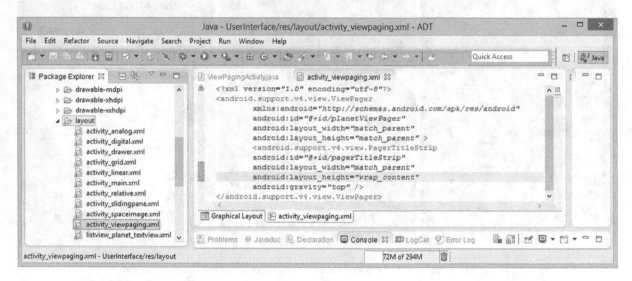

Figure 18-5.   Change the android:layout_height parameter to use a WRAP_CONTENT constant to solve problem

Now that the basic UI design is in place, you can use the methods that I outlined in Table 18-1 earlier in the chapter to configure the UI design.

You do this using Java method calls, as these parameters are not yet available in the XML editor helper dialog, and because you need experience with setting these UI design parameters using your Java code, in case you want to do it this way, or to make these settings interactive using Java!

Configuring the PagerTitleStrip: Using Java Methods

The first thing we will do is to instantiate your final access modifier (so it can't be altered) PagerTitleStrip object named pagerTitle and load it with your UI definition using the findViewById() method call. This can be done using the following line of Java code, as is shown in Figure 18-6:

```
final PagerTitleStrip pagerTitle = (PagerTitleStrip) findViewById(R.id.pagerTitleStrip);
```

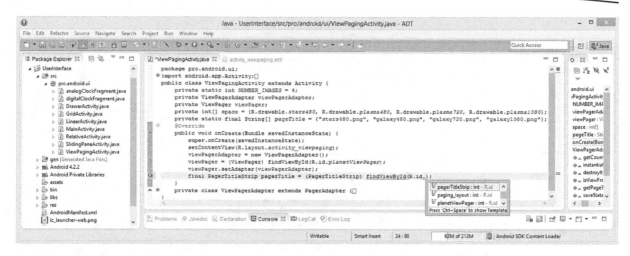

Figure 18-6. Adding a final PagerTitleStrip named pagerTitle and instantiating it using the findViewById() method

As you can see in Figure 18-6, if you type in the "**R.id.**" part of the path to your XML definitions, Eclipse will open a helper dialog, containing all your ID values for your project, which is dozens at this point in time.

Now that this final pagerTitle PagerTitleStrip object has been declared, instantiated, and loaded with the UI design base definition, the object can be used to call those four different methods that will allow you to set up your TextSize, TextColor, TextSpacing, and your Non-Primary (non-current title) Alpha Channel values for the PagerTitleStrip UI element for the ViewPager.

Set the TextSize Parameter

The first parameter we will set is your TextSize, as this is an important parameter for visibility for end-users. Add a line of space under the pagerTitle object declaration and type in the pagerTitle object name, and then add the **.setTextSize()** method call using dot notation.

This is done using the following line of Java, shown in Figure 18-7:

```
pagerTitle.setTextSize(TypedValue.COMPLEX_UNIT_SP, 12);
```

As shown in Figure 18-7 Eclipse opens a helper dialog containing the **TypedValue** constants for defining what method of Text sizing you would like to use. Find and select a **Standard Pixels SP** constant value as shown.

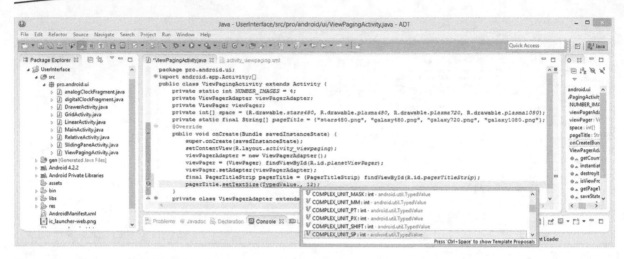

Figure 18-7. Use a pagerTitle PagerTitleStrip object to call the .setTextSize() method using TypedValue constant

Set the TextColor Parameter

The next most impactive parameter that you can set is the TextColor, using the **.setTextColor()** method call. You implement this in the same way, by calling it off the pagerTitle object using the following Java code:

```
pagerTitle.setTextColor(Color.CYAN);
```

In Figure 18-8, once you type the **Color** class and a **period** inside your method parameter area, Eclipse brings up a list of all the Android Color class color constant values from which you can select. I selected **CYAN** for readability, but GREEN would look great with your galaxy image content that you are using, as would YELLOW or WHITE.

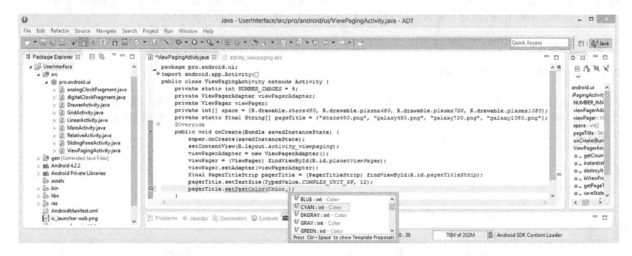

Figure 18-8. Use a pagerTitle PagerTitleStrip object to call the .setTextColor() method using a Color constant

Let's take a moment to use the **Run As ➤ Android Application** work process, and take a look at your **12SP** TextSize and **CYAN** TextColor setting results.

Testing Your 12SP TextSize and CYAN TextColor Setting Results

As you can see in Figure 18-9, in the left and center panes, the 12SP TextSize takes the title out of the way of the content, which is good, and the CYAN TextColor makes your title look a little bit more like it belongs in space. On the right side you can see the TextSpacing setting, which you will implement next, after you change your Alpha setting, from the default 50% opacity to a **64%** opacity setting. This makes (unused) image titles on either side of the current image title (label) more visible in your UI design. You can see the slight difference in the opacity setting among the left pane and the other (CYAN) pane images for the unused title opacity.

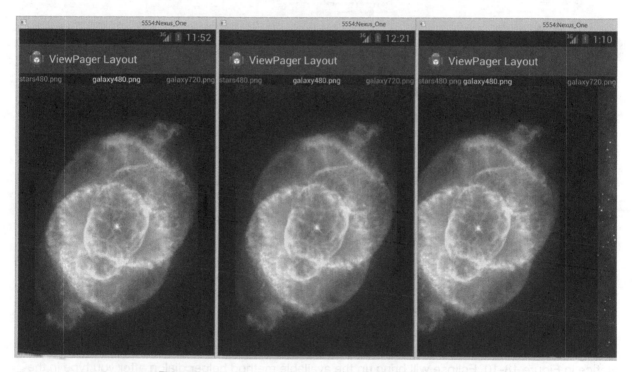

Figure 18-9. Testing the pagerTitle object's TextSize, TextColor, and TextSpacing parameters in the Nexus One

To set your **Non-Primary Alpha** value (your non-current titles dimming value) for your PagerTitleStrip UI element, use a float data value (0.64f) within the following single line of Java code, which can be seen in Figure 18-10:

```
pagerTitle.setNonPrimaryAlpha(0.64f);
```

Figure 18-10. *Use a pagerTitle PagerTitleStrip object to call a .setTextSpacing() method using a number of pixels*

Set the TextSpacing Parameter

Finally, we will set the TextSpacing parameter using a Java method call to the **.setTextSpacing()** method. On first glance, you might think that this parameter adjusts the spacing between the titles now located at the top of your UI design. However, it does not control this spacing, Android OS does this for you by splitting your titles hard left, center, and hard right, as you will see in Figure 18-9 on the left and center panes. What TextSpacing controls is the spacing between your primary (center) title and the side (non-primary) titles, **while your user is dragging the ViewPager**.

This can be seen in the right pane of Figure 18-9, and you can see in the screenshot that your ViewPager is being dragged (see image position).

Thus the integer pixel value is split in half (so use an even number) and placed on either side of the PagerTitle container. To get these titles to almost touch (a two pixel gap) I will use a value of **4** (pixels) in this **.setTextSpacing()** method call. The objective can be accomplished using the following simple line of Java code, which is shown in Figure 18-10:

```
pagerTitle.setTextSpacing(4);
```

Notice in Figure 18-10, Eclipse will bring up the available method helper dialog after you type in the **pagerTitle** object name, and then hit a **period** key. Find the **.setTextSpacing(int spacingPixels)** method and double-click it, to insert it into your Java statement, and then add a "4" value.

Next, test the completed PagerTitleStrip UI in the Nexus One so we can learn about how to implement a more interactive PagerTabStrip UI.

The PagerTabStrip Class: Horizontal Sliding Screen Tabs

The Android **PagerTabStrip** class is a **Tab-based UI** layout container class that was also introduced in Android Version 4.0, to provide support and enhancement for creating UI designs for the ViewPager viewpaging engine using ActionBar-like Tab UI elements.

This PagerTabStrip class provides developers with a Tab-based, **dynamic**, or **fully-interactive**, indicator of your current, next, and previous ViewPages in your ViewPager UI design and implementation. If you click one of the PagerTabStrip Tab UI elements, it will animate the swipe, which your users would have to do manually, if you were only using the PagerTitleStrip UI.

The PagerTabStrip class hierarchy begins with a Java Object master class, and progresses from the Android View class, to the Android ViewGroup class to the PagerTitleStrip UI class and finally to the PagerTabStrip UI class.

The Android PagerTabStrip class is also part of an **android.support.v4.view** package, and thus it is structured using the following class hierarchy:

```
java.lang.Object
  > android.view.View
    > android.view.ViewGroup
      > android.support.v4.view.PagerTitleStrip
        > android.support.v4.view.PagerTabStrip
```

This Android PagerTabStrip UI class is a **public class,** and it extends the **PagerTitleStrip** class that we learned about previously in this chapter. It is referenced using a specialized **support.v4.view** package, using an **import android.support.v4.view.PagerTabStrip** statement.

The import statement reference also indicates that the PagerTabStrip class is indeed a layout container, and not a UI widget. If it were a UI widget, it would be included as a part of the android.support.v4.widget package.

Like a PagerTitleStrip, a PagerTabStrip UI layout design is also commonly used in conjunction with the **PagerAdapter** class, which we learned about in Chapter 17 when we covered ViewPager related classes, constants, and layout parameters. Because the PagerTabAdapter builds on top of the PagerTitleStrip class and its methods and capabilities, it was logical for me to cover the PagerTitleAdapter first, so we can build on a Java programming structure that we have already put in place.

The PagerTabStrip UI container is also specified using XML as a child view of the ViewPager widget. It's also intended to be used underneath or under the control of your ViewPager viewpaging engine implementation. However as we now know, it is actually being placed "on top of" the ViewPager, in the UI design (z-order) sense, so we'll keep that in mind as we continue to UI design our ViewPager implemention during the rest of this chapter.

To implement the PagerTabStrip object for your ViewPager, simply add it as the child UI element inside your ViewPager. This is done using your XML layout container file definition, as you'll soon see in the next section.

Like the PagerTitleStrip, to locate a PagerTabStrip UI element at the top, or the bottom, of your ViewPager UI design, you set **android:layout_gravity** to the TOP or the BOTTOM constant value, respectively.

The Tabs for your ViewPages are supplied by using the method call to a **.getPageTitle()** method located within your custom PagerAdapter object. For your private ViewPagerAdapter class, such as the one that you supplied to your ViewPager object, this would represent adding an additional method to the ones that you created in Chapter 17.

Since you have already done this for the PagerTitleStrip, you will utilize this same infrastructure as you upgrade to a PagerTabStrip implementation.

I have compiled a table of the method calls that can be utilized with the PagerTabStrip class, shown in Table 18-3. I've left out the method calls that are inherited from the PagerTitleStrip class from this particular table, as those have already been listed previously in Table 18-1.

Table 18-3. *PagerTabStrip Public Method Calls and their Return Data Type, Along With What Each One Is Used For*

Method Type and Name	Method Used For
void setBackgroundColor()	Sets background Color for the PagerTabStrip UI element
void setBackgroundResource()	Sets background Drawable for PagerTabStrip UI element
void setTabIndicatorColor()	Sets the Color for the PagerTabStrip Tab indicator bar
void getTabIndicatorColor()	Gets the Color for the PagerTabStrip Tab indicator bar
void setPadding()	Sets up four Padding values for your PagerTabStrip UI
void setDrawFullUnderline()	Sets a full-width underline for your PagerTabStrip UI
Void getDrawFullUnderline()	Gets a full-width underline setting for PagerTabStrip
Boolean onTouch()	Implements for custom touchscreen motion event handling

I've also left out a currently deprecated **.setBackgroundDrawable()** method call, as it is no longer supported in Android. If you want to implement a Background Image Drawable–as you'll be doing a bit later on in the chapter–you will want to utilize the **.setBackgroundResource()** method call.

You'll be implementing the first four of these in the next section of this chapter, in order to further enhance your PagerTabStrip UI using your Java code foundation that you created for your PagerTitleStrip implementation.

Morph a PagerTitleStrip UI into a PagerTabStrip UI Design

Because you don't need both a PagerTitleStrip and a PagerTabStrip, you are going to "morph" your PagerTitleStrip implementation into a PagerTabStrip UI design. This is especially logical as a PagerTabStrip class is a close relative of (subclassed from) the PagerTitleStrip, so everything you have in place will work well, and all the code you have written so far will be necessary for your PagerTabStrip implementation.

This allows you to focus on those UI design elements for PagerTabStrip which differ from, or further enhance, the PagerTitleStrip UI design.

Morphing Your XML UI Definition

The first thing you will need to do is to edit your **activity_viewpaging** UI definition XML file, and change your PagerTitleStrip UI child tag, and its ID value, to be a PagerTabStrip child tag and ID as shown in Figure 18-11.

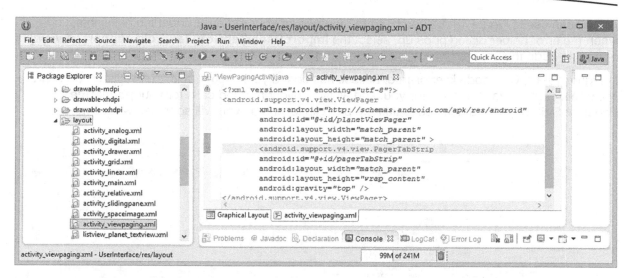

Figure 18-11. Change the PagerTitleStrip child tag into a PagerTabStrip child tag in your activity_viewpaging.xml

Morphing Your Java UI Definition

You'll make a similar modification in your Java code, changing your final PagerTitleStrip instantiation into a final PagerTabStrip instantiation, as shown in Figure 18-12. Notice that you keep your **pagerTitle** object name the same, so that all the method calls off this object do not need to be edited because the PagerTitleStrip methods are inherited by the PagerTabStrip class. This is one of the cool things with Java inheritance!

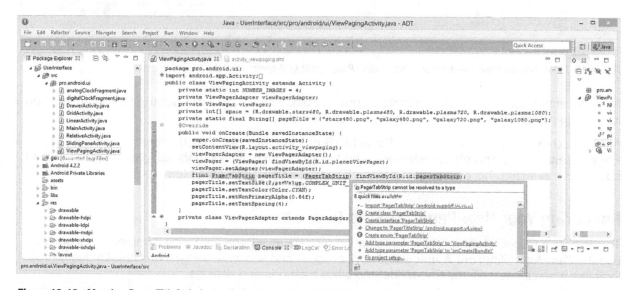

Figure 18-12. Morph a PagerTitleStrip instantiation into a PagerTabStrip instantiation referencing pagerTabStrip

As you can see in Figure 18-12, you need to mouse-over your red error underline highlights, and when the error helper dialog pops up, select the **Import PagerTabStrip (android.support.v4.view)** option, to code the import.

In Figure 18-13, your code is error-free, Eclipse has coded your import android.support.v4.view. PagerTabStrip; Java statement for you, and all five of your method calls for your **pagerTitle** PagerTabStrip object are deemed legitimate by Eclipse, and as you will soon see work perfectly.

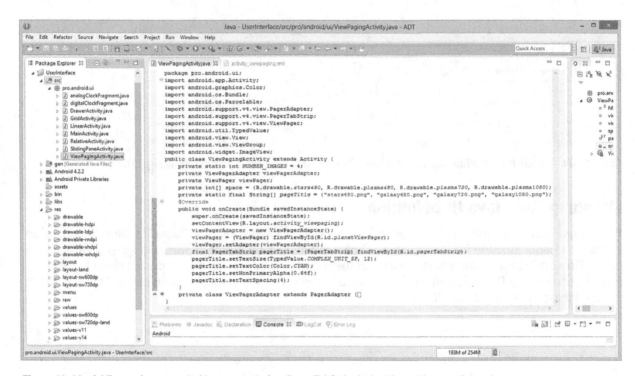

Figure 18-13. Adding an import android.support.v4.view.PagerTabStrip declaration at the top of the class

Now the entire code infrastructure that you put into place for your PagerTitleStrip UI implementation is working perfectly for your PagerTabStrip implementation.

All you had to do was to change your PagerTitleStrip class (and an object) reference to be a PagerTabStrip class and object reference, and to use the UI definition android:id pagerTabStrip (you could have even left this as a pagerTitleStrip ID value, if you had wanted to).

Rendering Your New PagerTabStrip UI

To see how a PagerTitleStrip UI implementation renders as a PagerTabStrip UI implementation, let's use the **Run As ➤ Android Application** work process and see what a PagerTabStrip UI design will look like when it use only the PagerTitleStrip class methods and settings.

As shown in Figure 18-14, the PagerTabStrip UI adds an ActionBar Tab "look and feel" to your UI design, as well as interactivity. To test this interactivity, click the other PagerTitle (now PagerTab) translucent UI elements, and watch the ViewPager screens animate on their own! As you can observe in Figure 18-14, some of the UI design elements that worked well with the PagerTitleStrip need to be fine-tuned for your PagerTabStrip UI.

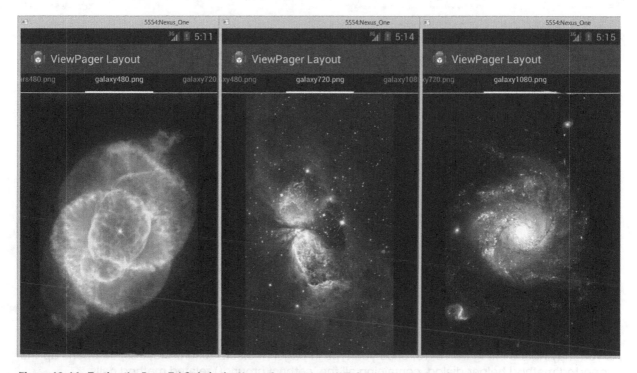

Figure 18-14. Testing the PagerTabStrip in the Nexus One emulator AVD for the three galaxy images

Let's start with the **.setBackgroundColor()** method call, since this is a UI design element that you might want to use to make your PagerTabStrip look more like an ActionBar filled with Tab UI elements.

To set the Background Color value for the PagerTabStrip, use the following line of Java code to invoke this method call, as is shown in Figure 18-15:

```
pagerTitle.setBackgroundColor(Color.DKGRAY);
```

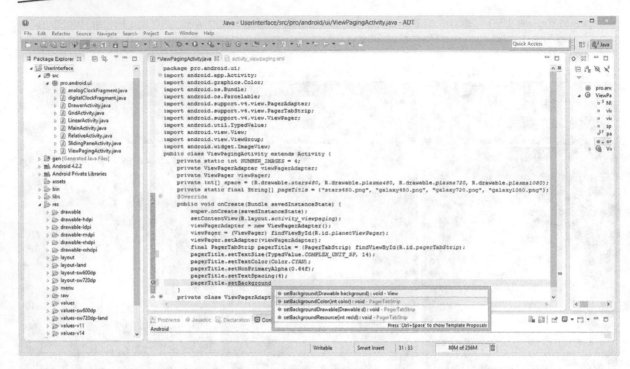

Figure 18-15. Use pagerTitle PagerTabStrip object to call .setBackgroundColor() method, using a Color constant

As you may notice in Figure 18-15, once you type in pagerTitle.setBackground, Eclipse opens up the supported method helper dialog, containing all the .setbackground() related method calls.

As you can see, this even includes the deprecated ones, which we will not be using, as they are no longer supported in Android. Double-click the .setBackgroundColor(int Color) method option to insert it, and then type **Color** inside it and a period, which brings up a helper dialog with all the OS supported Color class values. I selected the **DKGRAY** value, as that is the standard theme color value for an ActionBar UI element.

Defining Custom Colors for Your PagerTabStrip

Now that your PagerTabStrip has a dark gray background color, let's add a bit of color to your PagerTabStrip's Tab indicator UI element by using the **.setTabIndicatorColor()** method call. I am trying to include all the method calls to set UI design configuration parameters using Java for both the PagerTitleStrip and PagerTabStrip classes, so you are familiar with them.

Next, add another line of code, and type **pagerTitle.setT** that will open up a dialog in Eclipse which has all of the method calls that start with .setT, such as the **.setTabIndicatorColor()** method, as is shown in Figure 18-16.

Figure 18-16. *Use pagerTitle PagerTabStrip object and .setT to call .setTabIndicatorColor() method, using a Color constant*

It is important to notice that this Eclipse method helper dialog tells you exactly which classes these methods belong to–in this case it will be the View, ViewGroup, PagerTitleStrip, or PagerTabStrip class. These are from the PagerTabStrip class hierarchy we learned about in the previous section of this chapter.

Double-click the **.setTabIndicatorColor(int color)** method, and insert it into your Java code. Then type in the Color class reference, and a period, which brings up the Color constant helper dialog. Select **YELLOW** as the Android OS Color constant, as is shown In Figure 18-17.

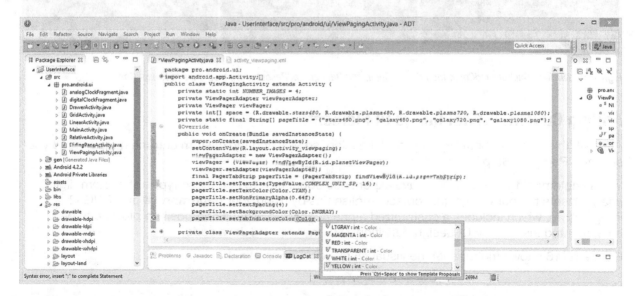

Figure 18-17. *Use pagerTitle PagerTabStrip object to call .setTabIndicatorColor() method with YELLOW constant*

Since you have added a couple of custom Color values to your UI elements, go ahead and use your **Run As ➤ Android Application** work process, and you can launch your app in the Nexus One emulator for a round of testing.

As you may notice in Figure 18-18, the dark grey background color (left pane) and the yellow indicator bar treatment (center pane) look great, and you can now proceed to add more custom UI elements, as well as tweak font size and spacing, to your PagerTabStrip UI design, which we are going to do in the next section regarding how to add custom image-based UI elements using image compositing work processes and parameters.

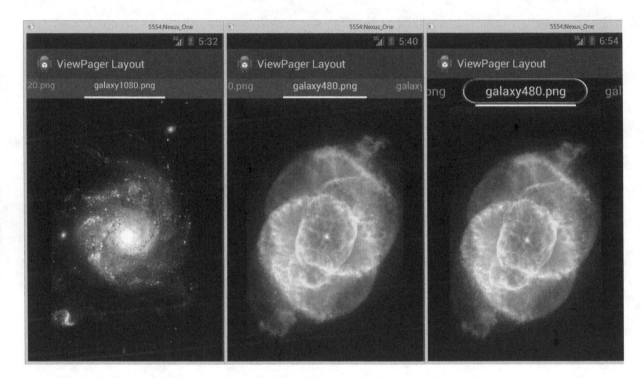

Figure 18-18. Test BackgroundColor, TabIndicatorColor, and BackgroundResource method calls in Nexus One

Adding Custom Digital Image UI Elements

After all, this book is about Pro Android UI design, so let's add the custom chrome hoop around your selected PagerTabStrip Tab indicator.

You'll implement this so that you have experience about how to add these types of custom digital image assets to your UI design. You accomplish this by using your **pagetaboval.png** PNG32 image asset, which includes a customized alpha channel to allow a compositing pipeline to be implemented inside your UI design definition XML markup and Java code.

Figure 18-18 shows (right pane) the visual result you'll be creating!

Using Image Compositing in Your PagerTabStrip UI Design

Add another line of Java code, and then type in **pagerTitle.setBackground** and find the **.setBackgroundResource(int resId)** method in the method helper dialog, as is shown in Figure 18-19.

Figure 18-19. Use pagerTitle PagerTabStrip object to call .setBackgroundResource() method, using a resId

Double-click this method call, and then type in an uppercase **R** denoting the Android OS Resource area, and then type in a **period**, which brings up yet another resource path helper dialog.

Find the **drawable** resource bucket or area, and double-click that to add it to the resource path, which you are creating through the use of Eclipse helper dialogs for this **.setbackgroundResource()** method call.

After this R.drawable has been added by your Eclipse resource path helper dialog, type in another period to bring up a list of all the drawable assets in your project. In this case, these are digital image assets, and in particular you are looking for the **pagetaboval.png** image asset. Be sure that you have copied this asset, from this book's resource files available on the Apress.com website. into your **/res/drawable-xhdpi** folder and then use the **Refresh** menu option so Eclipse can see that you have added this image asset into your project hierarchy.

Find your **pagetaboval** Drawable in the list in the pop-up helper dialog, as shown in Figure 18-20, and double-click it to add it to the path reference that you are creating for this .setbackgroundResource() method call.

Figure 18-20. Use pagerTitle PagerTabStrip object to call .setBackgroundResource() method, using pagetaboval

The final tweak we need to do to achieve the UI design shown on the right side of Figure 18-18 is to scale up your TextSize parameter to 24 pixels, to better fit inside of this new chrome oval UI decoration element.

You also need to add in some Padding, using the **.setPadding()** method call, to better center your Tab's title element within this chrome oval.

To accomplish this use a Padding Top value of 10 pixels. This is done using the **.setPadding(Left, Top, Right, Bottom)** method call format, using the following single line of Java code, as seen in Figure 18-21:

```
pagerTitle.setPadding(0, 10, 0, 0);
```

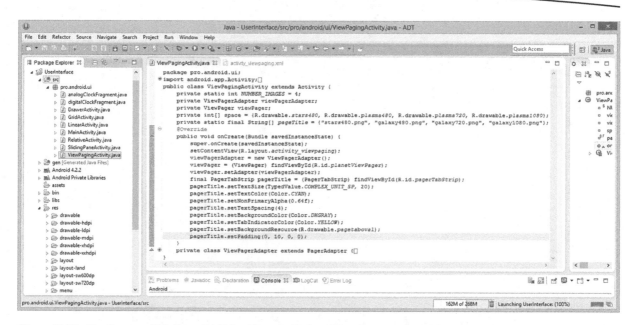

Figure 18-21. Use the pagerTitle PagerTabStrip object to call the .setPadding() method, using four integer values

Now you've fully implemented a PagerTabStrip for your ViewPager UI design!

Summary

In this final chapter, you learned all about the Android **PagerTitleStrip** and **PagerTabStrip** classes, and how they can be used to add to your ViewPager UI design.

You first looked at a **PagerTitleStrip** class, which was designed to provide title capabilities to a ViewPager class. You learned about 11 methods, which can be used to manage PagerTitleStrip content. You implemented four of these methods to create the PagerTitleStrip in your UserInterface app.

Next, you learned all about the **PagerTabStrip** class and its eight method calls, and you then morphed your PagerTitleStrip UI implementation into a PagerTabStrip implementation.

I that hope you all have enjoyed *Pro Android UI* and our exploration of some of the most popular Android User Interface classes, concepts, and implementations, as much as I've enjoyed writing it!

Index

W

X, Y, Z

Get the eBook for only $10!

> Now you can take the weightless companion with you anywhere, anytime. Your purchase of this book entitles you to 3 electronic versions for only $10.

This Apress title will prove so indispensible that you'll want to carry it with you everywhere, which is why we are offering the eBook in 3 formats for only $10 if you have already purchased the print book.

Convenient and fully searchable, the PDF version enables you to easily find and copy code—or perform examples by quickly toggling between instructions and applications. The MOBI format is ideal for your Kindle, while the ePUB can be utilized on a variety of mobile devices.

Go to www.apress.com/promo/tendollars to purchase your companion eBook.